## Study Guide to Accompany
### ALLOY / ACOCELLA / BOOTZIN

# ABNORMAL PSYCHOLOGY
## CURRENT PERSPECTIVES

### SEVENTH EDITION

# GARY BOTHE
# SUSAN JONES BOTHE
with the special assistance of

# PETER GRAM
*Pensacola Junior College*

The McGraw-Hill Companies, Inc.

New York   St. Louis   San Francisco   Auckland   Bogotá
Caracas   Lisbon   London   Madrid   Mexico City   Milan   Montreal
New Delhi   San Juan   Singapore   Sydney   Tokyo   Toronto

Study Guide to Accompany Alloy/Acocella/Bootzin
**ABNORMAL PSYCHOLOGY**: CURRENT PERSPECTIVES

2  3  4  5  6  7  8  9  0  SEM SEM  9  0  9  8  7  6

ISBN 0-07-006629-9

The editor was Brian L. McKean;
the production supervisor was Diane Ficarra.
Quebecor-Semline was printer and binder.

Cover
Paul Klee: Pompona, Overripe (slightly inclined),
1938/134 (J 14)
Oil on newspaper on burlap 26¼ X 20½  in.
Paul Klee Stifung. Kunstmuseum Bern.

# Contents

# How to use this Study Guide

The secret to effective learning is mental *activity*. Many students attempt to study by sitting down, usually on the night before the test, and reading the chapter through from beginning to end in one dull session. They would much rather be doing something else, and the attention they give to the material in the book is minimal and fleeting. Somehow, they hope, the information will just etch in their brains as their eyes drag over the words—after all, holding the book and forcing yourself to read must be good for something, isn't it?

Actually, this kind of passive, uninvolved study is one of the least effective ways to learn anything. On the other hand, active involvement stimulates effective learning that produces results on tests. Some of you may have hobby interests—hunting, cars, stamp collecting—and you may read magazines devoted to that interest. Did you ever notice how you can read an article one time on such a subject that interests you, and effortlessly remember just about everything in it, even weeks later? The reason you can do that is because you are actively involved in the learning process. You are interested, you put the words into action, and you *participate* in the information. If you could manage the same kind of interest and participation in connection with your college classes, you could learn and remember that kind of information just as easily. Unfortunately, many students find it difficult to generate the structure they need to accomplish this on their own. This is where a good study guide and good study methods come into the picture.

An *active* study method that is very effective is the **SQ3R Method**. The acronym stands for **Survey, Question, Read, Recite, Review**. It is a way of guiding yourself through text material in an organized, step-by-step manner, to produce effective learning and prolong retention. Let's take a few minutes to show you how you can apply this method to your textbook, and how you can use this Study Guide to help in the process.

**Survey** means that instead of reading a chapter through from beginning to end and hoping to get every detail you need to know in one sitting, you begin by glancing over the material quickly, just to get a feel for the content and the major issues. You begin by looking at the chapter title and major headings in the chapter, reading the chapter summary and the words in bold print, and even glancing at the first and last sentence of each paragraph. This survey should not take more than 5 or 10 minutes, and when you are done, you will know what you are going to be reading about in a general way. You will have gone on a reconnaissance, if you will, a scouting trip through the chapter. This Study Guide assists you in this survey by providing a list of **Objectives**, a **Chapter Outline, Concept Maps,** and lists of **Key Terms** and **Important Names**. These sections tell you what the major points of the chapter are, and give you a structured summary of the material. The **Names** are not highlighted in the text, but having them here gives you an opportunity to associate important concepts in abnormal psychology with the people who are responsible for them. **Textbook page numbers are in parentheses** to facilitate using the textbook and Study Guide together to produce the most effective results.

**Question** means to take the big ideas or major headings of the chapter and convert them into questions that you will need to answer. So if a heading in the text reads "Four assumptions of the behavioral approach," you simply convert that into a question: "What are the four assumptions of the behavioral approach?" By generating a question, you construct a framework for your study session—you build a structure that will guide you through the chapter in a step-by-step manner. This Study Guide helps you with this process by providing **Guided Self-Study** exercises in which questions similar to ones you might make up yourself are presented.

**Read** is the next step. But now, instead of just passively scanning the material, hoping that some of it will stick, you are reading *actively*, for a purpose. You are reading to find the answers to the questions that have been asked. For you to comprehend what you read, a good vocabulary is obviously a necessity. So, in addition to the terms highlighted by the authors of your text, we have also included a list of extra **Vocabulary Terms**. These extra words are not necessarily technical psychological terms, but are simply words often used in professional-level writing. Don't feel insulted if you already know what they mean—congratulate yourself on your knowledge! There are many college students who could really benefit from looking some of them up.

**Recite** means that as a result of your reading, you produce answers to the questions that have been posed. You may say them out loud, or write them down, but be sure you do something active in the recitation process. Just finding the answer and nodding your head in satisfaction is not enough. *Do something* that requires an effort; learning is much more effective that way. Writing the answers in the spaces provided in the study guide is an obvious approach, but consider writing the answers on a separate sheet of paper instead. This will allow you to repeat the exercise several times without giving away the answers to yourself. The **Helpful Hints** at the end of the exercise give additional information on content and study techniques that you may not have thought of yourself.

**Review** consists of going over the material again, after the study session is completed. This serves as a reality check, to see how much you really learned, and it also serves to rehearse or reinforce your new knowledge. One more run through the exercise portion of the study guide can help with this, but the big test of your knowledge is the **Practice Exam** provided at the end of the chapter. These questions are very similar to ones your instructor is likely to ask, and they provide a good measure of your ability to remember and integrate the information in the chapter. Here, as with the exercises, we would encourage you to write your answers on a separate sheet of paper, to permit retaking the test several times. We have even provided a tally box for you to record your success (or lack of it) in answering each question. We suggest that you keep reviewing until you can answer each question correctly twice in a row.

The **Answer** key at the end of each chapter allows you to check the accuracy of your responses to the exercises and the exam questions. Again, the **page numbers in parentheses** are for easy reference to the textbook page(s) where that specific information can be found.

Addendum to encourage Struggling Students from One Who Also Struggled (SJB).

1.      To those of you who do not find reading a textbook to be an easy means of learning, I have a recommendation: Use the SQ3R method intensively; use the study guide outline to preview each segment before you try to read from your textbook. This way you will not be tempted to wait until after you have heard the lecture to do your chapter reading. I, as a student, wanted to hear the lecture first. I wanted the teacher to tell me what I was going to read about before I read it because reading it cold was so slow for me.

I want to encourage those of you who are not expert readers. There is hope! I have several college degrees in spite of being a slow reader. If I can do it, so can you! You just have to learn how to work around your lack of reading expertise (that is a more positive way to state "reading problem"). Highlighting, underlining, and outlining allow me to get what reading alone does not provide. Yes, I have taken speed reading courses. As a result, my eyes can go faster, but my brain still just doesn't seem to keep up. What I need is *structure* so I can know what to expect when I am reading. That's why the outline in this study guide is so helpful. If provides the skeleton and then you use reading to flesh out the basics of the skeleton (outline).

2.      You will find that in the study exercises I emphasize basic concepts. I take this approach for two reasons: first, I want to *make very clear* what the most important facts are, and, second, I want to give you practice thinking about them. As basic concepts become established in your knowledge, you will then be able to use that knowledge. For example, in behaviorism, the answer is always "learning." Once you get that etched in your thinking, when you encounter a question about how the behaviorist is going to view a specific abnormal behavior, you will say to yourself

"How can this be seen as a learning situation?" After that line of thought becomes habitual for you, you'll start to say, "Okay, there are two types of learning, so which one is this?"

3.     You will find that sometimes I refer to an earlier chapter. This is because there are particular bits of information that you need to build on from that earlier chapter. I remind you of that material so you can check to make sure that you really know the information. If not, you will have that unsatisfactory feeling of "lostness"—wondering what is going on. You'll be saying, "Is there something I'm missing?" Yes! back on those pages in the earlier chapter.

I think it is important to become aware of that frustrated, lost feeling in studying so you can identify it and then develop study techniques to relieve it. That feeling, or the expectation of it, causes students to avoid studying or to stop before they have finished the assignment. Needless to say, that is the beginning of a negative, downward spiral. The less you study, the more lost and frustrated you feel, and that leads to even more avoided or aborted study experiences. Then you stop going to class because the lecture just reminds you of how far behind you are.

4.     Now I am going to nag a bit: Do not engage in what I call cop-out copying. Cop-out copying is mindlessly copying the answers from the text, the study guide answer key, or someone else's work. Cop-out copying gives you very little practice in anything but handwriting. If you have asked yourself the question, and realize that you don't know the answer, it is time to look up the answer. When you find it, read the info, and *then restate it in your own words!* That process makes clear whether you do or do not have the concept. If you can say it in your own words, you know what the idea is about and you are beginning to lock it into your memory. If you find that your statement of the concept is wordy and rambling, go back to the succinct terms of the textbook to more effectively articulate the concept. If you realize that you really don't know the concept, you can reread the text or your notes, look for a chart or graph, or ask your instructor or a classmate.

5.     If you did well in high school but are having trouble in college, your difficulty may be that college teachers do not drill (do repetitions of) the material. I have encountered students who were good high school students and who got by with doing almost no out-of-class study. They learned by hearing the repetitions that were done in class for those folks who needed them. When these students enter college, they try to do the same thing they did in high school. They are then at a complete loss when their grades are not as good as they were before.

College classes typically cover a book in one term, not in one year, which is the usual pattern in high school. With more material to cover, the college time frame does not allow the instructor to routinely do repetitions. The student hears the lecture on the topic, perhaps does a class experiment, group activity, or sees a film; the teacher then addresses students' questions and moves on to the next topic.

All except a few geniuses need to spend time outside of class doing some repetitions of the concepts just to lock them into memory. If you are not spending study time doing some drilling in addition to reading, you are probably not making the grades that you expect to make. This is another reason the SQ3R method is such an excellent study method. The recite and review parts give some repetitious rehearsal to lock the concepts into your memory.

## Using Concept Maps and Chapter Terms to Learn and Review - by P. C. Gram

This study guide has two special features, one old and one new. The old one is to provide Chapter Terms to help you drill vocabulary words. The pages are designed so that you can tear them out and cut the terms into a stack of small cards. Each card will have a term or concept in bold letters on one side and the corresponding definition on the other. You may drill by reading the definition and then saying the correct term (or vice versa), and checking your answer by flipping the card over.

The new technique involves using Concept Maps to deepen your understanding of the material in the chapter and providing a quick review of it. One topic discussed by psychologists is how people best learn new concepts, and how they organize what they know. Recently cognitive psychology has increased our awareness that knowledge is relational. By this we mean that we learn best by connecting ideas together, through analogy and in context. We learn most new words not by looking them up in the dictionary, but by seeing them in the context of a story or hearing them in a conversation. The same is true of concepts. We learn them best in relation to other ideas. Therefore this study guide uses a new technique called "Concept Mapping."

Concept maps are made of two parts: concepts and relationships. Boxes are used to identify concepts, and connecting lines to represent relationships or links between concepts. Note that many concepts may be connected to more than one other concept. These interconnections represent the richness of the human mind. For a student trying to learn new material, the more interconnections he or she makes, the easier it is to understand and remember a new concept.

In the maps in this study guide, major concepts are represented in **BOLD** print, general concepts are in SOLID CAPITALS in regular print, lesser concepts are in smaller type CAPITAL print, and examples of concepts are in lower case smaller print, i.e.:

**MAJOR CONCEPT**
GENERAL CONCEPT
LESSER CONCEPT
examples

The lines or links connecting the concepts go in the direction of top to bottom (broader concepts to more specific ones) except where noted by an arrow.

The following concept map could be a description of what a person might know about lobsters.

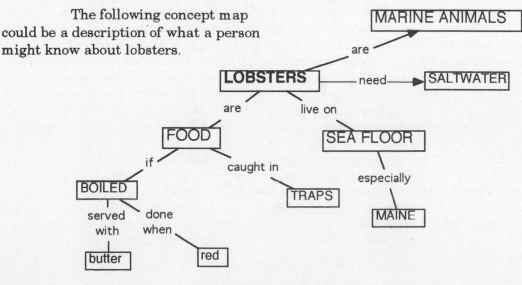

Note that some of these concepts may also be used in other maps (e.g., salt water may be a major concept in a related concept map with completely different associations). In some fashion all the concepts you know are interconnected, but, to represent a single major concept, you must limit the number of connections you draw.

Concept mapping is not limited to simple relationships, such as lobsters. Concept maps are <u>powerful tools</u> to teach new material. Here is another example from psychology. **LEARNING** has been studied by psychologists for a long time, and there have been various TYPES. These include specific theoretical positions (CLASSICAL, etc.), which have specific areas of interest or applicability (e.g. VOLUNTARY BEHAVIOR). Examples of these are then in lower case letters (e.g. reflexes).

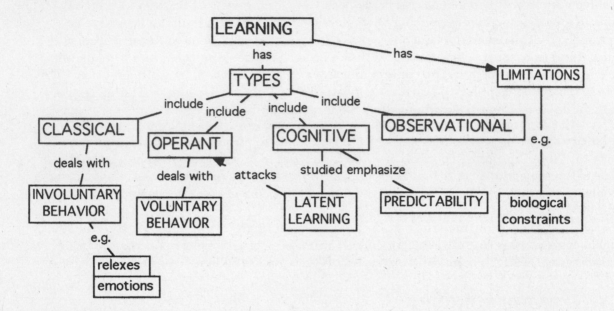

Each of the study guide chapters ends with a partial concept map or, in some cases, maps. Each map has a few blank boxes. You will be asked to fill in these boxes with the concept you believe belongs there. An answer key follows the concept map(s).

The most beneficial way for you to use concept maps is for you to <u>construct your own</u>, much the same way an instructor might ask students to take a blank sheet of paper and outline from memory the chapter they just read. In an attempt to work toward this goal, the concept maps in the beginning of the study guide will have most of the boxes filled with concepts. However, as you become more proficient with the concept mapping approach you might want to add to these concept maps with concepts of your own. The concept maps in the study guide can be checked by looking at the text, or on the answer page in the study guide. Please remember that there is <u>no single correct concept map</u>. Concept maps can be a very individual thing, since everyone has different arrangements of concepts in their memory. The answers are suggested by the author and fit with the chapter. Yours should approximate them, especially if you have the understanding of the material in the chapter to do well on evaluations.

Again, ideally, you should <u>construct your own concept map from scratch</u>, and then <u>revise</u> it. You might even use the cut-out Chapter Terms as concepts and arrange them into your own concept map. This gives you the best way of checking out your knowledge of the chapter. (I even know of one professor who assigns his students the task of making a concept map of the whole course as a final exam.) Hopefully, this new approach will prove helpful in developing a deeper knowledge, not only of psychology, but with any subject for which you use it.

## Chapter 1

# *Abnormal Behavior: Yesterday and Today*

## *LEARNING OBJECTIVES*
*By the time you are finished studying this chapter, you should be able to:*

### ABNORMAL BEHAVIOR AND SOCIETY
1. List and describe five criteria for defining abnormality (4-7).
2. List four categories of behavior that most societies consider indicative of mental disorder (7).
3. Describe the essential features of the medical model of abnormal behavior and list the advantages and criticisms of the medical model as presented in your text (7-9).
4. Name and describe six psychologically-based perspectives and one biologically-based perspective currently used to understand mental disorder (9).
5. List and explain three factors that influence how a culture will treat an individual with abnormal behavior (10).

### CONCEPTIONS OF ABNORMAL BEHAVIOR: A SHORT HISTORY
6. Describe three contributions of Hippocrates to the development of modern approaches to abnormal behavior (12).
7. Cite the contributions of Asclepiades and Galen to the study of abnormal behavior (13).
8. Discuss how the cultural atmosphere of the Middle Ages influenced attitudes and actions toward the mentally ill during that period (13-14).
9. Describe the European approach toward mental disorders during the Renaissance, including reference both to witch hunting and more moderate attitudes (14-15).
10. List the contributions of Pussin, Pinel, Esquirol, Tuke, Rush, and Dix to the reform of mental health care in the eighteenth and nineteenth centuries (16-18).
11. Define moral therapy and discuss its place in the development of modern psychotherapy (17-18).
12. List the contributions of Wundt, Kraepelin, Mesmer, Liebeault, Bernheim, Charcot, Breuer, and Freud to the development of modern psychotherapy (19-22).

### A MULTIPERSPECTIVE APPROACH
13. List three assumptions your text uses in constructing a multiperspective approach, and discuss the benefits of such an orientation toward abnormal behavior (22).

## *CHAPTER OUTLINE*

I. Abnormal behavior and society

    A. Defining abnormal behavior
       1. Criteria for abnormality
         a. Norm violation—behavior that most people in a society consider to be improper; varies from
           (1) Era to era within a society
           (2) Culture to culture
         b. Statistical rarity—behavior that does not occur often
         c. Personal discomfort—behavior that distresses the individual who has that behavior

1

      d.    Maladaptive behavior—behavior that causes the individual to be unable to do the things he/she needs to do

      e.    Deviation from an ideal—behavior that varies from an absolute standard

  2.  All above criteria depend to some extent on both facts and values

  3.  Most societies define the following categories of behavior to be a sign of mental disorder:

      a.    Behavior irrationally harmful to self or others

      b.    Behavior characterized by poor reality contact

      c.    Inappropriate emotional reactions

      d.    Erratic behavior

B.  Explaining abnormal behavior

  1.  Medical model says abnormal behavior is caused by physical (biological) illness or, at least, it can be understood in the same way a physical illness is understood

  2.  Psychological perspectives are based on intangible processes of the "mind" interacting with the environment

      a.    Psychodynamic perspective says behavior is the result of unconscious conflicts about sex and aggression

      b.    Behavioral perspective says abnormal behavior is the result of learning

      c.    Cognitive perspective says abnormal behavior is the result of irrational or counterproductive thinking

      d.    Humanistic-existential perspective says failure to take responsibility for one's own life causes abnormal behavior

      e.    Interpersonal perspective says abnormality is a product of disordered relationships

      f.    Sociocultural perspective says abnormality is a product of social forces and biases

  3.  Biological perspective says there are organic components of behavior, but unlike the medical model, it does not insist that mental disorder is essentially a medical problem requiring a medical approach to treatment

C.  Treating abnormal behavior depends on

  1.  Nature and structure of society

      a.    Small, traditional societies tend to have the family care for the deviant individual

      b.    Technological societies tend to isolate the deviant person from "normal" people

  2.  The criterion by which abnormality was identified

  3.  How society explains the cause of the abnormal behavior

II.  Conceptions of abnormal behavior: a short history

A.  Ancient societies often saw deviance as caused by the supernatural, that is, by evil spirits

B.  The Greeks were the first to take a scientific approach to studying and treating abnormal behavior

  1.  Hippocrates, a Greek physician, introduced a scientific approach to study abnormal behavior

      a.    He observed and recorded as objectively as possible

         (1)  He developed a biogenic explanation of abnormal behavior based on four bodily humors

         (2)  He attempted to develop a classification system for abnormal mental states

      b.    He used more humane treatment approaches than the exorcism-based therapies which addressed supernatural causes of abnormal behavior

  2.  Plato, a Greek philosopher, although still taking a quasi-supernatural approach to mental illness, said

      a.    Families should take care of their mentally ill

      b.    The mentally ill should not be held accountable for their actions

  3.  Asclepiades, a Greek physician practicing in Rome, described

      a.    Acute and chronic mental illnesses,

      b.    Hallucinations, delusions, and illusions

4. Galen, another Greek physician practicing in Rome, demonstrated that the arteries contained blood

C. Science declined with the fall of the Roman empire in the fifth century
   1. In the Middle Ages and the Renaissance (fifteenth to seventeenth centuries) both natural and supernatural explanations were used for abnormal behavior
   2. There was a revival of learning about natural phenomena
   3. The Christian church often had supernatural explanations (usually the devil)
   4. Witch hunts may have been motivated more by political and economic issues than by a desire to cope with people with abnormal behaviors

D. Eighteenth and nineteenth centuries
   1. Science dominates
   2. Reform of the asylums to more humane treatment by trying to elevate the patient's morale (called moral therapy)
      a. Vincenzo Chiarugi (Florence, Italy)
      b. Jean-Baptiste Pussin (Paris)
      c. Philippe Pinel (Paris)
      d. William Tuke (England)
   3. Mental health reforms in America
      a. Benjamin Rush wrote a treatise on mental health, organized first psychiatry course, was called the "father of American psychiatry"
      b. Dorothea Dix moved to establish mental hospitals to get the mentally ill out of jails and poorhouses
   4. Moral therapies declined because of
      a. Development of large hospitals which
         (1) Had inadequate staffing
         (2) Isolated and ostracized the mentally ill
      b. Lack of strong advocates to perpetuate the moral therapy movement
      c. Discrimination by Protestant establishment (in the U.S.) against poor Irish Catholic immigrants
      d. The rise of the medical model of mental disturbance

E. Foundations of modern abnormal psychology
   1. Experimental study of abnormal behavior
      a. Wilhelm Wundt established first psychological laboratory (1879)
      b. Emil Kraepelin established first laboratory for the study of psychopathology; founder of experimental abnormal psychology
   2. Biogenic theory—psychological dysfunction is due to organic dysfunction
      a. Griesinger—first systematic presentation of biogenic theory of mental disturbance
      b. Kraepelin—first comprehensive biogenic classification system, each disorder having different organic causes and symptoms
      c. Kraft-Ebing—discovered that syphilis (physical disease) causes general paresis (mental syndrome)
   3. Psychogenic theory—psychological disturbance is due primarily to emotional stress
   4. Mesmer's "animal magnetism" demonstrated the power of suggestion in disorder and cure
      a. The Nancy School—believed hysteria was a form of self-hypnosis and that other abnormal behavior could be entirely due to psychological causes
      b. Freud developed psychoanalysis

III. A multiperspective approach is the approach to be used in this text. It is based on the following three assumptions:

A. Human behavior can be studied scientifically
B. Most abnormal behavior results from psychological *and* biological processes
C. Each human being is unique

3

## KEY TERMS
*The following terms are in bold print in your text. Define them and practice their definitions using the flash cards at the end of the chapter.*

biogenic (8)
biological perspective (8)
clinical psychologist (10)
exorcism (11)
free association (22)
general paresis (20)
glove anesthesia (21)

humors (12)
hypnosis (20)
medical model (7)
moral therapy (17)
norms (4)
psychiatric social worker (10)

psychiatrist (10)
psychoanalysis (22)
psychoanalyst (10)
psychogenic theory (20)
psychopathology (19)
syndrome (20)

*Your text does not list the following terms as formal vocabulary; however, if you don't know what they mean, you will be unable to grasp the concepts of this chapter.*

adherents (21)
analogy (8)
cathartic (22)
criterion (criteria) (4)
custodial care (18)
deviation (6)

dysfunctional (7)
idiosyncratic (4)
intangible (9)
organic (8)
pathology (8)
prosaic (4)

Renaissance (14)
school of thought (9)
stigmatizes (5)
trephining (11)
unconscious (22)

## IMPORTANT NAMES
*Identify the following persons and their major contributions to abnormal psychology as discussed in this chapter.*

Asclepiades (13)
Hippolyte-Marie Bernheim (21)
Josef Breuer (21)
Jean-Martin Charcot (21)
Vincenzo Chiarugi (16)
Dorothea Dix (18)
Jean Esquirol (16)
Sigmund Freud (21)

Galen (13)
Wilhelm Griesinger (20)
Hippocrates (11)
Emil Kraepelin (19)
Richard von Krafft-Ebing (20)
Ambrose-Auguste Liebeault (21)
Franz Anton Mesmer (20)

Philippe Pinel (16)
Plato (12)
Morton Prince (19)
Jean-Baptiste Pussin (16)
Benjamin Rush (17)
Thomas Szasz (8)
William Tuke (17)
Wilhelm Wundt (19)

## GUIDED SELF-STUDY

ABNORMAL BEHAVIOR AND SOCIETY

1. List some behaviors that you have observed that seemed abnormal to you.

   a.

   b.

   c.

2. List the five criteria for defining abnormal behavior presented in your text.

   a.

   b.

   c.

   d.

   e.

   Make up your own memory trick for remembering these five criteria, or use the one given in the Answers section; however, if you make up your own, it will stay in your memory far better because you will have done mental exercise to create it.

3. Identify which definition would be used to define each of the following situations as abnormal.

    a. A three-year-old child who can read

    b. A person who can't hold a job due to chronic lateness

    c. A man who is depressed because he planned to be a millionaire by age 30, but isn't

    d. A man who has a wife *and* a girlfriend

    e. A student who feels a little queasy just signing up for algebra

    f. A woman who wrecks her new automobile while distracted by angry thoughts about the way her boss treats her at work

    g. A woman who decides to diet to attain the exact prescribed weight for her height

4. Determine which criterion for abnormal you used for each of your examples given for Question 1. Then, think up an example for the criteria you did not initially use. If you cannot, ask a classmate or your instructor so that you have a clear understanding of each of the criteria.

5. List some behaviors in which times and cultures would be critical factors as to whether the behaviors are seen as abnormal.

6. Each of the following statements is associated with one of the criteria for defining abnormal behaviors. From the three choices below each statement select its associated criteria.

    a. Lack of an objective standard is especially problematical
        **Norm violation / Deviation from ideal / Personal discomfort**
    b. Works fairly well in small, highly integrated societies
        **Statistical rarity / Norm violation / Maladaptive behavior**
    c. Favored by mental health professionals for its elasticity
        **Personal discomfort / Statistical rarity / Maladaptive behavior**
    d. Its major weakness is that it has *no* values considered
        **Statistical rarity / Norm violation / Deviation from ideal**
    e. Very practical view—survival
        **Maladaptive behavior / Deviation from ideal / Norm violation**
    f. *Everyone* is abnormal
        **Norm violation / Statistical rarity / Deviation from ideal**
    g. *Somebody* has to be abnormal
        **Maladaptive behavior / Personal discomfort / Statistical rarity**

7. Even though these criteria involve a variety of views, there actually is fairly clear agreement about what defines abnormal behaviors. Maher and Maher (1985) points out that in most societies four categories of behavior are seen as abnormal. Use the following terms to complete the four basic categories. Terms may be used more than once.

**erratic / poor / inappropriate / harmful**

    a. Behavior that is _____ to the self or that is _____ to others without serving the interests of the individual.

    b. _____ reality contact—for example, beliefs that most people do not hold, or sensory perceptions of things that most people do not perceive.

5

c.   Emotional reactions _____ to the person's situation.

d.   _____ behavior—that is, behavior that shifts unpredictably.

8.  After deciding which behaviors are abnormal we now turn to trying to explain what causes them.  Use the following words or phrases to fill in these blanks about the causes of abnormal behaviors: **multiperspective approach, supernatural, naturalistic, medical model, disturbances in human relationships, bodily chemistry, biological, psychological, bodily disease**.

The explanations used in this textbook are all (a)_____, which means they are

explained as events of nature, such as (b)_____.  During ancient times and

medieval times, (c)_____ explanations were common.  The three models of "natural"

scientific explanations of today are based on (d)_____, (e)_____, and (f)_____.

To use some combination of these approaches to explaining abnormal behavior is said to be a

(g)_____ approach.

9.  The psychological perspectives are theories based on intangible process in the individual's mind interacting with the individual's environment.  Each of the psychological perspectives focuses on different aspects of the mind as possible ways of explaining abnormal behavior.  Draw lines to match the following perspectives with their central concern:

Psychoanalytic              disordered relationships
Behavioral                  thinking
Cognitive                   unconscious conflicts
Humanistic-existential      body chemistry
Interpersonal               social forces
Sociocultural               self-acceptance
Biological                  learning

10.  How are the biological perspective and medical model alike, and how are they different?

11.  What three things determine how abnormal behavior will be treated?

12.  What therapeutic technique does each of the following perspectives use?

___ Cognitive            a.   Here YOU have to come to see that YOU and only YOU
___ Multiperspective          are responsible for your life.
___ Interpersonal        b.   Look at current interpersonal relationships for unsatisfactory
___ Sociocultural             habitual patterns and ineffective communication styles.
___ Humanistic-Exist.    c.   An exorcism
___ Biological           d.   An organic intervention to cure the causal disease (medicine,
___ Supernatural              surgery, or shock therapy)
___ Medical model        e.   Uncover and resolve your unconscious conflicts
___ Psychoanalytic       f.   Training new behaviors to replace your old "abnormal"
___ Behavioral                behaviors
                         g.   Make you aware of how you think and perceive and then
                              teach more productive, satisfactory thinking
                         h.   Find solutions for poverty and discrimination
                         i.   Organic and psychological interventions will be used to alter
                              your organic and behavioral problem areas.
                         j.   Select techniques from a variety of perspectives

6

# CONCEPTIONS OF ABNORMAL BEHAVIOR: A SHORT HISTORY

13. How did the ancient societies see abnormal behavior?

14. What dramatic change did the ancient Greeks bring about that influenced the course of how abnormal behavior was seen?

15. List three accomplishments with which Hippocrates is credited.

    a.

    b.

    c.

16. Would you have wanted Plato on your side if you were on trial for killing someone while you were temporarily experiencing a very abnormal mental state? Explain your answer.

17. Why is the fall of the Roman empire mentioned in this chapter?

    By the way, when was the fall of the Roman empire?

18. In the Middle Ages and the Renaissance both (a)_____ and

    (b)_____ explanations were used to explain abnormal behavior. The Christian church tended to encourage which explanation?

19. How did the witch hunts fit into the issue of abnormal behavior?

20. Where did science stand in the eighteenth and nineteenth centuries as compared to the supernatural approach?

21. Before considering the asylum reformers, fill in the following blanks for a brief historical review of early institutionalized care of the psychologically disturbed:

    In late Greek civilization, (a)_____ were established for the care of the mentally

    ill. In Alexandria, (b)_____ were set aside as asylums. In Arab countries, there

    were wards for the mentally ill within the general hospitals in the (c)_____ century. The

    first hospital set up exclusively for the insane was opened in Moslem Spain in the early

    (d)_____ century. Efforts to set up local community care for the mentally ill were seen in

    the Renaissance in England and (e)_____.

22. List some of the conditions that existed in the care of the mentally ill that needed to be changed.

23. Circle the names of four European mental asylum reformers.

**Wakefield / Szasz / Chiarugi / Hippocrates**
**Pussin / Boots / Galen / Pinel / Kraepelin**
**Wundt / Mesmer / Tuke / Krafft-Ebing**

24. **MORAL? or MORALE?  That is the question!** One of those words in each blank?

Even though the therapy which they advocated was called (a) _____ therapy it did NOT

address their (b)_____ behavior; its purpose was to try to raise their (c)_____.

25. If you were registered in the first psychiatry course in America, your teacher's name would

have been _____.  **(Anton Mesmer, Emil Kraepelin, Benjamin Rush, Ambrose Liebeault, or Wilhelm Wundt)**

26. Dorothea Dix's efforts to help the mentally disturbed eventually lead to a circumstance that she never intended.  What was it?
a.  Mental illness was declared to be illegal.
b.  Mental hospitals developed into large impersonal places.
c.  Mental patients became subjects in the first psychological laboratory.
d.  Hypnosis became the primary treatment for the mentally ill.

27. List four reasons for the decline of moral therapy?

a.

b.

c.

d.

28. (a)_____ established the first psychological laboratory in the city of

(b)_____ in the year (c)_____.  (d)_____ developed the first systematic presentation of the biogenic theory of mental disturbance. However,

(e)_____ moved it to the forefront of European psychiatric theory as the medical

model in his *Textbook of Psychiatry*. (f)_____ is also considered the founder of experimental abnormal psychology.

29. Why is syphilis listed as part of one of the milestones in the development of abnormal psychology?

30. Mesmer was trying to cure his patients by supposedly adjusting the (a)_____

in their bodies.  His technique was known as (b)_____. From this work came

Mesmer's great contribution to abnormal psychology: discovery of (c)_____.

Mesmer's technique was eventually to be known as (d)_____.

31. What was the Nancy School and where did it stand on the disorder known as hysteria?  Who was the opposition to the Nancy school?

32. Assign the correct order to the following events.

____        Freud found that everyone could not be hypnotized.
____        Freud became acquainted with Liebeault and Bernheim's ideas which were based on Mesmer's work that led to the development of hypnosis.
____        Freud went to Paris to study with the French neurologist Charcot.
____        Freud started using free association.
____        Freud started to work with Breuer who was experimenting with the use of hypnosis.

33. The discovery that hysteria could be cured or induced by (a)_____ suggested that, in general, (b)_____ could cause abnormal behavior.

A MULTIPERSPECTIVE APPROACH

34. Fill in the key words in the three assumptions about human behavior that underlie the multiperspective approach.
    a.   Human behavior can be studied _____.

    b.   Abnormal behavior results from both _____ and _____ processes.

    c.   Each human being is _____.

## *HELPFUL HINTS*

1. Learn and understand well the perspectives listed in this chapter, and save yourself trouble. They are not going to go away. They are ABCs of this course.
2. Since this chapter focuses on history, ask your instructor how much he/she expects you to know about specific dates and names.
3. *Anytime* you hear the word "behaviorism" translate it to "learning" until you become comfortable with behaviorism as a concept unto itself.
4. Translate the word "cognitive" to "thinking" until you become comfortable with the cognitive perspective.
5. Do not confuse the words "learning" and "thinking."
6. Be sure to distinguish among all the "*psych*"-something words. They all relate to the mind, but in a wide variety of ways. There are many of them: *psych*ology, *psych*ological, *psych*oanalytical, *psych*odynamic, *psych*ogenic, *psych*ometric, *psych*ologist, *psych*iatrist.
7. Be sure to get those *psych*-terms straight which are found in the box on page 10!
8. By the way, have you read "How to Use this Study Guide" found in the front of this workbook, right after the table of contents? If you haven't, you have already missed some more very important helpful hints.

## *PRACTICE TEST*
*Take the following test several times as you study the chapter. Write your answers on a separate sheet of paper and after each attempt, note in the tally box above each question whether your answer was correct or incorrect.*

| 1 | 2 | 3 | 4 |
|---|---|---|---|

1. "Abnormal" in the statistical sense means that
   a.   an individual has violated a social expectation.
   b.   there are many people who share the same problem.
   c.   the individual is in the minority in regard to that behavior.
   d.   the individual lives up to only a few of the ideals of his/her society.

| 1 | 2 | 3 | 4 |
|---|---|---|---|

2. The "personal discomfort" criterion for abnormality
   a.  depends on a person's belief and feelings that he/she has a problem.
   b.  refers to the difficulties that a mentally disturbed person causes others in society.
   c.  is used only by nonprofessionals.
   d.  is the most useful criterion because only the individual can tell if he/she really has a problem.

| 1 | 2 | 3 | 4 |
|---|---|---|---|

3. Which of the following is *not* one of categories of behavior assumed by most societies to indicate mental disorder?
   a.  Behavior that causes distress to the person engaging in it
   b.  Behavior indicating poor reality contact
   c.  Behavior that is harmful to the self or others
   d.  Emotional reactions inappropriate to the situation

| 1 | 2 | 3 | 4 |
|---|---|---|---|

4. Hippocrates is credited with which of the following?
   a.  Inventing trephining as a therapy technique
   b.  Describing and classifying abnormal behavior
   c.  Pointing out that "witches" were not mentally ill
   d.  Developing the first psychological laboratory

| 1 | 2 | 3 | 4 |
|---|---|---|---|

5. One of the first French reformers of lunatic asylums in the eighteenth century was
   a.  Pinel.
   b.  Mesmer.
   c.  Charcot.
   d.  Wundt.

| 1 | 2 | 3 | 4 |
|---|---|---|---|

6. A prominent figure in American mental health reform in the eighteenth century was
   a.  William Tuke.
   b.  Emil Kraepelin.
   c.  Nancy Charcot
   d.  Dorothea Dix

| 1 | 2 | 3 | 4 |
|---|---|---|---|

7. Which of the following statements is consistent with the ideas of moral therapy?
   a.  Upright moral character is the key to good mental health.
   b.  Evil influences must be driven out so that good can take their place.
   c.  You have to take the consequences of your own actions.
   d.  You need a break—go away for a while and get your head together.

| 1 | 2 | 3 | 4 |
|---|---|---|---|

8. Which of the following was a significant step in establishing the medical model as the dominant approach in European psychiatry in the nineteenth century?
   a.  Galen's discovery of blood rather than air in the arteries
   b.  Hippocrates' work on body types
   c.  Krafft-Ebing's discovery that syphilis could lead to general paresis
   d.  Mesmer's technique of having mentally distressed people relax in tubs of humors

| 1 | 2 | 3 | 4 |

9. One of the reasons moral therapy ultimately fell into disuse was
   a. the rise of the medical model of mental disorder.
   b. it's high cost.
   c. the early mental health reformers were against it.
   d. it focused on rigid morals that not all of society accepted.

| 1 | 2 | 3 | 4 |

10. One of the earliest major debates in the history of modern abnormal psychology was between Charcot and the "Nancy school." It was about
    a. hysteria.
    b. exorcism.
    c. humors.
    d. trephining.

| 1 | 2 | 3 | 4 |

11. Freud used which of the following techniques early in his career but abandoned it soon thereafter?
    a. Trephining
    b. Hypnosis
    c. Determinism
    d. Free association

| 1 | 2 | 3 | 4 |

12. Wundt was to Kraepelin as Charcot was to
    a. Pinel.
    b. Tuke.
    c. Freud.
    d. Mesmer.

13. The term "biogenic" means
    a. incurable.
    b. neuroscience.
    c. organically caused.
    d. all people have it to some extent.

| 1 | 2 | 3 | 4 |

14. Which of the following is one of the assumptions of the multiperspective approach to mental disorder?
    a. Abnormal behavior is a product of both biological and psychological processes.
    b. Some elements of human behavior are not appropriate for scientific study.
    c. Human behavior should be looked at in simple units for scientific clarity.
    d. The medical model is the basis for the study of all abnormal mental processes.

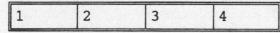

15. Hypnosis's effectiveness probably rests on
    a. the underlying principles of magnetism.
    b. the free association that it involves.
    c. Mesmer's use of the medical model.
    d. relaxation and suggestibility.

| 1 | 2 | 3 | 4 |
|---|---|---|---|

16. The psychodynamic perspective says behavior is the result of
    a. unconscious conflicts.
    b. social forces and biases working against the individual.
    c. misperception and misinterpretation of one's environment.
    d. too little "free association" during the first six years of life.

| 1 | 2 | 3 | 4 |
|---|---|---|---|

17. My therapist says that I read the wrong things into what people say.  My therapist has a
    _____ perspective.
    a. humanistic                               c. cognitive
    b. behavioral                               d. existential

| 1 | 2 | 3 | 4 |
|---|---|---|---|

18. My previous therapist tended to explain my behavior in terms of childhood conflicts that
    never got resolved.  My previous therapist took the _____ perspective.
    a. cognitive                                c. psychodynamic
    b. neuroscience                             d. behavioral

| 1 | 2 | 3 | 4 |
|---|---|---|---|

19. Which of the following mental health professionals has a Ph.D. or Psy.D. after four to six
    years in graduate school, followed by a year of clinical internship?
    a. A psychiatrist
    b. A clinical psychologist
    c. A psychiatric social worker
    d. A psychoanalyst

| 1 | 2 | 3 | 4 |
|---|---|---|---|

20. One of the most likely reasons for the witch hunts of the Renaissance was that
    a. mental disorder was assumed to be a contagious disease.
    b. unorthodox behavior was seen as a threat to Church authority.
    c. "witches" were better at curing mental cases than priests were.
    d. mental institutions were releasing too many uncured patients.

## ANSWERS
### Self-Study Exercise

1. Talking aloud to one's self, wearing bizarre clothing, biting fingernails down to nubs, falling
   asleep at a rock concert, cheating on one's mate, screaming at a newborn baby, driving a
   hundred miles per hour, watching the hanging of a criminal
2. a. Norm violation (4)                        d. Maladaptive behavior (6)
   b. Statistical rarity (5)                     e. Deviation from an ideal (6)
   c. Personal discomfort (6)
   Memory trick:  Underlined letters spell "rmind" to recall these five criteria.
3. a. Statistical rarity (5)                     e. Personal discomfort (6)
   b. Maladaptive behavior (6)                   f. Maladaptive behavior (6)
   c. Deviation from an ideal (6)                g. Deviation from an ideal (6)
   d. Norm violation (4)
   It is possible that there may be some debate over the correctness of one or more of answers to
   Question 3.  Read the answer to Question 4 to understand that the correctness of the answer
   will depend on the reason given for abnormality.  For example, situation "f" may also be listed

as "deviation from the ideal" of not having any problems with her boss, or "personal discomfort" because she is experiencing distress over his treatment of her. However, in view of the new problem created the best answer would most accurately be "maladaptive behavior" because her reaction to the situation has now contributed to more problems—hassle, expense, and perhaps loss of transportation.

4. Which criterion you used depends on the reasoning behind what you said. For example, biting fingernails down to nubs could fit any one of the criteria *depending on what reason you gave: Norm violation*, if you said *society says* one should not bite nails into the quick. *Statistical rarity*, if you said because *very few people* engage in nail biting. *Personal discomfort*, if you said the person who does it is *very unhappy* about it. *Maladaptive behavior*, if you said he *can't get a job or a date* because of it. *Deviation from an ideal*, if you said *the perfect* well-groomed individual will have neat, well-rounded nails with an eighth-inch tip showing.

5. Women wearing slacks
Deliberately inflicting pain on one's body
Breastfeeding infants in public places
A man or woman who has three spouses at one time

6. a. Personal discomfort (6)
   b. Norm violation (4)
   c. Maladaptive behavior (6)
   d. Statistical rarity (5)
   e. Maladaptive behavior (6)
   f. Deviation from an ideal (6)
   g. Statistical rarity (5)

7. a. harmful, harmful
   b. Poor
   c. inappropriate
   d. Erratic (7)

8. a. naturalistic (7)
   b. bodily chemistry, bodily disease, or disturbances in human relationships (7)
   c. Supernatural (10-11)
   d., e., and f. Medical model, psychological and biological, in any order (7-9).
   g. Multiperspective approach (9)

9. Psychodynamic - unconscious conflicts; Behavioral - learning; Cognitive - thinking; Humanistic-existential - self-acceptance; Interpersonal - disordered relationships; Sociocultural - social forces; Biological - body chemistry (9)

10. The medical model assumes medical causes (i.e. diseases) and medical treatments for psychological disorder; the biological perspective focuses the biological components to psychological disorders and treatments but does not insist on biology being the only factor (7-11).

11. The structure of the society, the definition of abnormality used, and the assumed causes of the abnormal behavior (i.e., What perspective is being used?) (10)

12. Cognitive—g
Multiperspective—j
Interpersonal—b
Sociocultural—h
Humanistic-existential—a
Biological—i
Supernatural—c
Medical model—d
Psychoanalytic—e
Behavioral—f (7, 9, 10-11)

13. A result of supernatural influence (11)

14. They began to consider mental disorder as a natural process (11)

15. a. Careful observation (12)
    b. Biogenic explanation (12)
    c. Unified mental disorder classification (12)

16. Yes. Plato believed that the mentally disturbed should not be held responsible for their acts (12).

17. The fall of Rome marked a change in the way mental disorder was viewed; Greek and Roman rationalism was replaced with a more supernatural approach (13); fifth century A.D. (13).

18. a. supernatural (13)
    b. natural (13)
    The Christian Church tended toward supernatural explanations (13).

19. Witch hunting was probably primarily economic and political maneuvering to eliminate rivals. Records indicate that some mentally ill individuals were persecuted by witch hunters, but the majority of the mentally ill were of little interest to them (14).

20. Science was beginning to edge out supernatural (13-19).

21. a. mental health retreats (12)
    b. temples of Saturn (12)
    c. eighth (15)
    d. fifteenth (15)
    e. Belgium (15)

22. Barbarous treatments thought to be therapeutic for abnormal behavior and horrid living conditions (13-16)
23. Chiarugi (16); Pussin (16); Pinel (16); Tuke (17)
24. a. moral (17)
    b. moral (17)
    c. morale (17)
25. Benjamin Rush (17)
26. b—Dorothea Dix worked to establish mental hospitals to care for the mentally ill so that they would not be put in jails and poorhouses. However, as these hospitals grew to become large, impersonal and costly, the principles of moral therapy which emphasized humane treatment were lost (18-19).
27. a. Failure of large hospitals to produce results (18)
    b. Lack of leadership (18)
    c. Ethnic discrimination against patients (18)
    d. Rise of medical model (18)
28. a. William Wundt (19)           d. Wilhelm Griesinger (20)
    b. Leipzig, Germany (19)        e. Emil Kraepelin (19-20)
    c. 1879 (19)                    f. Kraepelin (19-20)
29. Part of advanced syphilis can be a mental syndrome called general paresis. This discovery by Krafft-Ebing that general paresis was actually the result of the physical disease syphilis was dramatic evidence to support the medical model of disease processes as the causes of mental illnesses (20).
30. a. magnetism (20)              c. power of suggestion (20)
    b. mesmerism (20)              d. hypnosis (20)
31. The Nancy school, which started with Liebeault and Bernheim, believed hysteria had a psychological basis instead of an organic cause. Opposition came from the Paris school; it was made up of Charcot and his followers (21).
32. 4, 2, 1, 5, and 3 (21-22)
33. a. hypnosis (20-21)
    b. psychological factors (20-21)
34. a. scientifically
    b. psychological; biological
    c. unique (22)

## Practice Test

| | | | | | |
|---|---|---|---|---|---|
| 1. | c | (6) | 11. | b | (22) |
| 2. | a | (6) | 12. | c | (21) |
| 3. | a | (7) | 13. | c | (8) |
| 4. | b | (12) | 14. | a | (22) |
| 5. | a | (16) | 15. | d | (20) |
| 6. | d | (18) | 16. | a | (9) |
| 7. | d | (17) | 17. | c | (9) |
| 8. | c | (20) | 18. | c | (9) |
| 9. | a | (18) | 19. | b | (10) |
| 10. | a | (21) | 20. | b | (14) |

# CONCEPT MAP 1.1

Fill out the boxes marked with question marks (?) with the concepts or words you think belongs there. Possible answers suggested by the authors are on a following page.

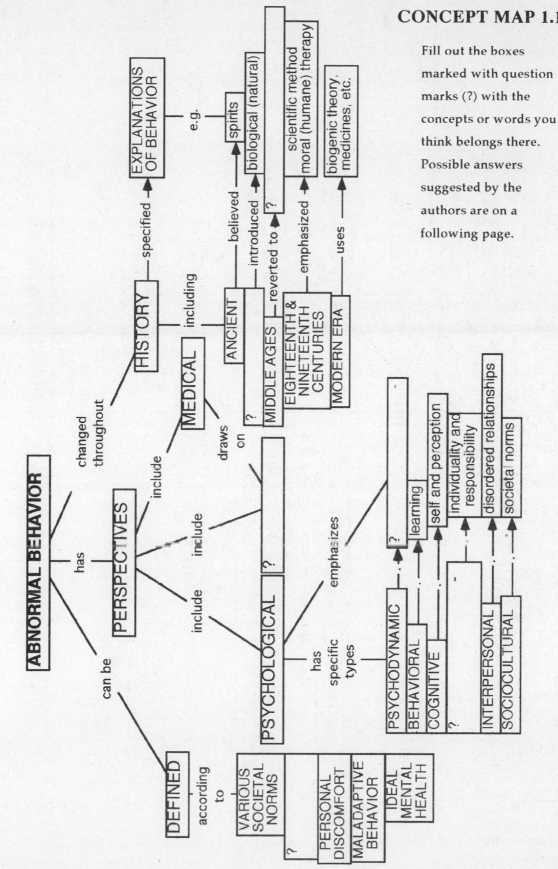

15

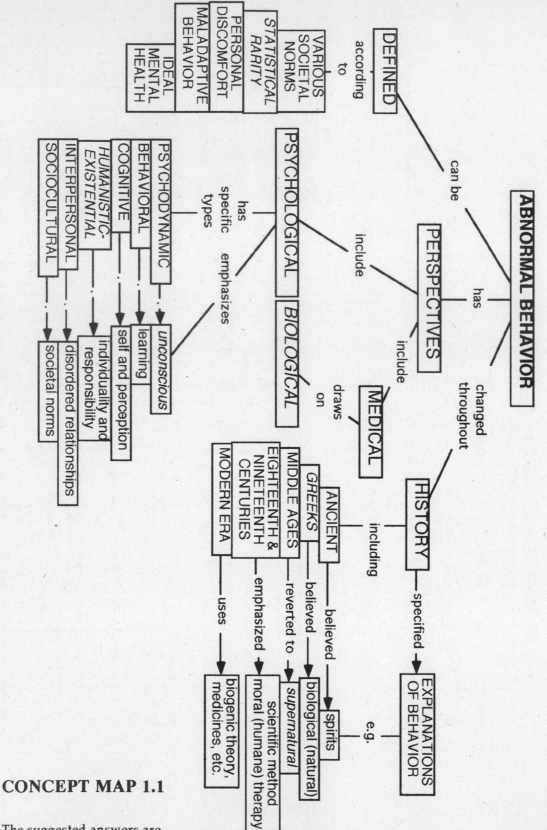

**CONCEPT MAP 1.1**

The suggested answers are
shown in *italics*.

16

# CHAPTER TERMS (Cut out on the lines to use as Flash Cards)

| | | |
|---|---|---|
| 1.1<br><br>**Biogenic** | 1.8<br><br>**Humors** | 1.15<br><br>**Psychoanalysis** |
| 1.2<br><br>**Biological Perspective** | 1.9<br><br>**Hypnosis** | 1.16<br><br>**Psychoanalyst** |
| 1.3<br><br>**Clinical Psychologist** | 1.10<br><br>**Medical Model** | 1.17<br><br>**Psychogenic Theory** |
| 1.4<br><br>**Exorcism** | 1.11<br><br>**Moral Therapy** | 1.18<br><br>**Psychopathology** |
| 1.5<br><br>**Free Association** | 1.12<br><br>**Norms** | 1.19<br><br>**Syndrome** |
| 1.6<br><br>**General Paresis** | 1.13<br><br>**Psychiatric Social Worker** | 1.20<br><br>*(You may fill in the remaining boxes with names, terms and definitions from text and lecture)* |
| 1.7<br>**Glove Anesthesia** | 1.14<br><br>**Psychiatrist** | 1.21 |

# DEFINITIONS (Cut out on the lines to use as Flash Cards)

| | | |
|---|---|---|
| 1.15 Method of therapy that relies heavily on techniques of free association, dream interpretation & analysis of resistance & transference. The aim is insight into patients' unconscious conflicts | 1.8 In Hippocrates' view, the four vital fluids possessed by humans: phlegm, blood, black bile, & yellow bile. The balance of these fluids in each individual was thought to influence personality | 1.1 A term used to describe abnormal behavior that results from some malfunction in the body. According to this theory, mental disturbance is due to organic disorders |
| 1.16 A postgraduate who has had special training in psychoanalysis and has undergone psychoanalysis himself | 1.9 Artificially induced sleep-like state in which the subject is highly susceptible to suggestion | 1.2 The conceptualization of psychological abnormalities which concentrates on the physical aspects of a disorder |
| 1.17 The view that mental disturbance is due primarily to emotional stress | 1.10 The conceptualization of psychological abnormality as a group of diseases analogous to physical diseases | 1.3 A Ph.D. or Psy.D. who has received training in clinical assessment and therapy, with at least a year long internship |
| 1.18 Abnormal psychology | 1.11 Treatment procedure developed in the early nineteenth century that is based on providing a pleasant and relaxed atmosphere for the mentally ill | 1.4 The practice of coaxing or forcing evil spirits from a person whom they possess |
| 1.19 The distinct cluster of symptoms that tend to occur in a particular disease | 1.12 The rules in any society that define "right" and "wrong." Norms guide most of our actions and are an important standard for defining abnormality | 1.5 A psychoanalytic technique in which the patient verbalizes whatever thoughts come to mind, without structuring or censoring the remarks |
| 1.20 | 1.13 A person who has earned an M.S.W. with an emphasis on psychological counseling | 1.6 An irreversible breakdown of physical and mental functioning which occurs in advanced stages of syphilis |
| 1.21 | 1.14 An M.D. who specializes in diagnosing and treating mental disorders. They are able to prescribe psychoactive medication | 1.7 A form of conversion disorder in which the individual reports a numbness in his or her hand from the tips of the fingers to a clear cutoff point at the wrist |

## Chapter 2

# *The Psychodynamic and Humanistic-Existential Perspectives*

## *LEARNING OBJECTIVES*
*By the time you are finished studying this chapter, you should be able to:*

### THE PSYCHODYNAMIC PERSPECTIVE
1. List three principles held in common by almost all psychodynamic theorists (26).
2. Describe the three levels of consciousness involved in Freud's theory and explain why Freud believed that behavior and experience need to be interpreted and not merely taken at face value (27).
3. Describe the functions and characteristics of the id, ego, and superego (27-29).
4. Define anxiety as Freud views it, and list and describe twelve defense mechanisms against anxiety (29-31).
5. List and describe four stages of personality development in Freudian theory (31-34).
6. Summarize Freud's view of normal and abnormal personality functions (34).
7. Name eight psychodynamic "descendants" of Freud and describe the contributions of each that distinguish them from Freud and from each other (34-40).
8. Describe four criticisms that have been leveled against the psychodynamic perspective, as well as three contributions that this perspective has made to psychology (40-42).

### THE HUMANISTIC-EXISTENTIAL PERSPECTIVE
9. List four assumptions held by both humanistic and existential psychology (42-43).
10. Name two major humanistic psychologists and describe the theoretical outlooks and major contributions of each (43-45).
11. Name three major existential psychologists and describe the theoretical outlooks and major contributions of each (46-48).
12. Discuss the impact of the humanistic-existential perspective on contemporary psychological theory and practice (48).
13. Compare and contrast the humanistic existential perspective to the psychodynamic perspective (48).
14. List and discuss two criticisms that have been leveled at the humanistic-existential perspective, and describe how humanistic-existential psychologists might respond to these criticisms (48).

## *CHAPTER OUTLINE*

I. The psychodynamic perspective

    A. Basic assumptions
       1. Behavior is determined by mental forces
       2. These mental forces are largely unconscious
       3. These forces are shaped by early childhood experiences

    B. Basic concepts of Freudian theory
       1. The depth psychology hypothesis assumes that most mental activity occurs on an unconscious level
       2. There are three levels of consciousness
         a. The perceptual conscious is present awareness

     b.    The preconscious is unaware but available

     c.    The unconscious proper is unaware and unavailable to awareness

3.   Most important mental activity is unconscious

4.   Much of what is unconscious has been pushed out of consciousness (repressed) because it is distressing

5.   Because of unconscious influences, most behavior must be interpreted
     a.    Outward appearances are manifest content
     b.    The true meaning is the latent content

6.   The structural hypothesis assumes three forces in the mind
     a.    The id
         (1)  Is present at birth
         (2)  Is driven by sexual and aggressive urges
         (3)  Operates on the pleasure principle
     b.    The ego
         (1)  Appears around the age of six months
         (2)  Connects the id with the real world
         (3)  Operates on the reality principle
     c.    The superego
         (1)  Begins to appears around the age of 5 or 6 years
         (2)  Represents the morals of society
         (3)  Holds up the standard of the ego ideal

7.   The ego must mediate between the demands of the id, the superego, and the outside world

8.   When the ego is threatened by these other forces, the result is anxiety

9.   Anxiety leads to the use of defense mechanisms
     a.    Repression pushes uncomfortable thoughts and feelings into the unconscious
     b.    Projection attributes uncomfortable thoughts and feelings to others
     c.    Displacement releases emotion against substitute targets
     d.    Rationalization is explaining and excuse making
     e.    Isolation separates feelings from situations
     f.    Intellectualization substitutes thinking for feeling
     g.    Denial refuses to acknowledge the existence of the problem
     h.    Reaction formation takes a position exactly opposite of true, but troubling feelings
     i.    Regression is a return to a more immature way of dealing with life
     j.    Undoing is ritual behavior or thought designed to cancel out the problem
     k.    Identification is psychological attachment to a person or group to relieve anxiety
     l.    Sublimation is the channeling of unacceptable impulses into socially acceptable directions

10.  Personality is formed during the childhood stages of psychosexual development
     a.    The oral stage
         (1)  First year of life
         (2)  Focus on mouth activities
         (3)  Symbolically related to stubbornness and dependency
     b.    The anal stage
         (1)  Second year of life
         (2)  Focus on eliminative functions
         (3)  Symbolically related to impulse control
     c.    The phallic stage
         (1)  Third to fifth or sixth year of life
         (2)  Focus on sexual gratification
         (3)  Symbolically related to self-concept
         (4)  Generates Oedipus (or Electra) complex because of unconscious sexual competition with same-sex parent for opposite-sex parent
         (5)  Conflict resolved through identification with same-sex parent
     d.    The latency period
         (1)  Roughly ages six through twelve years
         (2)  Sexual feelings go underground
     e.    The genital stage
         (1)  Age of puberty onward
         (2)  Focus on interpersonal relations rather than self-centered gratification

(3) Symbolically related to general personality maturity
11. The normal personality is characterized by
    a. A healthy balance between the id, ego, and superego
    b. Ego strength
12. The abnormal personality is characterized by
    a. A weakened ego
    b. A diminished ability to cope with the forces of the id, the superego, or the outside world

C. The descendants of Freud
1. Carl Gustav Jung
    a. "Spiritual" rather than sexual emphasis
    b. Saw the unconscious as a creative as well as a regressive force
    c. Proposed the existence of a collective unconscious representing inherited memory
    d. Healthy functioning requires the integration of opposites within the personality
2. Alfred Adler
    a. Emphasized the development of personal power rather than sexual desires as the driving force in the personality
    b. Emphasized relationships and social activism in the practice of psychology
3. Harry Stack Sullivan
    a. Emphasized parent-child relationship as critical in the development of the personality
    b. Pioneered work with severely disturbed patients
4. Karen Horney
    a. Emphasized "basic anxiety" which results from viewing the world as a cold and impersonal place. People cope with anxiety by
        (1) moving away from people
        (2) moving toward people
        (3) moving against people
    b. Pioneered in creating a female point of view in psychology
5. Heinz Hartmann
    a. Emphasized the ego rather than id or superego
    b. Developed an analytic focus on cognition
6. Erik Erikson
    a. Emphasized psychosocial rather than psychosexual development
    b. Considered personality development to be a lifelong process
    c. Focused on ego processes more than id processes
7. Margaret Mahler
    a. Emphasized a child's relationship with the mother
    b. Studied the separation-individuation process
8. Heinz Kohut
    a. Emphasized parent-child relationship in development of pathology

D. Evaluating the psychodynamic perspective
1. Criticisms
    a. Many psychodynamic concepts have not been verified scientifically because of their abstract nature or because of poor data
    b. The dependence on inference and interpretation makes analysis too subjective
    c. The application of psychodynamic ideas is limited by cultural bias and unrepresentative sampling
    d. The psychodynamic approach presents a reductive and pessimistic interpretation of life
2. Contributions of the psychodynamic approach
    a. It demythologized mental disorder
    b. It pioneered modern therapeutic practices
    c. It focused modern western society on the inner mental world

II. The humanistic-existential perspective

A. Underlying assumptions of the humanistic-existential perspective
1. The phenomenological approach, focusing on the subjective experience of the person

2. The uniqueness of the individual
3. Human potential, the idea that we are capable of more than we commonly achieve
4. Freedom and responsibility of the individual in the face of the world

B. Humanistic psychology
   1. Carl Rogers
      a. Took the optimistic position that all persons naturally strive to develop their unique potential (self-actualizing tendency)
      b. The degree to which we succeed at self-actualization depends on the extent to which the organism (the totality of our experience) and the self (the way we see ourselves) agree with each other
      c. A rigid self-image imposed by others in childhood makes congruence between self and organism impossible, thus stifling self-actualization
      d. Client-centered therapy allows development of a more genuine self and makes self-actualization more attainable
   2. Abraham Maslow
      a. Also proposes a self-actualization tendency
      b. Self-actualization is the last step up a hierarchy of human needs
         (1) Biological needs
         (2) Safety needs
         (3) Belongingness and love needs
         (4) Esteem needs
         (5) Self-actualization
      c. Abnormality results when one is kept from meeting these needs
      d. Psychology should help people overcome the obstacles that prevent self-actualization

C. Existential psychology
   1. Rollo May
      a. Asserts that an individual's mental problems have meaning only as one considers that individual's whole life
      b. The emergence of full self-consciousness is essential to therapy
   2. Viktor Frankl
      a. Asserts that people have a will to impose meaning on their lives
      b. Disorder results from a failure to discover such meaning
      c. Logotherapy is designed to foster the discovery of meaning
   3. R. D. Laing
      a. "Normal" living is a state of alienation from the self
      b. Mental disorder can be seen as a means of escaping from this pathological "normality"
      c. Therapy should not force the patient back into an alienated state but should foster the development of a true self

D. The impact of the humanistic-existential perspective
   1. Has been limited because the individuality of its proponents does not permit a united front in an effort to produce change
   2. But it has influenced the development of group therapies, and
   3. It has fostered a therapeutic focus on the here-and-now realities of the client's life

E. Comparing the humanistic-existential and psychodynamic perspectives
   1. Similarities
      a. Both emphasize the role of screening out parts of one's existence in the development of pathology
      b. Both emphasize insight as an essential part of therapy
   2. Differences
      a. The dynamic approach depends on insight provided by the therapist, while the humanistic-existential approach depends on insight provided by the client
      b. Dynamic therapists stress insight into the past while humanistic-existential therapists stress insight into the present
      c. While dynamic approaches strive to reduce problems, humanistic-existential approaches strive to go beyond the normal

F.  Criticisms of the humanistic-existential perspective
    1.  There is little emphasis on scientific research and verification
    2.  There is a dependence on unprovable assumptions such as free will and a tendency toward self-actualization
    3.  The insistence on phenomenology makes this approach too subjective

## KEY TERMS
*The following terms are in bold print in your text. Define them and practice their definitions using the flash cards at the end of the chapter.*

anal stage (31)
anxiety (29)
castration anxiety (37)
client-centered therapy (44)
clinical evidence (40)
collective unconscious (36)
conditions of worth (44)
defense mechanism (29)
denial (30)
depth hypothesis (26)
displacement (30)
ego (28)
ego ideal (28)
ego identity (38)
ego psychology (37)
Electra complex (32)
fixation (34)
genital stage (34)
hierarchy of needs (44)
humanistic-existential
    perspective (42)
id (27)
identification (30)
intellectualization (30)

interpretation (27)
isolation (30)
latency (32)
latent content (27)
libido (28)
logotherapy (47)
manifest content (27)
masculine protest (36)
neuroses (34)
object relations (39)
Oedipus complex (32)
oral stage (31)
penis envy (32)
perceptual conscious (27)
phallic stage (32)
phenomenological approach
    (43)
pleasure principle (28)
positive regard (44)
preconscious (27)
projection (29)
psychoanalysis (26)
psychodynamic perspective
    (26)

psychosexual development
    (31)
psychosis (34)
psychosocial development
    (38)
rationalization (30)
reaction formation (30)
reality principle (28)
regression (30)
repression (29)
self-actualization (43)
self psychology (39)
separation-individuation
    (39)
structural hypothesis (27)
sublimation (31)
superego (28)
unconscious (27)
undoing (30)
valuing process (43)
will-to-meaning (47)

*Your text does not list the following terms as formal vocabulary; however, if you don't know what they mean, you will be unable to grasp the concepts of this chapter.*

accessible (27)
alienated (45)
altruistic (32)
antagonizing (28)
autonomous (37)
chronological (38)
continuum (42)
corollary (43)
dichotomy (42)
dismal (41)
docile (44)
empathy (43)

extraneous (44)
incestuous (32)
ineradicable (33)
intransigent (28)
intrapsychic (27)
metaphors (29)
monopoly (42)
neurologist (26)
orthodox (42)
overt (41)
permeating (27)
psyche (27)

renounce (33)
repository (27)
resilient (39)
reverting (30)
siblings (38)
stratagem (47)
subsuming (28)
subterranean (42)
transcend (43)
validated (40)
vehemently (30)
vicariously (32)

## IMPORTANT NAMES
*Identify the following persons and their major contributions to abnormal psychology as discussed in this chapter.*

Alfred Adler (36)
Erik Erikson (37)
Viktor Frankl (47)
Sigmund Freud (26)
Heinz Hartmann (37)

Karen Horney (37)
Carl Jung (36)
Heinz Kohut (39)
R. D. Laing (47)
Margaret Mahler (39)

Abraham Maslow (44)
Rollo May (46)
Carl Rogers (43)
Harry Stack Sullivan (37)

## GUIDED SELF-STUDY

THE PSYCHODYNAMIC PERSPECTIVE

1. There is one man's name that I could mention that every one of you would probably recognize at once as a person in the field of psychology. Who do you think it is? (If you were correct, did you spell it correctly?)

2. If I had said his name, what would have been the first thing that popped into your mind?

3. Use following terms to fill the following blanks—**psychodynamic, psychoanalysis,** and **psychoanalytic.**

   (a)_____ is the name of Freud's theory; however, the whole line of thought that has

   developed out of his work is called the (b)_____ perspective. Freud is called the father

   of (c)_____ theory; however, many theorists have since altered some of Freud's

   theory and developed their own theories to add to this perspective. So, Freud's (d)_____

   theory is an example of (e)_____ theory, but all (f)_____ theory is **not**

   (g)_____ theory.

4. While the psychodynamic perspective on psychology may be interpreted in different ways by different psychologists, almost everyone who takes this point of view would agree on three basic ideas. Match these phrases to their explanations.
   a. **unconscious**              b. **early childhood**              c. **psychic determinism**

   ___ Behavior is not freely chosen by the individual
   ___ Individuals are unaware of most of their psychological processes
   ___ The most important time of psychological development

For Questions 5-9 use the following terms to complete the statements—**id, ego, superego, depth hypothesis, childhood, unconscious, preconscious, (perceptual) conscious, latent, manifest,** and **interpret**.

5. The key concept of psychoanalysis, which is said to be Freud's most important contribution to

   psychology, is the _____ _____ . This is Freud's idea that the causes of behavior are mostly unconscious.

6. Write in the appropriate level of consciousness next to its definition:

   (a) _____     The range of things you are aware of now
   (b) _____     Things you are not aware of but could recall if you tried
   (c) _____     Things you are not aware of and cannot recall even if you try

7. Freud believed that the most important mental processes are on the _____ level.

8. Therefore, Freud believed that it was necessary to (a) _____ what we say, dream, or do in order to understand what we really mean. In a dream, for example, the obvious plot that

   you tell about is the (b) _____ content. The symbolic meaning of the dream is the

   (c) _____ content.

9. Freud also believed that the personality consisted of three "structures." These are

   the (a)_____, the (b)_____, and the (c)_____.

10. Freud's personality theory is sometimes represented with the image of an iceberg. An iceberg (or an ice cube, for that matter) is mostly underwater, with only a little showing above the surface. The part above water is like the conscious mind, the part deeply under water is like the unconscious, and the part just below the surface is like the preconscious. The id, ego, and superego are then divided among these levels. Refer to the diagram as you write the name of the personality structure next to the characteristics that apply to it:

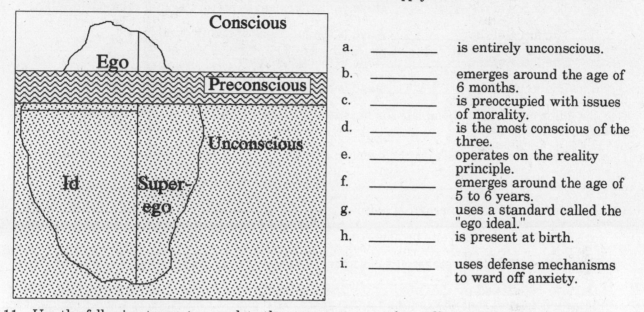

a. _____ is entirely unconscious.

b. _____ emerges around the age of 6 months.

c. _____ is preoccupied with issues of morality.

d. _____ is the most conscious of the three.

e. _____ operates on the reality principle.

f. _____ emerges around the age of 5 to 6 years.

g. _____ uses a standard called the "ego ideal."

h. _____ is present at birth.

i. _____ uses defense mechanisms to ward off anxiety.

11. Use the following terms to complete the statements—**anxiety, distort, id, ego, superego, and defense mechanism.**
In the normal individual, the (a)_____ is the personality structure that organizes the conscious life of the person. When this personality structure is threatened by reality, or by impulses

from the (b)_____, or by demands from the (c)_____, the result is (d)_____. An ego

(e)_____ _____ is what the ego uses to (f)_____ reality to reduce unbearable anxiety.

12. Write the name of the proper defense mechanism next to its definition:

| | | |
|---|---|---|
| **Rationalization** | **Sublimation** | **Displacement** |
| **Intellectualization** | **Denial** | **Isolation** |
| **Regression** | **Repression** | **Identification** |
| **Reaction formation** | **Projection** | **Undoing** |

a. _____ transforms unacceptable impulses into more socially appropriate forms.

b. _____ moves emotional reactions from an original situation or object to a different, safer situation or object.

c. _____ cuts emotional responses off from the events that cause them.

d. _____ is the refusal to acknowledge the existence of a source of anxiety.

e. _____ is the most fundamental defense mechanism. It pushes unacceptable material into the unconscious.

f. _____ attributes one's own unacceptable impulses to other people.

g. _____ finds socially acceptable reasons for doing what is unacceptable.

h. _____ replaces an emotional experience with an intellectual understanding.

i. _____ takes one back to a time of life when issues were more easily dealt with.

j. _____ handles unacceptable feelings by changing them into their opposites.

k. _____ is ritual behavior to erase effect of an unacceptable impulse.

l. _____ is attaching psychologically to a group to reduce anxieties.

13. In Freud's view, personality develops over the span of childhood in a number of stages. List Freud's stages and one period of psychosexual development in their proper order:

14. Use the stages that you listed in previous question as answers to be placed in the following blanks.
    a.  The focus of the _____ stage of development is mature sexual relationships.

    b.  The focus of the _____ stage is the functions of bodily elimination.

    c.  The focus of the _____ stage is mouth behavior.

    d.  The focus of the _____ stage is the sexual organs.

Use the following terms to complete the next two questions—**penis envy, fixated, castration anxiety,** and **phallic**.

15. The Oedipus complex is a crucial event in the (a)_____ stage. During this stage, boys

    experience (b)_____ _____, while girls experience (c)_____ _____.

16. If an individual fails to progress naturally through a given stage because of some traumatic

    experience, the person may become stuck, or _____ in that stage.

17. Since three of the four stages of development have occurred by age (a)_____ years, and since

    this age is followed by the (b)_____ period during which little of psychosexual significance occurs, it follows that the first half dozen years are the most important in the development of the personality.

These terms will complete the next three questions: **id, neuroses, superego, psychoses,** and **balance.**

18. In Freud's theory, the normal personality may have ongoing conflicts among the id, the ego, the superego, and the real world, but to remain normal the ego must be able to maintain a

    dynamic _____ among these forces.

19. In the abnormal personality, psychic energy is divided unevenly and the id or superego may

    gain disproportionate power. When the (a)_____ is dominant, the result may be an amoral,

    impulsive individual. When the (b)_____ dominates, excessive guilt or suspiciousness may be the result.

20. In the less severe forms of abnormality, an individual may be troubled and inefficient in

    living, but still retain reality contact. These types of problems are called (a)_____.
    In more severe disorders, reality contact may be lost because of overwhelming conflict and the

    breakdown of defenses. These problems are called (b)_____.

**REVIEW!  REVIEW!!  REVIEW!!!**

21. Freud's (a)_____ theory has expanded into a major line of thinking called the

    (b)_____ perspective which assumes that we are shaped by internal mental processes, although Freud's followers differ on the nature and relative importance of these mental processes. (This is a review of Question 3 material.)

22. For a further review, see if you can remember the three basic principles that psychodynamic theorists agree on. You considered these in Questions 4, 5, and 6. No fair looking back. Let's go for a reality check here. Do you or don't you know them? If you cannot remember them, you need to make up a memory trick to start etching them into your memory.

a.

b.

c.

23. Now list three directions that post-Freudian theorists have taken that depart from Freud substantially.

a.

b.

c.

24. Write the name of the appropriate post-Freudian thinker in front of each identifying phrase. Hint: the names are **Jung, Adler, Sullivan, Hartmann, Erikson, Mahler, Horney, and Kohut.**

a. _____ coined the term "inferiority complex."

b. _____ proposed eight stages of development.

c. _____ pioneered the treatment of severe disorders.

d. _____ was a major founder of "ego psychology."

e. _____ emphasized object relations theory.

f. _____ spoke of separation-individuation.

g. _____ believed that parents give child calmness and greatness.

h. _____ developed concept of collective unconscious.

i. _____ emphasized a striving for superiority.

j. _____ developed concept of narcissistic personality disorder.

k. _____ identified psychosocial, not psychosexual stages.

l. _____ proposed "basic" anxiety.

m. _____ was an early female psychoanalytic thinker.

25. Psychodynamic theory is criticized on a number of grounds and it is credited with a number of contributions to the field of psychology. Identify each of the following as a **credit** or a **criticism**.

a. _____ Demythologized mental illness
b. _____ Does not lend itself to straight forward experimental testing
c. _____ Stimulated advances in therapy
d. _____ Interpretations of the unconscious are subjective
e. _____ Based on unrepresentative, culturally biased sample
f. _____ Focused twentieth century thinking on the "inner" world
g. _____ A reductive interpretation of life

THE HUMANISTIC-EXISTENTIAL PERSPECTIVE

26. The humanistic-existential movement in psychology is largely a reaction against what was

    perceived as the sterile and deterministic positions of the _____ and behavioral
    (discussed next chapter) points of view.

27. Freud is seen as pessimistic about human nature, but the humanistic-existential psychologists

    believe that people are innately (a)_____, and they wanted to restore the study of the

    uniquely (b)_____ qualities to psychology.

28. Humanistic psychology and existential psychology share basic ideas but differ from each other
    because they emphasize different things. Write in **shared** or **humanistic** or **existential** for
    for each of the following concepts.

    a. _____ Takes exception to the concept of determinism
    b. _____ Sees uniqueness of the individual
    c. _____ Talks about alienation, defined as spiritual death
    d. _____ Takes the phenomenological approach
    e. _____ Is concerned about meaninglessness in life
    f. _____ Believes in human potential
    g. _____ Believes the individual has freedom and responsibility
    h. _____ Has an emphatically positive view of the human being

29. Write the name **Rogers** or **Maslow** in the space before each of the following identifying
    concepts:

    a. _____ Congruence between the self and the organism
    b. _____ The hierarchy of needs
    c. _____ Client-centered therapy
    d. _____ The "psychopathology of the normal"
    e. _____ Conditions of worth
    f. _____ The valuing process
    g. _____ Uses the term "self-actualization

30. Identify the following existential psychologists. Use the names **Laing**, **May**, or **Frankl** as
    answers for this question and for Question 31 as well.

    a. "I believe that life demands a response from us. We must find meaning for our existence.

       A life without meaning is a life not worth living. My name is _____."

    b. "I believe that what we sometimes call insanity is in fact real authenticity. It represents

       the refusal of the person to play along with a crazy culture. My name is_____."

    c. "I believe you cannot understand a person without stepping into that person's experience.
       You have to ask about the totality of the self to see the significance of a given event. My

       name is _____."

31. Write the appropriate name in the space before the following identifying concepts.

    a. _____ The ontological context
    b. _____ Social phenomenology
    c. _____ The will-to-meaning
    d. _____ The preservation of a center
    e. _____ Logotherapy
    f. _____ Mental disorder as a strategy for living the unlivable

32. Summarize how the humanistic-existential perspective has influenced each of the following issues in psychological therapies.

    a.  The client-therapist relationship

    b.  Group therapies

    c.  "Transpersonal" techniques in therapy

33. Determine which of the following concepts apply to the psychodynamic approach (**P**), the humanistic-existential approach (**H-E**), or to both (**B**), and mark the space before each statement accordingly.

    a.  ____ insight into the past
    b.  ____ insight provided by client
    c.  ____ insight in general
    d.  ____ insight provided by the therapist
    e.  ____ screening out experience leads to problems
    f.  ____ what the client says has heavy symbolic significance
    g.  ____ therapy corrects problems and makes you normal
    h.  ____ therapy frees you to develop your potential

34. Explain how mainstream scientific psychologists criticize the humanistic-existential perspective on each of the following points:

    a.  Scientific values and practices

    b.  The issue of free will

    c.  Phenomenology

35. Now explain how humanistic-existential psychologists would answer each of these criticisms.

    a.

    b.

    c.

## HELPFUL HINTS

1.  Be alert to learning the specific psychological definitions of textbook terms. Psychological terms have sometimes been adopted for general conversational use. Their conversational usages sometimes are quite different from their technical psychological definitions. Don't just glance at a vocabulary word, recognize it, and move on to the next term. Read the definition closely to see if that definition is consistent with the usage with which you are familiar. For instance, "his/her ego is bigger than it needs to be" does not relate to the way Freud used the term "ego."
2.  Do not let your personal opinions of the value of the different perspectives impair your learning. Frequently, I have students who totally reject "all that sexuality" in psychoanalytic theory. (Freud would say that was massive denial.) Because of this attitude, these students may not seriously study Freud's theory. Skipping over Freud's theory does not punish Freud; it only undermines the student's grade. Freudian theory is not going to go away. It is one of the major psychological theories. Even though my (SJB) viewpoint is not Freudian, over the years I have come to find some areas of Freudian theory to be very useful.
3.  Notice that there are two ego defense mechanisms that are very similar in spelling: repression and regression. Don't confuse them.
5.  Freud has *four stages* of psychosexual development. The latency period is termed a *period*,

not a stage.  So, when you learn Freud's four psychosexual stages in order, what you really have to know are Freud's *four stages* and *one period* in order.  If you are asked how many psychosexual *stages* Freud theorized, the answer is *four* even though you had to learn five terms in order to cover psychosexual development.

6.  Memory trick for three basic principles of psychodynamic theories:

D = Determinism,  U = Unconscious,  C = Childhood

Are you a *DUC*k, or *CUD* you remember those three psychodynamic principles?  Don't think my memory trick dumb, unless you make up a better one.  I just make them up on the spot.  That's what I hope you will learn to do if your memory is less than perfect.  Using memory skills actively can improve your grades.

## PRACTICE TEST
*Take the following test several times as you study the chapter.  Write your answers on a separate sheet of paper and after each attempt, note in the tally box above each question whether your answer was correct or incorrect.*

1.  Freud's "depth psychology hypothesis" refers to his belief that
    a.   deep brain structures are more important to thinking than the cortex.
    b.   the conscious mind is only the "tip of the iceberg," and much more lies beneath the surface.
    c.   we can understand ourselves by thinking deeply about our feelings and experiences.
    d.   hypnosis is the best way to probe the mind.

2.  According to Freud, the structures of the personality develop in which order?
    a.   Id, ego, superego
    b.   Ego, id, superego
    c.   Id, superego, ego
    d.   All three develop at the same time.

3.  Judy is having trouble living a happy life because she always seems to feel guilty about everything she does.  Freud would say she is suffering from
    a.   an uncontrollable id.                    c.   loss of reality contact.
    b.   an overactive superego.                  d.   an overinflated ego.

4.  Which defense mechanism is most likely to be socially productive?
    a.   Rationalization                          c.   Intellectualization
    b.   Reaction formation                       d.   Sublimation

| 1 | 2 | 3 | 4 |
|---|---|---|---|

5.  Waldo does some impulsive things now and then but he always manages to come up with a good reason or excuse for what he does.  This sounds like the defense mechanism called
    a.   rationalization.                         c.   regression.
    b.   projection.                              d.   denial.

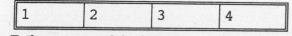

6. The manifest content of a dream is what you tell your psychoanalyst about. His job is to help you discover the
   a.  individual content.
   b.  latent content.
   c.  psychosocial content.
   d.  cathartic content.

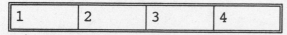

7. Erikson is noted for his
   a.  eight psychosexual stages.
   b.  belief that personality development continues throughout the lifespan.
   c.  departure from Freud's view on the structure of the unconscious.
   d.  focus on the separation-individuation process.

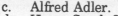

8. Freud thinks your problems all stem from sexual and aggressive conflicts left over from childhood. I disagree. I think you should view the matter in terms of a desire to be a competent and superior person. My name is
   a.  Carl Jung.
   b.  Heinz Kohut.
   c.  Alfred Adler.
   d.  Harry Stack Sullivan.

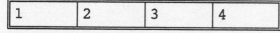

9. Which of the following criticisms has been leveled at the psychodynamic approach?
   a.  It depends too much on inference.
   b.  It doesn't take parental influence seriously enough.
   c.  It is not reductionistic enough.
   d.  It is influenced too much by Freud's religious beliefs.

| 1 | 2 | 3 | 4 |

10. Freud's theory is called "deterministic." This means that his ideas focus on
    a.  the biological causes of mental disorder.
    b.  developing the willpower needed to be your true self.
    c.  identifying unnecessary complications in life to control stress and improve mental health.
    d.  the things largely beyond our control that make us who we are.

| 1 | 2 | 3 | 4 |

11. When we say that the humanistic-existential approach to psychology assumes the phenomenological point of view, we mean that
    a.  it views a person's behavior from an external, objective point of reference.
    b.  it tries to experience the person's reality from the person's own point of view.
    c.  the behavior of people must be understood through a symbolic interpretation of the past.
    d.  it rejects the mental and tries to concentrate on physical processes only.

| 1 | 2 | 3 | 4 |
|---|---|---|---|

12. To an existentialist, being "alienated" means
    a. acting on every impulse, no matter how small.
    b. being haunted by a sense of meaninglessness in life.
    c. the belief that one has been abducted by aliens.
    d. finding one's assigned role in society and happily accepting it.

| 1 | 2 | 3 | 4 |
|---|---|---|---|

13. Cecil has had all the experiences that the rest of us normally have, good and bad, but for some reason all he can think about are his failures and his embarrassments. His mother was a very critical woman, and Cecil could never live up to her stern expectations. Rogers would say that there is little _____ between his organism and his self.
    a. consistency              c. congruence
    b. awareness                d. communication

| 1 | 2 | 3 | 4 |
|---|---|---|---|

14. Place Maslow's needs in the proper ascending order (most basic to most complex).
    a. Self-actualization, esteem, belongingness, safety, biological
    b. Esteem, self-actualization, safety, biological, belongingness
    c. Safety, biological, esteem, belongingness, self-actualization
    d. Biological, safety, belongingness, esteem, self-actualization

| 1 | 2 | 3 | 4 |
|---|---|---|---|

15. A central concept in Karen Horney's approach to psychology is
    a. the search for meaning.
    b. a striving for superiority.
    c. the quest for self-actualization.
    d. coping with basic anxiety.

| 1 | 2 | 3 | 4 |
|---|---|---|---|

16. The humanistic-existential perspective differs from the psychodynamic perspective in that the psychodynamic types are more
    a. future-oriented.
    b. concerned with immediate experience.
    c. likely to interpret a patient's problem for him or her.
    d. convinced of the client's ability to run his or her own life.

| 1 | 2 | 3 | 4 |
|---|---|---|---|

17. If I go to a humanistic-existential psychologist, I will quickly discover that the cure for my problem is expected to come from
    a. within me.
    b. learning new behaviors.
    c. adhering to social standards.
    d. understanding repressed information.

32

| 1 | 2 | 3 | 4 |

18. The humanistic-existential perspective has been criticized on which of the following grounds?
   a. It insists on treating people only in hospital settings.
   b. Its followers charge too much for their services.
   c. It is too new to have developed any methods of patient follow-up.
   d. It is unscientific.

| 1 | 2 | 3 | 4 |

19. Which of the following statements best reflects what the humanistic-existential perspective means by the concept of "human potential"?
   a. Optimum mental health means going beyond the normal and fully developing your capabilities.
   b. There is no limit to anything anyone can do. Even mind reading and ESP are possible.
   c. Our most human capability is to bear suffering. If you try hard enough you can endure anything.
   d. Intelligence can be increased beyond our present limits if we just learn how to use the 80% of the brain that presently lies dormant.

| 1 | 2 | 3 | 4 |

20. Which of the following is *not* one of the fundamental assumptions of the humanistic-existential perspective?
   a. The uniqueness of the individual
   b. Freedom and responsibility
   c. Human potential
   d. A striving for superiority

## ANSWERS
### Self-Study Exercise

1. Freud
2. Sex (if you are typical)
3. a. Psychoanalysis     e. psychodynamic
   b. psychodynamic     f. psychodynamic
   c. psychodynamic     g. psychoanalytic (26)
   d. psychoanalytic
4. c, a, b (26)
5. depth hypothesis (26)
6. a. (perceptual) conscious
   b. preconscious
   c. unconscious (27)
7. unconscious (27)
8. a. interpret
   b. manifest
   c. latent (27)
9. a. id (27)
   b. ego (28)
   c. superego (28)
10. a. Id (27)     f. Superego (28)
    b. Ego (28)     g. Superego (28)
    c. Superego (28)     h. Id (27)
    d. Ego (28)     i. Ego (28)
    e. Ego (28)
11. a. ego (28)     d. anxiety (28)
    b. id (27)     e. defense mechanism (29)
    c. superego (28)     f. distort or deny (29)

12. a.  Sublimation (31)
    b.  Displacement (30)
    c.  Isolation (30)
    d.  Denial (30)
    e.  Repression (29)
    f.  Projection (30)
    g.  Rationalization (30)
    h.  Intellectualization (30)
    i.  Regression (30)
    j.  Reaction formation (30)
    k.  Undoing (30)
    l.  Identification (30)
13. Oral stage, anal stage, phallic stage, latency period, genital stage (31-32)
14. a.  genital (32)
    b.  anal (31)
    c.  oral (31)
    d.  phallic (32)
15. a.  phallic
    b.  castration anxiety
    c.  penis envy (32)
16. fixated (34)
17. a.  six
    b.  latency (32)
18. balance (34)
19. a.  id (34)
    b.  superego (34)
20. a.  neuroses (34)
    b.  psychoses (34)
21. a.  psychoanalytic
    b.  psychodynamic (26,36)
22. Determinism, unconsciousness, childhood experience (26)
23. a.  an emphasis on the ego
    b.  an emphasis on social relationships
    c.  an extension of the developmental period (34-35)
24. a.  Adler (36)
    b.  Erikson (37-39)
    c.  Sullivan (37)
    d.  Hartmann (37)
    e.  Mahler (39)
    f.  Mahler (39)
    g.  Kohut (39-40)
    h.  Jung (36)
    i.  Adler (36)
    j.  Kohut (39-40)
    k.  Erikson (37-39)
    l.  Horney (37)
    m.  Horney (37)
25. a, c, and f are credits
    b, d, e, and g are criticisms  (41-42)
26. psychodynamic (42)
27. a.  positive, or good
    b.  human (42)
28. a.  Shared
    b.  Shared
    c.  Existential
    d.  Shared
    e.  Existential
    f.  Shared
    g.  Shared
    h.  Humanistic (42-43;45-46)
29. a.  Rogers (43-44)
    b.  Maslow (44-45)
    c.  Rogers (43-45)
    d.  Maslow (43-44)
    e.  Rogers (43-44)
    f.  Rogers (43-44)
    g.  Rogers and Maslow (43-44)
30. a.  Frankl (47)
    b.  Laing (47-48)
    c.  May (46-47)
31. a.  May (46-47)
    b.  Laing (47-48)
    c.  Frankl (47)
    d.  May (46-47)
    e.  Frankl (47)
    f.  Laing (47-48)
32. a.  The client-therapist relationship is now seen more as a partnership instead of one in which power is in the hands of the therapist (48).
    b.  The social emphasis of the humanistic-existential approach has increased the mental health profession's awareness of the potential for group treatment. The humanistic-existential approach has also pioneered many group techniques (48).
    c.  The humanistic-existential perspectives focus on the inner world has increased interest in many previously ignored techniques which manipulate or make use of the subjective experience of the person (48).

33. a. Psychodynamic (26-27)
    b. Humanistic-Existential (48)
    c. both (48)
    d. Psychodynamic (48)
    e. both (48)
    f. Psychodynamic (27)
    g. Psychodynamic (48)
    h. Humanistic-Existential (48)
34. a. Some humanists and existentialists are hostile to the scientific approach, and thus place themselves outside of the mainstream of psychological study.
    b. The humanistic-existential approach assumes the existence of free will, a concept that has no scientific evidence to support it.
    c. There is no way of knowing if the conclusions arrived at by the phenomenological approach are really pertinent to the client or merely the subjective interpretations of the therapist (48).
35. a. The scientific approach is an inappropriate way to study people. Since we have free will, we can choose not to obey scientific "laws" (42,48).
    b. Free will is assumed because it is a fact of subjective experience—it needs no scientific proof (48).
    c. The phenomenological approach is the only approach that will work with unique, free individuals (48).

## Practice Test

1.  b   (27)
2.  a   (28)
3.  b   (28)
4.  d   (31)
5.  a   (30)
6.  b   (27)
7.  b   (38)
8.  c   (36)
9.  a   (41)
10. d   (26)

11. b   (43)
12. b   (45-46)
13. c   (44)
14. d   (45)
15. d   (37)
16. c   (48)
17. a   (48)
18. d   (48)
19. a   (43)
20. d   (43)

# CONCEPT MAP 2.1

Fill out the boxes marked with question marks (?) with the concepts or words you think belong there. Possible answers suggested by the authors are on a following page.

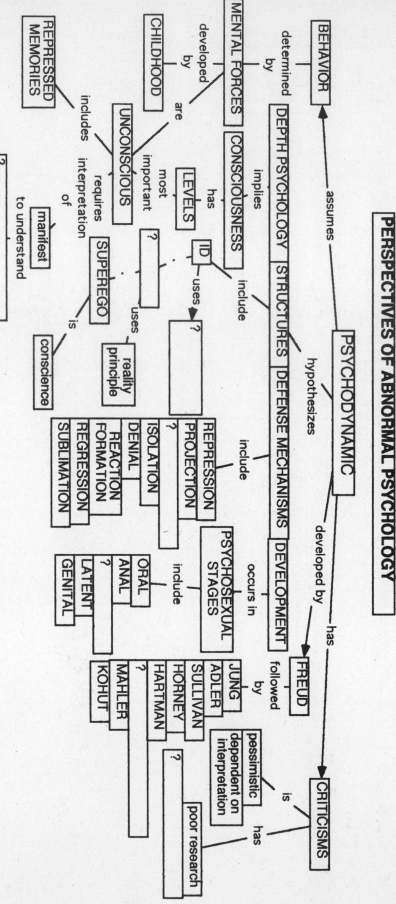

36

# CONCEPT MAP 2.2

Fill out the boxes marked with question marks (?) with the concepts or words you think belong there.  Answers suggested by the author are on a following page.

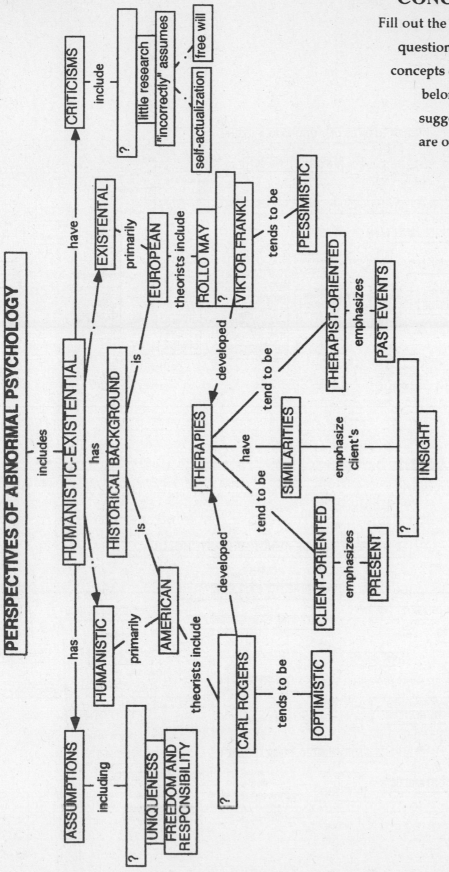

PERSPECTIVES OF ABNORMAL PSYCHOLOGY

includes → HUMANISTIC-EXISTENTIAL

have → CRITICISMS → include → [?], little research, "incorrectly" assumes → free will, self-actualization

HUMANISTIC-EXISTENTIAL → has → EXISTENTAL → primarily → EUROPEAN → theorists include → ROLLO MAY, [?], VIKTOR FRANKL → tends to be → PESSIMISTIC

developed → THERAPIES

HUMANISTIC-EXISTENTIAL → is → HISTORICAL BACKGROUND → is

HUMANISTIC-EXISTENTIAL → has → HUMANISTIC → primarily → AMERICAN → theorists include → CARL ROGERS → tends to be → OPTIMISTIC

CARL ROGERS → developed → THERAPIES

THERAPIES → have → SIMILARITIES → emphasize client's → [?]

THERAPIES → tend to be → THERAPIST-ORIENTED → emphasizes → PAST EVENTS

THERAPIES → tend to be → CLIENT-ORIENTED → emphasizes → PRESENT

INSIGHT

PERSPECTIVES OF ABNORMAL PSYCHOLOGY → has → ASSUMPTIONS → including → [?], UNIQUENESS, FREEDOM AND RESPONSIBILITY

37

## CONCEPT MAP 2.1

The suggested answers are
shown in *italics*.

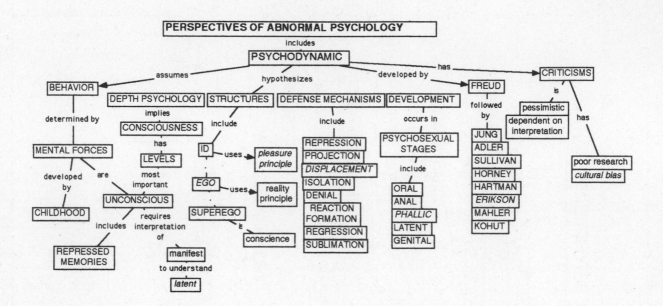

## CONCEPT MAP 2.2

The suggested answers are
shown in *italics*.

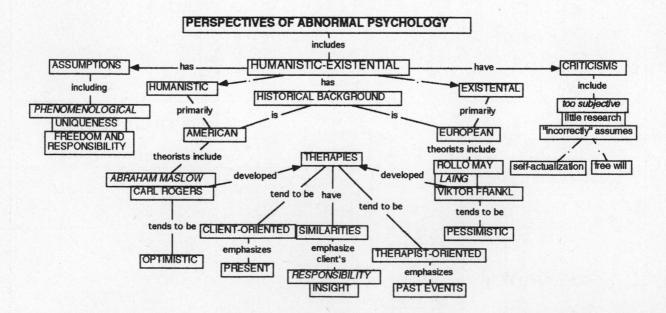

| | | |
|---|---|---|
| 2.1 **anal stage** | 2.8 **defense mechanism** | 2.15 **ego psychology** |
| 2.2 **anxiety** | 2.9 **denial** | 2.16 **Electra complex** |
| 2.3 **castration anxiety** | 2.10 **depth psychology hypothesis** | 2.17 **fixation** |
| 2.4 **client-centered therapy** | 2.11 **displacement** | 2.18 **genital stage** |
| 2.5 **clinical evidence** | 2.12 **ego** | 2.19 **hierarchy of needs** |
| 2.6 **collective unconscious** | 2.13 **ego ideal** | 2.20 **humanistic-existential perspective** |
| 2.7 **conditions of worth** | 2.14 **ego identity** | 2.21 **id** |

# DEFINITIONS (Cut out on the lines to use as Flash Cards)

| | | |
|---|---|---|
| **2.15** A post-Freudian school of thought which emphasizes less deterministic & less biologically oriented psychology; holds that the ego has its own energy and autonomous functions apart from the id. | **2.8** Any psychic stratagem that reduces anxiety by concealing the source of anxiety from the self and the world. | **2.1** In psychodynamic theory, the second stage of psychosexual development; a child focuses on the pleasurable feelings of retaining and expelling the feces; occurs in the second year of life |
| **2.16** According to Freud, the desire that female children have during the phallic stage to do away with their mother in order to take sexual possession of their father | **2.9** The refusal to acknowledge the source of distress | **2.2** A state of increased physiological arousal and generalized feelings of fear and apprehension |
| **2.17** A psychic mechanism in which a person experiences anxiety at a certain stage of development and fails to progress beyond that stage | **2.10** Freud's view that almost all mental activity happens unconsciously | **2.3** In psychodynamic theory, the male child's fear that his penis will be cut off as punishment for his sexual desire of his mother |
| **2.18** According to Freud, the final phase of mature sexuality, by which he meant heterosexual genital mating. | **2.11** A defense mechanism that involves the transfer of emotion from an unacceptable object to a safer one. | **2.4** Roger's therapeutic procedure in which a safe environment created by reflecting the patient's perceptions & offering unconditional positive regard allows the patient to confront feelings inconsistent with the self |
| **2.19** Maslow's concept of a series of needs that must be satisfied one by one in the process of development before the adult can begin pursuing self-actualization | **2.12** In Freudian theory, the psychic component of the mind which mediates between the id, reality, and the superego | **2.5** Observations of patients in therapy (e.g. case studies) |
| **2.20** A diverse approach to abnormal psychology whose proponents generally agree that behavior is both willed and purposive and that humans choose their lives and therefore are responsible for their lives. | **2.13** In Freudian theory, composite picture of values and moral ideals held by the superego | **2.6** According to Jung, the unconscious life of all human beings, which is composed of many common elements and not just sexual strivings as Freud contended |
| **2.21** According to Freud, the sum of the biological drives with which a person is born. | **2.14** Erikson's belief that the ego does more than just assimilate values of a parent, that it goes on to form an integrated, unique, and autonomous "self." | **2.7** According to Rogers, the values incorporated by the child that dictate which of his or her self-experiences are "good" and which are "bad." |

| 2.22 identification | 2.29 logotherapy | 2.36 penis envy |
|---|---|---|
| 2.23 intellectualization | 2.30 manifest content | 2.37 perceptual conscious |
| 2.24 interpretation | 2.31 masculine protest | 2.38 phallic stage |
| 2.25 isolation | 2.32 neuroses | 2.39 phenomenological approach |
| 2.26 latency | 2.33 object relations theorists | 2.40 pleasure principle |
| 2.27 latent content | 2.34 Oedipus complex | 2.41 positive regard |
| 2.28 libido | 2.35 oral stage | 2.42 preconscious |

# DEFINITIONS (Cut out on the lines to use as Flash Cards)

| | | |
|---|---|---|
| 2.36 In psychoanalytic theory, the female child's feeling that she has been born unequipped with a penis because of her sexual desire toward her father; counterpart of castration anxiety | 2.29 Frankl's technique for dealing with the spiritual aspect of psychopathology; the therapist confronts patients with their responsibility for their existence and their need to pursue life's values | 2.22 In psychodynamic theory, the incorporation of the same-sex parent's values, standards, sexual orientation, and mannerisms as part of the development of the superego |
| 2.37 In Freudian theory, the first level of the mind's consciousness, which contains whatever requires no act of recall | 2.30 In psychoanalytic theory, the content of a dream as seen and reported by the individual (Cf. latent content.) | 2.23 The avoidance of unacceptable feelings by repressing these feelings and replacing them with an abstract intellectual analysis of the problem |
| 2.38 In psychoanalytic theory, the 3rd stage of psychosexual development; pleasure is derived from masturbation, the stroking & handling of the genitals; occurs from the third to the fifth or sixth year of life | 2.31 Adler's name for the unwarranted belief that men are superior to women, due to unequal distribution of power in society | 2.24 Freud's primary technique for revealing a patient's hidden intrapsychic motives |
| 2.39 A therapeutic procedure in which the therapist attempts to see the patient's world from the vantage point of the patient's own internal frame of reference | 2.32 Conditions in which maladaptive behaviors serve as a protection against a source of unconscious anxiety | 2.25 In Freudian theory, a defense mechanism that separates feelings from the events to which they are attached. The feelings are repressed, and the events are viewed without emotion |
| 2.40 In Freudian theory, the tendency of the id to devote itself exclusively to the immediate reduction of tension | 2.33 Recent psychodynamic theorists who believe that the most powerful determinant of psychological development is the child's relationship with the mother. See separation-individuation | 2.26 The dormancy or hiddenness of a particular behavior or response. |
| 2.41 As defined by Rogers, people's need for affection and approval from those most important to them, particularly parents | 2.34 According to Freud, the desire all male children have during the phallic stage to do away with their father in order to take sexual possession of their mother | 2.27 In psychoanalytic theory, the unconscious material of a dream that is being expressed in disguised fashion through the symbols contained in the dream |
| 2.42 In Freudian theory, the second level of the mind's consciousness, which consists of whatever the person can remember without great difficulty | 2.35 In psychoanalytic theory, the first stage of psychosexual development, in which the mouth is the primary focus of libidinal impulses and pleasure; occurs in the first year of life | 2.28 In psychoanalytic theory, the energy of the life instinct, which Freud saw as the driving force of personality |

# CHAPTER TERMS (Cut out on the lines to use as Flash Cards)

| | | |
|---|---|---|
| 2.43 **projection** | 2.50 **reaction formation** | 2.57 **structural hypothesis** |
| 2.44 **psychoanalysis** | 2.51 **reality principle** | 2.58 **sublimation** |
| 2.45 **psychodynamic perspective** | 2.52 **regression** | 2.59 **superego** |
| 2.46 **psychosexual development** | 2.53 **repression** | 2.60 **unconscious** |
| 2.47 **psychosis** | 2.54 **self-actualization** | 2.61 **undoing** |
| 2.48 **psychosocial development** | 2.55 **self psychology** | 2.62 **valuing process** |
| 2.49 **rationalization** | 2.56 **separation-individuation** | 2.63 **will-to-meaning** |

# DEFINITIONS (Cut out on the lines to use as Flash Cards)

| | | |
|---|---|---|
| 2.57<br><br>Freud's belief that the mind can be divided into three basic forces: the id, the ego, and the superego | 2.50<br>A state in which a person represses feelings that are arousing anxiety and then vehemently professes the exact opposite of those feelings | 2.43<br><br>A defense mechanism whereby unacceptable impulses are first repressed and then attributed to others. |
| 2.58  A defense mechanism by which impulses are channeled away from forbidden outlets and toward socially acceptable ones | 2.51<br><br>In Freudian theory, the way in which the ego seeks to gratify the desires of the id, with safety as its main concern | 2.44  The psychodynamic therapy method that relies on techniques of free association, dream interpretation, & analysis of resistance and transference; the aim is insight into patients' unconscious conflicts & motives |
| 2.59<br>In Freudian theory, that part of the mind in which the person has incorporated the moral standards of the society | 2.52<br><br>A defense mechanism that involves the return to an earlier, less threatening developmental stage that one has already passed through | 2.45<br>A school of thought based on the assumption that human behavior is a function of events occurring within the mind and is explainable only in terms of those mental events |
| 2.60  In Freudian theory, the largest level of the mind's consciousness, which contains all memories not readily available to the perceptual conscious, because they have been forgotten or repressed | 2.53<br><br>A defense mechanism in which unacceptable id impulses are pushed down into the unconscious and thereby forgotten | 2.46  Freud's theory that personality development takes place in a series of stages, in each of which the child's central motivation is to gratify the drive for pleasure in a different bodily zone |
| 2.61<br><br>A defense mechanism in which ritualistic thought or behavior is designed to cancel out unacceptable impulses | 2.54<br>According to Rogers, the fulfillment of all an individual's capabilities | 2.47<br><br>Any severe psychological disorder in which a person's perception of reality is drastically distorted |
| 2.62<br>Rogers' theory that people judge experiences as self-enhancing or not; self-enhancing experiences are sought after, and negative experiences are avoided | 2.55  Kohut's view, based on his work with narcissistic personality patients, that development of the self depends on the child's receiving from parents confirmation of a sense of greatness, calmness & infallibility | 2.48<br>Erikson's theory of personality development, consisting of a series of chronological stages extending from birth to death |
| 2.63<br>In existential philosophy, the struggle of human beings to find some reason for their troubled, complicated, and finite existence | 2.56  Four-stage process, outlined by Mahler, by which an infant separates psychologically from the mother; beginning at five months, the infant undergoes differentiation, vacillating between pleasure and terror | 2.49  A defense mechanism in which socially acceptable reasons are offered for something that is done for unconscious and unacceptable reasons |

# Chapter 3

# The Behavioral, Interpersonal, Cognitive and Sociocultural Perspectives

## LEARNING OBJECTIVES
*By the time you are finished studying this chapter, you should be able to:*

### THE BEHAVIORAL PERSPECTIVE
1. Describe the major contributions of Pavlov, Watson, Thorndike, and Skinner to behavioral psychology (54-56).
2. List and explain four fundamental assumptions of the behavioral approach (56-57).
3. Briefly summarize the basic processes of respondent and operant conditioning (57-58).
4. Define reinforcement, and distinguish between primary, secondary, positive, and negative reinforcement (58).
5. Define punishment and distinguish between positive and negative punishment (58).
6. Describe the processes of extinction, generalization, discrimination, habituation, shaping, and modeling (59-61).
7. Summarize the behavioral view of mental disorder and treatment (61-63).
8. List and discuss three criticisms that have been leveled at the behavioral perspective, as well as three contributions attributed to this point of view (64-65).

### THE COGNITIVE PERSPECTIVE
9. Summarize the essential position of the cognitive perspective (65).
10. Describe the contributions of Ellis, Beck, Mischel, and Bandura to the cognitive perspective (66-68).
11. Discuss the role of selective attention, schemas, and beliefs in information processing (69).
12. Summarize the pros and cons of the cognitive perspective (69-70).

### THE INTERPERSONAL PERSPECTIVE
13. Summarize the essential position of the interpersonal perspective (70).
14. Explain communication theory, structural theory, the interpersonal circle, and complementarity as related to the interpersonal perspective (70-71).
15. Summarize the pros and cons of the interpersonal perspective (72-73).

### THE SOCIOCULTURAL PERSPECTIVE
16. List and discuss two ways in which the sociocultural perspective accounts for abnormal behavior (73-74).
17. Summarize the pros and cons of the sociocultural perspective (75).

## CHAPTER OUTLINE

I. The behavioral perspective

    A. The background of behaviorism
       1. Behaviorism is a reaction against introspective approaches to psychology
       2. Pioneering contributors
          a. Ivan Pavlov, a Russian neurophysiologist, *not* psychologist, discovered the (classical) conditioned reflex

      b.    John B. Watson developed Pavlov's ideas into a learning-based approach to psychology

      c.    Edward Thorndike formulated the "law of effect," stressing the impact of the consequences of behavior on learning

      d.    B. F. Skinner developed Thorndike's ideas into modern operant conditioning theory and refined the law of effect into the "principle of reinforcement"

B.   The assumptions of behavioral psychology
    1.   The proper focus of psychology is the study of behavior
    2.   The empirical method is the means by which behavior should be studied
    3.   The goal of psychology is the prediction and control of behavior
    4.   Behavior is acquired through learning

C.   The mechanisms of learning
    1.   Respondent (classical) conditioning examines how events (stimuli) elicit behaviors (responses) from an organism
       a.    Respondent behavior is behavior that occurs automatically in reaction to a stimulus
       b.    An unconditioned stimulus (UCS) produces an unlearned (reflexive) reaction
       c.    A conditioned stimulus (CS) comes to produce a learned reaction through pairing with a UCS
       d.    An unconditioned response (UCR) is the unlearned reaction produced by a UCS
       e.    A conditioned response (CR) is the learned reaction produced by a CS
    2.   Operant conditioning examines how the consequences of behavior affect the likelihood of that behavior occurring again
       a.    Operant behavior is behavior that operates on and produces reactions (consequences) from the environment
       b.    Reinforcers are consequences that increase the likelihood of behavior
          (1)   Primary reinforcers directly satisfy biological needs
          (2)   Conditioned (secondary) reinforcers are influential because they have been paired with primary reinforcers
          (3)   Positive reinforcers strengthen behavior when *presented* after the behavior
          (4)   Negative reinforcers strengthen behavior when *removed* after the behavior (avoidance learning)
       c.    Punishers are consequences that decrease the likelihood of behavior
          (1)   Positive punishers are desirable consequences that are earned by withholding a behavior
          (2)   Negative punishers are aversive consequences that are imposed following a behavior
       d.    Extinction decreases the likelihood of a behavior through removal of reinforcers
       e.    Generalization is the tendency to respond to similar stimuli in the same way
       f.    Discrimination (opposite of generalization) is the ability to distinguish between similar stimuli and respond to them individually
       g.    Habituation is a decrease of responding following repeated exposure to a stimulus
       h.    Shaping is the reinforcement of successive approximations to a desired behavior
       i.    Modeling is learning through imitation

D.   Abnormal behavior as a product of learning
    1.   Abnormal behavior is learned through the same processes as normal behavior
    2.   There is no need to assume an underlying "pathology"
    3.   Behavior therapy uses learning to help people acquire more adaptive patterns of responding
       a.    Respondent therapies tend to focus on emotional and motivational problems (e.g., systematic desensitization)
       b.    Operant therapies tend to focus on changing voluntary behaviors
       c.    Both approaches may combine direct conditioning with cognitive elements

E.   Evaluating behaviorism
    1.   Criticisms of behaviorism
       a.    A learning approach oversimplifies behavior

    b. It's deterministic stance offends some people's conceptions of themselves by denying free will

    c. Its frank discussion of control makes some fear the misuse of psychological knowledge

  2. Contributions of behaviorism

    a. Its objective orientation puts it on a solid scientific footing

    b. Its reluctance to label behavior as "abnormal" (only "maladaptive") can allow for more individualism among people

    c. A number of quite effective behavior therapies are in use

II. The cognitive perspective

  A. The background of the cognitive perspective

    1. It reflects a long-standing interest of psychologists in the mental process

    2. It is a reaction against the non-mental outlook of early behaviorism

  B. Cognitive behaviorism

    1. Albert Ellis

      a. Irrational beliefs, not events themselves, cause distress and maladaptive behavior

        (1) I *must* be successful

        (2) Others *must* be nice to me

        (3) Life *must* be fair

      b. Therapy consists of achieving a more rational view of life

    2. Aaron Beck

      a. Distorted thinking is associated with mental disorder

        (1) Magnification

        (2) Overgeneralization

        (3) Selective abstraction

      b. Therapy replaces distorted thoughts with more realistic ones

  C. Cognitive appraisal

    1. We do not simply react to stimuli but rather insert a mental (cognitive) interpretation of that stimulus between it and our response to it

    2. Attributions are the beliefs we have regarding the causes of behavior

    3. Cognitive variables affecting behavior

      a. Competencies—skills to be applied to the situation

      b. Encoding strategies—perceptual tendencies

      c. Expectancies—how we assume things will turn out

        (1) Outcome expectations (the situation)

        (2) Efficacy expectations (your own abilities)

      d. Values—things we like or dislike

      e. Plans and goals—intended patterns of action

  D. Self-reinforcement

    1. Many reinforcers come from within (self-talk)

    2. Self-reinforcement may account for learning in situations where external reinforcement is not present (e.g., modeling)

  E. Information processing

    1. Automatic processing—quick, well-learned responses

    2. Controlled processing—active integration of data to develop a response

    3. Selective attention allows us to "input" information for processing

    4. Organizing structures allow us to make sense out of information

      a. Schemas—structures that organize information about narrow areas of life

      b. Beliefs—things we assume to be true

  F. Evaluating the cognitive perspective

    1. Criticisms

      a. It is unscientific because it relies on inference about unobservable mental states

      b.    The mental states it studies may not be the important variables in a person's life
      c.    Its association with computer science leads to charges of oversimplification and sterility
   2.   Contributions
      a.    Much empirical data about cognition has been collected
      b.    Cognitive models are useful in understanding abnormality
      c.    Cognitive therapies are effective and useful

III.  The interpersonal perspective looks at relationships as a source of problems

   A.   Systems theories focus on habitual relationship patterns, typically in families
      1.   Communication theory focuses on faulty communication as a source of pathology
      2.   Structural theory (Minuchin) focuses on functional "units" within groups and how these units interact or mesh
   B.   The interpersonal circle plots interactions as functions of
      1.   Control (the dominant/submissive dimension) and
      2.   Affiliation (the friendly/hostile dimension)

   C.   Abnormal behavior is seen as resulting from destructive interpersonal behavior tendencies that support (complement) each other
      1.   Depression may result from one person's submissiveness being made worse by another person's dominance
      2.   Substance abuse or obesity may involve others who unwittingly perpetuate problem behavior in the substance/food abuser (identified patient)

   D.   Evaluating the interpersonal perspective
      1.   Contributions
         a.    It appeals to dynamic theorists because of its focus on relationships
         b.    It appeals to cognitive theorists because of its emphasis on mental processes
         c.    It encourages a broader treatment perspective of identified patient *plus* others who may also be affected
         d.    It encourages examination of the complications possible in the therapist/client relationship
      2.   Criticisms
         a.    Not all of its findings are solidly supported by repeated research
         b.    While relationship issues may be important in determining the direction or severity of a problem, there is little evidence that they are root causes

IV.  The sociocultural perspective

   A.   Psychopathology as the product of social pathology
      1.   Economic and other problems in society have their effects on individual functioning in general
      2.   When society treats certain groups or individuals less well than others, those at a disadvantage are more likely to show pathological effects

   B.   Psychopathology as a social institution
      1.   The mentally "ill" may have done nothing but violate social norms
      2.   Norm violators are labeled as "abnormal" to remove them from serious consideration by others
         a.    Labels place one into a social role with behavioral expectations attached
         b.    Labels are unfairly allocated based on social class

   C.   Evaluating the sociocultural perspective
      1.   Criticisms
         a.    The perspective oversimplifies things by placing problems in society and neglecting the person
         b.    Labeling in itself is insufficient to explain most problems
      2.   Contributions
         a.    This perspective forces us to look at larger causes for individual problems

## KEY TERMS
*The following terms are in bold print in your text. Define them and practice their definitions using the flash cards at the end of the chapter.*

attribution (67)
behavior therapy (63)
behavioral perspective (54)
cognition (65)
cognitive appraisal (67)
cognitive behaviorism (66)
cognitive perspective (65)
conditioned reflex (54)
conditioned reinforcers (58)
conditioned response (57)
conditioned stimulus (57)
contingency (58)
discrimination (59)

extinction (59)
generalization (59)
habituation (60)
interpersonal perspective (70)
law of effect (56)
learning (54)
modeling (61)
negative reinforcement (58)
operant behavior (57)
operant conditioning (57)
positive reinforcement (58)
primary reinforcer (58)

punishment (58)
reinforcement (58)
respondent behavior (57)
respondent conditioning (57)
schema (60)
selective attention (69)
shaping (60)
sociocultural perspective (73)
systems theories (70)
unconditioned response (57)
unconditioned stimulus (57)

*Your text does not list the following terms as formal vocabulary; however, if you don't know what they mean, you will be unable to grasp the concepts of this chapter.*

aversive (58)
coercion (64)
complementary (72)
continuum (61)
designate (74)
domain (69)
dysfunction (69)
efficacy (68)
empathetic (73)
endowment (61)
engender (63)

futile (64)
global (67)
inferred constructs (65)
inhibit (63)
inordinate (69)
intangibles (64)
intrinsically (74)
irrational (66)
maladaptive (61)
methodology (57)
nebulous (57)

prognosis (75)
provocation (73)
quibbles (64)
rigor (64)
schisms (71)
stereotypes (74)
suppression (58)
synonymous (57)
totalitarian (64)
transitory (74)

## IMPORTANT NAMES
*Identify the following persons and their major contributions to abnormal psychology as discussed in this chapter.*

Albert Bandura (68)
Aaron Beck (66)
Albert Ellis (66)
Mary Cover Jones (63)
Salvador Minuchin (71)

Walter Mischel (68)
Ivan Pavlov (54)
Thomas Scheff (74)
B. F. Skinner (56)
Edward Thorndike (56)

Edward Tolman (65)
John B. Watson (55)
Joseph Wolpe (63)

## GUIDED SELF-STUDY

1.  To get your mind geared up and your overview organized, list the seven perspectives that were listed in Chapter 1.


2.  Which perspectives were discussed in Chapter 2?

3.  Without looking, can you recall which perspectives are covered in this chapter? See how many you can recall.


4.  For closure, which one of the perspectives listed in Chapter 1 is still left to be covered?

5.  One more important point of review:

    Behaviorism = (a)_____     Cognition = (b)_____

Refer to Chapter 1 Helpful Hints in this study guide if you did not get this one correct; you have already missed some critical material.

THE BEHAVIORAL PERSPECTIVE

6. Behaviorism arose as a reaction to introspection, which was the predominant psychological

   investigative technique used in the late (a) _____ century.
   (b) Explain how introspection worked.


7. What did the behaviorists want to do instead of introspection?


8. Ultimately, the behaviorists were looking for changes in environmental stimulation that led to changes in behavior. This process of behavior change resulting from environmental influence

   is called _____.

9. Note which of four major behaviorists is associated with each of the following phrases. The answers are: **Ivan Pavlov, John B. Watson, Edward Thorndike,** and **B. F. Skinner**.

   a. _____ The Law of Effect
   b. _____ Scaring a baby with furry objects
   c. _____ Salivating dogs
   d. _____ Little Albert
   e. _____ Founded the behavioral movement
   f. _____ Established importance of consequences in learning
   g. _____ Renamed the Law of Effect as the Principle of Reinforcement

10. Use the following terms to complete the four basic assumptions of classical behaviorism: **process of learning, empirical method, observable behavior,** and **prediction and control of behavior**.
    a. The proper focus of psychology is the study of _____.

    b. The proper method of psychological study is the _____.

    c. The goal of psychology is the _____.

    d. Behavior is acquired through the _____.

11. What are the two types of learning that are the basis of behaviorism?

    a.                                    b.

RESPONDENT CONDITIONING

12. What Pavlov discovered surprised none of you who have pets: pets learn what events signal "food!" To what signals (stimuli) do your pets respond?


13. Now to get Pavlov's discovery into psychological terms. However, as we convert to psychological terms, don't scare yourself; it is still the same simple process that you already understand with your pets. Okay, here we go:

    **unlearned stimulus —> (leads to) unlearned behavior**
    **neutral stimulus + unlearned stimulus —> (leads to) unlearned behavior**

    When, through repeated pairings with an unlearned stimulus, the neutral stimulus comes to cause the specific behavior all by itself, that stimulus is no longer neutral; it has become a

    (a) _____. Also, since the response is no longer automatic, but occurs after a stimulus that had to be learned, the response is a (b) _____.

So now the situation looks like this:

**learned (previously neutral) stimulus —> learned (previously unlearned) behavior**

c.  Now write this whole process out, using the term "unconditioned" for unlearned and "conditioned" instead of learned.


Continue to write out this process using the correct terms until you can write it from memory.  If you are like most students, this page probably does not allow you enough practice spaces. You will need to work on a separate sheet of paper.


14.  MORE PRACTICE WORKING WITH CLASSICAL CONDITIONING TERMS!  Use each of these terms only once to make the best match with the following phrases.

**Reflex**       **Learning**      **Unconditioned**
**Reflexes**     **Neutral stimulus**    **Conditioned stimulus**
**Stimulus**     **Respondent conditioning**
**Response**     **Conditioned**

a.  _____ Event which triggers a behavior
b.  _____ Another name for classical conditioning
c.  _____ An automatic behavior that does not have to be learned
d.  _____ Behavior caused by a stimulus
e.  _____ Salivation, blink, sneeze, and knee jerk
f.  _____ Process of behavior change in response to the environment
g.  _____ Means "learned"
h.  _____ Means "not learned"
i.  _____ An event which triggers no particular response
j.  _____ Was originally the neutral stimulus

15.  For each of the following scenarios, decide which behavior or stimulus fits below each of the headings on the chart.

a.  An abused child has learned that when its parent starts to curse, it is going to be hit. The child now flinches when certain four-lettered words are said.

b.  A cat is fed Moist Munchies which come in individual cellophane packets.  The cat no longer has to be called to its food.  When cellophane paper wrappers are rattled in the kitchen, the cat appears—ready to eat.

c.  A cancer patient taking chemotherapy becomes nauseated at the sight of a physician on TV. (The side effects of some of the medications used for chemotherapy include nausea.)

d.  Watson's conditioning process with Little Albert

| Unconditioned Stimulus | Unconditioned Response | Neutral Stimulus | Conditioned Stimulus | Conditioned Response |
|---|---|---|---|---|
| a. | | | | |
| b. | | | | |
| c. | | | | |
| d. | | | | |

16. If you answered Question 15 correctly, whatever was written in the Neutral Stimulus column

was also written in the (a)_____ column, and whatever was written in the

Unconditioned Response column was also written in the (b)_____ column.

17. Now, if in Question 15, the conditioned stimuli are really the same as the neutral stimuli, and the conditioned responses are really the same as (or very similar to) the unconditioned responses, why are the terms changed?




18. If the cat in Question 15-b starts to salivate when Granny takes her peppermint candy from

its cellophane wrapper, the cat has (a)_____ its response to all crackling cellophane

sounds. In other words the response has (b)_____ to more than just the specific stimulus
with which it was originally paired.

19. Little Albert generalized when _____.

20. The process which is the opposite of generalization is (a)_____, which means you

(b)_____.

OPERANT CONDITIONING

21. **BEFORE or AFTER?** Stimuli can come either before a behavior or after a behavior. While

Pavlov and Watson looked at stimuli that came (a)_____ behavior, Thorndike

looked at stimuli that came (b)_____ behavior. Now we are going to look at operant conditioning. Don't tense up; remember how easy respondent conditioning was—the pet salivated when a learned stimulus signaled "food!" The only thing you had to remember was the terminology. This one is just as easy.

Okay! Here it is: Creatures do what they get paid to do. You knew that about people. That was no surprise. It is also true of other creatures: dogs, cats, birds, fish, flat worms, bears, seals, elephants, to name a few. The main idea is this: Behavior leads to a payoff. Stated in terms that psychologists use:

**Response   ->   Stimulus consequence**
**(or, in other words)**
**Behavior   ->   Payoff**

22. Use the following terms to identify the phrases. Terms may be used more than once.

| | | |
|---|---|---|
| **Shaping** | **Positive punishment** | **Instrumental** |
| **Reinforcer** | **Contingency** | **conditioning** |
| **Habituation** | **Primary reinforcers** | **Negative punishment** |
| **Modeling** | **Conditioned reinforcers** | **Extinction** |

a. _____ An aversive consequence that decreases the likelihood of a response
b. _____ Trophies, blue ribbons, money, and gold stars
c. _____ Rewards that satisfy biological needs
d. _____ Secondary reinforcers
e. _____ Another name for operant conditioning
f. _____ Food, water, and oxygen
g. _____ "Being able to sleep through anything" after living in a noisy dorm
h. _____ A bribe to stop biting one's fingernails
i. _____ Removing the consequence from a behavior

j. _____ Any stimulus consequence that increases the likelihood of a response
k. _____ Reinforcing successive approximations of the desired behavior
l. _____ The perceived association between an action and a consequence
m. _____ A caretaker who whispers so the children learn to speak softly

23. Number the following sequence for shaping a dog to rollover.  Number one will be the first behavior that you reinforce.
_____ Looks at trainer
_____ Head movement that starts body to roll
_____ Comes when called
_____ Rolls completely over
_____ Lays down
_____ Sits down

24. Mark the following instances as **Generalization** or **Discrimination**.

a. _____ Smiling only at the teachers who are giving you good grades
b. _____ Smiling only at the teachers from whom you need small miracles
c. _____ Smiling at all your teachers after smiling at the first one produced some "good attitude" points
d. _____ Taking a lost-looking freshman under your wing because he/she reminds you of your kid brother/sister back home

25. a. In behaviorism, what is always the "right" word?
b. So how do you think behaviorists explain abnormal behavior?????

(Please notice that behaviorists do acknowledge that one starts off with a genetic endowment.)

26. Here is an example of a behavior problem that can be understood from the point of view of operant conditioning: A kid gets choked on a piece of candy while at grandma's house and throws up.  After the choking is remedied, the grandma soothes the kid by telling him that he'll get an ice cream cone on the way home.  A few days later when visiting grandma again, the kid once more acts like he is choking and then throws up.  Grandma checks to see there are no symptoms of illness and no physical cause of choking.

Let's look at two possible scenarios for this situation:

Scenario A—Grandma cleans the kid up and then gives him a dish of his favorite ice cream.  What is going to happen here?

Scenario B—Grandma cleans the kid up, and instructs him to wash his mouth out to freshen his mouth after vomiting. What is going to happen here?

27. You have a problem.  You never manage to get to class registration early enough to get that required course that you dread taking.  What type of reinforcement is maintaining this problem behavior on your part?

28. The therapy that behaviorists do is called (a)_____. It is based on (b)_____

principles.  That means we can expect that these therapies will involve (c)_____and/or

(d)_____ conditioning.

29. For example, systematic desensitization uses (a)_____ conditioning to relieve anxiety by

pairing the (b)_____ with a (c)_____ state.

30. Mark each of the following as a **criticism** of behaviorism or a **contribution** to the field of psychology by behaviorism.
    a. _____ Made psychology more empirical
    b. _____ Looks only at small, isolated units of behavior and ignores intrapsychic events
    c. _____ Acknowledgement of the effects of slightly different environments encourages awareness of individual differences.
    d. _____ Determinism
    e. _____ Devised effective new alternatives to use in therapeutic treatments
    f. _____ External control of people
    g. _____ Oversimplification
    h. _____ Puts people under same principles of operation as animals or machines
    i. _____ Objectivity
    j. _____ Discounts any free will

COGNITIVE PERSPECTIVE

31. The interest in cognitive processes, such as (a)_____, _____,and_____ _____,

    has been around a long time. However, not until the decade of the (b)_____ did the cognitive perspective enter abnormal psychology. Cognition is an important part of abnormal psychology for two reasons:

    c.

    d.

After making all the fuss that I have, telling you cognition = thinking and behaviorism = learning, and never the two shall meet and don't confuse them, I am now going to tell you there are cognitive behaviorists!

32. Let's build on what you already know. There are psychologists who say that although they

    are not observable behaviors, thoughts, also called (a)_____, are internal events that operate according to learning principles. We also remember that "learning" translates to

    (b)_____. So what should we call these psychologists who combine cognition and

    learning???? We call them (c)_____ _____.

33. Use the following terms to complete the blanks: **appraisal, content, learning, intermediate steps.**

    Cognitive theorists are those theorists who are more interested in the (a)_____ of

    thoughts than how the principles of (b)_____ determine what thoughts will be maintained and which ones will be extinguished and which ones will serve as reinforcers for other internal

    or external behaviors. Cognitive behaviorists see thoughts as (c)_____ between

    stimuli and responses. The cognitive (d)_____ process explains why people respond to the same stimulus in different ways.

34. Cognitive theorists say the most powerful reinforcement is (a)_____, which is

    reinforcement that comes from (b)_____.

35. Cognitive theorists and behaviorists agree that behavior should be studied (a)_____, through observation and measurement; however, cognitive theorists think that

    (b)_____ is open to scientific study and behaviorists do not.

36. Edward Tolman went so far as to say that (a)_____ was not the be-all and end-all of learning. Oh! That is heresy to hard-line behaviorists! His theory has not wrecked basic behaviorism, but it does serve to point out where the cognitive behaviorists are going to part company from the plain behaviorists.

    b.     What did Tolman and Honig do to demonstrate that some learning does take place without payment?

37. Write in the name of the theorist associated with each of the following terms. **Ellis, Beck, Mischel,** and **Bandura** are the theorists from which to choose.
    a. _____ Competencies—things we do well
    b. _____ Distorted thinking
    c. _____ Irrational beliefs
    d. _____ Encodings—the way we perceive the world
    e. _____ Expectancies—how we think things will turn out
    f. _____ Outcome expectancies
    g. _____ Rational-emotive therapy
    h. _____ Efficacy expectancies
    i. _____ Magnification
    j. _____ Overgeneralization
    k. _____ Selective abstraction
    l. _____ Plans—intentions, rules and guidelines for behavior
    m. _____ Values—things we like and dislike

38. List the three dimensions of attributions.

## INFORMATION PROCESSING

39. (a)_____ is an area of cognitive research that considers how the mind takes in, stores, and uses information. This area of study has made a distinction between two types of processing that the mind does: controlled processing and automatic processing. List behaviors that you do that fit in each of these categories.

    b.     Automatic processing:

    c.     Controlled processing:

40. Although some people object to the human mind being compared with a computer, why might the computer also complain about the analogy?

41. Why is selective attention a critical function of our cognitive abilities?

42. Name the two organizing structures proposed in cognitive theory.

43. Give your schema for a fast food restaurant.

44. List one of your personal beliefs that serves as a structure for how you perceive and think.

## INTERPERSONAL PERSPECTIVE

The interpersonal perspective looks at an individual's behavior as part of interactions with other people. Interpersonal therapists are primarily concerned with the individual's current relationships. The text looks at three theoretical approaches within this perspective. (Two of them, communications theory and structural theory, are under a larger heading called systems theory.)

45. Complete the following chart for terms associated with each of the three approaches within this perspective: **Enmeshment, Ambiguous, Complementarity, Affiliation, Silent schisms, Disengaged relationships, Double-bind, Boundaries**, and **Control**.

| Interpersonal Circle | Communications theory | Structural theory |
|---|---|---|
| | | |

46. List contributions that the interpersonal perspective has made to the field of psychology.

    a.

    b.

    c.

47. List two criticisms of the interpersonal perspective.

    a.

    b.

## THE SOCIOCULTURAL PERSPECTIVE

48. What causes "abnormal" behavior, according to this group?

49. Use the following words to complete the following discussion of the sociocultural perspective: **labeling, stigmatizing, individual, limiting, lower, society**. Words may be used more than once.

    "Psychopathology as a social institution" basically says it is not the individual who cannot

    cope, but that it is (a)_____ which cannot cope with the individual. (b)_____ is assigning a person to some category that he/she seems to fit into for one reason or another. Whether labels are "good" or "bad" depends on the context of the situation; however, labels are always

    (c)_____. If the individual is labeled as fitting into a specific category, both that

    (d)_____ and (e)_____ may subtly cause that individual to come to behave more in accord with the labeling category. This is called a self-fulfilling prophecy. Also, research

    indicates there is discrimination in labeling against those individuals from (f)_____

    socioeconomic levels. They are more likely to be labeled with more (g)_____ labels.

50. Has having a label attached to you ever had any impact on your life?

51. State two criticisms and one contribution of the sociocultural perspective to the study of abnormal behavior.

52. What are reasons other than labeling that might cause more mentally ill people to be at the lower end of the socioeconomic ladder?

a.

b.

c.

## HELPFUL HINTS

1. In case you did not learn the following point from Helpful Hints in Chapter One, I am repeating it because it is even more critical to your being able to deal with this chapter.
   a. *Anytime* you hear the word "behaviorism," translate it to "learning" until you become comfortable with behaviorism as a concept unto itself.
   b. Translate the word "cognitive" to "thinking" until you become comfortable with the term cognitive.
   c. Do not mix up the words "learning" and "thinking."
2. Make sure you know all the names that respondent and operant conditioning are called; otherwise you may miss a question because you did not recognize what was being asked for.
3. Here are two different words that look similar: *elicit* and *illicit*. *Elicit* means to cause to come forth and is the term used repeatedly in connection with stimuli "eliciting" certain responses. *Illicit* means illegal.
4. This visual may help some of you with the concepts discrimination and generalization. If you had to place a > notation between the words generalization and discrimination, toward which word would you aim the point? The pointed end is aimed at discrimination because discrimination is very precise. The broad (open) end should be next to generalization because generalization is broad, not precise and sharp (pointed) as discrimination is. Now, if that makes sense to you, all that you have to remember is: discrimination < generalization.
5. Etch in your brain *REINFORCEMENT = INCREASE*. Anytime an increase in behavior is mentioned, we are talking reinforcement.
6. I (SJB) love a chart or flow diagram. There is a wonderful chart on page 62. Don't overlook it!
7. As I mentioned in earlier chapters, don't let your attitude about concepts prevent you from learning them. Sometimes I hear negative statements about behaviorism because of determinism and the issue of control. Regardless of your attitude, *learn* about the issues. If you still feel negatively about them later, then at least you will *know* something about the concepts you are rejecting.

## PRACTICE TEST
*Take the following test several times as you study the chapter. Write your answers on a separate sheet of paper and after each attempt, note in the tally box above each question whether your answer was correct or incorrect.*

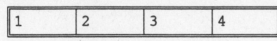

1. The law of effect was the work of
   a. Ivan Pavlov.
   b. John B. Watson.
   c. Edward Thorndike.
   d. David Premack.

2. "Conditioning" refers to the process of
   a. learning.
   b. generalizing.
   c. introspecting.
   d. thinking.

| 1 | 2 | 3 | 4 |

3. If you become tense when you hear a dentist's drill, you have been exposed to
   a. preparedness training.
   b. operant conditioning.
   c. respondent conditioning.
   d. instrumental learning.

| 1 | 2 | 3 | 4 |

4. I am participating in an experiment in which an apparatus buzzes briefly and then taps me gently just below the knee, causing my leg to jerk. This is repeated a number of times, and then the buzzing sound occurs alone, without being followed by the tap. Nevertheless, my leg moves anyway. The tap below the knee is
   a. an unconditioned stimulus.
   b. a neutral stimulus.
   c. a conditioned stimulus.
   d. an secondary stimulus.

| 1 | 2 | 3 | 4 |

5. Which of the following is true of positive and negative reinforcers?
   a. They are two words for the same thing.
   b. Positive reinforcers increase behavior while negative reinforcers decrease it.
   c. They can usually be identified only in laboratory conditions.
   d. They both increase the likelihood of behavior.

| 1 | 2 | 3 | 4 |

6. Which of the following is the best example of a secondary reinforcer?
   a. Food when you haven't eaten in 48 hours
   b. A warm blanket on a cold night
   c. Sexual contact when you are interested
   d. A paycheck after a week of hard work

| 1 | 2 | 3 | 4 |

7. Shaping is the process of
   a. controlling behavior by physical restraints.
   b. eliminating behavior by not reinforcing it.
   c. reinforcing successive approximations to a desired behavior.
   d. switching from primary to secondary reinforcement.

| 1 | 2 | 3 | 4 |

8. Eleanor goes to work each day, not because she gets anything great out of it, but because she needs the money to keep a roof over her head. Things would be worse if she didn't work. Eleanor is working for
   a. negative reinforcement.
   b. shaped consequences.
   c. extinction.
   d. positive reinforcement.

| 1 | 2 | 3 | 4 |

9. You wish to teach a dog a fairly complex trick that he is unlikely to do completely on the first try. Which learning technique would be the most appropriate?
   a. Modeling
   b. The Premack Principle
   c. Shaping
   d. Punishment

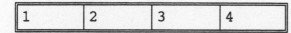

10. When Little Albert became afraid of a wide variety of white fuzzy objects after Watson scared him in the presence of the rat, he was demonstrating
    a. modeling.
    b. cognitive spread.
    c. discrimination.
    d. generalization.

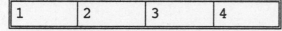

11. The behavioral approach has been criticized on all of the following *except*
    a. it is deterministic.
    b. it isn't objective enough.
    c. it oversimplifies things.
    d. its emphasis on control could be dangerous

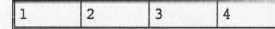

12. Which of the following is a contribution of the behavioral perspective?
    a. It has produced some efficient and effective treatment strategies.
    b. It has concentrated interest on the effects of early sexual abuse.
    c. It has removed the stigma associated with being a mental patient.
    d. It has proven the essential correctness of the medical model.

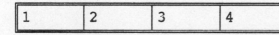

13. Cognitive psychologists differ from behaviorists in that they are
    a. more likely to investigate unseen mental processes.
    b. not as interested in viewing psychology as a science.
    c. still believers in the old Freudian analytical methods.
    d. more likely to perform controlled experiments on animal subjects.

| 1 | 2 | 3 | 4 |
| --- | --- | --- | --- |

14. Albert Ellis and Aaron Beck say the major cause of maladaptive behavior is
    a. a biologically based inability to perceive the world correctly.
    b. lack of appropriate learning before the age of three.
    c. marital and family conflict.
    d. irrational and self-defeating thoughts.

| 1 | 2 | 3 | 4 |
| --- | --- | --- | --- |

15. In the cognitive perspective, our beliefs about the causes of peoples' behavior are called
    a. appraisals.
    b. expectancies.
    c. attributions.
    d. encodings.

| 1 | 2 | 3 | 4 |
| --- | --- | --- | --- |

16. The interpersonal circle concept views relationships in terms of the two dimensions of
    a. operant and respondent learning.
    b. rational and irrational thinking.
    c. reinforcement and punishment.
    d. control and affiliation.

| 1 | 2 | 3 | 4 |
|---|---|---|---|

17. Betty says, "I used to think that a lot of mentally ill people were on the bottom of the socioeconomic ladder because they were too disturbed to make it in life. But now I think it is because poverty can drive people crazy." Betty is apparently a convert to
    a. the cognitive approach.
    b. the sociocultural perspective.
    c. Frankl's existential view.
    d. economic reductionism.

| 1 | 2 | 3 | 4 |
|---|---|---|---|

18. Bill drinks too much and is clearly in need of help. Which of the following statements is true?
    a. The behavioral perspective would see his drinking as a sign of deep personal issues.
    b. The sociocultural perspective would assume that he is thinking irrational thoughts.
    c. The interpersonal perspective would want his whole family in for treatment.
    d. The cognitive perspective would explain his problem in terms of labeling and social class.

| 1 | 2 | 3 | 4 |
|---|---|---|---|

19. One of the things the sociocultural perspective on mental disorder states is that
    a. society does its best to control behavior, but some people will go against cultural norms anyway.
    b. abnormal people cause abnormalities in society that can be corrected by intense concentration on individual behavior reform.
    c. The labeling of the mentally ill is the first step toward cure since it lets the person know that his or her behavior is wrong.
    d. if you call a person abnormal often enough, he or she might start acting that way.

| 1 | 2 | 3 | 4 |
|---|---|---|---|

20. Which of the following assertions about abnormal behavior offered by the sociocultural perspective is *least* supported by the evidence?
    a. Socioeconomic conditions contribute to psychological disturbance.
    b. Poor people often put off going for help until their problems get very bad.
    c. Psychological abnormalities are mainly an artifact of the labeling process.
    d. Economic status helps determine the quality of mental health care one receives.

## ANSWERS
### Self-Study Exercise

1. Psychodynamic, behavioral, cognitive, humanistic-existential, interpersonal, sociocultural, and biological (9)
2. Psychodynamic and humanistic-existential (25)
3. Behavioral, cognitive, interpersonal, and sociocultural (53)
4. The biological perspective, which is Chapter 4.
5. a. learning
   b. thinking
6. a. nineteenth
   b. Introspection is looking within one's own mind to see what is there. The subject was to report his/her ongoing conscious experience (54).
7. The behaviorists wanted to study something that was observable, objective, and verifiable by scientific methods. They wanted to observe behavior and the events surrounding it. These are phenomena that are observable and verifiable (54).
8. learning (54)
9. a. Thorndike (56)
   b. Watson (55)
   c. Pavlov (54)
   d. Watson (55)
   e. Watson (55)
   f. Thorndike (56)
   g. Skinner (56)

10. a. observable behavior
    b. empirical method
    c. prediction and control of behavior
    d. process of learning (56-57)
11. a. Respondent conditioning (57)
    b. Operant conditioning (57-58)
12. the sound of a can opener, the rattling of dishes, or the crumpling of a pet food bag
13. a. learned stimulus (57)
    b. learned response (57)
    c.

|  | Unconditioned Stimulus | -> | Unconditioned Response |
|---|---|---|---|
| Neutral stimulus + (becomes the) | Unconditioned Stimulus | -> | Unconditioned Response |
| Conditioned stimulus | - - - - - - - - - - - - - - - - - -> | | Conditioned response |

I hope you didn't look at a source until you made an effort. Did you get it right? What did you get wrong and why? Now try it again. Don't look at a source. How did you do this time? Do this process over and over until you can write it out perfectly. Ultimately you should be able to write:

$$
\begin{array}{rcl}
 & UCS & > & UCR \\
NS + & UCS & > & UCR \\
\overset{''}{CS} & \text{------------>} & & CR
\end{array}
$$

I REALLY DO RECOMMEND that you write this notation until you can do it effortlessly. If you just look at a source and copy it, you are aborting your learning experience. If you don't put your pencil to the paper and face that mental pain of realizing you don't know what to write, you have avoided that pain, yes, but you also have not learned.

14. a. Stimulus (57)
    b. Respondent (57)
    c. Reflex (57)
    d. Response (57)
    e. Reflexes (57)
    f. Learning (54)
    g. Conditioned (54, 57)
    h. Unconditioned (54, 57)
    i. Neutral stimulus (57)
    j. Conditioned stimulus (57)
15. a. Unconditioned stimulus—Hit
       Unconditioned response—Flinch
       Neutral stimulus—Curse
       Conditioned stimulus—Curse
       Conditioned response—Flinch (57)
    b. Unconditioned stimulus—Food
       Unconditioned response—Approaches food and salivates
       Neutral stimulus—Cellophane rattling
       Conditioned stimulus—Cellophane rattling
       Conditioned response—Approaches food and salivates (57)
    c. Unconditioned stimulus—Drug
       Unconditioned response—Nausea
       Neutral stimulus—Sight of doctor
       Conditioned stimulus—Sight of doctor
       Conditioned response—Nausea (57)
    d. Unconditioned stimulus—Loud noise
       Unconditioned response—Startle/fear
       Neutral stimulus—White rat
       Conditioned stimulus—White rat
       Conditioned response—Startle/fear (55, 57)
16. a. Conditioned Stimulus
    b. Conditioned Response (57)
17. The terms are changed because events are no longer really the same. The neutral stimuli are no longer neutral; they are learned because they now have the power to elicit responses all by themselves. And the unconditioned responses are no longer really unconditioned; they are being drawn out by new stimuli; so they are learned responses to the new stimuli (57).
18. a. generalized
    b. spread (59)
19. he responded to other white furry animals or objects with fear (55).

61

20. a. discrimination
    b. react to different stimuli in different ways (59).
21. a. before.
    b. after (56)
22. a. Negative punishment (58)         h. Positive punishment (58)
    b. Conditioned reinforcers (58)      i. Extinction (59)
    c. Primary reinforcers (58)          j. Reinforcer (58)
    d. Conditioned reinforcers (58)      k. Shaping (60)
    e. Instrumental conditioning (57)    l. Contingency (58)
    f. Primary reinforcers (58)          m. Modeling (60)
    g. Habituation (60)
23. 1, comes when called; 2, looks at trainer; 3, sits down; 4, lays down; 5, head movement that is the beginning of a roll; and 6, rolls over completely (60)
24. a. Discrimination                    c. Generalization
    b. Discrimination                    d. Generalization (59)
25. a. Learning (54)
    b. Learning! maladaptive behaviors (61)
26. a. The child is likely to continue to have vomiting episodes at grandma's house because the payoff (reinforcement) is getting a special treat.
    b. The child is not likely to continue to have the vomiting episodes if there is no physical cause and no payoff to maintain the response. If I paid you $500 every time you threw up, what would you do?
27. Negative reinforcement; this is avoidance learning (58).
28. a. behavior therapy                  c. respondent conditioning
    b. learning                          d. operant conditioning (63)
29. a. respondent
    b. anxiety producing stimulus
    c. relaxed (63)
30. a, c, e, and i are contributions; all the others are criticisms; If some of these looked very similar to you, great!! a and i are synonymous; b is the definition of g; and d, h, and j all refer to the same concept (64-65).
31. a. memory, reasoning, and problem solving
    b. 1970s
    c. Many abnormal disorders involve serious cognitive disturbances
    d. Certain cognitive patterns may actually cause some disorders instead of just being secondary symptoms (65).
32. a. cognitions
    b. behaviorism
    c. cognitive behaviorists (66)
33. a. content (65-69)                   c. intermediate steps (67)
    b. learning (66)                     d. appraisal (67)
34. a. self-reinforcement
    b. the things we say to ourselves about our own behaviors (68)
35. a. scientifically (66)
    b. subjective experience (54, 65)
36. a. reinforcement
    b. They conducted an experiment with rats which demonstrated that the rats learned while going through a maze without reinforcement. It was obvious they had learned because when given the opportunity to run the maze for "pay," they showed they could do it faster than naive rats (65).
37. a. Mischel (68)                      h. Bandura (68)
    b. Beck (66)                         i. Beck (66)
    c. Ellis (66)                        j. Beck (66)
    d. Mischel (68)                      k. Beck (66)
    e. Mischel (68)                      l. Mischel (68)
    f. Bandura (68)                      m. Mischel (68)
    g. Ellis (66)
38. global/specific, stable/unstable, internal/external (67)
39. a. Information processing (68)
    b. Automatic processing behaviors—driving in routine conditions, flipping the TV controller during commercials, dialing familiar phone numbers, searching for the car keys that you

chronically lose (68).
c. Controlled processing behaviors—learning to drive a car, ordering food from a restaurant's menu whose cuisine is unknown to you, deciding how you are going to tell your family that for the first time you are not coming home at all during vacation (68).

40. The computer might want to point out that it stores all information that it receives *and* stores it accurately. The human mind picks and chooses among which data bits it will store. The human mind also has serious problems with accuracy: it may store data bits to say what it wants them to say instead of recording them accurately (81).

41. We could not possibly process all the data that comes into our sensory channels. Selective attention directs the cognitive focus to those bits of data that are relevant for survival. For example, that little strange feeling about your ankle, your brain writes off as probably your pant leg. Your brain does not even mention it to you. However, when you are told someone has let a pet snake go in the library for "fun," your brain tells you to check out that little feeling about your ankle (78).

42. Schemas and beliefs (69)

43. Fast food restaurants—order at a central counter or drive-through, a standard menu, carry your own tray, no table cloths or table service, inexpensive fare (69)

44. Perhaps a religious or philosophical belief that influences how you see people

45. Communications theory - Double-bind, Ambiguous, Silent schisms (71)
Structural theory - Boundaries, Enmeshment, Disengaged relationships (71)
Interpersonal circle - Control, Affiliation, Complementarity (71)

46. a. Integrates a focus on underlying dynamics (the psychodynamic theorists) with a methodological approach of observable empirical measures of interpersonal exchanges which the cognitive behaviorists favor.
b. Brought attention to the necessity to treat a couple or family unit instead of just the "identified" patient
c. Brought attention to the innerworkings of the patient-therapist relationship (72).

47. a. Some of their theories have not seemed to be correct in view of experimental findings.
b. The view of the interpersonal perspective is too limited—interpersonal relationships are not the root cause of ALL! psychological disorders (73).

48. Problems in society cause individual people to have psychological problems (81).

49. a. society (73)          e. society (74)
    b. Labeling (74)         f. lower (74)
    c. limiting (74)         g. serious or stigmatizing (74)
    d. individual (74)

50. You probably have been: smart, slow, pretty, talented, rebellious, hyper, athletic, neat, messy, friendly, unfriendly, outgoing, or shy are some just to name a few. Whether labels are "good" or "bad" depends on the context you are in; however, labels are always limiting (74).

51. The contribution that the sociocultural perspective has made is to call attention to the fact that society exerts stress on individuals. This stress may cause or exacerbate psychological problems.
The sociocultural perspective is criticized for oversimplifying complex problems, neglecting the individual, and for attributing more to labeling than it can possibly explain (75).

52. a. Poor people have to cope with more serious threats.
b. Severely disturbed people tend to slip down the economic ladder because mental dysfunctions prevent them from holding jobs and working up to their skill potential.
c. Evidence suggest lower-class people resist getting mental health care and are, therefore, more advanced in pathology when they are finally diagnosed (75).

## Practice Test

| | | | | | | |
|---|---|---|---|---|---|---|
| 1. | c | (56) | | 11. | b | (64) |
| 2. | a | (54) | | 12. | a | (65) |
| 3. | c | (57) | | 13. | a | (65) |
| 4. | a | (57) | | 14. | d | (66) |
| 5. | d | (58) | | 15. | a | (67) |
| 6. | d | (58) | | 16. | d | (71) |
| 7. | c | (60) | | 17. | b | (73) |
| 8. | a | (58) | | 18. | c | (72) |
| 9. | c | (60) | | 19. | d | (74) |
| 10. | d | (59) | | 20. | c | (75) |

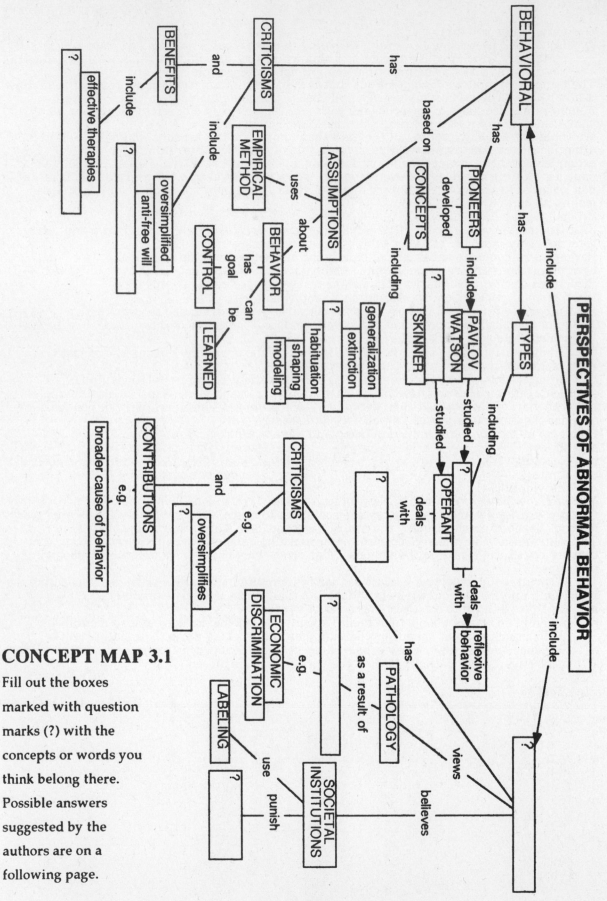

**CONCEPT MAP 3.1**

Fill out the boxes marked with question marks (?) with the concepts or words you think belong there. Possible answers suggested by the authors are on a following page.

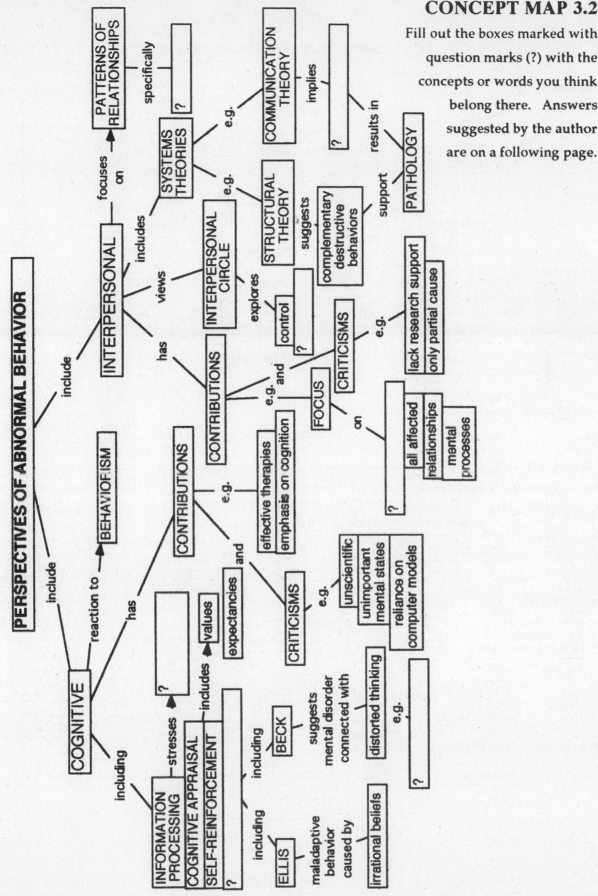

# CONCEPT MAP 3.2

Fill out the boxes marked with question marks (?) with the concepts or words you think belong there. Answers suggested by the author are on a following page.

**PERSPECTIVES OF ABNORMAL BEHAVIOR** include

- **INTERPERSONAL**
  - focuses on → PATTERNS OF RELATIONSHIPS — specifically → [?]
  - includes → **SYSTEMS THEORIES**
    - e.g. → **COMMUNICATION THEORY** — implies → [?] — results in → **PATHOLOGY**
    - e.g. → **STRUCTURAL THEORY** — suggests → complementary destructive behaviors — support
  - views → INTERPERSONAL CIRCLE — explores → control [?]
  - has → **CONTRIBUTIONS**
    - e.g. and → **FOCUS** — on → [?] all affected relationships, mental processes
    - **CRITICISMS** — e.g. → lack research support only partial cause

- reaction to → **BEHAVIORISM**

- **COGNITIVE**
  - has → **CONTRIBUTIONS**
    - e.g. → effective therapies emphasis on cognition
    - and → [?] — includes → values, expectancies
    - **CRITICISMS** — e.g. → unscientific, unimportant mental states, reliance on computer models
  - including → **INFORMATION PROCESSING** — stresses
  - **COGNITIVE APPRAISAL** — including → **ELLIS** — maladaptive behavior caused by → irrational beliefs
  - **SELF-REINFORCEMENT** [?] — including → **BECK** — suggests mental disorder connected with → distorted thinking — e.g. → [?]

65

## CONCEPT MAP 3.1

The suggested answers are
shown in *italics*.

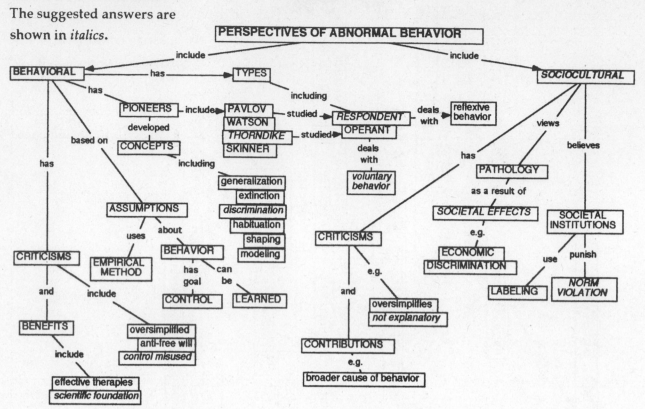

## CONCEPT MAP 3.2

The suggested answers are
shown in *italics*.

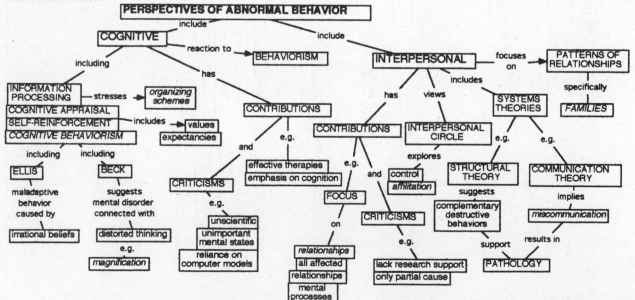

**CHAPTER TERMS** (Cut out on the lines to use as Flash Cards)

| | | |
|---|---|---|
| 3.1<br><br>**attribution** | 3.8<br><br>**conditioned reflex** | 3.15<br><br>**generalization** |
| 3.2<br><br>**behavior therapy** | 3.9<br><br>**conditioned reinforcers** | 3.16<br><br>**habituation** |
| 3.3<br><br>**behavioral perspective** | 3.10<br><br>**conditioned response** | 3.17<br><br>**interpersonal perspective** |
| 3.4<br><br>**cognition** | 3.11<br><br>**conditioned stimulus** | 3.18<br><br>**law of effect** |
| 3.5<br><br>**cognitive appraisal** | 3.12<br><br>**contingency** | 3.19<br><br>**learning** |
| 3.6<br><br>**cognitive behaviorism** | 3.13<br><br>**discrimination** | 3.20<br><br>**modeling** |
| 3.7<br><br>**cognitive perspective** | 3.14<br><br>**extinction** | 3.21<br><br>**negative reinforcement** |

# DEFINITIONS (Cut out on the lines to use as Flash Cards)

| | | |
|---|---|---|
| 3.15 The process by which an organism, conditioned to respond in a certain way to a particular stimulus, will also respond to similar stimuli in the same way | 3.8 A basic mechanism of learning whereby if a neutral stimulus is paired with a non-neutral stimulus, the organism will eventually respond to the neutral stimulus as it does to the nonneutral stimulus | 3.1 Our beliefs about the causes of peoples' behavior and life events; focus is on global/specific stable/unstable and internal/external |
| 3.16 Phenomenon whereby repeated exposure to a stimulus results in the lessening of the organism's response to it | 3.9 Stimuli or needs that one learns to respond to by associating them with primary reinforcer; also called secondary reinforcers | 3.2 A method of treatment for specific problems that uses the principles of learning theory |
| 3.17 Recent view that peoples' behavior is a function of their relationships with others; emphasis is placed on the social environment | 3.10 A simple response to a neutral stimulus that is the result of repeatedly pairing the neutral stimulus with a nonneutral stimulus that would have naturally elicited the response | 3.3 View that behavior is the sole result of learning; emphasizes scientific study of proximal environmental causes for our actions |
| 3.18 Thorndike's idea that responses with satisfying consequences are strengthened (likely to be repeated), while responses with unsatisfying consequences are weakened (not likely to be repeated) | 3.11 The neutral stimulus that elicits a particular response as a result of repeated pairings with a nonneutral or unconditioned stimulus that naturally elicits that response | 3.4 The act of knowing, including mental processes such as emotion, thought, expectation, and interpretation |
| 3.19 A relatively enduring change in behavior caused by experience or practice | 3.12 In operant-conditioning idea that the consequences of a response are associated with that response | 3.5 According to cognitive behaviorists, the process by which a person evaluates stimuli according to memories, beliefs, and expectations before responding; accounts for variation in responses to the same stimulus |
| 3.20 In behavioral theory, the learning of a new behavior by imitating another person performing that behavior | 3.13 The process of learning to distinguish among similar stimuli and to respond only to the appropriate one | 3.6 The school of behaviorism that proposes that the study of cognitive events should be incorporated into behavioral research |
| 3.21 A conditioning procedure in which a response is followed by the removal of an aversive event or stimulus (e.g. punishment), thereby promoting that response. | 3.14 A process in which a conditioned response is reduced to its preconditioned level; previously reinforced responses are no longer reinforced | 3.7 Recent view that behavior is the result of mental processes including memory, problem solving, and reasoining |

| 3.22 operant behavior | 3.29 selective attention | 3.36 |
|---|---|---|
| 3.23 operant conditioning | 3.30 shaping | 3.37 |
| 3.24 positive reinforcement | 3.31 sociocultural perspective | 3.38 |
| 3.25 primary reinforcer | 3.32 systems theory | 3.39 |
| 3.26 punishment | 3.33 unconditioned response | 3.40 |
| 3.27 reinforcement | 3.34 unconditioned stimulus | 3.41 |
| 3.28 schema | 3.35 *(You may fill in the remaining boxes with names, terms and definitions from text and lecture)* | 3.42 |

# DEFINITIONS (Cut out on the lines to use as Flash Cards)

| | | |
|---|---|---|
| 3.36 | 3.29 The ability of people to focus on specific sensory information and filter out the rest; some psychopathology may be the failure of this ability | 3.22 A behavior by which an organism acts upon the environment in order to achieve a desired result; all of these behaviors are the result of conditioning (Cf. respondent behavior) |
| 3.37 | 3.30 A type of operant conditioning used often with children whereby the subject is reinforced for successive approximations of target behavior | 3.23 The process by which an organism learns to associate certain results with certain actions it has taken; also called instrumental conditioning |
| 3.38 | 3.31 View that behavior is a product of broad social forces; emphasizes interaction, demographic research, and labeling | 3.24 A situation in which a response is followed by a positive event or stimulus, thereby increasing the probability that the response will be repeated |
| 3.39 | 3.32 Approach that says dysfunction is studied by analyzing relationships as systems of interlocking needs; variations emphasize communication, and boundaries between people | 3.25 A stimulus or need that one responds to instinctively, without learning |
| 3.40 | 3.33 A natural, unlearned response to a stimulus | 3.26 In behavioral theory, the process for suppressing behavior whereby a response is followed by an aversive stimulus |
| 3.41 | 3.34 A stimulus which elicits a natural or unconditioned response | 3.27 The process of following a behavior with something the organism desires (food, praise, desired activity, removal of punishment, etc.); roughly the same as rewarding the organism |
| 3.42 | 3.35 | 3.28 A structured body of information that is stored in the mind and helps a person to organize and process newly learned information |

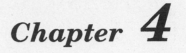

# The Biological Perspective

## LEARNING OBJECTIVES
*By the time you are finished studying this chapter, you should be able to:*

### THE BIOLOGICAL BASES OF BEHAVIOR
1. Define and briefly describe the field of behavior genetics (80).
2. Briefly explain the diathesis-stress theory of mental disorder (81).
3. Briefly explain the genetic research techniques involved in family studies, twin studies, and adoption studies (81-84).
4. Discuss the advantages and disadvantages of each of the preceding types of genetic research (81-84).
5. Describe the functions of the cell body, dendrites, axon, axon terminals, and the myelin sheath in the neuron (84-85).
6. List six common neurotransmitters and briefly describe their major functions as currently understood (86-87).
7. Name and describe the functions of the four lobes of the cerebral cortex (87-88).
8. List and define the functions of the brain structures noted in italics in your text (88-89).
9. Briefly describe the EEG, CT, PET, and MRI as tools for investigating the brain (89-90).
10. Describe the major functional differences between the right and left hemispheres of the cortex (91).
11. Generally describe the functions of the somatic and autonomic divisions of the peripheral nervous system (91-93).
12. Describe the contrasting functions of the sympathetic and parasympathetic divisions of the autonomic system (93).
13. Describe what hormones are and summarize their role in the functioning of the endocrine system (93).

### EVALUATING THE BIOLOGICAL PERSPECTIVE
14. List and discuss the advantages and criticisms of the biological perspective mentioned in your text (94-95).

## CHAPTER OUTLINE

I. The biological bases of behavior

    A. Mind-body problem examines the relationship between mental and physical processes
        1. Mental processes can affect the body
        2. Physical processes can affect the mind

    B. Behavior genetics studies the degree to which behavior is based on inherited predispositions
        1. Inherited characteristics are encoded in genes which are found on the chromosomes
        2. Diathesis-stress theory says that abnormality in behavior can result from a biological predisposition (diathesis) acted upon by environmental stressors
        3. Genetic studies examine how genotype (genetic blueprint) affects phenotype (observable characteristics)
            a. Family studies
                (1) Look at similarities in behavior among people who are related to each other
                (2) Do not adequately separate genetic and environmental effects

71

b. Twin studies
   (1) Compare behaviors of monozygotic (identical) and dizygotic (fraternal) twins
   (2) Still do not control for environmental similarities between twins raised together
   (3) May be difficult to perform because twins with specific disorders are relatively rare
c. Adoption studies
   (1) Look at adopted children whose biological mothers have behavioral problems (mothers are chosen because maternity is easier to prove than paternity)
   (2) Separate environment and heredity well

C. The central nervous system (CNS)
  1. Neurons process information in the body
    a. Cell body is the processor or "decision maker"
    b. Dendrites are "receivers" and handle input
    c. Axon is the "sender" and handles output
    d. Axon terminals are the "ends of the sender"
    e. Myelin sheath surrounds some axons and speeds neural transmission
    f. Synapse is the gap between axon of one neuron and dendrites of the next
  2. Neurotransmitters are chemicals that cross the synapse to convey information from cell to cell
    a. Acetylcholine
      (1) Causes muscle movement
      (2) Involved in Alzheimer's disease
    b. Dopamine
      (1) Regulation of motor behavior
      (2) Involved in schizophrenia
    c. Enkephalins
      (1) Naturally occurring opiates
      (2) Moderates pain experiences
    d. GABA (gamma-amino-butyric acid)
      (1) Inhibits neural activity in the brain
      (2) Tranquilizers increase GABA activity
    e. Norepinephrine
      (1) Autonomic nervous system transmitter
      (2) Fight or flight response
    f. Serotonin
      (1) Major transmitter in the brain
      (2) May interact with norepinephrine in cases of severe depression
  3. Anatomy of the brain
    a. Cerebral cortex (top of the brain) is divided into two parts or hemispheres
      (1) Longitudinal fissure separates the two hemispheres
      (2) Corpus callosum connects the two hemispheres
      (3) Central sulcus (fissure of Rolando) divides cortex roughly into front and back halves
      (4) Lateral sulcus (fissure of Sylvius) divides cortex roughly into top and bottom halves
      (5) Lobes of cerebral cortex
        (a) Frontal (many higher intellectual processes)
        (b) Parietal (motor control and integration of the senses)
        (c) Occipital (vision)
        (d) Temporal (hearing, vision and memory)
    b. Hypothalamus (hunger, thirst, sex, temperature, emotion)
    c. Limbic system (emotional reactions)
      (1) Amygdala ("fight or flight")
      (2) Hippocampus (emotions and memories)
    d. Thalamus (sensory relay station)
    e. Basal ganglia (execution of planned behavior)
    f. Cerebellum (posture and movement coordination)

g.  Brain stem
    (1)  Medulla (life support functions)
    (2)  Pons (relay station between spinal cord and brain)
    (3)  Reticular formation (sleep and arousal)
h.  Ventricles are spaces in the brain filled with cerebrospinal fluid
4.  Brain imaging techniques allow noninvasive investigation of the brain's structure and function
    a.  EEG (oldest noninvasive method) measures electrical fields
    b.  MEG (variation on EEG) measures magnetic fields
    c.  CT scans (computerized tomography) use x-rays
    d.  PET scans (positron emission tomography) use radioactive tracers
    e.  MRI (magnetic resonance imaging) uses radio waves
5.  Lateralization refers to the localization of functions in one hemisphere of the brain or the other; the two hemispheres have different specialties
    a.  Each hemisphere is wired to the opposite side of the body
    b.  Left brain controls most speech functions
    c.  Right brain seems more involved with emotion and spatial relations

D.  The peripheral nervous system (PNS)
1.  Somatic nervous system senses and acts on external world
2.  Autonomic nervous system (ANS) regulates smooth muscles, glands, and internal organs
    a.  Sympathetic n.s. does activation for "fight or flight"
    b.  Parasympathetic n.s. does deactivation and energy conservation

E.  The endocrine system (glandular system)
1.  Produces chemical messengers called hormones
2.  Influences emotions, sexual functioning, energy availability, and physical growth
3.  Master gland, or controlling gland, is the pituitary
4.  CNS controls pituitary through the hypothalamus

II.  Evaluating the biological perspective

A.  Difficulties with the biological perspective
1.  Methodological problems: what came first, the organic problem or the behavioral problem, or are they interactive with each other, or were they both caused by some third factor?
2.  Ethical questions
    a.  What genetic interventions should be made: mandatory sterilization, genetic counseling, genetic engineering?
    b.  Will "medicalized" psychology inappropriately lead to quick fixes and cause other types of therapy to be neglected?

B.  Contributions of the biological perspective
1.  Biological researchers tend to be careful scientists
2.  Effective psychoactive medications
3.  Increased understanding of the neurochemical side of abnormal behaviors

## KEY TERMS
*The following terms are in bold print in your text. Define them and practice their definitions using the flash cards at the end of the chapter.*

autonomic nervous system (ANS) (92)
behavior genetics (80)
brain plasticity (95)
central nervous system (CNS) (84)
chromosomes (80)
computerized tomography (CT) (90)
concordant (82)
co-twins (82)
diathesis (81)

diathesis-stress model (81)
dizygotic (DZ) twins (82)
electroencephalography (EEG) (89)
endocrine system (93)
genes (80)
genotype (81)
hormones (93)
index case (81)
lateralization (91)

magnetic resonance imaging (MRI) (90)
monozygotic (MZ) twins (82)
nervous system (84)
neurons (84)
neurotransmitters (85)
parasympathetic division (93)
peripheral nervous system (91)
phenotype (81)

polygenic (80)
positron emission tomography (PET) (90)
receptors (86)
reuptake (86)
somatic nervous system (91)
sympathetic division (93)
synapse (85)

*Your text does not list the following terms as formal vocabulary; however, if you don't know what they mean, you will be unable to grasp the concepts of this chapter.*

congenial (83)
enigma (88)
ethical (94)

fissures (87)
hypertension (80)
inferred (89)

intuitively (94)
joviality (91)
pragmatic (91)

## IMPORTANT NAMES
*Identify the following persons and their major contributions to abnormal psychology as discussed in this chapter.*

The "Minnesota Twins" (91)

## GUIDED SELF-STUDY

1. The biological perspective considers how the (a)_____ and the (b)_____ interact.

   This is called the (c)_____ _____ problem.

2. What are the possibilities for the way this interaction could go?

3. Where do you currently stand on this issue and why? (At the end of this course, see if your stand has changed any, and if so, why.)

4. Your textbook refers to the "organic environment" of the mind. What is the "organic environment" of the mind?

5. How does your body "know" how it is supposed to develop and what it is supposed to be like?

6. When was this "body plan" established in you?

7. Which cells of your body carry the entire plan?

8. Science has clearly demonstrated that genetic inheritance influences physical features and behavioral features of an individual. The big question now is *how much* do genes determine behavior, and how much does experience with the environment determine behavior.

   This is one of the big debates in psychology, called the (a)_____-_____ controversy.

   (b) _____ = genetic influences, and (c) _____ = environmental influences.

   **NOTICE!!!** In ecological concerns, TV commercials, etc., environment means nature, *but not* in a psychology course.

9. There is another perspective on the nature-nurture controversy. It is "nature via nurture." What does it mean?

10.  a.   At this point, what is your opinion on this issue:  Does nature or nurture have more impact on who *you* are?

b.   On a genetic level, how similar are you to each of your parents?

c.   List four behaviors in which you frequently engage.

d.   Do either of your biological parents have any of those behaviors?

e.   If they do, why does that not clearly support the nature side of the debate?

f.   In what situation would behavioral similarities between generations support the nature position?

11.  The theory that considers the interaction of environment and hereditary potential in the development of disorder is called the (a)_____-_____theory.

(b)_____ is the genetic influence (also called the constitutional predisposition).

(c)_____ is the influence that the environment exerts on the individual.

12.  Match the terms to the phrases.  Terms may be used more than once.

| **Chromosomes** | **Dizygotes** | **Index case** |
|---|---|---|
| **Co-twin** | **Genes** | **Monozygotes** |
| **Diathesis** | **Genotype** | **Phenotypes** |

a.   _____   Individual units of inheritance information
b.   _____   Constitutional predisposition
c.   _____   "Normal" humans have 23 pairs
d.   _____   Another name for a proband case
e.   _____   A "diagnosed" case
f.   _____   Identical twins
g.   _____   Fraternal twins
h.   _____   Observable characteristics
i.   _____   Twin of an index case
j.   _____   One's biological inheritance
k.   _____   String of genes that form a chain

13.  Describe your genotype.

14.  Describe your phenotype.

15.  Name three kinds of research studies that try to determine whether behavioral abnormalities are genetic.

16.  If you are the index case (also called proband case) in a family study, what does this mean to you and to your family?

17. a.  How are DZ twins different from MZ twins?

    b.  Do you know any DZ twins?  List their names.

    c.  Do you know any MZ twins?  List their names.

18. a.  What is a "co-twin?"  Would you want the position of being a co-twin?

    b.  What does concordant mean?  Would you want to be concordant with that twin?

19. What are the problems with working with the "genetically ideal" MZ twins?

20. What arrangement of adoption studies is the most fruitful to study and why?


CENTRAL NERVOUS SYSTEM
21. How could the nervous system be characterized in terms of function?

22. Label the **cell body, dendrites, axon, axon terminals,** and **myelin sheath** on this drawing of a  neuron.

    a.  _____

    b.  _____

    c.  _____

    d.  _____

    e.  _____

23. List six neurotransmitters.  Place stars by the four key ones thought to be particularly related to abnormal behavior.
    a.

    b.

    c.

    d.

    e.

    f.

24. Arrange the correct sequence for the message passing through the electrochemical neural transmission process. The starting and end points are already marked for you.

    1   Neurotransmitter released at the ends of axon terminals
    ___ Cell body tallies incoming excitatory and inhibitory messages
    ___ Excitatory messages pass critical all-or-none threshold
    ___ Message moves down axon
    ___ Message moves up the dendrite
    ___ Messages arrives at axon terminals
    ___ Neurotransmitter in the synapse
    ___ Neurotransmitter floats into receptors sites
    9   Neurotransmitter released at the ends of axon terminals

25. How do psychoactive drugs influence the activity of neurotransmitters?

26. Label the major features indicated in these drawings of the brain.

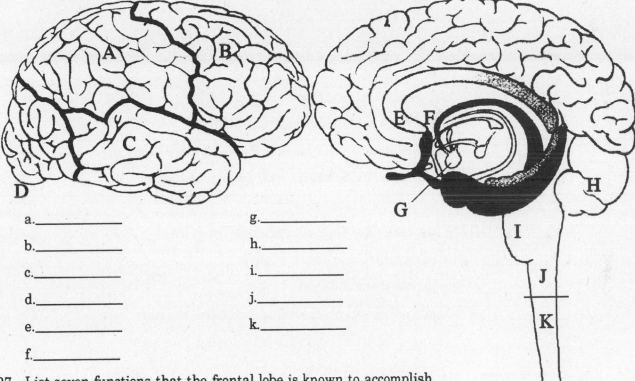

    a._____        g._____

    b._____        h._____

    c._____        i._____

    d._____        j._____

    e._____        k._____

    f._____

27. List seven functions that the frontal lobe is known to accomplish.

    a.

    b.

    c.

    d.

    e.

    f.

    g.

77

28. List the other three lobes of the brain. Give one or two functions that each of them serves.

   a.

   b.

   c.

29. What is the *total* number of lobes in a human brain?

30. Fill-in the blank with the correct brain structure.

   **Amygdala**              **Hippocampus**          **Reticular formation**
   **Brain stem**            **Hypothalamus**         **Thalamus**
   **Cerebellum**            **Limbic system**        **Ventricles**
   **Cerebral cortex**       **Medulla**
   **Corpus callosum**       **Pons**

   a. _____   controls hunger, thirst, and sexual drive

   b. _____   is the part of the limbic system dealing with fight/flight

   c. _____   is a pleasure center

   d. _____   is a sensory relay center

   e. _____   are cavities containing cerebrospinal fluid

   f. _____   controls posture, balance, and fine-motor coordination

   g. _____   is a system that interacts with the hypothalamus

   h. _____   regulates body temperature

   i. _____   is the center for fear and aggression reactions

   j. _____   is the memory and emotion center

   k. _____   regulates sleep and arousal

   l. _____   regulates heartbeat, breathing, and blood pressure

   m. _____   contains the pons, medulla, and reticular formation

   n. _____   relays messages between cerebellum, brain, and spinal cord

   o. _____   is the thin, convoluted layer of "gray matter"

   p. _____   connects the two hemispheres of the brain

31. For many years, the only way brain mapping could be done was by inferences drawn from debilitation of brain-damaged patients and patient reports during brain surgery. Today there are three noninvasive techniques. They are magnetic resonance imaging, positron emission tomography, and computerized tomography. Fill in each by its respective description.

   a. _____   based on radio waves in a magnetic field

   b. _____   based on radioactivity using x-rays

   c. _____   based on radioactive molecules using tracer substances.

d. _____ based on magnetic fields caused by brain's electrical reactions

32. When imaging techniques are used to look at the brain structure of schizophrenics, compared to nonschizophrenics, the brain ventricles appear to be (a)_____ and the frontal lobes appear to be (b)_____.

33. Lateralization means _____.

34. What abilities are usually found in the brain's
    a. left hemisphere?
    b. right hemisphere?

35. How can researchers tell which side of the brain does what?

36. Fill-in the correct division of the nervous system to complete the following thoughts.

**Autonomic nervous system**
**Central nervous system**
**Nervous system (in entirety)**

**Parasympathetic nervous system**
**Somatic nervous system**
**Sympathetic nervous system**

a. _____ was formerly called the involuntary nervous system.

b. _____ senses and acts on the external world.

c. _____ regulates heartbeat and respiration.

d. _____ contains the brain and spinal cord.

e. _____ specializes in "meeting emergencies."

f. _____ has fibers that emerge from top and bottom of the spinal cord.

g. _____ is a vast electrochemical conducting network.

h. _____ mainly stores and transmits information.

i. _____ is in general control of pupil dilation and bladder contraction.

j. _____ has nerve fibers that emanate from the middle of the spinal cord.

k. _____ plays a critical role in the stress response.

l. _____ decreases heart rate.

37. Fill in the following blanks. These terms may be used more than once: **endocrine, hormones, hypothalamus, pituitary gland,** and **controls.**

The (a)_____ system releases chemical messengers known as (b)_____ into the blood stream. The (c)_____ is called the "master gland" because it (d)_____ the other glands. It does this by release of its (e)_____which causes the other glands to release their (f)_____. The (g)_____ of the brain controls this "master gland."

38. Why are glands being discussed in connection with abnormal behavior?

39. What is the methodological problem in biological research that deals with determining the causes of mental disorder?

40. What are the possible relationships of the organic dysfunctions to abnormal behaviors?

41. What is the ethical question that comes with any scientific discoveries?

42. What are the four specific ethical questions about the discoveries in the biological perspective?

    a.

    b.

    c.

    d.

## *HELPFUL HINT*

This is *so* important that I put it in the study exercise so the people who don't read these helpful hints will still get it:

### NATURE = GENES
### NURTURE = ENVIRONMENT

**BEWARE!** In psychology, nature and environment are not equivalent as they are in ecology!

## *PRACTICE TEST*
*Take the following test several times as you study the chapter. Write your answers on a separate sheet of paper and after each attempt, note in the tally box above each question whether your answer was correct or incorrect.*

| 1 | 2 | 3 | 4 |
|---|---|---|---|
|   |   |   |   |

1. What is your text's position on the mind-body problem?
   a. Mind and body are totally independent of each other.
   b. Mind dominates body and controls it.
   c. Physical and mental events must be considered together.
   d. Physical ailments are byproducts of mental distress.

| 1 | 2 | 3 | 4 |
|---|---|---|---|
|   |   |   |   |

2. There is an idea about the causes of mental disorder that says it results from a combination of genetic predisposition and environmental triggering events. What is this idea called?
   a. Behavior genetics
   b. Diathesis-stress theory
   c. Nature-nurture hypothesis
   d. Proband principle

| 1 | 2 | 3 | 4 |
| --- | --- | --- | --- |

3. The unique combination of genes representing your biological inheritance from your parents is your
   a. phenotype.
   b. chromotype.
   c. somatotype.
   d. genotype.

| 1 | 2 | 3 | 4 |
| --- | --- | --- | --- |

4. Fran locates people with severe depression and then checks all their immediate relatives to see how many of them share the same problem. Then she compares the incidence of depression in these people with what would be expected in the general population. Fran is conducting a(n)
   a. family study.
   b. adoption study.
   c. twin study.
   d. genealogical study.

| 1 | 2 | 3 | 4 |
| --- | --- | --- | --- |

5. The major problem with the research conducted in question 4 is
   a. it is hard to separate the effects of shared heredity from shared environment.
   b. there aren't enough depressed people to make the results valid.
   c. one cannot predict the degree of genetic similarity in a person's relatives.
   d. ethical concerns do not permit us to inquire about mental problems in other people's families.

| 1 | 2 | 3 | 4 |
| --- | --- | --- | --- |

6. The type of genetic research that provides the best evidence on the heritability of disorder is
   a. family studies.
   b. concordate studies.
   c. twin studies.
   d. adoption studies.

| 1 | 2 | 3 | 4 |
| --- | --- | --- | --- |

7. Which of the following structures of the neuron mainly receives information from the outside of the cell?
   a. The cell body
   b. The axon
   c. The axon terminals
   d. The dendrites

| 1 | 2 | 3 | 4 |
| --- | --- | --- | --- |

8. Which of the following neurotransmitters is most involved in the "fight or flight" response of the autonomic nervous system?
   a. Enkephalin
   b. GABA
   c. Histamine
   d. Norepinephrine

| 1 | 2 | 3 | 4 |
| --- | --- | --- | --- |

9. As a tool for doing research on the brain, the letters MRI stand for
   a. Molecular Response Indicator
   b. Magnetic Resonance Imaging
   c. Micro-Reflective Interferometer
   d. Mass Replacement Index

10. A major division separating the cortex of the brain into right and left halves is the
    a. temporal sulcus.
    b. longitudinal fissure.
    c. central sulcus.
    d. fissure of Rolando.

11. Which of the following brain structures is mainly responsible for regulating vital functions such as breathing and blood pressure?
    a. The hypothalamus
    b. The reticular formation
    c. The medulla
    d. The thalamus

12. A stroke patient is brought to the hospital with total paralysis on his right side. What part of the brain has been affected?
    a. The right half
    b. Both frontal lobes
    c. The left hemisphere
    d. The lower cortex on both sides

13. What other symptom would we expect most patients like the one in Question 12 to show?
    a. Loss of language abilities
    b. Total blindness
    c. Inability to perceive music
    d. Total lack of emotion

14. Which of the following parts of the brain is most involved in sorting out information and the ordering or sequencing of behavior?
    a. The hypothalamus
    b. The occipital lobes of cortex
    c. The ventricles
    d. The frontal lobes of cortex

15. The autonomic nervous system is
    a. part of the central nervous system.
    b. responsible for the control of glands and internal organs.
    c. largely voluntary.
    d. not active in cases of extreme emotional arousal.

16. Which of the following nervous system divisions can be called an "emergency response system" in the body?
    a. Sympathetic division of the autonomic system
    b. Somatic division
    c. Parasympathetic division of the autonomic system
    d. Endocrine system

| 1 | 2 | 3 | 4 |
|---|---|---|---|

17. What is the purpose of the ANS's parasympathetic division?
    a. To regulate internal processes and conserve energy during nonstressful times
    b. To secrete hormones for the maintenance of growth, digestion and sexual potency
    c. To release intense bursts of physical energy when needed for survival
    d. To increase concentration in difficult problem-solving situations

| 1 | 2 | 3 | 4 |
|---|---|---|---|

18. The endocrine system is regulated by the central nervous system. At what point do the two systems come together?
    a. At the pons-medulla connection
    b. At the hypothalamus-thalamus connection
    c. At the corpus callosum-cortex connection
    d. At the pituitary-hypothalamus connection

| 1 | 2 | 3 | 4 |
|---|---|---|---|

19. If I go into therapy because of excess tension and anxiety, and the psychologist treats me with relaxation training to help me get my "stress response" under control. What part of my nervous system is being worked on?
    a. My cerebellum                     c. My autonomic nervous system
    b. My endocrine system               d. My spinal cord

| 1 | 2 | 3 | 4 |
|---|---|---|---|

20. Which of the following is a practical concern about the biological perspective?
    a. It may lead people to reject medical theories of abnormal behavior.
    b. It may lead to a psychology in which all problems will be dealt with by biological treatments.
    c. So far the results of biological research have simply not lived up to our expectations of success.
    d. Insurance companies will no longer pay for treatment unless done by a medical doctor.

## ANSWERS
### Self-Study Exercise

1. a. body
   b. mind
   c. mind-body (80)
2. The mind controls the body; the body controls the mind; the mind and body are not interactive; or the mind and body are different aspects of a single, complex entity (80).
3. Your opinion
4. The body (80)
5. There are individual units of information called genes along thread-like structures called chromosomes which form the recipe for your being (80).
6. At the moment of conception (80)
7. "Every cell of the human body" carries the entire plan. There is an exception which I will note for technical accuracy. The sex cells, eggs and sperm, carry only one half the genetic pattern of the individual (80).
8. a. nature-nurture
   b. Nature
   c. Nurture (80)
9. Genes dispose people to like certain kinds of stimulation meaning that genes dispose them to choose certain types of environments. The environment then exerts its influence but the genes have selected which environment the person will gravitate toward (83).

10. a. Your opinion; each of us has our own opinion, but in fact, it is a difficult question to answer, and arriving at the answer is precisely what we are discussing here. That is what behavior genetics is all about!
    b. On a genetic level you are 50 percent your biological mother and 50 percent your biological father (81).
    c. Your individual responses—possibilities include nail-biting, foot swinging, slow talking, being a "morning person," being athletic, loving craft work, loving hot pepper sauce
    d. Your individual responses
    e. Being like your biological parents does not give total support to the nature (genetic) side of the debate because you have also shared environment (nurture) with them to some extent (82).
    f. If you were removed from your parents at birth and never had any contact with them or knowledge of them, then similarities with them would support genetic theory (83-84).

11. a. diathesis-stress theory
    b. Diathesis
    c. Stress (81)

12. a. Genes (80)                     g. Dizygotes (82)
    b. Diathesis (81)                 h. Phenotypes (81)
    c. Chromosomes (80)               i. Co-twin (82)
    d. Index case (81)                j. Genotype (81)
    e. Index case (81)                k. Chromosomes (80)
    f. Monozygotes (82)

13. This is a trick question. Unless you had some condition that has required genetic counseling, you can probably only speculate about your genetic picture by looking at your phenotype. However, there is a growing population of people who can look at their chromosomal pictures (karyotypes) which were made when their mothers had amniocentesis (81).

14. Your phenotype is your observable characteristics (81).

15. Family studies, twin studies, adoption studies (81-84)

16. If you are an index case (proband case), you have some specific quality or condition that genetic researchers are studying. The researchers are looking to see if your family members show evidence of having a higher incidence of that same quality or condition than other people in your environment who are unrelated to you. Whether your family is going to be happy or not about a possible familial genetic potential all depends on whether the quality or condition is desirable to have (81).

17. a. Dizygotic (DZ) twins are no more genetically alike than regular brothers and sisters; monozygotic (MZ) twins have identical genetic material because they were actually only *one* person at conception. DZ twins were *always* two different people (82).
    b. Your knowledge. Listing their names may seem pointless, but it provides concrete cues for your memory of these concepts.
    c. Your knowledge

18. a. A co-twin is an individual who is twin to a person who has a certain quality or condition. Whether you want to be a co-twin to a person with a certain quality or condition would all depend on what the quality or condition was (82).
    b. Being concordant with your twin means having that same quality or condition that your twin does. Again, whether or not you want to be concordant with your twin will be determined by what the quality or condition is that your twin has (82).

19. MZ twins are rare; even rarer are MZ twins with mental disorder. Also, because MZ twins are so similar physically and are always the same sex, their life experiences may be more similar than DZ twins, who can look quite dissimilar and be of different sexes (82-83).

20. The most ideal arrangement of adoption studies is to compare adopted children whose biological mothers had no record of mental health problems to adopted children whose biological mothers had serious mental health problems. This pool of research subjects is more substantial than that of mentally ill MZ twins because mothers who are severely disturbed are likely to have to give their children up for adoption (84).

21. A vast electrochemical network for sending messages (84)

22. a. Dendrite                       d. Axon
    b. Cell body                      e. Axon terminal (85)
    c. Myelin sheath

23. *Acetylcholine                    *Serotonin
    *Dopamine                         Enkephalins
    *Norepinephrine                   GABA (86-87)

84

24. 1. Neurotransmitter released at the ends of axon terminals
    2. Neurotransmitter in the synapse
    3. Neurotransmitter floats into receptor sites
    4. Site message moves up the dendrite
    5. Cell body tallies excitatory and inhibitory messages
    6. Excitatory messages pass critical all-or-none threshold
    7. Message moves down axon
    8. Messages arrives at axon terminals
    9. Neurotransmitter released at the ends of axon terminals (84-86)

25. Psychoactive drugs alter neuronal firing patterns by affecting the level of neurotransmitter activity. Levels of neurotransmitter activity can be altered by a number of approaches. To increase neurotransmitter activity, increase the amount of neurotransmitter that is made, or cause the neurotransmitter to remain in the synaptic space longer for possible uptake by a dendrite. To decrease neuronal activity, either reduce the total quantity of neurotransmitter present or reduce the time that the neurotransmitter remains in the synaptic space (85).

26. a. Parietal lobe
    b. Frontal lobe
    c. Temporal lobe
    d. Occipital lobe
    e. Corpus callosum
    f. Thalamus
    g. Hypothalamus
    h. Cerebellum
    i. Pons
    j. Medulla
    k. Spinal cord (88)

27. a. Language ability
    b. Regulation of fine voluntary movements
    c. Ordering of stimuli
    d. Sorting of information
    e. Evaluation of one's own behavior for appropriateness and for the way it may be seen by others
    f. Getting one started on tasks
    g. Self-awareness (88)

28. a. Temporal lobes—auditory perception (hearing), some vision and memory
    b. Parietal lobes—intrasensory perception, motor (movement) and sensory somatic functions (knowing where in space your own body parts are). You cannot walk if your brain does not know where your foot is and what position it is in at every moment.
    c. Occipital lobes—visual discrimination and visual memory (88)

29. Although we speak of "the four lobes of the brain" in each hemisphere, both hemispheres together give eight lobes total (87).

30. a. Hypothalamus
    b. Amygdala
    c. Limbic system
    d. Thalamus
    e. Ventricles
    f. Cerebellum
    g. Limbic system
    h. Hypothalamus
    i. Amygdala
    j. Hippocampus
    k. Reticular formation
    l. Medulla
    m. Brain stem
    n. Pons
    o. Cerebral cortex
    p. Corpus callosum (87-89)

31. a. Magnetic resonance imaging (MRI)
    b. Computerized tomography (CT)
    c. Positron emission tomography (PET)
    d. Magnetoencephalography (MET) (89-90)

32. a. enlarged
    b. smaller (90)

33. "sidedness," the extent to which the different sides of the brain develop in different ways (91)

34. a. Motor control of the right side of the body, speech
    b. Left side motor control, visual imagery, musical abilities, expression and comprehension of emotions (91)

35. By looking at the deficits or behavioral changes that people display when they have damage or temporary anesthesia to specific areas of their brains (91)

36. a. Autonomic nervous system
    b. Somatic nervous system
    c. Autonomic nervous system
    d. Central nervous system
    e. Sympathetic nervous system
    f. Parasympathetic nervous system
    g. The (entire) nervous system
    h. Central nervous system
    i. Autonomic nervous system
    j. Sympathetic nervous system
    k. Sympathetic nervous system
    l. Parasympathetic nervous system (91-93)

37.  a. endocrine
     b. hormones
     c. pituitary gland
     d. regulates
     e. hormones
     f. hormones
     g. hypothalamus (93)
38.  Dysfunctions in certain glands are associated with some abnormal behaviors (93).
39.  The methodological problem is one of determining causality. When research finds biochemical abnormalities associated with abnormal behavior, that correlation alone *does not prove causality* (94).
40.  The organic dysfunction caused the abnormal behavior; the abnormal behavior caused the organic dysfunction; or there is some third underlying process that causes both the organic dysfunction and the behavioral abnormality. There is another possibility that they are only coincidentally related and neither has anything to do with the other. Notice this is the same answer as #2. So it seems we still have not resolved the mind-body problem (94).
41.  How will the scientific knowledge be used? (94)
42.  a. Should "wonder drugs" be used to try to eliminate abnormal organic dysfunctions or abnormal behaviors when definite direct causality has not been established?
     b. If hereditary factors are part of abnormal behavior, should reproduction be controlled?
     c. Should genetic counseling be done to warn people what genetic potentials their children may carry?
     d. If the genetic problem could be fixed, should it be? (Should you fool with Mother Nature?) (94)

## Practice Test

|     |   |      |     |   |      |
|-----|---|------|-----|---|------|
| 1.  | c | (80) | 11. | c | (89) |
| 2.  | b | (81) | 12. | c | (91) |
| 3.  | d | (81) | 13. | a | (91) |
| 4.  | a | (81) | 14. | d | (88) |
| 5.  | a | (82) | 15. | b | (92) |
| 6.  | d | (83) | 16. | a | (93) |
| 7.  | d | (84) | 17. | a | (93) |
| 8.  | d | (87) | 18. | d | (93) |
| 9.  | b | (90) | 19. | c | (92) |
| 10. | b | (87) | 20. | b | (94) |

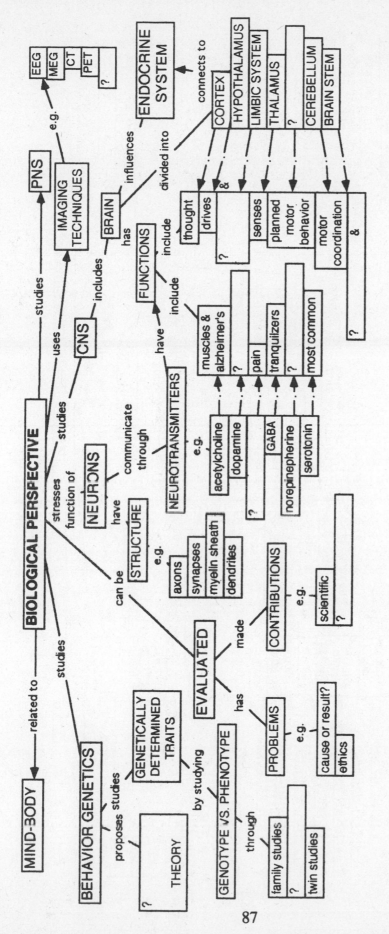

# CONCEPT MAP 4.1

Fill out the boxes marked with question marks (?) with the concepts or words you think belong there. Answers suggested by the author are on a following page.

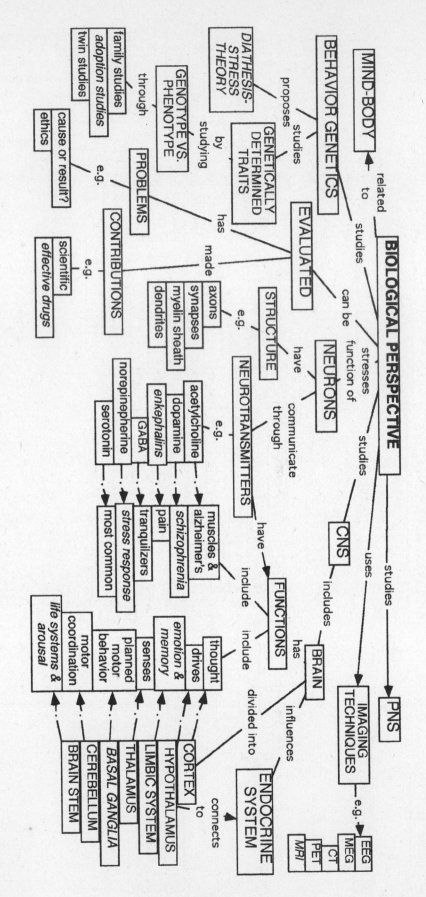

88

**CHAPTER TERMS** (Cut out on the lines to use as Flash Cards)

| | | |
|---|---|---|
| 4.1 **autonomic nervous system (ANS)** | 4.8 **co-twins** | 4.15 **genotype** |
| 4.2 **behavior genetics** | 4.9 **diathesis** | 4.16 **hormones** |
| 4.3 **brain plasticity** | 4.10 **diathesis-stress model** | 4.17 **index case** |
| 4.4 **central nervous system (CNS)** | 4.11 **dizygotic (DZ) twins** | 4.18 **lateralization** |
| 4.5 **chromosomes** | 4.12 **electro-encephalogram (EEG)** | 4.19 **magnetic resonance imaging (MRI)** |
| 4.6 **computerized tomography (CT)** | 4.13 **endocrine system** | 4.20 **monozygotic (MZ) twins** |
| 4.7 **concordant** | 4.14 **genes** | 4.21 **nervous system** |

# DEFINITIONS (Cut out on the lines to use as Flash Cards)

| | | |
|---|---|---|
| 4.15 The unique combination of genes which represents one's biological inheritance from one's parents | 4.8 A term used by genetic researchers to refer to the twins of the index cases | 4.1 That part of the nervous system which governs the smooth muscles, the heart muscle, the glands, and the viscera and controls their functions, inc. physiological responses to emotion |
| 4.16 Chemical messengers that are released directly into the bloodstream by the endocrine glands and that affect sexual functioning, physical growth and development, and emotional responses | 4.9 A constitutional predisposition toward a disorder | 4.2 The genetic study of psychological disorders |
| 4.17 In genetic family studies, the individual in the family who has the diagnosed case of the disorder being studied; also called proband case | 4.10 In schizophrenia research, an approach which holds that a predisposition to schizophrenia is inherited but that the disorder must be triggered by environmental stresses | 4.3 The concept that the brain is not static and is changed by influences from the environment (e.g. altering brain chemistry and brain processes) |
| 4.18 The localization of functions in either the left or the right hemisphere of the brain | 4.11 Twins who develop from two eggs fertilized by two different sperm and who have only approximately 50 percent of their genes in common (same as any siblings); also called fraternal twins | 4.4 That part of the nervous system made up of the brain and spinal cord |
| 4.19 The use of magnetic fields to produce a highly precise picture of the brain | 4.12 A record of brain-wave activity obtained by connecting sensitive electrodes to the skull which pick up and record the minute electrical impulses generated by the brain | 4.5 Twisted threadlike structures in all the cells of the body that carry genes in a linear order |
| 4.20 Twins who develop from a single fertilized egg and have the same genotype; they always have the same sex, eye color and blood type, etc.; also called identical twins | 4.13 The system of ductless glands such as the pituitary that is closely integrated with the central nervous system and is responsible for the production of hormones | 4.6 A series of X-rays of the brain, used in testing for organic impairment |
| 4.21 A vast electrochemical conducting network that extends from the brain through the rest of the body and carries information, in the form of electrical impulses, between the brain and the body | 4.14 The units on a chromosome that carry the instructions, inherited from the parents at conception, about the proteins that cells should produce and, in turn, determine physical characteristics | 4.7 A genetic term that means sharing the same disorder |

# CHAPTER TERMS (Cut out on the lines to use as Flash Cards)

| | | |
|---|---|---|
| 4.22<br><br>**neurons** | 4.29<br><br>**positron emission tomography (PET)** | 4.36 |
| 4.23<br><br>**neuroscience perspective** | 4.30<br><br>**receptors** | 4.37 |
| 4.24<br><br>**neurotransmitters** | 4.31<br><br>**reuptake** | 4.38 |
| 4.25<br><br>**parasympathetic division** | 4.32<br><br>**somatic nervous system** | 4.39 |
| 4.26<br><br>**peripheral nervous system** | 4.33<br><br>**sympathetic division** | 4.40 |
| 4.27<br><br>**phenotype** | 4.34<br><br>**synapse** | 4.41 |
| 4.28<br><br>**polygenic** | 4.35 *(You may fill in the remaining boxes with names, terms and definitions from text and lecture)* | 4.42 |

# DEFINITIONS (Cut out on the lines to use as Flash Cards)

| | | |
|---|---|---|
| 4.36 | 4.29 A means of examining the brain; the patient is injected with a radioactively labeled sugar solution, and the path of the radioactive particles through the brain is traced | 4.22 The cells of the nervous system; they connect motor and receptor cells and transmit information throughout the body |
| 4.37 | 4.30 Special proteins at the site of a post-synaptic neuron where the neurotransmitter molecule fits and, when stimulated, changes the voltage of the receiving cell | 4.23 A perspective that focuses on the biological aspects of abnormal behavior |
| 4.38 | 4.31 The process by which a neurotransmitter is reabsorbed by the presynaptic neuron's axon terminals to be reused | 4.24 A group of chemicals that facilitate the transmission of electrical impulses between nerve endings in the brain |
| 4.39 | 4.32 That part of the PNS that senses and acts on the external world, relaying to the brain sensory information and transmitting the brain's messages to the skeletal muscles, which move the body | 4.25 Division of the ANS which decreases physical arousal and is dominant under less emotional conditions; it regulates breathing, heart rate, blood pressure, stomach and elimination. (Cf. sympathetic)" |
| 4.40 | 4.33 The division of the ANS which becomes dominant in times of stress; it heightens the body's arousal, increasing blood pressure, perspiration, heart rate, & adrenaline; it dilates pupils and inhibits digestion | 4.26 The network of nerve fibers that leads from the CNS to all parts of the body and carries out the commands of the CNS; it has two branches: the somatic nervous system and the autonomic nervous system. |
| 4.41 | 4.34 The gap between two neurons across which nerve impulses pass by means of neurotransmitters | 4.27 The unique combination of observable characteristics that results from the combination of a person's genotype with the environment |
| 4.42 | 4.35 | 4.28 A term used to describe a trait that is the product of the interaction of many genes |

## Chapter 5

# Research Methods
# in Abnormal Psychology

## *LEARNING OBJECTIVES*
*By the time you are finished studying this chapter, you should be able to:*

### CHARACTERISTICS OF THE SCIENTIFIC METHOD
1. List and describe four objectives of the scientific method (100).
2. List three conditions that must be met before cause and effect can be established (101).
3. Distinguish between internal and external validity and describe the means by which each is obtained (101-102).
4. Discuss the process of developing and conducting an experiment, distinguishing between independent and dependent variables (102-103).
5. Distinguish between experimental and control groups, and describe three methods of experimental control (103).
6. Discuss the role of statistical analysis and inference in scientific research (104-105).

### RESEARCH DESIGNS
7. Define the case study method and list its advantages and disadvantages (105-108).
8. Distinguish between idiographic and nomothetic research (105-106).
9. Describe correlational research designs, and tell what one can and cannot conclude from them and why (108-110).
10. Define longitudinal studies, including high-risk designs, and discuss their advantages and shortcomings (110).
11. Define epidemiological studies and discuss the difference between incidence and prevalence (110-111).
12. Define analogue experimentation and tell when it is preferred over a true experiment (111-113).
13. Describe what is meant by the single-case study in experimentation (113).
14. Describe two variations on the single-case study mentioned in the text (113-115).

## *CHAPTER OUTLINE*

I. Characteristics of the scientific method

    A. A skeptical attitude is necessary because:
        1. The objects of scientific study are often very complex
        2. Fallible humans may not always understand things correctly

    B. Objectives
        1. Description—defining and classifying events in an objective manner
            a. Reliable descriptions are stable and consistent
            b. Valid descriptions describe what they claim to describe
        2. Prediction—anticipating outcomes on the basis of observations of events and their interrelationships
        3. Control—manipulating factors to produce a desired outcome
        4. Understanding—identifying and explaining causal factors
            a. The establishment of causality requires one to show:
               (1) Covariation of events

          (2)  A time-order relationship
          (3)  Elimination of other plausible explanations to decrease confounding and increase internal validity

  C.  Experimental Procedures
     1.  Development of a hypothesis (a tentative if-then proposition)
       a.  Hypotheses result from earlier observation
       b.  Hypotheses must be testable (falsifiable)
     2.  Operational definitions anchor concepts to observable criteria
     3.  Methods of control
       a.  Manipulation of variables allows one to see the effects of variable change
          (1)  Independent variables can be changed
          (2)  Dependent variables are measured
       b.  Holding other events constant (when possible) allows the effects of variable manipulation to be evaluated without confounding
       c.  Balancing by means of random subject selection and assignment diminishes confounding resulting from unanticipated and uncontrollable conditions
       d.  Effects of expectations by the subject can be minimized by:
          (1)  Keeping him/her in the dark about experimental conditions
          (2)  Using placebo control groups to ensure that all subjects are handled the same way
       e.  Effects of expectations by the experimenter can be minimized by:
          (1)  Double-blind techniques
          (2)  Use of the null hypothesis
          (3)  Use of inferential statistics to reduce subjective conclusions about results
             (a)  Statistical significance means that the result is probably not due to chance
             (b)  Clinical significance means that the result is meaningful in practice

II.  Research designs

  A.  The case study
     1.  Is idiographic (individual uniqueness-oriented) rather than nomothetic (general law-establishing)
     2.  Is useful in treating specific individuals
     3.  Is useful when disorders are very rare
     4.  Can provide the exception that challenges the rule
     5.  Cause and effect conclusions are limited
     6.  Individuals are unlikely to represent the population, resulting in low external validity

  B.  Correlational research designs (also called natural groups designs)
     1.  Correlational designs do not manipulate but only observe relationships between variables
     2.  The case-control version compares variables associated with cases (patients) with those associated with controls (nonpatients)
     3.  Correlational designs are good for description and prediction, but cannot be used to determine causality
       a.  Simple covariation does not tell which factor is causal
       b.  Alternative causes are not eliminated (third variable problem)
     4.  Correlational studies can provide ideas for controlled experiments which may reveal causality

  C.  Longitudinal studies
     1.  Study the same subjects repeatedly over time
     2.  Clarify time-order relationships
     3.  High risk versions of this approach make subject selection more efficient by studying persons thought most likely to develop a problem
       a.  Genetic high-risk design examines genetic predispositions
       b.  Behavioral high-risk design focuses on behaviors that tend to predict disorder

D. Epidemiology studies
   1. Epidemiology studies examine incidence and prevalence of disorders
      a. Incidence is the number of new cases in a given time period
      b. Prevalence is the frequency of the disorder in the population at any specific time
   2. Since epidemiological surveys take information from samples to draw conclusions about the population, representativeness of the sample is crucial for good results

E. Analogue experiments
   1. Attempt to recreate natural situations in controlled settings
   2. Uncontrolled variables can be minimized and causal conclusions may be more trustworthy (increased internal validity)
   3. Controlled laboratory conditions can substitute for conditions that would be unethical if created in uncontrolled real life
   4. Animals can be used in studies that would be unethical if done with humans
   5. One drawback is that external validity (generalizability) may be lost in the effort to gain internal validity

F. Single-case experimental designs
   1. Uses a single subject as his or her own control
   2. Types of single-case designs
      a. ABAB design compares treatment with no treatment
         (1) First A is initial baseline performance
         (2) First B is initial treatment performance
         (3) Second A is return to baseline
         (4) Second B is return to treatment
      b. Multiple baseline designs compare treatments for a variety of subjects, or for a variety of behaviors or situations in a single subject
   3. Limited in external validity because individual case may not be representative

## KEY TERMS
*The following terms are in bold print in your text. Define them and practice their definitions using the flash cards at the end of the chapter.*

ABAB design (113)
analogue experiments (111)
case-control design (108)
case study (106)
confounding (101)
control (100)
control techniques (103)
correlational research designs (108)
covariation of events (101)
demand characteristics (103)
dependent variables (103)
description (100)
double-blind (104)
elimination of plausible alternative causes (101)
epidemiology (110)
experimenter effects (104)
external validity (101)
generalizability (101)
high-risk design (110)
hypothesis (102)
idiographic research (106)

incidence (110)
independent variable (103)
internal validity (101)
longitudinal studies (110)
multiple-baseline design (114)
natural group designs (108)
null hypothesis (104)
operational definitions (102)
placebo control groups (104)
prediction (100)
prevalence (110)
random assignment (103)
random sample (102)
reliability (100)
representativeness (101)
single-case experiment (113)
statistical inference (104)
third-variable problem (108)
time-order relationship (101)
understanding (101)
validity (100)

*Your text does not list the following terms as formal vocabulary; however, if you don't know what they mean, you will be unable to grasp the concepts of this chapter.*

assess (104)
assessment (100)
complement (108)
compromised (111)
conjunctions (105)
debilitating (114)
deficits (112)

hypothetical (103)
inductive (104)
inert (104)
intervening (105)
linguistic (101)
meticulous (100)
mimic (112)

plausible (108)
precursors (112)
replicate (105)
spontaneous (113)
tentative (102)
unmethodical (100)
warrant (110)

## IMPORTANT NAMES
*Identify the following persons and their major contributions to abnormal psychology as discussed in this chapter.*

Sarnoff Mednick (110)

## GUIDED SELF-STUDY

1. First, can you name the topic of this chapter in two words? If you did not know the two words and you had to look them up, say them to yourself a couple of times to aid in recall.

2. What are the two topics discussed under research methods in this chapter?

3. What is difference between research designs and experimental designs?

4. Use the following terms to complete the blanks for the scientific method: **control, description, experimental, prediction, skeptical**, and **understanding**.

   The scientific method has a doubting attitude which means a (a)_____ attitude, and

   four objectives, which are: (b)_____, (c)_____, (d)_____, and (e)_____;

   and it uses (f)_____ procedures to test ideas.

5. Place a check by each of the following activities that you have ever done.

   _____ Bought a different shampoo and tried it out on your hair
   _____ Tried a different gasoline in your vehicle to see if it would give you better mileage
   _____ Tried a different gasoline to see if it would get rid of the "pinging" under the hood of your car
   _____ Bought a pair of running shoes to see if specialized shoes would help your legs feel less exhausted
   _____ Eaten breakfast in the morning instead of nothing or your usual cup of coffee to see if eating would give you more energy
   _____ Driven several different routes to school to check for the quickest route
   _____ Thrown away that bowl of furry-green-something that was in the refrigerator to see if that refrigerator smell would also go away
   _____ Tried sitting in a different area of the bus to see if you liked the ride any better there than in your "usual" place
   _____ Changed deodorants, looking for one that would make it through the day.

If you have ever engaged in any of these activities, you were doing informal experimentation yourself. You came up with a hypothesis, that is, whatever your idea was that you wanted to check out. Then you proceeded to engage in some activity and watch for the results. So, you already know how to do some of the things this chapter discusses!

6. Using the scientific method, we can state the underlying cause of a phenomenon only after three conditions have been met. The conditions are

   a.

   b.

   c.

7. Two more concerns that are very important to the scientific method are *reliability* and *validity*. These terms are used in scientific terminology the same way we use them in everyday conversation. Write a definition IN YOUR OWN WORDS of each of these terms.

   a. Reliability:

   b. Validity:

8. When you experiment with a new shampoo, you should do everything the same to your hair except the shampoo, so any differences could be attributed to ("blamed on") the one thing that was different, the shampoo. Sometimes in doing research it is impossible to get one factor to be the only difference. Whenever factors are hopelessly entangled together, they are said to

   be (a)_____, which means that bit of research will not have (b)_____.

   (c) What are the two entangled factors that are given as an example of this in your text?


   (d) Why can't they separate these two factors from each other?


9. You experiment with a new shampoo just for your own hair, but researchers are ultimately interested in being able to extend their experimental findings to others beyond the people in

   their experiment. This is called (a)_____. To the extent that this can occur

   the research is said to have (b)_____.

10. Generalizability depends on the (a)_____ of the sample.

    b. What does that mean? (Try putting it in terms of hair shampoo research findings).



11. When doing research that is to be extended to others, the test group (sample) should be representative of the entire group (population) to which you intend to generalize. Your text says you need a random sample of the population to which you were going to extend your research findings. Your text points out that one must "carefully" choose the random sample. Why do you have to be careful if you are going to be random?


12. Which of the following methods is most likely to result in a random sample for a shampoo experiment?
    a. Use the first 20 people that walk in to volunteer.
    b. Put all possible names in a hat and pull out 20 of them.
    c. Pick all the people who want to participate in the experiment the most.
    d. Use the people who have the unhealthiest looking hair.

13. Check your answer on Question 12 before answering this question. Give reasons why each of the other approaches may inadvertently include a selection bias.

14. After you have pulled the 20 names from the hat, how are you to decide who gets the "good" shampoo and who gets dreadful Brand X? What is the term for this process?

15. The above question has a scientific flaw. Did you spot it? How should this be handled?

16. What was the selection flaw in Brady's "executive monkey" research?

17. List three key elements in an experiment that indicate adherence to the scientific method.

    a.

    b.

    c.

18. When you turn in your research proposal, your instructor glances at it and then looks at you and says, "Your hypothesis is falsifiable." What will your reaction be?

19. The three methods of control of factors (variables) in research are

    a.

    b.

    c.

20. When a variable is "held constant," which of the following is true?
    a. None of the subjects are allowed to have it.
    b. A placebo is required.
    c. It is the same for all subjects.
    d. All subjects must have it in varying degrees.

21. To deal with factors that are uncontrollable, researchers use (a)_____ through

    (b)_____ assignment.

22. The third method of control is deliberate manipulation to see what effect the manipulation

    has. In an experiment, the (a)_____ variable is manipulated and the (b)_____ variable is measured.

23. In the shampoo experiment, the independent variable is (a)_____, and the

    dependent variable is (b)_____.

24. For the following research examples, list the independent variable and the dependent variable.

    a. Children with schizophrenic parents are being compared with children of nonschizo-phrenics on IQ tests.
    b. Music aptitude is being compared in left-handers and right-handers.
    c. Social perceptions of peers are being assessed before and after exposure to a class in formal manners.

|   | Independent variable | Dependent variable |
|---|---|---|
| a. | | |
| b. | | |
| c. | | |

25. We may like our friends to try to make us happy, but **WE DO NOT WANT OUR SUBJECTS IN OUR EXPERIMENT TO "TRY" TO DO ANYTHING!** However, human subjects in experiments develop ideas about what is going on and how they should act. Another name for these expectations that they may inadvertently start to display is (a)_____ _____. Also, you as experimenter may inadvertently see events the way you expect them to turn out. This would be termed (b)_____. To avoid both of these biases, a (c)_____ procedure can be used where neither the subjects nor the experimenter knows who is in what group. Explain this procedure.

26. In experiments where some subjects get the treatment and some do not, a _____ control group must be used to make those who got nothing think they got something.

27. An operational definition is specified by
    a. a set of objective criteria.
    b. two or more scientific terms.
    c. statistics based on the null hypothesis.
    d. expectations of demand characteristics.

28. Which of the following is a good operational definition for "tall"?
    a. People who never have trouble reaching top shelves
    b. People who are at least six feet in height
    c. People who describe themselves as tall
    d. People who are judged by others to be tall

29. Operational definitions are necessary for clear communication. What I call oily hair and what you call oily hair might be quite different. It doesn't matter which definition we work with as long as we are all working with the *same* exact one. Write an operational definition for "oily hair."

30. The hypothesis stated in a negative form (assuming that the independent variable has no effect) is called the (a)_____. If there is a difference between the groups that statistical analysis tells us could have happened by chance with a likelihood of only (b)_____, we reject the null hypothesis and call the results statistically significant. In other words, (c)_____ times out of (d)_____ we risk being wrong. We risk saying that the independent variable did have an effect when it really did not. See the Helpful Hints for more on this.

31. Since we are drawing conclusions on the whole population from data on a sample of that population, we say that our conclusions are based on _____.

32. Professional researchers would like to hear which of the following statements about their research?
    a. Your work does not need to be duplicated.
    b. Your work is so good that it will never be duplicated.
    c. I duplicated your work, but my findings are different from yours.
    d. I duplicated your work and found exactly the same results that you did.

33. We have now covered the basics of the scientific method. At this moment can you recall what those three basics steps in the scientific method were? Write them down and check your answer against the answer to Question 17.


RESEARCH DESIGNS
34. The second, and last, topic that you cover in this chapter about research methods is research designs. Different designs serve different purposes. Your textbook likened the researcher's selection of a design to a carpenter selecting which
    a. kind of wood to use.
    b. tool to work with.
    c. color of paint for the finish.
    d. assistant to hire.

35. List the five types of research designs that this textbook discusses. And here's my usual recommendation: Make up a memory trick so that they can be recalled with ease.

    a.

    b.

    c.

    d.

    e.

36. First of all, what is the name of the research design that is "the regular kind" with an experimenter doing an experiment?


37. How can research be done on "bad things"? Researchers can't abuse children and brainwash people for the sake of research. So how can they collect information on "bad things"?


38. Write the name of one of the listed designs next to the description with which it is *most* associated.

    **Analogue experiment**          **Longitudinal study**
    **Case study**                   **Multiple baseline**
    **Correlational study**          **Population surveys**
    **Epidemiology**                 **Single case experiment**

    a. _____ is also called a prospective study.

    b. _____ meets *only* the covariation requirement in trying to explain causes.

    c. _____ can provide the counterinstance.

    d. _____ is an experiment that imitates real life.

    e. _____ is useful in encouraging clinical innovation.

100

f. _____ is very useful for description and prediction.

g. _____ may gain internal validity at the cost of external validity by using tightly controlled investigations.

h. _____ can provide the extreme test of a theory which cannot be carried out experimentally.

i. _____ permits causality inferences.

j. _____ has the "third variable" problem possibility.

k. _____ is a correlational study that lasts over years.

l. _____ can deal with the ethical problem of removing or reversing a positive effect.

m. _____ is interested in "incidence" and "prevalence."

39. What research designs are likely to be the most applicable to the following circumstances? Explain your choice.

a. Access to records of a man (but not the man himself) who has broken his neck three times because he is certain that he can fly

b. Puppies who need paper training

c. Impact of parental divorce on children's emotional maturation according to age of child at time of divorce.

40. Use each of the following terms to complete these blanks.

+1.0                                   direction
-1.0                                   increase
decrease                              increases
decreases                            zero

The poorest correlation is (a)_____. This means there really is no correlation at all. The

highest possible correlation is (b)_____ or (c)_____. These mean a perfect correlation exists.

The pluses or minuses tell the (d)_____ of the correlation (i.e., together or opposite) not

the absolute value of it. In a positive correlation, the two variables either (e)_____

or (f)_____ together. In a negative correlation, one of the variables (g)_____

while the other (h)_____.

41. Which correlation in each of the following pairs is the strongest?
a. -0.5 or +0.2
b. +0.4 or +0.3
c -1.0 or +0.9

42. List possible third variables that could be responsible for the situations below:

a. Every time you are around one particular relative you get a severe headache. Otherwise you don't get many headaches.
**Erroneous causality conclusion:** That relative is so irritating that he/she actually causes you to be physically ill.
**Possible third factor:**

101

b. You study the most for your most difficult class, but you continue to make unsatisfactory grades on the tests. It even seems the harder you study, the worse your grade is.
**Erroneous causality conclusion:** Don't study; it only confuses you. Or, you are not bright enough, or the tests must be unfair.
**Possible third factor:**

c. Your cat has developed a rash when it started eating leaves off the bush in the back yard.
**Erroneous causality conclusion:** The bush caused the rash.
**Possible third factor:**

43. What is the difference between the case study and the single-case study design?

44. More terms--match the concepts to the associated phrases.

**ABAB**                               **High risk designs**
**Clinical significance**          **Idiographic**
**Control condition**            **Nomothetic**
**Counterinstance**              **Operational definitions**
**Experimental condition**

a. _____ More than statistical significance, it can be used and it works

b. _____ Law-establishing

c. _____ Based on one individual

d. _____ Violates a widely accepted principle

e. _____ Uses subjects who have a high probability of developing a disorder

f. _____ Reversal design

g. _____ The group that gets the treatment

h. _____ The group that does not get the treatment

i. _____ Used for clear communications

## HELPFUL HINTS

1. To keep independent variables and dependent variables separate, try some of these ideas if you can't come up with one yourself. (As always, ones you create yourself will be best for you.) To remember which variable is manipulated: The independent variable is manipulated (moved around) since independent people go where they want to go, *or*, dependent variables have to be watched (measured) just like dependent creatures (babies, pets, incompetent adults).
2. The first time I encountered the list of objectives for the scientific method, I thought someone had gotten them out of order. I thought "understand" should be before "predict" and "control." I was to learn later that there are many phenomena we can predict and exert some control over, but we still don't understand why they are happening. For example, in the 1950s some drugs were found to reduce symptoms in some mental patients. No one knew why they worked, but they did. So "predict" and "control" often come long before "understand" (100-101).
3. Find out from your instructor if you need to know the specific details of research examples in the text or if you just need to understand the general concept that they typify.
4. Even if your interests are not in doing research, you need to understand the basics of research design so you can deal with research findings intelligently. For example, a very important fact is that correlational studies *CANNOT* prove causality. In communications media, correlations

are sometimes reported with the implication that there is a cause and effect relationship between the two factors; as an informed listener, you should see the error in such an implication.

5. Beware two words that look very similar—*prospective* (p. 110) and *perspective*.
6. "Subjects" in this chapter are people or animals being analyzed or run in experiments. The subject in an experiment is never the "topic" of the research.
7. The concept of the null hypothesis is really not that complicated. Yes, the researcher really does believe he/she is studying something real; otherwise, there would be no reason to do the experiment. But to avoid getting carried away with his/her enthusiasm and coming to a falsely optimistic conclusion about the study, the researcher uses the null hypothesis in *evaluating* his/her data, and assumes that nothing of significance is happening until the data show otherwise. This is very much like the idea of "innocent until proven guilty" in a criminal court. The prosecutor really does believe the defendant is guilty, but the deck is stacked in the defendant's favor to avoid sending an innocent person to jail. In research, the deck is stacked to avoid the conclusion that something is there when it really isn't.

   Also, the statistics must be done from this negative perspective (i.e., there is no difference) because statisticians can figure the chance probability of outcomes when there actually is no difference. They cannot figure the chance outcomes if there is a difference.
8. There are two "random's" in this chapter: random sample of a population and random assignment of the subjects in the sample to the different groups in the experiment. In other words, the random sample will be randomly assigned in the experiment.

## PRACTICE TEST
*Take the following test several times as you study the chapter. Write your answers on a separate sheet of paper and after each attempt, note in the tally box above each question whether your answer was correct or incorrect.*

1. One of the personality characteristics that helps make a good scientist is
   a. skepticism.
   b. deviousness.
   c. loyalty.
   d. a belief in the supernatural.

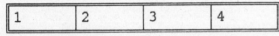

2. All of the following are goals of science *except*
   a. description.
   b. prediction.
   c. rationalization.
   d. explanation.

3. Covariation of events, a time-order relationship, and the elimination of other plausible alternative causes are the three conditions for
   a. proving a correlation.
   b. establishing causality.
   c. removing experimenter bias.
   d. demonstrating statistical significance.

4. Confounding occurs when
   a. experimental results do not come out the way you expect.
   b. experimenter bias produces fraudulent results.
   c. experimental subjects refuse to cooperate.
   d. two or more causal factors change simultaneously.

| 1 | 2 | 3 | 4 |
|---|---|---|---|

5. External validity is the degree to which
   a. research is free of confounding.
   b. research can be repeated by others.
   c. research findings can be generalized beyond the experimental situation.
   d. experimental results fit in with already established theories of psychology.

| 1 | 2 | 3 | 4 |
|---|---|---|---|

6. In selecting subjects for research, I try to be sure that all subgroups of the population are present in my sample in the proportion that they are found in the larger population. I am trying to get a _____ sample for my research.
   a. correlated
   b. representative
   c. idiographic
   d. null

| 1 | 2 | 3 | 4 |
|---|---|---|---|

7. Which of the following statements is true of hypotheses? Hypotheses are:
   a. statistical concepts for determining the likelihood of an event happening by chance.
   b. biased ideas that get in the way of experimental objectivity.
   c. the conclusions that are drawn from experiments.
   d. tentative explanations for things that research is designed to test.

| 1 | 2 | 3 | 4 |
|---|---|---|---|

8. A definition of something that is stated in terms of the procedures used to measure the thing is a(n)
   a. theoretical definition.
   b. conditional definition.
   c. empirical definition.
   d. operational definition.

| 1 | 2 | 3 | 4 |
|---|---|---|---|

9. Neither the researcher working with some experimental subjects nor the subjects themselves know to which group they have been assigned. This is a _____ experiment.
   a. randomized
   b. placebo control
   c. co-varied
   d. double-blind

| 1 | 2 | 3 | 4 |
|---|---|---|---|

10. What is the "third-variable problem" in correlational design?
    a. The possibility that an unknown variable may be influencing the two correlated variables
    b. The inability to deal with more than two variables at the same time
    c. The tendency to try to manipulate too many variables without adequate statistical control
    d. The problem of needing a third experimenter in double-blind experiments

| 1 | 2 | 3 | 4 |
|---|---|---|---|

11. I am doing research on the effects of adrenaline shots. I want all my subjects to be treated in exactly the same way, so even the control subjects are given injections, but of sterile water instead of adrenaline. I am making use of a procedure called
    a. placebo control.
    b. double-blind control.
    c. demand character variation.
    d. paired-associates control.

104

| 1 | 2 | 3 | 4 |

12. What is one thing you *cannot* do with a correlation?
    a. Determine the degree to which variables go together.
    b. Make statements about cause and effect.
    c. Measure the magnitude of the variables involved.
    d. Graphically plot out the relationships between variables.

| 1 | 2 | 3 | 4 |

13. The null hypothesis in an experiment is
    a. the idea that the experiment was designed to test.
    b. the assumption of internal validity.
    c. the idea that the independent variable has no effect.
    d. the belief that all biases and variability have been accounted for.

| 1 | 2 | 3 | 4 |

14. In the United States there were 15 new cases of purple hair syndrome in 1992. In Switzerland, there are roughly two cases per 100,000 people in the population. The first statement deals with _____, and the second deals with _____.
    a. reliability; validity
    b. prevalence; occurrence
    c. correlation; causality
    d. incidence; prevalence

| 1 | 2 | 3 | 4 |

15. The text speaks of idiographic and nomothetic approaches to psychological research. The idiographic approach
    a. concentrates on individual cases.
    b. rejects the scientific method.
    c. is interested in the formulation of general behavioral laws.
    d. is limited to the behavioral perspective.

| 1 | 2 | 3 | 4 |

16. Mednick's research on children of schizophrenic mothers is a good example of
    a. cross-sectional research.
    b. analogue experimentation.
    c. the case study method.
    d. longitudinal studies.

| 1 | 2 | 3 | 4 |

17. Which of the following is a real drawback to the case study approach?
    a. The experimenter is not dealing with real-life people.
    b. Case studies sometimes provide "counterinstances" to challenge accepted ideas.
    c. Case study results can only be applied to the "average" person.
    d. Cause-and-effect conclusions can rarely be drawn safely.

| 1 | 2 | 3 | 4 |

18. In an analogue experiment,
    a. different cultures are compared with regard to some problem.
    b. real-life situations are simulated in a controlled setting.
    c. external validity is maximized at the expense of internal validity.
    d. confounding is the most serious problem.

| 1 | 2 | 3 | 4 |
|---|---|---|---|

19. The "A" in an ABAB design refers to
    a. control groups.
    b. treatment conditions.
    c. baseline conditions.
    d. placebo conditions.

| 1 | 2 | 3 | 4 |
|---|---|---|---|

20. Terry designs a study to examine the effectiveness of a treatment for bedwetting. She only has access to four bedwetters, so after starting them all out with a no-treatment baseline, she introduces the treatment to one child at a time, three days apart. This is an example of a(n)
    a. case study.
    b. ABAB design.
    c. multiple-baseline design.
    d. population survey.

## ANSWERS
### Self-Study Exercise

1. **RESEARCH METHODS!** (99)
2. Characteristics of the scientific method and research designs (99)
3. All experimental designs are research designs, but all research designs are not experimental. Research designs are all those methods that collect information using the scientific method. The experimental designs are only those specific research designs that use manipulation of an independent variable to see if a dependent variable changes.
4. a. skeptical
   b. description
   c. prediction
   d. control
   e. understanding (99)
   f. experimental (102)
5. No right or wrong here, these are your own.
6. a. Covariation of events
   b. Time-order relationship
   c. Elimination of plausible alternative causes (101)
7. a. Dependable or consistent (100)
   b. Is really what it says it is (100)
8. a. confounded
   b. internal validity
   c. Being a mentally ill patient and taking medications for mental illness.
   d. It is impossible to separate these because people that have been hospitalized for mental illness are almost certainly on medications (101).
9. a. generalizability
   b. external validity (101)
10. a. representativeness (101)
    b. Your findings on your shampoo research on your hair will apply (i.e., will generalize) only to people who have hair like yours, or in other words, that your hair accurately represents.
11. You must be careful to use a selection technique in which each person has an equal chance of being selected (102).
12. "b" is the method to provide a random selection. All subjects are available for selection and in no particular order (102).
13. a. Maybe it is during the rainy season and all the curly haired people have hid out because they can't do a thing with their hair when it rains.
    b. This was the best answer.
    c. Maybe the people with the "wildest" hair are the most desperate for help and want to participate, *or*, maybe the people with "the great hair" want to participate to show off how great their hair can be.
    d. This is biasing toward problem types of hair.
14. Don't put that hat away. Put the 20 selected names back into the hat. Pull out ten for the good shampoo and ten for Brand X. This process is called "random assignment" (103).
15. By referring to the good shampoo and dreadful Brand X there may be an experimenter effect biased, perhaps unknowingly, toward the good shampoo. The shampoos should be simply Brand X and Brand Y (103-104).

16. Brady failed to use random assignment of subjects to the experimental groups (105).
17. a.  Develop a hypothesis (102)
    b.  Formulate operational definitions (102)
    c.  Establish methods of control (103)
18. You should be pleased.  A well formulated hypothesis is scientifically useful if it has testability (can be tested).  Ultimately, if a hypothesis cannot be tested for a yes or no answer, the hypothesis has no scientific usefulness (102).
19. a.  Manipulation
    b.  Balancing
    c.  Holding conditions constant (108)
20. "c" (103)
21. a.  balancing
    b.  random (103)
22. a.  independent
    b.  dependent (103)
23. a.  the different brands of shampoo
    b.  the condition of one's hair (103)
24. Independent variable
    a.  Having or not having schizophrenic parents
    b.  Handedness
    c.  Before and after etiquette class
    Dependent variable
    a.  IQ test scores
    b.  Musical aptitude test scores
    c.  Social perception ratings
25. a.  demand characteristics (103)
    b.  experimenter effects (104)
    c.  double-blind (104)
    In a double-blind experiment, the person who sets up circumstances (assigns subjects to test groups) is not the one who interacts with the subjects (104).
26. placebo (104)
27. "a" (102)
28. "b" (102)
29. Example: Oily hair is hair that leaves a one-quarter square inch oily spot on blotter paper when pressed against the hair for 30 seconds 24 hours after the hair has been shampooed (102).
30. a.  null hypothesis
    b.  0.05 percent
    c.  5
    d.  100 (104)
31. statistical inference (104)
32. "d" (105)
33. Develop a hypothesis, use operational definitions, establish methods of control (102)
34. "b" (105)
35. a.  Case study
    b.  Correlational research
    c.  Epidemiological studies
    d.  Experimental designs
    e.  Single-case study (99)
36. Experimental designs (111-113)
37. The researchers can use a natural group design which is a form of correlational research design.  In this they study the differences between groups of people who have had the bad experience during their lives and groups of people who have not had that specific bad experience (108).
38. a.  Longitudinal study (110)
    b.  Correlational study (108)
    c.  Case study (106)
    d.  Analogue experiment (111)
    e.  Case study (106)
    f.  Correlational study (108)
    g.  Analogue experiments (113)
    h.  Case study (105)
    i.  Analogue experiments (111)
    j.  Correlational study (108)
    k.  Longitudinal study (110)
    l.  Multiple baseline (114)
    m.  Epidemiology (110)
39. a.  Case study because your access is only to the records of this "weird bird" and it is a fairly safe bet that he is one of a kind (106)
    b.  Multiple baseline because whatever progress you make you want to keep (114)

c. Natural group design because you have to take the subjects as they come without doing any unethical manipulation (108)

40. a. zero      e. increase
    b. +1.0      f. decrease
    c. -1.0      g. increases
    d. direction      h. decreases (109)

41. a. -0.5
    b. +0.4
    c. -1.0 (109)

42. a. The relative has on some chemical (cologne, hair spray) to which you are allergic.
    b. Anxiety is most likely the third variable here. You may be so anxious about the course that your anxiety impairs your thinking skills while studying and/or while taking the test. Actually you may not be studying as much as you think, because anxious thoughts fill much of your study time.
    c. The cat has some dietary deficiency that is causing the rash and causing the cat to eat the leaves from that bush (108).

43. The case study is a research design which provides information through intensive description and intellectual analysis. The single-case design is an experimental research method because information is gathered through manipulating an independent variable in one subject to see what the dependent variable does. The single-case study is not in with the other experimental designs because it focuses on one subject. The other experimental designs are all based on multiple subjects (106, 113).

44. a. Clinical significance (105)      f. ABAB (113)
    b. Nomothetic (105)      g. Experimental condition (103)
    c. Idiographic (106)      h. Control condition (103)
    d. Counterinstance (106)      i. Operational definitions (102)
    e. High risk designs (110)

## *Practice Test*

1. a (100)      11. a (104)
2. c (100-101)      12. b (108)
3. b (101)      13. c (104)
4. d (101)      14. d (110)
5. c (101)      15. a (106)
6. b (103)      16. d (110)
7. d (102)      17. d (108)
8. d (102)      18. b (111)
9. d (104)      19. c (113)
10. a (108)      20. c (114)

**CONCEPT MAP 5.1**

Fill out the boxes marked with question marks (?) with the concepts or words you think belong there. Answers suggested by the author are on a following page.

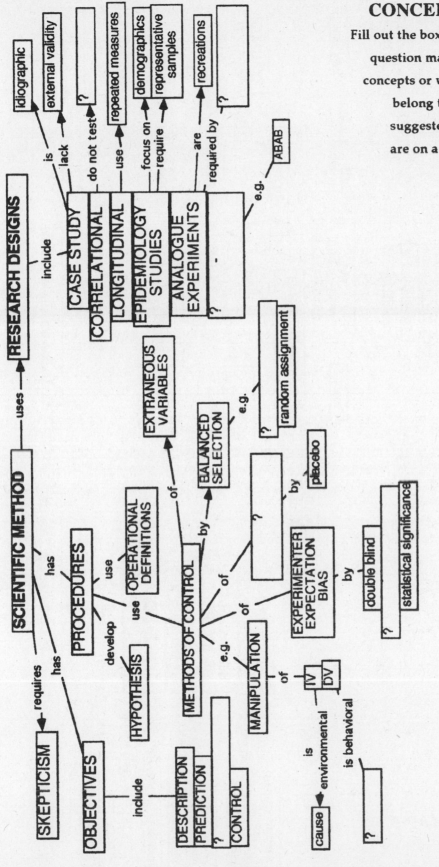

109

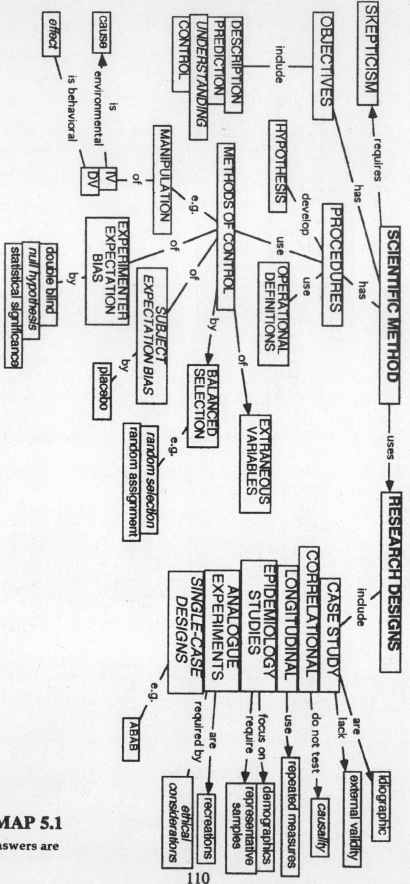

**CONCEPT MAP 5.1**

The suggested answers are shown in *italics*.

110

**CHAPTER TERMS** (Cut out on the lines to use as Flash Cards)

| | | |
|---|---|---|
| 5.1<br><br>**ABAB design** | 5.8<br><br>**correlational research designs** | 5.15<br><br>**epidemiology** |
| 5.2<br><br>**analogue experiments** | 5.9<br><br>**covariation of events** | 5.16<br><br>**experimenter effects** |
| 5.3<br><br>**case-control design** | 5.10<br><br>**demand characteristics** | 5.17<br><br>**external validity** |
| 5.4<br><br>**case study** | 5.11<br><br>**dependent variables (DV)** | 5.18<br><br>**generalizability** |
| 5.5<br><br>**confounding** | 5.12<br><br>**description** | 5.19<br><br>**high-risk design** |
| 5.6<br><br>**control** | 5.13<br><br>**double-blind** | 5.20<br><br>**hypothesis** |
| 5.7<br><br>**control techniques** | 5.14<br><br>**elimination of plausible alternative causes** | 5.21<br><br>**idiographic research** |

# DEFINITIONS (Cut out on the lines to use as Flash Cards)

| | | |
|---|---|---|
| 5.15 Study of the frequency and distribution of disorders within a population; emphasizes incidence and prevalence | 5.8 Research studies that seek to find the relationships between subjects' characteristics and their performance; they describe and predict-but do not identify causality | 5.1 An experimental research design that seeks to confirm treatment effects by showing that behavior changes systematically with alternate conditions of no treatment (A) and treatment (B) |
| 5.16 A methodological problem in which researchers inadvertently influence the subjects' responses or perceive the subjects' behavior in terms of their own biases | 5.9 The first condition to be met before causality can be demonstrated: two events must vary together; when one changes, the other must also change | 5.2 Experimental situations that attempt to reproduce, under controlled conditions, essential features of naturally occurring psychopathology or its treatment |
| 5.17 The degree to which research results can be generalized, or applied, to different populations, settings, and conditions. | 5.10 A methodological problem in which a subject's response is strongly determined by the research setting | 5.3 A research design in which cases, people diagnosed as having a mental disorder, are compared with people who have not been diagnosed with the disorder |
| 5.18 The ability of research results to be applied to different populations, settings, and conditions. | 5.11 In a research study, the factors that measure the behavior of the subjects; their results depend on what the subjects do in the experiment | 5.4 A research design that focuses on a single individual for description and analysis |
| 5.19 A form of longitudinal research which studies people who have a high probability of developing a disorder | 5.12 The first objective of the scientific method: the procedure by which events and their relationships are defined, classified, cataloged, or categorized | 5.5 In a research study, a phenomenon that occurs when two or more causal factors are affecting the DV simultaneously, interfering with accurate measurement of the causal role of the IV |
| 5.20 A tentative explanation for behavior that attempts to answer the questions how? and why?; a statement of relationship between variables | 5.13 A procedure in research that seeks to minimize the influence of subjects' and experimenters' expectations; both subject and experimenter are unaware of what treatment is being administered | 5.6 The third objective of the scientific method: the ability to influence behavior through treatment and preventive strategies |
| 5.21 Research built on the individual, such as the case study | 5.14 The third condition to be met before causality can be demonstrated: the proposed causal relationship can be accepted only after other likely causes have been ruled out | 5.7 Methods by which the effects of extraneous variables in an experiment can be reduced: manipulating, holding conditions constant, and balancing |

| | | |
|---|---|---|
| 5.22<br><br>**incidence** | 5.29<br><br>**operational definitions** | 5.36<br><br>**representativeness** |
| 5.23<br><br>**independent variable (IV)** | 5.30<br><br>**placebo control group** | 5.37<br><br>**single-case experiment** |
| 5.24<br><br>**internal validity** | 5.31<br><br>**prediction** | 5.38<br><br>**statistical inference** |
| 5.25<br><br>**longitudinal studies** | 5.32<br><br>**prevalence** | 5.39<br><br>**third-variable problem** |
| 5.26<br><br>**multiple-baseline design** | 5.33<br><br>**random assignment** | 5.40<br><br>**time-order relationship** |
| 5.27<br><br>**natural group designs** | 5.34<br><br>**random sample** | 5.41<br><br>**understanding** |
| 5.28<br><br>**null hypothesis** | 5.35<br><br>**reliability** | 5.42<br><br>**validity** |

# DEFINITIONS (Cut out on the lines to use as Flash Cards)

| | | |
|---|---|---|
| 5.36<br><br>The degree to which a research sample's characteristics match those of the population under study | 5.29<br><br>In science, definitions that provide a set of specific criteria to identify a concept; defining a concept by how it is created or measured | 5.22<br><br>The number of new cases of a disorder reported during a specific time period |
| 5.37 Research design that focuses on behavior change in one person but, unlike the case study, methodically varies and measures conditions affecting the person's behavior | 5.30 In a research study, a group of subjects given a treatment designed to affect only their expectations of change, thus minimizing the effects of expectations of subjects and experimenters | 5.23<br><br>In a research study, a manipulation or assignment that has been made before the experiment; it does not rely on anything the subjects may do |
| 5.38 Research technique to determine whether differences between experimental groups are due to the independent variable; it uses probability to determine the likelihood of rejecting the null hypothesis | 5.31<br><br>The second objective of the scientific method; the ability to identify a relationship between events | 5.24<br><br>The extent to which the results of an experiment can be confidently attributed to the effects of the independent variable |
| 5.39<br>In scientific research, an alternative factor, not considered by the researchers, that may be causing the covariation of the two factors being investigated | 5.32<br><br>The frequency of a disorder in a particular population | 5.25 Scientific research designs in which a group of subjects is studied several different times over an extended period of time; also called prospective studies |
| 5.40<br>The second condition to be met before causality can be demonstrated: the presumed cause must occur before the presumed effect | 5.33<br><br>A balancing control technique that involves assigning subjects randomly to the different groups in the experiment | 5.26 An experimental research design in which treatment is introduced at different intervals across subjects, behaviors, or situations |
| 5.41<br><br>The fourth objective of the scientific method: the identification of the cause or causes of a phenomenon | 5.34<br>A way of selecting subjects for research studies so that a representative sample is achieved; everyone has an equal chance of being in the sample | 5.27<br>Research studies designed to see whether systematic differences exist between groups of people who have been treated naturally |
| 5.42<br><br>The degree to which a description or test measures what it claims to be measuring | 5.35 In the scientific method, the degree to which a description remains stable over time and under different testing conditions; also in testing the degree of consistency in a measurement | 5.28<br>The assumption that the independent variable had no effect on the differences between experimental groups |

## Chapter 6

# Diagnosis and Assessment

*LEARNING OBJECTIVES*
*By the time you are finished studying this chapter, you should be able to:*

**ASSESSMENT: THE ISSUES**
1. Define psychological assessment and list two goals of the assessment process (121).
2. Define psychiatric diagnosis, list five criticisms of diagnosis, and explain why diagnosis is used in spite of these criticisms (122-123).
3. List and describe the five axes of diagnosis used in *DSM-IV* (123-125).
4. Define the concept of reliability in assessment and describe three types of reliability discussed in the text (125).
5. Define the concept of validity in assessment and describe two types of validity mentioned in the text (126-127).
6. Summarize the text's discussion of assessment problems and what can be done about them (129-130).

**METHODS OF ASSESSMENT**
7. Discuss the advantages and disadvantages of the interview as an assessment tool (130-131).
8. Name four currently-used intelligence tests and review the controversial aspects of using intelligence scores in psychological assessment (131-133).
9. List and briefly describe four personality tests (two projective and two self-report) discussed in the text (133-138).
10. Describe the use of psychological tests for the detection of organic impairment (138).
11. Describe five types of physiological lab tests highlighted in your text that are used in connection with psychological assessment (138-139).
12. Discuss the advantages and disadvantages of using observation in natural settings as an assessment tool (139-140).

**THEORETICAL PERSPECTIVES ON ASSESSMENT**
13. Discuss the essential attitude of each of the text's seven perspectives toward the concepts of diagnosis and assessment (140-144).
14. Describe the assessment techniques that each of the text's perspectives tend to favor and explain these preferences in terms of differing theoretical outlooks (140-144).

*CHAPTER OUTLINE*

I.  Assessment: The issues

   A.  Why assessment?
      1.  Assessment is the gathering, classifying, and interpreting of information
      2.  One goal is description, getting a clear picture
      3.  Prediction may also be possible if descriptions are accurate

   B.  The diagnosis of mental disorders
      1.  Psychiatric diagnosis is when the assessment process results in a person's behavior being classified within recognized categories of mental disorder

2. Diagnosis results in a description of the problem and a statement of prognosis, an outcome prediction
3. Reasons for using psychiatric diagnosis
   a. Research requires categorization of subject matter
   b. Clear communication requires a common vocabulary
   c. Government agencies, insurance companies, and others require evidence of organized knowledge
4. Criticisms of psychiatric diagnosis
   a. It can be used to gain power over people's lives
   b. It can make "problems" appear more different from ordinary behavior than they really are
   c. The problems encountered in real patients are not as clearly defined as the categories pretend
   d. The "naming" process gives the illusion of understanding
   e. Labels obscure individuality and stigmatize
5. The recognized categories of disorder used by American mental health professionals are found in the *DSM-IV*
   a. Specific diagnostic criteria of *DSM-IV*
      (1) Essential or defining features of a disorder
      (2) Associated features that accompany a problem
      (3) Diagnostic criteria that must appear in order for a label to be applied
      (4) Information on differential diagnosis
   b. The five axes of diagnosis in *DSM-IV*
      (1) Clinical syndrome (current symptoms)
      (2) Personality disorders in adults, or mental retardation in children and adolescents (long-term trends in behavior)
      (3) General medical (physical) disorders
      (4) Psychosocial and environmental problems (stressors)
      (5) Global assessment of functioning (coping)
   c. *DSM-IV* does not speculate on etiology (causes) of disorder; it just describes symptoms

C. Assessing the assessment: Reliability and validity
   1. Reliability is the ability to be consistent with repeated measurements
      a. Internal consistency tests if different parts of an assessment tool yield the same results (important if many items measure the same characteristic)
      b. Test-retest reliability looks at consistency over time (important for measuring presumably stable characteristics)
      c. Interjudge reliability looks at consistency over a variety of observers (important for categories that many people must use and agree on)
   2. Validity is the extent to which an assessment tool measures what it claims to measure
      a. Descriptive validity describes behavior meaningfully
      b. Predictive validity allows meaningful statements about causes and prognosis

D. Problems in assessment
   1. The assessor may unwittingly influence clients' responses
   2. The assessor may be unwittingly biased in his/her interpretation of the data
   3. The assessor may be influenced by nonprofessional pragmatic concerns
   4. Some assessors do not follow assessment procedures

II. Methods of assessment

A. The interview
   1. Structured interviews follow a prearranged format
   2. Unstructured interviews are more spontaneous
   3. Interviewer bias may easily influence conclusions, especially with an unstructured format

B. Psychological tests
   1. Intelligence tests
      a. Binet-based tests yield an intelligence quotient
      b. Wechsler tests give both verbal and performance scores
         (1) WAIS-R tests adults
         (2) WISC-III tests school-age children
         (3) WPPSI tests preschoolers
      c. Criticisms of intelligence tests
         (1) Intelligence scores can unduly influence a person's treatment in school and life
         (2) Intelligence tests may be defining intelligence too narrowly
         (3) Intelligence tests are culturally biased and therefore unfair to minorities
   2. Personality tests
      a. Projective tests allow creative responses to ambiguous stimuli
         (1) The Rorschach uses abstract inkblots
         (2) The TAT and CAT use ambiguous pictures to elicit psychologically significant themes
         (3) Projective tests allow creativity and may access important unconscious material
         (4) But projective tests involve much subjective interpretation
      b. Self-report inventories are like true-false or multiple-choice tests
         (1) The MMPI-2 requires true-false responses to over 500 statements
            (a) Client's answers are compared to those of others with specific diagnoses
            (b) Ten clinical scales are used
            (c) Control scales make it hard to fool the test
            (d) Response sets and acquiescence sets may be a problem
         (2) The MCMI-II is similar but is more oriented to specific DSM categories
   3. Psychological tests for organic impairment are used to detect neurological problems
      a. Bender Visual-Motor Gestalt Test asks client to reproduce printed designs
      b. Halstead-Reitan Neuropsychological Battery asks client to perform tasks which locate problems in the brain
   4. Laboratory tests evaluate nervous system functioning directly
      a. The EEG records brain waves from the scalp
      b. CT scans are computer-enhanced brain X-rays
      c. PET scans view radioactive tracers in the brain
      d. MRI uses magnetic fields to image the brain
      e. Polygraphs measure multiple physiological correlates of emotion
         (1) GSR reflects electrical conductance of skin
         (2) EMG reflects electrical activity in muscles
      f. Polysomnography records a variety of measures over a night's sleep

C. Observation in natural settings
   1. Natural observation assumes situation variables are more important than person variables
   2. Has the advantage of providing first-hand information through direct observation
   3. Eliminates many assessor influences and biases
   4. Leads to concrete, workable therapies
   5. But may be time-consuming and require deception

III. Theoretical perspectives on assessment

A. The psychodynamic approach favors methods that get at unconscious processes
   1. The depth interview
   2. The projective test
   3. But subjective methods used to evaluate unconscious processes result in serious validity problems

B. The behavioral approach favors methods that elicit samples of behavior for functional analysis
   1. Interviews
   2. Self-monitoring diaries

3. Direct observation
4. These techniques are seen by some as superficial

C. The cognitive approach favors methods that illustrate the thought processes of the client
   1. Perceptual tests
   2. Hopelessness scale
   3. Attributional Style Questionnaire
   4. Thought recording by client

D. The sociocultural approach worries about cultural biases in assessment
   1. Language differences between client and diagnostician may distort assessment
   2. What is normal behavior in one culture may be seen as abnormal in another
   3. Either ethnocentrism *or* extreme attempts to *avoid* ethnocentrism can distort assessment as well

E. The interpersonal approach focuses on relationships rather than individuals
   1. "Identified patient" not only assessed alone, but with significant others as well
   2. The "others," however, may not appreciate the implied association with the client's problem

F. The humanistic-existential approach favors methods that emphasize the client's individuality
   1. Any test instrument is seen as an opportunity for self-expression
   2. There is a problem with the degree to which clients' statements can be taken at face value

G. The biological approach favors methods that get at the organic components of behavior
   1. Laboratory tests are most commonly used
   2. Limited knowledge of brain processes requires these methods be supplemented by other, more psychological techniques

## KEY TERMS
*The following terms are in bold print in your text. Define them and practice their definitions using the flash cards at the end of the chapter.*

comorbidity (127)
depth interview (141)
description (121)
descriptive validity (126)
diagnosis (121)
*DSM-IV* (123)
electroencephalogram (EEG) (138)
electromyogram (EMG) (139)
functional analysis (142)
galvanic skin response (GSR) (139)
intelligence quotient (IQ) (131)
intelligence tests (131)
interjudge reliability (125)
internal consistency (125)
interview (130)
Minnesota Multiphasic Personality Inventory-2 (MMPI-2) (136)
person variables (139)

polygraph (139)
polysomnography (139)
prediction (121)
predictive validity (127)
prognosis (121)
projective personality tests (133)
psychological assessment (120)
psychological test (131)
psychometric approach (131)
reliability (125)
response sets (137)
Rorschach Psychodiagnostic Inkblot Test (133)
self-report personality inventories (136)
situational variables (139)
test-retest reliability (125)
traits (131)
validity (126)

*Your text does not list the following terms as formal vocabulary; however, if you don't know what they mean, you will be unable to grasp the concepts of this chapter.*

candor (130)
diagnostician (123)
explicitly (123)
idiosyncratic (122)

implicitly (123)
inadvertent (133)
infallible (137)
inferred construct (133)

proliferated (144)
reductive (142)
self-castigating (142)
surreptitious (140)

*Identify the following persons and their major contributions to abnormal psychology as discussed in this chapter.*

Emil Kraepelin (121)          D. L. Rosenhan (124)

## GUIDED SELF-STUDY

ASSESSMENT: THE ISSUES

1. Use these terms to complete the following blanks:

| | | |
|---|---|---|
| **behavior** | **educational plans** | **organized** |
| **career choices** | **experience** | **predict** |
| **control** | **future** | **psychological** |
| **decisions** | **hiring decisions** | **treatment plans** |
| **describe** | **interpreted** | **understand** |

   Psychological assessment is information about an person's (a)_____ and (b)_____

   that is (c)_____ and (d)_____ to form a (e)_____ portrait of the person.

   The goals of psychological assessment are (f)_____, (g)_____, (h)_____,

   and (i)_____.  Current psychological assessments are used for (j)_____ that are

   to be made about one's (k)_____, for example (l)_____, (m)_____,

   (n)_____, (o)_____, and treatment effectiveness.

2. Psychological assessments of people have been around a long time.  See if you can number the following assessments one to six with one being the earliest.

   ____    American Psychiatric Association (APA) published first *DSM*.
   ____    Babylonians started doing personalized horoscopes.
   ____    Chinese used written tests to select civil servants.
   ____    Greeks started to interpret character according to physique and bearing.
   ____    Hippocrates used his four humor theory.
   ____    Kraepelin publicized his biogenic classification system.

3. A (a)_____ is the classification of abnormal behavior into an accepted cataloging system.

   The most common form is the psychiatric diagnosis, which is a classification system of

   psychological disturbances defined by the (b)_____ in (c)_____

   which stands for (d)_____.

4. Indicate whether each of the following phrases is a **justification** or **criticism** of diagnosis.

   a.  _____ Abnormal as qualitatively different from normal
   b.  _____ Artificial clarity
   c.  _____ Grouping people for research studies
   d.  _____ Illusion of explanation
   e.  _____ Standardize terms for communications

5. Early editions of *DSM* had brief, vague descriptions of disorders.  But now, each diagnosis has the following information associated with it.  Draw a line from each feature to its definition.

   a.  Essential features          Define the disorder
   b.  Associated features         Distinguish among disorders
   c.  Diagnostic criteria         *Must* be present
   d.  Differential diagnosis      Usually present

6. Another important feature in *DSM-IV* is the five standard informational items that make up each diagnosis. These five areas of the individual's functioning are called the _____ of diagnosis.

7. List the five axes in order.

   I.                                          IV.

   II.                                         V.

   III.

8. Here are descriptions of the five axes. Identify them by their numbers.

   a. _____ Long-term trends in behavior not covered under clinical syndrome
   b. _____ Measure of coping
   c. _____ Medical problems
   d. _____ Patient's most serious current psychological problem
   e. _____ Things the patient has to cope with

9. Use the following terms to complete these blanks: **neurosis, non-Freudians, etiology, physiological, behavioral symptoms**.

   Another important aspect of DSM is the idea of unspecified (a)_____, which means there are no assumptions made as to causes of mental disorders. The 1980 edition deleted the use

   of the term (b)_____, which has psychoanalytic roots and therefore carried psychodynamic

   theoretical implications of anxiety caused by intrapsychic conflict. Many (c)_____ did not want to go on using a diagnostic term that implied concepts they did not use or accept.

   Thus, disorders are now categorized by (d)_____ instead of by assumed causes. The

   one exception is the organic disorders which are known to be (e)_____ in origin.

10. The usefulness of any assessment method depends on its reliability and its validity. From Chapter 5, you know the terms reliability and validity. Define them here in your own words.

    a. Reliability:

    b. Validity:

11. Here are the three conditions (criteria) for reliability in psychological assessment tools: Write in the name of each next to its description.

    a. _____ Each part of a measuring tool measures the same thing

    b. _____ Gives the same results with repeated uses

    c. _____ Gives the same results with different users

12. In psychiatric diagnoses, _____ is the most desired form of reliability.

13. When the *DSM* categories were broad and general, people "fit" into categories easily, perhaps too easily, and they often fit into too many categories for the diagnosis to be meaningful. With increased precision and specificity, that problem has been reduced; however, now more people

    are being diagnosed as "disorder not otherwise specified," which means _____

    _____.

14. The two kinds of validity that are discussed in Chapter 6 are (a)_____

    and (b)_____.

15. (a)_____ validity focuses on current behavior, and (b)_____ validity
    focuses on future behavior.

16. Fill in the following blanks with the correct term: **reliability** or **validity**.

    One can have (a)_____ without (b)_____, but one cannot have (c)_____

    without (d)_____.

17. List some of the problems associated with assessment that affect the reliability and validity
    of assessment tools.

    a.

    b.

    c.

    d.

    e.

18. List two ways the assessor's behavior can influence the client's assessment results.

    a.

    b.

19. With the reference to practical considerations, the diagnostician may want a diagnosis that is

    serious enough that (a)_____ and harmless enough not to (b)_____.

    Two popular disorders that fit these specifications are (c) _____ and

    (d)_____.

20. (a)_____ is term used for an individual who meets the diagnostic criteria for

    more than one Axis I diagnosis. Recent research reveals that it is (b)_____ (more/less)
    common to have two or more disorders than to have just one. This brings up the theoretical
    question of whether these are independently coexisting disorders or whether one is secondary
    to the other.

21. The study of comorbidity reveals some very interesting statistics. You fill in the blanks.

    a. One out of every _____ people will have serious psychological disorder.
    b. One out of every _____ people has had serious disorder within the last year.
    c. Less than _____ out of every ten of those people seek treatment.
    d. More than _____ percent of all the mental disorders are seen in 14% who had comorbidity
       on three or more disorders.
    e. What kinds of people tend to fall into this high-risk comorbidity population?

22. a. What was D. L. Rosenhan's experiment about?

    b. What were the results?

c. What was the point of this research?

d. Who were "fooled" and who were not?

23. Since diagnosticians are trained to detect abnormal behavior, diagnosticians are said to have a

_____ bias because they spot abnormality so readily and perhaps excessively.

## METHODS OF ASSESSMENT

24. List four categories of assessment methods discussed in this chapter.

a.

b.

c.

d.

Again, I recommend that you construct a memory trick so that you can recall these with little effort.

25. Match the phrases with the following assessment techniques: **Interview, Psychological testing, Laboratory testing**, and **Observation in natural settings**.

a. _____ may get at truths that people with problems can't or won't report.

b. _____ is a standard procedure of presentation of a series of stimuli.

c. _____ tends to provide workable answers to behavioral problems.

d. _____ can pinpoint the occurrence of stress reactions in an individual.

e. _____ is the oldest method of assessment.

f. _____ uses the psychometric approach as its dominant method.

g. _____ is the most commonly used method.

h. _____ requires tremendous investment of time.

i. _____ is the primary means of diagnosing organicity.

j. _____ involves watching things unfold without interference.

k. _____ can be structured or unstructured.

l. _____ may involve a polygraph (lie detector).

26. List four categories of psychological tests and two examples for each category.

a.

b.

c.

d.

27. Tell which category of psychological test or specific assessment tool is most accurately described by the following phrases. Here are the possible answers: **Bender Visual-Motor Gestalt Test, Intelligence tests, MCMI-II, MMPI, Projective tests, Psychological tests for organicity,** and the **Rorschach**.

    a. _____ are routinely used and may have major impact on the individual's life.

    b. _____ try to tap unconscious motives.

    c. _____ is the most widely used self-report personality inventory.

    d. _____ allow subjects the greatest freedom in expressing themselves.

    e. _____ is the most famous of the projective tests.

    f. _____ were the first kind of psychological test to be widely used.

    g. _____ are used to distinguish biogenic from psychogenic cases.

    h. _____ requires drawing of nine simple designs.

    i. _____ uses ten inkblots.

    j. _____ is specifically aimed at being consistent with disorder descriptions in the *DSM*.

28. The following terms are ones that you may commonly hear in connection with assessment of individuals with abnormal behaviors. Tell what each term means literally, what it assesses, and to what category of assessment technique it belongs.

    a. CT

    b. WAIS-R

    c. Bender-Gestalt

    d. MMPI

    e. PET

    f. WISC-III

    g. Stanford-Binet

    h. MRI

    i. Rorschach

    j. EEG

    k. CAT

    l. Halstead-Reitan Battery

    m. TAT

    n. IQ

## THEORETICAL PERSPECTIVES ON ASSESSMENT

29. List the seven theoretical perspectives on assessment discussed in this chapter.

    a.                                    e.

    b.                                    f.

    c.                                    g.

    d.

30. Since each perspective believes it knows what the most important contributing element to abnormal behavior is, each perspective tends to choose assessment methods that focus on that favorite element. Likewise, notice that whatever criticisms are leveled at a particular perspective are also frequently aimed at their favorite assessment techniques. Write in the name of the perspective that best goes with the following assessment techniques and their associated criticisms. Use your answers for question 29 as your choices.

    a. _____ Psychological tests for organicity and laboratory tests—knowledge about the intricate workings of the brain is still limited

    b. _____ Projective tests—subjective in scoring and interpretation

    c. _____ Laboratory tests on specific cognitive skills—still a relatively new perspective and its findings are still in preliminary stages

    d. _____ Interviews and questionnaires with identified patient and significant others—do not explain underlying psychological problem and significant others may be unwilling to cooperate

    e. _____ May use any assessment methods in whatever manner will help the client and therapist understand the subjective world of the client—assumes the client is telling the truth as she/he sees it

    f. _____ Concern for how assessment is influenced by cultural background

    g. _____ An interview that is a functional analysis of behavior—looks at the trivial and superficial while ignoring underlying causes

31. Tell which two approaches avoid labeling in the assessment process and tell why each of them does this.

    a.

    b.

32. A prediction of the future course of a patient's problem is called a _____.

33. What is the prognosis for your learning experience in this course?

## HELPFUL HINTS

1. At this point, if you have not read all of the first five chapters of the text and worked the corresponding study guide exercises, you should do so. Yes!!!! Even if you have already been tested on the first five chapters. The basics in those chapters are the foundation for the rest of the course. If you don't deal with those basics, you are on shaky ground. If you did do the work, you should now review it. Even two or three minutes of review per study session will make a difference. When you review, you don't just pick up bits of information that slipped by you the first time; you also have little insights into the information that you did not have the first time because now you have knowledge that you did not have when you went through the material earlier.

2. If your prognosis is not satisfactory, assess your study habits to see what changes you can make. List three changes that would either improve your grade or make your study time more efficient. The study methods section in the front of this study guide has a multitude of ideas for you to use in becoming a more efficient, productive learner. If you haven't read it, you are missing out on some of the benefits that you paid for when you bought this study

guide. If you read it at the beginning of the term, it is time to review it. What methods have you already incorporated into your study techniques? What other techniques could you try?

## PRACTICE TEST
*Take the following test several times as you study the chapter. Write your answers on a separate sheet of paper and after each attempt, note in the tally box above each question whether your answer was correct or incorrect.*

| 1 | 2 | 3 | 4 |
|---|---|---|---|

1. Psychological assessment can be defined as
   a. a background check to see if a person has ever been a mental patient before.
   b. the process of deciding on a course of treatment after a diagnosis has been made.
   c. the process of evaluating the effects of treatment at one-year intervals.
   d. collecting, organizing, and interpreting information about a person and a situation.

| 1 | 2 | 3 | 4 |
|---|---|---|---|

2. *DSM* stands for
   a. Demonologicum Segurum Mondum
   b. Diagnostic Standards and Methods
   c. Deviations, Symptoms, and Madness
   d. Diagnostic and Statistical Manual

| 1 | 2 | 3 | 4 |
|---|---|---|---|

3. The prediction of the future course of a problem is called
   a. etiology.
   b. prognosis.
   c. diagnosis.
   d. epidemiology.

| 1 | 2 | 3 | 4 |
|---|---|---|---|

4. Which of the following is *not* one of the objections to the diagnostic and assessment process mentioned in the text?
   a. Diagnostic techniques are obsolete because Kraepelin used them years ago.
   b. Diagnosis is a dehumanizing process that pigeon-holes people impersonally.
   c. Diagnostic labels give the illusion of an explanation even when there is none.
   d. Diagnostic labels stick with a person and become a blot on his or her record.

| 1 | 2 | 3 | 4 |
|---|---|---|---|

5. Waldo is seeing a psychologist for some of his problems. One of the things that has come out during the first meeting is that Waldo is sexually impotent as a result of injuries suffered in an accident five years ago. His injuries would be noted on axis _____ of *DSM-IV*.
   a. II
   b. III
   c. IV
   d. V

| 1 | 2 | 3 | 4 |
|---|---|---|---|

6. *DSM-IV* avoids specifying an etiology for the disorders it classifies. This means
   a. it tries not to place labels on people's problems.
   b. it makes no judgment about the severity of a problem.
   c. it doesn't make judgments about the causes of a problem.
   d. it avoids making suggestions about treatment.

| 1 | 2 | 3 | 4 |

7. Which of the following would be most likely to object to the classification of mental disorder?
   a.  A modern psychoanalyst
   b.  Thomas Szasz
   c.  Sigmund Freud
   d.  Emil Kraepelin

| 1 | 2 | 3 | 4 |

8. The kind of reliability that is shown when a test can be administered repeatedly with the same result is
   a.  internal consistency.
   b.  predictive reliability.
   c.  test-retest reliability.
   d.  interjudge reliability.

| 1 | 2 | 3 | 4 |

9. I am interested in hiring a new secretary, so I devise a test that each of the applicants must take. The test consists of taking a 1947 Dodge carburetor apart and reassembling it. Later, I find that the highest scorer on the test turns out to be a lousy secretary. What went wrong?
   a.  This test has no validity because what is being measured has nothing to do with secretarial skills.
   b.  I picked an old carburetor that I could hardly expect anyone to know about.
   c.  I need to retest several times to make sure the results are consistent.
   d.  When testing randomly selected skills like this, there is usually high validity but low reliability.

| 1 | 2 | 3 | 4 |

10. The psychometric approach to assessment uses psychological tests to measure
    a.  personality traits.
    b.  socioeconomic level.
    c.  electrical brain activity.
    d.  vocational skills.

| 1 | 2 | 3 | 4 |

11. Which of the following is an intelligence test?
    a.  MMPI-2
    b.  TAT
    c.  MCMI-II
    d.  WPPSI

| 1 | 2 | 3 | 4 |

12. In the Rorschach test, the subject is asked to
    a.  interpret vague photographs.
    b.  reveal the content of his or her dreams.
    c.  describe what he or she sees in inkblots.
    d.  answer a series of true-false questions.

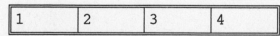

| 1 | 2 | 3 | 4 |

13. The most widely used self-report personality inventory is the
    a.  CAT.
    b.  MMPI-2.
    c.  WISC-III.
    d.  TAT.

| 1 | 2 | 3 | 4 |
|---|---|---|---|

14. Imogene is taking a self-report personality test. She has difficulty disagreeing with anybody and as a result she simply responds "true" to just about all the items. Her score is being distorted by a(n)
    a.  acquiescence set.
    b.  straight set.
    c.  positive transfer.
    d.  social desirability set.

| 1 | 2 | 3 | 4 |
|---|---|---|---|

15. The Bender Visual-Motor Gestalt test is used to
    a.  detect neurological impairment.
    b.  evaluate auditory perception.
    c.  test intelligence in preverbal children.
    d.  diagnose depression.

| 1 | 2 | 3 | 4 |
|---|---|---|---|

16. Which of the following physiological lab tests is able to detect emotional responses by monitoring muscle tension, pulse rate, and skin resistance?
    a.  Computerized axial tomography
    b.  The polygraph
    c.  The EEG
    d.  Positron-emission tomography

| 1 | 2 | 3 | 4 |
|---|---|---|---|

17. If you really want to know what Karen is like, you have to follow her around for a while. She tends to behave one way at work, another way at home and still another way when she is out with her friends. Such behavior variation can be explained as
    a.  acquiescence set effects.
    b.  a high MMPI "F" scale.
    c.  situational variable effects.
    d.  an unstable personality.

| 1 | 2 | 3 | 4 |
|---|---|---|---|

18. Assessment by direct observation is preferred by some psychologists because it
    a.  is easy to score by computer.
    b.  minimizes interpretation on the examiner's part.
    c.  reveals unconscious motivation very clearly.
    d.  can easily be done by the client him/herself.

| 1 | 2 | 3 | 4 |
|---|---|---|---|

19. A behavior therapist is likely to see the results of psychological testing as
    a.  indicators of underlying problems.
    b.  totally useless.
    c.  samples of behavior.
    d.  symptoms of an illness.

| 1 | 2 | 3 | 4 |
|---|---|---|---|

20. Ms. Wilson was telling her neighbor about her visit to the mental health center when she was depressed. She said "the doctor" made her look at all kinds of funny splotches on paper, and asked her many probing questions about her past. The doctor she saw was probably a(n)
   a.   psychoanalyst.
   b.   behaviorist.
   c.   humanist.
   d.   existentialist.

## ANSWERS
### Self-Study Exercise

1. a,b.          behavior and experience (any order)
   c,d.          organized and interpreted (any order)
   e.            psychological (120)
   f,g,h,i.      describe, predict, control, and understand (any order) (121)
   j.            decisions
   k.            future (121)
   l,m,n,o.   educational plans, career choices, hiring decisions, treatment plans (any order) (121)
2. 6, 2, 4, 1, 3, and 5
   Sixth century B.C.: Greeks started to interpret character according to physique and bearing.
   Fifth century B.C.: Babylonians started doing personalized horoscopes.
   Fourth century B.C.: Hippocrates used his four humor theory.
   Second century B.C.: Chinese used written tests to select civil servants.
   Late nineteenth century: Kraepelin publicized his biogenic classification system.
   1952: American Psychiatric Association (APA) published first *DSM* (120-121).
3. a.   diagnosis
   b.   American Psychiatric Association
   c.   DSM
   d.   Diagnostic and Statistical Manual of Mental Disorders (121)
4. a. criticism
   b. criticism
   c. justification
   d. criticism
   e. justification (121-122)
5. a.   Features that define the disorder
   b.   Features that are usually present in the disorder
   c.   Features that *must* be present for a diagnosis to be made
   d.   Data that help distinguish one disorder from another (123)
6. axes (123)
7. I.   Clinical syndrome
   II.   Personality disorders or mental retardation (children and adolescents)
   III.   General medical disorders
   IV.   Psychosocial and environmental problems
   V.   Global assessment of functioning
8. a.   Axis II
   b.   Axis V
   c.   Axis III
   d.   Axis I
   e.   Axis IV (124-125)
9. a.   etiology
   b.   neurosis
   c.   non-Freudians
   d.   behavioral symptoms
   e.   physiological (125)
10. a.   Consistency, stability, doing it the same way over and over (125)
    b.   Something that is what it says it is or measures what it says it measures (126)
11. a.   Internal consistency
    b.   Test-retest reliability
    c.   Interjudge reliability (125)
12. interjudge reliability (125)
13. those people do not fit anywhere in the well defined categories (126)
14. a.   descriptive validity
    b.   predictive validity (126-127)
15. a.   descriptive
    b.   predictive (126-127)

16. a. reliability      c. validity
    b. validity      d. reliability (127)
17. a. The test giver's personal demeanor may influence the person's behavior.
    b. Assessments that require interpretation by the diagnostician may be influenced by the diagnostician's perspective.
    c. Practical considerations influence the diagnoses: What disorders does this person's insurance cover? And who is going to have access to this information?
    d. Psychological disorders are very complex: Who is to say that the current criteria for diagnoses are really on the right track?
    e. Some clinicians simply do not follow the rules of diagnosis (129-130).
18. a. How the assessor behaves may influence how the person being assessed behaves.
    b. The assessor may have his/her own biases in interpreting behavior (136).
19. a. the insurance will pay      c. anxiety disorders
    b. stigmatize the individual      d. adjustment disorders (130)
20. a. Comorbidity
    b. more (128)
21. a. two
    b. three
    c. four
    d. fifty
    e. Female, white, 20-40 years old, urban, low-income, and poorly educated (128)
22. a. Rosenhan planted fake patients (pseudopatients) in a mental hospital and waited for them to be discovered.
    b. While discharged after varying periods of time, they were never discovered to be faking their problems.
    c. Rosenhan wanted to find out if mental health professionals could recognize "normality" when they saw it.
    d. The staff were fooled, but the mental patients were not fooled (124).
23. pathological (129)
24. a. The interview
    b. Psychological tests
    c. Laboratory tests
    d. Observation in natural settings (130)
25. a. Observation in natural settings (139-140)
    b. Psychological testing (131)
    c. Observation in natural settings (139-140)
    d. Laboratory testing (139)
    e. Interview (130)
    f. Psychological testing (131)
    g. Interview (130)
    h. Observation in natural settings (139-140)
    i. Laboratory testing (138)
    j. Observation in natural settings (139-140)
    k. Interview (130)
    l. Laboratory testing (139)
26. a. Intelligence tests (Stanford-Binet and the Wechslers) (131)
    b. Projective personality tests (Rorschach and TAT) (133-135)
    c. Self-report personality inventories (MMPI and MCMI-II) (136-138)
    d. Psychological tests for organic impairment (Bender-Gestalt and Halstead-Reitan) (138)
27. a. Intelligence tests (131-133)
    b. Projective tests (133)
    c. MMPI (136)
    d. Projective tests (135)
    e. Rorschach (133)
    f. Intelligence tests (131)
    g. Psychological tests for organicity (138)
    h. Bender Visual-Motor Gestalt Test (138)
    i. Rorschach (133)
    j. MCMI-II (137)

28. a. CT stands for computerized tomography; it provides an X-ray view of the brain; it is a laboratory test (139).
   b. WAIS-R stands for Wechsler Adult Intelligence Scale—Revised; it is a psychological test for the measurement of intelligence (133).
   c. Bender-Gestalt is a psychological test to detect organic impairment (138).
   d. MMPI stands for Minnesota Multiphasic Personality Inventory; it a self-report psychological test for assessing personality (136).
   e. PET stands for positron emission tomography; it is a laboratory test that gives a picture of neural activity in the brain (139).
   f. WISC-III stands for Wechsler Intelligence Scale for Children—3rd edition; it is a psychological test for the measurement of intelligence (133).
   g. Stanford-Binet is a psychological test for the measurement of intelligence (131).
   h. MRI stands for magnetic resonance imaging; it is a laboratory test that gives a detailed picture of internal brain structures (139).
   i. Rorschach is a projective psychological test using inkblots to assess personality (133-134).
   j. EEG stands for electroencephalogram; it is a laboratory test that measures electrical activity in the brain by means of scalp electrodes (138).
   k. CAT stands for Children's Apperception Test; it is a projective psychological test for assessing personality in children (135).
   l. Halstead-Reitan Battery is a psychological test for pinpointing neurological damage in the brain (138).
   m. TAT stands for Thematic Apperception Test; it is a projective psychological test that assesses personality with ambiguous pictures (134).
   n. IQ stands for intelligence quotient; it is a measure of intellectual ability (131).
29. a. Psychodynamic
   b. Behavioral
   c. Cognitive
   d. Sociocultural
   e. Interpersonal
   f. Humanistic-existential
   g. Biological
30. a. Biological (144)
   b. Psychodynamic (140)
   c. Cognitive (142)
   d. Interpersonal (144)
   e. Humanistic-existential (144)
   f. Sociocultural (142-144)
   g. Behavioral (141-142)
31. a. Behaviorists avoid labeling. Behaviorists view their assessments as samples of behavior. They are looking for the environmental contingencies that perpetuate the behaviors. They do not make any inferences about underlying traits or motivations so there is nothing to name (141).
   b. Humanistic-existential theorists also avoid labeling. They believe that each person is an individual so to put a label on a person and group him/her with other people flies in the face of this basic premise (144).
32. prognosis (130)
33. The point of this question is to have you work with the word "prognosis" in a personal context although this usage is stretching the use of the term which is more accurately used in connection with medical outcomes. See Helpful Hint Two.

### Practice Test

1. d (120)
2. d (121)
3. b (121)
4. a (122)
5. b (125)
6. c (125)
7. b (122)
8. c (125)
9. a (126)
10. a (131)
11. d (133)
12. c (133)
13. b (136)
14. a (137)
15. a (138)
16. b (139)
17. c (139)
18. b (140)
19. c (141)
20. a (141)

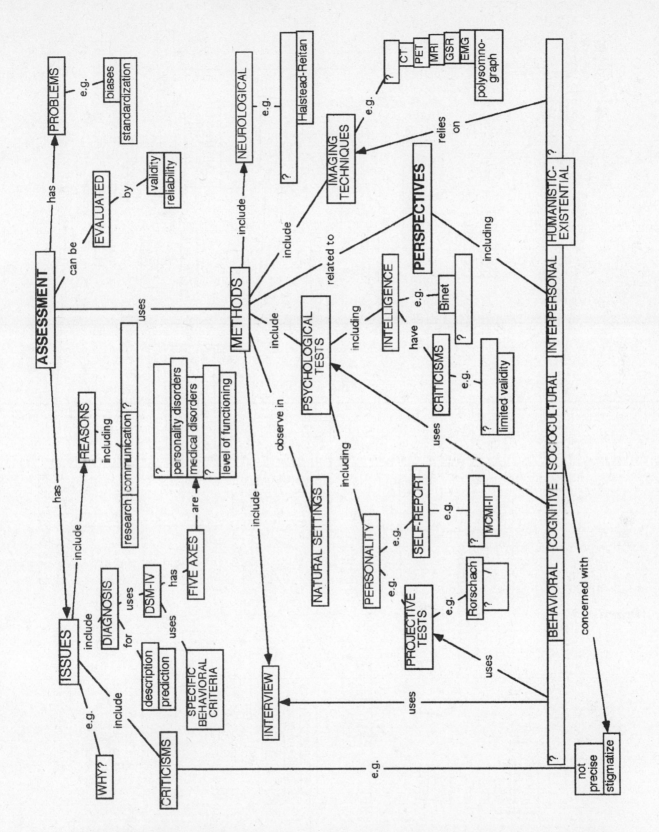

**CONCEPT MAP 6.1** Fill out the boxes marked with question marks (?) with the concepts or words you think belong there.          Suggested answers are on a following page.

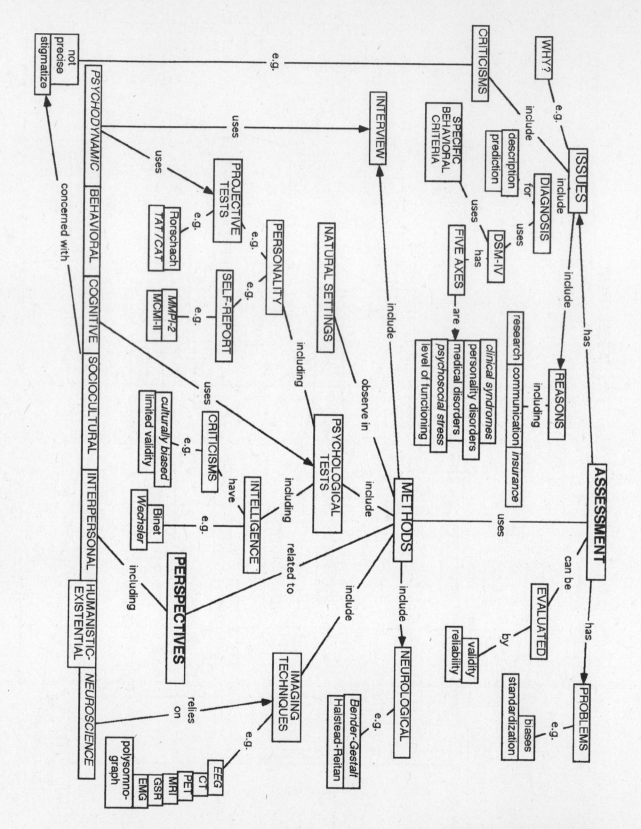

**CONCEPT MAP 6.1**
The suggested answers are shown in *italics*.

132

# CHAPTER TERMS (Cut out on the lines to use as Flash Cards)

| | | |
|---|---|---|
| 6.1<br><br>comorbidity | 6.8<br><br>electromyogram (EMG) | 6.15<br><br>interview |
| 6.2<br><br>depth interview | 6.9<br><br>functional analysis | 6.16<br>Minnesota Multiphasic Personality Inventory-2 |
| 6.3<br><br>description | 6.10<br><br>galvanic skin response (GSR) | 6.17<br><br>person variables |
| 6.4<br><br>descriptive validity | 6.11<br><br>intelligence quotient (IQ) | 6.18<br><br>polygraph |
| 6.5<br><br>diagnosis | 6.12<br><br>intelligence tests | 6.19<br><br>polysomnography |
| 6.6<br><br>DSM-IV | 6.13<br><br>interjudge reliability | 6.20<br><br>prediction |
| 6.7<br>electro-encephalogram (EEG) | 6.14<br><br>internal consistency | 6.21<br><br>predictive validity |

# DEFINITIONS (Cut out on the lines to use as Flash Cards)

| | | |
|---|---|---|
| 6.15 An assessment method consisting of a face-to-face conversation between subject and examiner | 6.8 A polygraph recording of the changes in the electrical activity of muscles | 6.1 The co-occurrence of depressive and anxiety disorders in a person, either simultaneously or at different times in his or her life |
| 6.16 Revision of most widely used objective personality test; compares statements of patients to a pattern of answers by various diagnostic groups (e.g. schizophrenics) | 6.9 A thorough analysis of the frequency of particular behaviors, the situations in which they occur, and their consequences | 6.2 A psychodynamic assessment method in which subjects are encouraged to talk about their past, particularly about sexual and aggressive impulses during childhood |
| 6.17 Each person's stable traits; adherents of this approach hold that personality comes mainly from person variables | 6.10 A polygraphic recording of the changes in the electrical resistance of the skin. | 6.3 The first goal of psychological assessment: the development of an accurate portrait of personality |
| 6.18 A recording device equipped with sensors which, when attached to the body, can pick up subtle physiological changes in the form of electrical impulses | 6.11 A score on an intelligence test that is computed by dividing the subject's mental age by his or her chronological age and then multiplying by 100 | 6.4 The degree to which an assessment device provides significant information about the current behavior of the people being assessed |
| 6.19 The all-night employment of a variety of measures including EEG, EMG, and respiration invaluable for measuring sleep | 6.12 Psychological assessment techniques effective in predicting success in school but questionable as a valid measure of intelligence | 6.5 The classification and labeling of a patient's problem within one of a set of recognized categories of abnormal behavior |
| 6.20 The second goal of psychological assessment: the development of hypotheses about future behavior, treatment, and statistical trends | 6.13 A criterion for judging the reliability of psychological tests; the test should yield the same results when scored or interpreted by different judges | 6.6 1994 revision of a system of categorizing mental disorders developed by the American Psychiatric Association; diagnoses individual on 5 axes |
| 6.21 The degree to which a test's findings are consistent with the subject's future performance | 6.14 A criterion for judging the reliability of psychological tests; different parts of a test should yield the same result | 6.7 Record of brain-wave activity obtained by connecting sensitive electrodes to the skull which pick up and record the minute electrical impulses generated by the brain |

| | | |
|---|---|---|
| 6.22<br><br>**prognosis** | 6.29 **Rorschach Psychodiagnostic Inkblot Test** | 6.36 |
| 6.23<br><br>**projective personality tests** | 6.30 **self-report personality inventory** | 6.37 |
| 6.24<br><br>**psychological assessment** | 6.31 **situational variables** | 6.38 |
| 6.25<br><br>**psychological test** | 6.32 **test-retest reliability** | 6.39 |
| 6.26<br><br>**psychometric approach** | 6.33 **traits** | 6.40 |
| 6.27<br><br>**reliability** | 6.34 **validity** | 6.41 |
| 6.28<br><br>**response sets** | 6.35 *(You may fill in the remaining boxes with names, terms and definitions from text and lecture)* | 6.42 |

# DEFINITIONS (Cut out on the lines to use as Flash Cards)

| 6.36 | 6.29 A projective test in which people respond to 10 cards depicting symmetrical inkblots through free association to investigate their unconscious | 6.22 The prediction of the course of a patient's illness. |
|---|---|---|
| 6.37 | 6.30 An assessment technique in which subjects are asked direct questions about their personality and feelings; thus, subjects assess themselves | 6.23 Assessment techniques used to draw out, indirectly, individuals' true conflicts and motives; presenting them with ambiguous stimuli and allowing them to put their private selves into the responses |
| 6.38 | 6.31 The environmental stimuli that precede and follow any given action by a person | 6.24 The systematic analysis of a person and his or her life situation. |
| 6.39 | 6.32 A criterion for reliability in psychological testing: the test should yield the same results when given to the same person at different times | 6.25 An assessment technique in which the subject is presented with a series of stimuli to which he or she is asked to respond |
| 6.40 | 6.33 Underlying characteristics that presumably exist in differing degrees in everyone | 6.26 A method of psychological testing that aims at locating and measuring stable underlying traits. |
| 6.41 | 6.34 The degree to which a description or test measures what it claims to be measuring | 6.27 The degree to which a measurement device yields consistent results under varying conditions. |
| 6.42 | 6.35 | 6.28 Test-taking attitudes that lead subjects to distort their responses, often unconsciously |

# Chapter 7

# *Anxiety Disorders*

## *LEARNING OBJECTIVES*
*By the time you are finished studying this chapter, you should be able to:*

### ANXIETY DISORDER SYNDROMES
1. List three characteristics of anxiety (150).
2. Explain the Freudian concept of "neurosis" and explain why this concept is no longer used as a diagnostic category in *DSM-IV* (151).
3. Describe two varieties of panic disorder and explain its possible relationship to agoraphobia (151-153).
4. Describe generalized anxiety disorder and distinguish it from panic disorder (153).
5. Define phobia and describe two categories of phobia mentioned in your text (153-155).
6. Define obsessive-compulsive disorder and distinguish between obsessions and compulsions (155-157).
7. Define posttraumatic stress disorder, list the factors associated with its occurrence and severity, and describe three phases of the disaster syndrome (157-161).
8. Discuss the problems associated with posttraumatic stress disorder as a diagnostic category (161).

### PERSPECTIVES ON THE ANXIETY DISORDERS
9. Explain how the psychodynamic perspective views the causes of anxiety disorders and how such disorders should be treated (161-164).
10. Explain how the humanistic-existential view understands and treats anxiety disorders (164).
11. Explain how the behavioral perspective accounts for and treats anxiety disorders, making specific reference to the two-process model of learning (165-167).
12. Explain the role of misperception in the cognitive understanding of anxiety disorders (167-170).
13. Describe the findings of genetic and biochemical research into anxiety disorders (170-172).

## *CHAPTER OUTLINE*

I. Anxiety

   A. Anxiety involves three basic components
      1. Subjective reports of fear
      2. Behaviors in reaction to perceived danger: avoidance, impaired speech, thinking, and motor behaviors
      3. Bodily responses to fear: muscle tension, increased heart rate and blood pressure, rapid breathing, dry mouth, nausea, diarrhea, and dizziness

   B. History of anxiety disorders begins with the history of the term neurosis
      1. Term originated with William Cullen because he believed rigid, self-defeating behaviors of "sane" people were caused by neurological dysfunction
      2. Then Freud used the term neurosis to mean anxiety about repressed memories and desires that broke through to consciousness from the unconscious mind
      3. Then DSM-III abandoned use of the term because its underlying psychodynamic assumptions were objectionable to other kinds of theorists

4. Term still used informally to mean less severe mental disorder in which reality contact is not impaired, but is no longer an official diagnostic category
5. Anxiety disorders are now classified according to their symptoms, obvious anxiety or behaviors to ward off anxiety

II. Anxiety disorder syndromes

A. Characterized by anxiety or behavior patterns to ward off anxiety

B. Can be classified into three groups:
  1. Those which have unfocused anxiety
    a. Panic disorder
    b. Generalized anxiety disorder
  2. Those which have focused anxiety (phobic disorders)
  3. Those disorders in which the person only experiences anxiety if he/she does *not* engage in certain thoughts or behavior (obsessive-compulsive disorder)

C. Panic disorder
  1. Characterized by panic attacks, which may be
    a. Unexpected (uncued), or
    b. Situationally bound (cued)
  2. Situationally bound attacks tend to go with phobias
  3. May be accompanied by agoraphobia, seen as an attempt to control further attacks
  4. More common in women than men
  5. Onset typically in early adulthood
  6. Hyperarousal of autonomic nervous system

D. Generalized anxiety disorder
  1. Characterized by chronic worry, dread, restlessness, irritability, insomnia
  2. Twice as common in women than men
  3. Onset typically early in life
  4. Hyperarousal of central nervous system

E. Phobic disorders
  1. Identifying characteristics
    a. Intense fear of some situation or object even though the individual intellectually knows there is no real threat
    b. Avoidance of the phobic stimulus
  2. Phobic disorders are divided into two types
    a. Specific phobias (fear of specific objects or circumstances)
      (1) More women than men
      (2) About 11 percent of population affected
      (3) Examples
        (a) Acrophobia (fear of heights)
        (b) Claustrophobia (fear of enclosed spaces)
        (c) Animal phobias
    b. Social phobias (fears involving social situations)
      (1) Men and women equally
      (2) About 13 percent of population affected

F. Obsessive-compulsive disorder
  1. Definitions
    a. Obsessions (recurring anxiety-provoking thoughts)
    b. Compulsions (recurring behaviors seen as rituals to control anxiety)
      (1) Cleaning compulsions and
      (2) Checking compulsions are the most common types
  2. Men and women equally at risk
  3. Affects 2-3 percent of population
  4. Not to be confused with obsessive-compulsive personality disorder
  5. Not to be confused with "compulsive" eating, gambling, etc.
  6. Trichotillomania (compulsive hair-pulling) may, however, be included here

G. Posttraumatic stress disorder
  1. Is currently classified as an anxiety disorder but is unlike the ones above because it is clearly a reaction to an intense external stressor
  2. Symptoms
     a. Reexperiencing the event or nightmares about it
     b. Avoidance of circumstances that bring the event to mind
     c. Overall psychic numbing to present environment
     d. Physical symptoms of heightened arousal such as insomnia and irritability
  3. Traumas that can cause posttraumatic stress disorder include
     a. Combat
     b. Civilian catastrophe: earthquakes, floods, assault, rape, fires, plane crashes, etc.
  4. Disaster syndrome stages
     a. Shock stage
     b. Suggestibility stage
     c. Recovery stage
  5. Survivors may experience guilt for having survived when others did not
  6. The role the individual had in the event also influences the form symptoms are likely to take
     a. Reexperiencing the event is more likely for those who have been victimized
     b. Denial or psychic numbing when the person took part in violence (as in combat)
  7. Factors that influence an individual's reaction to the stressor:
     a. Pretrauma adjustment
     b. Family psychiatric history
     c. Coping styles: problem focused better than emotion focused (wishful thinking, denial, emotional venting)
     d. Attribution styles: if a victim believes he/she has some control in the situation he/she is better off than one who feels totally helpless
     e. The cause of the event: events caused by human beings are more stressful than natural disasters
     f. How great the threat of death was
     g. The larger the number of victims involved the more stress incurred
     h. The amount of stress in the events leading up to the trauma
     i. The extent to which the victim's emotional support network and living circumstances are destroyed by the traumatic event
  8. Posttraumatic stress disorder has problems as a diagnostic category
     a. How to distinguish posttraumatic stress disorder from adjustment disorder?
     b. Should psychic numbing and denial elements of the disorder better place it among the dissociative disorders?

III. Perspectives on the anxiety disorders

  A. Psychodynamic perspective: Neurosis
     1. Anxiety is the root of neurosis
     2. "Defense style" determines the type of anxiety disorder the person will experience
     3. Treating neurosis
        a. Goal is to expose unconscious material that the ego is struggling to repress
        b. Treatment techniques try to break through the ego defense mechanisms with
           (1) Free association
           (2) Dream interpretation
           (3) Analysis of resistance
           (4) Analysis of transference

  B. Humanistic-existential perspective: Individual and society
     1. Anxiety is the result of conflict between individual and society
     2. Conflict results from discrepancy between the person's real self and his/her self-concept
     3. To rebuild the damaged self-concept the person must take responsibility for his/her own life so he/she can move toward wholeness and freedom
        a. Humanists emphasize self-actualization, which is fully developing the individual's unique inborn potential. Rogers' client-centered therapy assists the client with unconditional positive regard (listening to the client with a

nonjudgmental respect for the individual and without giving advice)
- b. Existentialists say anxiety comes from a discrepancy between one's authentic (real) self and inauthentic (society-shaped) self. Frankl developed paradoxical intention to help clients gain control over problem behaviors and express their authentic selves

C. Behavioral perspective: Anxiety results from learning
- 1. Behaviorists address anxiety that is observable rather than inferred
- 2. We learn anxiety through a two-stage process
  - a. Through respondent conditioning, a neutral stimulus becomes anxiety-arousing
  - b. The avoidance response is negatively reinforced when anxiety is reduced, and thus it becomes habitual
- 3. Although this theory has been supported by a number of studies, there are at least three problems
  - a. Some phobics cannot remember any traumatic encounters that could be the beginning of their phobias
  - b. Why should there be certain objects that are commonly the focus of phobias (read Seligman's theory on prepared learning)
  - c. Two-stage theory does not consider that thoughts may play a role
- 4. Techniques for unlearning anxiety
  - a. Systematic desensitization
    - (1) Learn deep muscle relaxation techniques
    - (2) Develop hierarchy of fears
    - (3) Relax in the presence of items on the hierarchy
  - b. In vivo desensitization
  - c. Modeling
  - d. Operant conditioning
- 5. Cognitive factors in behaviorism
  - a. Dealing with thoughts as behaviors: people are taught new cognitive strategies to replace self-defeating thinking patterns
  - b. Thought mediation (attitudes, personal goals, and mental images) plays some part in respondent and operant conditioning

D. Cognitive perspective: Misperception of threat
- 1. Anxiety results from misperception or misinterpretation of internal or external stimuli
  - a. A panic attack is misinterpretation of internal bodily stimuli when the body is experiencing some heightened arousal (compare to fear of fear theory in behaviorism)
  - b. Agoraphobia is seen as an extension of panic attack. A person low in self-efficacy believes he/she will be unable to cope with a panic attack in public.
  - c. The remaining anxiety disorders are seen as variations on the misinterpretation-of-threat theme
- 2. Reducing perceptions of threat: three-part program for panic disorder
  - a. Identifying patients' negative interpretations of "triggering" bodily sensation
  - b. Suggesting alternative, noncatastrophic interpretations
  - c. Helping patients test the validity of these alternative explanations

E. Biological perspective
- 1. Genetic research supports the possibility of some genetic predisposition to anxiety disorders, most strongly for panic disorder
- 2. Neurotransmitters may be involved with anxiety disorders because of the way certain drugs affect the symptoms
  - a. Benzodiazepines (some tranquilizer medications) are known to stimulate GABA (an inhibitory neurotransmitter) which reduces anxiety
  - b. There is apparently more than one kind of anxiety on a biochemical level
    - (1) Antidepressants are more effective with panic disorder
    - (2) Antianxiety medications are more effective for generalized anxiety disorder
  - c. Activity in the locus ceruleus in the brain stem leads to panic-like reactions
  - d. Basal ganglia may be involved in obsessive-compulsive disorder

## KEY TERMS
*The following terms are in bold print in your text. Define them and practice their definitions using the flash cards at the end of the chapter.*

acrophobia (154)
agoraphobia (152)
anxiety (150)
anxiety disorders (150)
claustrophobia (154)
client-centered therapy (164)
compulsion (155)
disaster syndrome (160)
dream interpretation (164)
free association (163)
generalized anxiety disorder (153)
in vivo desensitization (166)
obsession (155)

obsessive-compulsive disorder (155)
panic attack (151)
panic disorder (152)
paradoxical intention (164)
phobia (153)
posttraumatic stress disorder (157)
resistance (164)
social phobia (154)
specific phobia (154)
systematic desensitization (166)
transference (164)
trichotillomania (157)

*Your text does not list the following terms as formal vocabulary; however, if you don't know what they mean, you will be unable to grasp the concepts of this chapter.*

buttressed (169)
debilitating (151)
engendered (165)
incubation (159)

Oedipal conflict (163)
pervasive (155)
reiterated (160)
retrospective (162)

ruminate (156)
tenets (164)

## IMPORTANT NAMES
*Identify the following persons and their major contributions to abnormal psychology as discussed in this chapter.*

William Cullen (150)
Viktor Frankl (164)

Sigmund Freud (151)
Carl Rogers (164)

Joseph Wolpe (166)

## GUIDED SELF-STUDY

1. What do you personally experience when you are nervous or anxious?


2. List the three basic components of an anxiety response.

   a.

   b.

   c.

3. How does your account in Question 1 fit into the three basic components of Question 2? Did you list elements for each one of the components? If you did not, what did you not include? Give an example of that component.


Use the following terms to complete the blanks in Questions 4-10. Some are used more than once.

**Diagnostic and Statistical Manual**
**less severe**
**more serious and debilitating**
**neurosis**
**non-Freudian psychologists**
**nonpsychotics**
**organic problem in nerve cells**

**patterns of behavior**
**psychoanalytic**
**psychotic**
**repressed feelings and desires**
**severely impaired**
**symptoms**
**unconscious**

4. The history of anxiety disorders begins with the term (a)_____, coined by William Cullen. He used this term because he thought this group of abnormal behaviors was the result of (b)_____ in the nerve cells. Although these people had rigid, self-defeating behaviors, they were still "sane."

5. Freud then used the term (a)_____ to indicate that the patient was experiencing anxiety because feelings were coming into the conscious from the (b)_____. These feelings were about (c)_____.

6. *DSM-IV*, which stands for (a)_____, does not use the term (b)_____ as the earlier editions had, since this diagnostic classification system is used by (c)_____ who do not adhere to Freud's (d)_____ theory.

7. In *DSM-IV*, disorders are classified by (a)_____ that the individual displays. The disorders that were once labeled neurosis are now divided into several categories according to their (b)_____.

8. So, although the term (a)_____ is no longer used as a formal diagnostic label, it is still very much a part of Freud's (b)_____ theory. Also, many professionals use this term informally to indicate a disorder that is (c)_____.

9. In informal usage, the "opposite" of neurotic is (a)_____ which means the disorder is (b)_____ and reality contact is (c)_____.

10. When someone's reality contact is severely impaired, that person sees the world very differently from _____.

11. See if you can come up with an example of severely impaired reality contact.

12. People with anxiety disorders have relatively unimpaired reality contact; however, they do (a) mis-_____ or (b) over-_____ to stimuli that relate to their particular psychological problems.

13. Even though people with anxiety disorders have their problems, they are reasonably in touch with reality and are said to be "ambulatory." In this case "ambulatory" means (a)_____. While they are able to cope, their coping may be very (b)_____.

14. Although anxiety disorders are not so severe and debilitating as disorders that involve psychosis, there can be some serious consequences. Which of the following are true statements about the complications and consequences of anxiety disorders?

_____ Coping is very inefficient; too much energy for too little success.
_____ Largest mental health problem in the United States
_____ Can lead to more severe disorders, such as depression and alcoholism
_____ Can lead to physical disorders such as heart disease

142

ANXIETY DISORDER SYNDROMES
15. What are the three basic patterns for behaviors seen in the anxiety disorders?

a.

b.

c.

16. Fill in the blanks with the most specific correct term.  Here are your choices:

**Agoraphobia**                                 **Panic disorder**
**Claustrophobia**                              **Posttraumatic stress disorder**
**Generalized anxiety disorder**                **Specific phobia**
**Normal**                                      **Social phobia**
**Obsessive-compulsive disorder**

a. _____  Fear of purple pencils

b. _____  A man still re-experiencing horrors of combat 20 years after the war

c. _____  Chronic state of diffuse anxiety

d. _____  A mechanic who washes his hands five times an hour

e. _____  A dentist who washes her hands five times an hour

f. _____  A person suddenly, unaccountably, feels fearful and unreal to herself

g. _____  Fear of the marketplace

h. _____  Fear of leaving home

i. _____  A young executive who turns down a job that requires public speaking

j. _____  A cab driver panics when he loses count of the number of buses seen

k. _____  A student who will take only classes in auditorium-sized classrooms

l. _____  Going back four times to check to see if you unplugged the blow dryer

m. _____  Fear of encountering iced roads during a winter storm

17. How does panic disorder turn into agoraphobia?


18. Why is agoraphobia classified in two different places in *DSM-IV*?


19. How are panic attacks induced in the laboratory?


20. Besides the unpleasant experience of anxiety, what are other possible consequences of having generalized anxiety disorder?


21. What is "secondary anxiety"?

22. Generalized anxiety disorder and panic disorder are currently classed as two separate disorders. Why do some advocate classifying these two disorders as one?

23. List three research findings that suggest that generalized anxiety and panic disorder are separate entities.

    a.

    b.

    c.

24. Use these concepts to complete the following blanks: **avoidance, environment** and **real danger**.

    The difference between reasonable fear and a phobia is (a)_____. In a phobia, the

    person intellectually knows there is no (b)_____, but still reacts emotionally as

    though there were. The second element of the phobia is (c)_____ of the phobic
    stimulus. This is what determines the disruptive level of the phobia in the person's life.

    One's (d)_____ plays a significant roll in this element of the phobia.

25. a. A phobia for snakes (**is / is not**) a big problem if you live in New York City.
    b. A phobia for elevators (**is / is not**) a big problem if you live the a tropical jungle.
    c. A phobia for water (**is / is not**) a big problem if you live in a swamp.
    d. A phobia for speaking in public (**is / is not**) a big problem if you are a salesman.

26. (a)  List some common social phobias.

    (b)  Do you have any of these? Do they interrupt your life?

27. Use these terms to complete the blanks. Some terms are used more than once.

    | | | |
    |---|---|---|
    | **alcohol** | **drugs** | **social** |
    | **anxious** | **increases** | **social phobias** |
    | **clumsy** | **more** | **vicious cycle** |
    | **disapproval** | **specific** | |

    (a)_____ _____ often concern no more than fear of making small social blunders. When

    someone is a little (b)_____, he/she is more likely to stumble over words when speaking

    or to be a little (c)_____ in movement. Therefore, having the anxiety just (d)_____
    the likelihood that a social blunder will occur. Then when it does occur, the person's phobia

    (e)_____, which in turn (f)_____ the anxiety level, which then (g)_____ the
    likelihood that a little social blunder will occur *again*. Thus a social phobia becomes a

    (h)_____. In (i)_____ phobias, a person fears a particular stimulus. However, in

    (j)_____ phobias, the person usually fears a variety of social situations. However the

    underlying common element to social phobias is fear of the (k)_____ of other people;

    therefore, people with social phobias probably experience (l)_____ difficulty than people
    with specific phobias. Fifty percent of people with social phobias reported using

    (m)_____ and (n)_____ to try to cope with social situations.

144

28. When a person stays at home "excessively," the situation could be (a)_____ or

(b)_____. Distinguishing between the two may be quite difficult. One difference may

sometimes distinguish between the two disorders: (c)_____ are afraid of the terror they

experience and will actually seek out people for comfort in their anxiety. (d)_____ are
going to avoid having people see their anxiety.

29. What possible causes are proposed for social anxiety?

Use these terms to complete the blanks in Questions 30-32.

| | |
|---|---|
| **action** | **helplessness** |
| **anxiety** | **image** |
| **checking** | **mood** |
| **cleaning** | **obsessive-compulsive** |
| **depression** | **scandalous or violent** |
| **dominated** | **thought** |
| **guilt** | |

30. An obsession is a (a)_____ or an (b)_____. A compulsion is an (c)_____. The

purpose of the obsession or compulsion is to reduce or prevent (d)_____.

31. The most common compulsions fall into two categories: (a)_____ and (b)_____.

Pathological obsessions and compulsions often involve (c)_____ themes. If you

have an obsession, you are diagnosed as having (d)_____ disorder. If you have a

compulsion, you are diagnosed as having (e)_____ disorder. At its worst,
obsessive-compulsive disorder can be completely disabling because the person's life is totally

(f)_____ by the problem.

32. Since obsessions and compulsions are often accompanied by feelings of (a)_____,

there is debate that perhaps obsessive compulsive disorder should overlap both the

(b)_____ disorders and the (c)_____ disorders (where it is now).

33. Posttraumatic stress disorders (PTSD) are different from the other anxiety disorders because

the source of stress is from an objectively (a)_____ external stimulus. The level of
stress that the person will have experienced in connection with this event will be

(b)_____.

34. What are the symptoms that a person with posttraumatic stress disorder is likely to display?

a.

b.

c.

d.

35. Immediately after the trauma, a posttraumatic stress victim may seem rather normal, but may later get progressively more stressed out. What is said to come between the trauma and and the reaction in these cases?

36. What factors correlate with increased likelihood of developing posttraumatic stress disorder? List four that are features of the trauma and four that are features of the victim.

Features of the Trauma                     Features of the Victim

a.                                         e.

b.                                         f.

c.                                         g.

d.                                         h.

37. Name the two kinds of coping styles. Which one do you tend to use most in your life? Which one is more effective in averting PTSD?

a.

b.

38. What are some of the names given to posttraumatic stress disorder resulting from combat experience?

39. What factors in the Vietnam conflict made it particularly psychologically damaging?

a.

b.

c.

d.

40. Assign the correct numerical order to the three stages of disaster syndrome.

a. _____ Suggestibility state
b. _____ Shock stage
c. _____ Recovery stage

41. People that have suffered disaster syndrome may also then suffer _____ syndrome.

42. As mentioned in earlier chapters and in this chapter, categorization of behaviors is difficult because human behavior is very complex. Some researchers find similarities between PTSD

and (a)_____ disorders. There are some who debate that perhaps posttraumatic stress

disorder should be placed with the (b)_____ disorders because of the psychic

(c)_____ that accompanies it. People who have severe stress reactions to more ordinary

life experiences are diagnosed as having (d)_____ disorders.

PERSPECTIVES ON THE ANXIETY DISORDERS

43. Can you list, without looking at a source, the perspectives that you can expect to have explained here? Try it; test your memory. (The more you flex your memory, the stronger it will become.)

Use these terms for the blanks in Questions 44-49.

aggressive
anxiety disorder
anxiety
association
consciousness
defense mechanism
dream
ego
generalized anxiety disorder

id
obsessive-compulsive disorder
panic disorder
repressed
resistance
sexual
superego
transference
unconscious

44. For Freud, anxiety was caused by (a)_____ (b)____ impulses trying to break through into (c)_____.

45. According to Freud, these impulses were (a)_____ (defense mechanism) because they were of a (b)_____ or (c)_____ nature.

46. In this psychic conflict, the (a)_____ is trying to bring primitive urges to consciousness and the (b)_____ is concerned with keeping them unconscious because reality and the (c)_____ find them unacceptable.

47. When the ego is unsuccessful, the individual experiences intense (a)_____. The pattern of this manifest anxiety defines the (b)_____ which the individual experiences.

48. Sometimes the ego is successful in holding the anxiety off, but achieves this by using one (a)_____ mechanism to excess. The individual is impaired by being locked into this extreme effort with only one ego defense (b)_____; the abnormal behavior is the manifestation of this excessive effort. In Freudian terms, the nature of the disorder points out which (c)_____ is being used to excess, and the nature of this (d)_____ points to what the (e)_____ conflict is. Here are some examples: (f)_____ disorder would be the disorder for a chronic leaking out of anxiety; (g)_____ disorder would be the disorder for and occasional outburst of anxiety. (h)_____ disorder would likely be the disorder for someone who is struggling against letting some impulse out.

49. Through free (a)_____, (b)_____ interpretation, and analyses of (c)_____ and (d)_____, the orthodox psychoanalyst will try uncover the (e)_____ conflict that is causing the anxiety or requiring excess defensive effort on the part of the (f)_____.

50. I often ask questions to encourage you to relate your experiences to concepts in the chapter for enhanced learning. Why, in the course of these questions, haven't I asked you about your unconscious conflicts?

Use these terms in Questions 51-53.

| | |
|---|---|
| **analyzing, judging or advice giving** | **individual** |
| **anxiety** | **intrapsychic** |
| **client-centered** | **positive regard** |
| **concept** | **potential (164)** |
| **conditions of worth** | **self-actualization** |
| **ideal** | **should** |
| **ideal self** | **society** |

51. The humanistic-existential group always see anxiety as the result of conflicts between the

(a)_____ and (b)_____. This sounds rather like the socio-cultural perspective,

but the humanistic-existentialists are primarily focused on the (c)_____ conflict that

the individual experiences as a result of the (d)_____ society has imposed on her/him.

52. In the humanistic perspective, an impaired self-concept is the result of a discrepancy between

the self- (a)_____ and the (b)_____ self. According to the humanists, this

discrepancy is the result of upbringing that says you (c) "_____" be one way or another.

After years of this, the person may develop an (d)_____ _____ that is far removed from the individual's actual experience of living.

53. To rebuild the damaged self, humanistic psychologist Carl Rogers would engage in

(a)_____-_____ therapy and listen to the client without engaging in any

(b)_____. While giving the client this basic human respect called unconditional

(c)_____ _____, the client begins to sort out who he/she really is. Then, as the person begins to bring the ideal self and the self-concept closer together based on who he/she

really is, he/she begins to experiences less (d)_____. Finally, the client begins to

move toward the humanistic goal of (e)_____-_____; that is, he/she begins to bloom

and develop his/her unique human (f)_____ that humanists believe each of us possesses.

Use the following words and terms for blanks in Questions 54-56.

| | |
|---|---|
| **authentic** | **phenomenological subjective** |
| **decrease** | **self-actualization** |
| **increase** | **subjective** |
| **paradoxical intention** | **wholeness and freedom** |

54. Existentialists talk about becoming (a)_____ while the humanists talk about

(b)_____-_____.

55. Existentialists go even further in being nondirective by trying to lay aside even their own theoretical perspective. The idea is to let the client experience his/her own experience unencumbered by someone else's viewpoint. To refresh your memory from the chapter on the humanistic-existential perspective, this approach of trying to see things only from the client's point of view is called the (a)_____ approach. The goal is not an objective analysis, but participation in the client's (b)_____ world.

56. The existentialists, like the humanists, are more concerned with restoring the client's sense of (a)_____ than in dealing with troublesome symptoms. Viktor Frankl developed the technique called (b)_____, where the patient is told to indulge in his/her symptoms, even to exaggerate them. The purpose of this activity is to make the client aware that if he/she can (c)_____ the level of the symptoms, he/she can also (d)_____ them, thus demonstrating the freedom to make life choices.

57. Behaviorism *always* says the problem is a matter of_____.

58. Assign the correct order to the following sequence for two-stage anxiety learning.

_____Avoidance response to conditioned stimulus
_____Conditioned stimulus elicits fear
_____Negative reinforcement to avoidance behavior by anxiety reduction
_____Neutral stimulus paired with involuntary fear stimulus
_____Neutral stimulus becomes condition stimulus

Use the following terms and phrases for Questions 59-61.

deep muscle relaxation                    modeling
extinction                                most
in vivo desensitization                   systematic desensitization
least

59. List four techniques for "unlearning" anxiety. (Note: the acronym of first letters is SIME.)

a.

b.

c.

d.

60. To do systematic desensitization you must first learn (a)_____. Then you will begin with the (b)_____ feared item in the hierarchy of fears and work your way to the (c)_____ feared item.

61. If the process in Question 60 is done in actual real-life situations instead of through mental imagery, the technique is called _____ desensitization.

62. Put the following activities in a hierarchial order from 1 (least feared) to 7 (most feared).

_____Looking at a stuffed snake
_____Looking at a live snake
_____Seeing color pictures of a snake
_____Seeing black and white pictures of a snake
_____Seeing a child's simple drawing of a snake
_____Touching a live snake
_____Touching a stuffed snake

63. Cognition *always* refers to _____.

64. Bandura found that the best predictor of avoidance behavior was not the amount of anxiety experienced but rather one's (a)_____ expectations. These are expectations based on one's (b)_____ that are taken as indicators of how well you will be able to cope with a similar situation in the future.

Give one- or two-word descriptions of your personal efficacy expectations about the following situations:

Passing an advanced math class:

Driving a five-speed transmission:

Running a mile:

Identifying five microscopic plants:

Being able to spell "efficacy":

Staying on your diet:

65. What is a "self-defeating" thought? Give an example of one.

66. Research has revealed that panic attacks often follow events that raise the victim's bodily activity rate. This suggests that perhaps the panic attack begins as a _____ of bodily sensations. The victim's body then does react with a genuine intense alarm response because the victim thinks s/he is going to experience some catastrophe such as fainting or a heart attack.

67. However, if the situation in Question 66 is put in terms of the internal sensations becoming classically conditioned to cause the panic response, we are talking in terms of _____ theory, not cognitive theory.

68. In a Norwegian study, the concordance rate for panic disorder in MZ twins was (a)_____ percent and (b)_____ percent for DZ twins, which suggests (c)_____.

69. Benzodiazepines stimulate the neurotransmitter (a)_____, which stands for (b)_____. Stimulating this neurotransmitter reduces anxiety because this neurotransmitter is (c)_____, which means that it reduces or turns off neural activity.

70. Benzodiazepines are therapeutically effective for (a)_____ anxiety disorder; however, panic disorder responds to (b)_____. This suggests two points: generalized anxiety disorder and panic disorder are chemically (c)_____, and panic disorder may be more closely related to (d)_____ than it is to generalized anxiety disorder.

71. Three different lines of research have suggested that activity in the _____ of the brain is correlated with panic attacks.

72. When is "brain deterioration" happy news?

## HELPFUL HINTS

1. Don't be surprised if, when studying some of these disorders, you notice that you have some of the symptoms, and that you seriously suspect you actually have the disorder.
   This happens for two reasons. First, this is to be expected if you see abnormality as being on one end of a continuum that includes "normal." Everybody does some of these things some of the time. The question is *not* whether you do these things at all; rather, ask yourself how extreme are your symptoms? Do they disrupt your life? Are you dangerous to yourself or others? This is how we can tell if someone is really in need of assistance. See the criteria for abnormality in Chapter 1. The second reason students fear they have these disorders is called the "medical student syndrome." That is, students tend to become sensitive to the symptoms of whatever disorder they are studying at the time.
   Most of my (SJB) students usually happily conclude by the end of the course that they are no crazier than most of the rest of the people in the world. Interestingly, they do often conclude that some of their friends and family members are actually "nuts," just as they had always suspected. However, occasionally a student realizes that his/her anxiety level is higher than it needs to be and that some professional help could improve the quality of his/her anxious life. If, after taking this class, you decide that perhaps that you really do have a problem and may need help, seek out a professional opinion.
2. Many of the debates about where specific anxiety disorders should be listed in *DSM-IV* are mentioned in this chapter. To reduce confusion, be sure to learn the established categories before you try to understand the debates on categorization. Always learn the simple basics before you add any complications. Your instructor will definitely expect you to know the existing categories. Check with him/her to see how much information you need to know about the debates. *BUT BE SURE YOU KNOW THE ESTABLISHED SYSTEM FIRST!*

## PRACTICE TEST
*Take the following test several times as you study the chapter. Write your answers on a separate sheet of paper and after each attempt, note in the tally box above each question whether your answer was correct or incorrect.*

| 1 | 2 | 3 | 4 |
|---|---|---|---|

1. In current informal usage, neurosis refers to
   a. disorders characterized by unconscious conflict over repressed memories.
   b. disorders in which the individual has problems but is still in contact with reality.
   c. anxiety disorders only.
   d. problems that are limited to identifiable neurological impairment.

| 1 | 2 | 3 | 4 |
|---|---|---|---|

2. Which of the following is true of anxiety?
   a. It is always harmful.
   b. It plays no currently known role in compulsions and obsessions.
   c. Its presence is an indicator of serious underlying disorder.
   d. In the right amount, it can promote survival by acting as a powerful motivator.

| 1 | 2 | 3 | 4 |
|---|---|---|---|

3. Why has the use of the term neurosis been removed from recent editions of the *DSM*?
   a. The term implies a Freudian view of disorder and non-Freudians objected to its continued use as a diagnostic category.
   b. The term has acquired a social stigma that prevents many people from seeking help.
   c. The *DSM* was designed to be neutral with respect to theories, and the term was judged to be too medically oriented.
   d. The term implies a neurological cause for anxiety, and there is no evidence to support such a position.

| 1 | 2 | 3 | 4 |
|---|---|---|---|

4. If panic disorder is left untreated, it may progress to
   a. posttraumatic stress disorder.
   b. a total loss of emotional expression.
   c. agoraphobia.
   d. schizophrenia.

| 1 | 2 | 3 | 4 |
|---|---|---|---|

5. A major difference between generalized anxiety disorder and phobic disorder is
   a. a phobia has a specific focus, whereas generalized anxiety disorder is chronic and pervasive.
   b. phobias are always analyzed from the psychodynamic point of view, whereas generalized anxiety disorder need not be.
   c. phobias are seen as being symbolic of deeper conflicts, whereas generalized anxiety disorder can be taken at face value.
   d. a phobia is a neurosis, whereas generalized anxiety disorder is a psychosis.

| 1 | 2 | 3 | 4 |
|---|---|---|---|

6. Two distinct characteristics of a phobic response are
   a. avoidance and aggression.
   b. fear and anger.
   c. fear and avoidance.
   d. fear and depression.

| 1 | 2 | 3 | 4 |
|---|---|---|---|

7. Acrophobia is
   a. fear of open spaces.
   b. fear of water.
   c. fear of enclosed spaces.
   d. fear of heights.

| 1 | 2 | 3 | 4 |

8. Which of the following is true of social phobias, as compared to simple phobias?
    a. About 2 percent of the population; more women than men
    b. Men and women equally; about 13 percent of the population
    c. Onset around age 30; more likely in unindustrialized nations
    d. Less interference with normal living; more likely to have symbolic significance

| 1 | 2 | 3 | 4 |

9. Which of the following is the best example of an obsession?
    a. A constant mental preoccupation with public masturbation
    b. An unexplained paralysis
    c. An unrealistic fear of Ground Hog's Day
    d. A need to brush one's teeth every half hour

| 1 | 2 | 3 | 4 |

10. Waldo takes a long time getting off on trips because he constantly checks and rechecks the stove, the furnace, the door locks, the window latches, etc. He will even turn around after driving 10 miles just to check them again. It sounds like Waldo is suffering from
    a. generalized anxiety disorder.
    b. obsessive-compulsive disorder.
    c. a checking phobia.
    d. compulsive panic disorder.

| 1 | 2 | 3 | 4 |

11. One way to tell a true compulsion from an ordinary annoying habit is to prevent the person from engaging in the behavior. If it is a true compulsion, the person will probably become very anxious. This is because
    a. true compulsions are used to keep anxiety under control.
    b. the person will re-experience the childhood events that produced the problem.
    c. true compulsions are adaptive responses to the client's environment.
    d. the alternative to the compulsion is a descent into depression.

| 1 | 2 | 3 | 4 |

12. Posttraumatic stress disorder differs from other anxiety disorders in that
    a. it is an unreasonably strong reaction to a relatively minor event.
    b. it is a new disorder category that applies only to Viet Nam veterans.
    c. it is more or less understandable, given the events to which the victim has been exposed.
    d. the gene that produces the biological predisposition has been clearly identified.

| 1 | 2 | 3 | 4 |

13. Which of the following is *not* one of the stages of the disaster syndrome?
    a. Shock stage
    b. Active stage
    c. Suggestibility stage
    d. Recovery stage

14. According to a study of Australian firefighters, which of the following is the best predictor of an individual's psychological response to traumatic events?
    a. Intensity of the event
    b. Degree of perceived threat
    c. Extent of personal loss
    d. Pretrauma psychological adjustment

15. The nature of the disorder points to the defense mechanism, and the nature of the defense mechanism points to the underlying conflict. This statement reflects the _____ perspective on anxiety disorders.
    a. psychodynamic            c. cognitive
    b. humanistic               d. sociocultural

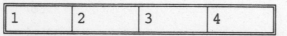

16. According to existential theorists, people with anxiety disorders
    a. are struggling with repressed inner conflicts.
    b. have had unfortunate, fear-related learning experiences.
    c. are experiencing the discomfort of an inauthentic existence.
    d. are the victims of their own negative thought processes.

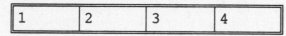

17. Luella has been late for her last four appointments with her analyst. The analyst suggests to her that this might be due to reluctance to discuss her relationship with her mother. The analyst thinks that her lateness is an example of
    a. repression.              c. inauthenticity.
    b. resistance.              d. neurotic interpretation.

18. The cognitive approach to anxiety disorders focuses on a person's
    a. interpretation of events and bodily processes.
    b. lack of authenticity and self-actualization.
    c. childhood conditioning of sexual and aggressive drives.
    d. emotional stability and biochemical balance.

19. The behavioral perspective sees anxiety developing in two stages. The two stages are
    a. generalization and discrimination.
    b. positive and negative respondent conditioning.
    c. modeling and internalization.
    d. respondent conditioning and avoidance learning.

| 1 | 2 | 3 | 4 |

20. Biochemically, panic disorder seems to be most closely related to
    a. generalized anxiety disorder.
    b. depression.
    c. schizophrenia.
    d. neurotic compression.

## ANSWERS
### Self-Study Exercise

1. Your own experience—some possibilities are sweating palms, tight stomach, general bodily tension, or mental preoccupation with your problem.
2. a. Subjective report
   b. Behavioral responses
   c. Physiological responses (150)
3. Subjective reports of tension and impending danger
   Behavioral responses such as talks too much, shaking knees, tremor in voice
   Physiological responses such as rapid heart rate, knot in stomach, sweaty palms (158)
4. a. neurosis
   b. organic problems (150-151)
5. a. neurosis
   b. unconscious
   c. repressed feelings and desires (151)
6. a. Diagnostic and Statistical Manual
   b. neurosis
   c. non-Freudian psychologists
   d. psychoanalytic (151)
7. a. patterns of behavior
   b. symptoms (151)
8. a. neurosis
   b. psychoanalytic
   c. less severe (151)
9. a. psychotic
   b. more serious and debilitating
   c. severely impaired (151)
10. nonpsychotics (151)
11. Little green men over in the corner of the room (yes, they are there now), or my belief that I am the queen of England
12. a. interpret
    b. react (151)
13. a. able to go about their daily lives
    b. poor (or inefficient) (151)
14. All of these are true of anxiety disorders. Memorize them all for the test (151).
15. a. Unfocused anxiety
    b. Fear of a particular object or situation
    c. A disruptive behavior designed to help keep anxiety down (151)
16. a. Specific phobia (154)
    b. Posttraumatic stress disorder (157-158)
    c. Generalized anxiety disorder (153)
    d. Obsessive-compulsive disorder (155)
    e. Normal (150, 155-157)
    f. Panic disorder (151)
    g. Agoraphobia (152)
    h. Agoraphobia (152)
    i. Social phobia (154-155)
    j. Obsessive-compulsive disorder (155-156)
    k. Claustrophobia (154)
    l. Obsessive-compulsive disorder (155-156)
    m. Normal (150, 155-157)

17. Panic involves a feeling of being out of control, so many panic disorder patients stay in an environment in which they feel they can control things—typically the home environment. Eventually, they may be unable to leave home (152).
18. It is classified differently depending on whether it exists alone or in combination with panic disorder (152).
19. Through pharmacological agents such as sodium lactate, yohimbine, or caffeine; through breathing procedures such as exercise, hyperventilation, or carbon dioxide inhalation; through confronting a phobic stimulus (153)
20. Development of secondary anxiety; difficulty in memory, concentration, and decision making; many physical complaints (153)
21. Fear of fear itself (153)
22. Some argue that generalized anxiety is the "resting state" of panic disorder (153).
23. a. Symptom profiles are different.
    b. Generalized anxiety disorder seems a more gradual process as compared to a faster course for panic disorder.
    c. Both disorders tend to run in families, but not the same families (153).
24. a. real danger      c. avoidance
    b. real danger      d. environment (153-154)

25. a. is not      c. is
    b. is not      d. is (154)
26. a. Possibilities include: speaking before groups, eating in public, using public bathrooms
    b. If you said "no," did you ever have to do a music recital as a child? Were you apprehensive? Do assignments involving oral reports give you a "knot in your stomach"? (154)
27. a. social phobias      h. vicious cycle
    b. anxious      i. specific
    c. clumsy      j. social
    d. increases      k. disapproval
    e. increases      l. more
    f. increases      m. drugs
    g. increases      n. alcohol (155)

28. a. agoraphobia      c. agoraphobics
    b. social phobia      d. social phobics (155)
29. Genetic causes: Shyness runs in families
    High-risk parenting styles:
    Parents who are overprotective yet emotionally unsupportive
    Parents who are overly concerned about dress, grooming, and manners
    Parents who discourage their children from socializing which prevents them from practicing their social skills (155)
30. a. thought      c. action
    b. image      d. anxiety (155)

31. a. cleaning      d. obsessive-compulsive
    b. checking      e. obsessive-compulsive
    c. scandalous or violent      f. dominated (155-156)
32. a. guilt, depression, and helplessness
    b. mood
    c. anxiety (156)
33. a. dangerous
    b. overwhelming, psychologically painful, and/or incapacitating (155)
34. a. Re-experiencing the trauma (flashbacks or nightmares)
    b. Avoidance of circumstances that bring the event to mind
    c. Numbness to their present surroundings
    d. Signs of increased arousal: difficulty sleeping and irritability (156)
35. The victim experiences an "incubation period" before the posttraumatic symptoms begin to appear (159).

36.    Features of the Trauma | Features of the Victim
        a.  Intensity of exposure          e.  Pretrauma Psychological adjustment
        b.  Duration of exposure           f.  Family history of psychopathology
        c.  Extent of threat               g.  Cognitive and coping styles
        d.  Nature of—natural vs manmade   h.  Feelings of guilt (158)
37.    a.  Problem focused (more effective in averting PTSD)
        b.  Emotion focused (158)
38. Shell shock, combat fatigue, combat exhaustion (159)
39.    a.  Little group identity among combatants
        b.  Opposition to war led to questioning of purpose
        c.  Military command's lack of all-out commitment to win
        d.  Abrupt transition from battle to home (160)
40.    a.  2
        b.  1
        c.  3 (160)
41. posttraumatic (161)
42.    a.  anxiety                          c.  numbing
        b.  dissociative                    d.  adjustment (161)
43. Psychodynamic, behavioral, cognitive, humanistic-existential, biological
44.    a.  unconscious
        b.  id
        c.  consciousness (161)
45.    a.  repressed
        b.  sexual
        c.  aggressive (161)
46.    a.  id
        b.  ego
        c.  superego (161)
47.    a.  anxiety
        b.  anxiety disorder (161)
48.    a.  defense                          e.  unconscious
        b.  mechanism                       f.  Generalized anxiety
        c.  defense mechanism               g.  Panic
        d.  defense mechanism               h.  Obsessive-compulsive (161, 163)

49.    a.  association                      d.  transference
        b.  dream                           e.  unconscious
        c.  resistance                      f.  ego (163-164)
50. By definition, you cannot know what your unconscious conflicts are.
51.    a.  individual                       c.  intrapsychic
        b.  society                         d.  conditions of worth (164)

52.    a.  concept                          c.  SHOULD!!
        b.  ideal                           d.  ideal self (164)

53.    a.  client-centered                 d.  anxiety
        b.  analyzing, judging or advice giving   e.  self-actualization
        c.  positive regard                f.  potential (164)
54.    a.  authentic
        b.  self-actualization (164)
55.    a.  phenomenological
        b.  subjective (164)
56.    a.  wholeness and freedom           c.  increase
        b.  paradoxical intention          d.  decrease (164)
57. learning (165)
58. 4, 3, 5, 1, and 2 (165)
59.    a.  Systematic desensitization (166)   c.  Modeling (167)
        b.  In vivo desensitization (166)      d.  Extinction (167)
60.    a.  deep muscle relaxation
        b.  least
        c.  most (166)

61. in vivo (166)
62. Hierarchies of fear are very subjective, because no two people fear the same things or fear them to the same extent. Therefore, though the following sequence makes sense to *me* (GGB), your arrangement may be slightly different:
4, 6, 3, 2, 1, 1, 7, and 5 (166)
63. thinking (167)
64. a. efficacy
    b. past performances (166)
65. One that causes you to fail because you have it. For example, if you say you are going to fail the English test, and you become so anxious about the test that you do not study effectively, you have caused yourself to fail because you scared yourself into not being able to study (167).
66. misperception (167)
67. behavioral (165)
68. a. 31
    b. 0
    c. some genetic predisposition to panic disorder (170).
69. a. GABA                                    c. inhibitory (171)
    b. gamma aminobutyric acid
70. a. generalized                             c. different
    b. antidepressants                         d. depression (171)
71. locus ceruleus (171)
72. Researchers have found there is a decline in anxiety disorders in middle age that may be the result of deterioration of certain areas in the brain (172).

## Practice Test

| | | | | | | |
|---|---|---|---|---|---|---|
| 1. | b | (151) | | 11. | a | (156) |
| 2. | d | (150) | | 12. | c | (158) |
| 3. | a | (151) | | 13. | b | (160) |
| 4. | c | (152) | | 14. | d | (158) |
| 5. | a | (153) | | 15. | a | (163) |
| 6. | c | (153) | | 16. | c | (164) |
| 7. | d | (154) | | 17. | b | (164) |
| 8. | b | (155) | | 18. | a | (167) |
| 9. | a | (155) | | 19. | d | (165) |
| 10. | b | (156) | | 20. | b | (171) |

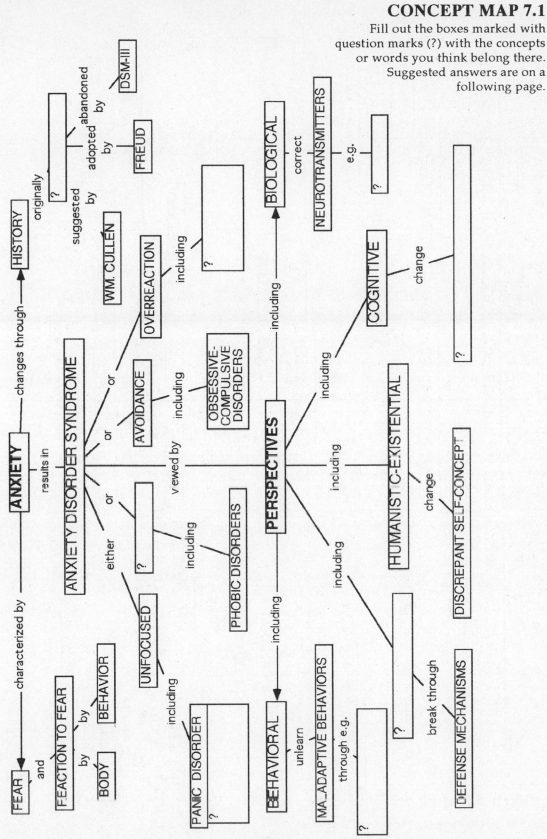

159

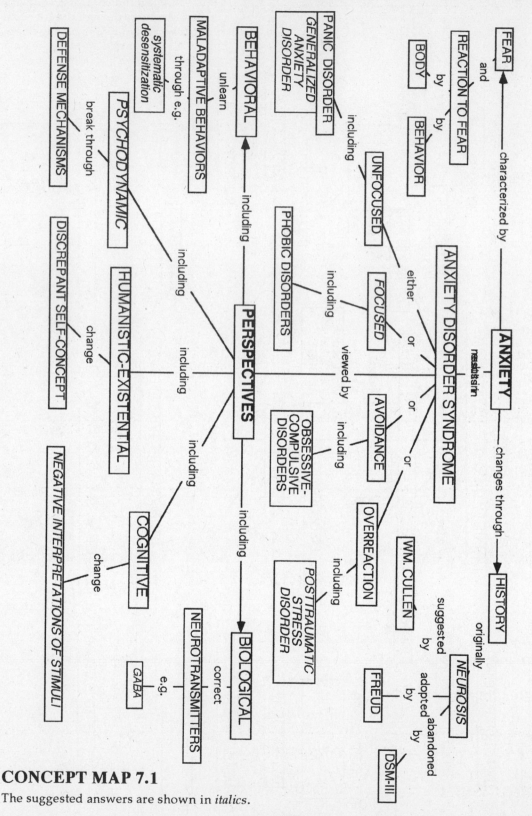

**CONCEPT MAP 7.1**

The suggested answers are shown in *italics*.

160

## CHAPTER TERMS (Cut out on the lines to use as Flash Cards)

| | | |
|---|---|---|
| 7.1<br><br>**acrophobia** | 7.8<br><br>**disaster syndrome** | 7.15<br><br>**panic attack** |
| 7.2<br><br>**agoraphobia** | 7.9<br><br>**dream interpretation** | 7.16<br><br>**panic disorder** |
| 7.3<br><br>**anxiety** | 7.10<br><br>**free association** | 7.17<br><br>**paradoxical intention** |
| 7.4<br><br>**anxiety disorders** | 7.11<br><br>**generalized anxiety disorder** | 7.18<br><br>**phobia** |
| 7.5<br><br>**claustrophobia** | 7.12<br><br>**in vivo desensitization** | 7.19<br><br>**posttraumatic stress disorders (PTSD)** |
| 7.6<br><br>**client-centered therapy** | 7.13<br><br>**obsession** | 7.20<br><br>**resistance** |
| 7.7<br><br>**compulsion** | 7.14<br><br>**obsessive-compulsive disorder** | 7.21<br><br>**social phobia** |

# DEFINITIONS (Cut out on the lines to use as Flash Cards)

| | | |
|---|---|---|
| 7.15 An attack of almost unbearable anxiety, beginning suddenly and unexpectedly and usually lasting several minutes though possibly continuing for hours | 7.8 A pattern of response to severe physical trauma involving three stages: shock, suggestibility, and recovery | 7.1 The fear of high places |
| 7.16 A disorder characterized by recurrent panic attacks or by persistent fear of subsequent attacks | 7.9 A psychoanalytic technique in which patients report their dreams and the therapist explores with the patient the elements of the dreams as symbols of unconscious wishes and conflicts | 7.2 The fear of open places away from a place of safety |
| 7.17 In existential therapy, a technique in which patients are asked to indulge or exaggerate their symptoms in order to prove to patients that they can control their symptoms | 7.10 A psychoanalytic technique in which the patient verbalizes whatever thoughts come to mind, without structuring or censoring the remarks | 7.3 A state of increased physiological arousal and generalized feelings of fear and apprehension |
| 7.18 An intense and debilitating fear of some object or situation that actually presents no real threat | 7.11 A chronic state of diffuse, unfocused anxiety | 7.4 Disturbances characterized either by manifest anxiety or by behavior patterns aimed at warding off anxiety |
| 7.19 Acute psychological reactions to intensely traumatic events, including assault, rape, natural disasters, and wartime combat | 7.12 Procedure in which phobic patients are led through the actual situations that arouse their anxieties, usually accompanied by a therapist to learn to relax in the presence of anxiety causing stimuli | 7.5 The fear of enclosed places |
| 7.20 In psychoanalytic theory, a defense mechanism used by the patient to avoid confronting certain memories and impulses e.g. argues with the therapist, changes subjects, misses appointments, etc. | 7.13 A thought or an image that keeps unwillingly intruding into a person's consciousness, though the person may consider it senseless or even unpleasant | 7.6 A therapeutic procedure developed by Rogers in which the therapist provides a safe environment for the patient by mirroring the patient's own perceptions and offering unconditional positive regard |
| 7.21 A phobic disorder in which the person's anxiety is aroused by one or more social situations and is related to the person's fear of being humiliated or criticized | 7.14 Involuntary dwelling on an unwelcome thought and/or involuntary repetition of an unnecessary action | 7.7 An action that a person feels compelled to repeat again and again in a stereotyped fashion, though he or she has no conscious desire to do so |

**CHAPTER TERMS** (Cut out on the lines to use as Flash Cards)

| 7.22 specific phobias | 7.29 | 7.36 |
|---|---|---|
| 7.23 systematic desensitization | 7.30 | 7.37 |
| 7.24 transference | 7.31 | 7.38 |
| 7.25 trichotillomania | 7.32 | 7.39 |
| 7.26 *(You may fill in the remaining boxes with names, terms and definitions from text and lecture)* | 7.33 | 7.40 |
| 7.27 | 7.34 | 7.41 |
| 7.28 | 7.35 | 7.42 |

# DEFINITIONS (Cut out on the lines to use as Flash Cards)

| | | |
|---|---|---|
| 7.36 | 7.29 | 7.22 Disorders in which the person's fear is often of something that suggests danger, such as animals or high places |
| 7.37 | 7.30 | 7.23 Behavior therapy technique in which the patient, while in a relaxed state, imagines increasingly more anxiety-provoking stimuli or is presented with the actual stimuli |
| 7.38 | 7.31 | 7.24 In psychoanalytic theory, the process by which patients identify the therapist with important people in their lives, usually with their parents, and project onto the therapist their relationship with those people |
| 7.39 | 7.32 | 7.25 The compulsive pulling out of one's own hair (generally head, but also eyebrow, pubic, etc.); linked to OCD and serotonin metabolism |
| 7.40 | 7.33 | 7.26 |
| 7.41 | 7.34 | 7.27 |
| 7.42 | 7.35 | 7.28 |

## Chapter 8

# Dissociative and Somatoform Disorders

## LEARNING OBJECTIVES
*By the time you are finished studying this chapter, you should be able to:*

**DISSOCIATIVE DISORDERS**

1. Compare and contrast dissociative and somatoform disorders, describing their similarities and differences (176-177).
2. Define dissociative amnesia and describe five patterns of this disorder mentioned in the text (177-179).
3. Define dissociative fugue and differentiate it from dissociative amnesia (179).
4. Define dissociative identity disorder and describe ways in which the personalities can manifest themselves (179-182).
5. Describe the problems with diagnosing dissociative identity disorder, and in determining the validity of cases of recovered childhood memories (183-186).
6. Define depersonalization disorder and describe the symptoms that accompany it (186-187).

**SOMATOFORM DISORDERS**

7. Describe the characteristics of body dysmorphic disorder (193-194).
8. Describe the characteristics of hypochondriasis (194-195).
9. Define somatization disorder and distinguish it from hypochondriasis (195).
10. Define conversion disorder and list the characteristics that distinguish it from a biologically based disability (195-198).

**PERSPECTIVES ON DISSOCIATIVE AND SOMATOFORM DISORDERS**

11. Describe how the psychodynamic perspective would explain and treat each of the disorders in this chapter (188-189, 198-199).
12. Describe how the behavioral and sociocultural perspectives would account for and treat the disorders in this chapter (189-191, 199-200).
13. Describe how the cognitive perspective would explain and treat each of the disorders in this chapter (191-192, 200-201).
14. Describe biological research on, and treatment of, the disorders in this chapter (192-193, 201-202).

## CHAPTER OUTLINE

I. Dissociative and somatoform disorders were both formerly called hysterical neuroses (a Freudian concept), but this terminology was discarded in 1980. We now classify these disorders simply by symptoms

   A. Both are psychological disorders that mimic biological problems, but no organic causes are found

   B. Dissociative disorders are psychological disorders that disrupt higher mental functioning by splitting apart normally integrated parts of the personality

   C. Somatoform disorders are psychological disorders that show themselves in the form of a physical symptom or disability

II. Dissociative disorders

    A. Dissociative amnesia (nonorganic forgetting)
       1. Appears suddenly following psychological trauma
       2. Often selective in its effects
       3. Patients show lack of distress over their condition
       4. Episodic—not semantic or episodic memories—are lost most often
       5. Lost memories can often be recovered later
       6. Types of psychogenic amnesia
          a. Localized amnesia blocks out all events during a specific period of time
          b. Selective amnesia characterized by "spot" losses
          c. Generalized amnesia is loss of entire past prior to traumatic event
          d. Continuous amnesia is loss of memory since the traumatic event
          e. Systematized amnesia is loss of certain categories of information only
       7. Persons accused of crime who claim to be suffering from amnesia raise legal issues such as competency to stand trial and the insanity defense

    B. Dissociative fugue (traveling amnesia)
       1. Appears suddenly following psychological trauma
       2. Patients relocate and assume a new identity
       3. Patients appear normal and purposeful during fugue state
       4. Upon remission, patients have no memory of events during the fugue state

    C. Dissociative personality disorder (multiple personality)
       1. Do not confuse with schizophrenia
       2. Personalities are often polar opposites of each other
       3. Most cases appear to be preceded by some form of childhood abuse
       4. Three to nine times more common in women than in men
       5. Disorder tends not to remit by itself
       6. Types of multiple personality
          a. Alternating type has each personality unaware of the other
          b. Coconscious type has dominant and subordinate personalities with the subordinate ones aware of the dominant one but not necessarily vice versa
       7. Diagnosis can be a problem because
          a. Symptoms of other disorders may also be present
          b. It is sometimes uncertain whether the disorder is *discovered* in treatment or *caused* by treatment
          c. Some patients may be malingering to avoid responsibility
          d. True and false cases of the disorder are not always easily distinguishable

    D. Depersonalization disorder (sense of unreal self)
       1. Major characteristic is disruption of personal identity
       2. The sense of strangeness may involve both mental and bodily experiences
       3. May occur temporarily after near-death experiences or severe stress or trauma
       4. May be accompanied by:
          a. Derealization, or a feeling of strangeness about the outside world as well
          b. Déjà vu, the feeling that what is being experienced has already happened
          c. Jamais vu, the feeling that what is being experienced has never happened before (although in fact, it has)
          d. Lack of emotionality and interest in life

III. Perspectives on the dissociative disorders

    A. The psychodynamic perspective: defense against anxiety
       1. Assumes common neurotic defenses carried to extremes
          a. Amnesia is repression
          b. Fugue and multiple personality are repression plus acting out
       2. However, these problems often violate traditional consciousness-unconsciousness distinction
       3. Treatment involves exposing the traumatic material that gives rise to the excessive defenses

B. The behavioral and sociocultural perspectives:
Dissociation as a social role
1. Dissociation is reinforced when troublesome aspects of life are avoided by doing it
2. Multiple personality may be "strategic enactment" that helps patient deal with difficult circumstances
3. Treatment involves not reinforcing dissociative behaviors

C. The cognitive perspective: Memory dysfunction
1. Retrieval failure
   a. State-dependent memory idea says that dissociation may occur because the high emotional state in which memories were formed does not recur in normal life
   b. Control elements idea says that key information, such as a name, triggers recall of associated information—if the key is lost, so is everything else
   c. Self-reference idea says that if a person's self-identification becomes fuzzy, information tied to that concept may be forgotten
2. Treatment attempts to trigger memories of key information or reinstate emotions that may have triggered the dissociation

D. The biological perspective: Brain dysfunction
1. Dissociative disorders may be related to undiagnosed epilepsy
   a. Seizures associated with multiple personality
   b. Dissociative symptoms associated with epilepsy
2. Naturally-present hidden parts in any of us may come out if the brain loses the ability to suppress or inhibit them

IV. Somatoform disorders

A. Body dysmorphic disorder
1. Preoccupation with imagined or exaggerated body defect
2. Patient may resort to unnecessary plastic surgery or other extreme remedies
3. Associated with social phobia and obsessive-compulsive disorder

B. Hypochondriasis (fear of disease)
1. Patients always on the lookout for signs of illness
2. May visit doctors frequently and medicate themselves heavily
3. Symptoms not consciously faked
4. May have had serious illness in the family as a basis for concern
5. May have had overprotective mother
6. Affects men and women equally

C. Somatization disorder (numerous and recurrent symptoms)
1. Do not confuse with hypochondriasis
   a. Hypochondriacs fear getting sick, and symptoms are merely indicators of impending disease
   b. Somatization patients focus on living out the sick role
2. Symptoms tend to be vague and varied
3. More common in women than in men

D. Conversion disorder (psychogenic physical disability)
1. Symptoms not medically justified but not consciously faked (not malingering)
2. Do not confuse with "psychosomatic" disorders, which are real physical problems brought on by stress
3. Conversion disorder contributed much to the development of psychoanalysis
4. Conversion disorder is one disorder for which many mental health professionals tend to agree with the dynamic perspective as an explanation—symptoms serve to:
   a. Block awareness of inner conflict (primary gain)
   b. Attract sympathy and attention (secondary gain)
5. Characteristic features
   a. Rapid appearance of symptoms following psychological trauma
   b. La belle indifférence (seemingly unconcerned about the problem)
   c. Selective symptoms (indicating problem is not organic)

6. May be more common than is realized due to inaccurate diagnosis as an organic problem

V. Perspectives on the somatoform disorders

   A. The psychodynamic perspective: Defense against anxiety
      1. Sexual and aggressive tendencies lead to anxiety and conflict
      2. Somatoform symptoms resolve the conflict by either symbolically (indirectly) releasing the energy associated with the wish (as in hypochondriasis or somatization disorder) or preventing the expression of the wish (as in conversion disorder)
      3. Treatment uncovers the true nature of the conflict and works it out
      4. Treatment is not dramatically successful

   B. The behavioral and sociocultural perspectives: The sick role
      1. "Sick" behaviors are maintained through reinforcement (what Freud called primary and secondary gains)
      2. Bodily processes can be respondently conditioned to anxiety-producing situations
      3. Culture influences the degree to which these disorders show themselves (implying social learning)
      4. Treatment involves removal of reinforcement for sick behavior while providing a "face-saving" means of resuming normal activities

   C. The cognitive perspective: Misinterpreting bodily sensations
      1. Patients have a cognitive style which predisposes them to pay too much attention to their bodies
      2. Patients tend not to express emotions directly
      3. Treatment involves challenging assumptions about the reality and rationality of symptoms

   D. The biological perspective: Genetics and brain dysfunction
      1. Genetic family research shows that first-degree relatives of somatization patients are more susceptible to either somatization disorder (females) or antisocial personality disorder (males)
      2. Brain studies show sensory inhibition in conversion patients
      3. Right brain is implicated in about 70 percent of somatoform problems
      4. Neuroscience findings are not conclusive, and are probably intertwined with psychological factors

## KEY TERMS
*The following terms are in bold print in your text. Define them and practice their definitions using the flash cards at the end of the chapter.*

alternating personality (181)
amnesia (177)
body dysmorphic disorder (193)
coconscious (181)
conversion disorder (195)
depersonalization disorder (186)

derealization (186)
dissociative amnesia (177)
dissociative disorders (177)
dissociative fugue (179)
dissociative identity disorder (179)
explicit memories (178)
hypochondriasis (194)
hysteria (176)

implicit memories (178)
la belle indifference (196)
malingering (183)
primary gain (196)
secondary gain (196)
somatization disorder (195)
somatoform disorders (193)

*Your text does not list the following terms as formal vocabulary; however, if you don't know what they mean, you will be unable to grasp the concepts of this chapter.*

| | | |
|---|---|---|
| catastrophize (200) | exacerbate (188) | premise(s) (185) |
| chronic (176) | incredulous (185) | remits (179) |
| circumscribed (178) | inhibit (192) | retrospective (178) |
| constellation (182) | integrated (177) | scenario (199) |
| demarcation (197) | irreproachable (185) | stratagem (182) |
| diagnostician (183) | mimics (176) | strategic enactments (191) |
| encapsulate (182) | misattributing (185) | subordinate (181) |
| enunciate (188) | paradoxical (196) | traumatized (176) |
| equanimity (196) | precipitated (178) | |

## IMPORTANT NAMES
*Identify the following persons and their major contributions to abnormal psychology as discussed in this chapter.*

Pierre Janet (188)

## GUIDED SELF-STUDY

1.  The introductory paragraphs to the chapter explain why the dissociative disorders and somatoform disorders are grouped together. These disorders were grouped together in the

    past as (a)_____. Dissociative disorders and somatoform disorders are alike

    in that they both mimic (b)_____. They are different in that (c)_____

    disorders disrupt only the higher cognitive functions; (d)_____ disorders affect *only* sensory and/or motor functions.

## DISSOCIATIVE DISORDERS
2.  List the four dissociative disorders discussed in your text.

    a.

    b.

    c.

    d.

3.  Label each of the following patterns of amnesia: **Continuous, Selective, Localized, Generalized,** and **Systematized**.

    a. _____ The person forgets his/her entire past life.

    b. _____ The person experiences spot erasures of memory for a certain period of his/her personal history.

    c. _____ A person forgets from a specific point forward, and has ongoing loss of memory for present events.

    d. _____ A person forgets all the events of a certain time period.

    e. _____ Only certain categories of information are forgotten.

4.  If a person's amnesia is not dissociative, what kind would it be?

5. Draw a line to connect each type of memory with its definition and circle the one that is usually affected by dissociative amnesia.

   a. Episodic                    How to do skills

   b. Semantic                    General knowledge

   c. Procedural                  Personal experiences

6. The text suggests three possible explanations for an accused person's claim to have no memory of committing the crime. What are these explanations?


7. If a person has true dissociative amnesia about a crime he/she has committed, then the person has forgotten because of the level of _____ about the crime.

8. The difference between dissociative fugue and dissociative amnesia is that in fugue the person not only (a)_____ stressful material, but also (b)_____. When the person recovers from the dissociative fugue, s/he will have (c)_____ about the time and events of the fugue.

9. Use the following terms to complete the blanks: **alternating personality, coconscious, multiple personality**, and **traumatically abusive**.

   Dissociate identity disorder, also known as (a)_____ _____, is more than just feeling outgoing one day and shy another day. Everyone has a variety of facets to his/her personality. In dissociative identity, the different personalities have entirely different identities. In the simplest form, called (b)_____ _____, there are two personalities, neither of which knows about the other. In some cases the individual may have a number of personalities, some dominant and some subordinate. The subordinate personalities may know about the dominant personalities, in which case the subordinate is said to be (c)_____ with the dominant personality. However, the dominant personality does not have conscious awareness of the subordinate personalities. Putnam's research suggests that (d)_____ _____experiences in childhood might be the cause of dissociate identity.

10. In the special interest box on "Who Committed the Crime? Subordinate Personalities and the Law" what two legal questions arise?

    a.

    b.

11. Depersonalization is like fugue and dissociate identity in that there is a disruption of (a)_____, but unlike these other two there is no (b)_____. With depersonalization there are feelings of a strangeness about the world; this is called (c)_____. Depersonalization experiences happen in a number of different circumstances. Some of the situations listed in your text include (d) _____.

12. The psychodynamic perspective talks about dissociative disorders in the context of "defense against anxiety." Explain that phrase.

13. What will the goal of psychodynamic therapy be with dissociative disorder?

14. Why is hypnosis used in psychodynamic therapy for dissociative disorders?

15. What is the prognosis on each of these dissociative disorders?

    a. Dissociative amnesia:

    b. Fugue:

    c. Dissociate identity:

16. In behaviorism, the bottom line is *always* (a)_____. An explanation for disassociation based on this approach says that there are two types of learning: (b)_____ (reflex), and (c)_____ (payoff). Since we do not know of any dissociation reflex, this must be a payoff situation. A person does what he/she gets paid or (d)_____ for doing. Dissociative disorders seem to be a response that is rewarded by escape or avoidance of something that is unpleasant (stressful) for that individual. This would be an example of (e)_____ reinforcement. There may also be some (f)_____ reinforcement in that the individual gets some attention and nurturance due to having some mental impairment. The situation is the same as when you have a hurt foot; some people start to be a little kinder to you than they would normally be.

17. In the sociocultural perspective, society reinforces or encourages certain roles. Spanos's research shows that not only the client may be reinforced for being a dissociate identity, but that the (a)_____ may also be reinforced. Spanos suggests that the use of (b)_____, as well as additional cues from the (c)_____ may actually encourage people to experience multiple personality.

18. What therapeutic approach will behavioral psychologists use for dissociative disorders?

19. Why is essentially the same therapeutic approach advocated by the sociocultural perspective?

20. What is supposed to pop into your mind when you see "the cognitive perspective"?

21. The three different cognitive theories proposed to explain dissociative disorders are each based on memory retrieval failures. Match each one to its key concept.

    a. State-dependent learning        Cues for some memories are personal facts
    b. Control elements               Memory that is cued by a mood
    c. Self-reference                 Personal identity is essential to retrieval

22. What do all three of these cognitive theories say that is the same? Answer: From a cognitive perspective the dissociative disorders are a result of _____ loss.

23. What cognitive therapies are done with dissociative disorders?


24. The biological perspective talks in terms of (a)_____. One biological theory proposes that some cases of dissociative disorder are cases of undiagnosed (b)_____. This theory is proposed very (c)_____ because there seems to be some correlation between epilepsy and experiences of dissociation and dissociative identity disorder. However, the extent to which these are related is still unknown.

25. The following terms complete the second biological theory. Terms may be used more than once: **activity, hemispheres, radical,** and **suppressed**.

    The second biological theory is really (a)_____: It says we have other parts to our

    personality that the brain keeps (b)_____; when there is a change in brain (c)_____ due to damage, disease, and/or stress causing neurochemical changes, these parts are no

    longer (d)_____. The result is the person appears to dissociate from his/her normal personality content as s/he displays this erupting mental material. This theory has some

    support with evidence that the different (e)_____ of the brain have different personalities.

Note: Do remember that the biological perspective does not claim that organic problems are the ultimate underlying cause of behavioral disorders. The biological perspective says only that organic correlates are part of the total picture. Instead of organic factors causing behavior to change, behavior may cause organic conditions to change as well.

SOMATOFORM DISORDERS
26. Somatoform disorders are mental problems manifested (played out) as bodily sicknesses where

    there is no (a)_____ _____ for the physical complaint. People with somatoform disorders are not consciously "faking" sickness; fakers are assigned to a category termed

    (b)_____. People with somatoform disorders mentally experience their bodily problems. Also, do not confuse somatoform disorders with the "real" organically based disorders that are caused or aggravated by mental health issues. You will study these in Chapter Nine.

27. Match the four following somatoform disorders to their definitions: **Body dysmorphic disorder, Conversion disorder, Hypochondriasis,** and **Somatization disorder**.

    a. _____ Preoccupation with imagined or exaggerated bodily defects

    b. _____ Fear of particular diseases

    c. _____ Manifested motor or sensory dysfunctions

    d. _____ Many varied, vague, and recurrent physical symptoms

28. Do you know someone who has body dysmorphic disorder?

29. Concern about bodily appearance is so pervasive in our society; how do you feel about your appearance? What of your features do you like least? Do you ever border on body dysmorphic disorder about that feature?

30. Differentiate between the three somatoform disorders discussed in the text by filling in the following blanks.

If a friend with somatization disorder telephones you, she is going to tell you all about

(a)_____. This person (more likely a woman than a man) may actually

have some organic problems which are the result of (b)_____. If your friend

with conversion disorder telephones you, you can expect to hear (c)_____

_____. If your hypochondriacal friend telephones you, you are going to hear

about physical conditions that *might be* (d)_____. By the way, the sex of

the hypochondriac is more likely to be a (e)_____ (**male / female / either sex**).

31. Why is a glove anesthesia almost certainly a conversion disorder?

32. What are the three circumstances that suggest dissociative rather than biogenic disability?

    a.

    b.

    c.

33. The primary gain in conversion disorder is the (a) _____, and the secondary gain is (b)_____.

PERSPECTIVES ON THE SOMATOFORM DISORDERS
34. Draw a line to connect the perspective to its explanation for somatoform disorders. **BE SURE TO CHECK THE ANSWER ON THIS QUESTION IMMEDIATELY AFTER YOU ATTEMPT IT.**

| Perspective | Explanation |
|---|---|
| Psychodynamic | The sick role |
| Behavioral | Genetics |
| Cognitive | Defense against anxiety |
| Sociocultural | Misinterpreting bodily sensations |
| Biological | Brain dysfunction |

35. What kind of therapy will each perspective suggest? Fill in the blanks with the perspectives: **Biological, Psychodynamic, Behavioral, Sociocultural,** and **Cognitive**.

    a. _____ will always want to uncover the unconscious problem so the person can work through it.

    b. _____ will try to stop the payoff, or the reinforcement.

    c. _____ will say society has to change of what it approves or disapproves.

    d. _____ will help the individual discover the error in his/her thinking and encourage him/her to deliberately change his thought pattern habits.

    e. _____ is not proposing any therapies, but has come up with some interesting preliminary findings that suggest there may be a genetic element to somatization disorder in women that has some correlation with antisocial personality disorder in men.

36. The biological perspective has suggested that conversion disorder is a suppression of sensory processing at the (a)_____level of the brain. Also, the (b)_____ hemisphere of the brain *may be* a significant player in somatoform disorders.

37. What two circumstances are necessary for the person to learn the role of "sick?"

    a.

    b.

38. Research indicates that somatization and conversion disorders are seen more in some cultures than others. What does this suggest?

39. Bits and pieces—do you recognize them as they connect to this chapter? The terms may be used more than once.

| | |
|---|---|
| **Anterograde** | **Hypoglycemia** |
| **Antisocial personality disorder** | **Hypoxia** |
| **Biogenic** | **Hysteria** |
| **Body dysmorphic disorder** | **Implicit** |
| **Corpus callostomy** | **Janet's désagrégation** |
| **Couvade** | **Neuroscience** |
| **Déjà vu** | **Paralysis** |
| **Diversiform somatizer** | **Somatic** |
| **Explicit** | **Source amnesia** |
| **Fugue** | |

    a. _____ Syndrome when husband experiences labor pains

    b. _____ Traveling amnesia

    c. _____ Area within biological perspective

    d. _____ Surgery to neurologically separate the two brain hemispheres

    e. _____ Having a biological beginning

    f. _____ Motor impairment

    g. _____ Moving forward

    h. _____ Clearly present

i.   _____    Present but not obvious

j.   _____    One explanation for recovery of false memories

k.   _____    Already seen

l.   _____    From Latin word for flight

m.   _____    Original conception of mental dissociation

n.   _____    Treatment for extreme cases of otherwise untreatable epilepsy

o.   _____    Caused by a wandering uterus

p.   _____    Chronic indifference to the rights of others

q.   _____    Individual has less physical symptoms, but they are more diverse in nature

r.   _____    Oxygen deprivation

s.   _____    Low blood sugar

t.   _____    Related to the physical body

u.   _____    Closely associated with obsessive-compulsive disorder

## HELPFUL HINTS

1. Notice that the term is "dissociative" not "disassociative." They are the same in meaning, but you do need to know that the name of the disorders that are the result of some mental disassociation is dissociative.
2. *Do not confuse dissociative identity disorder (multiple personality) with schizophrenia.* Multiple personality is commonly referred to as "split personality" and the term schizophrenia means "split mind." Other than the common connection of a loose usage of the word "split," these two disorders are not related. The person who suffers from schizophrenia has a serious problem testing reality accurately (an extreme example of problems with reality testing would be seeing little green men over in the corner of the room). In multiple personality, the person may have more than one personality, but at any given moment he/she is in touch with reality through the personality that is active.
3. Multiple-personality *is not a personality disorder*. It is a dissociative disorder. In Chapter 11 you will study about what a personality disorder is.
4. One of those interesting bits of trivia: Conversion disorder was originally called hysteria because it was thought to be caused by the uterus wandering unfulfilled in the body of childless women. That is in your text. You can connect this information together if you remember that surgery to remove a woman's uterus (womb) is called a hysterectomy.
5. I have found that people use the word "psychosomatic" disorder when they want to say that the health problem is really in the person's mind. That is incorrect. As you will learn in the next chapter, psychosomatic illnesses have observable physical problems that are caused or aggravated by psychological stress.
6. The term hypochondriasis is also often misused. It is often used to describe someone with varied, vague physical complaints. This is actually somatization disorder. The complaints of the hypochondriac are specific and related to his/her fears of a particular disease. If you choose to continue using these terms in the colloquial manner to communicate with others who misuse them in the same way, that is your choice. Just know that on a psychology test, you are going to need to know them as they are defined in psychology books.
7. There are numerous references in this chapter to movie characters and real life people who typify the disorders in this chapter. Check with your instructor to see if testing will cover the specific references to these characters and individuals.

*Take the following test several times as you study the chapter. Write your answers on a separate sheet of paper and after each attempt, note in the tally box above each question whether your answer was correct or incorrect.*

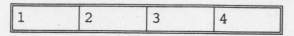

1. Dissociative disorders are defined as problems which affect
   a. physical health and abilities.
   b. higher cognitive functions.
   c. motor and sensory processes.
   d. emotional stability and control.

2. Dan was the victim of a hostage situation and now finds that he cannot remember anything of the four days he spent as a hostage. Dan is experiencing
   a. generalized amnesia.
   b. continuous amnesia.
   c. selective amnesia.
   d. localized amnesia.

| 1 | 2 | 3 | 4 |
|---|---|---|---|

3. Selective amnesia is when the person
   a. makes "spot erasures" within a given period of time.
   b. forgets all events before a certain point in time.
   c. forgets his or her entire past life.
   d. forgets everything after a critical incident in life.

| 1 | 2 | 3 | 4 |
|---|---|---|---|

4. Juanita is greatly distressed by what she calls an experience of "missing time." She found herself in Seattle one morning without knowing how she got there and discovered that six weeks of her life were unaccounted for. The disorder in this chapter that would be most likely to account for her experience is
   a. psychogenic amnesia.
   b. psychogenic fugue.
   c. conversion disorder.
   d. multiple personality.

| 1 | 2 | 3 | 4 |
|---|---|---|---|

5. Which of the following is true of psychogenic fugue?
   a. It is one criterion for diagnosing posttraumatic stress disorder.
   b. It is one of the most common somatoform disorders.
   c. It is characterized by more coherent and purposeful behavior than psychogenic amnesia.
   d. It is the one dissociative disorder that is classified as a psychosis.

| 1 | 2 | 3 | 4 |
|---|---|---|---|

6. Cases like *Sybil* and *The Three Faces of Eve* are examples of
   a. psychogenic fugue.
   b. selective amnesia.
   c. conversion disorder.
   d. dissociative identity disorder.

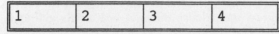

7. One characteristic that shows up very often in cases of dissociative identity disorder is
   a. a history of serious illnesses in the patient's parents.
   b. physical or sexual abuse in childhood.
   c. onset of the problem between the ages of 20 and 25.
   d. high resistance to hypnosis.

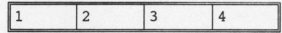

8. Which of the following is true of depersonalization?
   a. Its presence is a clear discriminator between normal and severely troubled individuals.
   b. It is mainly associated with chronic alcohol abuse.
   c. Trauma victims who show initial depersonalization may be at higher risk for posttraumatic stress disorder.
   d. While depersonalization disorder is fairly serious, the likelihood of recovery is nevertheless good.

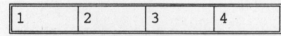

9. The defense mechanism psychodynamic theorists believe is operating in amnesia is
   a. projection.                          c. reaction formation.
   b. repression.                          d. displacement.

| 1 | 2 | 3 | 4 |

10. Which psychological perspective assumes that dissociative symptoms are a strategy for avoiding responsibility for unacceptable behavior, and that they are likely to be repeated when they are successful?
    a. The sociocultural perspective       c. The humanistic perspective
    b. The cognitive perspective           d. The psychodynamic perspective

| 1 | 2 | 3 | 4 |

11. One approach to dissociative disorders assumes that the major problem is memory failure. Specifically, highly emotional events may not be remembered in more normal, less emotional situations. This is the idea of
    a. control element failure.            c. state dependent memory.
    b. loss of self-reference.             d. episodic versus semantic recall.

| 1 | 2 | 3 | 4 |

12. Somatoform disorders are characterized by
    a. transformation of a psychological conflict into a physical symptom.
    b. psychological reactions to physical injuries and disabilities.
    c. lifelong personality traits that lead to physical illness.
    d. conscious faking of symptoms to gain sympathy and attention.

| 1 | 2 | 3 | 4 |
|---|---|---|---|

13. Betsy will tell you that she is not well.  She is convinced she has cancer, but the doctors tell her there is nothing wrong with her.  She is presently trying a variety of experimental cancer treatments on her own.  She is driving her family crazy with what they call her "sick act."  Betsy sounds like someone with
    a.  somatization disorder.
    b.  conversion disorder.
    c.  depersonalization disorder.
    d.  hypochondriasis.

| 1 | 2 | 3 | 4 |
|---|---|---|---|

14. All of the following are characteristics of conversion disorder *except*
    a.  sudden appearance of symptoms.
    b.  selective symptoms.
    c.  conscious faking of symptoms.
    d.  la belle indifference.

| 1 | 2 | 3 | 4 |
|---|---|---|---|

15. Jack, a victim of conversion disorder, appears to be paralyzed from the waist down. He has a handicapped sticker on his car and needs people to open doors for him in his wheelchair.  These consequences of his paralysis are what Freud would call
    a.  secondary gains.
    b.  primary gains.
    c.  symptom substitution.
    d.  transference neuroses.

| 1 | 2 | 3 | 4 |
|---|---|---|---|

16. Which of the following best describes a typical patient with somatization disorder?
    a.  Male, well educated, emotionally expressive, sexually active
    b.  Male, poorly educated, unemployed, convicted of sexual abuse
    c.  Female, easily hypnotized, assertive, verbally expressive
    d.  Female, depressed, emotionally unexpressive, poor education

| 1 | 2 | 3 | 4 |
|---|---|---|---|

17. Primary and secondary gains in a conversion disorder would be given a different name by behaviorists.  They would call these gains
    a.  reinforcers.
    b.  manifest content.
    c.  primary symptoms.
    d.  conditioned responses.

| 1 | 2 | 3 | 4 |
|---|---|---|---|

18. Antonello has been diagnosed as having a case of conversion disorder.  If you were a cognitive psychologist, you would be most interested in studying Antonello's
    a.  hidden desires and memories.
    b.  perceptions of his own body.
    c.  family medical history.
    d.  EEG and CAT scan results.

| 1 | 2 | 3 | 4 |
|---|---|---|---|

19. Genetic research seems to show a link between somatization disorder and
    a.  panic disorder.
    b.  antisocial personality disorder.
    c.  generalized anxiety disorder.
    d.  conversion disorder.

| 1 | 2 | 3 | 4 |
|---|---|---|---|

20. Which of the following best sums up the behavioral approach to treating somatoform disorders?
    a. As a man thinks, so is he.
    b. When you fall off a horse, get right back on.
    c. Ignore it and it will go away.
    d. Don't cross your bridges before you come to them.

## ANSWERS
### Self-Study Exercise

1. a. hysterical neurosis
   b. actual neurological disorders
   c. dissociative
   d. somatoform (176)
2. a. Dissociative amnesia
   b. Dissociative fugue
   c. Dissociative identity disorder
   d. Depersonalization disorder (175)
3. a. Generalized amnesia
   b. Selective amnesia
   c. Continuous amnesia
   d. Localized amnesia
   e. Systematized amnesia (178)
4. Organically based amnesias (also called biogenic amnesias), which are caused by a real head injury or brain disease (177).
5. a. Episodic memory is that of personal experiences.
   b. Semantic memory is that of general knowledge.
   c. Procedural memory is that of how to do skills (178).
   Episodic memory is the one usually affected by dissociative amnesia (178).
6. Drug-induced blackouts, faking, and dissociative amnesia (178-179)
7. stress or emotional arousal (179)
8. a. forgets
   b. makes a sudden, unexpected trip; in other words, physically moves away from the source of the stress
   c. amnesia (179)
9. a. multiple personality (179)
   b. alternating personality (181)
   c. coconscious (181)
   d. traumatically abusive (182-183)
10. a. Is the whole person guilty if one of his/her personalities commits a crime?
    b. If one personality consents, can another personality within that individual claim to have been victimized? (180)
11. a. personal identity
    b. amnesia
    c. derealization
    d. Brief experiences in the course of normal life; very tired; meditating; drug induced; as a component of a number of different mental disorders; or after a near-death experience (186-187)
12. In the psychodynamic perspective, the problem is always anxiety from deep "unacceptable" (sex and aggression) unconscious impulses from the id in conflict with reality from the ego and morals from the superego. The ego defense mechanisms are trying to keep the anxiety at a manageable level. In dissociative disorders, the defense mechanisms are very extreme and maladaptive; they have simply cut off parts of the mind to avoid or reduce anxiety (34, 188).
13. In the psychodynamic approach, the goal is always to uncover the unconscious conflict that is causing the problem (188).
14. Hypnosis is a technique that gets at unconscious material fairly readily. In dissociative disorders the challenge is to overcome the barriers that prevent awareness of the troubling material (188-189).

15. a. Dissociative amnesia tends to remit without treatment.
    b. Fugue tends to remit without treatment.
    c. Dissociate identity is much more difficult to overcome and may leave the individual vulnerable to relapse in future times of stress (189).
16. a. learning      d. reinforced
    b. respondent      e. negative
    c. operant      f. positive (189-191).
17. a. therapist
    b. hypnosis
    c. therapist (189-190)
18. In behaviorism, if you want someone to stop doing something, you stop paying (reinforcing) them to do it. So the therapist is going to figure out what is reinforcing the dissociation so that circumstances can be rearranged for the payment (reinforcement) to stop (189-191).
19. The sociocultural approach to treatment is very similar to the ideas advocated by the behaviorists. The sociocultural perspective says the person is behaving this way because society is reinforcing him/her (189).
20. Thinking!!!!
21. a. State-dependent learning: Memory that is cued by a mood, whatever mood you were in when the memory was stored
    b. Control elements: The cues for some memory retrieval are personal facts; the theorist who proposed this idea says that one's name may be a major control element. If you forget your name (obviously due to extreme circumstances) you then lose access to all the memory that your name could cue up.
    c. Self-reference: This idea says that it is not your name that helps you to recall your episodic memory, but whatever your sense of self (self-reference) is. If for some reason you lose that essence of you in your own thinking, then you lose all the memory that is cued to that self-reference (191-192).
22. memory (If you did not answer this question easily, did you miss the subheading on page 191? Did you read it? Did you just not remember it? Or perhaps you still do not readily understand the phrases "memory dysfunction" or "retrieval failure."
23. So far, not much cognitive therapy has been used on dissociative disorders. Some efforts that have been made are trying to access implicit memory, trying to cue up memories through moods, and trying to find control elements that would trigger recall of other memories (192).
24. a. organicity or brain dysfunction,
    b. epilepsy
    c. tentatively (192-193)
25. a. radical      d. suppressed
    b. suppressed      e. hemispheres (193)
    c. activity
26. a. organic basis (193)
    b. malingering (a fancy word for faking) (197)
27. a. Body dysmorphic disorder (193)      c. Conversion disorder (195)
    b. Hypochondriasis (194)      d. Somatization disorder (195)
28. You probably do know someone particularly if your associates are teens or young adults. This becomes a disorder when the concern about the bodily feature interferes with the living of the person's life (193).
29. Your personal response
30. a. a long list of physical complaints
    b. unnecessary hospitalization, surgery and medications (195). (This is the person that you learn never to ask "How are you?" The answer is at least half an hour long.)
    c. a seemingly unworried, even cheerful detailed account of his/her sensory and/or motor incapacitation (195-197).
    d. symptoms of a serious disease (194).
    e. Hypochondriacs are equally likely to be male or female (194).
31. A short glove pattern on the hand is inconsistent with the neurology of the hand and lower arm (197).
32. a. Rapid onset of symptoms, particularly after a psychological trauma
    b. La belle indifférence
    c. Selective symptoms (197)
33. a. reduction of mental conflict
    b. being relieved of responsibilities and gaining attention and sympathy (196).

34. By now I hope you are learning to spot the perspectives.
      Role—Sociological word! (200)
      Genetics—Organic word! must be biological (201)
      Anxiety—Freudian word! psychodynamic (198)
      Misinterpret—Cognitive word! (200)
      Brain—Organic word! biological again (201-202)
    *There was a trick* in this question, *not* to make you feel stupid but to call your attention to a fact if you have not already noticed it. There were two terms that went with biological, so that left one perspective with no explanation if you are using a process-of-elimination technique to figure out the answers. The point is this: in this chapter for both dissociative and somatoform disorders, the behavioral perspective shares a view that is very similar to the sociocultural perspective. So to solve the puzzle in this question you had to use "sick role" twice, once for the sociocultural perspective and again for the behavioral perspective. The reason the two perspectives are so similar here is that the coping response the behaviorists see as being learned (there's that behavioral word!) involves a whole complex pattern that is so elaborate as to overlap with what the sociocultural perspective calls a social role. Then, to make it even more similar, the sociocultural perspective says that society reinforces the individual in the role. To separate these two, see what the focus of the theory is. Is the focus the *learning* that the person does? Then you are dealing with the behavioral perspective. Or, is the focus learning what *society* (as a whole) is reinforcing? That is the sociocultural perspective.

35. a. Psychodynamic (199)        d. Cognitive (200-201)
    b. Behavioral (199)           e. Biological (201)
    c. Sociocultural (200)
36. a. cortical
    b. right (202)
37. a. First, the person must experience the role of sickness or see it modeled by someone else.
    b. Then, when the person tries out the role of sickness as a way of coping with life, it must pay off (206).
38. A sociocultural perspective! Cultures which have value systems that say physical illness is acceptable, but a show of emotional distress is not acceptable, can expect to see psychological problems expressed in physical symptoms (200).
39. a. Couvade (195)            l. Fugue (179)
    b. Fugue (179)            m. Janet's désagrégation (188)
    c. Neuroscience (192)      n. Corpus callostomy (193)
    d. Corpus callostomy (193)  o. Hysteria (196)
    e. Biogenic (176)          p. Antisocial personality disorder (201)
    f. Paralysis (176)          q. Diversiform somatizer (201)
    g. Anterograde (177)       r. Hypoxia (202)
    h. Explicit (178)          s. Hypoglycemia (202)
    i. Implicit (179)          t. Somatic (193)
    j. Source amnesia (184)    u. Body dysmorphic disorder (194)
    k. Déjà vu (187)

## Practice Test

| | | | | | |
|---|---|---|---|---|---|
| 1. | b | (176) | 11. | c | (191) |
| 2. | d | (178) | 12. | a | (193) |
| 3. | a | (178) | 13. | d | (194) |
| 4. | b | (179) | 14. | c | (195) |
| 5. | c | (179) | 15. | a | (196) |
| 6. | d | (181) | 16. | d | (195) |
| 7. | b | (182) | 17. | a | (199) |
| 8. | c | (187) | 18. | b | (200) |
| 9. | b | (188) | 19. | b | (201) |
| 10. | a | (189) | 20. | c | (200) |

# CONCEPT MAP 8.1

Fill out the boxes marked with
question marks (?) with the concepts
or words you think belong there.
Answers suggested by the author
are on a following page.

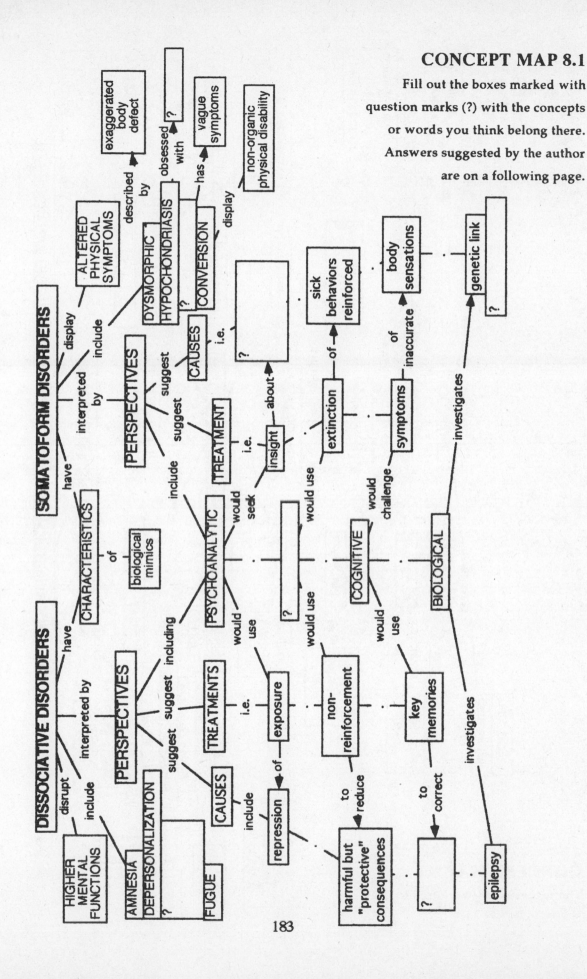

183

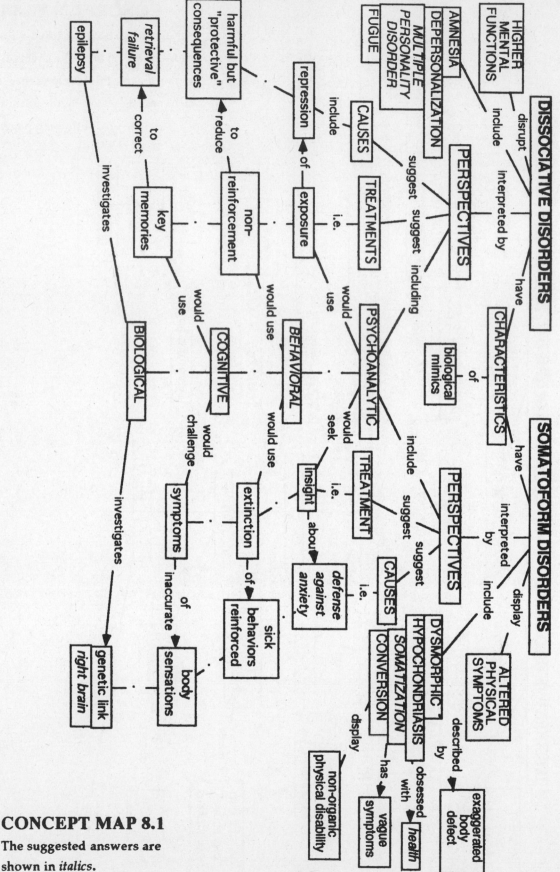

**CONCEPT MAP 8.1**

The suggested answers are
shown in *italics*.

# CHAPTER TERMS (Cut out on the lines to use as Flash Cards)

| | | |
|---|---|---|
| 8.1<br><br>**alternating personality** | 8.8<br><br>**dissociative amnesia** | 8.15<br><br>**implicit memories** |
| 8.2<br><br>**amnesia** | 8.9<br><br>**dissociative disorders** | 8.16<br><br>**la belle indifference** |
| 8.3<br><br>**body dysmorphic disorder** | 8.10<br><br>**dissociative fugue** | 8.17<br><br>**malingering** |
| 8.4<br><br>**coconscious** | 8.11<br><br>**dissociative identity disorder** | 8.18<br><br>**primary gain** |
| 8.5<br><br>**conversion disorder** | 8.12<br><br>**explicit memories** | 8.19<br><br>**secondary gain** |
| 8.6<br><br>**depersonalization disorder** | 8.13<br><br>**hypochondriasis** | 8.20<br><br>**somatization disorder** |
| 8.7<br><br>**derealization** | 8.14<br><br>**hysteria** | 8.21<br><br>**somatoform disorders** |

# DEFINITIONS (Cut out on the lines to use as Flash Cards)

| | | |
|---|---|---|
| **8.15** Those aspects of memory of which we are unaware; e.g. the memory of an emotion associated with an explicit memory | **8.8** The partial or total forgetting of past experiences; generally anterograde, selective, and causing little distress, it may be associated with organic brain syndromes or with psychological stress | **8.1** A form of multiple personality in which two identities shift between each other, each having amnesia for the thoughts and actions of the other |
| **8.16** A characteristic of conversion disorder in which the person does not seem at all disturbed by his or her disability | **8.9** Disorders resulting from the splitting off of some psychological function from the rest of the conscious mind | **8.2** The partial or total forgetting of past experiences; it can be associated with organic brain syndromes or with psychological stress |
| **8.17** The conscious faking of symptoms in order to avoid responsibility | **8.10** A form of amnesia in which the person forgets his past and also takes a sudden trip away from home; a traveling amnesia | **8.3** An excessive concern about a particular imagined or grossly exaggerated "defect" in one's appearance |
| **8.18** In conversion disorder, the relief from anxiety that is experienced by the person as a result of the conversion symptom, which blocks the person's awareness of internal conflict | **8.11** The pattern of personality breaks into two or more distinct personalities; also known as multiple personality disorder | **8.4** In multiple-personality disorder, the term used to refer to a subordinate personality that is fully aware of the dominant personality's thoughts and actions |
| **8.19** In conversion disorder, the "benefit" of being excused from responsibilities and attracting sympathy and attention, which accrue to the person as a result of the conversion symptom | **8.12** Memories that we are aware of as "memories"; e.g. the memory of an event such as graduation | **8.5** The loss or impairment of some motor or sensory function for which there is no organic cause. Formerly known as "hysteria" or "hysterical neurosis" |
| **8.20** A syndrome characterized by numerous and recurrent physical complaints, persisting for several years, for which no medical basis can be found | **8.13** A disorder in which a person converts anxiety into a chronic fear of disease; fear is maintained by the constant misinterpretation of physical signs and sensations as abnormal | **8.6** A disruption of personal identity that is characterized by a sense of strangeness or unreality in oneself, e.g., feeling that one is viewing oneself from the outside or is functioning like a robot |
| **8.21** Conditions in which psychological conflicts take on a somatic or physical form; include hypochondriasis, somatization disorder, and conversion disorder | **8.14** A psychogenic disorder that mimics a biogenic disorder | **8.7** A feeling of strangeness about the world. Other people seem robotic, dead, or somehow unreal |

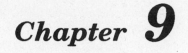

# Chapter 9

# Psychological Stress and Physical Disorders

## LEARNING OBJECTIVES
### By the time you are finished studying this chapter, you should be able to:

**MIND AND BODY**
1.  Summarize your text's position on the relationship between mind and body (206-208).
2.  Define stress, and list the effects of stress on illness, body regulatory processes, behavior, and the functioning of the immune system (208, 210-214).
3.  Define stimulus specificity and individual response specificity, and describe how they interact to determine a person's reaction to stress (208-210).

**PHYSICAL DISORDERS ASSOCIATED WITH PSYCHOLOGICAL FACTORS**
4.  Describe essential hypertension, and discuss its possible stress-related causes (214-216).
5.  Define migraine headache and discuss current thinking on the biogenic versus psychogenic nature of this disorder (216-217).
6.  Define obesity and discuss the biological and psychological factors assumed to be responsible for the problem (217-219).
7.  Define asthma, and discuss current thinking on the biogenic versus psychogenic nature of this disorder (219-220).
8.  Describe the physiological and psychological factors associated with sleep disorders such as insomnia and circadian rhythm disorder (220-221).
9.  Summarize research on psychological factors affecting patients' susceptibility to and survival of diseases like cancer and AIDS (221-223).

**PERSPECTIVES ON STRESS-RELATED PHYSICAL DISORDERS**
10. Discuss how behavioral psychologists explain and treat stress-related disorders through the mechanisms of learning (223-224).
11. Summarize the cognitive perspective's view of stress-related disorders (224-225).
12. Describe the psychodynamic perspective's concept of "organ neurosis" as an explanation for stress-related disorders, and discuss the usefulness of catharsis in treatment (225).
13. Explain how certain Type A personality traits have been connected with stress-related illness (225-227).
14. Describe the sociocultural understanding of stress-related disorders (227).
15. Summarize neuroscience research on genetic predispositions for the disorders in this chapter (227-228).

## CHAPTER OUTLINE

I.  Mind and body

    A.  Traditionally, mind and body were seen as separate entities (dualism of Plato and Descartes)

    B.  Gradually, it was noticed that mind can affect body and vice versa, so exceptions to the dualistic rule were made (psychophysiological disorders)

C. Today, the position of your text is that mind and body are a unity, just different aspects of the same thing

II. Psychological stress

    A. The autonomic nervous system (ANS) regulates the functioning of internal organs
        1. ANS parasympathetic division conserves energy in normal circumstances
        2. ANS sympathetic division expends energy to meet emergencies (stress reaction)
        3. In the general adaptation syndrome, the stress reaction consists of three stages:
            a. Alarm and mobilization
            b. Resistance
            c. Exhaustion

    B. Stress is variously defined as:
        1. A *stimulus* or environmental *demand* that leads to autonomic responses
        2. The autonomic *response* to environmental demands
        3. The *interaction* between a stimulus and the person's cognitive appraisal of it

    C. The way in which a given individual responds to stressful stimuli depends on the interaction between:
        1. Stimulus specificity, where particular types of stressors produce particular reactions
        2. Individual response specificity, where genetic and/or learned predispositions tend one toward one reaction or another

    D. How stress influences illness
        1. One idea is that stress disrupts critical parts of bodily processes (Schwartz); *or*
        2. Stress disrupts the timing of oscillations in bodily processes as a whole (Weiner)
        3. Stress may increase high-risk behavior through distraction or in attempts to feel better
        4. Stress may incline people to report symptoms earlier and more frequently
        5. Psychoneuroimmunology studies how stress depresses functioning of the immune system by looking at three types of stressors
            a. Naturalistic major events (that cause large disruptions in life)
            b. Naturalistic minor events (low-level daily hassles)
            c. Laboratory stressors (more experimental control—recall analogue experiments?)

III. Physical disorders associated with psychological factors

    A. Essential hypertension (high blood pressure with no known organic cause)
        1. Fifteen percent of population may be affected, but it produces no immediate discomfort, so many are not aware of their dangerous condition
        2. Environmental demands (particularly danger) can drive blood pressure up
        3. Individual response specificity may contribute through inherited or learned patterns of behavior (such as suppression of anger)
        4. Chronic high blood pressure may damage blood vessels or baroreceptors so they no longer work properly

    B. Headache
        1. Migraine differs from ordinary muscle-contraction headache because it:
            a. Is often more intense
            b. Is often localized on one side of the head
            c. May be preceded by an aura
            d. Seems unrelated to blood vessel constriction or dilation
        2. Migraines seem related to:
            a. Low serotonin activity in the brain
            b. Possible hormone imbalances (more women than men)
            c. Depression and sleep disturbances
            d. Possible genetic predispositions

    C. Obesity (overweight)
        1. Defined as being more than 20 percent overweight

2. Subjective, social definitions also apply in our attractiveness-conscious society
3. Some obesity is biogenic, relating to metabolism
4. Key psychological factors seem to be:
   a. Overresponsiveness to food stimuli
   b. Underresponsiveness to body feedback when eating
5. These factors may be related to disregulation caused by chronic dieting

D. Asthma (a breathing difficulty)
1. Some reactions are the result of allergies
2. In nonallergenic cases, psychological factors were long suspected, but recent research fails to demonstrate clear psychological connections
3. It may be that both psychogenic and biogenic factors are at work in nearly all cases of asthma

E. Sleep disorders
1. Insomnia (chronic inability to sleep)
   a. Three insomnia patterns:
      (1) Inability to fall asleep
      (2) Inability to stay asleep
      (3) Waking up too early in the morning
   b. Anticipatory anxiety can aggravate the condition
   c. A variety of stress and lifestyle factors can be involved
      (1) Drug use
      (2) Stress and anxiety
      (3) Physical or mental illness
      (4) Inactivity
      (5) Poor sleep environment
      (6) Poor sleep habits
   d. Physiological overarousal (hypervigilance) seems to be present
   e. Many sleeping drugs are ineffective in the long run and have serious side effects
2. Circadian rhythm disorders (biological clock disruptions)
   a. Shift workers may have their rhythms disrupted by their jobs
   b. Other people have waking and sleeping times that vary for no obvious reason
   c. Treatment may include
      (1) Chronotherapy, in which sleep times are shifted incrementally
      (2) Light therapy, where exposure to light at various times helps regulate waking and sleeping

F. Cancer
1. Long thought to be totally biogenic, new research shows psychogenic components
2. Psychological factors seem to include:
   a. Bottling up of emotions
   b. Helplessness/hopelessness
   c. Severe personal loss
3. One current focus of research involves supportive group therapy

G. AIDS (Acquired immune deficiency syndrome)
1. Relationship between psychological processes and survival of AIDS is unclear
2. Most psychological intervention goes toward reducing high-risk behavior

IV. Perspectives on stress-related disorders

A. The behavioral perspective
1. Autonomic responses can be conditioned
   a. Pairing an ANS response with neutral stimuli can result in respondent conditioning
   b. Following an ANS response with reinforcing consequences can maintain it by operant conditioning
2. Biofeedback training can teach people to gain voluntary control over ordinarily involuntary autonomic responses

3. Relaxation training can also lower the stress response
4. Exercise can relieve stress and lower the effect of stress on the immune system

B. The cognitive perspective
 1. Two factors that seem to influence the intensity of a stress response are the degree to which one can:
   a. Predict stress-producing stimuli
   b. Control stress-producing stimuli
 2. Lazarus, et al, emphasize six stages of cognition/stress interaction
   a. The environmental event (stressor)
   b. Primary appraisal (evaluation of the event)
   c. Secondary appraisal (evaluation of ability to deal with the event)
   d. Coping, which focuses on either
     (1) the event (problem-focused), or
     (2) emotional reactions to the event
   e. Outcomes of coping (biological, cognitive, or behavioral changes)
   f. Health outcomes (impairment or improvement of health, depending on coping success)
 3. Cognitive treatment emphasizes:
   a. Enhancing problem-solving skills
   b. Enhancing coping skills
   c. Enhancing belief in one's capabilities

C. The psychodynamic perspective
 1. The concept of "organ neurosis" assumes that stress-related disorders are anxiety disorders (Chapter 7) in which the defense leads to physical illness
   a. Choice of physical symptom may be related to the nature of the conflict
   b. Family interactions are seen as the key to understanding these problems
 2. Catharsis (getting it out of your system) is valuable in defusing stress

D. Personality theories
 1. There does not seem to be a single stress-reactive personality, but there may be some traits that put one at higher risk for stress-related problems (hostility, anger and aggression in Type A personalities)
 2. Treatment consists of teaching clients relaxation and self-control to change troublesome traits

E. The sociocultural perspective
 1. Low social support (as in single-parent households or disrupted marriages) may add to stress
 2. Cultural changes may be responsible for changes in susceptibility to certain problems
   a. Male-female ulcer ratio used to be 4:1; now it is 2:1
   b. Black-white hypertension ratio likely to change as well?

F. The biological perspective
 1. Genetic studies show that there may be inherited predispositions for:
   a. Migraines
   b. Hypertension
   c. Type A behavior
 2. Treatment involves identifying those with possible predispositions and helping them adjust their lives to prevent triggering of the problem

## KEY TERMS
*The following terms are in bold print in your text. Define them and practice their definitions using the flash cards at the end of the chapter.*

acquired immune deficiency syndrome (AIDS) (222)
asthma (219)
biofeedback training (223)
circadian rhythm disorder (221)

essential hypertension (215)
feedback (211)
health psychology (206)
human immunodeficiency virus (222)
hypertension (214)

immune system (212)
individual response specificity (210)
insomnia (220)
migraine headache (216)
mind-body problem (206)
muscle contraction headache (216)
negative feedback (211)
obesity (217)

oscillations (211)
psychoneuroimmunology (PNI) (212)
psychophysiological disorders (206)
relaxation training (223)
stimulus specificity (209)
stress (208)
Type A (226)

*Your text does not list the following terms as formal vocabulary; however, if you don't know what they mean, you will be unable to grasp the concepts of this chapter.*

aerobic (224)
anecdotal (206)
bidirectional (224)
catheters (214)
contradictory (223)
dander (219)
disregulated (211)

dualism (207)
efficacy (224)
entities (207)
grotesque (218)
heterogeneous (226)
hypervigilance (220)
intractable (217)

jet-lag (221)
metabolic rate (218)
problematic (222)
ramifications (220)
reciprocal (224)
synergistically (216)
trivial (225)

## IMPORTANT NAMES
*Identify the following persons and their major contributions to abnormal psychology as discussed in this chapter.*

W. B. Cannon (208)
Meyer Friedman (226)

R. H. Rosenman (226)
Gary Schwartz (211)

Hans Selye (208)
Herbert Weiner (211)

## GUIDED SELF-STUDY

1.  Use these terms to complete the following blanks:

asthma
behavioral
blood pressure
dualistic
emotional

health
heart rate
holistic
hypertension
migraine headaches

psychological
psychophysiological
psychosomatic
susceptibility
ulcer

A (a)_____ disorder is another name for a (b)_____ disorder, which means a real

physical disorder that is caused or heavily influenced by (c)_____ factors.  In the past,

only a few limited illnesses were listed in this group: (d)_____, _____,

_____, and _____ were among these disorders.  The mind-body problem was seen

from a (e)_____ perspective where the mind and body are separate entities.  In the 1960's

previously involuntary behaviors such as (f)_____ and _____ were found to be
responsive to voluntary control of the individual.  More recent research has demonstrated that

(g)_____ to disease and rate of progression of a disease is affected by (h)_____

factors.  This new (i)_____ concept sees the mind and body as a unified process—two

sides of the same coin.  This new approach has been named (j)_____ psychology, also

called (k)_____ medicine.

2. What are the three major historical trends of thought that have come together in this new discipline?

   a.

   b.

   c.

3. The autonomic nervous system is the link between higher brain functions (i.e., experiencing and thinking) to the body's responses to cope with the environment. Use these terms to complete the following blanks: **autonomic, constrict, dilate, increase, inhibition, parasympathetic,** and **sympathetic**.

   The (a)_____ nervous system controls smooth muscles, glands, and internal organs. It is

   divided into two subsystems: The (b)_____ division mobilizes the body to meet environmental demands. When stress is experienced and this system is activated, heart rate,

   blood pressure and breathing (c)_____, pupils (d)_____, blood vessels near the

   skin (e)_____, and there is (f)_____ of saliva production (e.g., dry mouth) and

   digestion. The (g)_____ division reverses these processes to bring the body back to a resting state so that it can rebuild its energy supply.

4. How do you personally know when you are stressed? In other words, what are your physical symptoms of stress?

5. Are you aware of someone else's physical stress reactions, maybe a family member, friend, roommate, or coworker? Are her/his stress reactions similar to yours, or quite different from yours?

6. Which of the following definitions of stress is the correct one?
   a. Environmental demands
   b. Autonomic nervous system activation
   c. Interaction between the stimulus and the person's appraisal of the stimulus

7. Use these terms and phrases to complete the following explanation:

| | |
|---|---|
| **brain-wave changes** | **individual response pattern** |
| **decreases** | **individual response specificity** |
| **facial expressions** | **innate tendencies** |
| **frontal** | **physiological** |
| **gastric** | **programmed pattern of responses** |
| **hemispherical asymmetry** | **stimulus specificity** |
| **hormone secretions** | **stressor** |
| **increased** | |

   According to your text, two factors determine what response an individual will make to stress:

   (a)_____ _____ and (b)_____ _____ _____. Stimulus specificity says that

   a particular type of (c)_____ causes particular kinds of autonomic responses. For

   example, a stressor that makes you angry causes increased flow of (d) _____ juices; a fear

   stimulus (e)_____ the flow of gastric juices. (f)_____ _____ _____
   means individuals each have their own patterns of reacting to specific stressors. Because of

learning or (g)_____ _____, one individual might respond more or less strongly, or might respond with a different kind of (h)_____ reaction. These two factors do not contradict or interfere with one another. Each contributes its own predispositions to reactions in a given situation. For any particular type of stressor there is a (i)_____ _____ ___ _____ that a human's body is inclined to make; this is the response specificity. However, that pattern is very complex; the degree to which one will display different parts of the patterns is determined by the individual's characteristic pattern: one individual may accent one part of the pattern while another person accents another part of the pattern. Let's say two people are angry. They both will tend to have (j)_____ flow of gastric juices and (k)_____ blood pressure. One may have his blood pressure shoot up very high while the other's blood pressure rises only moderately. However, the one with moderately elevated blood pressure may have higher levels of gastric juices than the other person. Thus each person has an (l)_____ _____ _____ within the general pattern they both share.

Update on stimulus specificity!! Weiner has gone on to show not only autonomic activity but also (m)_____, _____, and _____ have distinctive patterns of response according to which type stressor is the stimulus. There is an update for individual response specificity, too. EEG's can predict which people tend to respond more intensely to stress in general. Infants with (n)_____ _____, which means more activity on one side of the brain than on the other, particularly those with more activity in the right (o)_____ lobe of the brain are more likely to be generally more sensitive to stressors.

8. Identify the theorist whose name is associated with each of the following. Choose among

**Gary Schwartz**          **Holmes and Rahe**          **W. B. Cannon**
**Hans Selye**             **Lazarus**                  **Weiner**

One of the names is used twice.

a. _____ Described massive activation of the entire sympathetic division

b. _____ "General adaptation syndrome"

c. _____ Disregulation model

d. _____ Oscillation model

e. _____ Dynamic model

f. _____ The correlation between major life crises and illness

g. _____ The daily hassles of life significantly affect health

9. Assign the correct order to the stages of Hans Selye's general adaptation syndrome.

a. _____ Resistance
b. _____ Alarm and mobilization
c. _____ Exhaustion and disintegration

10. Schwartz's disregulation model is an explanation for how a (a)_____ disorder can develop.

(b) REVIEW! At this point can you remember the other name for this disorder?

11. Choose the correct alternative: Schwartz uses the term negative feedback to mean
    a. personal criticism as a destructive environmental stimulus.
    b. unpleasant physiological arousal.
    c. a cut-off arrangement in a body regulatory system.
    d. misinformation from a malfunctioning organ.

12. Match these terms to their definitions: **Immune, Lymphocytes, Mitogens, Psychoneuroimmunology,** and **Stressor**.

    a. _____ White blood cells that defend the body

    b. _____ System which defends body against invaders

    c. _____ Major life events that make demands on us

    d. _____ Compounds that mimic the action of foreign substances in the body

    e. _____ Study of stress, illness, and the immune system

    f. _____ Minor life events that make demands on us

PHYSICAL DISORDERS ASSOCIATED WITH PSYCHOLOGICAL FACTORS
13. Use these terms and phrases to complete the following blanks:

| | | |
|---|---|---|
| **constant alertness** | **environment** | **obvious discomfort** |
| **constricted** | **essential** | **organic** |
| **cut off** | **genetic** | **personality** |
| **dangerous** | **heart attack** | **relax** |
| **disregulation** | **hypertension** | **stroke** |
| **dietary** | **kidney trouble** | **suppress** |

(a)_____ means high blood pressure.   In a small number of cases of high blood pressure

there is an identifiable organic cause, usually (b) _____ _____. The vast majority of

cases are called (c)_____ hypertension for which there is no known (d)_____
cause for the person to have high blood pressure.  Research has shown that people who have

chronic hypertension have chronically (e)_____ blood vessels.  That is, their blood vessels

do not (f)_____ when arousal has passed, as blood vessels do in people who do not have

blood pressure problems.  This is consistent with Schwartz's (g)_____ model, which

says that there is a problem in that the constriction mode does not (h)_____.  The
text lists several different factors that could contribute to this state of chronically constricted

blood vessels.  Those factors are an (i)_____ with many stressors that require a

(j)_____ _____, a (k)_____ component, (l)_____ patterns, and

(m)_____ traits that tend to (n) _____ anger. The results of untreated

hypertension can be (o)_____ _____ and (p) _____.  High blood pressure is very

(q)_____ because those who have it go for years without treatment because there is no

(r)_____ _____ to signal the body's dysfunction.

14. What are the two types of headaches?

15. What are five characteristics that differentiate migraine headaches from other kinds of headaches?

    a.

    b.

    c.

    d.

    e.

16. The long dominant theory of migraine causation was stress-induced (a)_____ constriction

    and (b) _____ in the brain.  More recent research has led to a newer theory about

    (c)_____ disorder involving the neurotransmitter (d)_____.

17. "Obesity is a socially defined condition."  What does that mean?



18. What two physiological factors control weight?



19. Use these words to complete the following blanks.  Several words are used more than once.

| characteristic | eating patterns | lowers |
|---|---|---|
| cues | exercise | maintain |
| dieters | fat | moderately |
| dieting | genetically | more |

    Some obese people can eat (a)_____ and will still remain (b)_____.  Several factors

    contribute to this circumstance.  Metabolic rate is primarily (c)_____ determined.

    We need (d)_____ calories to gain weight than to (e)_____ that same amount of

    weight.  So once gained, fat stays on even more easily than it was gained.  Dieting (f)_____

    metabolic rate, too.  Very important information has been discovered in regard to weight

    control programs and how people respond to eating (g)_____.  Some behaviors thought

    to be (h)_____ of obese people in general are seen mostly in chronic (i)_____ and

    people of normal weight who are prevented from engaging in their normal (j)_____.
    Researchers had not taken into account the fact that many obese people are also chronic

    (k)_____.  When obesity and (l)_____ were separated, (m)_____ seems to be

    the causal factor.  Chronic (n)_____ seems to lead to disregulation.  This is why weight

    reduction programs have changed their emphasis from (o)_____ to (p)_____.

20. What is an asthma attack?

21. Which of the following best summarizes current thinking on the psychological aspects of asthma?
    a. Asthma is a prime example of a stress-related problem.
    b. Asthma is a biologically determined allergic reaction.
    c. Asthma attacks result from a biological predisposition and a stress trigger.
    d. Asthma, regardless of its cause, can create psychological issues that make the problem worse.

22. Who is more likely to get insomnia: Men or women?    Younger or older people?

23. What are the three different patterns of insomnia?

    a.

    b.

    c.

24. When studying sleep, researchers operationally define sleep as when a subject
    a. no longer responds to his name whispered at 60 db
    b. begins to have rapid eye movements
    c. relaxes the major muscle groups of the body
    d. shows an EEG brain pattern labeled as indicating sleep

25. Choose the correct terms for the following blanks. Not all are used. **Anterograde state, Sleep-state misperception, Hypoglycemic, Anticipatory anxiety,** and **Hypervigilance**.

    a. _____    Person can't sleep because he/she is worried that he/she will be unable to fall asleep
    b. _____    An individual's extreme underestimation of amount of sleep actually occurring
    c. _____    Remaining to some degree alert instead of relaxing into sleep

26. List four factors that cause or worsen insomnia.



27. Why are nightmares, night terrors, and sleepwalking not discussed here as sleep disorders?


28. Among the following words are the right answers to these blanks:

| active | helplessness | not |
|---|---|---|
| chemotherapy | humans | prevent |
| delay | less | rats |
| denial | little | social |
| die | longer | strong |
| fatalities | monkeys | support |
| financial | no | survival |

At this point there is (a)_____ suggestion that stress in and of itself causes cancer. However,

there is (b)_____ evidence that psychological factors play some part in cancer (c)_____:

Married cancer victims as a group survive (d)_____ than do their unmarried

counterparts. Cancer victims who have participated in peer (e)_____ groups survive

longer than their counterparts who did (f)_____. Research revealed that (g)_____ which

were placed in inescapable shock situations were more likely to (h)_____ from implanted

196

cancer cells than were those who were put in the same situation but could make a response to (i)_____ the shocks. From this researchers have postulated that the (j)_____ support benefit for humans encourages the cancer victims to make (k)_____ coping responses instead of sinking into a sense of (l)_____.

29. Why is AIDS included in this chapter since it comes not from stress but from a virus?

30. The current focus of psychological treatment in regard to AIDS is what?

31. Lagniappe—something a little extra: You might see some of these on the test. Find the term and fill in the blank.

a. _____ Cells that are sensitive to arterial pressure

b. _____ Most common physical disorder associated with stress

c. _____ Virus that destroys immune cells

d. _____ Having a psychological cause

e. _____ Biological clock

f. _____ Most dangerous physical disorder associated with stress

g. _____ A virus that remains in the body and flares up occasionally particularly under stress

h. _____ Progressive breakdown of mental functioning

i. _____ Twice as common among blacks

j. _____ Twice as common among women

k. _____ A stress-related disorder common in young children

l. _____ Speed at which the body converts food into energy

m. _____ Having to do with a life process

## PERSPECTIVES ON STRESS-RELATED PHYSICAL DISORDERS

32. Compare the list of perspectives in Chapter One to those in Chapter Nine. Connect the ones seen in both lists. Which ones are added for Chapter Nine and which ones will not be discussed in Chapter Nine?

Perspectives listed in Chapter One

Psychodynamic
Behavioral
Cognitive
Humanistic-existential
Interpersonal
Sociocultural
Biological

Perspectives listed in Chapter Nine

Behavioral
Cognitive
Psychodynamic
Personality
Sociocultural
Biological

33. a. What's the magic word for the behavioral perspective?

   b. From Chapter Three, what are the two mechanisms (or processes) for behaviorism should pop into the forefront of your memory after the "the magic word" for behaviorism?

   c. This means that behaviorists will attempt to explain psychophysiological disorders in terms of _____.

34. For many decades behavioral theorists believed that the stress responses from the autonomic nervous system were learned and controlled through (a)_____ conditioning only. Then, in the 1960's, research demonstrated that people could learn to control autonomic processes by (b)_____ conditioning as well. This discovery gave birth to a behavioral therapy technique known as (c)_____ training for dealing with stress.

35. Biofeedback is learning to listen to your body. What are you actually listening to during the training?

36. What other behavioral techniques are commonly used in teaching people to cope with stress?

37. List some bits of news that would cause you to have physical reactions. Also, consider exactly what physical reactions you experience.

38. What two cognitive variables have researchers found that make dramatic differences in stress reactions?

39. a. What is the name given to the training sessions that cognitive therapists use to help people learn to cope?

   b. What specific training is likely to be offered in these sessions?

40. Some research on catecholamine levels points out the importance of how you think. Low catecholamine levels have been associated with (a)_____ and subjective feelings of inability to (b)_____.

41. According to this research, which of the following students is going to have the highest catecholamine level?
   a. The very bright student who knows the material thoroughly but experiences very high test anxiety.
   b. The student who knows he/she doesn't understand the material, and accepts the reality that he/she will make a low C at best in the class
   c. The student who says, "I will schedule two hours of study time to this class every Thursday because the instructor always schedules tests on Fridays."
   d. The student who says, "This class is not worth the trouble. I am wasting my time and effort with it."

42. Assign the correct order to the following stages of Lazarus' interactive dynamic model of stress.

   a. _____ Coping
   b. _____ Environmental event
   c. _____ Health outcomes
   d. _____ Outcomes of coping
   e. _____ Primary appraisal
   f. _____ Secondary appraisal

43. The underlying problem from the psychodynamic perspective is always (a)_____ _____.

   Psychodynamic theorists refer to stress-related physical disorders as (b)_____ _____.

   Psychodynamic treatment tries to uncover the repressed material and emotionally get it out in

   the open, a process called (c)_____. PNI research verified that writing out one's
   stressful events did do something to relieve stress, as indicated by increased activity in the

   person's (d)_____ _____.

44. Complete the following blanks using one or more of these terms. Not all terms will be used.

   | aggressive achievers | highly competitive | more |
   | cardiovascular | hostility | personality |
   | cognitive | impatient | relaxation |
   | denial | less | self-control |
   | goal setting | liver | theory |

   When a psychologist is trying to predict who will get what psychosomatic disorder by the

   person's personality, this theorist is taking a (a)_____ theory perspective. Although
   these theories have been around most of the century, research findings have not supported
   them. The Friedman and Rosenman book *Type A Behavior and Your Heart* proposed that

   people called "Type A" were (b)_____ likely to develop hypertension and other

   (c)_____ disorders. This book describes Type As as people who are (d)_____,

   _____. Research has not found the drive to achieve to be as dangerous as Friedman and
   Rosenman's book suggested. However, the research has substantiated a correlation between

   level of (e)_____ and heart disease. The finding suggests that Type A's are
   extremely responsive to stress. Type A's are more likely to survive after one heart attack if

   they receive training in (f)_____, _____, and _____.

45. The (a)_____ perspective proposes that modern industrialized society causes stress

   which leads to physical illness. One effect industrialization has had is on (b)_____.

   Research leaves no doubt that people who do not have a social support network are (c) _____
   at risk for illness than people who *do* have a social support network.

46. Use the following terms to fill in the blanks. More than one term is used in some of the
    blanks. Each term will be used only once.

   | behavioral | genes | MZ |
   | DZ | genetic | organic |
   | emotional | immune | physical |

   The biological perspective always focuses on the (a)_____ elements. In the stress-related

199

disorders the biological perspectives emphasizes two organic contributors: they are (b)_____ and _____ . The (c)_____ element in some stress reactions is supported strongly in the comparison between (d)_____ twins. The role of the (e)_____ system is part of a complex, intricate system involving (f)_____, _____, and _____ causes.

47. Now we have covered all the perspectives for Chapter Nine. Do you recognize them? Label each of the following for its correct perspective. Here are your choices: **Behavioral, Cognitive, Psychodynamic, Personality, Sociocultural, Biological**.

a. _____ Organ neurosis
b. _____ Thinking
c. _____ Physical relaxation
d. _____ Respondent conditioning
e. _____ Onsite employment childcare
f. _____ Catharsis
g. _____ Biofeedback
h. _____ Type A's
i. _____ Prediction and control
j. _____ Genetics
k. _____ Unconscious conflicts
l. _____ Efficacy expectations
m. _____ Operant conditioning
n. _____ Progressive relaxation

## HELPFUL HINTS

1. I hope this hint will sound very familiar to you. It was mentioned in the previous chapter. I am including it here as well because it is fundamental to this chapter. I have found that people use the word "psychosomatic" when they want to say that someone's health problem is really in the person's mind. That is incorrect. As you learned in the last chapter, that would be either psychogenic pain disorder or a somatoform disorder. As you learn in this chapter, psychosomatic illnesses have observable physical problems that are caused or aggravated by mental issues. Also in common public usage, the term hypochondriasis is often misused. It is often used to describe someone with varied, vague physical complaints. This is actually somatization disorder. According to psychological definition, the hypochondriac has fears of particular diseases. If you choose to continue using these terms in the colloquial manner to communicate with others who misuse them in the same way, that is your choice. Just know that on a psychology test, you are going to need to know them as they are defined in psychology books.

2. Remember that respondent conditioning is always based on (involuntary) reflex responses. Yes, you are a puppet on a string in respondent conditioning (64). Operant conditioning is changing behavior because of the consequences the response brought. *You* are pulling the strings to bring the consequences you want (66). If at this point, you are swearing off being a puppet on a string (respondent conditioning), and are becoming a devotee to pulling your own strings (operant conditioning), reread "operant versus respondent conditioning" on pages 66 and 67. *You NEED BOTH kinds of conditioning to survive.* Being on a string that alerts you to danger is not bad!

3. Learning terminology used in a course, whether it is listed as formal vocabulary or not, is crucial! As a classroom teacher, I am often astounded when students demonstrate that they do not know basic terms from the text or terms that I commonly use in lecture. The opinion seems to be if it is not in the vocabulary list, it will not be on the test. **WRONG!!!!!** If it is not in the vocabulary list, the textbook author and/or the teacher believes that word to be in the student's working vocabulary.

4. Since you are taking this course, you are a college student; so by definition this chapter on **STRESS!!** is for you! Learn it not only for the test, but also for managing your own quality of life. I am not suggesting that you quit school; look into your time and stress management skills and your study skills. I have seen very few students (including myself) who do not benefit from a class or course or self-help book on these issues.

*Take the following test several times as you study the chapter. Write your answers on a separate sheet of paper and after each attempt, note in the tally box above each question whether your answer was correct or incorrect.*

| 1 | 2 | 3 | 4 |
|---|---|---|---|

1.  What research discipline emphasizes an integrated approach to mental and physical health?
    a.  Psychosomatic science
    b.  Behavioral medicine
    c.  Psychic healing
    d.  Psychophysics

| 1 | 2 | 3 | 4 |
|---|---|---|---|

2.  In discussing the mind-body problem, your text takes the position that
    a.  mind and body cannot be separated.
    b.  mind dominates the body and controls it.
    c.  mind and body are essentially unrelated.
    d.  physical disorders give rise to mental illness.

| 1 | 2 | 3 | 4 |
|---|---|---|---|

3.  Which of the following is *not* part of the general adaptation syndrome described by Hans Selye?
    a.  Alarm reaction
    b.  Resistance stage
    c.  Exhaustion stage
    d.  Recovery phase

| 1 | 2 | 3 | 4 |
|---|---|---|---|

4.  Heidi grew up in a highly competitive family where idleness was frowned upon and success was all-important. Wayne's family, on the other hand, was very relaxed about most things. As a result, Heidi and Wayne have learned very different physiological and behavioral responses to similar stimuli. Their different response patterns can be explained in terms of
    a.  stimulus specificity.
    b.  individual response specificity.
    c.  feedback specificity.
    d.  pathological bias.

| 1 | 2 | 3 | 4 |
|---|---|---|---|

5.  In the preceding question, Heidi's family shows what personality type?
    a.  Anal expulsive type
    b.  Type A
    c.  Passive-aggressive type
    d.  Type B

| 1 | 2 | 3 | 4 |
|---|---|---|---|

6.  Shift workers often experience trouble with sleeping, and may have other problems as well. According to Weiner, this is because
    a.  they are angry about their shift schedules and need catharsis to relieve their stress.
    b.  they have paired waking and sleeping with many different times of day in a respondent conditioning situation.
    c.  they have disrupted their natural rhythms or oscillations of sleep and waking.
    d.  they have accepted social expectations about sleeplessness in shift workers.

| 1 | 2 | 3 | 4 |

7. In a properly functioning negative feedback system, information about some component of the system
   a. is used by the system to exaggerate the activity of that component.
   b. is recorded by the system as data but no further effect is produced.
   c. is ignored by the rest of the system.
   d. is used by the system to decrease or balance the activity of that component.

| 1 | 2 | 3 | 4 |

8. Gary Schwartz's disregulation model states that
   a. organic problems occur because we cannot control external stressors.
   b. our way of thinking about our problems is the major cause of mental disorder.
   c. mental illness makes one more susceptible to physical disease.
   d. physical diseases may result from the failure of internal regulatory systems.

| 1 | 2 | 3 | 4 |

9. Psychoneuroimmunology research would support which of the following statements?
   a. Minor daily stressors can lead to problems even if no major issues are affecting your life.
   b. Susceptibility to stress related disorders is mainly a matter of genetic inheritance.
   c. Major stressing events are unlikely to cause problems as long as you eat and sleep well.
   d. AIDS is more a result of stress, not a virus.

| 1 | 2 | 3 | 4 |

10. Which of the following definitions of abnormality is most likely being referred to when your text says that obesity is a socially defined condition?
    a. Statistical rarity
    b. Maladaptive behavior
    c. Norm violation
    d. Personal discomfort

| 1 | 2 | 3 | 4 |

11. All of the following have been implicated in essential hypertension *except*
    a. a tendency toward bipolar disorder.
    b. an inability to express aggression and anger.
    c. a genetic predisposition to deal with stress with elevated blood pressure.
    d. dangerous and high-stress environments.

| 1 | 2 | 3 | 4 |

12. Which of the following is true of insomnia?
    a. It is helped by the long-term use of sleeping pills.
    b. It occurs in less than 10 percent of the population.
    c. It can be aggravated by anticipatory anxiety.
    d. It generally affects more men than women.

| 1 | 2 | 3 | 4 |

13. The effect of stress on the body's ability to resist disease is the subject of
    a. psychobiology.
    b. physiometrics.
    c. psychoneuroimmunology.
    d. neuropsychiatry.

14. Treatment of stress-related disorders by the use of biofeedback and muscle relaxation is most likely to be done by
    a. a behavior therapist.
    b. a psychoanalytically oriented therapist.
    c. someone in the cognitive perspective.
    d. an existential therapist.

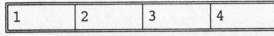

15. Your text refers to the field of health psychology as being "holistic." The term "holistic" means
    a. religion-based.          c. inferential.
    b. restricted.              d. unified.

16. For the psychodynamic theorists, stress-related disorders
    a. are just another example of symptoms produced by anxiety.
    b. must be interpreted differently from other neuroses.
    c. are best treated by medically alleviating the organic symptoms.
    d. are really the cause of anxiety and not the result of it.

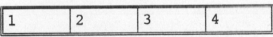

17. Chronotherapy and light therapy, as discussed in this chapter, are most often used to treat
    a. obesity.                 c. cancer.
    b. essential hypertension.  d. sleep disorders.

```
| 1 | 2 | 3 | 4 |
```

18. According to the sociocultural perspective, which of the following would be at highest risk for stress-related disorders?
    a. A happily married white female
    b. A divorced black male
    c. A married white male with a good job
    d. A dating, well-employed black female

```
| 1 | 2 | 3 | 4 |
```

19. According to the text, which of the following is evidence supporting a genetic connection in stress-related disorders?
    a. People with hypertensive parents are more likely to experience hypertension themselves.
    b. There is an identified gene associated with the development of breast cancer.
    c. MZ twins and DZ twins are equally likely to develop asthma.
    d. Insomnia can be induced in all members of any given family.

```
| 1 | 2 | 3 | 4 |
```

20. The most productive application of behavior therapy in the fight against AIDS is in
    a. training people in conscious control of their immune systems.
    b. reducing the likelihood of high-risk behavior.
    c. changing homosexuals into heterosexuals.
    d. reducing the public's fear of the human immunodeficiency virus (HIV).

# ANSWERS

## Self-Study Exercise

1. a. psychophysiological
   b. psychosomatic
   c. emotional (206)
   d. asthma, ulcer, hypertension, and migraine headaches (206)
   e. dualistic (207)
   f. blood pressure and heart rate (207)
   g. susceptibility (206)
   h. psychological (207)
   i. holistic (206)
   j. health (206)
   k. behavioral (206)

2. a. The focus is now holistic: state of mind and way of living affects physical well-being.
   b. Psychological factors and life-style factors can be used to prevent or treat physical illness.
   c. Behavioral training can help relieve stress-related physical illness (206).

3. a. autonomic (208)
   b. sympathetic (208)
   c. increase (208)
   d. dilate (208)
   e. constrict (208)
   f. inhibition (208)
   g. parasympathetic (208)

4. Your own experience
5. Your own observations
6. All of these are definitions of stress discussed in your text. This was a trick question to call your attention to the fact that there are different ways to define stress (208).

7. a. stimulus specificity (208-209)
   b. individual response specificity (209-210)
   c. stressor (208-209)
   d. gastric (209)
   e. decreases (209)
   f. Individual response specificity (209-210)
   g. innate tendencies (209)
   h. physiological (209)
   i. programmed pattern of responses
   j. increased
   k. increased
   l. individual response pattern (210)
   m. facial expressions, brain waves changes, and hormone secretions (209)
   n. hemispheric asymmetry
   o. frontal (210)

8. a. W. B. Cannon (208)
   b. Hans Selye (208)
   c. Gary Schwartz (211)
   d. Weiner (211)
   e. Lazarus (224)
   f. Holmes and Rahe (209)
   g. Lazarus (209)

9. a. 2
   b. 1
   c. 3 (208)

10. a. psychophysiological (211, 206)
    b. Psychosomatic. You could have these answers reversed. Just make sure you recognize both terms as the concept of physical illnesses influenced by emotional factors (206).

11. "c" (211)

12. a. Lymphocytes (212)
    b. Immune (212)
    c. Stressor (212)
    d. Mitogens (212)
    e. Psychoneuroimmunology (212)
    f. Stressor (212)

13. a. Hypertension (214)
    b. kidney trouble (215)
    c. essential (215)
    d. organic (215)
    e. constricted (215)
    f. relax (215)
    g. disregulation (214)
    h. cut off (211)
    i. environment (215)
    j. constant alertness (215)
    k. genetic (215)
    l. dietary (215)
    m. personality (215)
    n. suppress (215)
    o. heart attack (214)
    p. stroke (214)
    q. dangerous (215)
    r. obvious discomfort (215)

14. Migraine and tension headaches (also called muscle-contraction headaches) (216)

15. a. Localized on one side of the head
    b. More intense than other headaches
    c. Sometimes preceded by an aura
    d. Often accompanied by physical problems (nausea, vomiting), cognitive problems (confusion), and affective problems (depression, irritability)
    e. May involve intolerance to light and/or sounds (216)
16. a. blood vessel (216)       c. neurological (216)
    b. dilation (216)           d. serotonin (216)
17. All people must have some fat to carry out the required chemical processes of the body, but how much is the right amount to have "in storage" on the body is defined by the culture (217-218).
18. Metabolic rate and activity level (218)
19. a. moderately        i. dieters
    b. fat               j. eating patterns
    c. genetically       k. dieters
    d. more              l. dieting
    e. maintain          m. dieting
    f. lowers            n. dieting
    g. cues              o. dieting
    h. characteristic    p. exercise (217-219)
20. An asthma attack is when the airways into the lungs narrow, causing the person to feel he/she cannot get enough air.  In an extreme attack the person feels that suffocation is imminent (219).
21. "d" (220)
22. Women and older (220)
23. a. Taking a long time to fall asleep
    b. Awakening too early in the morning
    c. Going to sleep easily but waking up repeatedly during the night
    To summarize for easy recall—awake too long, too early, or too often (220)
24. "d" (220)
25. a. Anticipatory anxiety (220)
    b. Sleep-state misperception (220)
    c. Hypervigilance (220)
26. Drugs, alcohol, caffeine, nicotine, stress, anxiety, physical illness, psychological disturbance, inactivity, poor sleep environment, and poor sleep habits are all listed in the text (220).
27. Because they are primarily seen in children, they will be discussed in the chapter on childhood (221).
28. a. no            g. rats
    b. strong        h. die
    c. survival      i. prevent
    d. longer        j. social
    e. support       k. active
    f. not           l. helplessness (221-222)
29. Since one's immune system is weakened by stress, a disease attacking the immune system itself is likely to be worsened by stress also.  The research findings are mixed on this so far; however, the effect of stress on HIV and AIDS is still under study (223).
30. Teaching people to avoid high risk behaviors through education, assertiveness training, problem solving to anticipate and avoid risk factors, and reinforcement of behavior change (223).
31. a. Baroreceptors (211)        h. Dementia (213)
    b. Hypertension (214)         i. Hypertension (215)
    c. HIV (222)                  j. Migraine headache (216)
    d. Psychogenic (20)           k. Asthma (219)
    e. Circadian rhythm (221)     l. Metabolic rate (218)
    f. Hypertension (214)         m. Organic (dictionary, see Hint 3)
    g. Herpes (213)
32. The humanistic-existential and interpersonal perspectives are not discussed in Chapter Nine, and the perspective on personality theories is included in Chapter Nine (3, 205).
33. a. Learning!
    b. Respondent and operant conditioning!
    c. learning, specifically respondent and operant conditioning (223)

34. a. respondent (same as classical)
    b. operant
    c. biofeedback (see Helpful Hint number 4) (223)
35. For the training you actually hear a machine that monitors your body and tells you what is happening inside your body so that you can become aware of what a specific condition feels like within your sensory experience (223).
36. Progressive relaxation and physical exercise (223-224)
37. Your own experience, but here are some possibilities for bits of information that may cause a "sick feeling": News of disasters or personal tragedies, certainly, but on a less disastrous level, you've overdrawn your checking account; you are going to be forced to deal with someone you distinctly dislike (a parent, an in-law, an ex-roommate, or ex-boyfriend/girlfriend/spouse); and that always-dreaded word "test."
    Here are possibilities for physical sensations you might have listed: hit in the stomach; stomach goes into a knot; stomach seems to jump or to flip over; a sinking feeling in your stomach and/or heart; sense of heart stopping and then racing; pain in the head; tight jaw from teeth clenching; full body tension; or numbness in the sense of existing but not feeling.
38. Predictability and, (even more important) a sense of control (224)
39. a. Stress management programs
    b. Time management and/or assertiveness training as well as relaxation techniques (225)
40. a. depression
    b. cope
41. "c" (224)
42. a. 4          d. 5
    b. 1          e. 2
    c. 6          f. 3 (224)

43. a. unconscious conflicts (225)     c. catharsis (225)
    b. organ neurosis (225)            d. immune cells (225)

44. a. personality theory             d. highly competitive, aggressive achievers
    b. more                           e. hostility
    c. cardiovascular                 f. relaxation, self-control, goal setting (226)

45. a. sociocultural                  c. more (227)
    b. marriage and the family

46. a. organic                        d. MZ and DZ
    b. genes and the immune system    e. immune
    c. genetic                        f. physical, behavioral and emotional
                                         (227-228)

47. a. Psychodynamic (225)            h. Personality (226)
    b. Cognitive (224)                i. Cognitive (224)
    c. Behavioral (224)               j. Biological (227)
    d. Behavioral (223)               k. Psychodynamic (225)
    e. Sociocultural (227)            l. Cognitive (224)
    f. Psychodynamic (225)            m. Behavioral (223)
    g. Behavioral (223)               n. Behavioral (223)

**Practice Test**

1. b    (206)          11. a    (215)
2. a    (208)          12. c    (220)
3. d    (208)          13. c    (212)
4. b    (209-210)      14. a    (223)
5. b    (226)          15. d    (206)
6. c    (211)          16. a    (225)
7. d    (211)          17. d    (221)
8. d    (211)          18. b    (227)
9. a    (213)          19. a    (227)
10. c   (217)          20. b    (223)

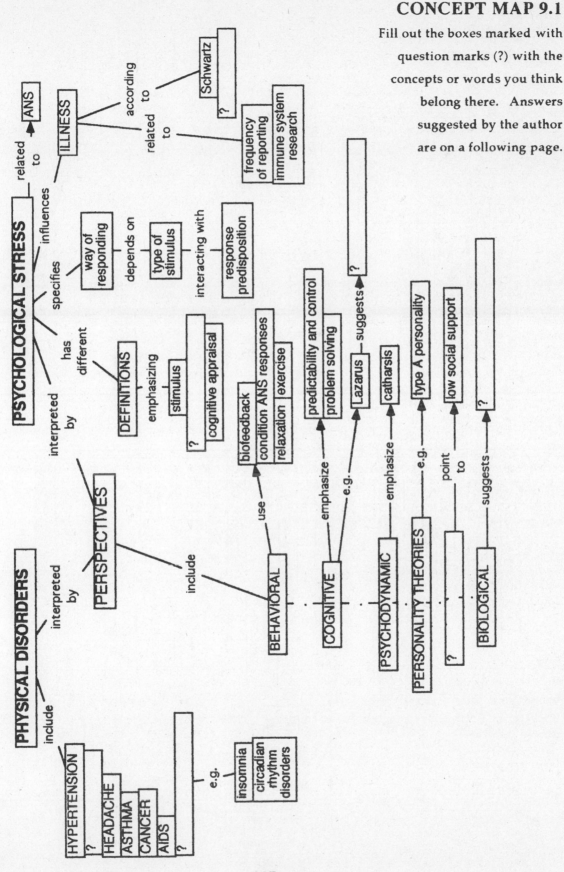

## CONCEPT MAP 9.1

Fill out the boxes marked with question marks (?) with the concepts or words you think belong there. Answers suggested by the author are on a following page.

207

# CONCEPT MAP 9.1

The suggested answers are shown in *italics*.

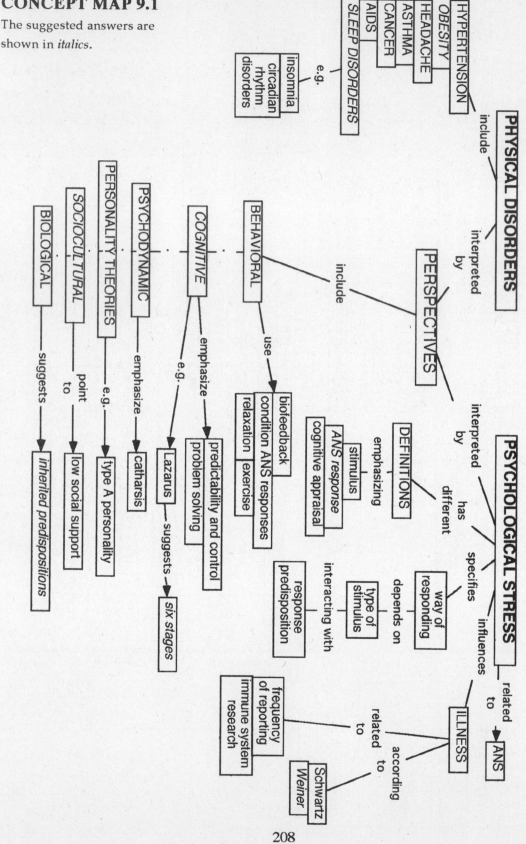

# CHAPTER TERMS (Cut out on the lines to use as Flash Cards)

| | | |
|---|---|---|
| 9.1<br><br>**acquired immune deficiency syndrome (AIDS)** | 9.8<br><br>**human immunodeficiency virus (HIV)** | 9.15<br><br>**muscle contraction headache** |
| 9.2<br><br>**asthma** | 9.9<br><br>**hypertension** | 9.16<br><br>**negative feedback** |
| 9.3<br><br>**biofeedback training** | 9.10<br><br>**immune system** | 9.17<br><br>**obesity** |
| 9.4<br><br>**circadian rhythm disorder** | 9.11<br><br>**individual response specificity** | 9.18<br><br>**oscillations** |
| 9.5<br><br>**essential hypertension** | 9.12<br><br>**insomnia** | 9.19<br><br>**psychoneuro-immunology (PNI)** |
| 9.6<br><br>**feedback** | 9.13<br><br>**migraine headache** | 9.20<br><br>**psychophysiological disorders** |
| 9.7<br><br>**health psychology** | 9.14<br><br>**mind-body problem** | 9.21<br><br>**relaxation training** |

**DEFINITIONS** (Cut out on the lines to use as Flash Cards)

| | | |
|---|---|---|
| 9.15 <br><br> Ordinary tension headaches | 9.8 Virus which is thought to cause AIDS; may remain dormant for decades before AIDS symptoms appear; transmitted sexually through body fluids (e.g. blood, semen, vaginal secretions. breast milk) | 9.1 <br> Sexually transmitted disease which attacks the immune system, leaving the person open to various lethal infections; caused by HIV |
| 9.16 <br><br> Feedback in which the turning on of one component of a system leads to the turning off of another component, in order to regulate the system | 9.9 <br> Chronic elevation of blood pressure due to constriction of the arteries; a stress related physical disorder. Also called high blood pressure | 9.2 A respiratory disorder in which the body's air passageways narrow, causing coughing, wheezing, and shortness of breath; usually associated with allergies or organic problems, but some cases may be related to stress |
| 9.17 An excessive amount of fat on the body; each culture sets its own standard for ideal body weight, so what is considered acceptable in one culture may not be in another | 9.10 <br><br> The system the body uses to protect itself against disease and invading organisms | 9.3 <br> A technique by which subjects, with the help of various machines, can monitor and control their own biological processes such as pulse, blood pressure, and brain waves |
| 9.18 <br> Rhythmic back and forth cycles of the various systems of the body; used in Herbert Weiner's theory | 9.11 The principle that people seem to have characteristic patterns of autonomic nervous system response which carry over from one kind of stress to another | 9.4 Disorder characterized by drowsiness and poor sleep caused by trying to rest at times not in synchronization with the body's cycles of sleep and wakefulness; treated by light therapy and chronotherapy |
| 9.19 <br><br> A specialty of health science linking the immune system and stress related illness | 9.12 <br><br> Chronic inability to sleep; the condition can stem from both physical and psychological factors | 9.5 <br><br> Chronically high blood pressure for which no organic cause can be found |
| 9.20 <br><br> Illnesses influenced by emotional and psychological factors; also known as psychosomatic disorders | 9.13 Severe form of stress-related chronic headache; usually localized on one side of the head and sometimes preceded by perceptual distortion (aura), accompanied by other symptoms such as nausea or confusion | 9.6 <br> A process in which information is returned to a system in order to regulate that system |
| 9.21 A technique by which a patient is taught to recognize the symptoms of stress or tension and to reduce them | 9.14 <br> The issue of the relationship between the psychic and somatic aspects of human functioning | 9.7 <br> A research discipline that focuses on the relationship between mental and physical health; also called behavioral medicine |

| | | |
|---|---|---|
| 9.22 <br><br> **stimulus** <br><br> **specificity** | 9.29 | 9.36 |
| 9.23 <br><br> **stress** | 9.30 | 9.37 |
| 9.24 <br><br> **Type A** | 9.31 | 9.38 |
| 9.25 | 9.32 | 9.39 |
| 9.26 | 9.33 | 9.40 |
| 9.27 | 9.34 | 9.41 |
| 9.28 | 9.35 | 9.42 |

# DEFINITIONS (Cut out on the lines to use as Flash Cards)

| | | |
|---|---|---|
| 9.36 | 9.29 | 9.22<br><br>The principle that different kinds of stress produce different kinds of physiological response |
| 9.37 | 9.30 | 9.23 The environmental demands that lead to ANS sympathetic responses; the physiological (ANS) response to an environmental stressor; or the interaction between a stimulus and a person's appraisal of it |
| 9.38 | 9.31 | 9.24<br>Personality pattern associated with aggressive achievers who have a chronic sense of time pressure and tend to stress their cardiovascular systems |
| 9.39 | 9.32 | 9.25 *(You may fill in the remaining boxes with names, terms and definitions from text and lecture)* |
| 9.40 | 9.33 | 9.26 |
| 9.41 | 9.34 | 9.27 |
| 9.42 | 9.35 | 9.28 |

# Chapter 10

## Mood Disorders

### LEARNING OBJECTIVES
*By the time you are finished studying this chapter, you should be able to:*

#### CHARACTERISTICS OF MANIC AND DEPRESSIVE EPISODES
1. List and describe nine characteristics of a major depressive episode (233-234).
2. List and describe eight characteristics of a manic episode (234).

#### MOOD DISORDER SYNDROMES
3. Describe the patterns of mood episodes that are characteristic of major depressive disorder and bipolar disorder (235-237).
4. Summarize the population data that differentiate major depression from bipolar disorder (236).
5. Define dysthymia and cyclothymia, and distinguish them from major depressive disorder and bipolar disorder (237).
6. Distinguish between neurotic versus psychotic disorders, endogenous versus reactive disorders, and the effects of early versus late onset (237-241).
7. Define comorbidity as it applies to the disorders in this chapter (241).

#### SUICIDE
8. Summarize the population data concerning suicide (241-243).
9. List the common myths about suicide presented in your text and summarize the major behavioral, environmental and cognitive predictors of suicide (243-246).
10. Describe and evaluate the effectiveness of attempts at suicide prevention (246).

#### PERSPECTIVES ON THE MOOD DISORDERS AND SUICIDE
11. Explain the "reactivated loss" and "anger in" hypotheses held by the psychodynamic perspective (246-248).
12. Explain how the concept of inauthenticity relates to mood disorders and suicide in the humanistic-existential perspective (248).
13. Explain how behavioral psychologists account for mood disorders and suicide in terms of learning processes and extinction (248-250).
14. Explain how cognitive theorists account for mood disorders and suicide in terms of destructive thinking, learned helplessness, and poor self-schemas (250-253).
15. Summarize sociocultural factors that may impact on mood disorders and suicide (253-254).
16. Summarize recent biological findings relating to mood disorder, making particular reference to genetic studies, seasonal affective disorder, and the catecholamine hypothesis (258-261).

### CHAPTER OUTLINE

I. Characteristics of depressive and manic episodes

    A. *Episodes* are *occurrences* of depressive or manic symptoms while mood *disorders* consist of one or (often) more of these episodes in various combinations

B. Major depressive episode
   1. Depressed mood
   2. Loss of pleasure or interest in usual activities
   3. Disturbance of appetite (increase or decrease)
   4. Sleep disturbance (increase or decrease)
   5. Psychomotor retardation or agitation
   6. Loss of energy
   7. Feelings of worthlessness or guilt
   8. Difficulties in thinking
   9. Recurrent thoughts of death or suicide

C. Manic episode
   1. Elevated, expansive, or irritable mood
   2. Inflated self-esteem
   3. Sleeplessness
   4. Talkativeness
   5. Flight of ideas
   6. Distractibility
   7. Hyperactivity
   8. Reckless behavior

II. Mood disorders: Individual syndromes

A. Major depressive disorder (may be psychotic or nonpsychotic)
   1. Consists of one or more depressive episodes
   2. Statistical data
      a. Overall lifetime risk in U.S. is about 17 percent
      b. Strikes women two or three times as often as men
      c. Single or divorced people at higher risk
      d. All age groups are susceptible, particularly the young
      e. About half of victims have only one episode
      f. Ranks second only to schizophrenia in mental hospital admissions
      g. Twelve to 48 percent of medical patients may be depressed
      h. Rates of depression have increased since World War II

B. Bipolar disorder (may be psychotic or nonpsychotic)
   1. Bipolar I disorder
      a. Typically begins with a manic episode, followed by:
         (1) Normality, followed by depression, followed by normality, followed by mania, etc. (typical pattern), or
         (2) Manic episodes may alternate with depressive episodes with no normal periods in between (rapid cycling type), or
         (3) Mania and depression may appear simultaneously (mixed type), or
         (4) Manic or mixed episodes can occur *alone* with no depression
   2. Bipolar II disorder
      a. Major depressive episode(s) and *hypomanic* episode(s) (not serious enough to be termed truly manic)
   3. Statistical data
      a. Typically appears late in adolescence
      b. Less common than major depression
      c. No sex differences in susceptibility
      d. Higher socioeconomic groups more at risk
      e. Relationship factors make no difference
      f. Typically more hyperactive premorbid history than in depression
      g. Episodes briefer and more frequent than in depression
      h. More likely to run in families than depression

C. Dysthymia and cyclothymia (nonpsychotic)
   1. Dysthymia is chronic, mild depression with symptoms similar to major depression but not as debilitating
   2. Cyclothymia is chronic, mild version of bipolar disorder

214

D. Dimensions of mood disorder
  1. Psychotic versus neurotic
     a. Psychotic disorders—impaired reality contact
     b. Neurotic disorders—reality contact unimpaired
     c. Traditionally, psychoses and neuroses are seen as different *kinds* of problems, but the continuity hypothesis argues that they may simply be different in *degree*
  2. Endogenous versus reactive
     a. Endogenous (coming from within) disorders were originally thought to be organic in origin, but evidence on this is mixed
     b. Reactive disorders were originally thought to be responses to personal loss, but this may be true of endogenous disorders as well
     c. Characteristics
        (1) Endogenous disorders show:
            (a) More vegetative symptoms (melancholia)
            (b) Better response to biological treatments
        (2) Reactive disorders show:
            (a) More emotional and cognitive symptoms
            (b) Less response to biological treatments
  3. Early versus late onset
     a. Early onset tends to go with a family history of mood disorder
     b. Early onset also tends to predict susceptibility to related disorders

E. Comorbidity: Mixed anxiety-depression
  1. Many patients show so many symptoms common to both anxiety and mood disorders that they could be diagnosed as having either one, either:
     a. At the same time (intraepisode comorbidity), or
     b. At different times (lifetime comorbidity)
  2. Comorbidity leads some researchers to wonder if anxiety disorders and depressive disorders are related and if a new combined diagnostic category is in order

III. Suicide

A. The prevalence of suicide
  1. Tenth most common cause of death in U.S.
  2. 30,000 suicides in U.S. in 1986
  3. Possibly eight attempts for every actual suicide
  4. Fifteen percent or more of fatal auto accidents may be suicides

B. Who commits suicide
  1. Modal suicide *attempter*
     a. Native-born Caucasian female
     b. Housewife in twenties or thirties
     c. Uses barbiturate overdose
     d. Cites marital difficulties or depression
  2. Modal suicide *committer*
     a. Native-born Caucasian male
     b. Aged 40 or older
     c. Uses shooting, hanging, or carbon monoxide
     d. Reasons are ill health, depression, or marital troubles
  3. There does not seem to be a typical suicide-prone personality

C. Myths about suicide
  1. Those who threaten it won't do it
  2. Suicide attempts aren't serious, just an attention getter
  3. Discussing suicidal thoughts with a depressed person will make it more likely he/she will do it

D. Suicide prediction
  1. Behavioral predictors
     a. Announcements of intent

      b.   Giving away valued possessions
      c.   Sudden improvement in a previously agitated person
      d.   Improvement after serious depression
   2.  Environmental predictors
      a.   Interpersonal conflicts (younger people)
      b.   Economic problems (older people)
      c.   "Exit" and "entrance" events
   3.  Cognitive predictors are possibly the most useful, especially feelings of hopelessness

  E.  Suicide prevention
    1.  Telephone hot lines
    2.  Education about warning signs
    3.  Minimal success with the above, however, suggests that dealing with root causes (drug abuse, family stress, teen pregnancy, etc.) may ultimately be more effective

## IV. Perspectives on the mood disorders and suicide

  A.  The psychodynamic perspective
    1.  "Anger in" idea says that depression or suicide results when a loss causes anger directed inward (possibly as a result of guilt) instead of outward at the loss itself
    2.  More recent ideas assume:
      a.   A person of low self-esteem who experiences
      b.   Loss or threatened loss during childhood,
      c.   Of someone or something toward which the person has ambivalent feelings,
      d.   Which is reactivated by a new loss in adulthood,
      e.   Producing helplessness and hopelessness,
      f.   Which may serve to express dependence on others
    3.  Treatment consists of uncovering the early loss and understanding the ambivalent feelings to see how the depression fits into current life needs

  B.  The humanistic-existential perspective: Depression is
    1.  A response to inauthentic living, or
    2.  A futile struggle against unavoidable aloneness
    3.  Suicide is seen as the final inauthentic act of an inauthentic life
    4.  Treatment focuses on being authentic and valuing independence as a motivator for individuality

  C.  The behavioral perspective
    1.  Extinction theory says that depression occurs as a result of nonreinforcement, and people lose reinforcers because:
      a.   They respond to only limited numbers of stimuli,
      b.   Reinforcers cease to be available to them, or
      c.   They have little skill in obtaining reinforcers
    2.  Interpersonal theory says depression results from an aversive interpersonal style that fails to get the reinforcers (love, affection, sympathy) the person wants
    3.  Treatment consists of teaching the person to acquire and enjoy reinforcers, both physical and social

  D.  The cognitive perspective
    1.  Learned helplessness theory says uncontrollable aversive situations may teach the person that he/she is helpless, which results in resignation and hopelessness
    2.  Such helpless/hopeless individuals see negative life events as
      a.   Permanent rather than temporary
      b.   General rather than specific
      c.   Their own fault
    3.  Negative self-schema theory says that depression results from a self-critical "loser" mentality
    4.  Unfortunately, depressives' view of life and the world may be more accurate than that of normals—in other words, a little self-deception may be good for your mental health
    5.  Therapy consists of making negative cognitions more optimistic

E.   The sociocultural perspective stresses the individual's relationship to society
     1.   Depression rates are lower in more "traditional" societies
     2.   May be related to lack of stability and social support in modern society

F.   The biological perspective
     1.   Genetic research shows that mood disorders have a hereditary component,
          particularly bipolar disorder (possibly, but not conclusively, chromosome 11)
     2.   Neurophysiological research
          a.   Depressives tend to have REM sleep abnormalities, possibly as a result of
               biological clock problems
          b.   Seasonal affective disorder
               (1)   Occurs during winter months when days are short
               (2)   May involve a disruption of circadian rhythms
               (3)   Treatment involves additional (morning) exposure to bright light
     3.   Biochemical research
          a.   Hormone imbalances
               (1)   Possible hypothalamus or pituitary defect may cause (among others) thyroid
                     imbalances
               (2)   Noted particularly in endogenous depression
               (3)   Dexamethasone suppression test (DST) can detect
               (4)   Hormone treatments can produce improvements
          b.   Neurotransmitter imbalances
               (1)   Catecholamine hypothesis says norepinephrine excess causes mania, deficit
                     causes depression
               (2)   Serotonin probably involved as well in both mood disorders and suicide
               (3)   L-tryptophan increases serotonin levels and is effective against both
                     depression and mania

## KEY TERMS
*The following terms are in bold print in your text. Define them and practice their
definitions using the flash cards at the end of the chapter.*

agitated depression (233)
anhedonia (233)
bipolar disorder (236)
catecholamine hypothesis (258)
comorbidity (241)
continuity hypothesis (239)
cyclothymic disorder (237)
depression (232)
dexamethasone suppression test (DST) (257)
dysthymic disorder (237)
endogenous (240)
helplessness-hopelessness syndrome (233)
hypomanic episode (234)

learned helplessness (250)
major depressive disorder (235)
major depressive episode (232)
mania (232)
manic episode (234)
mixed episode (235)
mood disorders (232)
premorbid adjustment (236)
reactive (240)
retarded depression (233)
seasonal affective disorder (SAD) (256)
social-skills training (250)
tricyclics (258)

*Your text does not list the following terms as formal vocabulary; however, if you don't
know what they mean, you will be unable to grasp the concepts of this chapter.*

abrogates (248)
anecdotal (239)
apocryphal (239)
debilitating (232)
demographic (236)
exacerbate (249)
feign (245)

grandiose (234)
insidious (237)
intrapsychic (246)
introverted (237)
melancholy (233)
morose (237)
pervasive (236)

pragmatic (248)
precipitating event (240)
precipitously (253)
rumination (235)
stupor (233)

## IMPORTANT NAMES
*Identify the following persons and their major contributions to abnormal psychology as discussed in this chapter.*

Karl Abraham (246)        Emile Durkheim (253)        Martin Seligman (250)
Aaron Beck (251)           Emil Kraepelin (238)

## GUIDED SELF-STUDY

Use the following terms to complete the blanks in Questions 1-6.

| | |
|---|---|
| **Abraham Lincoln** | **manic** |
| **affective** | **mild** |
| **Aretaeus** | **Roman emperor Tiberius** |
| **episodic** | **temporary** |
| **Louis XI of France** | **time pattern** |
| **Hippocrates** | **Winston Churchill** |

1. Variations in mood are quite normal when they are _____ and _____.

2. When mood variations become so extreme and prolonged that the victim's life is disrupted,

    that is a mood disorder, or an _____ disorder.

3. (a)_____ described depression and mania in the fourth century B.C.

    (b)_____ observed that sometimes manic and depressive behaviors occurred in the same person.

4. A distinctive characteristic of mood disorders is their _____ quality.

5. Whether the episode is (a)_____ or depressive, its severity and its (b)_____ will determine which mood disorder diagnosis is applied.

6. List four famous people from history that suffered with depression.

    a.                      c.

    b.                      d.

7. List nine characteristic features of a major depressive episode. Try to list these from memory to see which you already know. If you just copy them straight from the book first without trying to recall them or make them up yourself, you will not have "exercised" your neurons. Remember NO PAIN, NO GAIN (or no brain)!

    a.                      f.

    b.                      g.

    c.                      h.

    d.                      i.

    e.

8. What is the helplessness-hopelessness syndrome?

9. For those of you who are having trouble seeing how mania fits with depression, have you ever busied yourself so as not to think about something else? List some examples of activities that you use to get your mind off of upsetting topics.

10. Now list eight characteristics of a manic episode. (How many can you do from memory?)

a.                                          e.

b.                                          f.

c.                                          g.

d.                                          h.

11. How can you tell whether a person is manic or just very happy, self-confident, and energetic?

12. Mark each of the following timing factors as characteristic a manic episode or a depressive episode.

a. _____ Ends abruptly over a few days
b. _____ More gradual onset over weeks
c. _____ Shorter in duration, lasting only several days to several months
d. _____ Starts rather suddenly over a few days
e. _____ Subsides slowly over weeks or months

## MOOD DISORDER SYNDROMES

Use these terms to complete Questions 13 and 14.

| | | |
|---|---|---|
| **bipolar I disorder** | **cyclothymia** | **major depression** |
| **bipolar II disorder** | **depression** | **manic** |
| **bipolar disorder** | **depressive** | |
| **chronic** | **dysthymia** | |

13. There are typically two patterns (syndromes) in which people experience mood disorders.

There are people who have one or more episodes of (a)_____ or there are those who

have some combination of (b)_____ episodes and (c)_____ episodes. If

one has only depressive episodes, one is diagnosed as having (d)_____ disorder.

If one has the combination of episodes, the diagnosis is (e)_____. Then this category

is broken down into two types. (f)_____ are those people have had at least one manic

or mixed episode. (g)_____ are those people who have depression and only a hypomanic symptoms—but not full blown manic symptoms.

14. If one has one of the two patterns of mood disorders described in Question 13, but to a lesser degree, not disabling enough to merit a diagnosis of major depression or bipolar disorder; the

disorders are called (a)_____ and (b)_____ respectively. Although

these disorders are milder, they are particularly troublesome because they are (c)_____.

15. (a)_____ percent of the population will experience major depression at some time in their lives.

(b) Explain the textbook authors' quote that some experts believe "we are embarking on an 'age of depression.'"

16. What segments of the population are more likely to have depression?

17. What are three proposed explanations for why women are at higher risk than men for experiencing depression?

a.

b.

c.

18. If you have a major depressive episode, what are the chances that you will have another one?

19. How can one depressive episode contribute to another one occurring?

20. Give the appropriate diagnosis for each of the following mood patterns. Remember, in bipolar disorder, there is Type I, which can be mixed or rapid cycling, and there is Type II.

a. _____ Manic—depressive—normal—manic—depressive—normal

b. _____ Manic—normal—depressive—normal—manic—normal—depressive

c. _____ Manic—depressive—manic—depressive—manic—depressive

d. _____ Both manic and depressive symptoms at once

e. _____ One manic episode

f. _____ Manic—normal—manic—normal—manic—normal

g. _____ Depressive—hypomanic

h. _____ Depressive—normal—depressive—normal—depressive—normal

21. Write the correct disorder (either **major depression** or **bipolar disorder**) before each of the following descriptions that differentiate the two disorders.

a. _____ is the much less common of the two disorders.

b. _____ occurs in the two sexes equally.

c. _____ is not avoided by having close emotional relationships.

d. _____ typically have a normal premorbid personality.

e. _____ seems to be a pervasive slowing down.

f. _____ has episodes that tend to be briefer and more frequent.

g. _____ is very likely to run in the family.

22. Draw lines to connect the terms that go together in pairs with regard to the dimensions of mood disorders.

Endogenous      Psychotic
Neurotic        Early
Late         Reactive

23. By the way, what is the term for your condition before you became depressed?

24. The psychotic-neurotic dimension is used to indicate (a)_____ of impairment, which meant the person's ability to do (b)_____ testing. Psychosis can involve distortions in perceptions that are so drastic that the person can actually experience a false sensory experience called a (c)_____. If the person holds false beliefs, he/she is said to have (d)_____.

25. Draw a box around the following depressions which may possibly reach psychotic proportions. Encircle those that never reach psychotic proportions. Put a star next to those that are always at a psychotic level.

Dysthymia   Major depression   Cyclothymia   Bipolar disorder

a. How many boxes do you have? _____
b. How many circles do you have? _____
c. How many stars do you have? _____

26. Use these terms to complete the following blanks.

**cognitive**        **sleep disturbance**
**emotional**        **slowed bodily movements**
**exit**          **uncontrollable**
**melancholic**       **vegetative**
**people**         **weight loss**
**precipitating event**

Originally, the reactive-endogenous dimension indicated whether the depression was preceded by a (a)_____ which often is about (b)_____ loss, particularly of (c)_____. These are referred to as (d)_____ events. However, such a determination was often not so easy to make. Currently, the term reactive is assigned to people whose impairment is mainly characterized by (e)_____ and (f)_____ dysfunction. The term endogenous is assigned to those people who have primarily (g)_____ symptoms, which are physical symptoms such as (h)_____, _____, and _____. *DSM-IV* lists these as (i)_____ features.

27. Circle the best place to be on each of the three dimensions to produce the best prognosis.

Neurotic  .  .  .  Psychotic

Endogenous .  .  .  Reactive

Early onset .  .  .  Late onset

28. Use these terms to complete the following blanks: **Comorbidity, Intraepisode comorbidity**, and **Lifetime comorbidity**.

(a)_____ means two pathological events happening together in the same individual. When this happens at the very same time, the events are said to have

(b)_____. If a person's whole life is considered, then the term is

(c)_____. (d)_____ is also by definition

(e)_____, but (f)_____ may or may not be

(g)_____.

29. Two disorders that have a high rate of lifetime comorbidity and even intraepisode comorbidity are (a)_____ and (b)_____. There is so much comorbidity between these two disorders that a unitary view exists which says that they are really (c)_____.

Another proposal has suggested that a mixed (d)_____-_____ diagnosis be included in future *DSM*s.

SUICIDE

30. Why are accurate statistics on suicide really unknown?

31. a. Who commits more suicide, married or single people?

b. Who commits more suicide, men or women?

c. Who attempts more suicide, men or women?

d. What is one reason for the statistics of "b" and "c"?

e. Does the likelihood of suicide increase or decrease with age, or is it uncorrelated?

f. There has been a recent shift in which of the above factors?

32. Why is it important to know about the myths about suicide?

33. Here are some *myths* about suicide. Write the truth below the myth to lock the truth into your mind.

a. People who threaten won't actually do it.

b. People who attempt suicide are not serious or they would not have failed.

c. Don't talk about suicide; you might give somebody ideas.

34. If reports of suicide on TV do not actually *cause* suicides, what effect *do* they have?

35. Do people who are really suicidal give clues about what is going on in their thinking?

36. What are some behaviors that should make you think that someone is suicidal?

    a.

    b.

    c.

    d.

    e.

    f.

    g.

    h.

    i.

37. What percent of suicide attempters are sure they really do want to die?

38. What then is the issue with the rest of the suicide attempters?

## PERSPECTIVES ON THE MOOD DISORDERS

39. As the different perspectives consider the mood disorders, most attention is focused on the

    problem of (a)_____ because (b)_____ is far less common and is considered by

    some to be primarily a reaction to (c)_____ anyway. The one perspective which does not

    take this approach is the (d)_____ perspective.

40. Use these terms and phrases to complete the following blanks. Items may be used more than
    once.

| | |
|---|---|
| **affectionless control** | **love** |
| **ambivalent (or mixed)** | **parent** |
| **dependent** | **recent** |
| **esteem** | **rejection** |
| **grief** | **role** |
| **hopelessness-helplessness** | **sexual and aggressive** |
| **incorporated** | **social** |
| **interpersonal** | **unconscious** |
| **loss of a love object** | |

Unconscious conflicts are usually about (a)_____ impulses; however, Freud said that the

unconscious conflicts underlying depression are about anxiety over (b)_____.

Abraham added that if the individual had (c)_____ feelings about the love object, loss
of the love object would result in anger and guilt which the person directs inwardly because

the love object was emotionally (d)_____ into the individual's self-identity.  The

person commits suicide to kill the (e)_____ love object.  More modern psychoanalytic
thinkers have revised this early theory to center around some core ideas:  Early loss or

threatened loss of a (f)_____; this primal wound is then reactivated by some (g)_____ trauma; regression proceeds to a point of (h)_____; a focus more on the

(i)_____ feelings than the anger turned inward; loss of self (j)_____; and using

depression to form (k)_____ relationships with other people. Research somewhat
supports the ideas of depression as dependency or parental loss, or at least parenting patterns

termed as (l)_____, where there is too much protection yet too little emotional

nurturance. Psychoanalytic therapy as always looks for (m)_____ conflicts; in

depression the focus will be a primal trauma in childhood and reactivation of that event by a

more (n)_____ trauma. The latter is likely to be in one of four categories: (o)_____,

(p)_____ disputes, (q)_____ transition, or lack of (r)_____ skills. If the patient

is suicidal, the therapist will be careful to avoid doing anything that could seen as (s)_____

by the patient because current psychoanalytic theory sees suicide as an appeal for (t)_____.

41. Here are the terms for these blanks:

**aloneness**                                    **inauthentic**
**authentic**                                    **meaningless**
**confront her/his existence**                   **satisfaction**
**death**

Humanistic-existential (H-E) psychologists see depression as a very understandable reaction to

an (a)_____ existence. A H-E therapist tries to help the depressed patient see that

his/her pain is real; in fact the depression is a very (b)_____ reaction, given the
circumstances. The pain is the result of the patient living a very hollow life that holds no real

(c)_____ for her/him and, therefore, does feels empty and (d)_____. In H-E

terms, the patient must (e)_____; that is, look at his current life to

analyze it and see what about it is empty and (f)_____ to him/her so s/he can change

those parts. Existentialists are particularly focused on the (g)_____ a person

experiences within his/her own mind and the reality that one's (h)_____ gives life its
meaning by making it a limited, passing opportunity to use or lose.

42. After having taken an abnormal psych class, your roommate has now become an "expert."
When you appear depressed, he/she gives you his/her best humanistic-existential advice in a
nutshell. He/she tells you to

a. go out and buy one thing that you've always wanted.
b. deal with your feelings and get on with your life.
c. find someone to love.
d. take the weekend off.

43. Here are the answers.  Find their blanks.

anxiety
consequences
contingency
conversation
extinction
eye
death

interpersonal
learning
pleasurable activities
reinforcers
small
two

Behaviorism, or (a) _____ theories, have (b)_____ major approaches to explaining

depression.  The first theory is (c)_____, which means the person isn't getting any

good payoffs or (d)_____ in life.  The second theory is that depressed people have

aversive (e)_____ styles which cause them to get negative reactions from other people.

Behavior therapists treat depression by helping patients get goodies, or (f)_____

back into their lives; actually making dates with themselves for (g)_____ (Sounds good to

me).  Social skills training in (h)_____ contact, making (i)_____ talk, and ending

(j)_____ in a positive manner help depressives get more positive reactions, or

(k)_____, from other people.  Suicidal patients are also taught to do (l)_____

management and (m)_____ contracting, particularly with family members about

family disputes.  Behaviorists also point out that a person who sees no adequate (n)_____

in life and expects none in the future might see (o)_____ as reinforcing if the person sees
dying as a means to get attention, pity or revenge.  The problem with that plan is that the

person is not going to be around to enjoy these (p)_____.  Anticipating the impact of
suicide may be "fun," but the suicide is going to bring that anticipatory pleasure to an
unfulfilled and permanent end!

44. Here are the terms for the blanks for the cognitive perspective on depression and suicide:

accurate
attributions and inferences
change
control
depression
expectation
extinction
future
hopelessness

helplessness
learning
self schema
positive
think
thinking
thinks
two
world

Behaviorism means (a)_____ and the cognitive perspective means (b)_____.  From

the cognitive perspective, depression is the result of how we (c)_____ about ourselves, the

(d)_____, and the (e)_____.  The text discusses (f) _____ cognitive theories of

depression.  The first one is hopelessness-(g)_____.  This is different from the

(h)_____ theory in the behavioral perspective which focuses on an environment that
does not reinforce any behaviors, an operational definition of helpless.  In the cognitive

perspective the hopelessness-helplessness theory focuses on how the person (i)_____ from a helpless mind-set; that is, the individual has an (j)_____ that s/he will be unable to cope in a satisfactory way. This negative outcome expectancy is the result of

(k)_____ that the individual makes about his/her life. The people most at risk for depression see situations as the result of widespread personal shortcomings that are

never going to (l)_____. The cognitive theorists have found the best predictor of

attempted and completed suicides is the cognitive factor of (m)_____. It predicts even

more accurately than the presence of (n)_____. The second cognitive theory says

depression is the result of having a negative (o)_____, which means the person sees her/himself as a loser. Interestingly, research reveals that depressives make more

(p)_____ assessments than nondepressed individuals about how much (q)_____ they have in life and about how well they are doing. Apparently a cognitive perspective that

is biased in a (r)_____ manner and gives an "illusion of (s)_____" promotes better psychological health.

45. Considering research on attributions and inferences that people make regarding stressful events, which of the following people is the most likely to be depressed? A person who thinks:

   a. This is strange—a freak accident.
   b. It's my fault—I always make mistakes.
   c. Why are you always picking on me? I deserve better.
   d. This is a chain of uncommonly bad luck for me.

46. These are the terms for the sociocultural perspective:

   **earlier**                    **socioeconomic**
   **more**                       **stability**
   **restrictions**               **stressor**
   **society**                    **teens**

   The sociocultural perspective ALWAYS relates issues to factors in (a)_____. There is no

   doubt: suicide rates are directly affected by (b)_____ conditions. Research also

   indicates that depression is happening (c)_____ and at an (d)_____ age in the United States. Social change is proposed to be the cause because this trend to depression is not seen

   in traditional, tight-knit, nonindustrialized communities with stable social structures. Not all

   sociocultural theories are based on the benefits of (e)_____ in cultures. The text gives a partially sociological explanation for why women are more at risk for depression after they

   enter their (f)_____. However, in this theory, a stable social structure is a (g)_____: 

   according to this theory in adolescence young women begin to confront the (h)_____ of a sex-biased society.

47. Use these terms for the biological perspective:

bipolar
chromosome 11
circadian rhythms
depression
different
dream
genetic
hormone
hypothalamus
interpersonal relationship
light
mania

master gland
mood
neurotransmitter
norepinephrine
organic
relationship
seasonal affective disorder
serotonin
sleep
summer
unipolar
wintertime

Regardless of what other factors may be a part of depression, there is definitely an overall

(a)_____ element. Research indicates there is clearly a (b)_____, or inherited,

component which is much stronger in (c)_____ disorder than in (d)_____ disorder.

This is also evidence that these are two distinctly (e)_____ disorders. The Amish study

suggested bipolar disorder may be transmitted on (f)_____. Other studies have not
found this to be the case. Some scientists have suggested this contradictory evidence is the

result of (g)_____ disorder being a cluster of related disorders instead of one single
disorder. Two areas of research look for the organic component of depression: neuro-
physiological research looks for explanations in the area of biological rhythms (also called

(h)_____). Sleep research reveals that people who are depressed, have been
depressed, or are even close kin to a depressive have increased likelihood to have disturbances

in (i)_____ patterns: REM sleep, or (j)_____ sleep, comes on too quickly. A change

in an intimate (k)_____ can affect sleep patterns if one's sleeping times and
circumstances are altered by changes in the relationship. So then, did the disturbed

(l)_____ or the disturbed (m)_____ pattern cause the depression? (Or perhaps
some third variable affected both?) Along this same line of biological rhythms is

(n)_____ (SAD) where the time of year is the predictor of the

depression. Most suffers experience SAD in the (o)_____; however there are

(p)_____ sufferers as well. (q)_____ therapy, which affects sleep cycles and
circadian rhythms, gives some relief to three-fourths of SAD suffers. The second area of the

biological perspective is biochemical research which looks into (r)_____ and

(s)_____ imbalances. Since the (t)_____ of the brain controls the pituitary

gland, which is the (u)_____ of the endocrine system, the (v)_____ is a proposed
site of possible dysfunction to cause depression. Some cases of depression are responsive to

(w)_____ therapies. Neurotransmitter imbalance ideas focus on (x)_____ and

(y)_____. A deficiency in (z)_____ perhaps predisposes one to

(aa)_____ disorder. Then, if the level of (bb)_____ is too high, (cc)_____ is manifest;

if the level is too low, (dd)_____ is manifest.

48. Lithium carbonate is a medication that seems particularly effective for treating (b)_____ disorder.

49. The biological approach is exploring a "suicidal" neurochemical problem that is independent of depression. What is it?

50. See if you can identify the perspective associated with each of these terms.

a. _____ Sense of nonbeing

b. _____ Negative self-schema

c. _____ Learned helplessness

d. _____ Reactivated loss

e. _____ Chromosome 11

f. _____ Extinction

g. _____ Anger turned inward

h. _____ Catecholamine hypothesis

51. Imagine that you have just moved away from your long-time home to a town far away, and you are now feeling depressed. You go to consult a psychologist and the following information is gathered. Indicate which perspective would find each of the following details as being most important:

a. It will be a while before you develop new friends with which to have good times.

b. You doubt whether you will succeed at making new friends and adjusting to your new situation.

c. You "failed" the DST.

d. You can't really identify why you are depressed—it makes no sense.

e. You can't decide what you want out of life.

## HELPFUL HINTS

1. Major depression is also called unipolar disorder. Bipolar disorder is also commonly called manic-depression. Getting this terminology locked into your thinking is **VERY IMPORTANT** so you can follow lectures regardless of which terminology your teacher and fellow students use. To put this info into organized form: "Uni" means one. (A unicycle has one wheel.) Unipolar means one-ended; therefore, unipolar disorder means depression only, also called major depression. "Bi" means two. (A bicycle has two wheels.) Bipolar means two-ended; therefore, bipolar disorder means (usually) mania and depression, or manic-depression.
2. Look back in Chapter Three to remind yourself what a contingency is in contingency contracting and also for anxiety management skills.
3. Beware! Even though learned helplessness says "learned," its focus is an expectation, which is a cognitive term.

*Take the following test several times as you study the chapter. Write your answers on a separate sheet of paper and after each attempt, note in the tally box above each question whether your answer was correct or incorrect.*

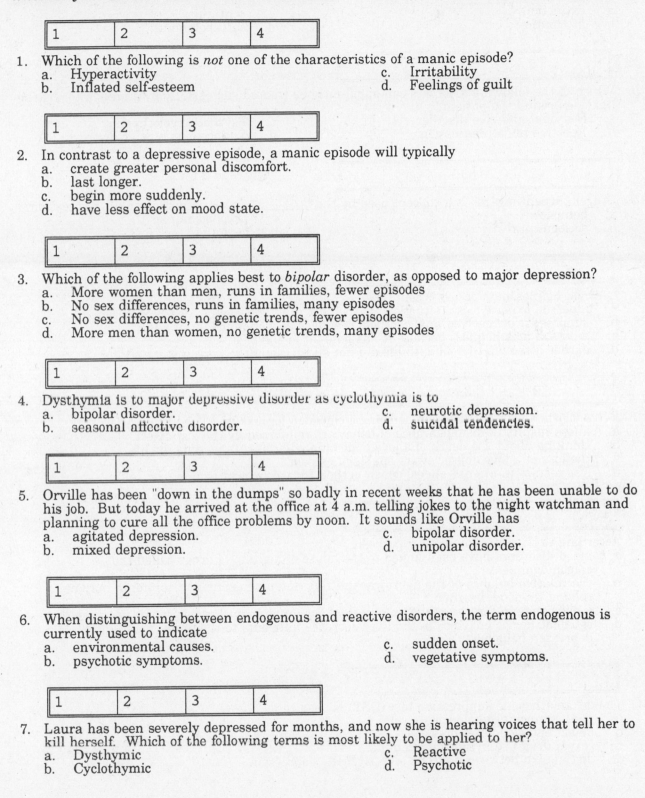

| 1 | 2 | 3 | 4 |
|---|---|---|---|

1. Which of the following is *not* one of the characteristics of a manic episode?
   a. Hyperactivity
   b. Inflated self-esteem
   c. Irritability
   d. Feelings of guilt

| 1 | 2 | 3 | 4 |
|---|---|---|---|

2. In contrast to a depressive episode, a manic episode will typically
   a. create greater personal discomfort.
   b. last longer.
   c. begin more suddenly.
   d. have less effect on mood state.

| 1 | 2 | 3 | 4 |
|---|---|---|---|

3. Which of the following applies best to *bipolar* disorder, as opposed to major depression?
   a. More women than men, runs in families, fewer episodes
   b. No sex differences, runs in families, many episodes
   c. No sex differences, no genetic trends, fewer episodes
   d. More men than women, no genetic trends, many episodes

| 1 | 2 | 3 | 4 |
|---|---|---|---|

4. Dysthymia is to major depressive disorder as cyclothymia is to
   a. bipolar disorder.
   b. seasonal affective disorder.
   c. neurotic depression.
   d. suicidal tendencies.

| 1 | 2 | 3 | 4 |
|---|---|---|---|

5. Orville has been "down in the dumps" so badly in recent weeks that he has been unable to do his job. But today he arrived at the office at 4 a.m. telling jokes to the night watchman and planning to cure all the office problems by noon. It sounds like Orville has
   a. agitated depression.
   b. mixed depression.
   c. bipolar disorder.
   d. unipolar disorder.

| 1 | 2 | 3 | 4 |
|---|---|---|---|

6. When distinguishing between endogenous and reactive disorders, the term endogenous is currently used to indicate
   a. environmental causes.
   b. psychotic symptoms.
   c. sudden onset.
   d. vegetative symptoms.

| 1 | 2 | 3 | 4 |
|---|---|---|---|

7. Laura has been severely depressed for months, and now she is hearing voices that tell her to kill herself. Which of the following terms is most likely to be applied to her?
   a. Dysthymic
   b. Cyclothymic
   c. Reactive
   d. Psychotic

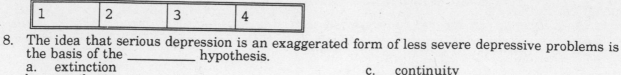

8. The idea that serious depression is an exaggerated form of less severe depressive problems is the basis of the _____ hypothesis.
   a. extinction
   b. attribution
   c. continuity
   d. catecholamine

9. Which of the following disorders can apparently be treated successfully by merely altering the lighting around the patient?
   a. Seasonal affective disorder
   b. Reactive major depression
   c. Psychotic cyclothymia
   d. Endogenous bipolar disorder

10. "Anger turned inward" is a concept used by the _____ perspective to explain depression.
    a. behavioral
    b. sociocultural
    c. psychodynamic
    d. cognitive

11. Learned helplessness occurs when
    a. a person experiences a situation for the first time and has no idea how to cope.
    b. supposedly unresolved anal conflicts reappear as symptoms in an adult.
    c. a person acts helpless because it has paid off in the past.
    d. earlier attempts to deal with life did not succeed and the person stops trying.

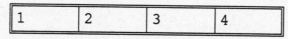

12. Behaviorists speak of extinction as being a cause of depression. This means that
    a. a loss results in disappearance of behaviors reinforced by the lost object.
    b. thinking about the death of a loved one created a loss of meaning for life.
    c. the loss of a love object lowers one's self-esteem.
    d. loss results in intense anger, which is then turned inward against the self.

```
| 1 | 2 | 3 | 4 |
```

13. According to the catecholamine hypothesis
    a. mood disorders have been linked to the abuse of a group of drugs called the catecholamines.
    b. the relative balance of the neurotransmitters norepinephrine and serotonin may be related to mood disorder.
    c. a deficiency in serotonin and an excess of dopamine may result in major depression.
    d. catecholenergic enzymes in the liver decrease nutrients to the brain, resulting in depressed behavior.

```
| 1 | 2 | 3 | 4 |
```

14. The dexamethasone suppression test (DST) is used to
    a. predict suicidal tendencies.
    b. detect endogenous depression.
    c. reveal drug use in suicide attempts.
    d. distinguish between neurotic and psychotic depression.

| 1 | 2 | 3 | 4 |

15. People who commit suicide usually
    a. threaten to take other people with them.
    b. tend to have an unrealistically high self-concept.
    c. give out subtle hints and calls for help.
    d. do so in the depths of psychotic depression.

| 1 | 2 | 3 | 4 |

16. Pick the most likely suicide *committer*.
    a. Eighteen-year-old black female with job problems
    b. Fifty-year-old white male in ill health
    c. Forty-five-year-old white female with marital difficulties
    d. Thirty-year-old unemployed black male

| 1 | 2 | 3 | 4 |

17. Mario has been openly threatening to kill himself. He has always been a loner with no friends and now he just does not see how he can cope with life. From what we know about predicting suicide we might conclude
    a. Mario is in serious danger and needs help right now.
    b. there is no real problem since immature people often try to get attention in this way.
    c. there is no danger since if he were really serious he would not be advertising his intentions.
    d. the risk is moderate, but action should not be taken unless he engages in two more predictive symptoms.

| 1 | 2 | 3 | 4 |

18. What biochemical findings give hope for possible future drug therapy for suicide attempters?
    a. Low epinephrine levels in the brains of suicide victims
    b. Low serotonin levels in the cerebrospinal fluid of suicide attempters
    c. Abnormal acetylcholine levels in the frontal cortex of suicide attempters
    d. High dopamine levels in the cerebrospinal fluid of suicide committers

| 1 | 2 | 3 | 4 |

19. The major difference between bipolar I disorder and bipolar II disorder is that
    a. bipolar I disorder does not have the depressive component.
    b. bipolar I disorder is only found in women.
    c. bipolar II disorder has less severe manic components.
    d. bipolar II disorder is generally endogenous.

| 1 | 2 | 3 | 4 |

20. The humanistic-existential perspective sees suicide as
    a. the last of a series of inauthentic choices in life.
    b. the logical outcome of living in an insane world.
    c. the result of losing most of the good things in life.
    d. neither good nor bad as long as it is the result of a conscious decision.

## ANSWERS
### Self-Study Exercise

1. mild and temporary (232)
2. affective (232)
3. a. Hippocrates
   b. Aretaeus (232)
4. episodic (232)
5. a. manic
   b. time pattern (232)
6. a. Roman emperor Tiberius
   b. Louis XI of France
   c. Abraham Lincoln
   d. Winston Churchill (232)
7. a. Depressed mood
   b. Loss of pleasure or interest in usual activities
   c. Disturbance of appetite
   d. Sleep disturbance
   e. Psychomotor retardation or agitation
   f. Loss of energy
   g. Feelings of worthlessness and guilt
   h. Difficulties in thinking
   i. Recurrent thoughts of death or suicide (233-234)
8. The helplessness-hopelessness syndrome is that pattern of thinking that deeply depressed people experience. They feel utter despair and believe they are going to feel that way forever; they are convinced that nothing will be able to lessen the mental anguish that they are experiencing (233).
9. Behaviors that people often engage in to get their minds off something are looking at a magazine, reading a book, going for a walk, engaging in some household chore that needs doing (scrubbing something or mowing the lawn), listening to music, watching TV, and the ever popular eating! The difference between healthy distraction and manic behavior is that the manic seems driven and pursues activity with a vengeance; the individual who uses distraction constructively becomes comfortably immersed in the distraction but then eventually gets on with his/her life.
10. a. Elevated or irritable mood
    b. Inflated self-esteem
    c. Sleeplessness
    d. Talkativeness
    e. Flight of ideas
    f. Distractibility
    g. Hyperactivity
    h. Reckless behavior (234)
11. A person with mania becomes extremely hyperactive over a short time, maybe even a few days. The behavior has a driven quality to it. There is unusual extremeness in the thinking and in the person's behavior: If he/she is spending money, the spending is likely to be with no regard for his/her actual financial condition. If the individual is driving a vehicle, the speed may be as fast as the vehicle will go with no concern to the dangers involved. Irritability in the individual is triggered very easily by anyone who interferes (234).
12. a. Manic
    b. Depressive
    c. Manic
    d. Manic
    e. Depressive (234)
13. a. depression
    b. depressive
    c. manic
    d. major depression
    e. bipolar disorder
    f. Bipolar I disorder
    g. Bipolar II disorder (235, 236)
14. a. dysthymia
    b. cyclothymia
    c. chronic (237)
15. a. Seventeen
    b. The prevalence of major depression is rising with each successive generation since World War II (235).
16. Divorced or maritally separated; women (1 and a half to 3 times higher than men); the young (women, 15 to 19 years; men 25 to 29 years) (235)
17. a. Hormonal differences between men and women
    b. The changing social role of women
    c. Sex differential in response to sadness: Women tend to ruminate about sadness which only makes the sadness worse, whereas men tend to distract themselves by engaging in a hobby or sport (235).

232

18. Fifty percent, or 5 chances out of 10 (235)
19. Recurrent episodes have a tendency to set up conditions for further episodes because the results of a major depressive episode are stressful in themselves: Lowered self-confidence; family and marital relationships are disrupted; progress in school or at work is interrupted; people's expectations of the depressed person are changed (235).
20. a. Bipolar I
    b. Bipolar I
    c. Bipolar I (rapid cycling type)
    d. Bipolar I (mixed episode)
    e. Bipolar I (Yes, one manic episode makes a bipolar disorder diagnosis.)
    f. Bipolar I
    g. Bipolar II (236)
    h. Major depressive disorder (235, 236)
21. All of these descriptions fit bipolar disorder (236).
22. Endogenous—Reactive (239-240)
    Neurotic—Psychotic (237-239)
    Late—Early (240-241)
23. Premorbid adjustment (236)
24. a. severity
    b. reality
    c. hallucination
    d. delusions (237-238)
25. a. 2 boxes, Major depression and Bipolar disorder
    b. 2 circles, Dysthymia and Cyclothymia
    c. No stars; there are no depressive disorders *defined* as psychotic (238).
26. a. precipitating event
    b. uncontrollable
    c. people
    d. exit
    e. emotional
    f. cognitive
    g. vegetative
    h. sleep disturbance
       weight loss
       slowed bodily movements
    i. melancholic (240)
27. Neurotic, Reactive, and Late onset (238-241)
28. a. Comorbidity
    b. intraepisode comorbidity
    c. lifetime comorbidity
    d. Intraepisode comorbidity
    e. lifetime comorbidity
    f. lifetime comorbidity
    g. intraepisode comorbidity (241)
29. a. anxiety
    b. depression
    c. different aspects of the same underlying disorder
    d. anxiety-depression (241)
30. Suicides are many times disguised as accidental deaths (242).
31. a. Single
    b. Men
    c. Women
    d. Men use more lethal methods (242)
    e. Increases
    f. Age (243)
32. So a myth will not cause you to overlook someone who is possibly suicidal (263-264).
33. a. People who threaten suicide are at higher risk of doing it (243).
    b. People who attempt suicide are at higher risk of doing it again and succeeding (243-244).
    c. Encouraging a person to talk about his feelings is therapeutic (244).
34. They may suggest methods of suicide to someone who is already considering it (246).
35. **YES**, in the majority of cases (245)
36. a. Comments about the futility of life in general or of his/her life in particular
    b. Becoming withdrawn
    c. Seeming to make preparations for a long trip
    d. Giving away treasured possessions
    e. Suddenly becoming tranquil after signs of depression
    f. High level of stress in the person's life
    g. Recent "exit" events in the person's life
    h. Recent "entrance" events
    i. A perspective of hopelessness (243-246)
37. Only 3 to 5 percent (246)
38. Thirty percent are ambivalent about dying. They are the "to be or not to be" group; people who aren't sure they want to die, but don't want to live the way they have been doing. Sixty-five percent are trying to say they are in emotional pain that seems unbearable to them (246).

39. a. depression
    b. mania

    c. depression
    d. biological (246)

40. a. sexual and aggressive (27)
    b. loss of a love object (246)
    c. ambivalent (or mixed)
    d. incorporated (246)
    e. incorporated (246)
    f. parent
    g. recent
    h. hopelessness-helplessness
    i. ambivalent
    j. esteem

    k. dependent (247)
    l. affectionless control (247)
    m. unconscious
    n. recent
    o. grief
    p. interpersonal
    q. role
    r. social (248)
    s. rejection
    t. love (248)

41. a. inauthentic
    b. authentic
    c. satisfaction
    d. meaningless

    e. confront her/his existence
    f. meaningless
    g. aloneness
    h. death (248)

42. "b" is correct. An inauthentic existence means you are going through the motions of life without really living (248).

43. a. **LEARNING!!** (54)
    b. two (248)
    c. extinction
    d. reinforcers (248)
    e. interpersonal (249)
    f. reinforcers
    g. pleasurable activities (249-250)
    h. eye

    i. small
    j. conversation
    k. reinforcers
    l. anxiety
    m. contingency (250)
    n. reinforcers
    o. death
    p. consequences (or reinforcers) (249)

44. a. learning!!!! (54)
    b. thinking!!!!!
    c. think
    d. world
    e. future (250)
    f. two (250-251)
    g. helplessness
    h. extinction
    i. thinks
    j. expectation

    k. attributions and inferences
    l. change
    m. hopelessness
    n. depression
    o. self schema (251)
    p. accurate
    q. control
    r. positive
    s. control (252)

45. "b" is correct. This statement suggests the idea that the individual sees the problem as internal to and widespread within the individual and permanent in duration (252).

46. a. society
    b. socioeconomic
    c. more
    d. earlier

    e. stability
    f. teens
    g. stressor
    h. restrictions (254)

47. a. organic (254)
    b. genetic
    c. bipolar
    d. unipolar
    e. different (254-255)
    f. chromosome 11
    g. bipolar (256)
    h. circadian rhythms
    i. sleep
    j. dream
    k. interpersonal relationship
    l. relationship
    m. sleep (256)
    n. seasonal affective disorder
    o. wintertime

    p. summer (256)
    q. Light (256-257)
    r. hormone (257)
    s. neurotransmitter (258)
    t. hypothalamus
    u. master gland
    v. hypothalamus
    w. hormone(257)
    x. serotonin
    y. norepinephrine
    z. serotonin
    aa. mood
    bb. norepinephrine
    cc. mania
    dd. depression (258)

48. a. bipolar (manic-depressive) (259)
49. Reduced serotonin activity between the brain stem and the frontal cortex (259)
50. a. Humanistic-existential (248)
   b. Cognitive (251-252)
   c. Cognitive (250) See Helpful Hint 3
   d. Psychodynamic (246-247)
   e. Biological (256)
   f. Behaviorism (248-249)
   g. Psychodynamic (246-247)
   h. Biological (258)
51. a. Extinction or drop in number of reinforcers = behaviorism (248-249)
   b. Negative self-schema = cognitive theory (251-252)
   c. An organic test = biological (257)
   d. Unconscious reasons = psychodynamic (246)
   e. Freedom and responsibility to choose direction in one's life = humanistic-existential (248)

## Practice Test

1. d (234)
2. c (234)
3. b (236)
4. a (237)
5. c (236)
6. d (240)
7. d (238)
8. c (239)
9. a (256)
10. c (247)

11. d (250)
12. a (249)
13. b (258)
14. b (257)
15. c (243)
16. b (243)
17. a (243-244)
18. b (259)
19. c (236)
20. a (248)

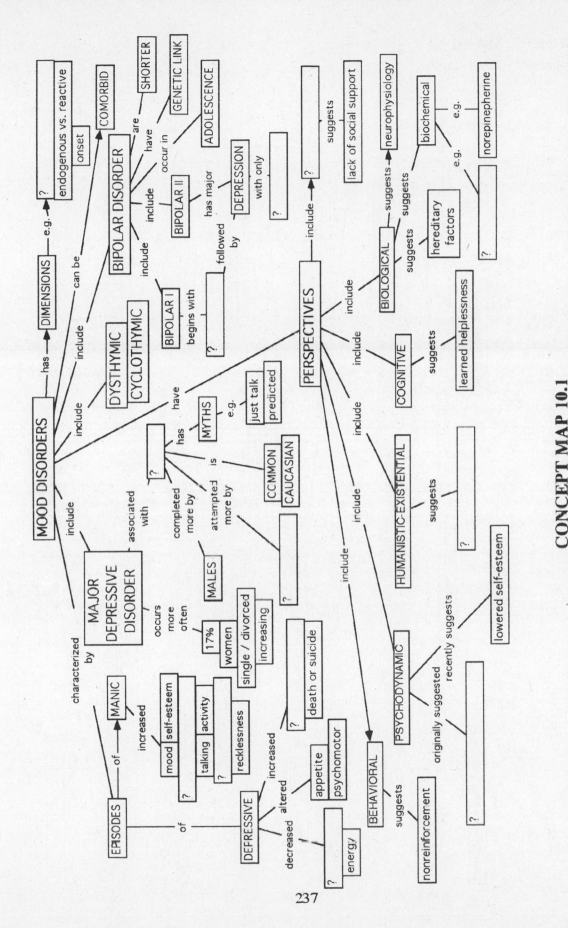

**CONCEPT MAP 10.1**

Fill out the boxes marked with question marks (?) with the concepts or words you think belong there. Suggested answers are on a following page.

237

# CONCEPT MAP 10.1

The suggested answers are shown in *italics*.

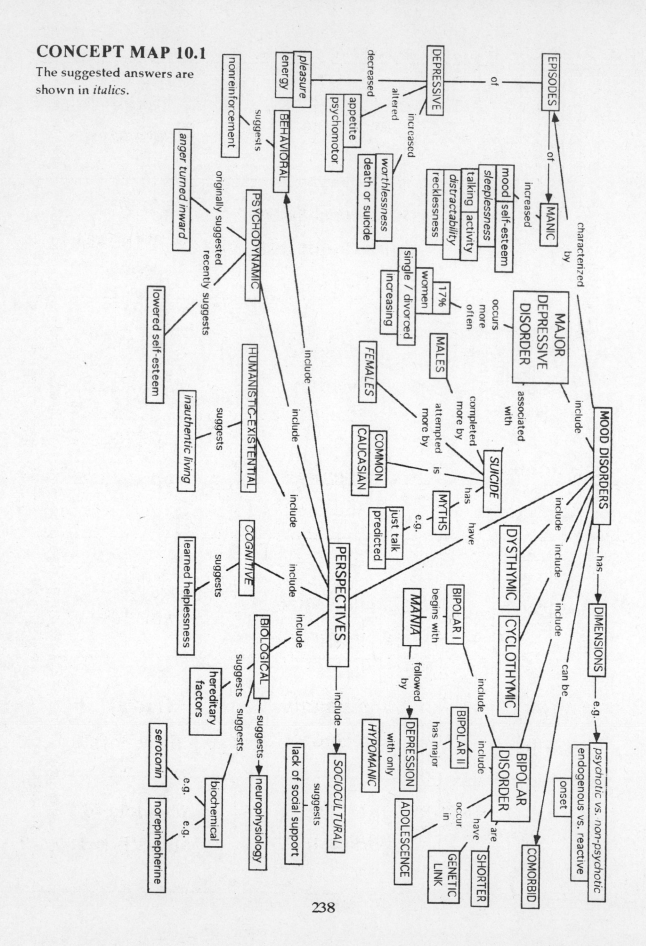

238

| | | |
|---|---|---|
| 10.1<br><br>**agitated<br>depression** | 10.8<br><br>**depression** | 10.15<br><br>**major<br>depression** |
| 10.2<br><br>**anhedonia** | 10.9<br><br>**dexamethasone<br>suppression test<br>(DST)** | 10.16<br><br>**major<br>depressive<br>episode** |
| 10.3<br><br>**bipolar<br>disorder** | 10.10<br><br>**dysthymic<br>disorder** | 10.17<br><br>**mania** |
| 10.4<br><br>**catecholamine<br>hypothesis** | 10.11<br><br>**endogenous** | 10.18<br><br>**manic<br>episode** |
| 10.5<br><br>**comorbidity** | 10.12<br><br>**helplessness-<br>hopelessness<br>syndrome** | 10.19<br><br>**mixed<br>episode** |
| 10.6<br><br>**continuity<br>hypothesis** | 10.13<br><br>**hypomanic<br>episode** | 10.20<br><br>**mood<br>disorders** |
| 10.7<br><br>**cyclothymic<br>disorder** | 10.14<br><br>**learned<br>helplessness** | 10.21<br><br>**premorbid<br>adjustment** |

# DEFINITIONS (Cut out on the lines to use as Flash Cards)

| | | |
|---|---|---|
| 10.15 A mood disorder characterized by the occurrence of major depressive episodes without intervening manic episodes | 10.8 An emotional state characterized by the exaggeration of negative feelings; the person becomes inactive and dejected and thinks nothing is worthwhile | 10.1 A form of depression characterized by incessant activity and restlessness |
| 10.16 An extended period of intense depression that usually begins and ends gradually and causes a radical change in most aspects of the individual's functioning | 10.9 A laboratory test used to identify people suffering from endogenous depression | 10.2 A mood abnormality among schizophrenics in which the person's experience of pleasure is reduced; inability to enjoy accustomed activities often experienced by people during major depressive episodes |
| 10.17 An emotional state characterized by the exaggeration of positive feelings; the person becomes feverishly active and excited and feels capable of accomplishing anything | 10.10 A mood disorder involving mild, persistent depression over an extended period of time | 10.3 A mood disorder involving both manic and depressive episodes |
| 10.18 An extended period of intense mania that usually begins and ends suddenly and causes a radical change in an individual's social functioning | 10.11 In depression, the term used to describe patients whose symptoms are primarily physical | 10.4 The biochemical theory that increased levels of the neurotransmitter norepinephrine produce mania, while decreased levels produce depression |
| 10.19 A period of a mood disorder in which symptoms of mania and depression occur simultaneously | 10.12 A thought process characteristic of deeply depressed persons; they regard their condition as irreversible, believing that they are unable to help themselves and unlikely to be helped by external forces | 10.5 The co-occurrence of depressive and anxiety disorders in a person, either simultaneously or at different times in his or her life |
| 10.20 Emotional conditions in which feelings of depression or mania become so extreme and prolonged that the person's life is completely disrupted (also called affective disorders) | 10.13 A less severe form of manic behavior | 10.6 A theory which holds that pathological depression and normal sadness are two points on a continuum of mood reactions |
| 10.21 The level of functioning that was normal for a person before the onset of a disorder | 10.14 In behavioral theory, the depressive's inability to initiate adaptive responses, possibly due to a helplessness conditioned by earlier, inescapable trauma | 10.7 A mood disorder involving a persistent pattern of moderately manic or depressive periods that occur at least every few months |

**CHAPTER TERMS** (Cut out on the lines to use as Flash Cards)

| | | |
|---|---|---|
| 10.22<br><br>**reactive** | 10.29 | 10.36 |
| 10.23<br><br>**retarded depression** | 10.30 | 10.37 |
| 10.24<br>**seasonal affective disorder (SAD)** | 10.31 | 10.38 |
| 10.25<br><br>**social-skills training** | 10.32 | 10.39 |
| 10.26<br><br><br>**tricyclics** | 10.33 | 10.40 |
| 10.27  *(You may fill in the remaining boxes with names, terms and definitions from text and lecture)* | 10.34 | 10.41 |
| 10.28 | 10.35 | 10.42 |

# DEFINITIONS (Cut out on the lines to use as Flash Cards)

| | | |
|---|---|---|
| 10.36 | 10.29 | 10.22 <br> In depression, the term used to describe patients whose symptoms are primarily emotional and cognitive |
| 10.37 | 10.30 | 10.23  A type of depression in which there is generally little spontaneous motor activity; movement is slow and deliberate, with a minimum number of gestures and little verbalization |
| 10.38 | 10.31 | 10.24 <br> A mood disorder characterized by depression that occurs only during the winter |
| 10.39 | 10.32 | 10.25 <br> A behavioral therapy that teaches people basic techniques for engaging in satisfying interactions with others |
| 10.40 | 10.33 | 10.26 <br> A class of antidepressants that seem to increase the level of certain neurotransmitters, including norepinephrine and serotonin |
| 10.41 | 10.34 | 10.27 |
| 10.42 | 10.35 | 10.28 |

## Chapter 11

# *Personality Disorders*

## LEARNING OBJECTIVES
*By the time you are finished studying this chapter, you should be able to:*

### PERSONALITY DISORDERS: INDIVIDUAL SYNDROMES
1. Define a personality disorder according to *DSM-IV* criteria (264-265).
2. List and describe the essential characteristics of each of the 10 established personality disorders (265-276).
3. Distinguish between paranoid personality disorder and paranoia and paranoid schizophrenia (265).
4. Distinguish between obsessive-compulsive personality disorder and obsessive-compulsive disorder (269).

### ANTISOCIAL PERSONALITY DISORDER
5. Distinguish between the concepts of "antisocial personality disorder" and "adult antisocial behavior" (270-272).
6. List the five criteria used by *DSM-IV* to diagnose antisocial personality disorder (272-273).
7. List four characteristics that are typical of antisocial personality disorder as described by Cleckley (273-275).
8. Describe the relationship between juvenile conduct disorder and antisocial personality disorder (276).

### PERSPECTIVES ON THE PERSONALITY DISORDERS
9. Discuss the psychodynamic perspective on personality disorders, emphasizing the role of the family in the development of personality (276-278).
10. Explain personality disorders from the behavioral and cognitive perspectives, with emphasis on the concepts of modeling and schemas (278-280).
11. Explain the sociocultural perspective's view of personality disorder, with specific reference to the concept of "anomie" (280-281).
12. Summarize the genetic and physiological research supporting the idea that antisocial personality disorder may have a biological basis (281-284).
13. Summarize the treatment techniques applied to personality disorders by each of the perspectives, and evaluate their effectiveness (277-284).

## CHAPTER OUTLINE

I. Personality disorders

    A. Since personality is a long-term trend in behavior, personality disorders are long-term trends in abnormal behavior, present since adolescence or earlier

    B. Individual syndromes
        1. Paranoid personality disorder
            a. Defining trait is suspiciousness
            b. Not to be confused with paranoia or paranoid schizophrenia (Chapter 14)
        2. Schizotypal personality disorder
            a. Defining trait is "oddness" in speech, behavior, thinking, or perception

b. Not serious enough for a diagnosis of schizophrenia
c. Victims may be more susceptible to schizophrenia
3. Schizoid personality disorder
a. Defining trait is social withdrawal
b. Stems from lack of interest in interaction
4. Avoidant personality disorder
a. Defining trait is also social withdrawal
b. Stems from fear of rejection
5. Dependent personality disorder
a. Defining trait is dependence on others
b. Fear of abandonment may be at the root
6. Borderline personality disorder
a. Defining traits are:
(1) Unstable sense of self
(2) Distrust of others
(3) Impulsive and self-destructive behavior
(4) Difficulty controlling emotions
b. May be related to abuse in childhood
7. Histrionic personality disorder
a. Defining trait is exaggerated emotionality
b. Emotional display is often used to manipulate others
8. Narcissistic personality disorder
a. Defining trait is an exaggerated sense of self-importance
b. Problem may serve to mask fragile self-esteem (reaction formation)
9. Obsessive-compulsive personality disorder
a. Defining trait is excessive preoccupation with trivial details
b. Not to be confused with obsessive-compulsive disorder (Chapter 7)

II. Antisocial personality disorder

A. The psychiatric classification of antisocial personality disorder
1. Defining trait is a predatory attitude toward others
2. Victims previously called psychopaths or sociopaths
3. Not to be confused with "normal" criminal behavior because here the antisocial behavior stems from a psychological disturbance, not just the greed or revenge of the "normal" criminal

B. Characteristics of antisocial personality disorder
1. According to *DSM-IV*
a. A history of problem behavior since before age 15 and continuing into adulthood
b. Irresponsibility in work, relationships, or finances
c. Irritability and aggressiveness
d. Reckless and impulsive behavior
e. Disregard for the truth
2. Additional characteristics by Cleckley
a. Motives and purposes are incomprehensible to others
b. Little ability to experience emotion
c. Poor judgment and inability to learn from experience
d. Good acting ability—can fake sincerity well

C. The case of Roberta
1. Roberta displays nearly all characteristics referred to above
2. Even the treatment process is seen as a "game" to be won at the expense of the therapist

D. Antisocial behavior in juveniles: The conduct disorders
1. While related to antisocial personality, *DSM-IV* lists these problems under disorders of childhood and adolescence (Chapter 17)
2. Conduct disorder in juveniles can be a good predictor of antisocial personality in adulthood

III. Perspectives on the personality disorders

    A. The psychodynamic perspective
        1. Personality disorders stem from disturbances in the early stages of psychosexual development (family deficiency)
        2. Individual syndromes result from disturbances at different stages and circumstances (e.g., lack of superego development in the antisocial personality)
        3. Result is a weak ego (stronger than in psychotics, but weaker than in neurotics) and poor coping abilities
        4. Psychotherapy is often ineffective (particularly with antisocial personalities)
            a. Little motivation to change
            b. Little voluntary cooperation
            c. Much manipulation of therapist and therapeutic situation

    B. The behavioral perspective
        1. Personality disorders are a result of inappropriate learning
        2. Individual syndromes are the result of specific kinds of inappropriate learning
            a. Poor learning of living skills or the learning of inappropriate skills
            b. Having inappropriate behavior (e.g., aggression for the antisocial personality) modeled in the environment
            c. Reinforcement of inappropriate behavior or the lack of reinforcement for appropriate behavior
            d. Noncontingent reinforcement in the case of conduct disorders
        3. Treatment focuses on learning appropriate behavior
            a. Social-skills training
            b. Regulation of emotions
            c. Toleration of stress and grief

    C. The cognitive perspective
        1. Personality disorders are the result of distorted (and rigid) information processing schemas
        2. Individual syndromes result from specific kinds of distorted schemas (e.g., "I must be perfect" in the obsessive-compulsive personality)
        3. Treatment consists of altering schemas

    D. The sociocultural perspective
        1. Tends to focus on the antisocial personality
        2. Emphasizes role of culture in promoting disorder
        3. Anomie (normlessness) leads to disregard for rules
        4. Treatment focuses on changing the society more than on changing the individual

    E. The biological perspective
        1. Growing evidence that genetic components may be more important in determining behavior than they were previously thought to be
        2. Antisocial personality studied most intensely
            a. XYY chromosome anomaly studies are inconclusive overall
            b. Twin and adoption studies indicate genetic component
            c. Many antisocial personalities show EEG abnormalities (slow wave activity)
            d. Autonomic underarousal is often present (temporarily reversible with adrenaline injections)
            e. Information processing abnormalities may prevent switching attention from reward to punishment

## KEY TERMS
***The following terms are in bold print in your text. Define them and practice their definitions using the flash cards at the end of the chapter.***

anomie (281)  
antisocial behavior (270)  
antisocial personality disorder (269)  
avoidant personality disorder (266)

borderline personality disorder (267)  
dependent personality disorder (266)  
histrionic personality disorder (268)  
impulse control disorder (274)

narcissistic personality disorder (268)
noncontingent reinforcement (278)
obsessive-compulsive personality disorder
(269)
paranoid personality disorder (265)

passive avoidance learning (274)
personality disorder (264)
schizoid personality disorder (266)
schizotypal personality disorder (266)

*Your text does not list the following terms as formal vocabulary; however, if you don't
know what they mean, you will be unable to grasp the concepts of this chapter.*

ambivalence (267)
apropos (270)
ceding (277)
critique (281)
derelictions (280)

dialectical (279)
eccentricity (266)
grandiose (268)
impetus (281)
masochistic (270)

nonchalance (268)
predatory (269)
sadistic (270)

## IMPORTANT NAMES
*Identify the following persons and their major contributions to abnormal psychology as
discussed in this chapter.*

H. M. Cleckley (273)

## GUIDED SELF-STUDY

1. Personality disorders differ from the other disorders discussed thus far in three ways.

   a. They have no history of "_____" predating the dysfunction.

   b. The personality disorder is pervasive, which means it affects _____ aspects of the
   person's life.

   c. They usually don't cause the patient as much _____ as they cause for the people
   around the patient.

2. Complete the following statements about the reliability of the personality disorder diagnostic
   category using these terms:

   **atypical**                **personality disorder**              **reliable**
   **different**               **reliability**

   As a diagnostic category, personality disorders has not been very (a)_____.

   Diagnosticians fairly well agree on the presence or absence of a (b)_____,

   but they often disagree as to which (c)_____ is being manifested in a

   particular patient. The problem is to make the categories (d)_____ enough among

   themselves to ensure high (e)_____, but they not so limiting as to cause too many

   people to be put in the "mixed" or (d)_____ categories.

3. Which of the personality disorders shows the most reliability as a diagnostic category?


4. The other problem with the personality disorder diagnosis is the assumption that stable
   personality traits exist. Which perspective objects to this assumption?

# PERSONALITY DISORDERS: INDIVIDUAL SYNDROMES

5. Some personality disorders have names that are similar to those of other psychiatric problems. It is important not to confuse the personality disorders with these other diagnoses. After each of the following personality disorders, list the other disorder or disorders from which it must be differentiated.

   a. Paranoid personality disorder:

   b. Schizotypal personality disorder:

   c. Schizoid personality disorder:

   d. Obsessive-compulsive personality disorder:

6. Draw a line from each personality disorder to the phrase that most closely defines the disorder. Use each disorder and each phrase only once.

| | |
|---|---|
| Paranoid | Withdraws fearing rejection |
| Schizotypal | "Odd" |
| Schizoid | Predatory attitude |
| Avoidant | Doesn't find social contact worthwhile |
| Dependent | Bogged down in details |
| Borderline | "Ego" maniac (not Freudian ego) |
| Histrionic | Puts decision making on someone else |
| Narcissistic | A "flake" (unstable) |
| Obsessive-compulsive | Suspicious |
| Antisocial | Self-dramatizing |

7. Find one or more "good jobs" for each of the following personality disorders. Consider the needs of the job and the characteristics of each of the disorders.

**Accountant**  **Forest ranger in a remote region**
**Auto body painting**  **Long-haul truck driver**
**Bookkeeping**  **Private detective**
**Cartoonist**  **Proofreading**
**Comedian**  **Security guard**

   a. _____ Obsessive-compulsive

   b. _____ Paranoid

   c. _____ Schizotypal

   d. _____ Schizoid

8. Place a check mark in front of each personality disorder in which the person in some way "uses" other people. Then, after the disorders you checked, tell how the person with the problem uses others.

| | |
|---|---|
| _____ Paranoid | _____ Borderline |
| _____ Schizotypal | _____ Histrionic |
| _____ Schizoid | _____ Narcissistic |
| _____ Avoidant | _____ Obsessive-compulsive |
| _____ Dependent | _____ Antisocial |

9. Place a check mark next to the personality disorders that tend to deliberately "distance" themselves from other people, and tell what the motive for seeking distance is.

| | |
|---|---|
| _____ Paranoid | _____ Borderline |
| _____ Schizotypal | _____ Histrionic |
| _____ Schizoid | _____ Narcissistic |
| _____ Avoidant | _____ Obsessive-compulsive |
| _____ Dependent | _____ Antisocial |

10. Check the personality disorders that are likely to have few to no warm friendships with other people. Then tell why they tend not to form good relationships with others.

| | |
|---|---|
| _____ Paranoid | _____ Borderline |
| _____ Schizotypal | _____ Histrionic |
| _____ Schizoid | _____ Narcissistic |
| _____ Avoidant | _____ Obsessive-compulsive |
| _____ Dependent | _____ Antisocial |

11. List four factors that contribute to the instability of the borderline personality.

a.

b.

c.

d.

ANTISOCIAL PERSONALITY DISORDER

12. _____ and _____ are two other names which have been used in the past for people with antisocial personality disorder.

13. There is a difference in motivation between someone with antisocial personality disorder and someone with adult antisocial behavior not attributable to a mental disorder. Ordinary

criminals (those without mental disorder) commit their crimes for _____ reasons: greed, revenge, etc. People with antisocial personality disorder do not seem to act in response to _____ motives.

14. List the five characteristics of the antisocial personality as described in *DSM-IV*.

    a.

    b.

    c.

    d.

    e.

15. Cleckley attributes four characteristics to people who have antisocial personalities. Use these terms to complete them:

    **anxiety**                    **judgement**
    **experience**                 **motivation**
    **guilt**                      **shallowest**
    **impulsive**

    a.  _____ to the point of no apparent understandable _____

    b.  Emotions on the _____ level

    c.  Poor _____ and failure to learn from _____

    d.  Since they lack _____ and _____, they can maintain poise when others could not.

16. Antisocial personality as a personality diagnosis is not applied to children and teenagers. Antisocial personality disorder is used only with adults. Juvenile antisocial behavior is

    diagnosed as (a)_____, which is listed under disorders of (b)_____. However, research reveals that conduct disorders are definitely related to a later diagnosis of

    (c)_____. Not all youngsters with conduct disorders go on to develop (d)_____

    _____, but by definition antisocial personality disorder which starts before age

    (e)_____ was originally a conduct disorder.

## PERSPECTIVES ON THE PERSONALITY DISORDERS

17. Of the seven perspectives introduced in Chapter One, which ones are not discussed in this chapter on personality disorders?

18. What do psychodynamic theorists call personality disorders?

19. In the disorders that have been discussed thus far, the psychodynamic perspective assumed

    that the problem was unconscious (a)_____. With these earlier disorders the (b)_____ is "overworked" by the quantity of anxiety it is trying to keep down. However, in the character disorders, the ego is not working well because of problems in the (c) **early / late** stages of

    (d)_____ development.

20. In regard to ego functioning, how do psychodynamic theorists rank **character disorders** with **neuroses** and **psychoses**? Write each disorder in the appropriate space.

    Best-functioning:_____/_____/_____:Worst-functioning

21. Psychodynamic theory says that different personality disorders result from different kinds of ego problems. Match each personality disorder with its ego problem.

    a. _____ Ego is unstable, person "falls apart" in times of stress

    b. _____ Ego cannot delay gratification

    c. _____ Ego forgoes own thinking skills in favor of thinking skills of others

    d. _____ Ego shifts all mental energy into planning

    e. _____ Ego directs all mental energy into scanning the environment

    f. _____ Ego cannot learn from experience

22. In the antisocial personality, the ego cannot delay gratification because ultimately the person's

    (a)_____ is inadequate, which in non-Freudian terms means s/he lacks a

    (b)_____. This lack of development is because the child never resolved his

    Oedipal (her Electra) complex by (c)_____ with his/her (d)_____ sexed parent in the

    (e)_____ psychosexual stage.

23. The prognosis for character disorders is quite (a) _____. People with character disorders are usually not distressed by their own personality quirks; and if they are distressed, they are

    likely to perceive the problem as (b)_____.

24. In treating personality disorders, psychodynamic therapists take a more (a)_____, parent-like role than psychoanalytic therapists do with other clients. These therapists are

    trying to provide an opportunity for the patient to rework the disrupted (b)_____-child

    relationship that is assumed to underlie (c)_____, as the psychoanalysts call these disorders.

25. Use these terms for behaviorism:

    **learning**                                        **personality**
    **traits**                                          **trends**

    Some behaviorists object to the concept of (a)_____ because these behaviorists are

    unwilling to talk in terms of fixed (b)_____. Some behaviorists see the

    individual as (c)_____ classes (types) of behaviors that lead to (d)_____ in

    behavior equivalent to the concept of (e)_____.

26. Circle four of the following to identify the learning processes that behaviorists believe explain personality disorders.

| | |
|---|---|
| **Invalidating syndrome** | **Noncontingent reinforcement** |
| **Anomie** | **Premorbidity** |
| **Prognosis** | **Direct positive reinforcement** |
| **Parasympathetic retraining** | **Disregulation syndrome** |
| **Modeling** | **Fugue** |
| **Biofeedback reinforcement** | **Schema alignment** |
| **Endogenous assertiveness** | |

Use the following terms for Questions 27 -30:

adult
adult-sized
approval and attention
behaviors
consequences
desensitized
emotional
invalidating syndrome
learning

parents
peers
reinforcement
reward
self-calming
social
television characters
unpredictable
useless

27. The (a)_____ is the behavioral pattern in which the parents dismiss a child's

emotional distress unless the distress comes from a problem of (b)_____ proportions. As

a result, the child does not get practice in (c)_____ and emotional problem-solving on

small, child-sized (d)_____ problems. For example, when a child is learning to
cope with the pain of a tiny hurt (often not visible to the parent's eye), that child is making

beginning steps toward (e)_____ to deal with the (f)_____ pain of personal
rejection or losing a job.

28. In modeling, the child copies the behavior that he/she sees _____, _____,

and _____ using.

29. Noncontingent reinforcement prevents the child from learning what (a)_____ bring

what (b)_____. In this process the child becomes (c)_____ to the (d)_____
stimuli around him/her. Noncontingent reinforcement teaches that the events are totally

(e)_____. On a learning level, the child gets the message that it is (f)_____ to

try to figure out a predictable system of what (g)_____ follow what (h)_____
when there really is not one.

30. In direct positive (a) _____ the person develops a pattern of behaviors for which

he/she receives some (b)_____, particularly peer and parental (c)_____.

Use the following terms in the blanks in Questions 31-34:

compelled
consideration
faulty
limit
rigid

schemas
schematic camouflage
store
unlikely
use

31. Cognitive psychologists talk in terms of (a)_____, which are the organizational

structures that individuals use to efficiently conceptualize and (b)_____ information in
memory. Instead of remembering every fast food restaurant as a separate place, most people
have a schema for a fast food restaurant. If a place is proposed for lunch and noted as a fast
food restaurant everyone knows what to expect without further description needed.

251

32. Circle the following concepts which are probably in most people's schemas for fast food restaurant.

| | |
|---|---|
| **Servers in formal attire** | **Drive through service** |
| **Valet parking** | **Filet mignon on the menu** |
| **Self serve areas** | **Economical prices** |
| **Menu over central counter** | **Necessity to make reservations** |
| **Cloth table napkins** | **Topless waitresses** |
| **Limited menu** | |

33. Cognitive theorists see personality disorders as the result of (a)_____ schemas. Many of us may hold beliefs that are counterproductive; however, these only become a major problem suitable of a diagnosis if we feel strongly (b)_____ to exercise the ideas and beliefs across circumstances without any (c)_____ for the particulars of any given situation. In other words. our thinking and behavior become very (d)_____.

34. The ambitious goal of cognitive therapists is to change faulty (a)_____. A more realistic and practical alternative to complete change, which is very (b)_____ to occur, is to help the person try to (c)_____ the use of his/her faulty schemas and to put them to as good (d)_____ as can be worked into the person life. The cognitive therapists may also teach some socially acceptable behaviors to be used within the otherwise "quirky" personality; this is called (e)_____.

35. Sociocultural theorists have focused primarily on (a)_____ personality disorder. Of course, they see it in terms of large-scale (b)_____ processes, just as they see everything else.

Merton suggests that our society places an unrealistically high value on (c)_____, access to which is then limited to the privileged few. Merton says this creates a state of (d)_____ in the underprivileged, which means there is no real societal norm for them to follow to reach what is essentially an unobtainable goal.

36. Biological research has dramatically demonstrated that there is a (a)_____ component to personality. How the inherited components are developed into the stable traits to define (b)_____ is still unknown. The publicized (c)_____ chromosomal abnormality of some criminals is interesting. It is found (d)_____ times more often among male criminals than males in general; however only about (e)_____ percent of male criminals have this abnormality and there are men who have it that have never been convicted of a crime. More likely men with this disorder are nonviolent, mildly (f)_____ individuals.

37. In looking for the organic elements of antisocial personality, no one distinctive element has been discovered, but a number of studies have contributed to building a picture of the physiology of antisocial personality. Fill in the blanks on these six summarized findings with these terms:

| | |
|---|---|
| **abnormalities** | **attention** |
| **adrenaline** | **autonomic** |
| **age** | **avoidance** |

a.  EEG _____

b.  Behavioral improvements with _____

c.  Poor performance in _____ learning

d.  Improved learning performance with _____ injections

e.  Signs of _____ underarousal

f.  Problem switching _____ from reward cues to punishment cues

## HELPFUL HINTS

1.  To have certain personality disorder tendencies and to use them to one's advantage is productive.  However, at the point when they would actually be diagnosed as a personality disorder, they have crossed over the line and are causing the person real problems, although they may still not be disabling (264).
2.  Noncontingent reinforcement means unpredictable payoff.
3.  Note that just because someone engages in some of the behaviors described in this chapter some of the time does not mean that person has a disorder.  You can identify first-time mothers because they boil the pacifier every time it hits the floor.  By the third kid the attitude is likely to change.  So what if the kid shares the pacifier with the dog? Pervasiveness, inflexibility and long duration are the key issues in defining these disorders.

## PRACTICE TEST
*Take the following test several times as you study the chapter.  Write your answers on a separate sheet of paper and after each attempt, note in the tally box above each question whether your answer was correct or incorrect.*

| 1 | 2 | 3 | 4 |
|---|---|---|---|

1.  Which of the following is true of personality disorders?
    a.  They are some of the most reliably diagnosed disorders.
    b.  They are all derived from the bipolar mood disorder.
    c.  In most cases the victim does not recognize the problem for what it is.
    d.  They tend not to appear until after the age of 30.

| 1 | 2 | 3 | 4 |
|---|---|---|---|

2.  Another way of stating the *DSM-IV* definition of personality disorder is
    a.  a lifestyle that creates difficulties for the person or others.
    b.  a limited behavioral quirk that irritates those around the patient.
    c.  a lack of emotional responding that takes that joy out of life.
    d.  a retreat from anxiety to the point that reality contact is lost.

| 1 | 2 | 3 | 4 |
|---|---|---|---|

3.  A likely underlying problem in avoidant personality disorder is
    a.  low self-esteem.
    b.  repressed hostility.
    c.  a fragile superego.
    d.  callousness toward other people.

| 1 | 2 | 3 | 4 |
|---|---|---|---|

4. An individual who overreacts to the slightest event with an outburst of melodramatic emotion is likely to be classified as having a(n)_____ personality disorder.
   a. paranoid
   b. histrionic
   c. dependent
   d. antisocial

| 1 | 2 | 3 | 4 |
|---|---|---|---|

5. The defining characteristic of paranoid personality disorder is
   a. overdramatization.
   b. preoccupation with detail.
   c. indirect resistance to the demands of others.
   d. suspiciousness.

| 1 | 2 | 3 | 4 |
|---|---|---|---|

6. The difference between the obsessive-compulsive personality disorder in this chapter and the obsessive-compulsive disorder in Chapter 7 is that the personality disorder is
   a. usually found in combination with a total loss of reality contact.
   b. restricted to one or two specific behaviors.
   c. more pervasive in all aspects of the person's life.
   d. regarded as an organic psychosis.

| 1 | 2 | 3 | 4 |
|---|---|---|---|

7. Waldo has always been somewhat strange. The questions he asks in class are usually way out in left field. He always wears dress shoes but no socks, and it doesn't appear that he has had a bath in weeks. Waldo might very well have a(n)
   a. antisocial personality disorder.
   b. dependent personality disorder.
   c. avoidant personality disorder.
   d. schizotypal personality disorder.

| 1 | 2 | 3 | 4 |
|---|---|---|---|

8. A major difference between the schizoid personality disorder and the avoidant personality disorder is that the schizoid personality disorder
   a. is accompanied by fairly low intelligence scores.
   b. is based on a fear of rejection by others.
   c. shows withdrawal because of a lack of interest in others.
   d. is characterized by more open aggression toward others.

| 1 | 2 | 3 | 4 |
|---|---|---|---|

9. Which of the following personality disorders is characterized by instability in emotion and behavior?
   a. Narcissistic
   b. Borderline
   c. Passive-aggressive
   d. Obsessive-compulsive

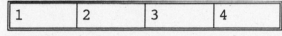

10. Daphne drives people up the wall because she is such a nit-picker. She spends more time organizing details than actually getting important things done, and on a recent trip to the beach with some friends she could hardly cope with the fact that the hotel had changed their room without telling them, and it no longer faced the water. This sounds like which personality disorder?
   a. Obsessive-compulsive
   b. Antisocial
   c. Sadistic
   d. Passive-aggressive

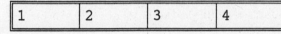

11. The difference between (1) antisocial personality disorder and (2) adult antisocial behavior is that
   a. (1) is a mental disorder and (2) is not.
   b. (1) is socially caused and (2) is organic.
   c. (1) refers to adolescents and (2) refers to adults.
   d. (1) does not involve criminal behavior and (2) does.

| 1 | 2 | 3 | 4 |

12. Another, older term for someone with antisocial personality disorder is
   a. cretin.
   b. intransigent.
   c. psychopath.
   d. imbecile.

| 1 | 2 | 3 | 4 |

13. All of the following are characteristics of antisocial personality disorder *except*
   a. lack of regard for truth or responsibility.
   b. lack of normal emotional experience.
   c. ability to maintain a pleasant and charming front.
   d. high self-awareness and insightfulness.

| 1 | 2 | 3 | 4 |

14. Which of the following is *not* true of antisocial personality disorder?
   a. It has the highest diagnostic reliability of all the personality disorders.
   b. It is more common in males than in females.
   c. All teens with juvenile conduct disorder become antisocial personalities, but not all antisocial personalities have a history of juvenile conduct disorder.
   d. Patients in this category seem to show cortical immaturity, autonomic underarousal, and difficulty with avoidance learning situations.

| 1 | 2 | 3 | 4 |

15. From the psychodynamic perspective, the antisocial personality
   a. is the same as the neurotic because the behavior results from anxiety defense.
   b. is the opposite of the neurotic because while the neurotic has poor control over the id, the antisocial personality cannot control the superego.
   c. is related to sexual frustration, leading to displaced aggression.
   d. is the opposite of the neurotic because while the neurotic has an overdeveloped superego, the antisocial personality has an underdeveloped superego.

| 1 | 2 | 3 | 4 |
|---|---|---|---|

16. There has been some largely inconclusive research that attempted to show a connection between antisocial behavior and the _____ chromosome abnormality.
   a. XXX
   b. XXY
   c. XYY
   d. YYY

| 1 | 2 | 3 | 4 |
|---|---|---|---|

17. Physiological research seems to indicate that there may be a connection between antisocial behavior and
   a. slow-wave EEG patterns.
   b. abnormal visual sensitivity.
   c. autonomic overarousal.
   d. male hormone deficiencies.

| 1 | 2 | 3 | 4 |
|---|---|---|---|

18. The term "noncontingent reinforcement" means
   a. reinforcement that has no effect on the person.
   b. the total absence of reinforcement.
   c. the use of punishment as the exclusive means of behavior control.
   d. reinforcement unrelated to behavior.

| 1 | 2 | 3 | 4 |
|---|---|---|---|

19. "Many poor people or minority people can't seem to make society's rules work for them as they try to make a living, and they see others getting rich through crime. No wonder we have so many antisocial personalities--we create them." This sounds like someone who would support the _____ perspective on antisocial personality disorder.
   a. psychodynamic
   b. existential
   c. cognitive
   d. sociocultural

| 1 | 2 | 3 | 4 |
|---|---|---|---|

20. Insight-oriented treatment programs for personality disorders
   a. are generally not very successful.
   b. are most effective when based on neo-Freudian theory.
   c. are as effective as the best biological treatments.
   d. are most successful when the client is forced to participate by the courts or other means.

## ANSWERS
### Self-Study Exercise

1. a. normal
   b. all
   c. distress (264)
2. a. reliable
   b. personality disorder
   c. personality disorder
   d. different
   e. reliability
   f. atypical (264-265)
3. Antisocial personality disorder (269)
4. Behaviorists (265)
5. a. Paranoia and paranoid schizophrenic (265)
   b. Schizophrenia (266)
   c. Schizophrenia (266)
   d. Obsessive-compulsive (anxiety) disorder (269)

6. Paranoid—Suspicious (265)
   Schizotypal—"Odd" (266)
   Schizoid—Doesn't find social contact worthwhile (266)
   Avoidant—Withdraws fearing rejection (266)
   Dependent—Puts decision making on someone else (266)
   Borderline—A "flake" (unstable) (267)
   Histrionic—Self-dramatizing (268)
   Narcissistic—"Ego" maniac (268)
   Obsessive-compulsive—Bogged down in details (269)
   Antisocial—Predatory attitude (269)
7. a. Obsessive-compulsive (attention to detail)—Accountant, auto body painting, proofreading (269)
   b. Paranoid (hypervigilant)—Private detective, security guard (265)
   c. Schizotypal (unusual perspective and behaviors)—Cartoonist, comedian (the ones who see the world from unusual perspectives are some of my favorites) (266)
   d. Schizoid (very content alone)—Accountant, security guard, forest ranger in a remote region, long-haul truck driver (266)
   Be sure to read Helpful Hint #1 on this issue.
8. Dependent—Puts responsibility for personal decisions on others (266)
   Histrionic—Uses others as an audience for attention and sympathy (268)
   Narcissistic—Uses others to obtain validation for "magnificent" self-image (268)
   Antisocial—Uses others to gratify self-centered impulses (269)
9. Paranoid—Withdraws to protect self from suspected ill intentions of others (265)
   Schizoid—Withdraws because he/she has no motivation toward other people (266)
   Avoidant—Withdraws fearing anticipated rejection from others (266)
10. Paranoid—Guardedness won't allow enough closeness to build a friendship (265)
    Schizotypal—May evoke avoidance from others because of odd behavior (266)
    Schizoid—Makes no effort to build friendships (266)
    Avoidant—Too apprehensive about rejection to risk a friendship (266)
    Dependent—Drives others away with clinging dependency (266)
    Borderline—Is so changeable that friendships are unstable (267)
    Histrionic—People tire of the dramatics and manipulation (268)
    Narcissistic—Self-involvement does not leave room for others as equals (268)
    Antisocial—Victims avoid them after discovering they are selfishly motivated (269-275)
11. a. Difficulties in establishing a secure self-identity
    b. Distrust
    c. Impulsive and self-destructive behavior
    d. Difficulty controlling anger and other emotions (267-268)
12. Psychopaths and sociopaths (271)
13. normal, normal (272-273)
14. a. Unacceptable behavior beginning before age 15 and continuing into adulthood
    b. Inconsistent and irresponsible in all areas of life
    c. Irritability and aggressiveness
    d. Reckless and impulsive behavior
    e. No regard for truth (272-273)
15. a. Impulsive, motivation
    b. shallowest
    c. judgement, experience
    d. anxiety, guilt (273-275)
16. a. conduct disorder
    b. childhood and adolescence
    c. antisocial personality disorder
    d. antisocial personality disorder
    e. fifteen (276)
17. Humanistic-existential and interpersonal (9, 263)
18. Character disorders (276)
19. a. conflicts
    b. ego (26-28)
    c. early
    d. psychosexual (276)
20. Best functioning: Neurotic / Character disorder / Psychosis :Worst functioning (277)
21. a. Borderline personality disorder
    b. Antisocial personality disorder
    c. Dependent personality disorder
    d. Obsessive-compulsive personality disorder
    e. Paranoid personality disorder
    f. Antisocial personality disorder (277)

22. a. superego
    b. moral conscience
    c. identification
23. a. poor
    b. external to them (277)
24. a. directive
    b. parent
25. a. personality
    b. traits
    c. learning
26. Invalidating syndrome, modeling, noncontingent reinforcement, and direct positive reinforcement (278-279)
27. a. invalidating syndrome
    b. adult
    c. self-calming
28. parents, peers, television characters (in any order) (278)
29. a. behaviors
    b. consequences
    c. desensitized
    d. social

30. a. reinforcement
    b. reward
31. a. schemas
    b. store (280)
32. Self serve
    Menu over central counter
    Limited menu
33. a. faulty
    b. compelled

34. a. schemas
    b. unlikely
    c. limit
35. a. antisocial
    b. social

36. a. genetic
    b. personality
    c. XYY

37. a. abnormalities
    b. age
    c. avoidance

d. same
e. phallic (Oedipal) (277)

c. character disorders (277-278)

d. trends
e. personality (278)

d. emotional
e. learning
f. adult-sized (278)

e. unpredictable
f. useless
g. consequences
h. behaviors (278-279) See Hint 2

c. approval and attention (279)

Drive through service
Economical prices (280)

c. consideration
d. rigid (280)

d. use
e. schematic camouflage (280)

c. material luxuries
d. anomie (281)

d. fifteen
e. two
f. mentally retarded (281-2)

d. adrenaline
e. autonomic
f. attention (282-284)

### Practice Test

| | | | | | | |
|---|---|---|---|---|---|---|
| 1. | c | (264) | | 11. | a | (272) |
| 2. | a | (264) | | 12. | c | (271) |
| 3. | a | (266) | | 13. | d | (272-275) |
| 4. | b | (268) | | 14. | c | (276) |
| 5. | d | (265) | | 15. | d | (277) |
| 6. | c | (269) | | 16. | c | (281) |
| 7. | d | (266) | | 17. | a | (282) |
| 8. | c | (266) | | 18. | d | (278) |
| 9. | b | (267-268) | | 19. | d | (281) |
| 10. | a | (269) | | 20. | a | (277) |

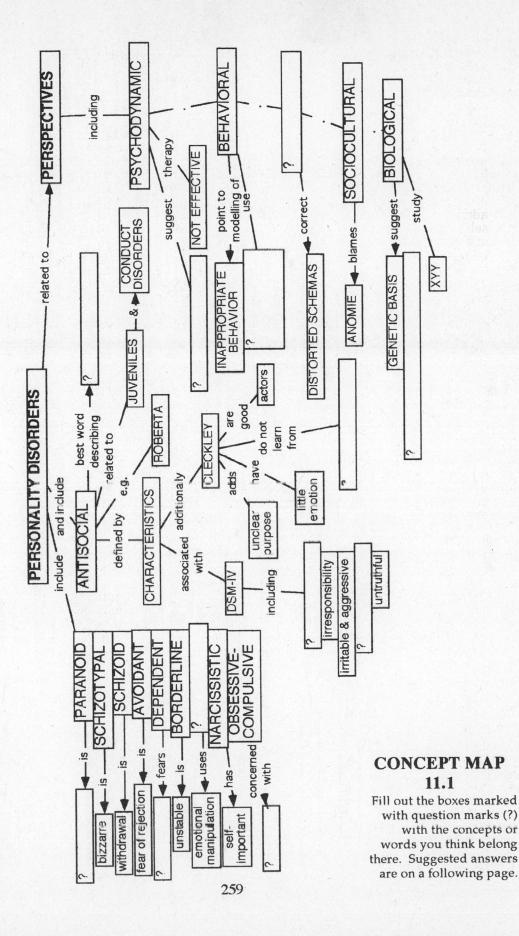

**CONCEPT MAP
11.1**

Fill out the boxes marked
with question marks (?)
with the concepts or
words you think belong
there. Suggested answers
are on a following page.

## CONCEPT MAP 11.1

The suggested answers are shown in *italics*.

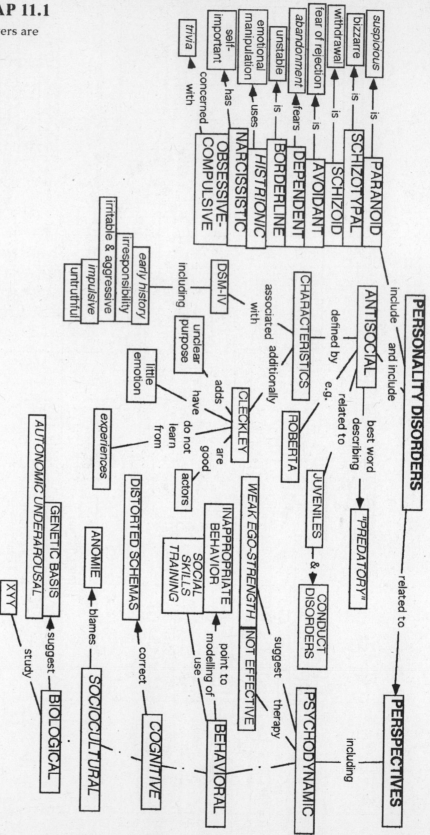

260

**CHAPTER TERMS** (Cut out on the lines to use as Flash Cards)

| | | |
|---|---|---|
| 11.1<br><br>**anomie** | 11.8<br><br>**impulse control disorder** | 11.15<br>**schizoid personality disorder** |
| 11.2<br><br>**antisocial behavior** | 11.9<br>**narcissistic personality disorder** | 11.16<br>**schizotypal personality disorder** |
| 11.3<br>**antisocial personality disorder** | 11.10<br><br>**noncontingent reinforcement** | 11.17 *(You may fill in the remaining boxes with names, terms and definitions from text and lecture)* |
| 11.4<br>**avoidant personality disorder** | 11.11<br>**obsessive-compulsive disorder** | 11.18 |
| 11.5<br>**borderline personality disorder** | 11.12<br>**paranoid personality disorder** | 11.19 |
| 11.6<br>**dependent personality disorder** | 11.13<br>**passive-aggressive personality disorder** | 11.20 |
| 11.7<br>**histrionic personality disorder** | 11.14<br><br>**personality disorders** | 11.21 |

# DEFINITIONS (Cut out on the lines to use as Flash Cards)

| | | |
|---|---|---|
| **11.15** <br><br> A disorder marked by social withdrawal and isolation | **11.8** <br><br> Class of disorders characterized by a person's inability to resist tendencies to act in a way harmful to oneself or others | **11.1** Merton's term for a feeling of normlessness that exists in disadvantaged groups; may contribute to the development of antisocial personalities found in members of such groups |
| **11.16** <br><br> A disorder marked by odd speech, behavior, thinking, and/or perception | **11.9** <br><br> Disorder characterized by a grandiose sense of self-importance, often combined with periodic feelings of inferiority | **11.2** <br><br> Behavior that violates the rights of others; usually associated with antisocial personality |
| **11.17** | **11.10** <br><br> Arbitrary reinforcement unrelated to behavior | **11.3** <br><br> A disorder marked by chronic indifference to and violation of the rights of others |
| **11.18** | **11.11** <br><br> Involuntary dwelling on an unwelcome thought and/or involuntary repetition of an unnecessary action | **11.4** <br><br> A disorder in which the individual withdraws from social contact out of fear of rejection |
| **11.19** | **11.12** <br><br> A disorder defined by suspiciousness in almost all situations and with almost all people. | **11.5** A disorder marked by defects in self-other individuation, distrust, impulsive and self-destructive behavior, and difficulty in controlling anger and other emotions |
| **11.20** | **11.13** <br><br> A disorder characterized by indirectly expressed resistance to demands made by others | **11.6** <br><br> A disorder marked by extreme dependence on others |
| **11.21** | **11.14** Long-standing habits of maladaptive thought and behavior that color the person's whole life and impair that life, either by making the person unhappy or by impeding his or her functioning or both | **11.7** <br><br> A disorder involving the exaggerated display of emotion |

## Chapter 12

# Substance-Use Disorders

*LEARNING OBJECTIVES*
*By the time you are finished studying this chapter, you should be able to:*

**THE NATURE OF SUBSTANCE DEPENDENCE AND ABUSE**
1. List seven criteria used by *DSM-IV* to diagnose psychoactive substance *dependence*, and four criteria used to diagnose psychoactive substance *abuse* (289).

**ALCOHOL DEPENDENCE**
2. Summarize the statistical data on the effects of alcoholism on society (290-292).
3. Summarize the behavioral and cognitive effects of various amounts of alcohol on the individual (290-292).
4. Summarize the development of alcohol dependence, comparing patterns of dependence typical of men and women (293).

**PERSPECTIVES ON ALCOHOL DEPENDENCE**
5. Explain the dependency and power-seeking hypotheses of alcohol dependence put forward by the psychodynamic perspective (294).
6. Describe the positive and negative reinforcement explanations of alcohol dependence proposed by the behavioral perspective (294-295).
7. Summarize three cognitive explanations for the development of alcohol dependence (296-297).
8. Summarize cultural and social-environmental research on alcohol dependence presented from the sociocultural perspective (297-300).
9. Summarize data suggesting genetic and biochemical predispositions for alcohol dependence (300-302).
10. Describe the various treatment methods that the perspectives in this chapter have applied to alcohol dependence, and define what is meant by multimodal treatment (294-303).

**NICOTINE DEPENDENCE**
11. Summarize the physical and psychological effects of nicotine and discuss nicotine dependence from the biological and the various psychological viewpoints (303-306).

**OTHER PSYCHOACTIVE DRUGS**
12. Describe the effects of depressant drugs, and distinguish among opiates, barbiturates, tranquilizers, and nonbarbiturate sedatives (307-310).
13. Describe the effects of stimulant drugs, and distinguish among amphetamines, cocaine, and caffeine (310-312).
14. Describe the effects of hallucinogenic drugs, and summarize research on the short-term and long-term effects of marijuana and hashish (312-315).

**PERSPECTIVES ON DRUG DEPENDENCE**
15. Relate the study of endorphins and dopamine to drug dependence (315-316).
16. Relate drug use to personality traits and social environmental influences (316-317).
17. Summarize the effects of drug use on society and outline typical multicomponent treatment programs and efforts to prevent relapse in recovering addicts (317-320).

# CHAPTER OUTLINE

I. The nature of substance dependence and abuse

    A. A psychoactive drug is a substance that alters one's psychological state

    B. Psychoactive substance *dependence* criteria (three needed for a diagnosis)
        1. Preoccupation with the drug
        2. Unintentional overuse
        3. Tolerance
        4. Withdrawal
        5. Persistent desire or efforts to control drug use
        6. Abandonment of important social, occupational, or recreational activities for the sake of drug use
        7. Continued drug use despite serious drug-related problems

    C. Psychoactive substance *abuse* criteria
        1. Recurrent drug-related failure to fulfill major role obligations
        2. Recurrent drug use in a physically dangerous situation
        3. Drug-related legal problems
        4. Continued drug use despite social or interpersonal problems

II. Alcohol dependence

    A. The social cost of alcohol problems
        1. Decreased work productivity is an issue because drinkers
            a. Are slower and less efficient
            b. Make poor decisions
            c. Have more accidents
            d. Cause morale problems on the job
        2. Alcohol abusers have higher medical costs
            a. $20 billion was spent in 1990 for services to alcoholics
            b. 40 percent of hospital patients have alcohol-related problems
            c. Alcoholic women risk giving birth to infants with fetal alcohol syndrome
        3. $12 billion lost annually due to alcohol-related motor vehicle accidents
            a. Intoxication is defined as a 0.10 percent blood alcohol level
            b. The amount of liquor needed to achieve 0.10 percent varies with body weight and sex
        4. Alcohol also contributes to physical assault and sexual offenses

    B. The personal cost of alcohol dependence
        1. Immediate effects of alcohol
            a. While alcohol may initially loosen inhibitions, giving rise to more active behavior, alcohol is actually a CNS depressant
            b. Stress and tension are forgotten
            c. Emotionally motivated behaviors emerge, because of
                (1) Released inhibitions
                (2) Expectations about the intoxicated state
                (3) The environmental context
        2. Long-term effects of alcohol
            a. Psychological effects include:
                (1) Loss of mental acuteness
                (2) Erosion of self-esteem
                (3) Disrupted relationships
                (4) Loss of jobs
                (5) Increased abuse of other people
                (6) Increased risk of psychiatric disorders
            b. Physical effects include:
                (1) Ulcers
                (2) Hypertension
                (3) Heart problems

        (4)  Cancer
        (5)  Brain damage
        (6)  Cirrhosis of the liver
        (7)  Malnutrition
        (8)  Memory loss (Korsakoff's psychosis)
        (9)  Delirium tremens (withdrawal symptom)

C.  The development of alcohol dependence
    1.  There is no clear-cut alcohol-dependent personality type
    2.  Most drinkers develop their addiction over a long period of drinking and show increased:
        a.  Blackouts
        b.  Sneaking of drinks
        c.  Morning drinking
        d.  Benders
        e.  Inability to abstain
    3.  Men are more prone to alcohol dependence than women and the sexes show different drinking patterns; *women* are more likely to:
        a.  Start drinking later in life
        b.  Come for help sooner
        c.  Cite a stressful event as the original cause for drinking
        d.  Have an alcohol-abusing spouse or lover
        e.  Drink alone
        f.  Have shorter, less intense drinking bouts
        g.  Combine alcohol with other drugs

III.  Perspectives on alcohol dependence

    A.  The psychodynamic perspective (two viewpoints)
        1.  Alcohol dependence is seen as an oral stage fixation
            a.  Problem drinkers seem to have more oral habits than nondrinkers
            b.  Problem drinkers also seem to have more dependency needs than nondrinkers
        2.  Alcohol dependence is seen as a drive for power (McClelland)
            a.  Alcohol gives the illusion of mastery and life confidence
            b.  Dependency needs may be an attempt to borrow power from others
        3.  Treatment attempts to deal with either:
            a.  Oral stage conflicts from childhood, or
            b.  Ways of gaining power in one's life without the need to drink

    B.  The behavioral perspective (two viewpoints)
        1.  Drinking is motivated by a desire for tension reduction
            a.  Drinking helps one to relax when under stress
            b.  Relaxation reinforces further drinking
            c.  Drinking causes additional problems
            d.  Drinking increases to deal with those problems as well
        2.  Drinking is motivated by a desire to generate pleasant states of mind
            a.  Release of dopamine and norepinephrine may be involved
            b.  Endorphins (natural opiates) are released as well
        3.  Treatment may involve:
            a.  Elimination of drinking behavior by aversive consequences
                (1)  Electric shock consequences
                (2)  Nausea-inducing drugs
            b.  Learning new skills to cope without alcohol
                (1)  Social skills training
                (2)  Relaxation and coping techniques
            c.  Best treatments eliminate drinking *and* train coping

    C.  The cognitive perspective (three viewpoints)
        1.  Drinking behavior is determined by our expectations regarding alcohol
            a.  If one expects beneficial results from drinking, drinking is more likely
            b.  Heavy drinkers seem to expect more from alcohol than light drinkers

265

2. Drinking is reinforced by its ability to dull self-awareness
   a. If self-image is poor, we drink to escape our negative self
   b. Dulling of self-awareness reduces inhibitions, which may result in fun (reinforcing) activities
3. Drinking is a self-handicapping strategy in which self-esteem is maintained by providing an excuse (alcohol) for failures and shortcomings
4. Treatment involves the teaching of more appropriate coping skills and increasing feelings of competence

D. The sociocultural perspective
   1. Higher educational and socioeconomic groups show higher rates of alcoholism
   2. In general, more men abuse alcohol than women, but the gap is closing
   3. Some ethnic groups are more susceptible to alcohol dependence (Native Americans, Latinos, Puerto Ricans, and Irish, especially), but gender and income effects mentioned above tend to override ethnic effects
   4. The more one's religious affiliation encourages drinking control, the less the risk of alcohol abuse
   5. Peer pressure and social norms can be important in determining drinking behavior

E. The biological perspective
   1. Genetic research shows that Asians may have less tolerance for alcohol than Caucasians
   2. Study of adopted sons of alcoholics shows more alcoholism in the children than would be expected by chance
   3. Family and twin studies also show a genetic factor
   4. More than one genetic pattern may be involved and at least one of them (Type 2) may be sex-linked (father-son)
   5. Rat studies show that alcoholism predisposition can be selectively bred
   6. The predisposition may take the form of increased sensitivity to pleasurable effects of alcohol

F. Multimodal treatments
   1. Detoxification (getting off alcohol)
   2. Rehabilitation (getting on with life)
      a. Occupational therapy
      b. Relaxation training
      c. Individual counseling
      d. Family or marriage therapy
      e. Alcohol aversion training (Antabuse)
      f. Support groups (such as Alcoholics Anonymous)
      g. Residential treatment programs

IV. Nicotine dependence

A. Nicotine dependence is the most common form of drug dependence in the U. S.

B. Nicotine is not particularly dangerous psychologically, but is very dangerous physically—it can lead to, among other things:
   1. Lung cancer
   2. Heart disease
   3. Emphysema

C. Recent legislation and social awareness efforts have decreased the use of nicotine in the U. S. from 45 percent of the population in 1954 to 29 percent in 1991

D. Perspectives on nicotine dependence are similar to those on alcoholism
   1. Psychodynamic theorists see it as another form of oral dependency
   2. Behaviorists focus on the reinforcing qualities of smoking (physical and social)
   3. Research on physiological and psychological effects of nicotine indicate that the reason most smokers continue smoking is to avoid withdrawal

4. Treatment is not particularly successful; best results go with:
   a. High intrinsic motivation
   b. High sense of self-efficacy
   c. Good coping skills
   d. Good social support
   e. Nonsmoking peer group

V. Other psychoactive drugs

A. Depressants (CNS downers)
   1. Opiates (opium, its derivatives, or synthetic relatives)
      a. Examples
         (1) Opium (the original opiate)
         (2) Morphine (derived from opium for use as pain killer)
         (3) Heroin (originally thought nonaddictive)
         (4) Methadone (used in heroin treatment)
      b. Effects of heroin
         (1) Pleasant effects are "rush" and feeling of well-being lasting three to five hours
         (2) Negative effects include nausea, tolerance, bad withdrawal
   2. Barbiturates (sedatives)
      a. Examples
         (1) Nembutal
         (2) Seconal
      b. Barbiturates sometimes prescribed as sleeping pills
      c. Often used in suicide attempts
      d. Effects similar to alcohol
      e. Synergistic (multiplying) effect with alcohol
   3. Tranquilizers (T) and nonbarbiturate sedatives (S)
      a. Examples
         (1) Dalmane (S)
         (2) Halcion (S)
         (3) Tranxene (T)
         (4) Librium (T)
         (5) Valium (T)
      b. Effects similar to barbiturates
      c. Dependence typically begins with attempt to deal with sleeping problems or stress
         (1) May result in drug-induced insomnia
         (2) REM sleep deprivation with use
         (3) REM rebound when discontinued

B. Stimulants (CNS uppers)
   1. Amphetamines
      a. Examples
         (1) Benzedrine (amphetamine)
         (2) Dexedrine (dextroamphetamine)
         (3) Methedrine (methamphetamine)
      b. Effects
         (1) High energy
         (2) Sleeplessness
         (3) Loss of appetite
         (4) Autonomic arousal
         (5) Improved motor coordination
         (6) Irritability
         (7) Hostility
         (8) Anxiety
         (9) Confusion
      c. High dosages and continued use pose addiction problems
      d. Effects of amphetamine abuse resemble those of paranoid schizophrenia

2. Cocaine
    a. Available in powder or "crack" forms
    b. Effects
        (1) Euphoria
        (2) Excitement
        (3) Impaired judgment
        (4) Irritability
        (5) Agitation
        (6) Impulsive sexual behavior
    c. Addiction with regular use (faster with crack)
    d. Severe withdrawal symptoms
    e. Cravings may continue indefinitely after use is stopped
3. Caffeine
    a. Effects
        (1) Nervousness
        (2) Excitement
        (3) Rambling thoughts
        (4) Motor agitation
        (5) Insomnia
        (6) Muscle twitches
        (7) Irregular heartbeat
        (8) Flushed skin
        (9) Increased need to urinate
    b. Can cause withdrawal in chronic users when use is stopped
    c. *DSM* refers to caffeine "intoxication," but not to abuse, dependence, or withdrawal

C. Hallucinogens (alter CNS information processing)
    1. Examples
        a. Mescaline
        b. Psilocybin
        c. PCP
        d. LSD
    2. Effects
        a. Changes in sensory perception
        b. Changes in body image
        c. Alterations in time and space perception
        d. Altered states of awareness
    3. "Bad trips" may result in psychologically unstable individuals
    4. Flashbacks of drug experience may occur after use is stopped

D. Marijuana and hashish (minor hallucinogens)
    1. America's most popular illegal drug
    2. Medically useful in cancer and glaucoma therapy
    3. Short-term effects (increase with dosage)
        a. Increased heart rate
        b. Reddening of eyes
        c. Decreased motor coordination and response time
        d. Euphoria
        e. Sensory changes
        f. Alterations in time sense
        g. Relaxed passivity
    4. Long-term effects
        a. Regular use may lead to lower testosterone level, but does not seem to affect sexual functioning of males with well-established sex lives
        b. Clinically nonsignificant impairment of immune system
        c. Possible carcinogens may lead to lung cancer in heavy users
        d. Personality effects are inconclusive

VI. Perspectives on drug dependence

    A. Drugs and brain chemistry
        1. Endorphin theory
            a. Opiates appear to fit neurotransmitter receptors of endorphins (naturally occurring opiates)
            b. Continued use may cause brain to reduce its own production of endorphins, leading to tolerance effects
            c. Ceasing of use results in endorphin/opiate deficit, resulting in withdrawal
        2. Dopamine theory says that drugs stimulate the production of dopamine, which increases reinforcing effects of drug, leading to addiction

    B. Drugs and personality factors
        1. Even though a number of traits have been associated with drug use, there is no one single "drug personality"
        2. Drug use among peers is a good predictor of use in an individual
        3. For adolescents, times of confusion and transition may predict drug use

    C. Drugs and society
        1. Effects of drugs on society include:
            a. Lost work productivity
            b. Drug-related accidents
            c. The spread of AIDS (needles)
            d. Crime (to support a habit)
        2. Legalization of drugs is sometimes suggested as a solution, but many fear this may just increase the problem

    D. Drug rehabilitation
        1. Withdrawal is the first step (detoxification)
        2. Most effective programs take a multifaceted approach
            a. Job skills training
            b. Individual therapy
            c. Family and marriage therapy
            d. Stress management training
            e. Group support
            f. Therapeutic residential communities

    E. Relapse prevention
        1. Relapse rates across all drugs range from 50 to 90 percent
        2. Getting off drugs involves:
            a. Decision and commitment (to quit)
            b. Making the initial change
            c. Maintaining the change
         3. Failure to maintain change can be due to:
            a. Individual (intrapersonal) factors
                (1) Negative emotional states
                (2) Lack of motivation and commitment
                (3) Lack of self-efficacy beliefs
            b. Environmental factors
                (1) Absence of social support
                (2) Exposure to negative environments
            c. Physiological factors
                (1) Withdrawal effects
                (2) Drug cravings
        4. Substituting harmful addictions with positive ones, such as exercise, may also prevent relapse

## KEY TERMS
*The following terms are in bold print in your text. Define them and practice their definitions using the flash cards at the end of the chapter.*

addiction (289)
amphetamines (310)
barbiturates (308)
blood alcohol level (290)
cocaine (310)
delirium tremens (293)
depressant (307)
detoxification (302)
drug-induced insomnia
   (309)

hallucinogens (312)
heroin (307)
methadone (307)
morphine (307)
opiates (307)
opium (307)
psychoactive drug (288)
psychological dependence
   (289)
stimulants (310)

substance abuse (289)
substance dependence (289)
synergistic effect (308)
tolerance (289)
tranquilizers (309)
withdrawal symptoms (289)

*Your text does not list the following terms as formal vocabulary; however, if you don't know what they mean, you will be unable to grasp the concepts of this chapter.*

acupuncture (315)
acute (289)
antecedent (294)
belligerent (292)
concurrently (302)
consequent (294)

corroborated (292)
discordant (301)
extrinsic (306)
in remission (303)
index group (301)
insidious (299)

intrinsic (306)
mandate (288)
proliferation (288)
quell (296)
reverie (307)
sporadic (308)

## IMPORTANT NAMES
*Identify the following persons and their major contributions to abnormal psychology as discussed in this chapter.*

Albert Hoffman (312)      David McClelland (294)      Stanley Schachter (305)

## GUIDED SELF-STUDY

NATURE OF SUBSTANCE DEPENDENCE AND ABUSE

1.  Psychoactive substances are those that _____.

2.  In the past, definitions of drug dependence were divided into two categories: (a)_____

    and (b)_____.  They are no longer separate.  In *DSM-IV*, they now form one

    category called (c)_____.

3.  Fill in the seven *DSM-IV* criteria for substance dependence.  Here are the missing terms to be used:

    **abandonment**          **preoccupation**          **withdrawal**
    **control**                **tolerance**
    **drug-related**          **unintentional**

    a.  _____ with the drug

    b.  _____ overuse

    c.  _____ developed

    d.  _____ symptoms with decreased levels of the substance

    e.  Persistent desire or efforts to _____ drug use

    f.  _____ of social, occupational, or recreational activities

g.   Continued use despite _____ problems

4.  How many of these criteria must be met to allow the diagnosis of psychoactive substance dependence?

5.  If an individual does not meet enough criteria to be diagnosed as substance dependent, yet

"obviously" has a drug-related problem, the diagnosis can be (a)_____.  The text lists four criteria in connection with this:

Failure to take care of major (b)_____

Creates physically (c)_____ situations

Drug related (d)_____ problems

Drug related (e)_____ problems

ALCOHOL DEPENDENCE

6.  Alcohol is a depressant; that means it (a)_____.

b.   If it is a depressant, why do some people perceive that they feel more "up" at a party after a drink?

7.  a.   At what blood alcohol level will mood and social behavior be affected?

b.   What is the blood alcohol level at which a person is considered to be "intoxicated" in all states?

c.   Exactly what does that number mean?

8.  About how much alcohol would it take to raise your blood alcohol to 0.10 percent? (Look up your statistic in Table 12.1).

9.  To determine the answer to the previous question you had to look on the chart which

considered your (a)_____ and your (b)_____.  Your weight

determines how much (c)_____ you have in which to distribute the alcohol.

Your sex must be considered because females have less (d)_____ per pound of body weight in which to dilute the alcohol.

10.  What does Table 12.2 (page 291) indicate could be a really bad outcome for "winners" in an alcohol chug-a-lug (drinking) contest?

11.  Beyond the chemical depression of cortical tissues, what else influences how the person will behave when consuming alcohol?

12. Do you know the dimensions of the alcohol problems in the United States? First, give your best estimate on each of the following statistics. Then look up the correct statistic to see how close your estimate was.

Your guess     Correct data

a. _____     _____ Total alcohol-related cost in 1990

b. _____     _____ Percentage of auto accidents that are alcohol related

c. _____     _____ Percentage of occupied hospital beds filled with alcohol-related illnesses

13. Rank the three major areas of economic loss due to alcohol: (a-most costly to c-least costly)

_____ Motor vehicle accidents
_____ Health problems
_____ Decreased work productivity

14. What are some physical illnesses that habitual overuse of alcohol can cause or aggravate?

15. Babies born to mothers who drank during pregnancy may have a disorder called

(a)_____. Characteristics of this disorder are (b)_____ retardation,

(c)_____ development and a particular pattern of bodily (d)_____.

16. While individuals may follow different paths toward the development of an alcohol addiction, Jellinek's famous study on the development of alcoholism describes a common pattern of behavior. List the order from *a*, the beginning, to *f*, the end.

_____ Benders
_____ Discovering and then relying on the tension-reducing properties of the drug
_____ Experiencing blackouts
_____ Living to drink and drinking to live
_____ Morning drinking
_____ Sneaking drinks

17. What kind of time frame did Jellinek's research indicate most commonly existed around this pattern of decline from heavy drinking to complete defeat?

18. There are people who have serious problems with alcohol, yet they do not drink every day.

This pattern of drinking is called (a)_____ drinking. Individuals can stay sober for

periods of time, then some event will trigger an alcoholic binge or (b)_____.

19. What other behavioral disorder seems to follow the same sequence that Jellinek found in alcoholics?

20. There are predictable differences in behaviors between male and female alcoholics.

a. Women usually begin drinking _____ in their lives.

b. Women are more likely than men to cite a _____ as the beginning of their drinking problems.

c. Women are more likely to be associated with a problem-drinking _____ or _____.

d. Socially, women are more likely to drink _____.

e.  Women are more likely to have a _____ pattern where they combine other

drugs with _____.

PERSPECTIVES ON ALCOHOL DEPENDENCE

21.  Here are the seven perspectives introduced in Chapter One. Mark out the ones that will not be addressed for alcohol dependence.  Are there any new ones added?  (Also, see Hint 2.)

**Psychoanalytic**          **Interpersonal**
**Behavioral**              **Sociocultural**
**Cognitive**               **Biological**
**Humanistic-existential**  **New?** _____

22.  Here are terms for the psychoanalytic perspective on alcoholism:

**control**        **primary**
**fixation**       **unconscious**
**oral**

In psychodynamic theory, the "problem" is always an (a)_____ emotional conflict.  In the case of alcoholism, it has caused fixation in the early oral stage, so the individual is still

trying to cope with needs for (b)_____ gratification.  The alcoholic is still emotionally a young infant who is quite dependent, even to wanting to suck on a bottle.  In contrast to this

dependency resulting from oral (c)_____, another psychoanalytic theory says that alcoholism is a drive for power.  According to this theory people use alcohol trying to gain

(d)_____ over themselves and their world.  These theorists think the drive for power is

the (e)_____ motivation, not merely reaction formation against oral dependence which the other psychoanalytic theorists propose.

23.  The behaviorists explain alcohol abuse as a learned method of anxiety relief.  This is

explained in the (a)_____ model.  This theory fails to explain the increased anxiety that some people experience after drinking.

24.  Here are the terms for the behavioral perspective on alcoholism:

**aversion**                  **elicit**
**respondently**              **problem-solving**
**electric shock or nausea**  **social**
**suppress**                  **stress**

Behavior therapies initially centered on (a)_____ therapy, which involves the individual

being (b)_____ conditioned so that an aversive stimulus such as (c) _____

_____ is paired with alcohol.  Current behavioral treatment programs go beyond

aversion therapy.  Even though aversion therapy works to (d)_____ drinking, it does

not deal with all the stimuli that strongly (e)_____ drinking behaviors.  Behavioral

programs for alcoholism now teach (f)_____ skills and (g)_____

skills to help cope with problems of life.  Relaxation techniques are taught to directly address

bodily (h)_____ reactions.  Alcoholics are taught to recognize cues and situations that lead to drinking, and to practice dealing with these situations without drinking.

Here are the terms for the cognitive perspective in Questions 25 and 26:

| | | |
|---|---|---|
| **restructuring** | **positive** | **thinking** |
| **defeatist** | **recovery** | **thinks** |
| **painful** | **relapse** | **total** |
| **planned** | **self-handicapping** | |

25. The three cognitive theories, of course, focus on how the person (a)_____. The first theory is about (b)_____ expectancies; the second one, about trying to reduce (c)_____ self-awareness; and the third, about setting up a (d)_____ strategy to explain anticipated failures.

26. Therapy from the cognitive view is always based on changing thinking habits. In addition to this cognitive (a)_____, the cognitive therapists address (b)_____ prevention in an aggressive manner. They teach how to deal with inevitable slip ups in the (c)_____ process and even practice (d)_____ relapses. The goal of this approach is still focused on (e)_____ process. They do not want a little slip up to cause (f)_____ thinking and lead the person to have a (g)_____ relapse.

27. The _____ perspective suggests that socioeconomic factors are a significant force in determining alcoholism problems because different rates of alcoholism are seen in different social groups.

28. In the each of the following categories, circle the factor that produces the *highest* risk for alcohol dependency.

   a. Education level:      **Low / Moderate / High**

   b. Economic level:      **Low / Moderate / High**

   c. Ethnic group:      **Latino / Native American / Irish**

   d. Sex:      **Men / Women**

29. Besides religious and cultural affiliations, what is the major predictor of alcohol consumption among adolescents?

30. Here are the terms for the biological perspective for alcoholism:

| | | |
|---|---|---|
| **adolescence** | **genetic** | **quiet-living** |
| **adulthood** | **low** | **reinforcing** |
| **alpha** | **nine** | **sexes** |
| **autonomic** | **ninety** | **stressor** |
| **driving** | **personality** | **two** |
| **father-to-son** | **predisposition** | |

Biological research has demonstrated that a susceptibility to alcoholism is (a)_____. In looking for what is actually inherited, the researchers have found that the children of alcoholics have increased physiological response to alcohol that enhances the (b)_____ effects of alcohol. The actual physiological component may be in the (c)_____ nervous system or perhaps in (d)_____ brain wave activity. This evidence also suggests that there are (e)_____ different patterns for this inheritance of a (f)_____ to alcohol dependence. Type 1 generally begins in (g)_____ and affects both (h)_____ following diathesis-stress predictors; that is, the person is likely to succumb to alcoholism after a major (i)_____. Type 1 seems to be more common in (j)_____ income level groups and among rather (k)_____ people. Type 2 generally begins in (l)_____. It follows a sex-linked pattern: (m)_____. The sons that inherit this pattern are at (n)_____ percent risk. In other words if the father fits this pattern, the son has (o)_____ out of ten chances to also be alcoholic. There is a (p)_____ pattern also associated with Type 2 alcohol dependence: impulsiveness, aggression, risk-taking, brawling, reckless (q)_____ and other criminal behavior.

31. Here are the terms for the multimodal treatment approach:

| | | |
|---|---|---|
| detoxification | peer support | truth |
| fluids | relaxation | understand |
| marital | social | variety |
| nausea | stressors | withdrawal |

Multimodal treatment uses a (a)_____ of therapeutic approaches. First, (b)_____ helps the individual withdraw from physical dependency on alcohol. Medication is used as needed to ease the (c)_____. There is also an emphasis on returning the person to physical health—vitamins and plenty of (d)_____. Once "detox" is complete, problem areas are assessed and treatment addresses the many problem areas in the alcoholic's life: occupational therapy, family and (e)_____ therapy, (f)_____ skills training, problem resolution techniques to reduce existing and/or future (g)_____, and (h)_____ techniques that directly address bodily stress. Involvement in a (i)_____ network such as Alcoholics Anonymous gives the individual opportunities to develop relationships based on (j)_____ and with people who really do (k)_____. Antabuse may help the person's will power against impulsive drinking because (l)_____ occurs if alcohol is consumed within two days after taking Antabuse.

NICOTINE DEPENDENCE

32. Here are the terms for reviewing nicotine dependence:

| | | |
|---|---|---|
| aggressive | heart | paradoxical |
| calming | increasing | physiological |
| cancer | mental | secondhand |
| chewing tobacco | mild | stimulant |
| death | mouth | stress |
| decreased | nicotine | vitamin C |
| elevate | normal | |

Nicotine has a seemingly contradictory effect on the body called a (a)_____ effect. Not only does nicotine elevate blood pressure and heart rate, which is the effect of a (b)_____, but at the same time it has a (c)_____ effect. This effect is not just in the minds of smokers; rats became less (d)_____ when injected with nicotine. Nicotine does not seem to impair (e)_____ functioning; however, once a nicotine level in the blood is established, a drop in that nicotine level does lead to (f)_____ performance. This research finding contradicts the hypothesis that nicotine dependence is perpetuated by a continuing (g)_____ reinforcement effect for the smoker. Schachter's research found that smoking does not calm established smokers nor (h)_____ their moods, nor does nicotine improve their performance over nonsmokers. So basically smokers seem to smoke to maintain blood (i)_____ level just to keep them feeling (j)_____, since habitual use eliminates the initial paradoxical effects of nicotine. Circumstances such as increased (k)_____ intake or (l)_____ exposure, both of which lower blood nicotine levels, lead to increased smoking. This blood nicotine level research indicates (m)_____ addiction. However, on the other, hand smokers do not develop tolerance in which an ever (n)_____ level of nicotine is required to maintain the same level of effect.

Withdrawal symptoms are said to be (o)_____ compared to the physical withdrawal of alcohol. (See Hint 3.) The distinct drawback associated with nicotine use is the possibility of (p)_____ eventually. Cigarette smoking is associated with higher death rates from (q)_____, (r)_____ disease, and other illnesses. Recent evidence has also revealed that inhaling (s)_____ smoke (from someone else's cigarette) is harmful to one's health. Smokeless tobacco such as snuff and (t)_____, is associated with cancer of the throat and (u)_____.

33. From the psychodynamic perspective, the person's unconscious conflicts have caused him/her to become fixated at the _____ stage.

34. Use these terms to review the behavioral perspective on nicotine:

**learned**                                    **sophistication**
**reinforcers**                                **tension**

Behaviorists propose four possible explanations for maintenance of smoking behavior as a

(a)_____ behavior: Stimulant effects of nicotine, pleasure associated with inhaling and

exhaling the smoke, (b)_____ reduction in social situations and/or an enhanced

self-image of (c)_____. Schachter's research that demonstrated that the drug
enhancement effects of nicotine are lost to established smokers contradicts actual physical

effects as (d) _____. Schachter's research demonstrates that smokers smoke to
maintain blood nicotine level to ward off withdrawal effects. See Hints.

35. Use these terms in the following blanks:

**coping**                                     **number**
**extrinsic**                                  **self-efficacy**
**intrinsic**                                  **support**
**motivation**

Here are six factors that affect the likelihood of success in being able to stop smoking:

The individual's (a) _____ level; whether the motivation is (b)_____ (doing it for

yourself) or (c)_____ (doing it to please someone else); the (d)_____ level which
the person experiences; that is, does the person believe he/she can successfully stop smoking;

how many alternative (e)_____ mechanisms the person has as resources; (f)_____

by compliments and encouragements from others; (g)_____ of smokers in one's social
environment.

OTHER PSYCHOACTIVE DRUGS

36. Here are the categories of drugs discussed in this chapter under "Other Psychoactive Drugs."
Match each one to its effects.

**Depressants**                                **Marijuana and hashish**
**Hallucinogens**                              **Stimulants**

a. _____ "Downers"--decrease brain activity

b. _____ "Uppers"--increase brain activity

c. _____ Cause distortions in sensory processes

d. _____ Euphoria, passivity, intensified sensory perceptions

37. List three physiological effects common to all depressant drugs.

a. _____ develops

b. _____ symptoms occur

c. _____ functions in vital organs, such as respiration; death can result

38. The _____ effect in depressant drugs is the cumulative potentiating effect (combined multiplied effect) seen as depressant drugs interact with each other in the body:

$$1 \text{ drug} + 1 \text{ drug} = \text{more than the 2 drugs just added together}$$

For example, alcohol to help you swallow your barbiturate sleeping med could give you four times the effect of either the alcohol or barbiturate alone; you could end up permanently "asleep."

39. When using tranquilizers and nonbarbiturate sedatives, about how long does the individual use the drug before tolerance develops and the dosage needs to be increased to get the same desired effect?
    a. Two days
    b. Two weeks
    c. Two months
    d. Two years

40. Assign the probable order to the following sequence for drug-induced insomnia.

    _____ Habitual use of sleeping aid
    _____ Higher dose of medication required to achieve sleep
    _____ Person takes sleeping aid to avoid bad dreams
    _____ Person tries to stop the medication
    _____ Problem with disrupted, fitful sleep
    _____ REM rebound occurs filled with unpleasant dreams and nightmares
    _____ Use of sleeping aid medication begins

41. Identify to which category of drugs (**Depressant, Stimulant,** or **Hallucinogen**) each of the following belongs:

    Amphetamines—                          Tranquilizers—

    Alcohol—                               Caffeine—

    Opiates—                               Cocaine—

    LSD—                                   Barbiturates—

42. List the source of each of the following drugs.

    Narcotics—                             Cocaine—

    Nicotine—                              Marijuana—

    Caffeine—                              Hashish—

43. Which drug is:

    a. America's most common form of drug dependence?

    b. America's number one drug problem?

    c. America's most popular illicit drug?

    d. America's most widely used illegal narcotic?

44. Amphetamine abuse creates symptoms that resemble those of another serious mental disturbance. What is it?

45. Circle the active ingredient in marijuana and hashish.

CHT　DLS　HCT　LSD　SLD　TCH THC

46. The two consistent physiological effects caused by marijuana and hashish use are

(a)_____ heart rate and (b)_____ of the whites of the eyes.

47. What are four physical effects from long-term use of marijuana?

a.　Reduction of _____ (male sex hormone) in males

b.　Possible suppression of the _____ system which protects the body from disease

c.　Effect of marijuana smoke on the _____—it has 50 percent more carcinogenic hydrocarbons than tobacco smoke

d.　Impaired judgment, apathy, and an existence centered around _____

48. After your experience with the information in this chapter, see how much of a complete drug list by categories and subcategories you can construct from memory. After you've attempted this reality check to see how much you really do know, then add the rest from the answer key so you memorize the listings. See Hint #1.

I'll give you a hint by starting you off with the four major categories of abused drugs. (I count 35 subcategories and names for you to fill in on this chart using the information provided in the text.)

Depressants (4 subcategories,　　　　　　　　Stimulants (4 subcategories,
17 total entries)　　　　　　　　　　　　　　　12 total entries)

Hallucinogens (4 entries)

And the last two?

PERSPECTIVES ON DRUG DEPENDENCE
49. Where do the psychological perspectives stand on the other types of drug abuse besides alcohol?

50. Two theories of brain chemistry are proposed to try to explain drug dependence.

a.　Opiates decrease _____ production, creating a craving for external opiates.

b.　Most drugs of abuse increase _____ activity which has a positive reinforcement effect that the person becomes driven to seek.

51. No single addictive personality characteristic has been found that determines drug abuse and addiction; however, a number of personality traits seem to have some relationship to drug abuse. List at least five.




52. The foremost predictor of drug usage by adolescents is _____.

53. Use these terms for the following blanks:

**opiate**                                          **naltrexone**
**methadone**                                   **withdrawal**

Two drugs, (a)_____ and _____ are possibilities for the treatment of heroin

addiction because they both affect (b)_____ receptor sites.  (c)_____, a synthetic

opiate, is itself highly addicting.  But, (d)_____ does not create the euphoria of heroin,

so it satisfies the addict's craving without enticing others to use it to get high. (e)_____
causes the individual to no longer respond to opiates.  The individual can neither get high on

heroin nor even use it to stave off (f)_____.  Thus, by administering (g)_____
to the person, one eliminates the physiological impact of heroin.

54. What are the current relapse rates in connection with drug addiction?


55. Relapse prevention specialists point to a difference between a lapse and a relapse.  A

(a)_____ does not have to become a full-fledged (b)_____.  A (c) _____ can be
an opportunity for learning, coping, and renewing commitment to recovery.

56. List the three-stage process to change an addictive behavior.

    a.

    b.

    c.

57. Categorize each of the following as possible factors that could lead to drug lapse or relapse according to Schachter's factors: **Intrapersonal, Environmental,** or **Physiological**.

    a.   Angry at spouse—

    b.   Noisy neighbors—

    c.   Fourth of July Beer and Brats celebration—

    d.   Feelings of inadequacy—

    e.   Old army buddies reunion—

    f.   A lot of physical tension—

    g.   Spouse out of town—

## HELPFUL HINTS

1. Ask your instructor what level of detail you need to know about the individual drugs referred to in the chapter. Do you need to know specific brand names and/or their generic names? Is an ability to recognize the names in each category sufficient, or will you have to recall them without prompting?
2. I (SJB) hope by now you are using the overview at the beginning of each chapter to scan the line-up on perspectives for each chapter. I am frequently contrasting those to the list on page 9 of the seven perspectives introduced in Chapter One. My approach here is based on the idea that you are more likely to get where you are going if you have some idea in advance what your destination is. That is why I keep urging you to overview which perspectives are discussed in any one chapter before you begin to wander vaguely through the perspectives with no direction.
3. Death is one possible outcome of alcohol withdrawal if medical support therapies are not available. Perhaps no one has ever died from nicotine withdrawal, but the person in withdrawal is sometimes irritable enough to provoke death threats from friends and co-workers.
4. The explanation of Schachter's findings in behavioral terms is that smoking is maintained by a negative reinforcer. The smoker smokes to escape or to avoid the unpleasant feeling of low blood nicotine level.

## PRACTICE TEST

*Take the following test several times as you study the chapter. Write your answers on a separate sheet of paper and after each attempt, note in the tally box above each question whether your answer was correct or incorrect.*

| 1 | 2 | 3 | 4 |

1. Tolerance to a drug means
   a. you don't need as much to get the same effect.
   b. severe allergic reactions begin to occur.
   c. you need more to get the same effect.
   d. the drug ceases to effect the body at all.

| 1 | 2 | 3 | 4 |

2. In all states, it is illegal to drive with more than _____ blood alcohol level.
   a. 0.01 percent
   b. 0.10 percent
   c. 1.00 percent
   d. 10.0 percent

| 1 | 2 | 3 | 4 |

3. Alcohol is pharmacologically classified as a
   a. depressant.
   b. stimulant.
   c. hallucinogen.
   d. narcotic.

| 1 | 2 | 3 | 4 |

4. From the cognitive point of view, one of the reasons that fights occur more commonly in bars than at private parties is that
   a. it is acceptable to drink larger quantities in bars.
   b. "nicer" people tend to avoid bars and attend private parties.
   c. people have lower expectations for "proper" behavior in bars.
   d. the atmosphere of bars tends to draw a higher proportion of males.

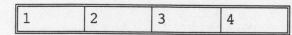

5. In developing alcohol dependence, which of the following applies more to females?
   a. Begins drinking earlier, solitary drinker, drinks longer before treatment
   b. Starts drinking later, solitary drinker, shorter drinking time before treatment
   c. Starts drinking later, solitary drinker, unlikely to use alcohol with other drugs
   d. Social drinker, likely to use alcohol with other drugs, drinks to deal with stress

6. George used to drink when exams were coming up or when a term paper was due. Now George drinks whenever anything goes wrong in his life and he is having trouble controlling it. How might a behaviorist account for his *initial* drinking?
   a. Power needs
   b. Low self-esteem
   c. Childhood dependency needs
   d. Tension reduction

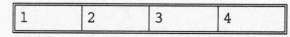

7. A psychodynamic therapist might say that George's problem in Question 6 is
   a. an avoidance learning situation.
   b. repressed hostility against his parents.
   c. an anal retentive personality.
   d. fixation in the oral stage.

8. Which of the following has the greatest risk of becoming a problem drinker?
   a. An Italian farmer
   b. A conservative Protestant female librarian
   c. A Native American college student in a fraternity
   d. A poorly educated Orthodox Jewish shopkeeper

```
| 1 | 2 | 3 | 4 |
```

9. Which of the following is most true of alcohol treatment programs?
   a. They need to have strong follow-up components after detoxification.
   b. They are most successful if tied to a single psychological theory.
   c. They are generally more successful than programs treating other mental disorders.
   d. They need to be led by recovering alcoholics if they are to achieve solid reputations.

```
| 1 | 2 | 3 | 4 |
```

10. Which is true of "multimodal" treatment programs?
    a. They are mainly biological in orientation.
    b. They are generally the least effective approach.
    c. They have largely been replaced by behavior therapy.
    d. They attack a problem from a variety of angles.

```
| 1 | 2 | 3 | 4 |
```

11. The psychoactive ingredient in tobacco is
    a. nicotine.
    b. caffeine.
    c. mescaline.
    d. THC.

| 1 | 2 | 3 | 4 |

12. Which of the following does *not* fit with the others?
   a. Morphine
   b. Heroin
   c. Methadone
   d. Cocaine

| 1 | 2 | 3 | 4 |

13. When drug combinations show a "synergistic" effect, it means that they
   a. cancel each other out.
   b. have opposite effects that make nervous system response unpredictable.
   c. multiply their effects and produce a very strong reaction.
   d. require larger and larger doses to get the same effect.

| 1 | 2 | 3 | 4 |

14. Cocaine is to the coca plant as THC is to the
   a. opium poppy.
   b. LSD mushroom.
   c. cannabis plant.
   d. coffee bean.

| 1 | 2 | 3 | 4 |

15. Repeated doses of sedatives as a sleeping aid can cause
   a. Korsakoff's syndrome.
   b. drug-induced insomnia.
   c. delirium tremens.
   d. formication.

| 1 | 2 | 3 | 4 |

16. Which of the following is *not* a stimulant?
   a. Cocaine
   b. Dexedrine
   c. Nicotine
   d. Mescaline

| 1 | 2 | 3 | 4 |

17. Which of the following is true of marijuana?
   a. It is a fairly powerful hallucinogen.
   b. It may impair sexual functioning in sexually inexperienced teens.
   c. It biochemically leads to a craving for stronger drugs.
   d. It has been linked to AIDS in its effects on the immune system.

| 1 | 2 | 3 | 4 |

18. Which of the following is true of endorphins?
   a. They are stimulants related to amphetamines.
   b. They are the active ingredients in marijuana.
   c. They are a part of natural brain chemistry.
   d. They are a class of hallucinogenic drugs.

| 1 | 2 | 3 | 4 |
|---|---|---|---|

19. Which of the following is the best predictor of drug use among teens?
    a. A genetic history of alcoholism on the mother's side
    b. Low socioeconomic status and poor education
    c. A lack of organized recreational activities and employment
    d. Peer pressure and life stress

| 1 | 2 | 3 | 4 |
|---|---|---|---|

20. With regard to personality factors predicting drug dependency, the text reports that
    a. there is no one single key personality trait.
    b. a tendency toward manic disorders is seen in most cases.
    c. most addicts tend to have IQs under 90.
    d. almost all addicts are extreme introverts.

## ANSWERS
### Self-Study Exercise

1. alter one's psychological state (288)
2. a. psychological
   b. physiological
   c. psychoactive substance dependence (289)
3. a. preoccupation
   b. unintentional
   c. tolerance
   d. withdrawal
   e. control
   f. abandonment
   g. drug-related (289)
4. Any three (289)
5. a. substance abuse
   b. role responsibilities
   c. dangerous
   d. legal
   e. social or interpersonal (289)
6. a. slows activity starting in the higher brain centers first and moving downward
   b. The first things that are depressed are a person's (cortical) inhibitions (292).
7. a. 0.05
   b. 0.10 percent (291)
   c. 1/1000 of your blood is alcohol (290)
8. Your own findings from Table 12.1 (291)
9. a and b. weight and sex
   c. mass
   d. fluid (290-291)
10. Death (If a person gets enough alcohol into his/her system to raise his/her blood alcohol level to 0.35 to 0.40 percent, he/she will die. Yes, it has happened (291).
11. Aside from the brain's lowered activity level, the person will play out the expectations he/she has about what the alcohol is "supposed" to do to behavior (292).
12. a. $121 billion (not million) (290)
    b. Fifty (291)
    c. Forty (290)
13. a. Decreased work productivity
    b. Health problems
    c. Motor vehicle accidents (290)
14. Stomach ulcers, hypertension, heart failure, cancer, cirrhosis of the liver, brain damage, and malnutrition, leading to Korsakoff's psychosis (292-293)
15. a. fetal alcohol syndrome
    b. mental
    c. delayed
    d. malformations (290)
16. a. Discovering and then relying on the tension-reducing properties of the drug
    b. Experiencing blackouts
    c. Sneaking drinks
    d. Morning drinking
    e. Benders
    f. Living to drink and drinking to live (293)

17. 12 to 18 years (293)
18. a. spree
    b. bender (293)
19. Compulsive gambling (293)
20. a. later
    b. stressful event
    c. spouse or lover
    d. alone or with someone close to them
    e. polydrug, alcohol (293)
21. Two perspectives from Chapter One are not covered--Humanistic-existential and Interpersonal. Also, the multimodal treatment approach is added; it combines ideas and techniques from the other perspectives (9, 287, 302).
22. a. unconscious
    b. oral
    c. fixation
    d. control
    e. primary (294)
23. a. tension-reduction (305-306)
24. a. aversion (295)
    b. respondently (57, 295)
    c. electric shock or nausea (295)
    d. suppress
    e. elicit
    f. problem-solving
    g. social
    h. stress (295)

25. a. thinks
    b. positive
    c. painful
    d. self-handicapping (296)

26. a. restructuring
    b. relapse
    c. recovery
    d. planned
    e. thinking
    f. defeatist
    g. total (297)
27. sociocultural (297)
28. a. High education level
    b. High socioeconomic level
    c. American Indian
    d. Men (297-298)
29. Peer-group behavior (299-300)
30. a. genetic (301)
    b. reinforcing (302)
    c. autonomic (301)
    d. alpha (302)
    e. two
    f. predisposition
    g. adulthood
    h. sexes
    i. stressor
    j. low
    k. quiet-living
    l. adolescence
    m. father-to-son
    n. ninety
    o. nine
    p. personality
    q. driving (301)
31. a. variety
    b. detoxification
    c. withdrawal
    d. fluids
    e. marital
    f. social
    g. stressors
    h. relaxation
    i. peer support
    j. truth
    k. understand
    l. nausea (302-303)

32. a. paradoxical
    b. stimulant
    c. calming
    d. aggressive
    e. mental
    f. decreased
    g. physiological
    h. elevate
    i. nicotine
    j. normal
    k. vitamin C
    l. stress
    m. physiological
    n. increasing
    o. mild
    p. death
    q. cancer
    r. heart
    s. secondhand
    t. chewing tobacco
    u. mouth (303-305)
33. oral (instead of sucking on a bottle, the sucking is now on a cigarette) (305)

34. a. learned
    b. tension
    c. sophistication
    d. reinforcers (305)

35. a. motivation
    b. intrinsic
    c. extrinsic
    d. self-efficacy
    e. coping
    f. support
    g. number (306)

36. a. Depressants (307)
    b. Stimulants (310)
    c. Hallucinogens (312)
    d. Marijuana and hashish (313)

37. a. Tolerance
    b. Withdrawal
    c. Lowered or decreased (307)

38. synergistic (308)
39. "b" Two weeks (309)
40. 7,3,6,4,1,5,and 2 (309-310)
41. Amphetamines—Stimulant (310)    Tranquilizers—Depressant (309)
    Alcohol—Depressant (292)         Caffeine—Stimulant (311)
    Opiates—Depressant (307)         Cocaine—Stimulant (310)
    LSD—Hallucinogen (312)           Barbiturates—Depressant (308)
42. Narcotics—opium (from the opium poppy plant), opium derivatives, and synthetic drugs
        designed to copy the effects of opium (307)
    Nicotine—tobacco (304)
    Caffeine—found in coffee, tea, cola drinks, cocoa, and chocolate (312)
    Cocaine—from the coca plant (310)
    Marijuana—leaves of the cannabis plant (313)
    Hashish—resin from the cannabis plant (313)
43. a. Nicotine (304)
    b. Alcohol (290)
    c. Marijuana (313)
    d. Heroin (308)
44. Paranoid schizophrenia (310)
45. THC, which stands for delta-9, tetrahydrocannabinol (313)
46. a. accelerated
    b. reddening (313)
47. a. testosterone
    b. immune
    c. lungs
    d. drug use (314)

48. Depressants:                     Stimulants:
        Alcohol                          Nicotine
        Narcotics                        Caffeine
            Opium                            Coffee
            Morphine                         Tea
            Heroin                           Cola drinks
            Methadone                        Cocoa
        Sedatives                            Chocolate
            Barbiturates                 Cocaine
                Nembutal                 Amphetamines
                Seconal                      Benzedrine
            Nonbarbiturates                  Dexedrine
                Dalmane                      Methedrine
                Halcion              Hallucinogens:
        Tranquilizers                    Mescaline
            Librium                      Psilocybin
            Valium                       PCP
            Tranxene                     LSD
                                     Marijuana and hashish

49. Abuse of any drug, regardless of which one, is considered in the same way as all other drug
    abuse. The alcohol perspectives are applicable to all drugs of abuse (315).
50. a. endorphin
    b. dopamine (315-316)

286

51. Impulsivity
    Sensation-seeking
    Nonconformity
    Feelings of alienation from society
    Lack of respect for social values
    Depressive tendencies
    Dependent behavior
    Focus on short-term goals at the expense of long-term goals
    Low frustration tolerance
    Sense of heightened stress
    History of childhood antisocial behavior (316-317)
52. drug use by one's peers (316)
53. a.  methadone and naltrexone      e.  Naltrexone
    b.  opiate                        f.  withdrawal
    c.  Methadone                     g.  naltrexone (316-317, 319)
    d.  methadone
54. 50 to 90 percent (319)
55. a.  lapse
    b.  relapse
    c.  lapse (327)
56. a.  Decision and commitment
    b.  Initial change
    c.  Maintaining the change (319)
57. a.  Intrapersonal                 e.  Environmental
    b.  Environmental                 f.  Physiological
    c.  Environmental                 g.  Environmental (319)
    d.  Intrapersonal

## Practice Test

| | | | | | |
|---|---|---|---|---|---|
| 1. | c | (289) | 11. | a | (304) |
| 2. | b | (291) | 12. | d | (310) |
| 3. | a | (292) | 13. | c | (308) |
| 4. | c | (292) | 14. | c | (313) |
| 5. | b | (293) | 15. | b | (309) |
| 6. | d | (295) | 16. | d | (312) |
| 7. | d | (294) | 17. | b | (314) |
| 8. | c | (298) | 18. | c | (315) |
| 9. | a | (302) | 19. | d | (316-317) |
| 10. | d | (302) | 20. | a | (316) |

# CONCEPT MAP
## 12.1

Fill out the boxes marked with question marks (?) with the concepts or words you think belong there. Suggested answers are on a following page.

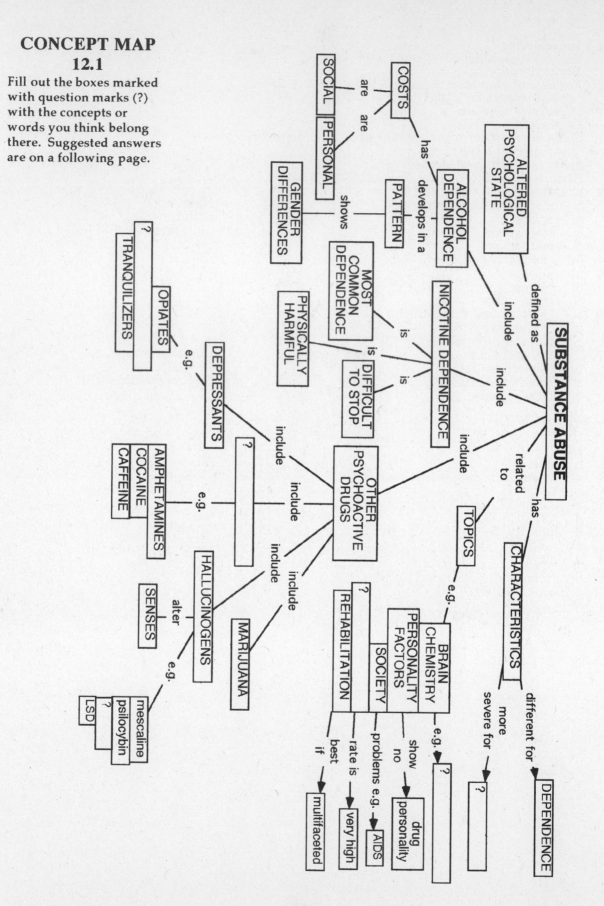

288

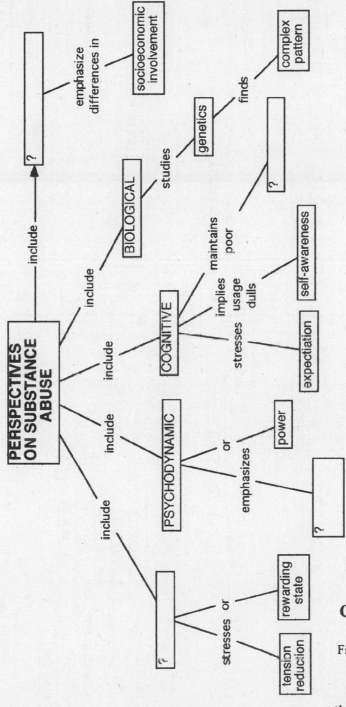

**CONCEPT MAP 12.2**

Fill out the boxes marked with question marks (?) with the concepts or words you think belong there. Suggested answers are on a following page.

# CONCEPT MAPS

## 12.1 & 12.2

The suggested answers are shown in *italics*.

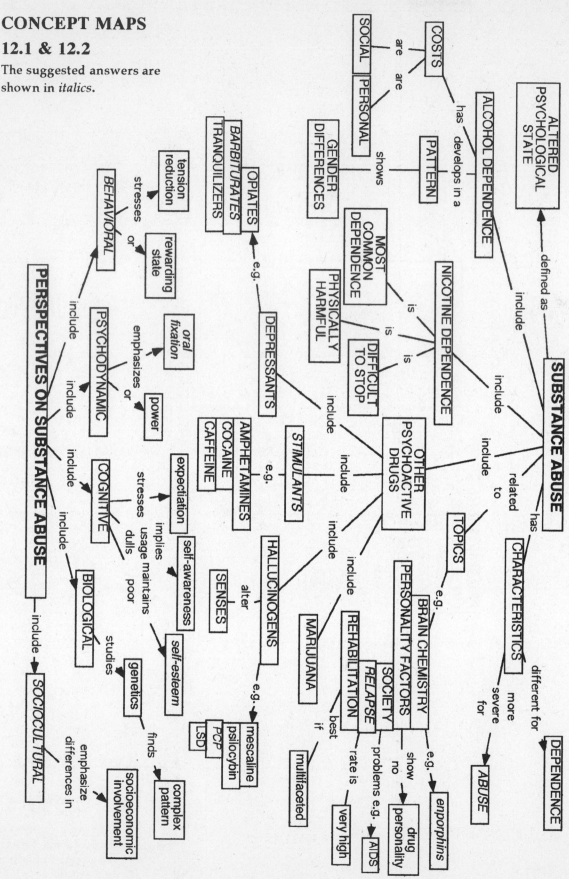

| 12.1 addiction | 12.8 detoxification | 12.15 opium |
|---|---|---|
| 12.2 amphetamines | 12.9 drug-induced insomnia | 12.16 psychoactive drug |
| 12.3 barbiturates | 12.10 hallucinogens | 12.17 psychological dependence |
| 12.4 blood alcohol level | 12.11 heroin | 12.18 stimulants |
| 12.5 cocaine | 12.12 methadone | 12.19 substance abuse |
| 12.6 delirium tremens | 12.13 morphine | 12.20 substance dependence |
| 12.7 depressant | 12.14 opiates | 12.21 synergistic effect |

# DEFINITIONS (Cut out on the lines to use as Flash Cards)

| | | |
|---|---|---|
| 12.15 <br><br> Chemically active substance derived from the poppy plant | 12.8 <br> Medical treatment for alcoholism that consists of getting the alcohol out of the alcoholic's system and seeing him or her through the withdrawal symptoms. | 12.1 <br> Physiological dependence on a drug in which the drug use has altered the body's chemistry to the point where its "normal state" is the drugged state |
| 12.16 <br><br> A drug that alters one's psychological state | 12.9 <br> Pattern of disrupted slumber without any deep sleep; created by prolonged barbiturate use | 12.2 <br> A group of synthetic stimulants, the most common of which are Benzedrine, Dexedrine, and Methedrine |
| 12.17 <br> The nonphysiological dimension of drug abuse, characterized by the abuser's growing tendency to center his or her life on the drug | 12.10 <br> Class of drugs that act on the central nervous system and cause distortions in sensory perception | 12.3 <br> A group of powerful sedative drugs used to alleviate tension and bring about relaxation and sleep |
| 12.18 <br> Class of drugs that provide energy, alertness, and feelings of confidence | 12.11 <br> An addictive narcotic derived from morphine | 12.4 <br> Amount of alcohol in the bloodstream, expressed in terms of the number of milligrams of alcohol per 100 ml of blood |
| 12.19 <br> Pattern of maladaptive drug use that is less severe than dependence | 12.12 <br> Synthetic chemical that satisfies the craving for narcotics but does not produce narcotic euphoria | 12.5 <br> Natural stimulant, made from the coca plant, that produces feelings of euphoria and omnipotence |
| 12.20 Pattern of severe maladaptive drug use; includes 3 of following: preoccupation, overuse, tolerance, withdrawal, attempts to control, reduced social involvement, health problems | 12.13 <br> An addictive narcotic derived from opium by isolating its ingredients | 12.6 Severe withdrawal symptom experienced by alcoholics when their blood alcohol level drops suddenly; known as the DTs, consists of trembling, perspiring, disorientation, and delusions |
| 12.21 <br> Combined impact of two drugs, which is greater than the effect of either drug when taken alone | 12.14 <br> Chemically active substance derived from the opium poppy; one of the narcotics | 12.7 <br> Drug that acts on the central nervous system to reduce pain, tension, and anxiety, to relax and disinhibit, and to slow down intellectual and motor reactivity |

**CHAPTER TERMS** (Cut out on the lines to use as Flash Cards)

| | | |
|---|---|---|
| 12.22 <br><br> **tolerance** | 12.29 | 12.36 |
| 12.23 <br><br> **tranquilizers** | 12.30 | 12.37 |
| 12.24 <br><br> **withdrawal symptoms** | 12.31 | 12.38 |
| 12.25 *(You may fill in the remaining boxes with names, terms and definitions from text and lecture)* | 12.32 | 12.39 |
| 12.26 | 12.33 | 12.40 |
| 12.27 | 12.34 | 12.41 |
| 12.28 | 12.35 | 12.42 |

# DEFINITIONS (Cut out on the lines to use as Flash Cards)

| 12.36 | 12.29 | 12.22 Physiological condition in which the usual dosage of a drug no longer provides the desired "high" |
|---|---|---|
| 12.37 | 12.30 | 12.23 Group of drugs that produce mild calm and relaxation; they can be addictive and have side effects; most popular are Tranxene, Librium, and Valium |
| 12.38 | 12.31 | 12.24 Temporary psychological and physiological disturbances resulting from the body's attempt to readjust to the absence of a drug |
| 12.39 | 12.32 | 12.25 *(You may fill in the remaining boxes with names, terms and definitions from text and lecture)* |
| 12.40 | 12.33 | 12.26 |
| 12.41 | 12.34 | 12.27 |
| 12.42 | 12.35 | 12.28 |

## Chapter 13

# Sexual and Gender Identity Disorders

*LEARNING OBJECTIVES*
*By the time you are finished studying this chapter, you should be able to:*

**DEFINING SEXUAL DISORDERS**
1. Discuss the difficulties involved in defining sexual disorder, making specific reference to the issue of homosexuality as an example (324-325).

**SEXUAL DYSFUNCTION**
2. Describe three categories of sexual dysfunction grouped by phases of the sexual response cycle (326-329).
3. Define the sexual pain disorders, dyspareunia and vaginismus (329).

**PERSPECTIVES ON SEXUAL DYSFUNCTION**
4. Discuss the psychodynamic perspective on sexual dysfunction, stressing the role of the Oedipal conflict (329-331).
5. Explain the learning-based view of sexual dysfunction as proposed by the behavioral and cognitive perspectives (331-333).
6. Summarize the components of a multifaceted treatment approach to sexual dysfunction (333 334).
7. List and describe possible organic causes of sexual dysfunction, and describe treatments for dysfunction based on the biological perspective (334-335).

**PARAPHILIAS**
8. Define paraphilias according to *DSM-IV* (335).
9. List eight paraphilias and give a brief description of each (335-341).
10. Discuss how each of the paraphilias might present problems in living for the client or interfere with the lives or rights of others (335-341).

**GENDER IDENTITY DISORDER (TRANSSEXUALISM)**
11. Define gender identity disorder and distinguish it from homosexuality (341).
12. Discuss treatment for gender identity disorder, including sex reassignment surgery (341-342).

**INCEST AND RAPE**
13. Define incest and rape, profile the typical perpetrators of these crimes, and discuss the psychological impact on the victims (342-345).

**PERSPECTIVES ON THE PARAPHILIAS AND GENDER IDENTITY DISORDERS**
14. Explain the psychodynamic perspective on these problems, with special emphasis on the role of Oedipal fixation (346).
15. Explain the behavioral and cognitive understanding of these disorders, and give examples of treatment strategies (354-356).
16. Explain the biological view of and treatment for these disorders (348-349).

# CHAPTER OUTLINE

I. Defining sexual disorders

    A. While interest in sex is biologically based, attitudes on how sex is expressed in behavior are determined by culture (learning)
        1. Extreme attitudes in Inis Beag and Mangaia
        2. Publicly stated cultural norms are not always adhered to in private life

    B. Cultural norms on sexuality change with time
        1. What was shocking in the 1950s is not shocking today
        2. Homosexuality is more accepted today than years ago and is no longer considered a disorder by the *DSM*
        3. This shows how the mental health profession generally does not impose standards of behavior on a culture, but reflects and functions within that culture

II. Sexual dysfunction

    A. Criteria for labeling
        1. Must cause marked distress or interpersonal difficulty
        2. Must persist over time (isolated incidents do not qualify)
        3. Does not apply to young people still establishing their sex lives

    B. Forms of sexual dysfunction
        1. Sexual desire disorders
            a. Hypoactive sexual desire disorder (lack of interest in sex)
            b. Sexual aversion disorder (disgust, repulsion, anxiety)
                (1) Many people with this problem were molested as children, and if so,
                (2) It can be seen as a variation on posttraumatic stress disorder
        2. Sexual arousal disorders
            a. Male erectile disorder
            b. Female sexual arousal disorder
        3. Orgasmic disorders
            a. Premature ejaculation (male orgasm too soon)
            b. Male orgasmic disorder (orgasm delayed or absent)
            c. Female orgasmic disorder (delayed or absent)
        4. Sexual pain disorders
            a. Dyspareunia (painful intercourse)
            b. Vaginismus (vaginal muscle spasms)

    C. Categorizing the forms of dysfunction
        1. Lifelong dysfunction (has always been there)
        2. Acquired dysfunction (develops after some normal functioning has been demonstrated)
        3. Generalized dysfunction (present in all sexual situations)
        4. Situational dysfunction (present in only certain situations)

    D. Prevalence of sexual dysfunction
        1. 4 to 20 percent of men with erectile disorder
        2. 3 to 10 percent of men with orgasmic disorder
        3. 5 to 15 percent of women with orgasmic disorder
        4. One third of men have premature ejaculation

III. Perspectives on sexual dysfunction

    A. The psychodynamic perspective: Oedipal conflict
        1. Male dysfunctions are generally seen as failure to separate psychologically from mother
        2. Female dysfunctions are generally seen as a result of penis envy
        3. Psychoanalysis has had some good success in dealing with sexual dysfunction, but the process is long and expensive

B.  The behavioral and cognitive perspectives
    1.  Based on the respondent conditioning of negative experiences to the sexual situation, such as:
        a.  Performance anxiety
        b.  Shame
        c.  Pain
        d.  Fear of discovery
    2.  Treatment consists of deconditioning the negative reactions and reconditioning more pleasurable ones
        a.  Sensate focusing in nonthreatening situations
        b.  Paradoxical instruction to relieve performance anxiety
        c.  Autoerotic training (masturbation)
        d.  Improving communication
    3.  The cognitive perspective attempts to reveal and change attitudes and beliefs that interfere with normal sexual functioning
        a.  Performance anxieties
        b.  Negative body attitudes
        c.  Goodness or badness of sexual expression

C.  Multifaceted treatment assumes multiple causes of dysfunction, both in the present and in the past
    1.  Kaplan: Immediate and remote causes
        a.  Immediate causes are here-and-now problems
            (1)  Performance anxiety
            (2)  Overconcern about partner's pleasure
            (3)  Poor technique
            (4)  Poor communication
            (5)  Marital conflict
        b.  Remote causes are holdovers from previous learning
            (1)  Infantile needs
            (2)  Deep-seated guilt
            (3)  Oedipal struggles
        c.  Therapy consists of both direct intervention into immediate causes and insight therapy directed at remote causes
    2.  Systems theory focuses on interlocking needs in a relationship, often power and control issues

D.  The biological perspective
    1.  There are a variety of organic causes for sexual dysfunction
        a.  Diabetes
        b.  Heart disease
        c.  Kidney disease
        d.  Alcoholism
        e.  Medical treatment side effects
        f.  Infections and diseases of the sexual organs
        g.  Hormone and/or neurotransmitter imbalances
        h.  Neurological impairment
    2.  Treatments
        a.  Vascular dilation agents to promote erections
        b.  Aphrodisiac drugs (yohimbine)
        c.  Penile prostheses
    3.  Often, the problem may be both psychological *and* biological, each requiring its own treatment

IV.  Paraphilias

    A.  Males affected disproportionately

    B.  Pathology is determined *not* by whether or not the behavior is *ever* done, but by the extent to which it harms others and/or interferes with the living of a normal life

C.  Forms of paraphilias
    1.  Fetishism
        a.  Reliance on inanimate objects as major focus for gratification
        b.  May not be a problem unless partner is disturbed
    2.  Transvestism
        a.  Gratification through cross-dressing
        b.  Does not imply other mental disturbances, but may result in marital problems
        c.  Thought to be rare, but apparent rarity may be a result of acting out only in private
        d.  Not to be confused with homosexuality
    3.  Exhibitionism
        a.  Gratification through observing others' reaction to sexual display
        b.  Most exhibitionists are not dangerous
        c.  Typical exhibitionist is sexually insecure
    4.  Voyeurism
        a.  Gratification through clandestine sexual observation of others
        b.  Most voyeurs are harmless and sexually insecure
    5.  Sadism and masochism
        a.  Sadism is gratification through inflicting pain on others
            (1)  May indicate a basic interaction between aggressive and sexual predispositions with aggression expressed sexually
        b.  Masochism is gratification through experiencing of pain
        c.  Sadists and masochists may find one another and form a sadomasochistic relationship
        d.  May involve heterosexual or homosexual relationships
        e.  Much variation in "style" and severity
    6.  Frotteurism is gratification through touching or rubbing against a nonconsenting person
    7.  Pedophilia (child molestation)
        a.  Ten to 15 percent of children have been sexually victimized, mostly female
        b.  Most pedophiles are related to their victims
        c.  Many pedophiles have themselves been molested
        d.  Preference molesters do it as a sexual way of life
        e.  Situational molesters act on impulse and find their actions repulsive
        f.  Molestation is rarely reported by victim because of fear or guilt
        g.  Victims may suffer a variety of long-term psychological and behavioral problems

D.  Gender identity disorder
    1.  Gender identification with opposite sex
    2.  Do not confuse with homosexuality or transvestism
        a.  Since the individual identifies with the opposite biological sex, sexual attraction to the same biological sex is *not* seen as homosexual in the true sense
        b.  Since the individual identifies with the opposite biological sex, dressing in the clothes of that sex is not seen as transvestism
    3.  Some clients resort to biological sexual reassignment to make the body match the mind

E.  Incest
    1.  Sex with immediate relatives
    2.  Prohibitions against nuclear incest exist in all known cultures
    3.  Rate of occurrence in population from 7 to 17 percent
    4.  Perpetrators may be hyperreligious and in a troubled marital relationship
    5.  Victims may suffer a variety of long-term psychological and behavioral problems

F.  Rape
    1.  Sex with a nonconsenting partner
    2.  Many rapists are sexually insecure
    3.  Many rapes are more motivated by aggression than sexual desire
    4.  High incidence of rape may be result of the culture's frequent pairing of sex and violence

5. Cognitive variables influencing likelihood of committing rape
   a. Motivation (sexual or aggressive arousal)
   b. Disinhibition (hostility, antisocial characteristics)
   c. Opportunity (mainly situational factors)
6. Many rapes are not reported because of fear or guilt on the part of the victim
7. Victims may suffer a variety of long-term psychological and behavioral problems

V. Perspectives on paraphilias

  A. The psychodynamic perspective
    1. Polymorphous perversity may be the cause (a tendency to find many forms of sexual expression pleasurable)
    2. Fixation in the pregenital stages allows polymorphous perversity to carry over into adulthood
    3. The form a paraphilia takes is symbolically related to the person's specific developmental problem
    4. Therapy consists of working through the underlying unconscious conflicts
    5. Therapy for paraphilias is often unsuccessful because of lack of motivation and coerced participation in treatment

  B. The behavioral perspective
    1. Paraphilias are respondently conditioned, sexual arousal being paired with stimuli characteristic of the various paraphilias
    2. Therapy involves unlearning old responses and relearning new ones
      a. Stimulus satiation "wears one out" on deviant stimuli and encourages response to appropriate stimuli
      b. Covert sensitization creates an aversive response to inappropriate stimuli
      c. Shame aversion therapy creates embarrassment for deviant behavior
      d. It is not sufficient to eliminate undesirable behavior, but desirable responses must be learned to replace them

  C. The cognitive perspective
    1. Deviant attitudes are the cause of deviant behavior
    2. Deviant beliefs are challenged in treatment and replaced with more productive ones

  D. The neuroscience perspective
    1. Emphasis is on search for possible biological causes for deviant behavior
    2. Treatment may include hormone therapy to alter sex drive

## KEY TERMS
*The following terms are in bold print in your text. Define them and practice their definitions using the flash cards at the end of the chapter.*

acquired dysfunction (329)
covert sensitization (347)
dyspareunia (329)
exhibitionism (335)
female orgasmic disorder (329)
female sexual arousal disorder (329)
fetishism (335)
frotteurism (335)
gender identity disorder (341)
generalized dysfunction (329)
hypoactive sexual desire disorder (327)
incest (343)
lifelong dysfunction (329)
male erectile disorder (329)
male orgasmic disorder (329)
masochism (335)

paraphilias (335)
pedophilia (335)
premature ejaculation (329)
rape (343)
sadism (335)
sadomasochism (339)
sexual aversion disorder (327)
sexual dysfunctions (327)
shame aversion therapy (347)
situational dysfunction (329)
spectator role (331)
stimulus satiation (347)
transsexualism (341)
transvestism (335)
vaginismus (329)
voyeurism (335)

*Your text does not list the following terms as formal vocabulary; however, if you don't know what they mean, you will be unable to grasp the concepts of this chapter.*

| | | |
|---|---|---|
| aberrations (336) | covertly (340) | overtly (340) |
| acquiesce (340) | cunnilingus (343) | pejorative (327) |
| adversarial (344) | disinhibition (345) | predilection (337) |
| clandestine (335) | ecstasy (329) | prosthesis (335) |
| clitoris (330) | engorge (335) | sensate focus (331) |
| collaboration (332) | fellatio (343) | *sine qua non* (336) |
| collusion (341) | gregarious (324) | supplanted (324) |

## IMPORTANT NAMES
*Identify the following persons and their major contributions to abnormal psychology as discussed in this chapter.*

| | |
|---|---|
| Havelock Ellis (324) | Richard von Krafft-Ebing (324) |
| Virginia Johnson (327) | The Marquis de Sade (339) |
| Helen Singer Kaplan (333) | William Masters (327) |
| Alfred Kinsey (343) | Leopold von Sacher-Masoch (339) |

## GUIDED SELF-STUDY

DEFINING SEXUAL ABNORMALITY

1. As you will notice, in this chapter I will not ask you to note your own personal experiences to facilitate your memory for chapter information. What do you think is the explanation for this obvious change in approaching the chapter?

Here are the terms for the blanks of Questions 2 and 3:

| | | |
|---|---|---|
| **hobby** | **orgasm** | **vaginal** |
| **minimalist** | **puberty** | |
| **opposite** | **reproduce** | |

2. Western hemisphere cultures have very specific ideas about what is "normal" sexual

   interaction between people: penile-(a)_____ intercourse with a member of the

   (b)_____ sex to reach (c)_____.

3. The Irish island (Inis Beag) people have a (a)_____ attitude toward sex. Their sexual

   activity seems to be the absolute minimum to (b)_____ the species. The Polynesian

   island (Mangaia) people seem to have sex as their (c)_____ for everyone past the age of

   (d)_____. How you personally would "characterize" these vastly different attitudes will

   depend on your own ideas about sex. (Some of my (GGB) students think the Mangaian attitude is shocking; others want to know how to get there.)

4. What do the differences between these two societies' sex practices point out most clearly?

Here are the terms for Questions 5 - 10.

| | | |
|---|---|---|
| **actually doing** | **harmless** | **phase** |
| **communication** | **information** | **response** |
| **desire** | **limited** | **safety** |
| **excitement** | **orgasm** | **techniques** |
| **gratification** | **performance** | |

5. The 1953 Kinsey reports indicated that social norms were much more (a)_____ than what people were (b)_____.

6. The current American approach to sexuality is interest in sexual (a)_____ with particular interest in (b)_____ for achieving gratification. AIDS has now added (c)_____ to the concerns in sexual behavior.

7. Here are some of the benefits of this current approach to sexuality.

   a. Increased flow of _____ about sex

   b. Better _____ between partners on sexual matters

   c. Dispelled anxiety and guilt over _____ sexual practices

8. The down side of the new focus in sexuality is anxiety about one's sexual _____.

SEXUAL DYSFUNCTION

9. Sexual dysfunction means that what one does is not working out satisfactorily. There is either pain or repeated failure in the sexual response cycle. Failure problems are grouped according to the (a)_____ of the sexual (b)_____ cycle in which they occur.

10. Here are descriptions of the three phases of the sexual response cycle that Kaplan used to organize sexual dysfunctions. Give the name of each phase.

   a. _____ The want-to

   b. _____ Physiological responses of want-to

   c. _____ Moving to completion on the want-to and the physiological arousal

11. Name the problems seen in the desire stage. (No hints this time)

   a. _____ Lack of interest in sex

   b. _____ Negative emotions about sex

12. What are the difficulties seen in the arousal stage?

   a.

   b.

13. In the third and last stage, orgasm, the male problem is likely to be one of timing; the most common sexual dysfunction for men is (a)_____. For women, the problem will be delayed or absent orgasm, termed (b)_____, although in the U. S., orgasm is a "never" for (c)_____ percent of women and "rarely" to "sometimes" for (d)_____ percent.

14. What was Freud's opinion about female orgasms? What kinds? What was the "normal" desirable one?

15. What is the current attitude on female orgasms, neurologically and psychologically?

16. Use these terms to complete the following blanks:

**dyspareunia**               **vaginal**                              **women**
**men**                      **vaginismus**

The two sexual dysfunctions involving pain are dyspareunia and vaginismus. (a)_____,

pain during intercourse, can be complaint of either gender, but is seen more frequently in

(b)_____ than (c)_____. (d)_____, a female difficulty that causes

intercourse to be painful or impossible, is caused by (e)_____ muscle spasms that
prevent penetration.

Here are the terms for the following discussion of sexual dysfunction (17 and 18):

**acquired dysfunction**                        **lifelong dysfunction**
**distress**                                   **quite normal**
**generalized dysfunction**                   **situational dysfunction**
**interpersonal**

17. Along with categorizing sexual dysfunction according to phase of sexual response cycle, there
    are other critical elements of information to complete the diagnosis. If a person has always

    had the problem since sexual activity began, the problem is termed (a)_____;
    however, if the person functioned satisfactorily for a time and then developed the problem, the

    diagnosis is (b)_____. Also, one needs to note whether the problem occurs in all
    sexual circumstances or just specific types of circumstances. If it happens all the time, it is

    called (c)_____; however, if it happens only in certain kinds of circumstances, it

    diagnosed as (d)_____.

18. The term "sexual dysfunction" is applied **ONLY** to sexual problems that persist over time.

    Occasional, random episodes of sexual failure are (a)_____. Also whatever the person's

    sexual response cycle is is not an issue unless it causes that individual (b)_____ or

    (c)_____ difficulty.

19. List at least five reasons that occasional, random episodes of sexual failure can
    happen.
    a.

    b.

    c.

    d.

    e.

20. Why, when discussing sexual dysfunction, does a distinction need to be made between
    individuals who are fairly inexperienced sexually and those that have established regular
    patterns of sexual activity?

21. Use these phrases to complete the following explanation of how one insignificant sexual failure can be magnified to make disaster!

**it does**                    **one random**                    **performance**
**no**                         **one failure**

One episode of sexual "failure" can lead to future failure due to (a)_____ anxiety.  A

person can develop significant sexual problems that started out as (b)_____ episode of

sexual "failure" that really should have been of (c)_____ significance.  However, once there is

(d)_____ experience, the person is so afraid another failure is going to happen that

(e)_____.

PERSPECTIVES ON SEXUAL DYSFUNCTION

22. Psychodynamic theory says one develops mature sexuality only after he/she has resolved his

(a)_____ complex (Electra for women), which is the issue of being in love with the

parent of the opposite sex during the (b)_____ stage of psychosexual development.  Female

orgasmic disorder is also seen as continued penis envy, also in the (c)_____ stage.

23. Behaviorism explains how one failure can lead to another through learning.  When someone is anxious about failure, he/she can stop enjoying the experience of sex and adopt what is called

the (a)_____ role.  To learn to get back into normal sexual function (b)_____

focus is used.  It is sexual "petting" exercises with no (c)_____ allowed.  It gets

the couple in touch with (d)_____ experiences without pressure to perform sexually.

24. For whom is sensate focus likely to be disturbing?

25. Paradoxical instruction aims at getting the (a)_____ outcome from what "seems" to be the desired outcome.  Paradoxical instruction tends not to work on patients that

(b)_____ that it is being used.

26. What is the goal of cognitive therapy in dealing with sexual dysfunction?

27. Complete these thoughts and attitudes that can lead to problems in sexual expression.  Here are the phrases you need:

**A person**                   **Letting**                    **Wondering**
**Good girl**                  **Right**

a.  _____ and wrong behaviors

b.  _____ -bad girl dichotomy

c.  _____ must be aroused to begin any sexual exchange

d.  _____ if one looks attractive to one's partner

e.  _____ one's mind wander to nonsexual topics

303

28. Complete these statements about the activities and goals of a multifaceted treatment program for sexual dysfunction. Here are the terms to use:

**exercises**         **issues**         **reassurances**
**inform**         **performance**         **stimulation**

a. Symptom directed _____

b. Exploration of cognitive and relationship _____

c. Activities that _____ and instruct

d. Emotional support through _____ from therapists

e. Increase couple's range of sexual _____

f. Lowering of _____ demands

29. Mark each of the following as to whether it is an **immediate** or **remote** cause for sexual dysfunction according to Kaplan.

a. _____ Deep-seated guilt
b. _____ Intrapsychic conflicts about infantile needs
c. _____ Lack of communication between partners
d. _____ Poor technique
e. _____ Marital conflict
f. _____ Overconcern about pleasing one's partner
g. _____ Performance anxiety
h. _____ Unresolved Oedipal struggles

Here are the terms to complete the blanks for Questions 30 and 31. One of them is used twice.

**before**         **needs**         **unconscious**
**combination**         **payoffs**
**immediate**         **resistance**

30. Kaplan suggests a (a)_____ of therapeutic techniques to address immediate and remote problem areas. First, direct therapy is used to address (b)_____ causes; however, just (c)_____ success is reached, it is typical for unresolved conflicts to flood in, causing anxiety and (d)_____ to further progress. At this point some psychodynamic exploration and interpretation to help the patient gain some insight into his/her (e)_____ is required so that direct therapy techniques can again become effective.

31. The systems approach contends that sexual dysfunction usually has an important, though unsuspected, role in maintaining the couple's relationship. Systems theorists expect to encounter (a)_____ as they start to work with sexual issues between their clients (a couple). They do an analysis of the relationship as a system of interlocking (b)_____. They must discover what the secret (c)_____ are for each of the areas of dysfunction. If the systems therapist tries to remove the dysfunctions without seeing that the needs of each individual are met in a satisfactory manner, emotional chaos within the couple will result.

32. From the biological perspective, what is a primary question about sexual dysfunctions?

33. List five physical problems that can cause erectile dysfunction.

a.                                          d.

b.                                          e.

c.

34. List four physical problems that can cause female dyspareunia.

a.                                          c.

b.                                          d.

35. What are some more subtle organic problems that could be present in some cases of sexual dysfunction where there is no known physical cause?

36. What does NPT "stand for"? How does it help?

## PARAPHILIAS

37. With regard to gender differences, paraphilias are far more common among (a)_____. Most are almost exclusively found in (b)_____.

38. In most of the paraphilias the problem is _____.

39. List what brings sexual gratification in each of the following deviations.

a. Fetishism:

b. Transvestism:

c. Exhibitionism:

d. Voyeurism:

e. Sadism:

f. Masochism:

g. Frotteurism:

h. Pedophilia:

40. What is a common difficulty seen in men who are transvestites?

41. What are the two sex offenses most often reported to the police?

a.                                          b.

42. How physically dangerous are typical exhibitionists and voyeurs (beyond the psychological trauma they may inflict on their victims)?

43. Here are the terms to complete the blanks about the typical exhibitionists:

**masculinity**　　　　　　　　　　　　　　　**puritanical**
**masturbation**　　　　　　　　　　　　　　　**inadequacy**

The typical exhibitionist is likely to be a shy, submissive, immature man who has very

(a)_____ ideas about sex, particularly about (b)_____. He may experience

feelings of social or sexual (c)_____ and have serious doubts about his (d)_____.

44. When dealing with an episode of exhibitionism, what are some other factors that may need to be considered as possible explanations?


45. Select the correct answer. An exhibitionist is the most likely to be sexually gratified when exposing himself if the victim reacts with
    a. indifference.
    b. anger and scorn.
    c. shock and dismay.
    d. sexual arousal her/him self.

46. What is the more realistic portrait of a pedophile instead of the mythological "dirty old man" from Somewhere Else? Circle the most common profile.

    Age:　　　　　　　　　　20　30　40　50　60　70
    Marital status:　　　　　Single / Married / Divorced
    Parental status:　　　　 Has children / Has none
    Relation to victim:　　　Known / Unknown to the victim

Use these terms in the blanks for the next two questions about pedophiles.

**anger or accusation**　　　　　　　　　**other children**
**closely related**　　　　　　　　　　　**repeated episodes**
**cooperated**　　　　　　　　　　　　　**too shy**
**counter**　　　　　　　　　　　　　　**violence or penetration**
**most comfortable**

47. There are at least four possible reasons for why a person becomes a pedophile:

    a. Arrested emotional development, so that the individual is _____ relating to a child

    b. _____ to establish adult sexual relationships, so turns to children as substitutes

    c. Due to early sexual experience with _____, the individual may have fixated on children and still experiences arousal to children

    d. The perpetrator was molested as a child, and now replays the scene as the adult in the

       control role to _____ the feelings of being the helpless child victimized

48. Complete these five factors that contribute to the psychological damage done to a child by a molester:

    a. If there are _____ over time

    b. If _____ is involved

    c. If the molester is _____ to the child (particularly father or stepfather)

306

d.  If the child feels he/she _____ in any way

e.  If disclosure is met by parental _____ at the child

49. According to Diana Russell's survey of women in the San Francisco area, what relatives were most likely to commit incest?  Mark the order for the four following relations from 1 (most likely) to 4 (less likely).

_____  Brothers
_____  Fathers
_____  First cousins
_____  Uncles

Use these terms and phrases for the blanks in the Questions 50 and 51:

**aggressor-controlling**          **justifiable**
**antisocial**                     **moralistic**
**force**                          **rejection**
**fundamentalist religious**       **unsatisfactory**

50. The typical incestuous father is likely to be a man who limits his extramarital sexual contact

to his daughters; he is likely to be highly (a)_____ and devoutly attached to

(b)_____ doctrines.  His relationship with his wife is (c)_____.

51. Give five reasons why a man might engage in rape even if there were some potentially willing female in the environment.

a.  A timid, submissive male with grave doubts about his masculinity may rape to avoid

risking _____.

b.  _____ personalities just follow their impulses at another's expense.

c.  Some men must use _____ as the prerequisite for sexual arousal.

d.  Victims of child abuse may want to be in the _____ role.

e.  Normal men may be culturally indoctrinated to link sex and violence and may believe

rape is _____ under some circumstances.

52. Use these terms to complete these blanks about coercive sex:

**adversarial**        **opportunity**        **want to be raped**
**disinhibiting**      **stereotyped**        **women**
**motivation**         **tolerant**
**normal**             **twenty-six (26)**

Men who were the most likely to engage in coercive sex had common lines of thinking.  Their

pattern of thinking had certain themes: (a)_____ ideas about sex roles; male-female

relationships as fundamentally (b)_____ relationships; the idea that (c)_____ are

responsible for preventing rape; the rape "myth" that women unconsciously (d)_____;

these men are also more aggressive and more (e)_____ of aggression.  Since many rapists

are found to be (f)_____ men with no particular psychological abnormality and with

307

adequate sexual relationships, a cultural explanation is strongly suggested: The culture

socializes men toward a sexual predator role. This is evidenced by the finding that (g)_____

percent of college men interviewed admitted having attempted to force sexual intercourse on
women who were actively resisting the assault. A combination of three variables is suggested

as a predictor of who will rape: Someone who has (h)_____, (i)_____ factors

which tend to just augment the primary motivation, and then (j)_____.

53. The transsexual's problem is not one of object of attraction, but rather one of (a)_____.
Transvestites get a sexual thrill from dressing in clothes of the opposite sex while

transsexuals cross-dress because that clothing seems (b)_____ to them. The first sexual

reassignment surgeries (sex change operations) were done in the (c)_____. By 1977,

(d)_____ Americans had had the surgery. The current estimated rate per year in the

United State is (e)_____.

PERSPECTIVES ON THE PARAPHILIAS

Use these terms to answer Questions 54, 55, and 56:

castration                              Oedipal
fixation                                polymorphous perverse
model                                   respondent conditioning

54. As with the psychodynamic perspective on sexual dysfunction, the psychodynamic perspective

on paraphilias is explained by (a)_____ in the (b)_____ stage. The psychodynamic
perspective explains the variation seen in sexually deviant behaviors as the result of

psychosexual immaturity. Freud said that children are (c)_____; that is, they
get sexual (sensual) pleasure from many different kinds of stimulation. Ultimately,
paraphilias move the person away from actual sexual intercourse (coitus), which is very

threatening to a male with (d)_____ anxiety.

55. The simplest behavioral learning mechanism can readily explain sexual deviance. What is it?

56. Bandura points out that parents may knowingly or unknowingly _____ deviant sexual
behavior for their children.

57. Use these terms to complete the blanks describing behavioral therapy:

arousal                 interrupt               shame
avoid                   satiation               temporary
follow through          sensitization

Behavioral programs for paraphilia are multifaceted. Treatment begins by steps to get

the deviant behavior under (a)_____ control. Behavioral techniques will then be

employed to eliminate the deviant (b)_____ response. Three of these techniques are

stimulus (c)_____, covert (d)_____, and (e)_____ aversion. Then, relapse is prevented by teaching the person to (f)_____ situations that put them at risk for the

deviation, showing the person how to (g)_____ the chain of event that leads to commission of the offense, and by persuading the person that having the impulse does not

mean that one must (h)_____ by committing the act.

58. Write in the name of the perspective on paraphilias that fits these descriptive phrases.

a. _____     "Objectification" of victims

b. _____     Is associated with castration anxiety

c. _____     Myths say that women want to be raped

d. _____     Involves early respondent conditioning

e. _____     Involves modeling of deviant sexual behavior

f. _____     Involves fixation in early Oedipal stage

59. Use these terms to complete the biological perspective:

**antiandrogen**                **plethysmography**
**antidepressants**             **testosterone**

Biological research into the causes of paraphilias has been inconclusive. However, one

treatment that has been provided by the biological perspective is the use of (a)_____ drugs

which decrease the level of (b)_____, a hormone essential for male sexual function.

Another biological technique is the penile (c)_____ to see if a man experiences arousal to children. This test does not always work, but does offer some information. Also

(d)_____ give some relief to those whose deviant patterns are reactions to shame and guilt.

## HELPFUL HINTS

1. I have heard students indicate that they assume homosexuals are pedophiles. This is an incorrect assumption. Homosexuality and pedophilia are unrelated topics except that pedophiles can be heterosexual, homosexual, or bisexual. The vast majority of pedophiles are men, and girls are twice as likely to be molested as boys. That makes pedophiles more likely to be heterosexual than homosexual (349).
2. For those of you who are uninformed on the subject, baby boys sometimes have erections; it's a perfectly normal autonomic nervous system arousal. It does not mean they are going to grow up to be "perverts." Little boys engaging in any exciting activity may experience some degree of erection.

*Take the following test several times as you study the chapter. Write your answers on a separate sheet of paper and after each attempt, note in the tally box above each question whether your answer was correct or incorrect.*

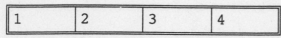

1. Which of the following is the most accurate?
   a. Kinsey found that most people tend to follow closely the sexual norms established by society.
   b. *DSM-IV* defines masturbation as a psychologically damaging practice.
   c. *DSM-IV* includes all forms of homosexual behavior under the heading of sexual deviance.
   d. Different cultures vary greatly in what they consider normal sexual behaviors and attitudes.

2. Sexual dysfunction is
   a. another term for male impotence.
   b. a problem that prevents a person from enjoying sex.
   c. a term used only for biogenic sex problems.
   d. an indicator of homosexual tendencies.

| 1 | 2 | 3 | 4 |

3. According to Kaplan, inability to have an erection is a sexual _____ disorder.
   a. desire
   b. arousal
   c. orgasmic
   d. resolution

| 1 | 2 | 3 | 4 |

4. Which of the following is an orgasmic disorder?
   a. Premature ejaculation
   b. Dyspareunia
   c. Erectile disorder
   d. Vaginismus

| 1 | 2 | 3 | 4 |

5. What is the difference between a generalized and a situational dysfunction?
   a. Generalized means under all circumstances; situational means it depends on conditions.
   b. Generalized means lifelong; situational means acquired.
   c. Generalized means either sex; situational means male.
   d. Generalized means learned; situational means biogenic.

| 1 | 2 | 3 | 4 |

6. An arousal disorder that has developed recently as a result of stress from impending final exams would be described as
   a. lifelong.
   b. dyspareunic.
   c. acquired.
   d. deviant.

| 1 | 2 | 3 | 4 |

7. The psychodynamic perspective on sexual dysfunction sees most difficulties as resulting from unresolved problems in the _____ stage.
   a. oral
   b. anal
   c. phallic
   d. genital

| 1 | 2 | 3 | 4 |

8. One aspect of Masters and Johnson's treatment for dysfunctions is called "paradoxical instruction." This involves
   a. telling the clients to avoid some aspect of sexual activity in the hope that reduction in performance anxiety will make it more likely to happen.
   b. telling the clients to reverse their sex roles in order to better experience what the other person is feeling.
   c. encouraging a lot of sexual experimenting in order to reduce the desire for other less acceptable behaviors.
   d. instructions given by a pair of doctors together in order to decrease doubts and increase hopeful expectations.

| 1 | 2 | 3 | 4 |

9. Recent research has indicated that
   a. there is a clear difference between vaginal and clitoral orgasms in the female.
   b. women have more satisfactory sexual experiences if they can manage to avoid clitoral contact during intercourse.
   c. sixty percent of the female population does not achieve orgasm.
   d. the manner of achieving orgasm says little or nothing about the normality of a woman's sexual experience.

| 1 | 2 | 3 | 4 |

10. Norm and Vera decide to seek help for their faltering sex life. They enroll in a two-week program involving a medical workup, behavior modification, and couple counseling on sexual attitudes and communication skills. They are enrolled in a
    a. psychodynamic treatment program.
    b. multifaceted treatment program.
    c. Havelock Ellis Sexual Workshop.
    d. Differential Diagnostic Therapy Program.

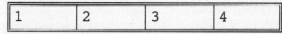

11. When systems theorists speak of the "function of dysfunction," they are referring to
    a. the biological problem underlying the dysfunction.
    b. the repressed superego component of the dysfunction.
    c. the social attitudes about sex that the client is responding to.
    d. the role the dysfunction plays in larger relationship issues.

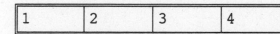

12. One of *DSM-IV*'s two criteria for *non-paraphilic* sexuality is that
    a. the behavior does not violate social norms.
    b. sexual desire is focused only on members of the opposite sex.
    c. the focus of attraction should be a consenting adult.
    d. the behavior is not illegal where the person lives.

13. Arnold has the habit of going about the house nude with the curtains open. He feels sexual excitement at the idea of being at the window just as the lady next door passes by. Arnold may be classified as a(n)
    a. fetishist.
    b. exhibitionist.
    c. transvestite.
    d. transsexual.

14. The lady who lives next door to Arnold in the previous question plans her activities so she can secretly watch Arnold in his house. She would be a(n)
    a. masochist.
    b. frotteurist.
    c. voyeur.
    d. exhibitionist.

15. Which of the following is true of gender identity disorder?
    a. It is another term for transvestism.
    b. It is a variety of fetishism.
    c. It is an early stage of homosexuality.
    d. It is a case of being in a body that doesn't match one's mental sex.

| 1 | 2 | 3 | 4 |
|---|---|---|---|

16. The typical male exhibitionist
    a. may have serious doubts about his own masculinity.
    b. is advertising for a sex partner in socially unacceptable ways.
    c. is usually happily married and has several children.
    d. simply does not grasp the social inappropriateness of his behavior.

| 1 | 2 | 3 | 4 |
|---|---|---|---|

17. In cases of pedophilia, the victim is most often molested by
    a. a known sex offender.
    b. an acquaintance or relative.
    c. a male with a history of homosexual contacts.
    d. the parent of the same sex.

| 1 | 2 | 3 | 4 |
|---|---|---|---|

18. Generally, psychological treatment for sexual deviants
    a. is complicated because many patients have no choice about seeking treatment.
    b. clearly works best when a psychodynamic approach is used.
    c. has a better success rate as compared to treatment for sexual dysfunction.
    d. is now limited to those whose behavior is "ego dystonic."

| 1 | 2 | 3 | 4 |
|---|---|---|---|

19. According to your text, many rapes are the result of
    a. marital discord and jealously.
    b. our cultural mixing of sex and aggression.
    c. glandular disturbances in the perpetrator.
    d. a desire to return to a "mother figure."

| 1 | 2 | 3 | 4 |
|---|---|---|---|

20. The current position of the mental health profession on homosexuality is that
    a. all homosexuals are candidates for psychotherapy.
    b. homosexuality validates the concept of polymorphous perversity.
    c. only "ego dystonic" homosexuals are candidates for treatment.
    d. homosexuality as such is not pathological and is not listed in the *DSM*.

## ANSWERS
### Self-Study Exercise

1. We have a very strong cultural norm that says we do not publicize the details of our sexual experiences (*unless* they have been with famous people—movie stars, politicians, or royal families. Then you can tell all and make big money!)  If I asked you questions as I have in some of the other chapters, this study guide would need an X-rating.
2. a. vaginal
   b. opposite
   c. orgasm (324)
3. a. minimalist
   b. reproduce
   c. hobby
   d. puberty (325)
4. Sex drive is inborn, but how it is acted upon is determined by the society (325).
5. a. limited
   b. actually doing (325)
6. a. gratification
   b. techniques (326)
   c. safety (327)
7. a. information
   b. communication
   c. harmless (327)
8. performance (327)
9. a. phase
   b. response (327)
10. a. Desire (327)
    b. Excitement (329)
    c. Orgasm (329)
11. a. Hypoactive sexual desire disorder
    b. Sexual aversion disorder (327-328)
12. a. Erectile disorder (men)
    b. Female sexual arousal disorder (women) (329)
13. a. premature ejaculation
    b. inhibited female orgasm
    c. 5 to 15
    d. 30 (329)
14. There were two kinds—clitoral and vaginal.  According to Freud, the vaginal orgasm was the "normal" psychologically mature one (330).
15. Neurologically, all orgasms are the same, regardless of what stimulation elicits them.  If a woman finds her sexuality satisfying, then she has no reason to seek professional help looking for "the normal" female pattern (330).
16. a. Dyspareunia
    b. women
    c. men
    d. Vaginismus
    e. vaginal (329)
17. a. lifelong dysfunction
    b. acquired dysfunction
    c. generalized dysfunction
    d. situational dysfunction (329-330)
18. a. quite normal
    b. distress
    c. interpersonal (329)
19. a. Fatigue
    b. Illness
    c. Emotional upset
    d. Mental distraction
    e. Too much to drink (That is something else psychoactive depressant drugs take down besides higher cortical functions.) (329)
20. Contrary to myths, sexual expertise does not just come naturally to men or women. Until skills have been perfected, there are likely to be performance difficulties and anxieties that practice will eventually eliminate.  Remember when your parent would tell you to practice, practice, practice in order to get a thing right—well, they were right! (329)

21. a. performance        d. one failure
    b. one random        e. it does (330)
    c. no
22. a. Oedipal (330)        c. phallic (32)
    b. phallic (32)
23. a. spectator        c. intercourse
    b. sensate        d. sensory (331)
24. Victims of rape or incest may experience "flashbacks" or panic in sensate focus exercises. They need help to deal with their victimization before the current sexual problems can be addressed (331).
25. a. opposite
    b. understand, or are aware (332)
26. As always, the cognitive perspective sets out to discover the thoughts and attitudes a person holds. In this particular chapter, it will be thoughts and beliefs that the person holds about sexuality and how they influence that individual's sexual response and interactions (332).
27. a. Right        d. Wondering
    b. Good girl        e. Letting (333)
    c. A person
28. a. exercises        d. reassurances
    b. issues        e. stimulation
    c. inform        f. performance (334)
29. a, b, and h are remote cause. All others are immediate causes (333).
30. a. combination        d. resistance
    b. immediate        e. unconscious (333-334)
    c. before
31. a. resistance        c. payoffs (334)
    b. needs
32. Is it organic or is it psychological? There is still much debate about the underlying causes of sexual dysfunctions. Researchers are currently considering that perhaps the causes are not either-or, but a very intricate pattern of both (334).
33. a. Diabetes        d. Alcohol problems
    b. Heart disease        e. Medication side effects (334)
    c. Kidney disease
34. a. Vaginal infections
    b. Ovarian cysts
    c. Lacerations or scar tissue resulting from childbirth
    d. Hormonal deficiencies (334)
35. Hormonal deficiencies, neurological impairment, or low levels of neurotransmitters are all possibilities (334).
36. Nocturnal penile tumescence. Since men have erections during REM sleep cycles several times a night, checking to see if the penis is physiologically working is a simple matter (334).
37. a. males
    b. males (336)
38. the object of attraction (335)
39. a. Fetishism—inanimate object or bodily part to exclusion of person as a whole
    b. Transvestism—dressing in clothes of opposite sex
    c. Exhibitionism—exposing one genitals to an unwilling viewer
    d. Voyeurism—clandestine viewing of body parts or sexual activity without the consent of those being viewed
    e. Sadism—inflicting pain on others
    f. Masochism—experiencing pain or humiliation oneself
    g. Frotteurism—touching and rubbing a nonconsenting person
    h. Pedophilia—sexual contact with children (335)
40. Marital problems if the cross-dressing is discovered (337)
41. Exhibitionism and voyeurism (338)
42. Typically not dangerous, *but* ten percent of child molesters started out as exhibitionists, eight percent of rapists began as exhibitionists (338), and ten to 20 percent of voyeurs go on to rape the women they peep at (339).
43. a. puritanical        c. inadequacy
    b. masturbation        d. masculinity (338)
44. Schizophrenia, psychomotor epilepsy, senile brain deterioration, or mental retardation (338)

45. "c" (338)
46. A man in his thirties or forties, married with children of his own, and who is acquainted with the victim and/or the victim's family (340)
47. a. most comfortable          c. other children
    b. too shy                    d. counter (341)

48. a. repeated episodes          d. cooperated
    b. violence or penetration    e. anger or accusation (341)
    c. closely related
49. Most likely uncles, then first cousins, after that fathers and then brothers (343)
50. a. moralistic                 c. unsatisfactory (343)
    b. fundamentalist religious
51. a. rejection                  d. aggressor-controlling
    b. Antisocial                 e. justifiable (344-345)
    c. force
52. a. stereotyped                f. normal (345)
    b. adversarial                g. 26 (344)
    c. women                      h. motivation
    d. want to be raped           i. disinhibiting
    e. tolerant (334)             j. opportunity (345)

53. a. gender identity (341)      d. 2,500
    b. normal                     e. 1000 (342)
    c. 1930's
54. a. fixation                   c. polymorphous perverse
    b. Oedipal                    d. castration (346)
55. Respondent conditioning. Whatever accidentally gets paired with sexual arousal during an early experience of arousal may become a conditioned stimulus for arousal in the future (346). Read Helpful Hint 2.
56. model (347)
57. a. temporary                  e. shame
    b. arousal                    f. avoid
    c. satiation                  g. interrupt
    d. sensitization              h. follow through (347-348)

58. a. Cognitive (348)            d. Behavioral (346)
    b. Psychodynamic (346)        e. Behavioral (347)
    c. Cognitive (348, 344)       f. Psychodynamic (346)

59. a. antiandrogen              c. plethysmography
    b. testosterone (348)        d. antidepressants (349)

## Practice Test

| | | |
|---|---|---|
| 1. d (325) | 11. d (334) |
| 2. b (327) | 12. c (335) |
| 3. b (329) | 13. b (338) |
| 4. a (329) | 14. c (338) |
| 5. a (329) | 15. d (341) |
| 6. c (329) | 16. a (338) |
| 7. c (330) | 17. b (340) |
| 8. a (332) | 18. a (346) |
| 9. d (330) | 19. b (345) |
| 10. b (333) | 20. d (326) |

# CONCEPT MAP 13.1

Fill out the boxes marked with question marks (?) with the concepts or words you think belong there.  Answers suggested by the author are on a following page.

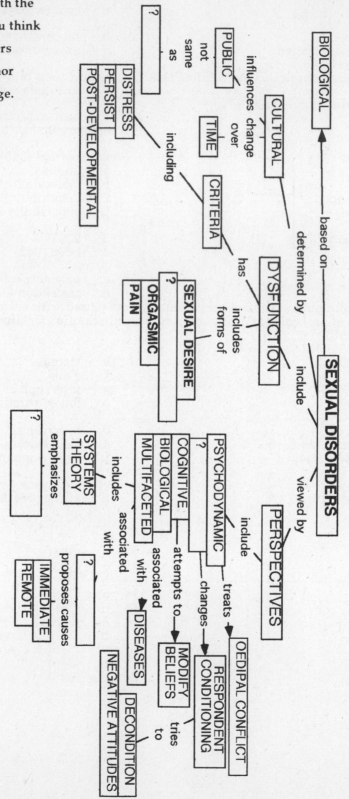

316

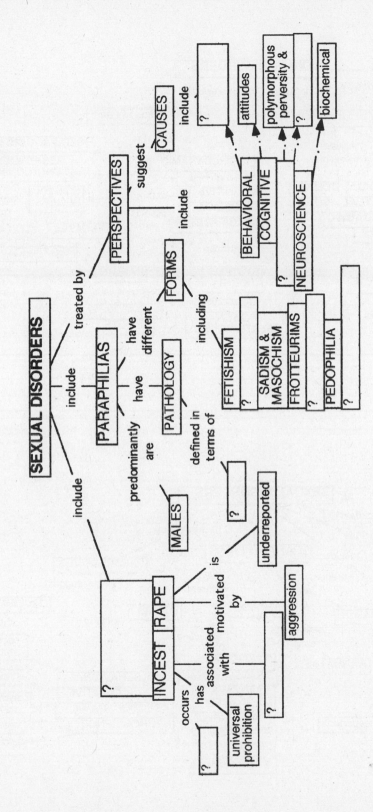

**CONCEPT MAP 13.2**

Fill out the boxes marked with question marks (?) with the concepts or words you think belong there.  Answers suggested by the author are on a following page.

CAUSES —include→ ?

attitudes

polymorphous perversity & ?

biochemical

PERSPECTIVES —suggest

—include→ BEHAVIORAL  COGNITIVE  NEUROSCIENCE  ?

FORMS

SEXUAL DISORDERS —treated by

—include→ PARAPHILIAS —have different

have predominantly are—MALES

PATHOLOGY —defined in terms of

including→ FETISHISM  SADISM & MASOCHISM  FROTTEURIMS  PEDOPHILIA  ?  ?

?

—include→ ?  INCEST  RAPE

is—underreported

motivated by—aggression

occurs —universal prohibition

has associated with—?

?

317

## CONCEPT MAP 13.1

The suggested answers are
shown in *italics*.

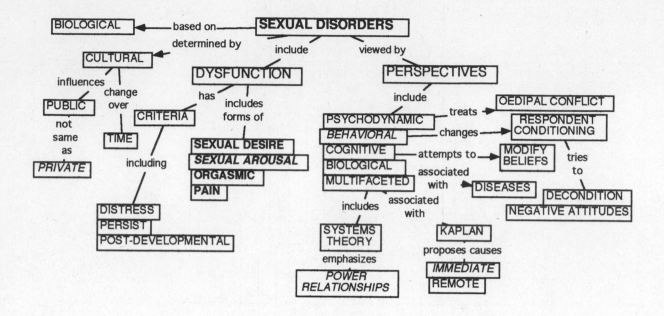

## CONCEPT MAP 13.2

The suggested answers are
shown in *italics*.

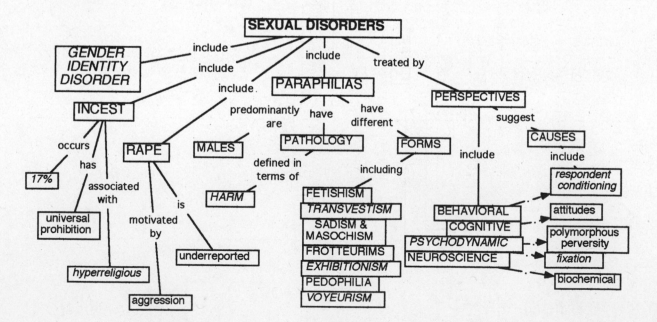

**CHAPTER TERMS** (Cut out on the lines to use as Flash Cards)

| | | |
|---|---|---|
| 13.1 **acquired dysfunction** | 13.8 **frotteurism** | 13.15 **masochism** |
| 13.2 **covert sensitization** | 13.9 **gender identity disorder** | 13.16 **paraphilias** |
| 13.3 **dyspareunia** | 13.10 **hypoactive sexual desire disorder** | 13.17 **pedophilia** |
| 13.4 **exhibitionism** | 13.11 **incest** | 13.18 **premature ejaculation** |
| 13.5 **female orgasmic disorder** | 13.12 **lifelong dysfunction** | 13.19 **rape** |
| 13.6 **female sexual arousal disorder** | 13.13 **male erectile disorder** | 13.20 **sadism** |
| 13.7 **fetishism** | 13.14 **male orgasmic disorder** | 13.21 **sadomasochistic** |

# DEFINITIONS (Cut out on the lines to use as Flash Cards)

| | | |
|---|---|---|
| 13.15<br><br>Sexual gratification through pain inflicted on oneself. | 13.8<br><br>Sexual gratification through touching and rubbing against a nonconsenting person | 13.1<br><br>A sexual dysfunction that develops after at least one episode of normal functioning |
| 13.16   Sexual patterns that deviate from the standard of normal sexuality as defined by nondestructive interplay between consenting adults; includes fetishism, transvestism, etc. | 13.9<br>Condition in which people identify with the opposite sex so completely that they feel they belong to that sex and that their biological gender is a mistake; also called transexualism | 13.2<br><br>A behavioral technique in which the effect of a stimulus is changed by pairing an imagined stimulus with imagined dire consequences. |
| 13.17<br><br>Child molesting; i.e., sexual gratification, on the part of the adult, through sexual contact with children | 13.10<br><br>A chronic lack of interest in sex | 13.3<br>A sexual dysfunction characterized by pain during intercourse; men may suffer from this disorder, but it is more typically a female problem |
| 13.18<br><br>A sexual disorder in which the rapidity of ejaculation interferes with the couple's enjoyment | 13.11<br><br>Sexual relations between members of the immediate family | 13.4<br><br>Sexual gratification through displaying one's genitals to an involuntary observer |
| 13.19<br><br>Forced sexual intercourse with a nonconsenting partner | 13.12<br><br>A sexual dysfunction that has existed, without relief, since the person's earliest sexual experiences | 13.5<br><br>A recurrent lengthy delay or absence of orgasim in a woman |
| 13.20<br><br>Sexual gratification through infliction of pain on others | 13.13<br><br>In men, the absence or weakness of the physiological changes or feelings of sexual excitement that normally occur in the arousal phase of sexual response | 13.6<br><br>In women, the absence or weakness of the physiological changes or feelings of sexual excitement that normally occur in the sexual arousal phase |
| 13.21   Term applied to sexual patterns in which either a sadist and a masochist pair up to satisfy their complementary needs or both enjoy both sadism and masochism and switch between the two | 13.14<br><br>A recurrent lengthy delay or absence of ejaculation and orgasim in a man | 13.7<br><br>Sexual gratification via inanimate objects or some part of the body to the exclusion of the person as a whole |

**CHAPTER TERMS** (Cut out on the lines to use as Flash Cards)

| | | |
|---|---|---|
| 13.22<br><br>**sexual aversion disorder** | 13.29<br><br>**transvestism** | 13.36 |
| 13.23<br><br>**sexual dysfunctions** | 13.30<br><br>**vaginismus** | 13.37 |
| 13.24<br><br>**shame aversion therapy** | 13.31<br><br>**voyeurism** | 13.38 |
| 13.25<br><br>**situational dysfunction** | 13.32 *(You may fill in the remaining boxes with names, terms and definitions from text and lecture)* | 13.39 |
| 13.26<br><br>**spectator role** | 13.33 | 13.40 |
| 13.27<br><br>**stimulus satiation** | 13.34 | 13.41 |
| 13.28<br><br>**transsexualism** | 13.35 | 13.42 |

# DEFINITIONS (Cut out on the lines to use as Flash Cards)

| 13.36 | 13.29 Sexual gratification through dressing in the clothes of the opposite sex | 13.22 Active avoidance of sex as a result of feelings of disgust or fear about it |
|---|---|---|
| 13.37 | 13.30 Sexual dysfunction in which the muscles surrounding the entrance to the vagina undergo involuntary spasmodic contractions, making intercourse either impossible or painfully difficult | 13.23 Disorders that prevent the individual from having or enjoying coitus |
| 13.38 | 13.31 Sexual gratification through clandestine observation of other people's sexual activities or sexual anatomy | 13.24 A behavioral technique in which deviant sexual arousal is eliminated by having the patient perform a deviant act in the therapist's office while the therapist observes and comments |
| 13.39 | 13.32 | 13.25 A sexual dysfunction that occurs only in certain situations |
| 13.40 | 13.33 | 13.26 Sexual dysfunction in which a person is unable to relax or experience pleasure because he or she is constantly judging his or her sexual performance; sexual stimuli are often blunted |
| 13.41 | 13.34 | 13.27 A behavioral technique in which the attractiveness of a stimulus is reduced by providing an overabundance of it |
| 13.42 | 13.35 | 13.28 Gender identification with the opposite sex |

## Chapter 14

# Schizophrenia and Delusional Disorder

## LEARNING OBJECTIVES
*By the time you are finished studying this chapter, you should be able to:*

### SCHIZOPHRENIA
1. Define psychosis, and list three varieties of psychosis referred to in the text (354).
2. Summarize the history of the disorder now called schizophrenia, with reference to the contributions of Kraepelin and Bleuler (355).
3. Summarize population data on schizophrenia (354-355).
4. Define and give examples of the following cognitive symptoms of schizophrenia: delusions, loosened associations, poverty of content, neologisms, clanging, word salad (355-362).
5. Define and give examples of the following perceptual symptoms of schizophrenia: breakdown in selective attention, hallucinations (362-364).
6. Summarize the disorders of mood, behavior, and social interaction that can accompany schizophrenia (364-366).
7. Describe the course of schizophrenia, defining the prodromal, active, and residual phases of the disorder (366-367).
8. Describe the five subtypes of schizophrenia and the characteristic symptom patterns that accompany each (367-370).
9. Explain the process-reactive, positive-negative symptoms, and paranoid-nonparanoid dimensions of schizophrenia (370-372).
10. Define brief psychotic disorder and schizophreniform disorder, and distinguish each of them from schizophrenia (373-374).

### DELUSIONAL DISORDER
11. Define delusional disorder and distinguish it from paranoid personality disorder and paranoid schizophrenia (374-375).
12. List and describe five categories of delusional disorder contained in *DSM-IV* (374-375).

## CHAPTER OUTLINE

I. Schizophrenia

    A. The prevalence of schizophrenia
        1. 1 or 2 percent of U.S. population affected
        2. Schizophrenia accounts for half of mental hospital population
        3. Half of schizophrenics discharged will relapse
        4. 10 to 13 percent of homeless people are schizophrenic

    B. The history of the diagnostic category
        1. Kraepelin first called the disorder "dementia praecox" in 1896
        2. Bleuler renamed it schizophrenia in 1911 because Kraepelin's term was a poor description
        3. Schizophrenia (split mind) refers to the loss of unity in the personality
        4. Do not confuse schizophrenia with multiple personality

C. The symptoms of schizophrenia
  1. Disorders of thought and language (thought is inferred from language)
     a. Delusions (beliefs unsupported by reality)
        (1) Found in three-quarters or more of schizophrenics
        (2) Characterized by airtight self-contained logic (can't talk them out of it)
        (3) Types
            (a) Delusions of persecution
            (b) Delusions of control or influence; may be related to:
                i) Delusions of thought broadcasting
                ii) Delusions of thought insertion
                iii) Delusions of thought withdrawal
            (c) Delusions of reference
            (d) Delusions of sin and guilt
            (e) Hypochondriacal delusions
            (f) Nihilistic delusions
            (g) Delusions of grandeur
     b. Loosening of associations (derailed train of thought)
     c. Poverty of content (speech without substance)
     d. Neologisms (making up new words)
     e. Clanging (use of words for their sounds more than for their meaning)
     f. Word salad (completely disorganized speech)
  2. Disorders of perception
     a. Breakdown of selective attention (inability to focus concentration)
     b. Hallucinations (perceptions without stimuli)
        (1) About 75 percent of schizophrenics hallucinate
        (2) Hallucinations mainly auditory (70%), then visual, then other senses
        (3) May reflect inability to distinguish reality from fantasy (internal versus external stimuli)
        (4) Do not confuse hallucinations with *delusions* or *illusions*
  3. Disorders of mood
     a. Blunted or flattened affect (lack of emotion)
     b. Inappropriate affect
     c. Therefore, the mood component of schizophrenia differs from that of the mood disorders—not "up and down" (mania or depression) but "horizontal" (flat or out in left field)
  4. Disorders of motor behavior
     a. Stereotypy (purposeless repetitive actions)
     b. Extremes of high activity or inactivity (catatonia)
  5. Social withdrawal
  6. Disturbance in sense of self (depersonalization)
  7. Lack of volition (inability to self-start)

D. The onset and course of schizophrenia
  1. Onset usually in late adolescence or early adulthood
     a. Mid-twenties for men
     b. Late-twenties for women
     c. Early onset goes with poor prognosis
  2. Prodromal phase (downhill slide into disorder)
  3. Active phase (full-blown symptoms present)
  4. Residual phase (uphill climb toward normality, but not all patients make it, and many relapse)

E. The subtypes of schizophrenia (based on symptoms)
  1. Disorganized (hebephrenic) schizophrenia, characterized by:
     a. Pronounced incoherence of speech
     b. Disturbed (usually inappropriate) affect
     c. Also many other symptoms described above
  2. Catatonic schizophrenia, characterized by:
     a. Speech disturbances
        (1) Mutism (lack of speech)
        (2) Echolalia (parroting the speech of others)

      b.   Movement disturbances
          (1)   Catatonic stupor (immobility)
          (2)   Catatonic posturing (strange body positions)
          (3)   Waxy flexibility
          (4)   Catatonic rigidity
          (5)   Echopraxia (imitating the movements of others)
          (6)   Catatonic negativism (doing the opposite)

   3.   Paranoid schizophrenia, characterized by:
      a.   Delusions (often of persecution or grandeur)
      b.   Hallucinations (complementing the delusions)
      c.   More common occurrence than disorganized or catatonic schizophrenia
      d.   Better prognosis than catatonic or disorganized schizophrenia
   4.   Undifferentiated schizophrenia (leftover category for those who cannot be cleanly fitted into the first three types)
   5.   Residual schizophrenia (patients in the residual phase)

F.   The dimensions of schizophrenia
   1.   Process-reactive (good-poor premorbid)
      a.   Process schizophrenia
          (1)   Can be called chronic disorder
          (2)   Slow onset (long prodromal phase)
          (3)   Poor premorbid adjustment
          (4)   Poor prognosis
      b.   Reactive schizophrenia
          (1)   Can be called acute disorder
          (2)   Shows rapid onset (short prodromal phase)
          (3)   Good premorbid adjustment
          (4)   Good prognosis
   2.   Positive-negative symptoms
      a.   Positive symptoms are presence of things that should not be there (e.g., hallucinations)
          (1)   Tends to go with good premorbid category
          (2)   Tends to respond to medication
          (3)   Also called Type I schizophrenia
          (4)   Women more susceptible
      b.   Negative symptoms are absence of things that should be there (e.g., social withdrawal)
          (1)   Tends to go with poor premorbid category
          (2)   Tends not to respond to medication
          (3)   Also called Type II schizophrenia
          (4)   Men more susceptible
   3.   Paranoid-nonparanoid dimension
      a.   Paranoid characterized by presence of delusions of persecution and/or grandeur
          (1)   Better in cognition and maturity
          (2)   Better prognosis
      b.   Nonparanoid lacks these symptoms
          (1)   Poorer in cognition and maturity
          (2)   Poorer prognosis

G.   Two related categories: Brief psychotic disorder and schizophreniform disorder
   1.   Brief psychotic disorder
      a.   Symptoms similar to schizophrenia
      b.   Lasts less than one month
      c.   Falls into reactive category (good premorbid) by definition
      d.   Good prognosis
   2.   Schizophreniform disorder
      a.   Symptoms similar to schizophrenia
      b.   Lasts between one and six months (more than six months is schizophrenia)
      c.   May or may not be reactive
      d.   Prognosis may not be as good as with brief reactive psychosis, but is generally better than with schizophrenia

II. Delusional disorders (paranoid disorders)

    A. Main symptom is delusions
       1. Other symptoms of schizophrenia are largely absent
       2. Delusions tend to be less extreme than with paranoid schizophrenia (things that *could* be true)
       3. Sort of a middle ground between paranoid personality disorder (Chapter 11) and paranoid schizophrenia
       4. More common in women than in men
       5. Less common than schizophrenia (but this may be because less severe symptoms result in less contact with mental health professionals)

    B. Delusional types
       1. Persecutory type (people are out to get me)
       2. Grandiose type (I know something you don't)
       3. Jealous type (you are running around on me)
       4. Erotomanic type (somebody very important loves me)
       5. Somatic type (I have severe physical problems)

## KEY TERMS
*The following terms are in bold print in your text. Define them and practice their definitions using the flash cards at the end of the chapter.*

active phase (366)
acute (371)
anhedonia (362)
blocking (357)
blunted affect (365)
brief psychotic disorder (373)
catatonic schizophrenia (368)
catatonic stupor (369)
chronic (371)
clanging (361)
delusional disorders (374)
delusions (356)
disorganized schizophrenia (367)

echolalia (369)
echopraxia (369)
flat affect (365)
hallucinations (363)
inappropriate affect (365)
loosening of associations (357)
mutism (369)
negative symptoms (371)
neologisms (361)
paranoid-nonparanoid dimension (372)
paranoid schizophrenia (369)
positive symptoms (371)
poverty of content (361)

process-reactive dimension (370)
process schizophrenia (370)
prodromal phase (366)
psychoses (354)
reactive schizophrenia (370)
residual phase (367)
schizoaffective disorder (364)
schizophrenia (354)
schizophreniform disorder (373)
stereotypy (365)
Type I schizophrenia (371)
Type II schizophrenia (371)
word salad (362)

*Your text does not list the following terms as formal vocabulary; however, if you don't know what they mean, you will be unable to grasp the concepts of this chapter.*

atrophy (369)
delineate (370)
dichotomy (371)
disconsonance (355)

dissipated (367)
frenetically (365)
gamut (368)
incipient (366)

insidious (366)
juxtaposition (361)

## IMPORTANT NAMES
*Identify the following persons and their major contributions to abnormal psychology as discussed in this chapter.*

Eugen Bleuler (355)
Emil Kraepelin (355)

Milton Rokeach (356)
The Three Christs of Ypsilanti (356)

## GUIDED SELF-STUDY

1. Both schizophrenia and delusional disorder are psychoses, which means they have

    (a)_____ reality contact; that is, they interrupt one's abilities to perceive, process, and (b)_____ to the environmental stimuli in an adaptive manner.  They are the most

(c)_____ of all psychological disorders.

2. List the three main groups of psychoses.

   a.

   b.

   c.

## SCHIZOPHRENIA

3. Schizophrenic disorders are characterized by three major types of symptom patterns:

   a.

   b.

   c.

4. Schizophrenia is a collective name given to what is probably more accurately described as the

   (a)_____ disorders.  Schizophrenia has such a wide variety of possible (b)_____

   patterns within the these three major problem areas that there is likely to be (c)_____
   one underlying disorder.  See Helpful Hint #1 for this chapter.

5. In 1896, Kraepelin called schizophrenia (a) _____, which means premature
   mental deterioration.  In 1911 Bleuler said that in some cases it was not premature and in
   some cases it was obviously not a permanent deterioration because some people recovered.  So

   Bleuler called the disorder (b)_____, which means "split mind."  Split-mind

   described the separation of (c)_____ processes within the schizophrenic person's mind.

6. As a person in the United States, what are the chances that you will ever have a
   schizophrenic episode in your life?

7. (a)_____ of all beds in mental hospitals are occupied with someone who has

   schizophrenia; (b)_____ percent of all homeless people are schizophrenic.

8. Schizophrenia typically involves a variety of symptoms, including disorders of (a)_____

   and language, disorders of (b)_____, which refers to the way stimuli are interpreted

   and attended to, disorders of (c)_____ or emotions, bizarre (d)_____ behavior,

   social (e)_____, a disturbed sense of (f)_____, and a lack of goal directedness,

   called a disturbance in (g)_____.

9. Identify these two symptoms of thought disorder.

   a.  _____  Firmly held beliefs that have no basis in reality

   b.  _____  Thoughts that are related but stray from the original intended
       direction of thinking

10. List the eight patterns of delusional thought given in your text.

    a.                                                 e.

    b.                                                 f.

    c.                                                 g.

    d.                                                 h.

11. Apply the information from the listing in the previous question, and write in the name of the delusional pattern that goes with each description.

    a.  _____  My mother-in-law is trying to poison me.

    b.  _____  I feel myself slipping away. Some days I just don't exist.

    c.  _____  My boss at the store where I work is having me followed by the CIA.

    d.  _____  It was so terrible. I caused that last earthquake in California.

    e.  _____  The national news reporters always smile at me; they know when I am watching the TV.

    f.  _____  My husband won't let me spend any money. When I try to, he paralyzes me by remote control.

    g.  _____  I'm your guardian angel, and I'm writing this exercise just for you because I can read your mind and I know what you don't understand in this chapter.

    h.  _____  My bladder doesn't work because I have rust in my pipes.

    i.  _____  I can't talk on the telephone while the television is on because my voice goes out through the TV antenna.

12. Sometimes it is hard to tell if beliefs are real or delusional. List three examples in which it would be hard to be sure if you were dealing with a fact or a delusion.

    a.

    b.

    c.

13. There is evidence that suggests that delusions are some people's efforts to try to explain some very unusual sensation or experience they have had. Some delusional experiences have been

found to be explainable in terms of a physical (a)_____ that the person really had.

Also, *non*delusional subjects will give (b)_____ explanations when put in situations that seemingly make no sense to them.

14. List schizophrenic symptoms that reflect disorder of language.

    a.                                                 c.

    b.                                                 d.

15. List two manifestations of disordered perception in schizophrenia.

    a.

    b.

16. (a)_____ hallucinations are most frequently experienced and (b)_____ hallucinations are the second most frequently occurring type.

17. By definition, the mood symptoms in schizophrenia are considered secondary because

otherwise schizophrenia would be in Chapter 10 with the (a)_____ disorders (where emotion is the primary problem). Schizophrenics commonly have one of two mood abnormalities. They

either have (b)_____ affect or (c)_____ affect.

18. Typically, schizophrenics show (a)_____ physical activity. If this trend is carried to

the extreme, the individual may lapse into a catatonic (b)_____.

19. _____ is the purposeless repetitive activity that some schizophrenics may engage in for hours at a time.

20. If you sit and observe a schizophrenic ward for an hour, you may see many normal and many unusual and maybe socially inappropriate behaviors. The one behavior that will be noticeably

lacking is _____.

21. List the three phases of schizophrenia in order from beginning to end.

a.

b.

c.

22. List the five subcategories of schizophrenia discussed in *DSM-IV*.

a.                                           d.

b.                                           e.

c.

23. Define each of the following behavior patterns seen in catatonic schizophrenia.

**Catatonic negativism**          **Catatonic stupor**
**Catatonic rigidity**            **Mutism**
**Catatonic posturing**           **Waxy flexibility**

a. _____ Complete immobility

b. _____ Cessation of speech

c. _____ Assuming a pose and remaining in that pose for hours at a time.

d. _____ Staying in whatever pose someone arranges

e. _____ When the pose is rigidly held and resistant to the efforts of someone else trying to alter it

f. _____ Doing the opposite of what is being asked

24. Position yourself in front of a clock, standing with your arms held straight out to the sides. How long can you stand there without moving? Did you find the experience more exhausting than you would have imagined?

25. You enter a room and find four people there. Determine which one most represents each of the following categories of schizophrenia: **Catatonic, Paranoid, Disorganized**, and **Residual**.

   a. _____ One claims to be the President of the United States and claims an assassin is looking for him.

   b. _____ When I introduce myself, one of them responds quite appropriately; she is clearly the most normal person in the group.

   c. _____ One sits at attention, staring out the window with one hand held up in the "live long and prosper" salute.

   d. _____ One wanders about the room singing a nonsense rhyme and occasionally hopping as though he is playing a childhood game.

26. List the dimensions of schizophrenia.

   a. _____ vs. _____

   b. _____ vs. _____

   c. _____ vs. _____

27. Now take the dimensions of schizophrenia and write each part under "good prognosis" or "poor prognosis" where they belong.

   Good Prognosis                    Poor Prognosis

   a. _____        —

   b. _____        —

   c. _____        —

28. Circle the following behaviors that are "positive" symptoms.

   **delusions**        **speech with little meaning**        **social withdrawal**

   **hallucinations**        **flat affect**        **bizarre behavior**        **apathy**

29. Women are more likely to have the (a)_____ prognosis symptom pattern and men are more likely to have the (b)_____ prognosis symptom pattern. There is also a differential response to (c)_____ between the two patterns. Good prognosis patterns are (d)_____ responsive to medication than poor prognosis patterns.

30. What impact has the discovery of these patterns and correlations (things that go together) had on our understanding of schizophrenia?

31. What did they name the two new patterns of schizophrenic disorders?

32. Answer the following questions about the long-term outlook for patients with schizophrenia.

   a. What percentage of schizophrenics continue to be schizophrenic?

   b. What percentage alternate between residual and active phases?

   c. What percentage return to and maintain normal functioning?

DELUSIONAL DISORDERS
33. Here are other disorders that have some similarity to schizophrenia. Assign their names to their descriptions.

**Brief psychotic disorder**             **Schizoaffective disorder**
**Delusional disorders**               **Schizophreniform disorder**

a. _____ Same symptom pattern as schizophrenia, following a recognizable stressor, but lasting less than a month

b. _____ Same symptom pattern lasting more than a month but less than six months, with or without a precipitating trauma

c. _____ The person seems entirely normal except for the presence of a delusional system

d. _____ The person shows symptoms of schizophrenia but the mood component also seems to be primary with mania or major depression

34. What is another name give to the delusional disorders?

35. Identify the category for each of the following delusions:

**Erotomanic type**             **Persecutory type**
**Grandiose type**              **Somatic type**
**Jealous type**

a. _____ My teacher hates me. No matter what I do in this class, she is going to fail me.

b. _____ Don't worry, Mom. I don't have to study. I've got this term under control.

c. _____ My girlfriend (who's been in the coma ever since the accident) is cheating on me with her doctor. I can tell by that sneaky look on her face when I visit.

d. _____ Michael Jackson is in love with me. He is doing all those hang-ups on my telephone. He's just too shy to speak to me.

e. _____ The cafeteria food is causing my guts to rot.

36. Even though paranoia is a popular topic in story lines, it is really extremely rare, occurring in

_____ individuals per thousand.

## *HELPFUL HINTS*

1. Your text points out that even after all the decades of research on the subject, very little is known about schizophrenia—what the fundamental symptoms are, or even if it is actually more than one disorder. As a comparison, imagine how things might have been before knowledge had accrued about the respiratory system. All the people who had "breathing problems" might have been put into one group. In spite of the common term used to diagnose all these people, there would have been a wide range of symptoms: nasal congestion, restricted air flow, coughing, sneezing, noisy breathing, fever, head and/or chest pain, and even death. Now, with current knowledge, many different respiratory disorders can be recognized: colds, allergies, asthma, bronchitis, emphysema, tuberculosis, and lung cancer. Perhaps some day the schizophrenic disorders will be a list of many quite individual disorders too.

2. **DO *NOT* CONFUSE "SPLIT-MIND" (SCHIZOPHRENIA) WITH SPLIT (MULTIPLE) PERSONALITY.** Other than the use of the term "split," they are totally unrelated concepts! Review multiple personality in Chapter 8 if this is not perfectly clear. (I say "perfectly clear" with humor: I was often still in a total fog when others assumed that concepts should be "perfectly clear").

3. Be alert that in the schizophrenic disorders, those that are reactive (acute, good premorbid, positive symptoms, Type I) are *more* responsive to medication (371). That is just the reverse of the mood disorders, where reactive depression is *less* responsive to medication.

4. Beware of people who throw around the terms "schizo" and "paranoid." By now I hope you know that those terms relate to several different diagnoses that encompass a wide variety of behavioral abnormalities.

Paranoid:   Paranoia (delusional disorder)—unreasonable belief systems
            Paranoid schizophrenia—unreasonable beliefs + other psychotic symptoms
            Paranoid personality disorder—suspicious outlook on life
Schizo:     Schizophrenia—psychotic thought/mood/behavior symptoms
            Schizotypal personality disorder—very unusual behavioral quirks
            Schizoid personality disorder—profound social withdrawal (a loner)

## PRACTICE TEST

*Take the following test several times as you study the chapter. Write your answers on a separate sheet of paper and after each attempt, note in the tally box above each question whether your answer was correct or incorrect.*

| 1 | 2 | 3 | 4 |
|---|---|---|---|

1. The original term for schizophrenia was
   a. general paresis.
   b. delirium tremens.
   c. hysteria.
   d. dementia praecox.

| 1 | 2 | 3 | 4 |
|---|---|---|---|

2. The main type of delusion exhibited by the "three Christs of Ypsilanti" is
   a. delusion of control.
   b. nihilistic delusion.
   c. delusion of grandeur.
   d. hypochondriacal delusion.

| 1 | 2 | 3 | 4 |
|---|---|---|---|

3. Delusions of reference means
   a. the feeling that people are out to get you.
   b. the belief that any communication between others is about you.
   c. the belief that you are an important person, like Napoleon.
   d. the feeling that you have committed an unpardonable sin.

| 1 | 2 | 3 | 4 |
|---|---|---|---|

4. If, in describing a scene, I invent a new word that obviously conveys a lot of meaning for me, but means little or nothing to you, I have illustrated
   a. clanging.
   b. neologism.
   c. word salad.
   d. delusional references.

| 1 | 2 | 3 | 4 |
|---|---|---|---|

5. Clear speech, with good grammatical sentences and good vocabulary, but that nevertheless conveys no real information is an example of
   a. poverty of content.
   b. word salad.
   c. thought withdrawal.
   d. blocking.

| 1 | 2 | 3 | 4 |
|---|---|---|---|

6. Which of the following is the best description of word salad?
   a. Using language mainly for the way it sounds or rhymes
   b. The invention of new words to suit individual purposes
   c. The kind of language that results from thought broadcasting
   d. A meaningless and random arrangement of words

| 1 | 2 | 3 | 4 |
|---|---|---|---|

7. A hallucination can be defined as
   a. a belief system for which there is no evidence.
   b. a sensory experience for which there is no stimulus.
   c. misinterpretation of a sensory stimulus.
   d. bizarre behavior in inappropriate circumstances.

| 1 | 2 | 3 | 4 |
|---|---|---|---|

8. Mood abnormality for schizophrenic patients usually takes which of the following forms?
   a. An unusually elevated mood (mania)
   b. Uncontrollable aggression or rage
   c. Inappropriate or blunted emotional expression
   d. An unusually depressed mood that is chronic

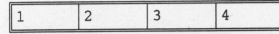

9. The act of engaging in purposeless actions repetitively for hours at a time is called
   a. catatonic stupor.
   b. stereotypy.
   c. somnambulism.
   d. waxy flexibility.

10. Ernestine has just been released from inpatient mental health care. She is feeling much better and is not suffering from the delusions and hallucinations she experienced before treatment. Ernestine is in the _____ phase of schizophrenia.
   a. prodromal
   b. active
   c. post-critical
   d. residual

| 1 | 2 | 3 | 4 |
|---|---|---|---|

11. Which of the following is true of the typical "reactive" schizophrenia?
   a. Premorbid adjustment is good, onset is sudden, and good recovery is likely.
   b. Premorbid adjustment is good, onset is slow, and good recovery is likely.
   c. Premorbid adjustment is poor, onset is slow, and good recovery is unlikely.
   d. Premorbid adjustment is poor, onset is sudden, and good recovery is unlikely.

| 1 | 2 | 3 | 4 |
|---|---|---|---|

12. Negative symptoms are described as
   a. a pessimistic or depressed outlook on life.
   b. resistance to the demands made by other people.
   c. the absence of a normal behavior or quality.
   d. symptoms that get progressively worse.

333

| 1 | 2 | 3 | 4 |

13. The distinguishing feature of catatonic schizophrenia is
    a.  delusions of grandeur or persecution.
    b.  disturbance in motor behavior.
    c.  vague psychotic symptoms that do not fit neatly into any pattern.
    d.  visual hallucinations.

| 1 | 2 | 3 | 4 |

14. Which type of schizophrenia is characterized mainly by incoherent and silly language, giggling, funny faces and the like?
    a.  Catatonic          c.  Residual
    b.  Paranoid           d.  Disorganized

| 1 | 2 | 3 | 4 |

15. Marjorie's husband died suddenly and she completely "flipped out." She talked to him as though he were still there and claimed to hear him talking to her. This shocked her friends since she always seemed so stable. Her problem would be seen as
    a.  process.           c.  reactive.
    b.  neurotic.          d.  endogenous.

| 1 | 2 | 3 | 4 |

16. Marjorie's prognosis (see the previous question) is probably
    a.  pretty bad.                       c.  catatonic schizophrenia.
    b.  paranoid schizophrenia.           d.  fairly good.

| 1 | 2 | 3 | 4 |

17. Assuming that Marjorie recovers from her loss and returns to normal life after a period of six weeks (see previous questions), her disorder would be called
    a.  paranoid schizophrenia.           c.  paranoid personality disorder.
    b.  brief psychotic disorder.         d.  schizophreniform disorder.

| 1 | 2 | 3 | 4 |

18. Brief psychotic disorder shows basically the same symptoms as schizophrenia and schizophreniform disorder except
    a.  there are no delusions.
    b.  there are only delusions of grandeur or persecution.
    c.  it doesn't last as long as schizophrenia or schizophreniform disorder.
    d.  it doesn't last as long as schizophrenia but longer than schizophreniform disorder.

| 1 | 2 | 3 | 4 |

19. Delusional disorders are characterized by
    a.  simple suspiciousness only.
    b.  delusions without any other schizophrenic symptoms.
    c.  delusions plus hallucinations.
    d.  all schizophrenic symptoms plus delusions.

| 1 | 2 | 3 | 4 |
|---|---|---|---|

20. A difference between the paranoid personality disorder and paranoid schizophrenia is that paranoid schizophrenia
    a. carries suspiciousness to the point of full-blown delusions.
    b. is a neurosis, while paranoid personality disorder is a psychosis.
    c. involves fewer but more serious symptoms.
    d. involves simple suspiciousness only.

## ANSWERS
### Self-Study Exercise

1. a. impaired
   b. respond
   c. serious (354)
2. a. Mood disorders
   b. Schizophrenia
   c. Delusional disorder (354)
3. a. Bizarre behavior
   b. Social withdrawal
   c. Distorted thought, perception and mood (354)
4. a. schizophrenic
   b. symptom
   c. more than (354)
5. a. dementia praecox
   b. schizophrenia
   c. mental—emotions, ideas, and perceptions, to be more specific (355)
6. Between one and two chances out of 100 (354)
7. a. One-half
   b. ten to thirteen (354)
8. a. thought
   b. perception
   c. mood
   d. motor
   e. withdrawal
   f. self
   g. volition (355-366)
9. a. Delusions (356-357)
   b. Loose cognitive associations (357-361)
10. a. Persecution
    b. Control or influence
    c. Reference
    d. Sin and guilt
    e. Hypochondriacal
    f. Nihilistic
    g. Grandeur
    h. Thought tampering (356-357)

11. a. Persecution
    b. Nihilistic
    c. Persecution
    d. Sin and guilt
    e. Reference
    f. Control or influence
    g. Grandeur
    h. Hypochondriacal
    i. Thought tampering (356-357)
12. Here are some possibilities:
    a. My house is sinking into the ground.
    b. I was kin to Elvis Presley.
    c. One bee sting and I'll be dead.
    d. After that happened, the police were everywhere.
    e. I won a million dollar lottery ten years ago.
    f. I've been in the private living quarters of the White House without anyone knowing it. (357)
13. a. disease
    b. irrational (359)
14. a. Poverty of content (361)
    b. Neologisms (361)
    c. Clanging (361-362)
    d. Word salad (362)
15. a. Breakdown of selective attention (362-363)
    b. Hallucinations (363-364)

16. a. Auditory
    b. visual (363)
17. a. mood, or affective (374)
    b. blunted or flat
    c. inappropriate (365)
18. a. decreased
    b. stupor (365)
19. Stereotypy (365)
20. normal interpersonal interaction (366)
21. a. Prodromal (366)
    b. Active (366-367)
    c. Residual (367)
22. a. Disorganized (367-368)                    e. Residual (367)
    b. Catatonic (368-369)
    c. Paranoid (369-370)
    d. Undifferentiated (367)
23. a. Catatonic stupor                          d. Waxy flexibility
    b. Mutism                                    e. Catatonic rigidity
    c. Catatonic posturing                       f. Catatonic negativism (368-369)
24. Your time and experience. This activity was to make you aware of how much energy a
    catatonic posture requires.
25. a. Paranoid                                  c. Catatonic
    b. Residual                                  d. Disorganized (367-370)
26. Process-reactive (370-371)
    Positive-negative symptoms (371-372)
    Paranoid-nonparanoid (372)
27. a. Reactive: Good        Process: Poor
    b. Positive symptoms: Good    Negative symptoms: Poor
    c. Paranoid: Good        Nonparanoid: Poor (370-372)
28. Delusions, hallucinations, bizarre behavior (372)
29. a. good                                      c. medication
    b. poor                                      d. more (372)
Note: If you haven't noticed Table 14.1 on the bottom of page 372, you have missed out. It
summarizes the material from the last three questions.
30. Researchers now propose that there may be two different disorders (371).
31. Type I and Type II schizophrenia (371)
32. a. 10 percent
    b. 50-65 percent
    c. 25 percent (367)
33. a. Brief psychotic disorder
    b. Schizophreniform disorder (373)
    c. Delusional disorders (374)
    d. Schizoaffective disorder (see bottom of page 364)
34. Paranoia (374)
35. a. Persecutory type                          d. Erotomanic type
    b. Grandiose type                            e. Somatic type (374)
    c. Jealous type
36. three (375)

## Practice Test

| 1. | d | (355) | | 11. | a | (371) |
|----|---|-------|--|-----|---|-------|
| 2. | c | (356) | | 12. | c | (371) |
| 3. | b | (356) | | 13. | b | (368) |
| 4. | b | (361) | | 14. | d | (367) |
| 5. | a | (361) | | 15. | c | (371) |
| 6. | d | (362) | | 16. | d | (371) |
| 7. | b | (363) | | 17. | d | (373) |
| 8. | c | (365) | | 18. | c | (373) |
| 9. | b | (365) | | 19. | b | (374) |
| 10. | d | (367) | | 20. | a | (375) |

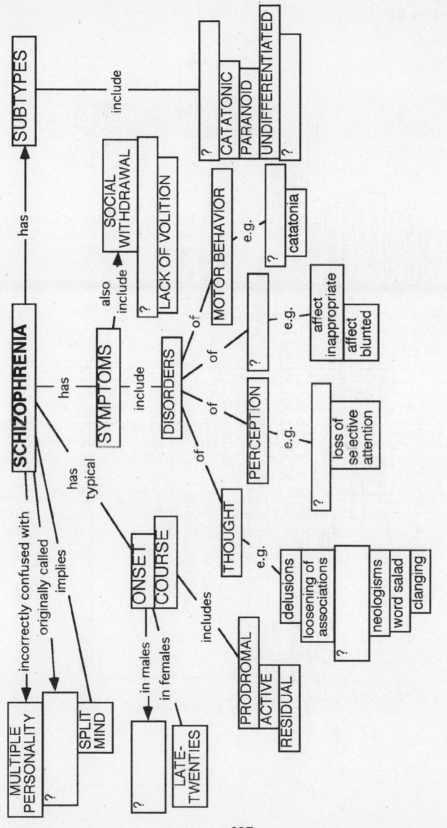

**CONCEPT MAP 14.1**

Fill out the boxes marked with question marks (?) with the concepts or words you think belong there. Suggested answers are on a following page.

337

# CONCEPT MAP

## 14.1

The suggested answers are
shown in *italics*.

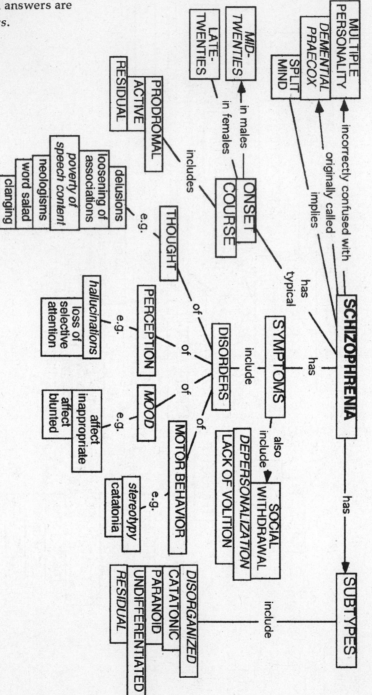

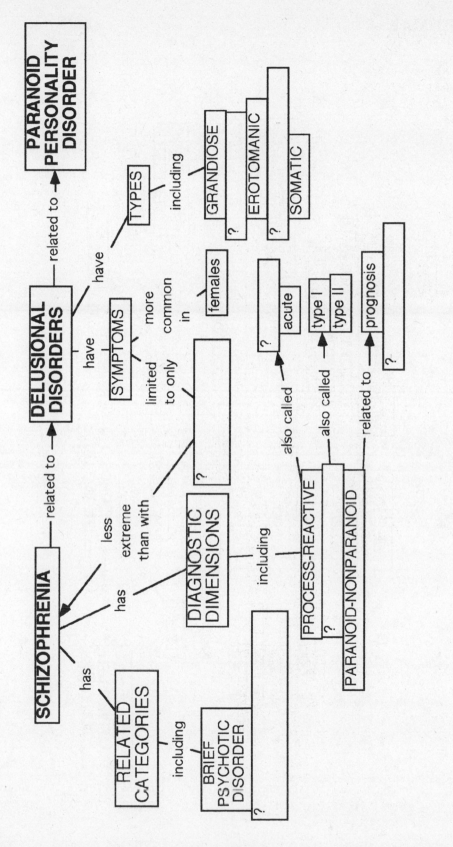

**CONCEPT MAP 14.2**

Fill out the boxes marked with question marks (?) with the concepts or words you think belong there. Suggested answers are on a following page.

# CONCEPT MAP

## 14.2

The suggested answers are shown in *italics*.

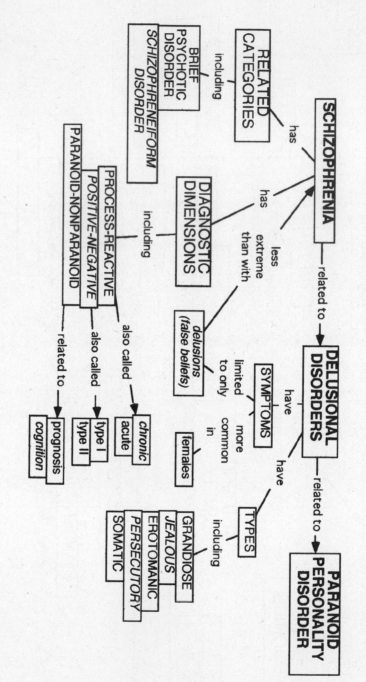

340

# CHAPTER TERMS (Cut out on the lines to use as Flash Cards)

| | | |
|---|---|---|
| 14.1<br><br>**active phase** | 14.8<br><br>**catatonic stupor** | 14.15<br><br>**echopraxia** |
| 14.2<br><br>**acute** | 14.9<br><br>**chronic** | 14.16<br><br>**flat affect** |
| 14.3<br><br>**anhedonia** | 14.10<br><br>**clanging** | 14.17<br><br>**hallucinations** |
| 14.4<br><br>**blocking** | 14.11<br><br>**delusional disorders** | 14.18<br><br>**inappropriate affect** |
| 14.5<br><br>**blunted affect** | 14.12<br><br>**delusions** | 14.19<br><br>**loosening of associations** |
| 14.6<br><br>**brief psychotic disorder** | 14.13<br><br>**disorganized schizophrenia** | 14.20<br><br>**mutism** |
| 14.7<br><br>**catatonic schizophrenia** | 14.14<br><br>**echolalia** | 14.21<br><br>**negative symptoms** |

# DEFINITIONS (Cut out on the lines to use as Flash Cards)

| | | |
|---|---|---|
| 14.15<br><br>Imitation of the movements of others; associate with catatonic schizophrenics | 14.8<br>An extreme form of withdrawal in which the individual retreats into a completely immobile state, showing a total lack of responsiveness to stimulation | 14.1<br><br>The second stage of schizophrenia, during which the patient begins showing prominent psychotic symptoms |
| 14.16<br><br>A mood abnormality among schizophrenics in which the person shows no emotion | 14.9<br><br>Referring to schizophrenics who have long-standing severe deficits | 14.2<br><br>Referring to patients who are in the midst of the short-term active phase of their first schizophrenic episode |
| 14.17<br><br>Sensory perceptions that occur in the absence of any appropriate external stimulus | 14.10<br><br>A characteristic speech pattern of schizophrenics in which words are used together because they rhyme or sound similar, without regard to logic | 14.3 Mood abnormality among schizophrenics in which the experience of pleasure is reduced; often associated with major depressive episodes; lowered enjoyment leads to a lowered interest in activities |
| 14.18 Mood abnormality among schizophrenics in which the person's emotional responses seem totally unsuitable to the immediate context | 14.11<br><br>A group of psychoses in which the delusional system is the basic or even the only abnormality | 14.4<br><br>A condition sometimes experienced by schizophrenics in which the person falls silent in the midst of talking, with no recollection of what he or she was talking about |
| 14.19<br><br>Rambling, disjointed quality that characterizes schizophrenic speech | 14.12 Irrational beliefs that a person will defend with great vigor despite overwhelming evidence that they have no basis in reality; delusions are among the most common schizophrenic thought disorders | 14.5<br><br>A mood abnormality among schizophrenics in which the person shows little emotion |
| 14.20<br><br>The cessation of speech; often a characteristic of catatonic schizophrenia | 14.13 Form of schizophrenia characterized by incoherence of speech and childlike disturbed affect, such as giggling wildly and assuming absurd postures (also called hebephrenic schizophrenia) | 14.6 Condition in which a person with no history of schizophrenic symptoms has an episode of such symptoms that is marked by rapid onset, a clear precipitating event, and a duration of less than a month |
| 14.21 In schizophrenia, the absence of something that is normally present, including poverty of speech, flat affect, withdrawal, and inattention | 14.14<br>A speech deficit, characteristic of autistic children, in which the child aimlessly repeats what other people say | 14.7 Form of schizophrenia characterized by a marked disturbance in motor behavior, decreases in motion, complete immobility, cessation of speech, or alternating periods of immobility and extreme agitation |

**CHAPTER TERMS** (Cut out on the lines to use as Flash Cards)

| | | |
|---|---|---|
| 14.22<br><br>**neologisms** | 14.29<br><br>**prodromal<br>phase** | 14.36<br><br>**stereotypy** |
| 14.23<br><br>**paranoid-<br>nonparanoid<br>dimension** | 14.30<br><br>**psychosis** | 14.37<br><br>**Type I<br>schizophrenia** |
| 14.24<br><br>**paranoid<br>schizophrenia** | 14.31<br><br>**reactive<br>schizophrenia** | 14.38<br><br>**Type II<br>schizophrenia** |
| 14.25<br><br>**positive<br>symptoms** | 14.32<br><br>**residual phase** | 14.39<br><br>**word salad** |
| 14.26<br><br>**poverty<br>of content** | 14.33<br><br>**schizoaffective<br>disorder** | 14.40 *(You may fill in the remaining boxes with names, terms and definitions from text and lecture)* |
| 14.27<br><br>**process-reactive<br>dimension** | 14.34<br><br>**schizophrenia** | 14.41 |
| 14.28<br><br>**process<br>schizophrenia** | 14.35<br><br>**schizophreniform<br>disorder** | 14.42 |

**DEFINITIONS** (Cut out on the lines to use as Flash Cards)

| | | |
|---|---|---|
| 14.36 The act of engaging in purposeless actions repetitively for hours; a behavior sometimes shown by schizophrenics | 14.29 The initial stage of schizophrenia, during which the person generally becomes withdrawn and socially isolated | 14.22 Schizophrenic speech pattern in which new words are formed by combining parts of two or more regular words or in which common words are used in a unique fashion |
| 14.37 A dimension of schizophrenia characterized by the presence of something that is normally absent (positive symptoms) | 14.30 Any severe psychological disorder in which a person's perception of reality is drastically distorted | 14.23 The classification of schizophrenics according to the presence (paranoid) or absence (nonparanoid) of delusions of persecution and/or grandeur |
| 14.38 A dimension of schizophrenia characterized by the absence of something that is normally present (negative symptoms) | 14.31 Schizophrenia in which onset is sudden and apparently precipitated by some traumatic event | 14.24 Form of schizophrenia characterized by delusions and/or hallucinations, often related to themes of persecution and grandeur |
| 14.39 A schizophrenic speech pattern in which words and phrases are combined in a disorganized fashion, seemingly without logic or meaning or even associations | 14.32 The third phase of schizophrenia, during which behavior is similar to that seen during the prodromal phase | 14.25 In schizophrenia, the presence of something that is normally absent, including hallucinations, delusions, bizarre behavior, and incoherent thought patterns |
| 14.40 | 14.33 Syndrome intermediate between schizophrenia and the mood disorders in which individuals suffer a manic or a depressive episode while showing the symptoms of schizophrenia | 14.26 A characteristic of schizophrenic speech in which words are used correctly but communication is poor |
| 14.41 | 14.34 Group of psychoses marked by severe distortion and disorganization of thought, perception, and mood, by bizarre behavior, and by social withdrawal | 14.27 The classification of schizophrenics according to whether the onset of symptoms is gradual, or abrupt and precipitated by some traumatic event |
| 14.42 | 14.35 Disorder in which a person with no history of schizophrenic symptoms has an episode of such symptoms that is marked by rapid onset, with or without a precipitating event, and a duration of 1 to 6 months | 14.28 Schizophrenia in which onset is gradual |

## Chapter 15

# *Perspectives on Schizophrenia*

## *LEARNING OBJECTIVES*
*By the time you are finished studying this chapter, you should be able to:*

**PROBLEMS IN THE STUDY OF SCHIZOPHRENIA**
1. Discuss why schizophrenia is difficult to diagnose, and cite the problems that imprecise diagnosis poses for research (380).
2. Describe how standard research techniques are of limited usefulness in the study of a disorder like schizophrenia (380-381).
3. Describe what is meant by the "chicken and the egg" problem and the third variable problem (380-381).

**PERSPECTIVES ON SCHIZOPHRENIA**
4. Summarize genetic research on schizophrenia, citing the results of family studies, twin studies, adoptions studies, and high-risk research (381-388).
5. Describe brain structure abnormalities and evidence of prenatal brain injury found in some schizophrenics (388-389).
6. Explain the dopamine hypothesis in schizophrenia, and describe the relationship of dopamine to Type I and Type II schizophrenia and to Parkinson's disease (389-391).
7. Discuss the pros and cons of chemotherapy for schizophrenia (391-392).
8. Summarize the cognitive perspective's ideas on the role of attention problems as a factor in schizophrenia (392-394).
9. Summarize the role of pathological interpersonal relationships in the development of schizophrenia according to the family theory approach (394-397).
10. Summarize the psychodynamic view of the causes of schizophrenia (397).
11. Summarize how humanistic-existential psychologists explain schizophrenia (397-398).
12. Summarize the behavioral position on the causes of schizophrenia (399).
13. Briefly describe how each of the preceding psychological perspectives would approach the treatment of schizophrenia (396-400).
14. Explain the diathesis-stress theory of schizophrenia and describe the problems with using the diathesis-stress theory as an explanation for schizophrenia (400-401).

## *CHAPTER OUTLINE*

I.  Problems in the study of schizophrenia

    A.  What is to be studied
        1.  Accurate diagnosis of schizophrenia is difficult
            a.  Agreement on a general diagnosis of schizophrenia was only 53-74 percent as recently as the 1960s
            b.  Psychiatrists in different parts of the world diagnose things differently (London versus New York)
            c.  With *DSM-IV*, however, agreement is improving
        2.  There is also disagreement over what the primary pathology is in schizophrenia; which symptoms reflect causes and which are byproducts

B. Problems in experimentation
   1. Direct, controlled experimentation on causes of schizophrenia cannot be done for ethical reasons
   2. This leaves only uncontrolled means of collecting data, which prevents cause and effect conclusions
      a. Chicken and egg problem (are variables being studied causes or effects?)
      b. Third variable problem (are variables being studied all the result of something else?)
   3. Schizophrenics being studied in research are almost invariably hospitalized and on medication, possibly disguising the true symptoms of the problem
   4. Differential deficits (ones specific to schizophrenia) are hard to identify

II. Perspectives on schizophrenia

A. The biological perspective (emphasizing biological diathesis, or predisposition)
   1. Genetic studies look for inherited predispositions
      a. Family studies show that schizophrenia runs in families
      b. Twin studies show MZ twins have higher concordance rate than DZ twins (3:1 or 5:1 rates)
         (1) Type II (negative symptom) schizophrenia seems more heritable than Type I
         (2) Children of MZ and DZ twins show occurrences of the disorder consistent with genetic predisposition idea
      c. Adoption studies looking at biological children of schizophrenics show higher rates of disorder than predicted in normal population
      d. The mode of genetic transmission is still unclear, but is most likely a polygenic characteristic interacting with environmental stressors
      e. Genetic high-risk studies look at children of schizophrenic mothers on a longitudinal basis (Mednick)
         (1) Advantages
            (a) Research efficiency; more potential subjects at lower cost
            (b) Subjects are identified prior to the start of disorder (premorbid)
            (c) Therefore bias toward subjects is not a major factor
            (d) Current information at any age or stage of disorder
            (e) Built-in control groups
         (2) Results show that "deviant" subjects have
            (a) More greatly disturbed mothers and more unstable home lives
            (b) More history of institutionalization
            (c) More criminal behavior and school discipline problems
            (d) More problems tuning out irrelevant environmental stimuli
            (e) More pregnancy or birth complications
         (3) In general, research like this supports the idea of genetic predisposition
   2. Behavioral high-risk studies look at behaviors in nonschizophrenics that are associated with schizophrenia
      a. Perceptual Aberration-Magical Ideation Scale (Per-Mag) is applied to college students
      b. High Per-Mag scorers show more psychosis than low scorers
   3. Brain structure studies look for abnormalities in the brains of schizophrenics
      a. Enlarged brain ventricles are associated with Type II schizophrenia
      b. Frontal lobe atrophy (degeneration) goes with Type II schizophrenia
      c. Temporal lobe or limbic system atrophy goes with Type I schizophrenia
      d. Basal ganglia may be involved with either Type I or II
   4. Biochemical research looks for chemical imbalances in brains of schizophrenics
      a. The dopamine hypothesis
         (1) Schizophrenic symptoms often result from abnormally high dopamine activity in the brain
         (2) Antipsychotic drugs that control schizophrenic symptoms lower dopamine activity
         (3) Drugs which raise dopamine activity make psychotic symptoms worse
         (4) Dopamine also implicated in Parkinson's disease, but in the opposite way
         (5) Still a problem with the fact that Type II schizophrenia seems related to dopamine *underactivity*, particularly in limbic system

        (6)   Also, dopamine affects symptoms of other psychotic disorders besides schizophrenia

        (7)   So, the biochemical basis of schizophrenia is likely to be more complex than is currently understood (perhaps involving serotonin as well)

    b.   Chemotherapy

        (1)   Antipsychotic drugs (such as phenothiazines) have revolutionized care of psychotics

        (2)   But, the drugs do not "cure" schizophrenia, they just control symptoms

        (3)   If drugs are discontinued, relapse often occurs

        (4)   Side effects, such as tardive dyskinesia, can be quite serious

B.   The cognitive perspective (emphasizing attention problems as a diathesis)

   1.   Overattention/underattention in schizophrenic patients

      a.   Type I (positive symptom) schizophrenics are unable to screen out stimuli effectively

         (1)   Auditory distraction experiments show high distractibility

         (2)   Orienting-brainwaves experiment shows large response to distractors

         (3)   Related to high dopamine levels

      b.   Type II (negative symptom) schizophrenics are unable to orient toward stimuli effectively

         (1)   Physiological orienting response lacking

         (2)   Backward masking experiment shows schizophrenics process more slowly

         (3)   Related to low dopamine levels

   2.   Remitted schizophrenics, relatives of schizophrenics, and others at risk for the disorder tend to show attention problems as well

C.   Family theories (emphasize early relationship problems as causes of schizophrenia)

   1.   Schizophrenogenic mothers are cold, domineering, rejecting, and yet overprotective (an idea taken less seriously today)

   2.   Negative and emotionally charged family atmosphere (high expressed emotion (EE)) may cause schizophrenia

   3.   Faulty communication in a family may lead to schizophrenia

      a.   Double-bind communication gives conflicting messages

      b.   Families of schizophrenics often show vague, muddled, or fragmented communication styles, called communication deviance (CD)

   4.   Family theories still cannot explain why one child will be schizophrenic and another will not

   5.   Family problems may be one part of a cause and effect network that includes inherited predispositions

   6.   Treatment focuses on

      a.   Positive working relationships between patient, family, and therapist

      b.   Stable, structured therapy format

      c.   Here-and-now problem solving orientation

      d.   Behavioral problem solving techniques

      e.   Improving communication skills

      f.   Encouraging respect for personal boundaries

      g.   Providing information about schizophrenia

D.   The psychodynamic perspective (also emphasizes family issues)

   1.   Sullivan emphasizes a damaging mother-child relationship which leaves the person unable to cope with interpersonal relations

   2.   Sullivan also pioneered analysis for schizophrenics—a more supportive and active role for the therapist than is done with neurotics

E.   The humanistic-existential perspective (emphasizing the search for authenticity)

   1.   Schizophrenics are unable to live inauthentic lives, so they create their own reality (Laing)

   2.   By doing so, they are in some respects more "sane" than the so-called normals who judge them

   3.   Antipsychiatric movement sees traditional ways of understanding schizophrenia as a way of imposing society's rules on nonconformists

4. Milieu therapy emphasizes self-responsibility in treatment rather than standards imposed from the outside (still rather traditional in setting, however)
5. Kingsley Hall-type therapies are more radical in that staff have little authority and symptoms not seen as pathological, but as attempts to break through inauthenticity
6. While useful as a "reality check" on traditional psychiatric methods, these therapies are being overshadowed by increasing evidence of organic factors in schizophrenia

F. The behavioral perspective (emphasizes the learning process)
   1. Ullman and Krasner's learned nonreponsiveness
      a. Deviant environment prevents person from learning to respond normally to stimuli
      b. Idiosyncratically chosen response patterns produce bizarre behavior
      c. If reinforced through attention or sympathy, bizarre behavior can become habitual
   2. Therapy consists of relearning normal behavior
      a. Direct reinforcement changes behavior
      b. Token economies simulate a real-life situation in which responsible behavior is needed to "earn a living"
      c. Social-skills training can deal with the withdrawal commonly seen in schizophrenics
   3. Behavior therapy can enhance functioning, but to the extent that there is a biological component, it does not "cure" schizophrenia

G. The diathesis-stress model (emphasizing a combination of environmental and biological causes)
   1. Diathesis (biological predisposition) must be present for stress to work on
   2. Stress (environmental factor) must be present for predisposition to be activated
   3. Exact nature of predisposition or the stressor is not well understood at this time
   4. Confusion exists as to primary or secondary factors contributing to disorder

## KEY TERMS
*The following terms are in bold print in your text. Define them and practice their definitions using the flash cards at the end of the chapter.*

behavioral high-risk design (387)
communication deviance (CD) (396)
diathesis-stress model (381)
differential deficits (381)
dopamine hypothesis (389)
double-bind communication (395)
expressed emotion (EE) (395)

genetic high-risk design (386)
milieu therapy (398)
mystification (398)
social-skills training (400)
tardive dyskinesia (392)
token economy (399)

*Your text does not list the following terms as formal vocabulary; however, if you don't know what they mean, you will be unable to grasp the concepts of this chapter.*

chronology (382)
exacerbate (396)
first-degree relatives (382)
impetus (396)
incontrovertible (401)
pernicious (395)

posits (389)
postmortem (388)
precursors (387)
stringent (380)
tangible (399)

## IMPORTANT NAMES
*Identify the following persons and their major contributions to abnormal psychology as discussed in this chapter.*

Loren and Jean Chapman (387)
Frieda Fromm-Reichmann (395)
R. D. Laing (398)
Mednick and Schulsinger (386)

David Rosenthal, et. al. (384)
Harry Stack Sullivan (397)
Ullman and Krasner (399)

# GUIDED SELF-STUDY

## PROBLEMS IN THE STUDY OF SCHIZOPHRENIA

1. The two problem areas that have hampered research into the causes of schizophrenia are

   a. Disagreement on _____, and

   b. Data must be collected in an ex_____ manner, which means after the fact.

2. The issues that complicate the diagnosis of schizophrenia are

   a. Uncertainty about whether schizophrenia is _____ one disorder

   b. Debate about what the _____ symptoms of schizophrenia are

   c. Questions about who fits into which diagnostic category because of the _____ of the symptom pattern from person to person

3. To more clearly define schizophrenia, recent editions of the *DSM* have tried to eliminate some of the diagnostic difficulties by establishing more _____ criteria for what behavioral patterns will be diagnosed as schizophrenia.

4. What other diagnoses need to be distinguished from schizophrenia to improve diagnostic accuracy? See how many you can list. There are at least six of them.

5. Why must data on schizophrenia be collected in an ex post facto manner?

6. Since direct experimentation into schizophrenia cannot be done, two research complications that arise are:
   a. A correlation does not prove _____.

   b. There may be an underlying _____ that is the cause of the two correlated factors.

7. What confounding variables are troublesome in research with schizophrenics?

## PERSPECTIVES ON SCHIZOPHRENIA

### BIOLOGICAL

8. Biological research on schizophrenia is currently one of the most (circle the best answer) **underrated** / **productive** / **disappointing** / **simplistic** areas in abnormal psychology.

9. List five biological approaches used to study schizophrenia.

   a.                                    d.

   b.                                    e.

   c.

10. List six different areas of genetic research on schizophrenia.

    a.                                          d.

    b.                                          e.

    c.                                          f.

11. Family studies have revealed that the closer you are related to a schizophrenic person, the more likely you are to have a schizophrenic episode yourself. Fill in the following statistics on your risk for schizophrenia. If you have

    a. No schizophrenic relatives          _____ in 100
    b. One schizophrenic parent            _____ in 100
    c. Two schizophrenic parents           _____ in 100
    d. A schizophrenic MZ twin             _____ in 100

12. Twin studies support the hypothesis that there are two different types of schizophrenia;

    Type I is characterized by (a)_____ symptoms, and Type II typically has

    (b)_____ symptoms. The one with the greater genetic component is (c)_____.

13. Use the following terms to complete the four advantages that longitudinal "high-risk" studies offer in research about the development of schizophrenia? (Mednick's list summarizes these nicely.)

    bias                                        control
    confounding                                 memories

    a. Data is collected before the _____ effects of hospitalization and medications have occurred.
    b. It eliminates the _____ of using data from patients whose clinical outcome is already known.
    c. Data is collected on an ongoing basis instead of depending on people's _____.

    d. This approach provides two _____ groups: the low risk children and the high risk children who did not develop schizophrenia.

14. Studies using genetically "high-risk" subjects are used to increase the odds that they will eventually have a group of schizophrenics large enough to make the study worthwhile. If researchers chose a random sample of children from the population, they would get only

    (a)_____ schizophrenics for every 100 children they followed. By using a group that is more at risk, the researchers know they will get more cases of schizophrenia. When one parent is

    schizophrenic, the person's chances increase to about (b)_____ in 100. Thus, the number that

    is going to develop schizophrenia has increased by (c)_____ times.

15. Use the following terms to complete the five critical differences found in Mednick's study for the high-risk children who did become mentally ill.

    complications                               troubled
    distractions                                unmanageable
    institutions

    a. Home life and family relationships were more _____.

    b. They had spent more time in _____.
    c. These children were more likely to have displayed extremely _____ behavior in school.

d. These children were more vulnerable to _____ from the environment.

e. The children were much more likely to have had _____ during pregnancy or childbirth.

16. What other high-risk research, besides genetic research, does your book mention? What does this research study?


17. What are some of the behaviors thought to be associated with schizophrenia?


18. What did home movies reveal about children who became mentally ill versus their siblings who do not become mentally ill?
    a. They tended to play "the clown" within the family dynamics.
    b. They showed atypical emotional expressions and poorer motor coordination.
    c. They showed aggression even in infancy, which is most unusual in a child under the age of eighteen months.
    d. They all were phobically afraid of the movie cameras.

19. If you are asked to identify pictures of the brains of schizophrenics versus pictures of the brains of people who did not have schizophrenia, you would look at the size of the

    (a)_____; those having the (b)_____ ones are more likely to be the brains of people who were schizophrenics.

20. Brain activity tests during cognitive tasks suggest that the schizophrenics with negative

    symptoms show abnormally low levels of activity in the (a)_____ lobes of the brain. The schizophrenics with positive symptoms are likely to have abnormally high levels of activity in

    the (b)_____ system or in the (c)_____ lobes of the brain. These different patterns of brain activity for the positive and the negative symptoms further supports the

    hypothesis that (d)_____.

21. Use the following terms to complete this summary of prenatal brain injury:

    **asymmetrical**                    **gliosis**
    **discordant**                      **second**
    **flu**

    Research into some prenatal brain injury points to the (a)_____ trimester. In normal development, the two hemispheres of the brain have different patterns during this time.

    Schizophrenic brains do not show this (b)_____ pattern. Brain injuries usually show

    evidence of (c)_____, which is the brain's healing process; however this process does not start to operate until the third trimester. Autopsies on the brains of people who were schizophrenic show brain damage that does not have this healing process. Identical twins

    who are (d)_____ for schizophrenia (one has it, one does not) also have more variation between their fingerprints, which also develop during this time. Another bit of

    support for this being a critical period is research showing that women who had (e)_____ during their second trimester of pregnancy had offspring who were more likely to become schizophrenic in later life.

22. Biochemical research has given attention to the (a) _____ hypothesis for the last two decades. This hypothesis is substantially supported by the fact that the (b)_____ medications block the brain's receptor sites for (c)_____ which is a neurotransmitter that carries the neural impulse across the (d)_____ (gap) between neurons.

23. Amphetamines are known to increase dopamine activity in the brain. This information would lead us to predict that _____-like symptoms can result from abuse of amphetamines.

24. Why do people with Parkinson's disease sometimes show schizophrenia-like symptoms?

25. The most common form of treatment for schizophrenia is (a)_____. A very troublesome side effect with most of these medications is (b)_____, which is a muscle disorder that causes the person to make uncontrollable movements of the facial muscles. The major criticism about antipsychotic medications is that they (c)_____.

26. We know that schizophrenia is not entirely determined by genetic factors because (a)_____ twins do not have 100 percent concordance. Their concordance rate is (b)_____ percent.

COGNITIVE

27. The cognitive theorists believe that the root cause of schizophrenia is biological, which causes a primary symptom of (a)_____ dysfunction. The problem is one of extremes: Either (b)_____ or (c)_____. Whichever way the problem exists, the problem increases the person's difficulty in coping with environmental (d)_____.

28. Use the following terms to discuss this matter of attention. One of them is used twice.

**delusions**
**focus**
**I**

**II**
**negative**
**stimuli**

The last question suggests there is a "just right" amount of attention for coping adaptively with life. Too much is confusing, and too little makes a person unresponsive. Overattention becomes a problem when there is a breakdown of selective attention. The person is so flooded with internal and external (a)_____ that he/she cannot think straight. He/she is confused and disorganized due to lack of ability to sort among sensations, perceptions, and thoughts, and to (b)_____ on selected ones. Meanwhile, more sensations are pouring in to further distract and confuse the individual. The result of all this unstructured stimulation can be hallucinations, (c)_____, and incoherent speech, which are termed positive symptoms and which are seen in Type (d)_____ schizophrenia. With inadequate attention, there is inadequate reaction to environmental (e)_____. Such people fail to make the normal orienting responses to moderate intensity stimuli. It is not just a matter of not showing a response. Their bodies give no indication that their brains have even seen or heard the stimuli. This lack of brain orienting response is correlated with the (f)_____ symptoms of flat affect and social withdrawal. Underattention is the type problem seen in

Type (g)_____ schizophrenics.

29. Use the terms **masking** and **target** to complete these blanks for the sequence of events in backward-masking research.

    a. _____ stimulus presented

    b. _____ stimulus presented

    c. Person is asked to recall the _____ stimulus

30. Choose the correct answer: In backward-masking paradigm research, Type II schizophrenics
    a. need more time to mentally process the masking stimulus.
    b. need more time to mentally process the target stimulus.
    c. can remember the target stimulus for only a short time.
    d. can remember the masking stimulus for only a short time.

## FAMILY THEORIES

31. Use these terms to complete the blanks:

**domineering**                                        **overprotective**
**father**                                             **schizophrenogenic**
**mother**

From the perspective of family theories, Frieda Fromm-Reichmann has suggested that the

actual problem in the family is the (a)_____, who is emotionally cold and rejecting,

yet (b)_____ and (c)_____. Later research has revealed that the

(d)_____ also actively contributes to the hostile, aggressive environments in these

families. This type mother was said to be a (e)_____ mother, that is, one that caused a child to develop schizophrenia.

32. Assessment of family dynamics was originally based on subjective judgments about the global interactions within the family. Family theorists later moved to a more precise approach which better lends itself to scientific, objective measures. Two different communications dynamics

within families have been described and researched. The first pattern, (a)_____, considers the level of criticism and emotional overinvolvement among family members.

(b)_____ considers the level of coherence and clarity in interpersonal exchanges; fragmented, garbled nature, blurred statements are noted. Another type of communication deviance has complete, coherent statements, but the statements and accompanying behaviors are inconsistent. When a child is given a statement that contains mutually contradictory material, with the parent implicitly forbidding this contradiction to be pointed out, the

statement is called a/an (c)_____ communication.

33. Identify the following communications patterns:

    a. Mom has written to a college-aged child to say that she and Dad love the child very much, but they are sorry that they both are going to miss her graduation day. Each parent has appointments "that can't be missed."

b. Mom and Dad tend to be perfectionists, and want the very best from their children. They have encouraged their children to participate in many extracurricular activities. The parents are always right there with "helpful criticism" (with the emphasis on criticism), telling the children how to improve their performances.

c. Dad: "Here today, gone tomorrow."
Son: "Could we?"
Dad: "I've been planning..."
Son: "You never listen to me!!"

34. Use the following terms to complete the components found in most effective family treatments:

**boundaries**                              **step-by-step**
**communication**                       **structured**
**problems**                               **therapist**
**schizophrenia**

a. A good working relationship between the _____ and the family

b. A stable, _____ therapeutic process

c. Focus on solutions to current family _____

d. Behavioral analysis to set up _____ sequences to work toward goals

e. Practicing improved _____ skills

f. Teaching the importance of personal _____ among family members

g. Providing information about _____ to reduce blame and guilt

## PSYCHOANALYTIC

35. Psychoanalytic theory has primarily addressed neurotic disorders. However, Harry Stack Sullivan, has focused on the (a)_____ disorder, schizophrenia. Sullivan said the cause of the schizophrenic's anxiety was a damaged (b)_____-_____ relationship. In the treatment of schizophrenia, instead of probing the unconscious as the psychoanalytic therapist usually does, he/she develops a supportive relationship almost as a second (c)_____ by offering support and esteem to help clients develop trust, confidence, and skills to allow them to build better (d)_____ relationships.

## HUMANISTIC-EXISTENTIAL

36. Use these terms to discuss Laing's thoughts on schizophrenia (one is used twice):

**alienation**                              **hypersane**
**antipsychiatric**                      **milieu**
**humanistic-existential**           **phenomenological**

R. D. Laing has been very outspoken about schizophrenia. He has reached what would seem to be the ultimate extreme of using the phenomenological approach of the (a)_____-_____ perspective. For quick review, the (b)_____ approach stresses seeing a person's life experience through his/her own eyes—thoughts, perceptions, and beliefs. Laing proposes that in industrial societies, "normal" people suppress their true feelings and accept

the trivial goals and distorted values of society. This is called a state of (c)_____.
According to Laing, a person who can no longer continue the masquerade that society insists
on is labeled "schizophrenic"! Quite to the contrary, Laing insists that this person is not

*in*sane but (d)_____; that is, he/she has started on the journey to rediscover his/her

real self. Those who agree with Laing are called members of the (e)_____ movement.

These theorists don't believe in sending a person to a psychiatrist because the psychiatrist's

goal is to help the person learn to wear the mask of (f)_____ again so that society

can deal with this person again. These theorists advocate (g)_____ therapy, where the
person goes into a warm, nurturing environment with few restraints on behavior. The person
is responsible for his/her own behavior as he/she strives to discover and express his/her real
feelings and self.

BEHAVIORISTS

37. The behaviorist sees the schizophrenic as someone having inadequate (a)_____ skills
and who needs (re)training for those skills. The one area that has received much attention is

learned (b)_____ problems. According to behaviorists, the schizophrenic has been in a

situation where he/she has received little or no reinforcement for socially (c)_____

responses. He/She may also have received strong reinforcement for some very (d)_____
behaviors. To counter the effect of these experiences, the behaviorist is likely to use direct

reinforcement and then a (e)_____economy situation to reinforce behaviors being taught

in a (f)_____ skills training program.

38. What skills are part of social skills training?


DIATHESIS STRESS

39. What are the three possible explanations for schizophrenia (or any disorder, for that matter)?

  a.

  b.

  c.

40. In the diathesis-stress model, diathesis refers to the _____.

41. Your text points out that the diathesis-stress model is only a model. It does not answer some
important questions. What are these questions?


42. Use the following terms to complete the blanks in the list of stressors that Mirsky and Duncan
hypothesize to be associated with the development of schizophrenia.

**attention**                              **expressed emotion**
**communication**                          **hospitalization**
**dependence**                             **organic**

  a.  Feelings of clumsiness and being "different" as a result of _____ deficits

355

b.  Increased _____ on parents as a result of being impaired

c.  Poor academic performance and poor coping skills resulting from the basic biological (or

_____) impairment

d.  Stressful family interactions, including high _____

e.  _____ deviance in the family, leading to difficulty in communicating with people outside the family, which leads to increased isolation

f.  Frequent _____ of a parent or other family member

## HELPFUL HINT

Review the parts of Chapter 5 (Research Methods in Abnormal Psychology) that relate to research methodology with schizophrenics. It is advantageous to refresh the learning that you have already done on that material. The most directly related material in Chapter 5 is "Correlational Research Designs" and "Longitudinal or Prospective Studies," which includes genetic and behavioral high-risk designs.

## PRACTICE TEST
*Take the following test several times as you study the chapter. Write your answers on a separate sheet of paper and after each attempt, note in the tally box above each question whether your answer was correct or incorrect.*

| 1 | 2 | 3 | 4 |
|---|---|---|---|

1.  In discussing research on schizophrenia, the text mentions the "chicken or the egg" problem. This means that
    a.  since poultry products have been implicated in schizophrenia, diet must be considered as a factor.
    b.  a simple correlation between two variables does not tell us which one caused the other.
    c.  the major issue in schizophrenia research is biological versus genetic causation.
    d.  poor definitions of disorder prevent accurate diagnoses.

| 1 | 2 | 3 | 4 |
|---|---|---|---|

2.  Some years ago, more schizophrenics were diagnosed in the United States than in England because
    a.  U.S. psychiatrists used fewer antipsychotic drugs.
    b.  English and American psychiatrists were not making diagnoses according to the same standards.
    c.  schizophrenia is a diagnosis limited to *DSM-IV* and this system is not used in England.
    d.  English families have better double-bind communication skills than the average U.S. family.

| 1 | 2 | 3 | 4 |
|---|---|---|---|

3.  Which of the following genetic research methods best separates genetic and environmental effects?
    a.  Adoption studies
    b.  Family studies
    c.  Twin studies
    d.  Correlation studies

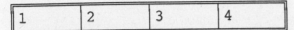

| 1 | 2 | 3 | 4 |

4. Which of the following can be derived from genetic studies of schizophrenia?
   a. The parents of schizophrenic children seem less likely to develop the disorder themselves.
   b. It is a sex-linked characteristic passed from mothers to daughters.
   c. Type II schizophrenia may have a larger genetic component than Type I schizophrenia.
   d. Males are more likely to have Type I schizophrenia and females are more likely to have Type II.

| 1 | 2 | 3 | 4 |

5. The dopamine hypothesis is primarily based on findings that
   a. schizophrenics show the same symptoms as victims of Parkinson's disease.
   b. Type II schizophrenia can be converted to Type I schizophrenia by dopamine therapy.
   c. drugs that lower dopamine activity can reduce symptoms of schizophrenia.
   d. schizophrenic symptoms result from a deficiency of L-dopa.

| 1 | 2 | 3 | 4 |

6. Mednick's "high-risk" study of schizophrenia uses as its main group of subjects children who have
   a. been diagnosed as schizophrenic.
   b. a number of behaviors associated with schizophrenia.
   c. schizophrenic mothers.
   d. schizophrenic brothers and sisters.

| 1 | 2 | 3 | 4 |

7. Which of the following brain abnormalities has been associated with negative symptom Type II schizophrenia?
   a. Low frontal lobe brain activity
   b. Shrunken brain ventricles
   c. Increased endorphin activity
   d. Damage to the cerebellum

| 1 | 2 | 3 | 4 |

8. Studies on brain asymmetry, fingerprint patterns in twins, and a brain-repair process called gliosis all are aimed at investigating whether schizophrenia can be connected to
   a. abnormalities on chromosome 11.
   b. brain damage in the teenage years.
   c. oxygen deprivation during the birth process.
   d. brain trauma prior to birth.

| 1 | 2 | 3 | 4 |

9. The "Per-Mag" scale, used in predicting psychotic behavior, measures
   a. magnetic disturbances in brain activity.
   b. abnormalities of perception and thinking.
   c. the presence of paranoid personality disorder.
   d. behavioral habits in school and work settings.

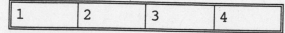

| 1 | 2 | 3 | 4 |

10. Harry Stack Sullivan saw schizophrenia originating from
    a.  a poor mother-child relationship.
    b.  inherited insanity.
    c.  the tendency of society to label and stigmatize nonconformists.
    d.  biologically-based thinking and perceptual deficits.

| 1 | 2 | 3 | 4 |

11. Which of the following statements is most true of family theories of schizophrenia?
    a.  They most clearly demonstrate the inheritance of schizophrenia.
    b.  They are a variation on humanistic-existential theory.
    c.  They have recently been discredited as a result of organic research.
    d.  They provide a focus on the environmental factors involved in schizophrenia.

| 1 | 2 | 3 | 4 |

12. Which of the following is true of positive-symptom, Type I schizophrenics?
    a.  They tend to be easily distracted by irrelevant stimuli in their environment.
    b.  They tend to have low dopamine activity in subcortical brain areas.
    c.  They need long processing intervals in the backward-masking experiment.
    d.  They exhibit poorer premorbid adjustment and a poorer prognosis.

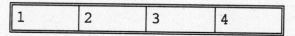

| 1 | 2 | 3 | 4 |

13. A family with a high expressed emotion (EE) score would tend to
    a.  be cold, rejecting, and uncaring.
    b.  be dominated by one parent to the exclusion of the other.
    c.  be critical and emotionally overinvolved.
    d.  produce more female schizophrenics than males.

| 1 | 2 | 3 | 4 |

14. The concept of double-bind communication means that
    a.  neither the patient nor the therapist knows if a placebo is being administered.
    b.  no matter what you say, you will be criticized for it.
    c.  the therapist suggests the opposite behavior from what is really desired.
    d.  behavior and its consequences are essentially unrelated.

| 1 | 2 | 3 | 4 |

15. In view of their attitudes about traditional mental health practices, humanistic-existential psychologists tend to prefer treatment programs that are
    a.  strongly structured to produce quick results so the patient can resume independent living as soon as possible.
    b.  emphatic about the measurement and documentation of results.
    c.  operated by M.D.s and not Ph.D.s.
    d.  loosely arranged to allow the maximum amount of freedom for the client.

16. According to Ullman and Krasner, schizophrenia is the result of
    a. lack of reinforcement for normal behavior.
    b. a refusal to conform to the demands of others.
    c. double-bind communication in the family.
    d. inconsistently applied punishment during childhood.

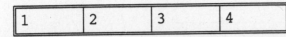

17. The token economy approach to treatment of schizophrenia involves
    a. immediate food reinforcers for appropriate behavior.
    b. primarily the extinguishing of unwanted behavior through nonreinforcement.
    c. forcing the patient to get a job in order to promote responsible living.
    d. symbolic reinforcers that can be traded in for other wants at a later time.

18. Which perspective on schizophrenia would be most likely to make the following statement: "Schizophrenics don't need a 'cure' so much as they need practical ways of coping with life."
    a. Psychodynamic
    b. Behavioral
    c. Humanistic-existential
    d. Family theories

| 1 | 2 | 3 | 4 |

19. A prominent and rather outspoken supporter of the antipsychiatric movement was
    a. Harry Stack Sullivan.
    b. Thomas Szasz.
    c. Karl Abraham.
    d. Stanley Friedman.

| 1 | 2 | 3 | 4 |

20. The diathesis-stress model of schizophrenia attributes the causes of the disorder to
    a. a combination of triggering and predisposing factors.
    b. environmental events in the stage of early adulthood.
    c. genetic biological factors resulting from dietary deficiencies.
    d. developmental crises in the family.

## ANSWERS
### Self-Study Exercise

1. a. diagnosis
   b. post facto (380)
2. a. more than
   b. primary
   c. variation (380)
3. specific (380)
4. Brief reactive psychosis (373)
   Schizophreniform disorder 373)
   Schizoid and schizotypal personality disorders (266)
   Paranoia (delusional disorders) (354)
   Mood disorders of a psychotic type (354)
   Schizoaffective disorders that involve both schizophrenia and mood problems (364)
5. Schizophrenia is one of those bad things that researchers cannot deliberately try to inflict on people for the sake of discovery and testing (380).
6. a. causality (cause and effect relationship) (380)
   b. third variable (381)

7. Hospitalization and antipsychotic drugs. Almost all diagnosed schizophrenics have had both, and those factors may influence research results (381).
8. productive (381)
9. a. Genetic studies
   b. Brain imaging studies
   c. Investigation of prenatal brain injury
   d. Biochemical research
   e. Chemotherapy (382-392)
10. a. Family studies
    b. Twin studies
    c. Adoption studies
    d. Studies looking for the specific nature of the genetic transmission
    e. Genetic high-risk studies
    f. Behavioral high-risk studies (404-409)
11. a. 1 to 2          c. 46
    b. 13              d. 48 (382)
12. a. positive
    b. negative
    c. Type II (383)
13. a. confounding     c. memories
    b. bias            d. control (386)
14. a. 1 or 2
    b. 13
    c. 6 to 13 (386)
15. a. troubled        d. distractions
    b. institutions    e. complications (386)
    c. unmanageable
16. Behavioral high-risk research studies people who have demonstrated thoughts and behaviors thought to be associated with schizophrenia (387-388).
17. Perceptual abnormalities and magical thinking (387)
18. "b" (387)
19. a. ventricles
    b. larger (388)
20. a. frontal
    b. limbic
    c. temporal
    d. there are at least two different types of schizophrenia (388).
21. a. second          d. discordant (389)
    b. asymmetrical    e. flu (390)
    c. gliosis
22. a. dopamine        c. dopamine (389)
    b. antipsychotic   d. synapse (389, 85)
23. schizophrenia (389)
24. People with Parkinson's disease take medications to increase dopamine activity in the brain; increased dopamine activity can produce schizophrenia-like symptoms (391).
25. a. chemotherapy (drug therapy) with antipsychotic medications
    b. tardive dyskinesia
    c. do not cure schizophrenia, they only reduce some of the symptoms (390-391).
26. a. MZ (monozygotic)
    b. 38 (383)
27. a. attention
    b. and c. overattention or underattention
    d. stressors (392-394)
28. a. stimuli         e. stimuli
    b. focus           f. negative
    c. delusions       g. II (394)
    d. I (393)
29. a. target
    b. masking
    c. target (394)
30. "b" (394)

31. a. mother
    b. domineering
    c. overprotective
    d. father
    e. schizophrenogenic (395)
32. a. expressed emotion (EE)
    b. communication deviance (CD)
    c. double-bind (395-396)
33. a. Double-bind communication—We love you but you are not very important to us (395)
    b. Expressed emotion—overinvolvement with child and very critical (395)
    c. Communication deviance—fragmented, incomplete non sequiturs (396)
34. a. therapist
    b. structured
    c. problems
    d. step-by-step
    e. communication
    f. boundaries
    g. schizophrenia (397)
35. a. psychotic
    b. mother-child
    c. parent
    d. interpersonal (397)
36. a. humanistic-existential
    b. phenomenological (43)
    c. alienation
    d. hypersane
    e. antipsychiatric
    f. alienation (397-398)
    g. milieu (398)
37. a. coping
    b. attention
    c. appropriate
    d. bizarre
    e. token
    f. social (399)
38. Conversation, eye contact, appropriate physical gestures, smiling, and improved voice intonation (399-400)
39. a. Genetic causation
    b. Environmental causation
    c. A combination of genetics and environment (381)
40. genetic potential or genetic predisposition (381)
41. a. What is the nature of the genetic defect? (384-387)
    b. What stressors are most likely to cause (to trigger) schizophrenia to develop? (400-401)
42. a. attention
    b. dependence
    c. organic
    d. expressed emotion
    e. communication
    f. hospitalization (401)

## Practice Test

| | | | | | | |
|---|---|---|---|---|---|---|
| 1. | b | (381) | 11. | d | (396) |
| 2. | b | (380) | 12. | a | (393) |
| 3. | a | (384) | 13. | c | (395) |
| 4. | c | (383) | 14. | b | (396) |
| 5. | c | (389) | 15. | d | (398) |
| 6. | c | (386) | 16. | a | (399) |
| 7. | a | (388) | 17. | d | (399) |
| 8. | d | (389) | 18. | b | (400) |
| 9. | b | (387) | 19. | b | (398) |
| 10. | a | (397) | 20. | a | (401) |

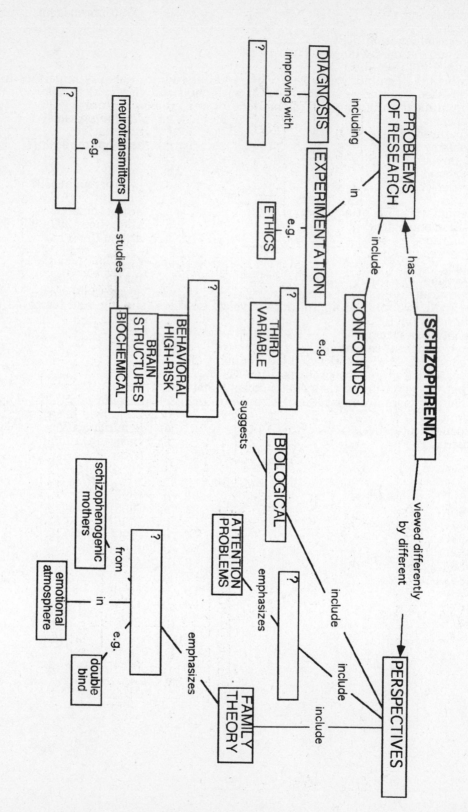

## CONCEPT MAP 15.1

Fill out the boxes marked with question marks (?) with the concepts or words you think belong there. Suggested answers are on a following page.

362

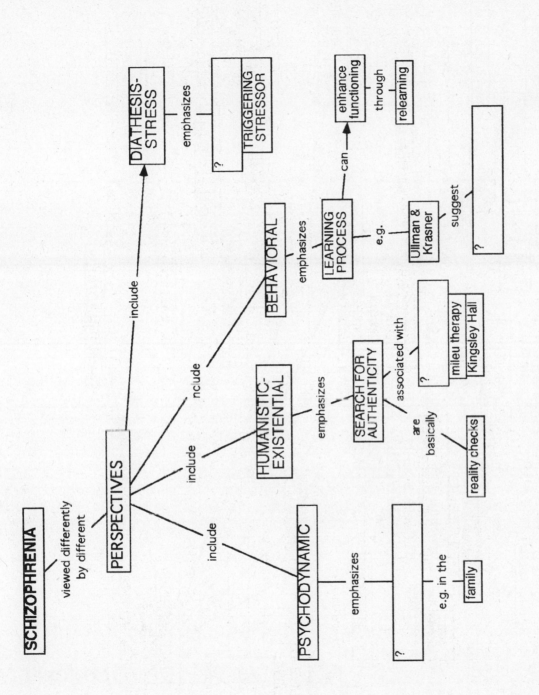

**CONCEPT MAP 15.2**

Fill out the boxes marked with question marks (?) with the concepts or words you think belong there. Suggested answers are on a following page.

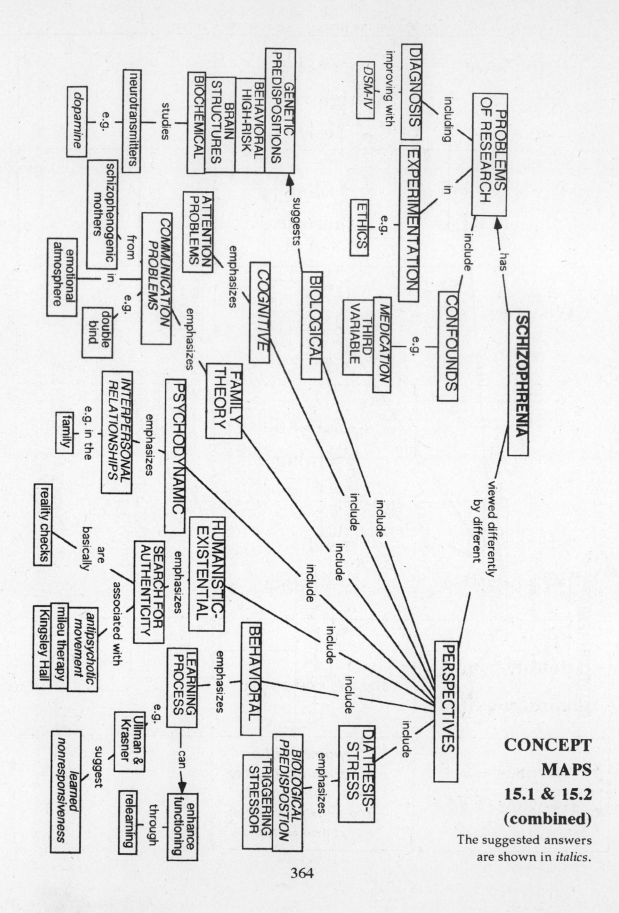

CONCEPT
MAPS
15.1 & 15.2
(combined)

The suggested answers
are shown in *italics*.

| | | |
|---|---|---|
| **15.1**<br><br>**behavioral high-risk design** | **15.8**<br><br>**genetic high-risk design** | **15.15** |
| **15.2**<br><br>**communication deviance (CD)** | **15.9**<br><br>**milieu therapy** | **15.16** |
| **15.3**<br><br>**diathesis-stress model** | **15.10**<br><br>**mystification** | **15.17** |
| **15.4**<br><br>**differential deficits** | **15.11**<br><br>**social-skills training** | **15.18** |
| **15.5**<br><br>**dopamine hypothesis** | **15.12**<br><br>**tardive dyskinesia** | **15.19** |
| **15.6**<br><br>**double-bind communication** | **15.13**<br><br>**token economy** | **15.20** |
| **15.7**<br><br>**expressed emotion (EE)** | **15.14** *(You may fill in the remaining boxes with names, terms and definitions from text and lecture)* | **15.21** |

**DEFINITIONS** (Cut out on the lines to use as Flash Cards)

| 15.15 | 15.8 A research design in which high-risk subjects are selected on the basis of genetic factors associated with the disorder in question | 15.1 A research design in which high-risk subjects are selected on the basis of behavioral traits thought to be associated with the disorder in question |
|---|---|---|
| 15.16 | 15.9 Residential community therapy in which patients take responsibility for their behavior, participate in their rehabilitation and that of others, and help in making decisions that affect the community, maximizing their independence | 15.2 A measurement of parental deviant or idiosyncratic test responses used to predict the potential for their children's future schizophrenic behaviors |
| 15.17 | 15.10 As used by Laing, a habitual mode of interaction between parent and child that causes the child to doubt the adequacy of his or her own thoughts, feelings, and perceptions | 15.3 In schizophrenia research, an approach which holds that a predisposition to schizophrenia is inherited but that the disorder must be triggered by environmental stresses |
| 15.18 | 15.11 A behavioral therapy that teaches people basic techniques for engaging in satisfying interactions with others | 15.4 Problems or characteristics which are specific to a disorder in question and presumably central to it; not found in other disorders |
| 15.19 | 15.12 A muscle disorder that causes uncontrollable grimacing and lip smacking; caused by the phenothiazine antipsychotic drugs | 15.5 Theory that schizophrenia is associated with excess activity of those parts of the brain that use dopamine as a neurotransmitter |
| 15.20 | 15.13 Behavior modification procedure, based on operant-conditioning principles; patients are given conditioned reinforcers for performing target behaviors and which can be exchanged for backup reinforcers | 15.6 Situation in which a mother gives mutually contradictory messages to her child while implicitly forbidding the child to point out the contradiction; believed by some to be a causative agent in schizophrenia |
| 15.21 | 15.14 | 15.7 Measurement of key relatives' level of criticism and emotional over involvement used in determining the family type of a hospitalized schizophrenic |

## Chapter 16

# *Cognitive Disorders of Adulthood*

*LEARNING OBJECTIVES*
***By the time you are finished studying this chapter, you should be able to:***

**PROBLEMS IN DIAGNOSIS**
1. Distinguish between biogenic and psychogenic disorders and list six characteristics of organic brain disorders (406-407).
2. Discuss the difficulties involved in determining organic causation and in specifying the site and nature of the damage (407-409).
3. Describe aphasia, apraxia, and agnosia (409-411).

**ORGANIC BRAIN DISORDERS CLASSIFIED BY CAUSE**
4. Name and describe four types of cerebral infection discussed in the text (411-412).
5. Name and describe three types of brain trauma discussed in the text (412-416).
6. List and describe the effects of two types of vascular accidents discussed in the text (416-417).
7. Discuss the effects of brain tumors on mental and behavioral processes (417-418).
8. Describe the following degenerative brain disorders: AIDS dementia, Alzheimer's disease, vascular dementia, Huntington's chorea, Parkinson's disease, and delirium (418-424).
9. Describe the causes and effects of Korsakoff's psychosis (424-425).
10. Name and describe two thyroid syndromes and two adrenal syndromes discussed under the heading of endocrine disorders (425-426).
11. Name and describe the effects of five substances that can lead to toxic disorders (426).

**THE EPILEPSIES**
12. Distinguish between symptomatic and idiopathic epilepsy (427).
13. Distinguish among simple partial, complex partial, absence, and tonic-clonic seizures (427-428).
14. Discuss psychological factors associated with epilepsy and current treatments for epilepsy (428-429).

*CHAPTER OUTLINE*

I.  Problems in diagnosis

   A.  Biogenic versus psychogenic disorders
      1.  Major symptoms of organic brain disorder
         a.  Impairment of orientation
         b.  Impairment of memory
         c.  Impairment of intellectual functioning
         d.  Impairment of judgment
         e.  Lability or shallowness of affect (emotion)
         f.  Loss of mental and emotional resilience
      2.  Many of these symptoms apply to psychogenic disorder as well
      3.  Some symptoms may be psychogenic *in response to* the organic problem
      4.  Clinicians need to rule out organic problems (often using sophisticated brain-imaging techniques) before diagnosing a problem as psychogenic

B.  Specifying the organic impairment is important (in order to apply proper treatment), but it is difficult because:
1.  There is much overlap among symptoms of various organic brain disorders
2.  The same disorder may produce different symptoms, depending on brain location
3.  Many individual personal factors influence how a given disorder will manifest itself
4.  Researchers still know fairly little about many of the structures and functions of the nervous system

C.  Specifying the site of the damage
1.  Brain imaging, physiological measures, or behavioral observation can be useful
2.  Some disorders (e.g., Alzheimer's disease) may produce diffuse damage
3.  Some disorders are characterized by localized damage and produce "focal" symptoms
    a.  Aphasia (a language impairment) is related to left hemisphere damage in most people
        (1)  Fluent aphasia has damage toward the rear of the language hemisphere
        (2)  Nonfluent aphasia has damage toward the front of the language hemisphere
    b.  Apraxia (a voluntary movement problem)
    c.  Agnosia (a perception-recognition problem)

II.  Organic brain disorders classified by causes (etiology)

A.  Cerebral infection
1.  Cerebral abscess
    a.  Caused by germs entering the brain
    b.  Less common today with improved infection control
2.  Encephalitis (inflammation of the brain)
    a.  Caused by a virus
    b.  Epidemic encephalitis (sleeping sickness) produces lethargy alternating with hyperactive behavior and personality changes
3.  Meningitis (inflammation of membranes around brain and spinal cord)
    a.  Caused by bacteria, viruses, protozoa, or fungi
    b.  May produce drowsiness, confusion, irritability, impairments of concentration, memory or sensory problems
4.  Neurosyphilis (about 3 percent of cases of untreated syphilis)
    a.  Previously called general paresis (Chapter 1)
    b.  Caused by spirochete *treponema pallidum* acquired through sexual contact
    c.  Produces slovenliness, tremors, disturbed speech and writing, shuffling, disturbed vision, memory loss, personality changes, and ultimately death
    d.  Juvenile paresis occurs when unborn child is infected by mother
    e.  Has been treated successfully since the 1940s with penicillin

B.  Brain trauma
1.  Concussion (jarring of the brain)
    a.  Produces temporary loss of consciousness, headaches, dizziness, apathy, depression, irritability, and disturbances of memory, sleep, or concentration
    b.  Successive concussions can produce a cumulative effect
2.  Contusion (bruising of the brain)
    a.  Produces a coma lasting hours or days, convulsions, disorientation, or permanent deficits
    b.  Boxers, football players, and others engaged in violent activities susceptible
    c.  Successive contusions can produce a cumulative effect
3.  Laceration (cuts or punctures)
    a.  Produces symptoms that vary according to the site and severity of damage
    b.  Phineas Gage is a classic and famous case

C.  Cerebrovascular accidents (CVA): Strokes
1.  Causes of CVAs
    a.  Infarctions (blocking of blood vessels)
    b.  Hemorrhages (breaking of blood vessels)
2.  Both produce physical symptoms varying with site and extent of damage

3. Psychological symptoms may result from the person's mental reaction to physical impairments
4. Risk increases with age; men more at risk than women

D. Brain tumors
1. Technical classification of brain tumors
   a. Primary tumors originate in the brain
   b. Metastatic tumors typically originating in cancers elsewhere in the body
   c. Intracerebral tumors grow within the brain
   d. Extracerebral tumors grow between skull and brain
2. Symptoms vary depending on location and size
3. Surgery and/or radiation can be used to treat

E. Degenerative disorders
1. Degenerative disorder used to be considered a normal consequence of aging, but now it is realized that such cases are actually in the minority (still only about 30 percent over age 85)
2. Technical classification of degenerative disorders
   a. Cortical degeneration (e.g., Alzheimer's disease) is characterized primarily by
      (1) Memory disturbance
      (2) Comprehension problems
      (3) Naming difficulties
      (4) Environmental disorientation
   b. Subcortical degeneration (e.g., Huntington's chorea and Parkinson's disease) is characterized chiefly by
      (1) Poor problem solving
      (2) Forgetfulness
      (3) Mood changes
      (4) Motor disturbances
   c. Degeneration of both cortical and subcortical areas
      (1) Vascular problems (e.g., vascular dementia) characterized by
         (a) Abrupt onset
         (b) Step-wise deterioration of function
         (c) Focal (specific) symptoms
      (2) Diffuse damage (such as by HIV virus in AIDS dementia) characterized by a variety of symptoms listed so far, with progressive deterioration over time
3. Alzheimer's disease
   a. Post-mortem brain analysis reveals
      (1) Neurofibrillary tangles
      (2) Senile plaques
   b. These same brain abnormalities appear in Down syndrome patients, suggesting a connection with chromosome 21 (see below)
   c. Symptoms
      (1) Cognitive (particularly memory) deficits starting with complex behaviors and progressing to simpler ones over time
      (2) Eventual physical weakening and total debilitation and death
   d. Possible causes
      (1) Excitotoxicity theory blames toxic levels of excitatory neurotransmitters possibly related to head injuries
      (2) Chromosome abnormalities (14, 19, and 21 may all be involved) related to buildup of beta amyloid
   e. At present, there is no cure and treatment is mainly custodial care, although manipulation of acetylcholine levels may temporarily relieve symptoms

4. Vascular dementia
   a. Cumulative effect of many small strokes
   b. Symptoms step-wise and progressive, their exact nature depending on site and extent of damage
5. Huntington's chorea
   a. Genetically transmitted
   b. No sex link—either parent to any child

      c.   Damages basal ganglia of brain
      d.   Symptoms
          (1)  Slovenliness
          (2)  Mood disturbance
          (3)  Intellectual disruption
          (4)  Psychotic symptoms
          (5)  Loss of motor control
          (6)  Death after about 14 years
  6.  Parkinson's disease
      a.   No precise cause known
      b.   Also affects basal ganglia
      c.   Symptoms
          (1)  Tremor (4-8 cycles per second)
          (2)  Lack of facial expression
          (3)  Slow, stiff, crouching walk
          (4)  Memory, learning, judgment, concentration problems
          (5)  Delusions, depression, suicidal tendencies
      d.   Drugs that increase dopamine levels can reduce symptoms but there is no cure
  7.  Delirium
      a.   Temporary global disorder of cognition and attention
      b.   Older people at greater risk
      c.   Possible causes
          (1)  Medication intoxication
          (2)  Surgery
          (3)  Drug withdrawal
          (4)  Head injury
          (5)  Sleep loss
          (6)  Malnutrition
          (7)  Stress (retirement, poverty, loneliness, physical changes, particularly in the elderly)
          (8)  Physical illness (good indicator of disorder in the elderly)
      d.   Symptoms
          (1)  Profound confusion
          (2)  Hallucinations and delusions
          (3)  Sleep disturbances
          (4)  Emotional instability

F.  Nutritional deficiency
  1.  Korsakoff's psychosis
      a.   Caused by deficiency of vitamin $B_1$ (thiamine)
      b.   Victims invariably have history of alcoholism
      c.   Symptoms
          (1)  Anterograde amnesia (can't form new memories)
          (2)  Confabulation (filling in memory gaps with fantasy)

G.  Endocrine disorders
  1.  Thyroid syndromes
      a.   *Hyper*thyroidism (Graves disease)
          (1)  Caused by overactive thyroid gland
          (2)  Symptoms resemble those of anxiety
      b.   *Hypo*thyroidism (myxedema)
          (1)  Caused by underactive thyroid gland, possibly a result of iodine deficiency
          (2)  Symptoms include depression, sluggishness, poor memory and concentration
  2.  Adrenal syndromes
      a.   Addison's disease
          (1)  Underactivity of adrenal cortex
          (2)  Symptoms vary with premorbid adjustment, usually degrees of depression
      b.   Cushing's syndrome
          (1)  Overactivity of adrenal cortex
          (2)  Usually affects young women
          (3)  Symptoms include obesity, muscle weakness, and emotional instability

H. Toxic disorders
   1. Lead encephalopathy (lead poisoning)
      a. Typical causes are eating lead-based paint or lead-contaminated food
      b. Fluid pressure builds in the brain
      c. Symptoms
         (1) Abdominal pain
         (2) Constipation
         (3) Facial pallor
         (4) Convulsions
         (5) Bizarre behavior
         (6) Hallucinations and other psychotic behavior
   2. Other heavy-metal toxins (mainly mercury and manganese)
      a. Typical causes are industrial waste or pollution
      b. Mercury poisoning symptoms
         (1) Memory loss
         (2) Irritability
         (3) Difficulty in concentration
         (4) Tunnel vision
         (5) Loss of motor coordination
         (6) Hearing and speaking problems
         (7) May go to paralysis, coma, and death
      c. Manganese poisoning symptoms
         (1) Motor and speech impairments
         (2) Restlessness
         (3) Emotional instability
   3. Psychoactive drugs
      a. Symptoms related in detail in Chapter 12
      b. Chemicals may accumulate and cause organ (including brain) damage
   4. Carbon monoxide
      a. Typical source is auto exhaust fumes
      b. Results in rapid oxygen deprivation
      c. Often used as a means of suicide
      d. If not successful, suicide attempters may suffer permanent brain damage

III. The epilepsies

A. Epilepsy is a generic term referring to disorders involving irregularly occurring disruptions of consciousness (seizures)
   1. Symptomatic epilepsy is seizures resulting from a variety of other disorders known to cause seizures
   2. Idiopathic epilepsy has no known "other" cause and is what is usually referred to by the term "epilepsy"
   3. There is no single epileptic "type" of personality
   4. Common causes of seizures (and age at which the cause is most common)
      a. Head injury (at any age)
      b. Trauma or oxygen deprivation at birth
      c. Brain tumors (middle age)
      d. Cerebral vascular disease (old age)
   5. Some seizures are preceded by an aura, typically an odd sensory experience
   6. Medication is a common treatment (80% success rate); surgery is a last resort

B. Types of seizures
   1. Partial seizures
      a. Simple partial
         (1) Cognitive functioning remains intact
         (2) Mainly characterized by sensory and motor changes
      b. Complex partial (most common form)
         (1) Cognitive functioning interrupted
         (2) Preceded by an aura
         (3) Temporary loss of reality contact
         (4) Victim may engage in bizarre behavior with no later memory of the seizure

2. Generalized seizures
   a. Absence (formerly *petit mal*)
     (1) Brief, almost unnoticeable lapse of consciousness
     (2) More common in children than in adults
   b. Tonic-clonic (formerly *grand mal*)
     (1) Aura (may or may not occur)
     (2) Tonic phase (no breathing, muscles rigid)
     (3) Clonic phase (rhythmic muscles contractions)
     (4) Coma phase (relaxation while unconscious)

## KEY TERMS
*The following terms are in bold print in your text. Define them and practice their definitions using the flash cards at the end of the chapter.*

absence seizures (428)
agnosia (410)
Alzheimer's disease (419)
aphasia (409)
apraxia (410)
brain trauma (412)
brain tumors (417)
catastrophic reaction (416)
cerebral abscess (411)
cerebrovascular accident (CVA) (416)
complex partial seizure (427)
concussion (413)
contusion (413)
degenerative disorders (418)
delirium (424)
dementia (418)
embolism (416)
encephalitis (411)
endocrine glands (425)
epilepsy (427)
general paresis (412)
generalized seizures (428)

hemorrhage (416)
Huntington's chorea (423)
idiopathic epilepsy (427)
infarction (416)
Korsakoff's psychosis (424)
laceration (415)
lead encephalopathy (426)
meningitis (411)
metastatic brain tumors (417)
neurosyphilis (411)
organic brain disorders (406)
Parkinson's disease (423)
partial seizures (427)
primary brain tumors (417)
senile dementias (418)
simple partial seizure (427)
stroke (416)
symptomatic epilepsy (427)
thrombosis (416)
tonic-clonic seizures (428)
traumatic delirium (413)
vascular dementia (421)

*Your text does not list the following terms as formal vocabulary; however, if you don't know what they mean, you will be unable to grasp the concepts of this chapter.*

affable (425)
camaraderie (408)
chagrined (408)
encapsulated (411)
exacerbated (417)

gamut (424)
heterogeneity (420)
hyperalert (424)
lability (407)
lethargy (411)

piqued (420)
ramifications (408)
resilient (409)
slovenliness (412)

## IMPORTANT NAMES
*Identify the following persons and their major contributions to abnormal psychology as discussed in this chapter.*

Phineas Gage (415)

## GUIDED SELF-STUDY

1. To make the concepts of this chapter concrete and relevant to you, list, on the next page, the people that **you know** who have had an organic brain disorder. (Also include the famous people mentioned in the chapter.) Ask older family members about *your family tree* to increase your number of examples and to further provoke your interest. When you know some disorder is in your biological family, the text material about which disorders are genetically based becomes interesting!

**Cerebral infection** (abscess, encephalitis, meningitis, neurosyphilis):

**Brain trauma** (concussion, contusion, laceration):

**Cerebrovascular accidents** (strokes):

**Brain tumors**:

**Degenerative disorders** (Huntington's chorea, Parkinson's disease, Alzheimer's, vascular dementia):

**Nutritional deficiency** (Korsakoff's psychosis [Alcoholics]):

**Endocrine disorders**
  **Thyroid** (Graves' disease [hyperthyroidism] and myxedema [hypothyroidism]):

  **Adrenal** (Addison's disease and Cushing's syndrome):

**Toxic disorders** (heavy metals, psychoactive drugs, carbon monoxide):

**Epilepsy**:

PROBLEMS IN DIAGNOSIS

2. Use the following terms to fill in the blanks on the three reasons that biogenic problems are discussed in a psychology textbook: **differential, physical,** and **psychological**.

   a. Organically caused behavior problems can look just like _____ behavior

   problems, so the first issue involving psychological disorder is making a _____ diagnosis between organic cause and psychological cause.

   b. How a _____ disease affects a person's behavior is influenced by the person's

   personality, experiences, and environment, which are all _____ factors.

   c. Onset of organic brain disorders can cause the person to have secondary _____ problems as a reaction to the primary physical problem.

3. Organic brain disorders are a _____ health problem in the United States; _____ of all first admissions to mental hospitals turn out to be organic brain disorders.

4. What are the four major questions to be answered in diagnosing an organic brain disorder?

   a.

   b.

   c.

   d.

5. What are the six major symptoms of organic brain disorder?

   a.                                    d.

   b.                                    e.

   c.                                    f.

6. There is just one tiny little problem with those six major symptoms of organic brain disorder. What is that "little" problem?

7. Fill in the blanks to form a list of some information sources a diagnostician uses to make a differential diagnosis.

**brain wave**                                    **interviews**                              **observation**
**cerebrospinal**                               **magnetic**                                   **x-rays**
**emission**                                       **neurological**
**history**                                          **neuropsychological**

a. Direct _____ of the patient

b. Detailed _____ of the onset and progress of the symptoms

c. _____ with the patient's family and physician

d. A series of _____ tests to assess reflexes

e. EEG's (electrical _____ readings from the face and scalp)

f. Brain CT scans (a series of _____ of the brain)

g. Chemical analyses of _____ fluid

h. _____ tests such as the Halstead-Reitan Battery

i. PET (positron _____ tomography)

j. MRI (_____ resonance imaging)

8. Beyond determining organicity, more difficulties are encountered in diagnosing specific organic brain disorders. Complete the following summary of the difficulty of symptom overlap:

(a)_____ disorders sometimes have same symptoms and

(b)_____ disorder can have different symptoms in different patients.

9. Name seven factors that determine which symptoms a patient will manifest with an organic brain disorder.

a.                                             e.

b.                                             f.

c.                                             g.

d.

10. What is the difference between a disorder that is diffuse and one that is localized?

11. What does the symptom pattern of an organic disability often indicate?

12. Write the name of the problem next to the appropriate symptoms.

**Apraxia**                                           **Nonfluent aphasia**
**Fluent aphasia**                                **Visual agnosia**

a. _____ Unable to make sense out of visual perceptions

b. _____ Great difficulty initiating speech and enunciating words

c. _____ Unable to perform ordinarily simple voluntary tasks

d. _____ Can form words but does so with a lack of meaning

13. Where is the damage if the average right-handed person

    a. cannot move left arm and leg?
    b. has fluent aphasia?
    c. has nonfluent aphasia?

ORGANIC BRAIN DISORDERS CLASSIFIED BY CAUSE
14. Identify the four types of cerebral infection mentioned in your text: **General paresis, Cerebral abscess, Meningitis,** and **Encephalitis.**

a. _____ Infection encapsulated by connective tissue

b. _____ Infection that inflames the brain

c. _____ Infection that inflames the covering of the brain and spinal cord

d. _____ Brain deterioration as a result of long-term (10-30 years) syphilitic infection

15. What fraction of all AIDS patients will experience dementia, usually in the later stages of the disease?

16. Identify the three kinds of brain trauma: **Laceration, Concussion,** and **Contusion.**

a. _____ Brain is jarred with brief loss of consciousness

b. _____ Exterior head trauma causes brain to slosh against inside of skull, causing neural bruising, coma, and possibly convulsions or delirium
c. _____ Injury from a foreign object entering the brain and destroying brain tissue

17. Traumatic (a)_____ is a state of disorientation that sometimes occurs when a person

awakens from a coma after a (b)_____. The patient may even seem to be in a paranoid delusional state, such as believing that the hospital staff are kidnappers or enemies.

Traumatic delirium usually clears up within a (c)_____ or so. The length of time that the

(d)_____ lasts is a good predictor of the posttraumatic symptoms. If damage is serious

enough or repeated enough, permanent (e)_____ instability and (f)_____ impairment

can result. This is seen in *dementia pugilistica*, better known as being (g)_____.

18. Organize the three types of brain trauma from least serious to most serious.

    Least serious — _____ / _____ / _____ — Most serious

19. Serious head trauma occurs at a rate of about (a)_____ people per 100,000. That means

yours chances of serious head trauma are about (b)_____ in 1,000; however, if you are a

young (c) **male / female**, your chances are greatly increased because these people tend to engage in riskier behavior.

20. Phineas P. Gage is a famous character in psychology books. Would you want his claim to fame??? Why?

21. Use the following terms to complete this summary of CVA's (one is used twice):

| | | |
|---|---|---|
| air | cerebrovascular | slow |
| aneurysms | embolism | small |
| blocking | fat | stroke |
| blood pressure | hemorrhage | strokes |
| blood clot | infarction | sudden |
| breaking | less | thrombosis |
| central | silent | twenty-five |

CVA's are commonly called (a)_____; CVA stands for (b)_____ accidents. A CVA is injury to the brain caused by vascular interruption which is either a

(c)_____ or (d)_____ of blood vessels in the brain. When brain tissue dies

because the blood supply to the area is cut off, the damaged area is called a/an (e)_____.

A cerebral (f)_____ is the CVA which is a ruptured blood vessel. The blockage that

causes an infarction is either a/an (g)_____ or a/an (h)_____. An (i)_____ is a floating ball of substance that eventually lodges in a vessel that is too narrow for it to pass.

The substance of the ball can be a (j)_____, (k)_____, or a piece of (l)_____. In the case of an infarction caused by a slow build up of fatty coating within a blood vessel, the

blockage is called a (m)_____. The onset of this kind of problem will be (n)_____ because of the slow build up of the material inside the blood vessel. The onset of a CVA

caused by an embolism will be (o)_____. When a CVA is a hemorrhage inside the

brain, it is usually traced to hypertension, which means high (p)_____; if it is in the

space around the brain, it is usually due to (q)_____. (r)_____ syndrome is evidence that a CVA has occurred because of acute onset of specific disabilities involving the

(s)_____ nervous system. Silent strokes are (t)_____ CVAs in (u)_____ critical areas of the brain that have little noticeable effect on the person's behavior. Evidence of CVAs

are found in (v)_____ percent of routine autopsies. Many of these were unnoticed (w)_____ strokes.

22. The clearest risk factor for stroke is (a)_____. A person's emotional state after the stroke is partly organically determined and partly psychologically determined. Left hemisphere strokes

tend to display the (b)_____ reaction. Right hemisphere stroke victims may show

(c)_____ or even joke about their condition. The victim's premorbid (d)_____ is also going to be a major factor in determining the response to CVA debilitation.

23. The two categories of brain tumors are (a)_____ tumors and (b)_____ tumors.

24. List the three different classifications of brain tumors beside their definitions.

    a. _____ tumors grow within the brain, destroy normal brain tissue and replace it with abnormal tumor cells

b. _____ tumors grow outside the brain, but inside the skull

c. _____ tumors develop in some other area of the body and travel to the brain via body fluids

25. Give examples of degenerative brain disorders with deterioration in the following locations:

a. Cerebral cortex:

b. Subcortical areas:

c. Both cortical and subcortical regions:

26. Use these terms to complete this discussion of dementia:

| | | |
|---|---|---|
| **Alzheimer's** | **physical** | **symptoms** |
| **both** | **medications** | **thirty** |
| **depression** | **senile dementias** | **vascular** |
| **four to seven** | **deterioration** | |

Dementia is severe mental (a)_____; the degenerative disorders of

late life are known collectively as (b)_____. These are the results of

pathological processes. They are not part of the normal aging process. Only (c)____ to _____ percent of people over the age of sixty-five have signs of dementia. In the age group eighty-

five and above, (d)_____ percent have dementia. The two most common senile dementias are

(e)_____ disease and (f)_____ dementia. The differential diagnosis between these two is difficult; there is no absolute medical test with which to diagnose them. The differential

diagnosis is further complicated because they can both show the same clinical (g)_____

and a patient may actually have (h)_____ kinds of deterioration. There are many treatable

problems that can mimic the symptoms of dementias, such as (i)_____ illnesses,

reactions to (j)_____, and (k)_____. These are very important differential diagnoses to make since treatable disorders are not permanent if treated correctly.

27. What kind of events do old people have to depress them? They don't have to take exams and they don't have parents hassling them. They get a pension check and they don't even have to go to work!

28. Autopsies of Alzheimer's patients show these people had twisted, distorted nerve fibers called

(a)_____ and microscopic lesions in their neurons called (b)_____.

29. Complete the blanks in the sequence of deterioration seen in Alzheimer's patients:

| | | |
|---|---|---|
| **bed** | **daily living skills** | **physical** |
| **complex** | **distant** | **recent** |

a. Loss of memory for _____ events

b. Loss of memory for _____ events

c. Loss of _____ behaviors for managing one's business affairs

d.  Loss of _____ (for instance, bathing and dressing)

e.  _____ weakness

f.  Become _____ patients

30. The cause of Alzheimer's disease is still unknown.  Draw a line to connect the theory on the left with its essential concept on the right.

Genetic                             Multiple contributing factors
Amyloid-cascade hypothesis          Build up of toxins
Excitotoxicity                      21, 14, 19
Threshold model                     Excess neurotransmitters

31. What is the relationship between head injury and the development of Alzheimer's disease?

32. What is the relationship between Down syndrome and Alzheimer's?

33. How did this Down connection influence genetic research for Alzheimer's?

34. What evidence suggests there may actually be more than one kind of Alzheimer's disease (like there seems to be more than one kind of schizophrenia)?

35. Early-onset Alzheimer's disease occurs between the ages of _____ and _____.

36. Huntington's chorea is a (a)_____ gene disorder; that is, if a person has even one

gene for it, the person will develop the disorder in (b)_____ or _____ adulthood.

37. The cause of Parkinson's disease is (a)_____.  It appears most often in people

between the ages of (b)_____ and _____.  The primary symptom of Parkinson's disease is

(c)_____.  The Parkinson's victim is likely to have a/an (d)_____ facial

appearance and walk in a/an (e)_____ manner.  Parkinson's symptoms can be treated for a

while with a medication that boosts the neurotransmitter (f)_____.

38. **DELIRIUM vs DEMENTIA**: Sudden onset of delirium in elderly people is not uncommon.

The person is profoundly confused and maybe even psychotic, having (a)_____ and

_____.  The condition is likely to pass within a/an (b)_____, leaving the

individual totally (c)_____.  The underlying problem in delirium seems to be a widespread
disruption of cerebral metabolism and neurotransmission.  Delirium should not be confused

with dementia, which is (d)_____; delirium can be the symptom that indicates a
treatable medical problem that needs attention.  Some of the causes of delirium in the elderly

are: Medication (e)_____, withdrawal from (f)_____, physical (g)_____,

surgery, (h)_____ loss, poor (i)_____, (j)_____ injury, or psychological

(k)_____.

39. Use these terms to complete the blanks for nutritional deficiencies that cause psychological disturbances.

**alcoholics**             **Korsakoff's**             **vitamins**
**beriberi**               **pellagra**

Nutritional deficiencies occur because of a lack of essential (a)_____. Thiamine deficiency

leads to (b)_____, and niacin deficiency causes (c)_____. These are still seen in less industrialized nations but have been largely eliminated in America. The one organic brain syndrome caused by a nutritional deficiency still commonly seen in the U. S. is

(d)_____ psychosis, which results from inadequate diets in people who are (e)_____.

40. After reading about Korsakoff's psychosis, you now understand why your long-term alcoholic relative is like s/he is. S/he can never remember your new spouse's name or even who the

current U.S. president is. (a)_____ amnesia is the term for this inability to learn new information. S/he will tell outrageous stories that could not possibly be true which is termed

(b)_____. When the individual cannot see how outrageous the story is, the rest of the family is irritated at the "obvious lying."

41. Why are endocrine glands mentioned in a chapter on brain disorders that cause psychological disturbance? Which endocrine glands are discussed?


42. List the disorders resulting from overactivity and underactivity for these two glands.

Gland               Underactivity                    Overactivity

Thyroid:

Adrenal:

43. What are some toxic agents that can affect the brain and, therefore psychological health?


44. Lead poisoning, called (a)_____, causes an accumulation of (b)_____ in the brain.

The most frequent victims of lead poisoning are (c)_____ who may become mentally

(d)_____ as a result of the poisoning. Lead is in the environment in the forms of

(name at least four) (e)_____.

45. Mercury and manganese poisoning are seen most often in people who _____ on a daily basis. Other people may suffer from these toxins as a result of industrial waste contamination, such as by eating fish from polluted waters.

46. A failed suicide attempt with carbon monoxide may leave a person (a)_____, (b)_____

and with (c)_____ deficits in addition to the issues that were involved in the suicide

attempt. These symptoms may clear up within (d)_____; however, for some people they are permanent.

THE EPILEPSIES
Use the following terms to complete Questions 47 and 48 about epilepsy:

**Absence seizure**          **idiopathic**              **Tonic-clonic**
**Complex partial**          **Simple partial**
**disruption**               **symptomatic**

47. Epilepsy is a (a)_____ in the normal electrical activity of the brain. Epilepsy that

    has a known cause is classified as (b)_____, and epilepsy that has no known cause is

    classified as (c)_____.

48. Identify each of the following types of epileptic seizures:

    a. _____ Loss of contact with reality for a brief time while engaging in
                       mechanical behavior
    b. _____ Loss of consciousness and convulsions

    c. _____ Brief loss of awareness

    d. _____ Muscle spasms in part of the body

49. Identify the correct order of events for a grand mal epileptic seizure:

    _____ Confused and sleepy
    _____ Aura phase
    _____ Clonic phase
    _____ Tonic phase

50. Although there is no particular personality and no mental illness associated with epilepsy, the
    epileptic may experience a secondary psychological disturbance because of the loss of

    _____ that goes with being temporarily unable to willfully control one's own body.

51. Lagniappe—a little something extra. Just in case it's on the test. Use the following terms to
    match the following phrases:

**Absence seizure**                    **Differential diagnosis**
**Aura**                               **Encephalitis**
**Automatisms**                        **Head-hunter**
**Biogenic**                           **Impairment in orientation**
**Caretaker**                          **Lability**
**Cushing's syndrome**                 **Meninges**
**Delirium**

    a. _____ Means has an organic cause

    b. _____ Person does not know where s/he is and what day it is

    c. _____ Moving from one emotion to another quickly and inappropriately

    d. _____ Choice between disorders when there is overlap of symptoms

    e. _____ Sleeping sickness

    f. _____ Membrane covering brain and spinal cord

    g. _____ Particularly responsible for head injuries in football

    h. _____ Hidden victim of Alzheimer's disease

i. _____ Acute confusion (not "a cute confusion")  See Helpful Hint 2.

j. _____ Possible diagnosis for an abnormally emotional, obese young woman

k. _____ Repetitive, purposeless movements of a complex partial seizure

l. _____ A strange sensation that warns a seizure may be coming

m. _____ Same as petit mal

## HELPFUL HINTS

1. A memory device for the first five of the six symptoms for organic brain disorder: the "word" **MOIJE**.  That word has worked for me for years when I need to do a quick, orderly recall.  Perhaps you can make a word that works better for you: jimoe, mijoe, emjoi?

   **M** = memory
   **O** = orientation
   **I** = intellect
   **J** = judgment
   **E** = emotions

2. These are the kind of associations, silly comments, jokes, and sometimes sick comments that I can use when studying or tutoring that will facilitate memory. (I can think of a lot of them with the term "head hunter" in a chapter about diseased brains.  Sorry if I grossed you out.  A laugh or a gross-out can really lock information into memory (sometimes better than serious, straight-faced effort.)

## PRACTICE TEST
*Take the following test several times as you study the chapter.  Write your answers on a separate sheet of paper and after each attempt, note in the tally box above each question whether your answer was correct or incorrect.*

1. Uncle Joe has Alzheimer's disease.  In addition to all the problems resulting directly from the disorder, he is also depressed and suicidal.  The depression and suicidal tendencies would be termed
   a. reactive schizophrenia.
   b. secondary emotional disturbances.
   c. biogenic psychoses.
   d. biochemical side effects.

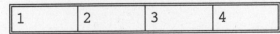

2. What is apraxia?
   a. The inability to perform voluntary movements in an otherwise normal person
   b. The inability to recognize common objects
   c. A speech disability in which one can read but not understand spoken language
   d. The inability to read or write

| 1 | 2 | 3 | 4 |
|---|---|---|---|

3. Albert was perfectly healthy until one day at lunch he became weak in his right arm and leg and found he could speak only very slowly and with great difficulty, even though he knew what he wanted to say.  Chances are that Albert is suffering from
   a. a cerebral laceration.          c. a cerebrovascular accident.
   b. general paresis.                d. encephalitis.

381

| 1 | 2 | 3 | 4 |

4. Albert's speech difficulty in the previous question would probably be termed
   a.  verbal agraphia.
   b.  fluent aphasia.
   c.  agnosia.
   d.  nonfluent aphasia.

| 1 | 2 | 3 | 4 |

5. Brain damage that occurs as a result of penetration by a foreign object is called
   a.  concussion.
   b.  laceration.
   c.  contusion.
   d.  auscultation.

| 1 | 2 | 3 | 4 |

6. When Laura fell off her bicycle she hit her head on the street and was unconscious for several minutes. Since then, she seems to have recovered with no permanent aftereffects. Laura apparently suffered a
   a.  contusion.
   b.  concussion.
   c.  laceration.
   d.  cerebrovascular accident.

| 1 | 2 | 3 | 4 |

7. A problem characterized by blockage of arteries carrying blood to the brain is called
   a.  a cerebral hemorrhage.
   b.  senility.
   c.  Korsakoff's psychosis.
   d.  a cerebral infarction.

| 1 | 2 | 3 | 4 |

8. Which of the following is a subcortical degenerative disorder?
   a.  Parkinson's disease
   b.  Alzheimer's disease
   c.  Addison's disease
   d.  Grave's disease

| 1 | 2 | 3 | 4 |

9. A disorder in which there is gradually increasing disability resulting from the cumulative effects of many small strokes is called
   a.  Korsakoff's psychosis.
   b.  vascular dementia.
   c.  Huntington's chorea
   d.  senile gravida.

| 1 | 2 | 3 | 4 |

10. The term for a brain tumor that is the result of cancer originating in another part of the body and spreading to the brain is
    a.  metastatic tumor.
    b.  aneurysm.
    c.  extracerebral tumor.
    d.  cerebral thrombus.

| 1 | 2 | 3 | 4 |

11. Which of the following disorders has been linked to chromosome 21 and may be related to Down's syndrome?
    a.  Parkinson's disease
    b.  cretinism
    c.  Alzheimer's disease
    d.  hyperthyroidism

12. A disorder associated with a deficiency of vitamin $B_1$ and characterized by anterograde amnesia and confabulation is
a. myxedema.
b. Grave's disease.
c. juvenile paresis.
d. Korsakoff's psychosis.

13. Which of the following disorders is somewhat successfully treated with drugs that increase dopamine levels in the brain?
a. Pick's disease
b. Addison's disease
c. Parkinson's disease
d. Grave's disease

```
| 1 | 2 | 3 | 4 |
```

14. Aunt Mary has Korsakoff's psychosis. What might we also guess about Aunt Mary?
a. She has had a drinking problem for some time.
b. She is in the early stages of Alzheimer's disease.
c. She is only of borderline intelligence.
d. She is probably of Eastern European Jewish descent.

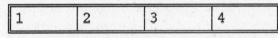

15. Which of the following is true of lead encephalopathy?
a. It may result in mental retardation.
b. It is another term for cretinism.
c. It involves low intracranial fluid pressures.
d. It is more common today than decades ago.

```
| 1 | 2 | 3 | 4 |
```

16. Which of the following is an endocrine disorder?
a. Senile dementia
b. Cushing's syndrome
c. Idiopathic epilepsy
d. Neurosyphilis

```
| 1 | 2 | 3 | 4 |
```

17. Fred is in his eighties. He lives alone, barely surviving on his social security check. He seems very depressed, talks to himself, and rarely takes a bath. Given his situation, your text suggests that the most likely cause of his mental state is
a. his environment and living conditions.
b. lead poisoning from the old paint in his apartment.
c. long-term personality disorder of the schizoid type.
d. inevitable cumulative loss of brain cells with age.

```
| 1 | 2 | 3 | 4 |
```

18. Which type of epilepsy is characterized by intact cognitive functioning, sensory changes, and strange motor symptoms?
a. Petit mal
b. Tonic-clonic
c. Complex partial
d. Simple partial

| 1 | 2 | 3 | 4 |
|---|---|---|---|

19. Randolph, age ten, has begun suffering from seizures. He passes out and exhibits muscle spasms. His doctor says he has idiopathic epilepsy. The cause of Randolph's seizures is
    a. head injury.
    b. lead encephalopathy.
    c. a toxic reaction.
    d. cannot tell for sure—idiopathic epilepsy has no certain cause.

| 1 | 2 | 3 | 4 |
|---|---|---|---|

20. Tonic-clonic seizures used to be called
    a. *petit-mal* seizures.
    b. Jacksonian seizures.
    c. *grand mal* seizures
    d. temporal lobe seizures.

## ANSWERS
### Self-Study Exercise

1. Infection (neurosyphilis): Henry VIII, probably Christopher Columbus (412)
   Brain trauma:    Concussion—Merril Hoge, Adrian Guitterez, Al Toon (414)
                         Laceration—Phineas Gage (415)
   Brain tumor: George Gershwin (407)
   Degenerative disorders: Parkinson's disease—Eugene O'Neill (423)
   Endocrine disorder: Graves' disease—former President and Mrs. Bush and their dog (425)
   Epilepsy: Julius Caesar, Feodor Dostoevsky, and Vincent van Gogh (428)
2. a. psychological; differential
   b. physical; psychological
   c. psychological (406)
3. major; one-fourth (406)
4. a. Is the disorder organically caused?
   b. If so, what is the nature of the brain pathology?
   c. Where is it located in the brain?
   d. How are psychosocial problems influencing the organic disorder's symptoms, and is psychotherapy needed? (406)
   ("Is it? If so, what kind and where?"—summaries the first three questions for easy memory facilitation.)
5. a. Impairment in orientation
   b. Impairment of memory
   c. Impairment of general intellectual functioning
   d. Impairment of judgment
   e. Emotional lability or shallowness of affect
   f. Loss of mental and emotional resilience (406-407)
6. The six major symptoms for organic brain disease are the same as the symptoms for many psychogenic disorders (407).
7. a. observation
   b. history
   c. Interviews
   d. neurological (408)
   e. brain wave (89)
   f. x-rays (90)
   g. cerebrospinal
   h. Neuropsychological
   i. emission
   j. magnetic (408-409)
8. a. Different
   b. the same (409)
9. a. Specific location of the pathology in the brain
   b. The patient's age
   c. The patient's general physical condition
   d. The patient's prior level of intellectual development
   e. The patient's premorbid personality
   f. The patient's emotional stability
   g. The patient's social situation (409)

384

10. *Diffuse* is scattered out over many different areas.
    *Localized* is clearly affecting specific locations within the brain without affecting other
    locations (409). (For ease of memory: diffuse = scattered; localized = limited)
11. The specific areas of the brain that are affected by the pathology (409)
12. a. Visual agnosia      c. Apraxia
    b. Nonfluent aphasia      d. Fluent aphasia (409-410)
13. a. Right hemisphere (91)
    b. Left hemisphere, toward the rear (410)
    c. Left hemisphere, toward the front (410)
14. a. Cerebral abscess
    b. Encephalitis
    c. Meningitis
    d. General paresis (neurosyphilis) (411-412)
15. Fifteen percent (419)
16. a. Concussion
    b. Contusion
    c. Laceration (412-416)
17. a. delirium      e. emotional
    b. contusion      f. intellectual
    c. week      g. punch drunk (413)
    d. coma
18. Least serious— concussion / contusion / laceration —Most serious (413)
19. a. 200      c. male (412)
    b. 2
20. No, Phineas's claim to fame is not one to be envied. He had a huge metal rod blown into his
    skull in the 1840's. His survival of such a trauma would be surprising even with modern
    medicine, to say nothing of the medicine of the 1840's. His personality was profoundly
    changed by the head trauma (415).
21. a. strokes      m. thrombosis
    b. cerebrovascular      n. slow
    c. blocking (or breaking)      o. sudden
    d. breaking (or blocking)      p. blood pressure
    e. infarction      q. aneurysms
    f. hemorrhage      r. Stroke
    g. thrombosis (or embolism)      s. central
    h. embolism (or thrombosis)      t. small
    i. embolism      u. less
    j. blood clot      v. 25
    k. air      w. silent (416-417)
    l. fat
22. a. age      c. indifference
    b. catastrophic      d. personality (416-417)
23. a. primary
    b. metastatic (417)
24. a. Intracerebral
    b. Extracerebral
    c. Metastatic brain (417)
25. a. Alzheimer's disease
    b. Huntington's chorea and Parkinson's disease
    c. Vascular dementia and AIDS demential (418)
26. a. deterioration      g. symptoms
    b. senile dementias      h. both
    c. 4 to 7      i. physical
    d. 30      j. medications
    e. Alzheimer's      k. depression (418-419)
    f. vascular
27. In retirement, they may miss their friends from the workplace and the satisfaction they got
    from their work. The incomes to which they were accustomed are reduced in retirement.
    They may be widowed and they experience death of their peers. They are likely to have
    health problems that are chronic, and they live in a society where people of old age are not
    valued (408).

28. a. neurofibrillary tangles
    b. senile plaques (419)
29. a. recent
    b. distant
    c. complex
    d. daily living skills
    e. Physical
    f. bed (419)
30. Genetic: 21, 14, 19 (chromosomes)
    Amyloid-cascade hypothesis: Build-up of toxins
    Excitotoxicity: Excess neurotransmitters
    Threshold model: Multiple contributing factors (420-421)
31. There is increased risk for developing Alzheimer's disease due to head trauma; however, head trauma is neither necessary nor sufficient to lead to the development of Alzheimer's (420).
32. Almost all people born with Down syndrome develop Alzheimer's disease if they live long enough (420).
33. The chromosomal basis of Down syndrome was known. Therefore, researchers looked at chromosome 21 for a genetic basis of Alzheimer's (420).
34. Besides the implications for genetic abnormalities on chromosome 21, early-onset Alzheimer's seems to be connected to chromosome 14; late onset Alzheimer's seems to be controlled by chromosome 19 (420).
35. 40 and 60 years old (419)
36. a. dominant
    b. young or middle (425)
37. a. unknown
    b. 50 and 70
    c. tremor
    d. expressionless, mask-like
    e. slow, stiff
    f. dopamine (423-424)

38. a. hallucinations and delusions
    b. month
    c. unharmed
    d. irreversible
    e. intoxication
    f. medications
    g. illness
    h. sleep
    i. nutrition
    j. head
    k. stress (424)
39. a. vitamins
    b. beriberi
    c. pellagra
    d. Korsakoff's
    e. alcoholics (424-425)
40. a. Anterograde
    b. confabulation (424)
41. Endocrine glands are discussed with organic brain disorders because they are the other area of organic dysfunction that causes very definite psychological disturbance. The disorders of the thyroid and adrenal glands are discussed (425-426).

42.
| Gland | Underactivity | Overactivity |
|---|---|---|
| Thyroid | hypothyroidism, or myxedema | hyperthyroidism, or Graves' disease |
| Adrenal | Addison's disease | Cushing's syndrome |

(425-426)
43. Lead, psychoactive drugs, carbon monoxide, heavy metals such as mercury and manganese (426)
44. a. lead encephalopathy
    b. fluid
    c. children
    d. retarded
    e. lead-based paints, lead-lined water pipes, old plaster walls, clay pottery, candles with lead-core wicks, exhaust from leaded gasoline in autos, and industrial pollution (426)
45. work with these (426)
46. a. apathetic
    b. confused
    c. memory
    d. two years (426)
47. a. disruption
    b. symptomatic
    c. idiopathic (427)
48. a. Complex partial
    b. Tonic-clonic
    c. Absence seizure
    d. Simple partial (427-428)
49. 4, 1, 3, and 2 (428)

50. self esteem (428)
51. a. Biogenic (406)
    b. Impairment in orientation (406)
    c. Lability (407)
    d. Differential diagnosis (407)
    e. Encephalitis (411)
    f. Meninges (411)
    g. Head-hunter (414)
    h. Caretaker (422)
    i. Delirium (424)
    j. Cushing's syndrome (426)
    k. Automatisms (427)
    l. Aura (427)
    m. Absence seizure (428)

## Practice Test

1. b (407)
2. a (410)
3. c (416)
4. d (409)
5. b (415)
6. b (413)
7. d (416)
8. a (418)
9. b (421)
10. a (417)

11. c (420)
12. d (424)
13. c (424)
14. a (424)
15. a (426)
16. b (426)
17. a (408)
18. d (427)
19. d (427)
20. c (428)

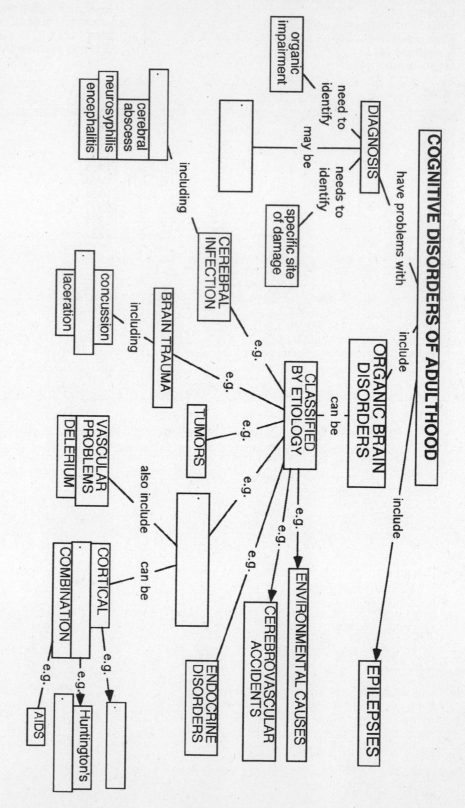

# CONCEPT MAP 16.1

Fill out the boxes marked with question marks (?) with the concepts or words you think belong there. Suggested answers are on a following page.

**COGNITIVE DISORDERS OF ADULTHOOD**

have problems with

include

include

**DIAGNOSIS**

need to identify → organic impairment

may be

needs to identify → specific site of damage

including → cerebral abscess, neurosyphilis, encephalitis

**ORGANIC BRAIN DISORDERS**

can be

**CLASSIFIED BY ETIOLOGY**

e.g. → **CEREBRAL INFECTION**

e.g. → **BRAIN TRAUMA**
including → concussion, laceration

e.g. → **TUMORS**

e.g. → **ENDOCRINE DISORDERS**

e.g. → **CEREBROVASCULAR ACCIDENTS**

e.g. → **ENVIRONMENTAL CAUSES**

also include
can be → **CORTICAL**, **COMBINATION**

**VASCULAR PROBLEMS**, **DELERIUM**

e.g. → AIDS
e.g. → Huntington's
e.g.

**EPILEPSIES**

388

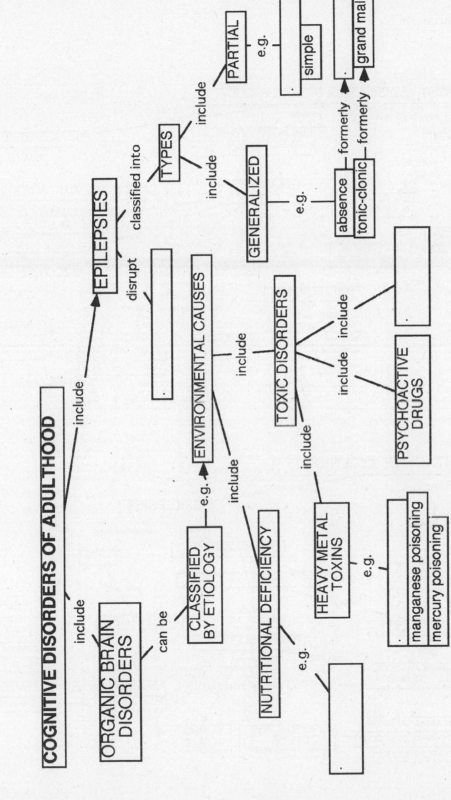

## CONCEPT MAP 16.2

Fill out the boxes marked with question marks (?) with the concepts or words you think belong there. Suggested answers are on a following page.

## CONCEPT MAPS

## 16.1 & 16.2

The suggested answers are
shown in *italics*.

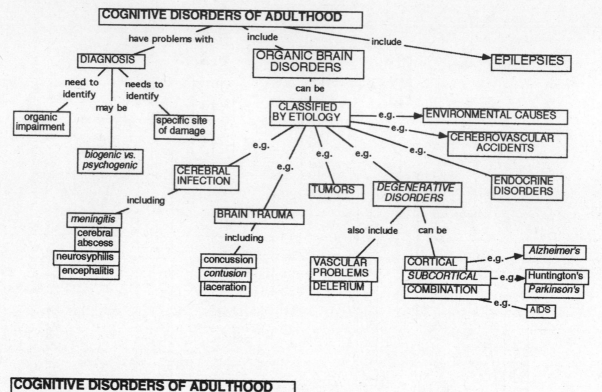

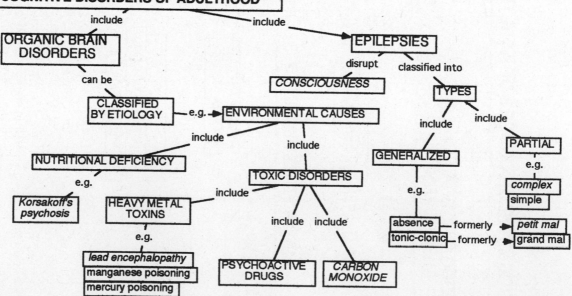

# CHAPTER TERMS (Cut out on the lines to use as Flash Cards)

| | | |
|---|---|---|
| 16.1<br><br>**absence seizures** | 16.8<br><br>**cerebral abscess** | 16.15<br><br>**dementia** |
| 16.2<br><br>**agnosia** | 16.9<br><br>**cerebrovascular accident (CVA)** | 16.16<br><br>**embolism** |
| 16.3<br><br>**Alzheimer's disease** | 16.10<br><br>**complex partial seizure** | 16.17<br><br>**encephalitis** |
| 16.4<br><br>**aphasias** | 16.11<br><br>**concussion** | 16.18<br><br>**endocrine glands** |
| 16.5<br><br>**apraxia** | 16.12<br><br>**contusion** | 16.19<br><br>**epilepsy** |
| 16.6<br><br>**brain trauma** | 16.13<br><br>**degenerative disorders** | 16.20<br><br>**general paresis** |
| 16.7<br><br>**catastrophic reaction** | 16.14<br><br>**delirium** | 16.21<br><br>**generalized seizures** |

# DEFINITIONS (Cut out on the lines to use as Flash Cards)

| | | |
|---|---|---|
| 16.15<br><br>Severe mental deterioration | 16.8<br><br>A brain infection that becomes encapsulated by connective tissue; one of the four major categories of brain infection | 16.1<br><br>Brief generalized epileptic episodes during which patients, usually children, seem unaware of their surroundings |
| 16.16<br><br>Obstruction of a blood vessel by a ball of a substance such as fat, air, or clotted blood, thus cutting off the blood supply; a common cause of infarction | 16.9<br>A blockage of or break in the blood vessels in the brain, resulting in injury to brain tissue<br>Commonly called stroke | 16.2<br><br>Disturbed sensory perception |
| 16.17<br><br>Inflammation of the brain; one of the four major categories of brain infection | 16.10<br><br>A partial epileptic episode in which cognitive functioning is interrupted | 16.3<br>Organic brain disorder characterized by cognitive deficits such as failure of concentration and memory; the disease can occur as early as age forty, but its prevalence increases with age |
| 16.18<br>Glands responsible for the production of hormones that, when released into the blood, affect various bodily mechanisms such as physical growth and development | 16.11<br><br>A head injury caused by a blow to the head that jars the brain and momentarily disrupts functioning | 16.4<br><br>Language impairments generally attributable to damage in the dominant hemisphere of the brain |
| 16.19<br>Generic term for a variety of organic disorders characterized by irregularly occurring disturbances in consciousness in the form of seizures or convulsions | 16.12<br><br>A head injury in which the brain is shifted out of its normal position and pressed against one side of the skull, thus bruising the neural tissue | 16.5   Impairment of the ability to perform voluntary movements in a person who has normal primary motor skills and who understands the nature of the movement to be performed |
| 16.20<br><br>A final stage of syphilis, involving the gradual and irreversible breakdown of physical and mental functioning | 16.13   Organic brain syndromes characterized by a general deterioration of intellectual, emotional, and motor functioning as a result of progressive pathological change in the brain | 16.6<br><br>Injury to the brain as a result of jarring, bruising or cutting |
| 16.21<br>Epileptic episodes that either involve the entire brain at the outset (primary) or soon spread from one point to the entire brain (secondary) | 16.14   A global disorder of cognition and attention that begins suddenly and remits quickly, leaving most patients unharmed. Symptoms include confusion, hallucinations, and emotional lability | 16.7   An emotional disturbance sometimes accompanying organic brain disorder; the person, bewildered by the inability to perform simple tasks, responds with disorganization and sometimes violent fury |

# CHAPTER TERMS (Cut out on the lines to use as Flash Cards)

| 16.22<br><br>**hemorrhage** | 16.29<br><br>**meningitis** | 16.36<br><br>**senile dementias** |
|---|---|---|
| 16.23<br><br>**Huntington's chorea** | 16.30<br><br>**metastatic brain tumors** | 16.37<br><br>**simple partial seizures** |
| 16.24<br><br>**idiopathic epilepsy** | 16.31<br><br>**neurosyphilis** | 16.38<br><br>**symptomatic epilepsy** |
| 16.25<br><br>**infarction** | 16.32<br><br>**organic brain disorders** | 16.39<br><br>**thrombosis** |
| 16.26<br><br>**Korsakoff's psychosis** | 16.33<br><br>**Parkinson's disease** | 16.40<br><br>**tonic-clonic seizures** |
| 16.27<br><br>**laceration** | 16.34<br><br>**partial seizures** | 16.41<br><br>**traumatic delirium** |
| 16.28<br><br>**lead encephalopathy** | 16.35<br><br>**primary brain tumor** | 16.42<br><br>**vascular dementia** |

# DEFINITIONS (Cut out on the lines to use as Flash Cards)

| | | |
|---|---|---|
| 16.36 The pathological degenerative diseases of later life resulting from severe organic deterioration of the brain | 16.29 Brain infection involving an acute inflammation of the meninges and characterized by drowsiness, sensory impairments, irritability, and confusion; one of the four major categories of brain infection | 16.22 A cerebrovascular accident in which a blood vessel in the brain ruptures, causing blood to spill out into the brain tissue |
| 16.37 A partial epileptic episode in which cognitive functioning remains intact | 16.30 Secondary tumors, usually developing from cancer of the lungs, breast, stomach, or kidney, that are spread to the brain by body fluids | 16.23 A fatal organic brain disorder which is transmitted genetically; symptoms include spasmodic jerking of the limbs, bizarre behavior, and mental deterioration |
| 16.38 Label applied to convulsions that are a function of brain damage caused by pathologies such as alcohol or drug intoxication neurosyphilis, tumors, encephalitis, trauma, or strokes; "acquired epilepsy" | 16.31 Deterioration of brain tissue as a result of syphilis, which begins with infection by the spirochete *Treponema pallidum*; one of the four major categories of brain infection | 16.24 A convulsive disorder for which there is no known cause; the disorder usually has its onset between the ages of ten and twenty |
| 16.39 Obstruction of a blood vessel by a buildup of fatty material coating the inside of the vessel, thus blocking the flow of blood; a common cause of infarction | 16.32 Behavioral problems that are directly traceable to the destruction of brain tissue or to biochemical imbalance in the brain | 16.25 A cerebrovascular accident in which the supply of blood to the brain is cut off, resulting in the death of brain tissue fed by that source |
| 16.40 Generalized epileptic seizures that typically begin with a rigid extension of the arms and legs followed by jerking movement throughout the body | 16.33 Organic brain disorder involving damage to the basal ganglia; symptoms include stiff gait, tremors, a mask-like countenance, and psychological disturbances of a general mental deficit and social withdrawal | 16.26 An irreversible nutritional deficiency due to vitamin B, deficiency associated with alcoholism; characterized by anterograde amnesia and confabulation |
| 16.41 The state of disorientation that a patient suffering from contusion may experience upon awakening from the coma | 16.34 Epileptic episode that originates in one part of the brain (may be simple or complex) | 16.27 The most serious form of brain trauma, in which a bullet or piece of metal enters the skull and directly ruptures and destroys brain tissue |
| 16.42 The impairment of many of the brain's faculties as a result of many infarctions | 16.35 Tumors that originate either within the brain or inside the skull | 16.28 A toxic disorder due to excessive ingestion of lead, which causes fluid to accumulate in the brain and results in extraordinary intracranial pressure |

# Chapter 17

# Disorders of Childhood and Adolescence

## LEARNING OBJECTIVES
*By the time you are finished studying this chapter, you should be able to:*

### GENERAL ISSUES IN CHILDHOOD PSYCHOPATHOLOGY
1. Summarize information presented in the text on prevalence of childhood disorders (434-435).
2. Explain the classification system *DSM-IV* uses for childhood disorders (435).
3. Describe the degree to which childhood disorders predict adult disorders and the degree to which treatment of childhood disorders can prevent adult disorders (435-437).

### DISRUPTIVE BEHAVIOR DISORDERS
4. Describe the three varieties of attention deficit hyperactivity disorder (437-438).
5. Describe two varieties of conduct disorder based on age of onset, and explain how they relate to adult antisocial behavior and antisocial personality disorder (439-441).

### DISORDERS OF EMOTIONAL DISTRESS
6. Name and describe three varieties of anxiety disorder in children (441-442).
7. Summarize information presented in your text on childhood depression (442-443).

### EATING DISORDERS
8. Name and describe two varieties of eating disorder in children and adolescents (443-445).

### ELIMINATION DISORDERS
9. Name and describe two varieties of elimination disorder in children (445-446).

### SLEEP DISORDERS
10. Name and describe three varieties of sleep disorder in children (446-447).

### LEARNING DISORDERS
11. Summarize information presented in your text on learning disorders (447-448).

### COMMUNICATION DISORDERS
12. Summarize information presented in your text on problems with stuttering and with language articulation, reception, and expression (448-449).

### PERSPECTIVES ON THE DISORDERS OF CHILDHOOD AND ADOLESCENCE
13. Summarize the explanations of and recommended treatments for the disorders of childhood and adolescence as presented by psychodynamic, humanistic-existential, behavioral, cognitive, interpersonal, and sociocultural perspectives (449-456).
14. Discuss the degree to which the disorders in this chapter can be accounted for in terms of biological processes, with specific reference to the treatment of attention deficit hyperactivity disorder (456-457).

## CHAPTER OUTLINE

I.  General issues in childhood psychopathology

    A.   Prevalence
        1.   Possibly one out of four or five children in U.S. has some form of psychological disorder
        2.   Admissions for treatment begin to rise at age six or seven (beginning of school)
        3.   More boys affected than girls (except for eating disorders and disorders of emotional distress)

    B.   Classification and Diagnosis
        1.   *DSM-IV* method of classification is by symptoms (same as with adult disorders)
        2.   Empirical method of classification by common occurrence or common age is another variation and is used in this text
            a.   Disruptive behavior disorders (bother others more than the child)
            b.   Disorders of emotional distress (bother the child more than others)
            c.   Habit disorders
            d.   Learning and communication disorders

    C.   The long-term consequences of childhood disorders
        1.   Disorders of childhood can lead to
            a.   Disorder carrying over into adulthood with little or no change (stability)
            b.   Development of maladaptive behavior patterns leading to additional, different problems in adulthood (continuity of developmental adaptation)
            c.   Sensitivity to certain stressors which might make the person more susceptible to disorder as an adult
        2.   Treatment of childhood disorders may or may not prevent adult problems, but it certainly can't hurt, and it eases life for the child

II.  Disruptive behavior disorders (lack of self-control; diagnosis based on observable behavior)

    A.   Attention deficit hyperactivity disorder (ADHD)
        1.   Affects 3 to 5 percent of elementary school children
        2.   Boys outnumber girls about 9 to 1
        3.   Three subtypes are specified
            a.   Predominantly inattentive type
            b.   Predominantly hyperactive/impulsive type
            c.   Combined type (most common)
        4.   Symptoms
            a.   Restlessness
            b.   Poor attention span
            c.   Impulsive and disorganized behavior
            d.   Poor social adjustment
        5.   Prognosis better if disorder is situational rather than occurring in all settings
        6.   ADHD children more at risk for conduct disorders, drug use, antisocial personality, and continued cognitive problems

    B.   Conduct disorders (antisocial behavior)
        1.   Diagnostic criteria
            a.   Aggression against people or animals
            b.   Destruction of property
            c.   Deceitfulness or theft
            d.   Other serious violations of rules
        2.   Diagnosis requires three violations in any category in the past year while under the age of 18, and accompanied by generally poor adjustment at home or school
        3.   Subtypes
            a.   Childhood onset type (one symptom prior to age 10)
               (1)   Characterized by lack of emotional attachments and aggressive antisocial behavior
               (2)   Tends to predict antisocial personality disorder as an adult

       b.   Adolescent onset type (no symptoms prior to age 10)
          (1)  More or less normal emotional attachments to family or gang
          (2)  Tends to predict ordinary adult criminality
   4.  Prognosis is poor—continued criminal activity in adulthood is common

III.  Disorders of emotional distress (may be hard to diagnose because children do not always communicate well)

   A.  Anxiety disorders
      1.  Separation anxiety disorder
         a.  Is normal in infants but disappears after first year of life
         b.  Is a disorder when it persists or reappears later, typically after a period of stress
         c.  Symptoms
           (1)  Clinging to parents
           (2)  Fear of disaster if separated
           (3)  Sleeping problems
           (4)  Refusal to go to school or other places
      2.  Social phobia (fear of strangers)
         a.  Is also normal in infants but disappears by about age two or three
         b.  Is a disorder when it persists
         c.  Symptoms
           (1)  Not warming up to strangers, even with prolonged exposure
           (2)  Social withdrawal
           (3)  Few friends
      3.  Generalized anxiety disorder
         a.  Parallels adult version of same disorder (and may be the beginning of it)
         b.  Symptoms
           (1)  Diffuse anxiety
           (2)  Anticipatory fears
           (3)  Severe self-doubt
           (4)  Lack of spontaneity
           (5)  Chronic failure experiences

   B.  Childhood depression
      1.  2 to 5 percent of children may be depressed
      2.  More males than females in childhood years
      3.  More females than males in adolescent years
      4.  Tends to predict mood disorder in adult years
      5.  Symptoms
         a.  Typical adult symptoms (Chapter 10), and/or
         b.  Clinging to parents
         c.  Refusing to go to school
         d.  Exaggerated fears
         e.  Withdrawal
         f.  Slovenliness
         g.  Trouble in school
         h.  Delinquent behavior
         i.  Suicidal thoughts or tendencies (1 percent of school-age children)

IV.  Eating disorders

   A.  Anorexia nervosa (self-starvation for fear of gaining weight)
      1.  Extremely rare and 85 to 95 percent of cases are young females
      2.  Typical onset between ages 12 and 18
      3.  Symptoms
         a.  Aversion to food, or
         b.  Severe weight loss
         c.  Amenorrhea (ceasing of menstruation)
         d.  Distorted body image
         e.  In extreme cases, death

      4.   Possible causes
          a.   May be a way of avoiding sexuality
          b.   May be a way of rebelling against the family

  B.  Bulimia nervosa (binge-purge pattern)
      1.   More common than anorexia (1 to 3 percent of adolescent females)
      2.   Typical onset in late adolescence or early adulthood (usually during a diet)
      3.   Episodes may come and go for several years

V.  Elimination disorders

  A.  Enuresis (lack of normal bladder control past age 5)
      1.   Much more common in boys than in girls
      2.   Types of enuresis
          a.   Primary (bladder control never achieved)
            (1)  May well be biogenic
          b.   Secondary (control achieved and lost again)
            (1)  Almost always a result of stress
            (2)  Usually temporary
      3.   Most serious consequences are loss of self-esteem and social embarrassment

  B.  Encopresis (lack of normal bowel control)
      1.   Much less common than enuresis
      2.   More common in boys than in girls
      3.   Types of encopresis
          a.   Primary (control never achieved)
          b.   Secondary (control achieved and then lost)
      4.   Encopresis more serious than enuresis
          a.   Usually appears as part of larger pattern of disorder
          b.   May accompany child abuse

VI.  Sleep disorders

  A.  Nightmares
      1.   Common in periods of stress (10 to 50 percent occurrence at ages 3 to 5)
      2.   Occurs in REM sleep
      3.   Not necessarily an indicator of pathology

  B.  Night terrors
      1.   Worse than ordinary nightmares
      2.   Affects 1 to 6 percent of children (rare in adulthood)
      3.   Occurs in non-REM sleep
      4.   Symptoms
          a.   Extreme autonomic arousal
          b.   Confusion, disorientation, and agitation after awakening

  C.  Sleepwalking (somnambulism)
      1.   Affects 15 to 30 percent of children at least once
      2.   Peaks around age 12; rare in adults
      3.   Occurs in non-REM sleep
      4.   Not necessarily an indicator of pathology

VII. Learning disorders

  A.  Types
      1.   Reading disorder (dyslexia)
      2.   Disorder or written expression
      3.   Mathematics disorder

B. These problems are defined to exclude difficulties caused by sensory, motor, environmental, or intelligence deficiencies
    1. Affects five to 15 percent of population, with boys outnumbering girls
    2. May be associated with, or complicated by, ADHD
    3. Associated behaviors suggesting biological causes:
        a. Visual or auditory *perception* (not sensory) problems
        b. Problems with memory, sequential thinking, and organizing information
        c. Short attention span and hyperactivity
    4. Consequences
        a. Falling behind in school
        b. Social rejection
        c. Poor self-esteem
    5. Exact causes are not understood, treatment is varied, and outcome is not easily predicted

VIII. Communication disorders

A. Delayed speech and other communication gaps
    1. Prolonged delay past age 2 or so may indicate
        a. Autism
        b. Deafness
        c. Retardation
        d. Other neurological problems
        e. Environmental deficiencies
    2. Other types of language problems
        a. Articulation (enunciation) problems
        b. Expressive language problems
        c. Receptive (comprehension) language problems

B. Stuttering
    1. Affects about 1 percent of population with 4:1 ratio of boys to girls
    2. Most likely to appear between ages 2 and 7
    3. Most children overcome the problem by late adolescence
    4. Organic issues are possibly involved, but stress and anxiety clearly aggravate the problem if they do not cause it

IX. Perspectives on the disorders of childhood and adolescence

A. The psychodynamic perspective
    1. Basic idea is conflict between sexual and aggressive impulses and the restrictions of ego and superego
        a. Sleep disorders may result from unconscious urges coming too close to the surface during sleep
        b. Encopresis may be an expression of hostility against parental control
        c. Enuresis may be regression in the face of stress
        d. Anorexia may be regression in the face of sexual development (ego psychologists would rather talk about a need for autonomy, to control one's own life even if in a destructive way)
    2. Treatment may involve working through the problem by play therapy, in which the child will typically act out the nature of the problem in a naturalistic setting; parents often brought into the process

B. The humanistic-existential perspective
    1. Main idea is that problems result when child denies his/her own unique self to obtain the approval of others, or takes the views of others to be more important and legitimate than his/her own (mystification)
    2. Play therapy is used as a means of helping the child discover his/her own likes, needs, and means of self-expression

C. The behavioral perspective
   1. Main idea is that maladaptive behavior is acquired by either
      a. Inadequate learning (failure to pick up on relevant cues for desirable behavior, e.g., enuresis), or
      b. Inappropriate learning (actively learning undesirable behavior, e.g., conduct disorders)
   2. Treatment involves relearning more appropriate behaviors
      a. Respondent conditioning of bladder control with use of Mowrer pad
      b. Systematic desensitization of anxiety problems
      c. Modeling for the treatment of phobias
      d. Operant conditioning for attention deficit disorder or anorexia nervosa
      e. Token economy for conduct disorders

D. The cognitive perspective
   1. Basic idea is that problems result from faulty beliefs about the self and the world
      a. Depression may result from adult modeling of depression as the "normal" way to behave
      b. Children may erroneously believe that they are responsible for family breakup or other problems
   2. Treatment consists of constructing more reasonable ways of thinking
      a. Self-instructional training for ADHD
      b. Attributional training to find the true causes of a problem instead of internalizing it

E. The interpersonal perspective
   1. Main assumption is that the problem behavior of the child is just a symptom of a larger family pathology
   2. Treatment involves the entire family to work out the interpersonal dynamic of the problem (e.g., parent-child grievances are discussed in anorexia nervosa)

F. The sociocultural perspective
   1. Thai children have more disorders of overcontrol and American children have more problems with undercontrol
   2. Social problems within a culture can influence type and severity of pathology
      a. Conduct disorder related to poverty, unemployment, divorce, etc.
      b. Anorexia and bulimia related to body appearance pressures on women

G. The biological perspective
   1. All disorders discussed in this chapter may have some organic component
   2. The most convincing evidence is in the case of attention deficit hyperactivity disorder
      a. Approximately 75 percent of children with ADHD improve dramatically when given stimulants
      b. Drugs do not "cure" the problem, however, and other approaches to therapy should be considered as well

## KEY TERMS
*The following terms are in bold print in your text. Define them and practice their definitions using the flash cards at the end of the chapter.*

anorexia nervosa (443)
attention deficit hyperactivity disorder (ADHD) (438)
bulimia nervosa (444)
childhood depression (443)
conduct disorder (439)
disruptive behavior disorders (437)
encopresis (446)
enuresis (445)
generalized anxiety disorder (442)

learning disorders (447)
night terrors (446)
nightmares (446)
play therapy (449)
self-instructional training (452)
separation anxiety disorder (441)
sleepwalking (446)
social phobia (441)
stuttering (448)

*Your text does not list the following terms as formal vocabulary; however, if you don't know what they mean, you will be unable to grasp the concepts of this chapter.*

| | | |
|---|---|---|
| antecedents (451) | precipitated (452) | throes (446) |
| enunciate (448) | repertoire (451) | ubiquitous (440) |
| exponent (450) | surreptitiously (453) | |

## IMPORTANT NAMES
*Identify the following persons and their major contributions to abnormal psychology as discussed in this chapter.*

| | | |
|---|---|---|
| Anna Freud (450) | Meichenbaum and Goodman (452) | O. H. Mowrer (451) |

## GUIDED SELF-STUDY

GENERAL ISSUES IN CHILDHOOD PSYCHOPATHOLOGY
Use these terms to complete the lists of issues in Questions 1 and 2:

| | | |
|---|---|---|
| **age** | **disruption** | **onset** |
| **children** | **equivalents** | **outcome** |
| **developmental** | **intervention** | **temporary** |

1. List four general areas of childhood disorders.

   a. Failure to pass a _____ milestone "on time"

   b. _____ of a developmentally acquired skill

   c. Disorders that normally have their _____ prior to adulthood

   d. Disorders that adults have and that also appear in _____

2. List the reasons childhood disorders need to be studied separately from adult disorders. In other words, tell why we don't just study the disorder and list the age of the individual who has it.

   a. Some childhood disorders have no _____ in adult psychopathology.

   b. _____ is more critical in determining the problem in a child than in an adult.

   c. Childhood is a time of many changes, so even normal children may have _____ problems that will just pass with time as development continues.

   d. Course and _____ of a disorder is very different in children than in adults.

   e. Adults need to know about childhood difficulties because children only get help or

      _____ through adults.

3. Use the following terms to discuss the prevalence of childhood disorders:

| | | |
|---|---|---|
| **adolescence** | **boys** | **six or seven** |
| **age** | **develop** | **twenty-five** |
| **assessment** | **formal education** | |

   (a)_____ percent of children and adolescents are believed to have some form of

   psychological disorder. Children often first get treatment about age (b)_____ years. This

   does not necessarily mean that this is the age when children's mental illnesses actually (c)_____. This is the age at which children are in the beginnings of (d)_____

_____. This first exposes the child to (e)_____ by adults outside the home. Also, what might be marginally acceptable in a younger child becomes increasingly

unacceptable with (f)_____. Going to school can also be a major stressor in a child's life.

In childhood, (g)_____ are far more likely to manifest psychological disorders. At

(h)_____, psychological problems in females tend to become more apparent.

4. Fill in the following blanks to complete the listing of concerns about the relationship between childhood disorders and adult disorders:

**continuity**             **reactivity**             **treatment**
**predict**                **stability**

a. Do childhood disorders _____ adult disorders?

b. If so, can _____ in childhood avoid adult disorder?

c. _____ of disorders: Will a childhood disorder persist into adulthood in a similar form?

d. _____ of developmental adaptation: Does having a childhood problem cause later development be screwed up (skewed) so that eventual normal adult adjustment can never be attained?

e. _____ to particular stressors: If a child has had a problem in childhood, will he/she have a weak spot that will be very vulnerable to disorder in his/her adult emotional life?

5. Want to try a TV game show? The category is environmental factors that put children and teenagers at increased risk for psychological disturbance (Hint: Look at the box on p. 436).

a. P_v__ty

b. Ch_ld__n   h__ing   ch_ld__n

c. H_mele_sn__s

d. No   h__lth   __s_r_nce

e. _n_de__te   pr_sc__ol   _r_g_ams

f. La_qu__e   _ay   c_re

g. D__pp__g   o_t   _f   sch__

6. Use these terms to discuss which disorders are *most* predictive of adult maladjustment:

**ADHD**                   **developmental**          **educational**
**conduct**                **disruptive behavior**    **relationships**

The disorders of childhood that are most predictive of adult maladjustment are the

(a)_____ disorders. These two disorders are (b)_____ and (c)_____ disorders. When children and adolescents have these disorders, they are more at risk for

problems with (d)_____ with family and friends and for deficits in their (e)_____ progress. Thus the disorder not only exerts its pathology but it also brings in the

402

compounding effect of disrupting the whole (f)_____ sequence for the child or adolescent.

## DISRUPTIVE BEHAVIOR DISORDERS

7. Children with disruptive behavior disorders are very impulsive. They act without thinking of

   (a)_____. They behave in ways that are quite inappropriate to their (b)_____.

8. List some of the behaviors that are necessary for the totally un-self-controlled, impulsive infant to develop in order to become a self-controlled elementary school student. I can think of at least eight.

9. Children with attention deficit hyperactivity disorder often have (a)_____ motor

   activity and a very short (b)_____ _____. Some children do not have the high activity level. These children display their attention deficits as inattentive spaciness.

   Three subtype patterns of attention deficit disorder are: Predominantly (c)_____ type,

   predominantly (d)_____ / _____ type, and the (e)_____ type. (f)_____ to

   _____ percent of elementary school children are believed to have this problem. Boys

   outnumber girls (g)____ to one in having it. By adult standards, all children are

   "hyperactive;" the quality that makes the ADHD child different from the average child is the

   (h)_____ nature of the activity, moving from one focus to another on a moment-to-moment basis.

10. Here are the terms for discussing the conduct disorders (one of them is used twice):

    | | | |
    |---|---|---|
    | **adolescence** | **childhood** | **severe** |
    | **adolescent** | **criminals** | **temporary** |
    | **aggression** | **deceitfulness** | **ten** |
    | **antisocial** | **destruction** | |

    Conduct disorders include four categories of behaviors: (a)_____ against people or

    animals, (b)_____ of property, (c)_____ or theft, or other serious violation of

    rules. There are two types of conduct disorders determined by age of onset: (d)_____-

    onset type and (e)_____-onset type. If there is at least one symptom before age (f)_____

    years, the diagnosis is childhood-onset type. Research suggests that antisocial behavior is

    most common in (g)_____. However to study those who are likely to become problems to

    society in adulthood, one needs to focus the study on those who have (h)_____ -onset

    disorders. Earlier onset correlates with more (i)_____ disorder. Earlier onset tends to

    produce (j)_____ personality disorder or at least "ordinary" (k)_____. For those whose antisocial acts appear first in adolescence, the pattern is much more likely to be a

    (l)_____ rebellious pattern in the process of moving toward the adult role in society.

# DISORDERS OF EMOTIONAL DISTRESS

11. In the disorders of emotional distress the child is not acting out aggressively toward the
    outside world. He/she has turned the stress and conflict (a)_____. This type of disorder
    includes (b)_____ disorders and childhood (c)_____. In younger children, these
    disorders are difficult to diagnose because the child does not have the conceptual skills to
    understand his/her own (d)_____, nor the (e)_____ skills to communicate
    them in order to get help.

12. Adults may make incorrect inferences leading to an incorrect diagnosis when dealing with a
    child who cannot verbalize his/her inner conflicts. The text gives the example of a child who
    refuses to go to school and who is diagnosed as being "school phobic," when in reality the child
    just finds home a more fun place to be. Can you think of any other possible reasons why a
    child may not want to go to school? Why is accurate diagnosis important?

13. Separation anxiety is a child's distress when separated from (a)_____.

    "Separation anxiety" is *normal* in a child about (b)_____ of age. Children then gradually
    grow out of it. If they have not grown out of it by school age or it disappears and reappears, it
    becomes a significant concern.

14. Here are terms to complete the summary of childhood depression:

    | | | |
    |---|---|---|
    | **accurate** | **exaggerated** | **older** |
    | **altered** | **interest** | |
    | **clinging** | **mood** | |

    Depressed children do not necessarily act like depressed adults. Depressed adults usually
    show sad or hopeless (a)_____, loss of (b)_____ in usual activities, fatigue,
    insomnia, and (c)_____ (poor or excessive) appetite. Children may or may not show
    these symptoms of depression. Psychologists that deal with depressed children find that
    children may show depression by (d)_____ to parents, refusing to go to school, or
    by expressing (e)_____ fears, perhaps about their parents' deaths. (f)_____
    children may seem sulky, withdrawn, or retreat to their rooms. They may have school
    problems, get in trouble, or develop a slovenly manner of self-presentation. Again, an
    (g)_____ diagnosis is very important.

15. Here are terms to complete the following discussion of eating disorders. One is used twice.

    | | | |
    |---|---|---|
    | **amenorrhea** | **death** | **females** |
    | **anorexia nervosa** | **eighteen** | **large** |
    | **binge-eating/purge** | **fat** | **restricting** |
    | **body image** | **female** | **twelve** |

    (a)_____ is self-starvation for fear of gaining weight. The individual seems to be
    (b)_____ phobic. It is most often found in (c)_____, with typical age of onset being
    between ages (d)_____ and _____ years old. In some cases, the patient will simply stop

eating—termed the (e)_____ type of anorexia, but some anorexics eat some food, but then purge it from their bodies. This pattern is anorexia, (f)_____ type. When weight loss is severe enough, menstruation may cease, an event called (g)_____. Some cases are severe enough to cause (h)_____. One characteristic of these patients is a distorted (i)_____, in which they always see themselves as too (j)_____, no matter what their actual weights. The other eating disorder is bulimia nervosa. In it a person, again probably (k)_____, does a binge and purge pattern, but in this case the binge will be of inordinately (l)_____ quantities of food.

16. Use the following terms for the blanks for learning disorders.

| | | |
|---|---|---|
| **birth** | **esteem** | **normal** |
| **dietary** | **genetics** | **social** |
| **educational** | **mathematical** | |
| **environmental** | **mentally retarded** | |

If a child is professionally diagnosed as being learning disordered, by definition you automatically know that the child is not (a)_____. Even though the child displays (b)_____ intelligence, the child has a handicapping deficit in reading, written expression, or (c)_____ skills. The resultant academic problems may cause low self-(d)_____, anxiety, and frustrations which in turn compound into problems in (e)_____ relationships. The causes of learning disabilities are not known: Some of the possibilities are (f)_____, injuries during the (g)_____ process, and (h)_____ deficiencies. Technically, deficiencies caused by (i)_____ problems and inadequate (j)_____ opportunities are not supposed to be included in the diagnostic category of learning disorders; however, the reality is that they often are included since one cannot say with certainty what the cause of a child's deficiency may be. See Hint 1.

17. Use these terms in identifying the sleep disorders and communication disorders (more than one term is appropriate in some cases):

| | | |
|---|---|---|
| **Autism** | **Mental retardation** | **Sleep walking** |
| **Brain damage** | **Night terrors** | **Stuttering** |
| **Deafness** | **Nightmares** | |

a. Possible diagnosis for delayed speech:

b. Interruption of fluent speech:

c. Somnambulism:

d. "Regular" scary dreams that are common in children:

e. Extremely terrifying dreams that cause a physiological panic response

18. Write the name of the disorder in the space before the identifying phrase. Choose your answers from the following list, and use each answer only once.

**Anorexia nervosa**              **Conduct disorder—childhood onset type**
**Articulation disorder**         **Conduct disorder—adolescent onset type**
**Bulimia**                       **Generalized anxiety disorder**
**Dyslexia**                      **Attention deficit hyperactivity disorder**
**Encopresis**                    **Learning disorder**
**Enuresis**                      **Night terrors**
**Social phobia**                 **Nightmares**
**Somnambulism**                  **School phobia**
**Stuttering**                    **Separation anxiety disorder**

a. _____ Interruption of fluent speech by blocked, prolonged, or repeated sounds

b. _____ Dreams he/she was kidnapped by "bad people" who wore green shirts

c. _____ Very haphazard, non-goal-oriented behavior

d. _____ Devoted member of a gang

e. _____ Does not want to leave parent(s)

f. _____ Aggressive and extremely calloused toward the feelings of others

g. _____ Vomits due to stress of having to give a public piano recital

h. _____ Cannot do math concepts by the expected age

i. _____ Kid worries about everything

j. _____ Loss of 25 percent of body weight, amenorrhea, and severely distorted body image

k. _____ Uncontrolled binge eating of huge quantities followed with self-induced vomiting

l. _____ Lack of bladder control

m. _____ Happily goes anywhere but school

n. _____ Lack of bowel control

o. _____ Sleepwalking

p. _____ Violent thrashing in bed, difficult to waken and calm, doesn't remember the next morning

q. _____ Can't respond to printed visual code (reading) by the expected age

r. _____ Talks baby talk in second grade

19. In a (a)_____ disorder, normal function has never existed; in a (b)_____ disorder, normal function existed and then disappeared. These terms are used with the

(c)_____ disorders.

PERSPECTIVES ON THE DISORDERS OF CHILDHOOD AND ADOLESCENCE
20. Have you already checked out which perspectives are reported in this chapter? Take your best shot; how many can you recall?

# THE PSYCHODYNAMIC PERSPECTIVE

21. **ID, EGO,** or **SUPEREGO???** The "general rule" for the psychodynamic interpretation of childhood developmental disorders is the child's sexual and aggressive impulses from the

    (a)_____ are in conflict with the parents and the developing (b)_____.

22. Now, how does that general rule apply to each of the following disorders?

    | **Anorexia** **Encopresis** | | **Enuresis** **Nightmares and night terrors** |
    |---|---|---|
    | a. | _____ | Unconscious conflicts coming out in disguised (latent) form |
    | b. | _____ | Expression of hostility toward parents |
    | c. | _____ | Regression, likely motivated by envy of a younger sibling |
    | d. | _____ | Regression to avoid maturing sexuality in adolescence |

23. Since children lack the conceptual and verbal skills to engage in traditional psychoanalytic talk therapy, what approach do the psychoanalysts use?

# THE HUMANISTIC EXISTENTIAL PERSPECTIVE

24. Like the psychodynamic theorists, the humanistic-existential theorists think that

    (a)_____ holds the origins of adult problems. Humanistic-existential theory proposes that because of the conditions of worth that the child had to conform to in order to be loved,

    the child had to (b)_____ his/her own experience. Humanistic-existential therapy will want to provide an environment where the child can start to experience his/her own

    (c)_____ again, so that he/she can become a real, feeling person again instead of just someone else's puppet with denied emotions.

# THE BEHAVIORAL PERSPECTIVE

25. Behaviorists look at the problem behavior to see what (a)_____ process has brought it

    about and what environmental variables are (b)_____ it in less than acceptable form.

    For behaviorism, therapy is always (c)_____.

# THE COGNITIVE PERSPECTIVE

26. What does the cognitive theorist always "think!!" the primary problem is?

27. In the case of ADHD, cognitive therapists try to teach the student to guide his/her own thinking instead of letting his/her thoughts range free at the whim of whatever grabs the attention at any given moment. List self-talk statements that an ADHD child might learn to use in self-instructional training in order to increase self-direction for completing a task. I can think of at least six.

# THE INTERPERSONAL PERSPECTIVE

28. The interpersonal theorist sees the child's developmental disorder as a symptom of a

    (a)_____ problem. In family therapy, one branch of the (b)_____ perspective, the therapist, is going to be very interested in seeing how family members (c)_____ with each other.  Here to cure the child, one must cure the (d)_____.

## THE SOCIOCULTURAL PERSPECTIVE
29. There is no doubt that there are (a)_____ between child abuse and socioeconomic and cultural factors.  The circumstances of poverty undermine a child's physical and

(b)_____ health.  Studies of different cultures point out how even children who violate

their cultures' (c)_____ do so in a way that is characteristic of the culture.

## THE BIOLOGICAL PERSPECTIVE
30. The biological perspective thinks at least some developmental disorders are biological because

they tend to be seen in the same (a)_____ and some of them respond to (b)_____.

31. a.  What disorder(s) in particular respond(s) to medication?


    b.  What medications are used?


32. There are three strong arguments against using drugs to treat psychological disorders in children; what are they?

    a.

    b.

    c.

33. Complete the following list of factors that help predispose a person to abuse a child.

| abuse | male | self-confidence |
| abused | marital | unemployment |
| inappropriate | personality | violence |
| isolation | punishment | |

    a.  Having been _____ as a child

    b.  Immaturity, dependency, rigidity, lack of _____

    c.  _____ expectations of parenthood

    d.  Drug and alcohol _____

    e.  _____ disorders

    f.  Poverty and _____ or low income, with low education

    g.  _____ discord

    h.  Approval of physical _____

    i.  Family history of _____

    j.  Families dominated by a _____

    k.  Social _____

408

34. In your own experience, were you abused?  Are you aware of children that were abused in the environment in which you grew up?  Are you aware of children that are being abused today?


## HELPFUL HINTS

1.  I think one of the most frequent misconceptions that I find among students is that "learning disabled" is a nice way to say mentally retarded.  In fact, the professional diagnosis of learning disabilities *guarantees* that the child is *not mentally retarded*.  One can find children in gifted programs for high IQs who are learning disabled.
2.  A young child becoming afraid of strangers and becoming afraid of being separated from a primary caretaker reflects no psychological problem at all.  These developments are the result of baby getting smarter.  Developing thinking skills allows a child to identify a person as "not-my-caretaker" or to realize that separation from primary caretaker is about to happen.  Before, baby wasn't afraid because conceptual development was not adequate for realizations and expectations.  Even at this point baby is not actually thinking this phrase to him/herself because he/she is still preverbal, but there are some neurons "clicking" that let the kid know he/she is not happy.
3.  If you are a parent worried that your child's problem might be serious, seek professional counsel so you will know whether to get therapy for the child or to stop worrying.

## PRACTICE TEST
*Take the following test several times as you study the chapter.  Write your answers on a separate sheet of paper and after each attempt, note in the tally box above each question whether your answer was correct or incorrect.*

| 1 | 2 | 3 | 4 |
|---|---|---|---|

1.  Clinic admissions for treatment of childhood disorders begin to rise when
    a.   puberty occurs.
    b.   children begin to go to school.
    c.   language development is obviously defective.
    d.   children finish the genital stage of development.

| 1 | 2 | 3 | 4 |
|---|---|---|---|

2.  A child who shows emotional callousness, has no friends and no loyalties, and who began engaging in antisocial behavior at the age of nine, would be diagnosed as having
    a.   juvenile antisocial personality disorder.
    b.   conduct disorder, adolescent-onset type.
    c.   conduct disorder, childhood-onset type.
    d.   conduct disorder, undifferentiated type.

| 1 | 2 | 3 | 4 |
|---|---|---|---|

3.  A disorder that used to be called "minimal brain dysfunction" and that is characterized by a paradoxical response to amphetamines is
    a.   attention deficit hyperactivity disorder.
    b.   enuresis.
    c.   juvenile conduct disorder.
    d.   pavor nocturnus.

| 1 | 2 | 3 | 4 |

4. Normal separation anxiety is children is greatest at about the age of
    a.  birth.                                c.  two years.
    b.  one year.                             d.  three years.

| 1 | 2 | 3 | 4 |

5. Eating disorders are thought to reflect deep-seated emotional problems because
    a.  schizophrenics are known to have a problem with low blood sugar.
    b.  eating is connected to feelings about those who are responsible for nurturing us.
    c.  some mental patients will respond to primary reinforcers (food) and nothing else.
    d.  Western culture emphasizes the social process of eating.

| 1 | 2 | 3 | 4 |

6. Anorexia nervosa is defined as
    a.  failure to eat because of nervous tension.
    b.  failure to eat for fear of gaining weight.
    c.  a brain disturbance leading to "nervous" behavior.
    d.  a phobic refusal to eat meat.

| 1 | 2 | 3 | 4 |

7. In general, when there is a sexual differential in childhood disorders, it is that boys are more affected than girls.  An exception to this trend is with
    a.  anorexia nervosa.
    b.  enuresis and encopresis.
    c.  attention deficit hyperactivity disorder.
    d.  stuttering and learning disabilities.

| 1 | 2 | 3 | 4 |

8. Which of the following is true of primary enuresis?
    a.  The child loses bladder control after having once attained it.
    b.  Bed-wetting is confined to certain anxiety-provoking situations.
    c.  Toiled training has never been successfully accomplished.
    d.  Children must be 6 years old or younger.

| 1 | 2 | 3 | 4 |

9. Drucilla has anorexia nervosa.  When she looks in the mirror, she sees herself as
    a.  severely underweight.                  c.  being of normal weight.
    b.  slightly underweight.                  d.  overweight.

| 1 | 2 | 3 | 4 |

10. Which of the following is seen almost exclusively in children and rarely in adults?
    a.  Social phobia                          c.  Depression
    b.  Somnambulism                           d.  Generalized anxiety disorder

| 1 | 2 | 3 | 4 |
|---|---|---|---|

11. A particularly disturbing sleep disorder that affects children more than adults and is characterized by extreme autonomic arousal and occurrence in non-REM sleep is
    a. night terrors.
    b. somnambulism.
    c. anxiety nightmare.
    d. insomnia.

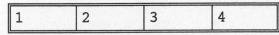

12. Which of the following is true of stuttering?
    a. It affects males and females equally.
    b. It almost always has its onset after the age of 12.
    c. It is associated with attention deficit disorder.
    d. It is usually "outgrown" by late adolescence.

| 1 | 2 | 3 | 4 |
|---|---|---|---|

13. A child who is diagnosed as having dyslexia will have problems with
    a. childhood depression.
    b. reading.
    c. impaired vision and hearing.
    d. antisocial conduct.

| 1 | 2 | 3 | 4 |
|---|---|---|---|

14. The Freudian interpretation of encopresis usually involves
    a. the disguised expression of dependency.
    b. a disguised expression of hostility toward the parents.
    c. obvious symptoms of regression.
    d. a reaction formation to oral fixation.

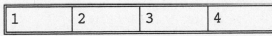

15. Which of the following is a characteristic of play therapy as practiced by the psychodynamic perspective?
    a. Many learning techniques are borrowed from the behavioral perspective.
    b. The therapist sees play as an opportunity for the child to learn who he or she really is.
    c. The child gets emotional support from the therapist while the therapist interprets play content.
    d. The child is encouraged to move around actively to release instinctive urges.

| 1 | 2 | 3 | 4 |
|---|---|---|---|

16. Which perspective on childhood disorders would be likely to employ such methods as the Mowrer pad or tokens in the process of therapy?
    a. Psychodynamic
    b. Behavioral
    c. Humanistic
    d. Cognitive

| 1 | 2 | 3 | 4 |

17. Which of the following situations is the most direct expression of the cognitive perspective of childhood disorders?
    a. Jennifer is depressed because she blames herself for her parents' divorce.
    b. Billy wets his bed nightly ever since his baby sister was born—he's competing with her.
    c. Nicole's is three years old and still won't leave her mother's side.
    d. Mario goes sleepwalking occasionally but his parents cannot relate it to anything stressful in his life.

| 1 | 2 | 3 | 4 |

18. Humanistic play therapy differs from psychodynamic play therapy in that humanistic psychologists see play as
    a. the symbolic expression of hidden desires.
    b. a sample of behavior from which to gain information.
    c. a means of expressing individual feelings.
    d. an opportunity to encourage more appropriate behavior.

| 1 | 2 | 3 | 4 |

19. One factor commonly associated with child abuse is
    a. parental alcohol or drug dependency.
    b. psychosis in one of the parents.
    c. a matriarchal family structure.
    d. a high sense of parental power.

| 1 | 2 | 3 | 4 |

20. According to your text, which of the following disorders can be most convincingly discussed from the biological point of view?
    a. Obesity
    b. Stuttering
    c. Secondary enuresis
    d. Attention deficit hyperactivity disorder

## ANSWERS
### Self-Study Exercise

1. a. developmental
   b. Disruption
   c. onset
   d. children (434)

2. a. equivalents
   b. Age
   c. temporary
   d. outcome
   e. intervention (434)

3. a. Twenty-five (1 in 4) (434)
   b. six or seven
   c. develop
   d. formal education
   e. assessment
   f. age
   g. boys
   h. adolescence (435)

4. a. predict
   b. treatment
   c. Stability
   d. Continuity
   e. Reactivity (435-436)

5. a. Poverty
   b. Children having children
   c. Homelessness
   d. No health insurance
   e. Inadequate preschool programs
   f. Inadequate day care
   g. Dropping out of school (436)

6. a. disruptive behavior
   b. ADHD
   c. conduct (439)
   d. relationships
   e. educational
   f. developmental (439, 441)
7. a. consequences
   b. ages (437)
8. Sit still
   Direct attention
   Wait for turn
   Inhibiting aggressive behavior
   Control temper
   Responding to adult supervision—inhibiting or exhibiting behaviors as directed
   Complete tasks
   Consider the feelings of others (437)
9. a. excess
   b. attention span
   c. inattentive
   d. hyperactive/impulsive
   e. combined
   f. 3 to 5 percent
   g. nine
   h. random or haphazard (437-438)

10. a. aggression
    b. destruction
    c. deceitfulness
    d. childhood (or adolescent)
    e. adolescent (or childhood)
    f. ten
    g. adolescence
    h. childhood
    i. severe
    j. antisocial
    k. criminals
    l. temporary (438-441)

11. a. inward
    b. anxiety
    c. depression
    d. emotions
    e. verbal (441)
12. School itself may not frighten the child; the problem may be the teacher, riding the bus, some particular activity during the day, an upset stomach from lunch in a hurried, noisy cafeteria environment, modeling a parent who was once overhead to say s/he always hated school or who laughingly retells stories of cutting school him/herself. If the school avoidance behavior is to be addressed successfully, the problem's nature must be precisely defined (441).
13. a. a parent or primary caretaker
    b. one year (441)
14. a. mood
    b. interest
    c. altered
    d. clinging
    e. exaggerated
    f. older
    g. accurate (442-443)
15. a. Anorexia nervosa
    b. fat
    c. females
    d. 12 and 18
    e. restricting
    f. binge-eating/purge
    g. amenorrhea
    h. death
    i. body image
    j. fat (443-444)
    k. female
    l. large (444-445)

16. a. mentally retarded (447)
    b. normal
    c. mathematical
    d. esteem
    e. social
    f. genetics
    g. birth
    h. dietary
    i. environmental
    j. educational (447-448)
17. a. Autism, Deafness, Mental retardation, Brain damage (448)
    b. Stuttering (448)
    c. Sleep walking (446)
    d. Nightmares (446)
    e. Night terrors (446)

18. a. Stuttering (448)
    b. Nightmares (446)
    c. Attention deficit hyperactivity disorder (438)
    d. Conduct disorder—adolescent onset type (439)
    e. Separation anxiety disorder (441)
    f. Conduct disorder—childhood onset type (439)
    g. Social phobia (441)
    h. Learning disorder (447)
    i. Generalized anxiety disorder (442)
    j. Anorexia nervosa (443)
    k. Bulimia (444)
    l. Enuresis (445)
    m. School phobia (441)
    n. Encopresis (445-446)
    o. Somnambulism (446)
    p. Night terrors (446)
    q. Dyslexia (447)
    r. Articulation disorder (448)
19. a. primary
    b. secondary
    c. elimination (445-446)
20. Glance at the list on page 433 to see which ones you omitted.
21. a. id (27)
    b. superego (449)
22. a. Nightmares and night terrors
    b. Encopresis
    c. Enuresis
    d. Anorexia (449)
23. Play therapy, where the child acts out what is in his thoughts (449)
24. a. childhood
    b. deny
    c. feelings (450-451)
25. a. **LEARNING!!!!!!**
    b. maintaining
    c. relearning (464)
26. **THINKING!!!!!!** As always, the cognitive psychologist is going to be looking at the child's thinking, particularly negative beliefs and faulty attributions routinely applied to him/herself in an across the board manner (452).
27. Defining the problem—What do I have to do?
    Focusing attention—Keep working at it.
    Guiding performance—Now I have to do thus and so.
    Evaluating performance—Did I do it right?
    Correcting errors—That's wrong; let's go back.
    Rewarding oneself for good performance—I did a good job! (452)
28. a. family
    b. interpersonal
    c. interact
    d. family (452-453)
29. a. correlations
    b. mental
    c. norms (453-454)
30. a. families
    b. medications (456)
31. a. Attention deficit disorder
    b. Amphetamines: Dexedrine or Ritalin (456)
32. a. Drugs have adverse side effects.
    b. These medications do not cure the disorder.
    c. The pattern of medicating problems when what is needed is a more appropriate academic challenge, or psychotherapy, or family counseling, would be an abuse of prescribed drugs (456-457).

33.
  - a. abused
  - b. self-confidence
  - c. Inappropriate
  - d. abuse
  - e. Personality
  - f. unemployment
  - g. Marital
  - h. punishment
  - i. violence
  - j. male
  - k. isolation (455)

34. These questions are designed to make you think about child abuse just in case you are one of those people who has never seriously considered the issue.  If you were an abused child, please take whatever action is necessary for you to psychologically heal from the experience.

## *Practice Test*

1. b (435)
2. c (439)
3. a (456)
4. b (441)
5. b (443)
6. b (443)
7. a (443)
8. c (445)
9. d (444)
10. b (446)

11. a (446)
12. d (448)
13. b (447)
14. b (449)
15. c (450)
16. b (451)
17. a (452)
18. c (451)
19. a (455)
20. d (456)

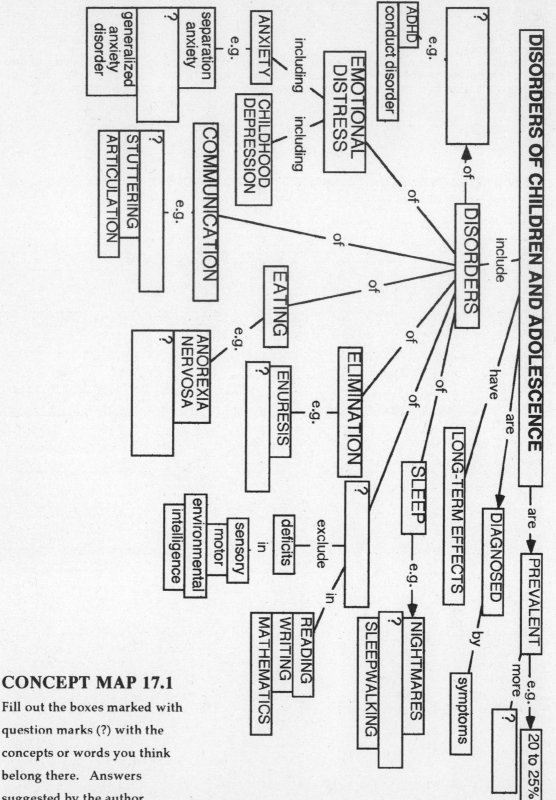

## CONCEPT MAP 17.1

Fill out the boxes marked with question marks (?) with the concepts or words you think belong there. Answers suggested by the author are on a following page.

**CONCEPT MAP 17.2**

Fill out the boxes marked with
question marks (?) with the
concepts or words you think
belong there.   Answers
suggested by the author
are on a following page.

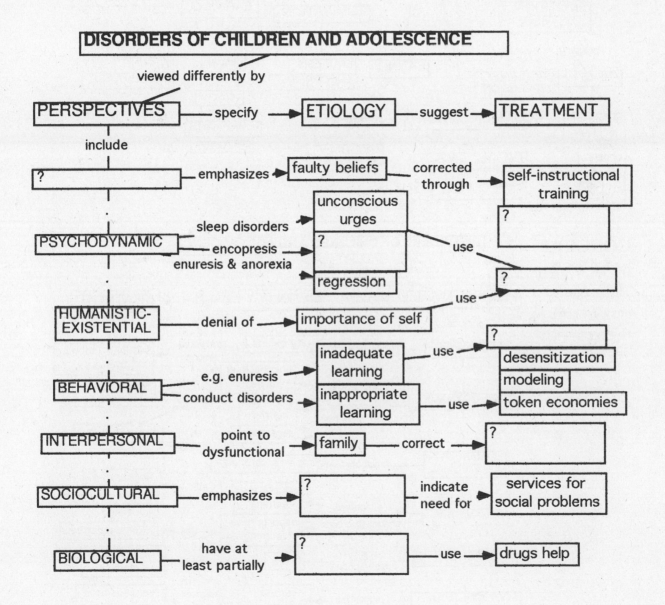

417

# CONCEPT MAP 17.1

The suggested answers are shown in *italics*.

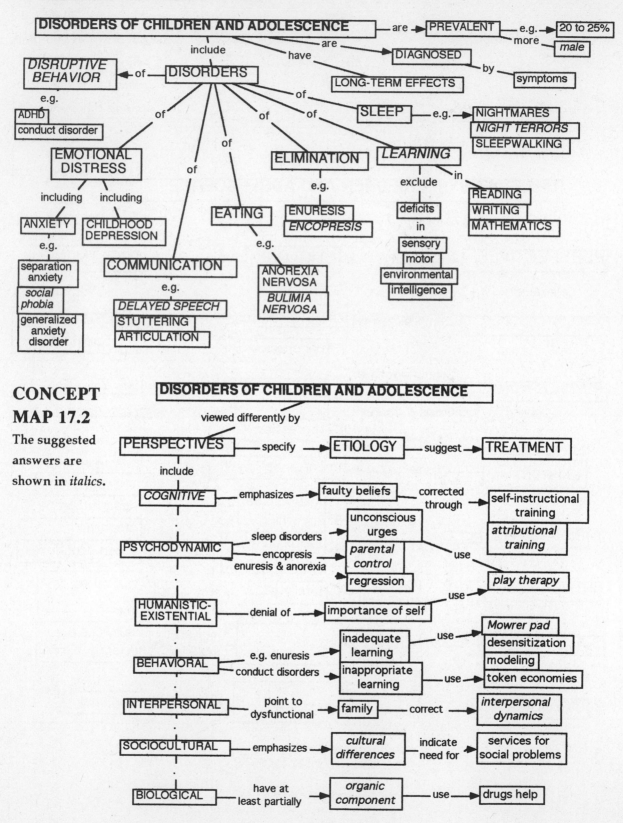

## CONCEPT MAP 17.2

The suggested answers are shown in *italics*.

# CHAPTER TERMS (Cut out on the lines to use as Flash Cards)

| | | |
|---|---|---|
| 17.1 **anorexia nervosa** | 17.8 **enuresis** | 17.15 **separation anxiety disorder** |
| 17.2 **attention deficit hyperactivity disorder (ADHD)** | 17.9 **generalized anxiety disorder** | 17.16 **sleepwalking** |
| 17.3 **bulimia nervosa** | 17.10 **learning disorders** | 17.17 **social phobia** |
| 17.4 **childhood depression** | 17.11 **night terror** | 17.18 **stuttering** |
| 17.5 **conduct disorder** | 17.12 **nightmares** | 17.19 *(You may fill in the remaining boxes with names, terms and definitions from text and lecture)* |
| 17.6 **disruptive behavior disorders** | 17.13 **play therapy** | 17.20 |
| 17.7 **encopresis** | 17.14 **self-instructional training** | 17.21 |

## DEFINITIONS (Cut out on the lines to use as Flash Cards)

| | | |
|---|---|---|
| 17.15 A childhood disorder characterized by intense fear and distress upon being separated from parents or other caretakers | 17.8 Lack of bladder control past the age when such control is normally achieved; primary implies never having achieved bladder control, secondary implies having lost the control they once had | 17.1 Chronic failure to eat for fear of gaining weight; occurs among adolescent girls and young women; the disorder results in severe malnutrition, semistarvation, and sometimes death |
| 17.16 A dissociative disorder in which the person walks and performs some complex action while asleep; it is much more common in children than in adults (also called somnambulism) | 17.9 A chronic state of diffuse, unfocused anxiety | 17.2 A childhood disorder characterized by incessant restlessness and an extremely poor attention span, leading to impulsive and disorganized behavior |
| 17.17 Phobic disorder in which the person's anxiety is aroused by one or more social situations and is related to the person's fear of being humiliated or criticized | 17.10 Three conditions characterized by deficits in one of the categories of educational skills: reading, writing, mathematics | 17.3 Excessive overeating or uncontrolled binge eating followed by self-induced vomiting |
| 17.18 The interruption of speech fluency through blocked, prolonged, or repeated words, syllables, or sounds | 17.11 Harrowing variety of bad dreams experienced by children, who show extreme autonomic arousal and violent movements during the dream and are confused, disoriented, and upset when awakened | 17.4 Childhood disorder of emotional distress with symptoms of sadness, hopelessness, etc. expressed in behaviors (e.g. clinging as children; delinquent acts as adolescents) |
| 17.19 | 17.12 A frightening dream that is not as physically arousing as night terrors; generally occurs in children during REM sleep | 17.5 Childhood disorder in which a preadolescent or an adolescent persistently violates social norms through behavior such as stealing, lying, or committing assault |
| 17.20 | 17.13 Psychodynamic technique in which the therapist provides young patients with drawing materials and toys, rather than asking them questions; assumes that they will expressed their troubles in their games | 17.6 Childhood disorders characterized by poorly controlled, impulsive, acting-out behavior in situations in which self-control and focused behavior are expected |
| 17.21 | 17.14 Cognitive therapy technique that teaches people to control their behavior by controlling what they say to themselves before, during, and after their actions | 17.7 A lack of bowel control past the age when such control is normally achieved |

Chapter *18*

# Mental Retardation and Autism

**LEARNING OBJECTIVES**
*By the time you are finished studying this chapter, you should be able to:*

**MENTAL RETARDATION**
1. Define mental retardation according to the American Association on Mental Retardation (462).
2. Describe four levels of retardation, giving IQ levels and representative behaviors for each (462-463).
3. Summarize the research findings on the genetic causes of retardation (463-465).
4. Describe the prenatal environmental effects that can result in retardation (465-467).
5. Describe the postnatal environmental effects that can result in retardation (467).
6. Define pseudoretardation, list some environmental variables associated with it, and relate it to the concept of brain plasticity (467-468).
7. Discuss the physical and psychological effects of retardation on adult victims, making specific reference to Alzheimer's disease (469-470).

**AUTISM**
8. Define autism and describe four symptom categories characteristic of this disorder (470-473).
9. Summarize how genetics, congenital defects, biochemical imbalances, and neurological problems may play a role in autism (473-475).
10. Summarize the cognitive perspective's position on the role of sensory and attention deficits in autism (475-476).

**SOCIETY, MENTAL RETARDATION, AND AUTISM**
11. Summarize five basic principles of public policy toward the mentally retarded that have evolved over the past 25 years (476-478).
12. Define supported living arrangements, community living facilities, and intermediate care facilities (479).
13. Discuss parental reactions to retardation and the problems associated with raising a retarded child (479-480).

**PREVENTION, EDUCATION, AND TREATMENT**
14. Describe prevention and early intervention techniques for minimizing the effects of mental retardation (480-481).
15. Summarize current trends in the education of mentally retarded persons, and describe the problems in implementing effective programs (481-483).
16. Describe how behavioral and cognitive therapies have been useful in the treatment of autistic and retarded persons (483-484).
17. Describe five controversial approaches to the treatment of autism, and discuss the degree to which they have been effective (484-486).

# CHAPTER OUTLINE

I. Mental retardation

    A. Mental retardation is defined as:
        1. Significantly subaverage general intellectual functioning combined with
        2. Deficits in adaptive behavior,
        3. Showing up prior to the age of 18

    B. Levels of retardation
        1. Mild retardation
            a. IQ 50-55 to 70
            b. Composes 85 percent of retardation cases
            c. Functioning may be quite adequate in less complex environments with occasional advice from others
        2. Moderate retardation
            a. IQ 35-40 to 50-55
            b. Functional level does not permit total independence, but with supervision many tasks in living can be managed
        3. Severe retardation
            a. IQ 20-25 to 35-40
            b. Basic self-care and simple work may be achieved under considerable supervision
        4. Profound retardation
            a. IQ below 20 or 25
            b. Extensive supervision and help required for almost all activities

    C. Genetic factors in retardation
        1. Chromosomal anomalies
            a. Fragile X syndrome
                (1) Caused by weak spot on X chromosome
                (2) More serious in men because they only have one X; women have another one to offset the effect
            b. Down syndrome
                (1) Also called trisomy-21
                (2) Almost always shows three chromosomes in chromosome pair 21
                (3) Related to ovum defects in older mothers
                (4) Typically shows an IQ of 50 or less
        2. Metabolic disturbances
            a. Phenylketonuria (PKU)
                (1) Caused by defective recessive gene
                (2) Victims cannot metabolize phenylalanine
                (3) Results in severe retardation
                (4) Special diet can help if detected early
            b. Tay-Sachs disease
                (1) Caused by recessive gene
                (2) Brain lacks hexosominidase A
                (3) Victims mostly of Eastern European Jewish ancestry
                (4) Usually fatal by age six

    D. Environmental factors in retardation
        1. Prenatal environment
            a. Congenital disorders
                (1) Rubella (German measles)
                (2) Congenital syphilis
                (3) Thyroxine deficiency
            b. Drugs
                (1) Thalidomide
                (2) Alcohol (fetal alcohol syndrome)
                (3) Crack cocaine
            c. Maternal malnutrition
                (1) Women on enriched diets give birth to more alert babies

           (2)  Malnutrition may adversely affect myelination process in the fetus
    2.   Postnatal environment
       a.   Toxins
           (1)  DPT (diphtheria, pertussis, tetanus) vaccine
           (2)  Lead poisoning (usually from old paint)
       b.   Physical trauma
           (1)  Head injuries during childbirth
           (2)  Oxygen deprivation during childbirth
           (3)  Trauma from early child abuse
       c.   Environmental deprivation (in the home)
           (1)  Related to poverty and its effects
           (2)  Lack of stimulation fails to take advantage of brain plasticity and the brain's development may be impaired
           (3)  May be responsible for cases of mild retardation where direct biological causes are less obvious
           (4)  Contributing factors
              (a)  Unstable home environment
              (b)  Inadequate parental care
              (c)  Low intellectual stimulation (important)
              (d)  Inadequate language models (very important)
              (e)  Low life expectations
              (f)  Atmosphere of hopelessness
              (g)  Inadequate food and medical care
           (5)  Many or all of these factors are common in cases of single teenage mothers
       d.   Institutionalization often results in a deprived learning environment
           (1)  Orphanage research by Spitz and Skeels & Dye
           (2)  Kibbutz research, however, shows that poor quality care is not inevitable

E.   Mental retardation in adults
    1.   With improved care, many retarded persons are living longer lives
    2.   Down syndrome patients almost inevitably develop Alzheimer's disease by their 40s
    3.   Depression is common in retarded persons because of:
       a.   Poor treatment by other members of society, and
       b.   Their own awareness of their limitations
    4.   Psychotherapy for retarded persons is now more available, but few receive it

## II.  Autism

A.   Term coined by Leo Kanner in 1943, disorder characterized by inability to relate to others

B.   The symptoms of autism
    1.   Social isolation in an extreme form; total rejection of attempts by others to interact
    2.   Mental retardation (70 percent have IQ below 70)
    3.   Language deficits
       a.   More than half of autistics do not speak at all
       b.   Echolalia is common (simple repetition of what others say)
       c.   The more severe the language deficit, the poorer the prognosis
    4.   Stereotyped behavior
       a.   Endless repetition of simple movements
       b.   Self-injurious behavior not uncommon
       c.   Preservation of sameness (change is not tolerated)

C.   Perspectives on autism
    1.   Psychodynamic view that pointed to cold, rejecting parents as the cause was popular in the 1950s and 1960s, but is discredited today
    2.   The biological perspective is the most influential today
       a.   Genetic research with twins tends to show a genetic component and a relationship to fragile X
       b.   Biochemical studies
           (1)  Autistic children may have abnormally high levels of serotonin and dopamine

    (2) Drugs which reduce the activity of these neurotransmitters reduce symptom severity

  c. Congenital disorders and birth complications
    (1) More than 7 percent of cases related to rubella
    (2) Medical problems in pregnancy, birth and infancy seem related to severity of symptoms

  d. Neurological studies
    (1) Many autism symptoms are related to central nervous system functioning
    (2) Many autistics have seizure disorders
    (3) Neurological testing of autistics often shows abnormalities of function
    (4) Many autistics have abnormal EEGs
    (5) Autopsies reveal abnormalities in cerebellum and limbic system

 3. The cognitive perspective—basic hypotheses
  a. Autistic children cannot modulate and integrate information from the senses
  b. Autistic children cannot process sounds normally
  c. Autistic children are overselective in attention
  d. Autistic children cannot take a point of view outside the self
  e. There is not a single problem, but a cluster of cognitive deficits

## III. Society, mental retardation, and autism

A. Public policy and retardation
 1. Within the past 25 years, citizens groups have made great strides in improving the lot of retarded people
 2. Basic principles of public policy
  a. Free and appropriate education
  b. Individualization of treatment
  c. Timely progress reviews to evaluate treatment
  d. Community integration (least restrictive environment concept)
    (1) "Mainstreaming" in local schools
    (2) Supported living arrangements (SLA)
    (3) Community living facilities (CLF)
    (4) Intermediate care facilities (ICF)
  e. Human rights focus to prevent abuse and to provide legal representation

B. Supporting the family
 1. Counseling can be provided to help families cope with the reality of having a retarded or autistic child
 2. Parents often need training in the practical aspects of caring for and raising a retarded or autistic child
 3. Families need advice in planning for a retarded or autistic person's future needs, such as capacity for independence and expression of sexuality

C. Employment
 1. Laws require retarded citizens to be given opportunities for useful employment
  a. Retarded people often make dedicated workers
  b. Sheltered workshops can provide the structure that is often needed

## IV. Prevention, education, and treatment

A. Prevention
 1. Genetic analysis and counseling
 2. Amniocentesis

B. Early intervention
 1. Diets and other medical treatment where effective
 2. Early stimulation programs to capitalize on young brains' flexibility
 3. Parent training to provide for child's needs, especially for the poor

C. Education
 1. Individualized education programs (IEP) treat each child uniquely

2. Cascade system fosters upward mobility through the educational system
3. Autistic children require different approaches to education than children with simple retardation
4. Self-instructional training gives cognitive tools to clients to help them stay on task

D. Behavior therapy
1. Behavioral techniques are useful for retarded or autistic children in a variety of settings and for a variety of training purposes
2. The more severely retarded the person, the more behavior therapy becomes the treatment of choice
3. Basic techniques
    a. Shaping (reinforcing successive approximations)
    b. Chaining (tying individual tasks into sequences)
    c. Stimulus control (discriminating under which conditions a behavior is reinforced)
4. In autistic clients, extinction and (as a last resort) punishment can eliminate inappropriate behaviors
5. Progress made in one setting may be lost if training is not carried over (generalized) to other settings
6. Behavior therapy does not "cure" retardation or autism, but it can help the individual make best use of whatever potential he or she possesses

E. Controversial treatments for autism
1. Punishment can be effective in reducing self-mutilating behavior, but some object
2. Facilitated communication claims to help clients express themselves, but facilitators may be greatly shaping the clients' expressions
3. Auditory training attempts to overcome an assumed auditory processing deficit, but effectiveness is doubtful
4. Megavitamin therapy is unproven and may even be dangerous ($B_6$ overdose)
5. Drug treatments (serotonin reducers) have had mixed results

## KEY TERMS
*The following terms are in bold print in your text. Define them and practice their definitions using the flash cards at the end of the chapter.*

amniocentesis (465)
brain plasticity (467)
congenital disorders (465)
Down syndrome (464)
early infantile autism (471)
echolalia (471)
fetal alcohol syndrome (466)
fragile X syndrome (464)

mental retardation (462)
phenylketonuria (PKU) (465)
savant syndrome (477)
sheltered workshops (480)
Tay-Sachs disease (465)
theory of the mind (476)
trisomy 21 (464)

*Your text does not list the following terms as formal vocabulary; however, if you don't know what they mean, you will be unable to grasp the concepts of this chapter.*

conjectural (486)
covertly (483)
enigmatic (477)

facilitate (478)
inconsolable (471)
incontinence (483)

lipid (465)
metabolic (465)
modulating (475)

## IMPORTANT NAMES
*Identify the following persons and their major contributions to abnormal psychology as discussed in this chapter.*

Langdon Down (464)
Leo Kanner (470)

H. A. Lubs (464)
René Spitz (469)

Alfred A. Tomatis (485)

MENTAL RETARDATION

1. Name the three elements of the most widely used definition of mental retardation.

   a.

   b.

   c.

2. In the past, an (a)_____ cause was also part of the criteria for a mental retardation diagnosis. Now that is not the case, as is apparent in the three elements in the previous answer. Your textbook points out that mental retardation can result from many different causes and some experts believe that it can come as a result of intellectual or social

   (b)_____ in childhood. Both organic and (c)_____ causes will be covered in this chapter.

3. Mental retardation affects about ____ percent of the population.

4. There are (a)_____ levels of retardation. These levels are based on the degree of intellectual

   limitation and the individual's ability to (b)_____ within society.

5. Fill in the following chart:

   | | Name of Level | IQ Range | Skills Level |
   |---|---|---|---|
   | a. | | | |
   | b. | | | |
   | c. | | | |
   | d. | | | |

6. For each of the following skills, check the level(s) of retardation that would permit that skill to be performed reliably with no supervision.

   | Mild | Moderate | Severe | Profound | |
   |---|---|---|---|---|
   | ___ | ___ | ___ | ___ | Do self-feeding |
   | ___ | ___ | ___ | ___ | Ride a bike |
   | ___ | ___ | ___ | ___ | Attend when called by his/her name |
   | ___ | ___ | ___ | ___ | Swing on a swing |
   | ___ | ___ | ___ | ___ | Balance a checkbook |
   | ___ | ___ | ___ | ___ | Brush teeth |
   | ___ | ___ | ___ | ___ | Tie shoes |
   | ___ | ___ | ___ | ___ | Buy a month's supply of groceries |
   | ___ | ___ | ___ | ___ | Buy a list of five items |
   | ___ | ___ | ___ | ___ | Dial a telephone number |
   | ___ | ___ | ___ | ___ | Cross a residential street alone |
   | ___ | ___ | ___ | ___ | Plan a budget |
   | ___ | ___ | ___ | ___ | Work as a grocery store bagger |
   | ___ | ___ | ___ | ___ | Work carrying out scrap lumber |
   | ___ | ___ | ___ | ___ | Sort two sizes of nails |

Use the following terms in the blanks for questions 7 and 8:

| | | |
|---|---|---|
| 1500 | ears | muscle tone |
| 21 | extra | nervous system |
| 30 | eyelid | respiratory |
| 300 | face | short |
| 50 | flat | small, round |
| 900 | fragile X | testicles |
| amniocentesis | heart | tongue |
| autism | males | trisomy 21 |
| corners | mechanism | X |

7. The American Association of Mental Retardation (AAMR) lists more than (a)_____ organic or genetic anomalies that are associated with mental retardation. Often, even when the cause for the mental retardation can be named, the actual (b)_____, or process that causes the damage to the central (c)_____ is still unknown. This is the case for the most common chromosomal anomaly, (d)_____ syndrome. People with this problem, which occurs about once in every 870 births, tend to have large, prominent (e)_____, an elongated (f)_____, and in males, enlarged (g)_____. Many of these people are also hyperactive and show behaviors similar to those found in (h)_____. The problem is more severe in (i) **males / females** because females will have another (probably normal) (j)____ chromosome to moderate the effects of the disorder, but males only have one such chromosome to begin with.

8. A Down syndrome person is almost always retarded, usually with an IQ of (a)_____ or less. The person will have a (b)_____ head, eyes with an extra fold of skin on the upper (c)_____, (d)_____ nose, mouth with down-turned (e)_____, and a thick protruding (f)_____. The fingers are usually (g)_____ and stubby, and there is poor bodily (h)_____. This child has an increased risk of (i)_____ and (j)_____ problems. In 1959, Jerome Lejeune found that Down syndrome was almost always correlated with having an (k)_____ chromosome on the chromosome pair number (l)_____. This is called a (m)_____. The approximate occurrence of Down syndrome is one in every (n)_____ births. The mother's age is a major factor. In women 29 and under, the chances are one in (o)_____ births. For women over the age of 45, the chances are one in (p)_____ births. This is why (q)_____ is routinely recommended for pregnant women over the age of 35.

9. Down syndrome and Fragile X syndrome are both the result of (a)_____ abnormalities.

   (b)_____ (PKU) and (c)_____ disease are both the result of recessive genes. Remember, for a recessive gene to show itself, both parents must contribute that same recessive gene. This is where genetic counseling is of tremendous value to people who know they are at risk for carrying certain "problem" genes.

10. (a)_____ disorders are those that occur during prenatal development but are not the manifestation of chromosomal anomalies or undesirable genes. The two most common

    congenital causes of mental retardation were from the mother having (b)_____ or

    (c)_____ during the pregnancy. These are not common now because of immunizations

    against (d)_____ and penicillin for the (e)_____. Another problem, thyroxine

    deficiency, (also called (f)_____), can be caused by a shortage of (g)_____ in the mother's diet.

11. Identify the problem that could lead to mental retardation.

    a. _____ Eating "sweet bits" that are picked off of the walls by little children

    b. _____ Common in third world countries and with drug-addicted mothers

    c. _____ Mother toured the wine country and drank heavily during pregnancy

    d. _____ Possible result of a long, complicated delivery of the baby

12. Environmental deprivation is believed to contribute the most to which level of retardation?

13. Environmental deprivation can interfere with development of intellectual potential. One form

    of deficit may result from emotional disturbances brought on by a poor environment; this is

    sometimes called (a)_____-retardation.

14. List some of the things that can harm a child in an impoverished home and background.



15. When all of the poverty factors that can contribute to lowered intellectual abilities are

    evaluated, the one that seems to be the most important is a decreased level of (a)_____,

    in the form of fewer opportunities for varied (b)_____ experiences, (c)_____

    communication, and one-on-one (d)_____ interactions. All of these problems are

    more likely to occur in a family headed by a single (e)_____ mother. A study
    comparing the IQs of children of teenage mothers to those of adult mothers showed that the

    children of the teenage mothers scored (f) **lower than / the same as / higher than** children of adults.

16. The idea that early experiences in life alter the structure and functioning of the brain is called
    a. pseudo-development.
    b. brain plasticity.
    c. postnatal encephalopathy.
    d. cerebral atrophy.

17. According to the idea in question 16, if the brain is shaped and programmed during early childhood, then a deprived childhood environment can produce a poorly programmed brain. This problem **may be / may not be** reversible later on.

18. Institutionalization has a profound effect on intelligence; institutionalization can (a)_____

intelligence perhaps as much as (b)_____ IQ points. How much effect each actual situation

has depends on the (c)_____ and (d)_____ of the institutional care. High quality care,

such as is found in well-staffed residences and in Israeli (e)_____ settings, show few
problems. In traditional institutional care, the aspect of development that suffers most is

usually (f)_____.

19. Just from what you have read in this chapter, if you were designing an institution for children
or picking out day-care for your own child, what features would you want to counter the
effects of institutionalization?


20. a.   What disorder that we studied in the chapter on organic brain problems is associated
with Down syndrome?

    b.   Mentally retarded adults are also generally susceptible to another emotional problem we
discussed in another chapter. What is it?

AUTISM
21. Up until 1943, many profoundly disturbed children were labeled (a)_____; however, at
that point Leo Kanner said the group whose main symptom was inability to relate to anyone

should be diagnosed as having early (b)_____, coming from the Greek word *autos*

which means (c)"_____." Kanner said that it was an (d)_____ disorder that manifested

before the age of (e)_____ years. See Hint 3.

22. "About (a)_____ of every 10,000 children are diagnosed as being autistic. Of those,

(b)____ out of 5 autistic children will be male.

23. The four basic symptoms of autism are:

    a.                                                      c.

    b.                                                      d.

24. What percentage of autistic children have an IQ lower than 70?

25. Describe the difference between a "normal" retarded pattern of cognitive impairment and the
retardation seen in autism.


26. Let's discuss some of the peculiarities seen in the speech of autistic children. Less than

(a)_____ of all autistic children speak at all. Some whine, scream or repeat fragments of

overhead dialogue. This meaningless repetition is called (b)_____. Some have

unusual use of pronouns, referring to themselves as (c)"_____" or "_____/_____." Autistic

children (d) **can / cannot** engage in give-and-take conversation.

27. A child's level of (a)_____ development is a good indicator of prognosis. If speech is used

   meaningfully by age (b)_____ years, a more positive prognosis is likely.

28. List some of the patterns of seemingly purposeless repetitive motor behaviors that autistic children perform.


29. Autistic children who are institutionalized spend up to _____ percent of their time in this ritualistic motor activity.

30. At what age do normal children tend to insist on an unvarying environment?

31. For two decades, the (a)_____ perspective had proposed that autism was caused by cold, rejecting parents. However, today the two dominant lines of research are in the

   (b)_____ and _____ perspectives.

32. List four different approaches the biological perspective has taken in studying autism.

   a.

   b.

   c.

   d.

33. When doing twin studies (comparing concordance rates for DZ and MZ twins), researchers are

   looking for a (a)_____ component in autism. One of the difficulties with trying to do

   twin studies for autism is the (b)_____ of the disorder. Despite these

   difficulties, genetic research has concluded that there (c) **is / is not** some genetic component to

   autism. There may be more than one variety of the disorder. One type, with severe

   retardation, is correlated with having siblings who are (d)_____, and another
   type, typically the better functioning patients, is associated with a family history of

   (e)_____.

34. Many autistic children have high levels of what two neurotransmitters?

35. What specific congenital disease is definitely seen at a higher rate in autistic children than in nonautistic children?

36. What five pieces of research support the idea that whatever the problem is in autism, it is within the central nervous system?

   a.

   b.

   c.

   d.

   e.

37. Obtaining EEGs for autistic children is very difficult because
    a. they usually come from very dysfunctional families.
    b. they have very few brain waves.
    c. they are very phobic about electrical equipment.
    d. they cannot cooperate well enough for testing.

38. Cognitive theorists say that _____ problems are primary in autism and cause the social problems that go along with the disorder.

39. Cognitive researchers argue about exactly what is the primary cognitive problem in autism. List three possibilities mentioned in your text.

    a.

    b.

    c.

40. The doll-hiding-the-marble experiment demonstrated that the large majority of autistic children cannot imagine another person's perspective.

    a.   Give the sequence of events that makes up the experiment.



    b.   Explain what the results suggest.


SOCIETY, MENTAL RETARDATION AND AUTISM
41. What are the five principles that have been established to guarantee full citizens' rights to retarded people?

    a.                                          d.

    b.                                          e.

    c.

42. These principles are designed to bring to an end the (a)_____ (or separation) of services that kept retarded citizens from participating in life as fully as they might. The

    principle of community (b)_____ says the retarded should live life right along with

    everyone else to the extent they are capable. They now go to school in their (c)_____

    schools. Some of the mildly retarded are (d)_____ in that some of their classes are with nonretarded children when it is appropriate.

43. Many mildly retarded adults are self-supporting and live independently. There are a variety of levels of supervised living circumstances. Identify the type of living circumstance represented by each description. Your choices are **Supported living arrangement (SLA),** **Community living facility (CLF),** and **Intermediate care facility (ICF).**

    a.   _____   (Ideally) a closely supervised environment for the severely retarded

    b.   _____   Small group home with supervision provided in the evenings for the mildly retarded
    c.   _____   Medium-sized residential center with round-the-clock supervision for the moderately retarded and the mildly retarded with emotional and/or behavioral problems

44. Where parents were encouraged in the past to institutionalize retarded children, today they are encouraged to raise their child in the (a)_____. These parents will need supportive (b)_____ and (c)_____.

45. What are some issues that parents of retarded children are going to have to cope with more than the parents of nonretarded children? (There are at least five.)

46. State and federal laws mandate opportunities for useful "employment" for the retarded. What does "employment" encompass in connection with retarded citizens?

47. What does research indicate about the employment record of retarded people? What factor seems most influential when a retarded person loses a job?

## PREVENTION, EDUCATION, AND TREATMENT

48. What are some of the measures being used to prevent mental retardation?

49. What are some of the early interventions that can reduce the severity of retardation in children who are already affected?

50. What are infant stimulation programs about, and why are they important?

51. Only a small percentage of the children who need early stimulation get it. Why?

52. Use the following terms in the blanks:

**cascade**
**education**
**funding**
**individualized educational program**
**multidisciplinary**

**nine**
**reevaluations**
**retailored**
**Rowley**
**upward (highest)**

In the year 1975, Public Law 94-142 established nationwide free public (a)_____ for everyone. This new law provided a graduated step system called a (b)_____ system that provides (c)_____ levels of education from the traditional classroom in a regular school to the most basic provision which is a hospital placement for those profoundly retarded people who must have total physical care. With periodic (d)_____, the structure is designed to place the retarded individual within the structure to best address his/her needs. Attaining the optimally (e)_____ level of function is the goal. Children who get any kind of special educational services have an IEP. IEP stands for (f)_____. This is drawn up at a (g)_____ conference where specialists from all the different areas of services that the child needs are present. As the individual develops, the program is (h)_____ to fit the person's specific needs. This ideal plan is rarely fully implemented because of lack of (i)_____. The (j)_____ case has ruled that the child is to be given a "basic floor of opportunity," but it does not clarify how extensively a child's needs must be met.

53. What was the issue in *Board of Education of the Hendrick Hudson School District v. Rowley?*

54. Designing education programs for autistic children is especially difficult. List some of the difficulties that have to be circumvented to foster learning in an autistic person.

55. Behavior therapy has been quite (a) **successful / unsuccessful** in a variety of settings for teaching skills and for (b)_____ management with both retarded children and adults.

56. Define the three basic techniques for teaching behaviors in behavior therapy.

   a.  Shaping:

   b.  Chaining:

   c.  Stimulus control:

57. Upon what type of learning are all these techniques based?

58. Which of the behavior modification techniques listed in question 56 is being used in each of the following situations?

   a.  Terry is taught not to undo her clothing until she is inside the bathroom door. There are places where undoing one's clothing is appropriate and places where it is not.

   b.  Now that Terry has mastered making peanut butter sandwiches, the next challenge will be to pack those sandwiches in a bag and add some fruit and a drink.

   c.  Terry is very socially withdrawn. She comes in late and lingers in the locker room. Her supervisor makes a point of reinforcing any inclination toward social interaction on her part. Terry now spends less time in the locker room.

59. Two of the most important skills for a retarded person to develop are (a)_____ training and the use of (b)_____. The behavior modification focus for autistic children is in the area of developing (c)_____ skills.

   d.  Why are these skills so important?

60. (a)_____ and (b)_____ are used to reduce inappropriate behaviors. Behavior can be maintained by either external or internal reinforcers. When behaviors are maintained by

(c)_____ rewards they are very difficult to suppress.

61. Self-instructional training teaches a person to _____ him/herself through a task.

62. Over the years, some controversial treatment approaches have been proposed and publicized for retarded and autistic people. Draw a line from the treatment to the controversy surrounding it:

a. Punishment:                  Trainer may produce most of the result, not the patient

b. Auditory training:          May not only be useless but can cause nerve damage

c. Drug treatment:             Follow-up studies have not shown it to be effective

d. Megavitamin therapy:      May be just a very expensive placebo effect

e. Facilitated communication:   Disturbed children simply should not be treated that way

## HELPFUL HINTS

1. I find likening the severely retarded adult individual to the mental age of a five- or six-year-old very helpful for understanding what can be expected from an individual at this level. If you are experienced with children and not with mentally retarded individuals, you can still quickly grasp the level of behavioral expectations.
2. Inappropriate orientation to the present is an excessive focus on here and now with none of the future-based consideration which is required for any planning (even planning for ten minutes from now).
3. Autism refers to self-absorption or aloneness. If it helps you to remember, cars are called *auto*mobiles because they are *self*-propelled vehicles.
4. Just in case I need to say this—notice the difference between autistic and artistic. They are very different concepts! And to confuse matters a little more—there are extremely rare autistic children who have an extraordinary *artistic* ability. See the article on savant syndrome (477).
5. I hope you remember from the chapter on organic brain disorders that two major issues are locating the site of dysfunction and determining exactly what kind of pathology exists in that area. As you can see, autism is still very much a mystery. Neither the exact pathology nor the site of the pathology is known.
6. If you do not know the word cascade, connect it with the common idea of the "cascading waterfall." That is an excellent concrete example of a step-wise sequential gradation.
7. An autistic child learns that the letter D written on the classroom blackboard says a "d" sound, but he is unable to carry that over to the letter D printed in a book. Or if he/she learns it for the letter D on a printed page in a particular book at school, that fact has no connection with the letter D in a book at home. The child is learning to discriminate between situations where no discrimination is appropriate.

## PRACTICE TEST
*Take the following test several times as you study the chapter. Write your answers on a separate sheet of paper and after each attempt, note in the tally box above each question whether your answer was correct or incorrect.*

| 1 | 2 | 3 | 4 |
|---|---|---|---|
|   |   |   |   |

1. A retarded person who may be able to carry out simple tasks, but always with supervision, who has little or no language ability, and who will probably be institutionalized permanently would be classified as
   a. mildly retarded.                  c. severely retarded.
   b. moderately retarded.        d. profoundly retarded.

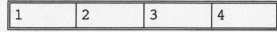

| 1 | 2 | 3 | 4 |

2. An IQ of 45 is associated with which category of retardation?
   a.  Mild retardation
   b.  Moderate retardation
   c.  Severe retardation
   d.  Profound retardation

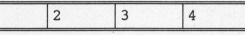

| 1 | 2 | 3 | 4 |

3. Which of the following is true of Down syndrome?
   a.  There are three chromosomes in pair 21 instead of two.
   b.  There is an abnormality in the sex chromosomes.
   c.  There is an XXY chromosome pattern.
   d.  Chromosome pair 21 is missing.

| 1 | 2 | 3 | 4 |

4. Which of the following is limited largely to those of Eastern European Jewish ancestry and is marked by the absence of hexosominidase A in cerebral tissue?
   a.  Phenylketonuria
   b.  Klinefelter's syndrome
   c.  Tay-Sachs disease
   d.  Grave's disease

| 1 | 2 | 3 | 4 |

5. Rubella and syphilis are discussed in the text under the heading of
   a.  chromosome anomalies.
   b.  metabolic disturbances.
   c.  congenital disorders.
   d.  toxic reactions.

| 1 | 2 | 3 | 4 |

6. Pseudoretardation is a term for
   a.  retardation resulting from genetic inbreeding.
   b.  poor IQ performance due to consciously faking a retarded condition.
   c.  apparent retardation due to poverty and lack of environmental stimulation.
   d.  autistic behavior in the face of family conflict and domineering parents.

| 1 | 2 | 3 | 4 |

7. Research by Skeels, Spitz, and others on the effects of institutional environments and social deprivation has indicated that
   a.  intelligence is more heredity than was originally thought.
   b.  as long as minimal physical needs are met, there is no problem with intellectual development.
   c.  group child-rearing practices, such as those found in the Israeli kibbutz, can lower IQ scores.
   d.  environmental deprivation, if severe and prolonged, may result in permanent disabilities.

| 1 | 2 | 3 | 4 |

8. Echolalia is
   a.  the inability to speak.
   b.  mindless repetition of whatever one hears.
   c.  speaking random words without meaning.
   d.  hallucinatory perception of echoes.

9. A good indicator of prognosis in autism is
   a. language abilities.
   b. IQ score.
   c. memory skills.
   d. the age of onset.

10. A disorder that almost always appears in cases of Down syndrome if the person lives into his/her 40s is
    a. thripsichordia.
    b. fragile X syndrome.
    c. autism.
    d. Alzheimer's disease.

11. Genetic evidence on the causes of autism
    a. is totally lacking on either side of the issue.
    b. indicates possible genetic links but is not conclusive at this time.
    c. is solidly against heredity as a cause.
    d. indicates that autism is a sex-linked disorder.

12. Your book mentions which of the following in connection with neuroscience research into the causes of autism?
    a. Serotonin and dopamine problems
    b. A correlation with high birth weight
    c. A degenerated corpus callosum
    d. High intracranial fluid pressure

13. Which of the following statements is true?
    a. The incidence of pregnancy and birth complications is higher in autistic children than in the general population.
    b. There is some evidence that autism may be transmitted by a virus.
    c. Neurological impairment has largely been ruled out as a cause of autism.
    d. Autism is more common among illegitimate children than among children of married couples.

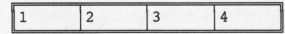

14. Which of the following is *not* one of the cognitive hypotheses in regard to autism?
    a. The major problem is an inability to modulate and integrate sensory information.
    b. The major problem is an inability to see the world from another person's viewpoint.
    c. Autistic children are reacting to rejection from their parents.
    d. Autistic children are overselective in their attention processes.

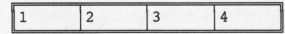

15. The researcher who first identified and named early childhood autism was
    a. René Spitz
    b. Leo Kanner
    c. Bruno Bettelheim
    d. Alfred A. Tomatis

| 1 | 2 | 3 | 4 |
|---|---|---|---|

16. In view of the increasing evidence that there may be organic involvement in autism, the behavioral viewpoint
    a. takes the position that even with organic deficits, behavioral treatment can improve behavior.
    b. is now seen as a pointless and ineffective approach to treatment.
    c. asserts that even organic problems can be corrected through intense behavior modification.
    d. is used only in cases where organic involvement is known not to be present.

| 1 | 2 | 3 | 4 |
|---|---|---|---|

17. All of the following are principles of current public policy on the treatment of the mentally retarded *except*
    a. free and appropriate education.
    b. timely progress reviews.
    c. community integration.
    d. the right to institutional custodial care.

| 1 | 2 | 3 | 4 |
|---|---|---|---|

18. Bill is severely retarded and needs constant supervision. Which of the following community residential alternatives to total institutionalization would be most appropriate for him?
    a. SLA
    b. ICF
    c. CLF
    d. HMO

| 1 | 2 | 3 | 4 |
|---|---|---|---|

19. Public Law 94-142 regarding the education of the mentally retarded mandates that
    a. states may decide for themselves whether public school education is practical for retarded children.
    b. all states must provide special institutional classes for the retarded instead of using the public schools.
    c. the retarded are a special class of persons not required to attend school.
    d. states must provide public school opportunities for the retarded appropriate to the child's needs.

| 1 | 2 | 3 | 4 |
|---|---|---|---|

20. Self-instructional training is
    a. a form of correspondence school designed for retarded children who cannot attend public schools.
    b. a guidebook provided by mental health professionals for parents of autistic children.
    c. a cognitive process by which a retarded person keeps him/her self focused on a task.
    d. a training method used to develop savant skills in autistic children.

## ANSWERS
### Self-Study Exercise

1. a. Significantly subaverage general intellectual functioning
   b. Related deficits in adaptive functioning
   c. Onset before the age of 18 (462)
2. a. organic
   b. deprivation
   c. environmental (462)

3. one (462)
4. a. four
   b. function (462)
5. 

| Name of Level | IQ Range | Skills Level |
|---|---|---|
| Mild | 50-55 to 70 | Productive and perhaps independent living |
| Moderate | 35-40 to 50-55 | Can do self-care but not live independently |
| Severe | 20-25 to 35-40 | Some self-care and simple skills in sheltered setting |
| Profound | 20-25 and below | Requires extensive supervision; very little speech, if any (462-463) |

6. Do self-feeding—yes for everyone except profound
   Ride a bike—yes for mild
   Response to own name—yes for everyone except profound
   Swing on a swing—yes for everyone except profound
   Balance a checkbook—no one
   Brush teeth—yes for mild and moderate
   Tie shoes—yes for mild and moderate
   Buy a month's supply of groceries—no one
   Buy a list of five items—yes for mild
   Dial a telephone number—yes for mild and possibly moderate
   Cross a residential street alone—yes for mild and moderate
   Plan a budget—no one
   Work as a grocery store bagger—yes for mild
   Work carrying out scrap lumber—yes for mild and moderate
   Sort two sizes of nails—yes for everyone except profound
       If there is debate over some of these skills, it is probably a matter of how simply the task is structured for the individual to perform. For instance, carrying scrap lumber between two boxes in a very limited and safe, well-supervised environment could be a task that some severely retarded individuals could perform (462-463). See Hint 1.

7. a. 300
   b. mechanism
   c. nervous system
   d. fragile X
   e. ears
   f. face
   g. testicles
   h. autism
   i. males
   j. X (464)

8. a. 50
   b. small, round
   c. eyelid
   d. flat
   e. corners
   f. tongue
   g. short
   h. muscle tone
   i. heart (or respiratory)
   j. respiratory (or heart)
   k. extra
   l. 21
   m. trisomy 21
   n. 900
   o. 1500
   p. 30
   q. amniocentesis (464-465)

9. a. chromosomal (464)
   b. Phenylketonuria
   c. Tay-Sachs (465)

10. a. Congenital
    b. rubella (German measles)
    c. syphilis
    d. German measles
    e. syphilis
    f. cretinism
    g. iodine (465-466)

11. a. Lead poisoning
    b. Malnutrition
    c. Fetal alcohol syndrome
    d. Hypoxia (466-467)

12. Mild level (467)
13. pseudo- (467)
14. Lack of a stable home environment
    Lack of proper parental care
    Lack of intellectual stimulation
    Lack of adequate language models
    Low expectations for life advancement
    Feelings of hopelessness
    Substandard housing
    Inferior education
    Discrimination (467)

15. a. stimulation
    b. sensory
    c. verbal
    d. parent-child
    e. teenaged
    f. lower than (467-469)
16. "b" brain plasticity (467)
17. may not be (468)
18. a. lower
    b. 50
    c. kind
    d. quality
    e. Kibbutz
    f. language (469)
19. An environment that is varied and stimulating without being noisy. An environment where there is an abundance of verbal interaction with the children from adults who "believe in" children (giving them respect and dignity) and have adequate vocabulary themselves. These adults recognize the importance of enrichment and are eager to provide it (467-469).
20. a. Alzheimer's disease (469)
    b. Depression (470)
21. a. schizophrenic
    b. infantile autism
    c. self
    d. inborn
    e. 2 1/2 (470-471)
22. a. 16-20
    b. 4 (471)
23. a. Social isolation as though other people do not exist
    b. Mental retardation, although a different pattern from other retarded children
    c. Language deficits
    d. Stereotyped behavior; doing repetitive self-stimulatory movements and the preservation of sameness in the environment (471-472)
24. Seventy percent of autistic people have IQs below 70 (471).
25. Autistic children have a distinctly uneven pattern of capabilities compared to the "normal" retarded child who shows cognitive function evenly depressed across all capabilities (471).
26. a. half
    b. echolalia
    c. you or he/she
    d. cannot (471-472)
27. a. language
    b. 5 (472)
28. Twirling, tiptoeing, hand flapping, rocking, tensing parts of the body, head banging, self-hand biting, chewing fingers (472)
29. 90 (482)
30. 2 1/2 years (473)
31. a. psychodynamic
    b. biological and cognitive perspective (473)
32. a. Genetic/chromosome research
    b. Biochemical research
    c. Congenital disorders and complications in pregnancy and birth
    d. Neurological studies (473-475)
33. a. genetic
    b. statistical rarity (2/1000; when combined with the rarity of twinning, this make twins with autism very hard to find)
    c. is
    d. retarded or autistic
    e. mood disorder (473-474)
34. Serotonin and dopamine (474)
35. Congenital rubella (German measles) (474)
36. a. Most characteristic signs of autism involve central nervous system activity.
    b. Many autistic children develop seizure activity in adolescence.
    c. Neurological exams of autistic kids often find other evidence of central nervous system dysfunction.
    d. There are reports of abnormal EEGs and ERPs for autistic children
    e. Autopsies reveal damage in the limbic system and cerebellum (475).
37. "d" (475)
38. cognitive—thinking! (If that answer was a surprise to you, you need h-e-l-p at this point, serious help!) (475)
39. a. Inability to modulate and integrate input from the different senses
    b. A sound-processing language disorder like aphasia
    c. Overselective attention (475-476)

40. a. The children watch the following scene played out with dolls: Sally puts her marble in the basket and leaves the scene. Ann then takes it out of the basket and hides it. The child is then asked where Sally will look for the marble when she returns.
    b. Most normal and retarded children say "in the basket" because they realize that although they saw Ann hide the marble, Sally did not see Ann hide the marble. The autistic child fails to realize that Sally did not see Ann hide the marble as the child him/herself did, so his/her response is that Sally will look for it in the hiding place (476).
41. a. They are entitled to a free and appropriate education.
    b. Services should be individualized.
    c. Progress should be regularly evaluated.
    d. Lives should be integrated into that of the community.
    e. They should be protected from abuse and deprivation (478).
42. a. segregation       c. local
    b. integration      d. mainstreamed (478)
43. a. Intermediate-care facility (ICF)
    b. Supported living arrangement (SLA)
    c. Community living facility (CLF) (479)
44. a. home environment      c. counseling (479)
    b. training
45. a. These children learn more slowly and benefit from whatever enhanced teaching skills the parents can give.
    b. In addition to mental handicaps, they may also have physical handicaps.
    c. They have to cope with being "different."
    d. They will have to cope with their age peers leaving them behind cognitively.
    e. Two major topics of adolescence for any teen are growing independence and developing sexuality. These topics are going to be more complicated if the individual has less cognitive skills to bring to bear on trying to cope with these teen challenges (479-480).
46. Their daytime activities are to have some purposefulness for them. "Employment" varies according to the needs and capabilities of each retarded individual. For the more severely impaired the "employment" may be a planned daytime program. For the mildly retarded and some moderately retarded this employment may be in the more traditional sense; they may have paying jobs in the competitive work market or in sheltered workshops which are special work centers tailored to meet the capabilities of their employees (480).
47. Studies indicate that when retarded citizens are properly placed in work that is appropriate to their skill levels, they make good employees. Research indicates that when they are fired, the reason is more likely to be one of lacking social skills related to the job than inability to do the job itself (480).
48. a. Genetic counseling and improved prenatal care
    b. Some blood tests can identify carriers for some disorders. Genetic analyses can be done on the developing fetus (480).
49. a. Low-phenylalanine diets for PKU children
    b. Thyroid medications for children with damaged or missing thyroid glands
    c. Stimulation therapy for babies at increased risk for mental impairment, such as Down syndrome children, infants of poverty and mothers with low IQs (490)
50. Infant stimulation programs take advantage of the fact that the brain is plastic, or flexible in early development (480). Some aspects of such programs are:
    a. Language acquisition (talking to and making eye contact)
    b. Problem-solving experience with a variety of sensory stimuli (sounds, colors, shapes, textures, and tastes, fine and gross motor manipulation of objects)
    c. Achievement motivation
    d. Teaching mothers to help infant with stimulation, exercise, and encouragement (480-481)
51. It requires an intensive effort on the part of the parents, four or five mornings a week, every week, until the child is ready for preschool at about age 2 1/2. Particularly for families struggling to survive in poverty, this much time, energy, and patience is hard to come by (481).
52. a. education      f. individualized educational program
    b. cascade (See Hint 6)      g. multidisciplinary
    c. nine      h. retailored
    d. reevaluations      i. funding
    e. upward (highest)      j. Rowley (481-482)
53. Whether a school system has to provide a sign-language interpreter for a deaf child (482).

54. a. Their obsession with sameness
    b. The ritualized motor behaviors that consume their attention
    c. The fact that they are not socially responsive and therefore do not respond to social reinforcers
    d. Hyperconcentration or overselective attention prevents the autistic person from generalizing learning to other areas of the person's life (482). See Hint 7.
55. a. successful
    b. behavior (483)
56. a. Shaping: Reinforcing successive approximations of desired behavior
    b. Chaining: Linking a series of simple tasks together to form a more complex sequence
    c. Stimulus control: Teaching what behaviors should occur in the presence of what stimuli (483)
57. Operant conditioning, based on reinforcement of responses (483, Chapter 3)
58. a. Stimulus control
    b. Chaining
    c. Shaping (483)
59. a. toilet (483)
    b. language (483)
    c. social (484)
    d. All of these skills relate to basic abilites that will determine the person's level of functioning in the social world.
60. a. Extinction
    b. punishment
    c. internal (484)
61. talk (482)
62. a. Punishment: Disturbed children simply should not be treated that way
    b. Auditory training: May be just a very expensive placebo effect
    c. Drug treatment: Follow-up studies have not shown it to be effective
    d. Megavitamin therapy: May not only be useless but can cause nerve damage
    e. Facilitated communication: Trainer may produce most of the result, not the patient (484-486)

## Practice Test

| | | | | | | |
|---|---|---|---|---|---|---|
| 1. | d | (463) | | 11. | b | (474) |
| 2. | b | (463) | | 12. | a | (474) |
| 3. | a | (464) | | 13. | a | (474) |
| 4. | c | (465) | | 14. | c | (476) |
| 5. | c | (465) | | 15. | b | (470) |
| 6. | c | (467) | | 16. | a | (484) |
| 7. | d | (469) | | 17. | d | (478) |
| 8. | b | (471) | | 18. | b | (479) |
| 9. | a | (472) | | 19. | d | (482) |
| 10. | d | (470) | | 20. | c | (482) |

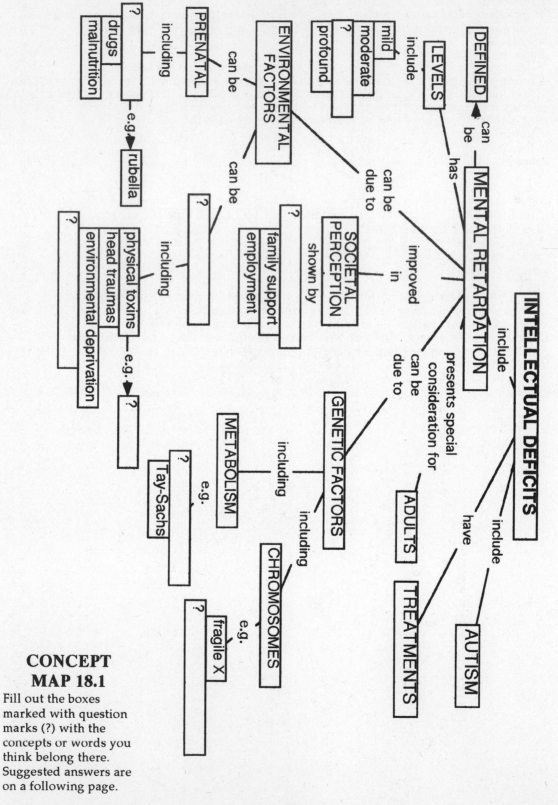

**CONCEPT MAP 18.1**

Fill out the boxes marked with question marks (?) with the concepts or words you think belong there. Suggested answers are on a following page.

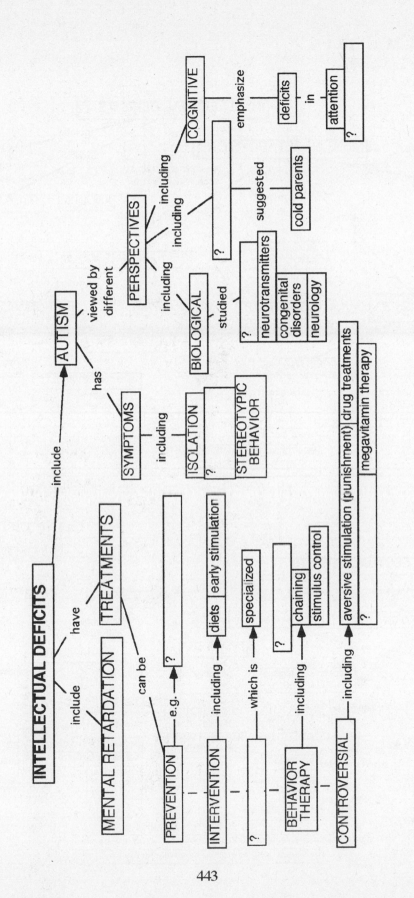

**CONCEPT MAP 18.2**

Fill out the boxes marked with question marks (?) with the concepts or words you think belong there. Suggested answers are on a following page.

443

## CONCEPT MAP 18.1

The suggested answers are
shown in *italics*.

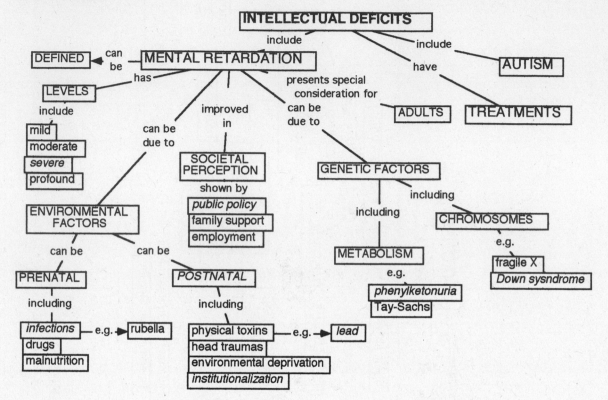

## CONCEPT MAP 18.2

The suggested answers are
shown in *italics*.

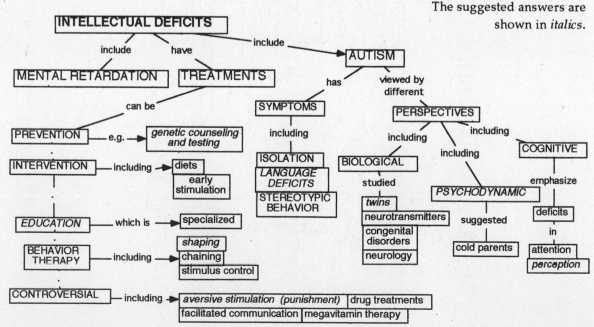

**CHAPTER TERMS** (Cut out on the lines to use as Flash Cards)

| | | |
|---|---|---|
| 18.1<br><br>**amniocentesis** | 18.8<br><br>**fragile X<br>syndrome** | 18.15<br><br>**trisomy 21** |
| 18.2<br><br>**brain<br>placticity** | 18.9<br><br>**mental<br>retardation** | 18.16<br>*(You may fill in<br>the remaining boxes<br>with names, terms<br>and definitions from<br>text and lecture)* |
| 18.3<br><br>**congenital<br>disorders** | 18.10<br><br>**phenylketonuria<br>(PKU)** | 18.17 |
| 18.4<br><br>**Down<br>syndrome** | 18.11<br><br>**savant<br>syndrome** | 18.18 |
| 18.5<br><br>**early infantile<br>autism** | 18.12<br><br>**sheltered<br>workshops** | 18.19 |
| 18.6<br><br>**echolalia** | 18.13<br><br>**Tay-Sachs<br>disease** | 18.20 |
| 18.7<br><br>**fetal alcohol<br>syndrome** | 18.14<br><br>**theory of<br>the mind** | 18.21 |

# DEFINITIONS (Cut out on the lines to use as Flash Cards)

| | | |
|---|---|---|
| 18.15 Condition in which there is an extra chromosome in pair 21 in the human cell; the genetic basis of Down syndrome | 18.8 Condition in which an individual's X chromosome shows a weak spot; most common genetic cause of mental retardation | 18.1 A clinical procedure that can identify abnormal chromosomes in a developing fetus |
| 18.16 | 18.9 Condition that is manifested during the developmental period and is characterized by subaverage intellectual ability and by serious deficits in adaptive behavior | 18.2 The ability of the infant's brain to be altered by environmental stimulation |
| 18.17 | 18.10 Genetic defect caused by a deficiency in a liver enzyme, phenylalanine 4-hydroxylase, which results in severe retardation, hyperactivity, and erratic behavior | 18.3 Disorders acquired during prenatal development but not transmitted genetically |
| 18.18 | 18.11 Disorder in which a person with greatly diminished mental skills will show extraordinary proficiency in one isolated skill | 18.4 Form of mental retardation caused by an extra chromosome; individuals with this condition usually have IQs of 50 or less and distinctive physical characteristics |
| 18.19 | 18.12 Special work centers designed to meet the needs of the retarded people who are employed in them | 18.5 Disorder in children in which the primary symptom, apparent from infancy, is the inability to relate to anyone outside of oneself |
| 18.20 | 18.13 Genetic disorder of lipid metabolism marked by the absence of the enzyme hexosominidase A in brain tissues; causes mental retardation, muscular deterioration, convulsions, and death before the age of six | 18.6 Speech deficit, characteristic of autistic children, in which the child aimlessly repeats what other people say |
| 18.21 | 18.14 Ability (lacking in autistim) to appreciate mental states (e.g. beliefs or desires) and to understand behavior based on these states | 18.7 Complex of physical and behavioral defects found in many children of alcoholic mothers; they have distinctive facial features, retarded physical growth and often mental retardation |

## Chapter 19

# *Individual Psychotherapy*

## LEARNING OBJECTIVES
*By the time you are finished studying this chapter, you should be able to:*

### THE DIVERSITY OF PSYCHOTHERAPIES
1. Distinguish between insight therapy and action therapy (492).
2. Explain what is meant by art versus science in psychotherapy (492-494).

### THE PSYCHODYNAMIC APPROACH TO TREATMENT
3. Summarize the basic purpose of therapy as Freudian therapists see it (495).
4. Describe how free association, dream interpretation, analysis of resistance, and analysis of transference are used in Freudian therapy (495-496).
5. Summarize the views of modern psychodynamic therapists, with specific reference to the ego psychologists, and describe how their approaches differ from that of Freud (496-497).

### THE HUMANISTIC-EXISTENTIAL APPROACH TO TREATMENT
6. Summarize the basic purpose of therapy as a humanistic-existential therapist would view it (498).
7. Describe the client-centered therapy of Carl Rogers, and list two factors he believes are necessary for its success (498-499).
8. Describe the variations on humanistic-existential therapy as practiced by Frankl, May, and Perls (499-500).

### THE BEHAVIORAL APPROACH TO TREATMENT
9. Summarize the basic purpose of therapy as a behavior therapist would view it (501).
10. Describe how the operant techniques of contingency management and stimulus control are used in behavior therapy (502).
11. Describe how the respondent techniques of systematic desensitization, flooding, aversion therapy, and covert sensitization are used in behavior therapy (503-504).

### THE COGNITIVE APPROACH TO TREATMENT
12. Describe self-instructional training and the cognitive restructuring techniques of Ellis, Beck, Meichenbaum, and Mahoney (505-507).

### EFFECTIVENESS: WHAT WORKS BEST?
13. Summarize the criticisms that have been leveled at each of the forms of therapy presented in this chapter, and how proponents of each approach would answer those criticisms (497-498, 500-501, 505, 507-508).
14. Summarize research on the effectiveness of the various therapies (508-510).

### INTEGRATION AND ECLECTICISM
15. Define "eclectic" psychotherapy, and discuss the value of integrating the different therapeutic approaches (510-511).

# CHAPTER OUTLINE

I. The diversity of psychotherapies

    A. Insight therapies aim at self-understanding
        1. Psychodynamic therapy focuses on insight into past causes
        2. Humanistic-existential therapy focuses on insight into present circumstances
        3. Cognitive therapies can also stress a degree of insight
        4. Insight therapists are more likely than others to see their work as at least partially an art

    B. Action therapies aim at direct changes in behavior
        1. Behavior therapies change behavior through learning
        2. Cognitive therapies change behavior by changing the thinking process
        3. Action therapists are more likely to see their work as an applied science

    C. Regardless of approach, most therapies agree that:
        1. The nature of the relationship between therapist and client is crucial to success
        2. Now, more than ever, the effectiveness of treatment must be clearly demonstrated

II. The psychodynamic approach to treatment

    A. Freudian psychoanalysis
        1. Is a rarely-used form of therapy today, but is of great historical importance because of its influence on many therapies that have followed it
        2. The goal of psychoanalysis is to bring the unconscious into consciousness
        3. Techniques
            a. Free association is uncensored talk about whatever comes to mind
            b. Dream interpretation gets at unconscious motives that the person cannot face while awake
                (1) Manifest content is the obvious story of a dream
                (2) Latent content is the symbolic meaning
            c. Analysis of resistance identifies "sore toes" that the person is unwilling to deal with
            d. Analysis of transference identifies emotional baggage from past relationships that is being brought into the relationship with the therapist

    B. Post-Freudian variations in psychodynamic therapy
        1. Characteristics of current psychodynamic therapy
            a. Therapist is more active in client-therapist relationship
            b. There is more of a here-and-now orientation to analysis
            c. Therapy is briefer and less intensive
        2. Ego psychology
            a. The ego stands on its own and does not derive its energy from the id
            b. Interpersonal relationships are the crucial variables in personality
            c. Traditional Freudian techniques are still used, but theoretical view differs

    C. Psychodynamic therapy: Pros and cons
        1. Criticisms
            a. Scientific validation is difficult due to highly abstract concepts and dependence on inference
            b. Goals of therapeutic insight vary with different theorists, clouding evaluations of success
            c. Psychodynamic therapy is elitist (it helps those best who need it the least)
                (1) Expensive
                (2) Time consuming
                (3) Requires good reality contact (not too serious a problem)
                (4) Good verbal abilities an asset
        2. Contributions
            a. Psychodynamic therapy has been the starting point for many other therapies

    b.    Regardless of the accuracy of theoretical details, many clients have gained valuable personal insights

    c.    Elitist or not, those whom it helps are still helped

III.  The humanistic-existential approach to treatment

    A.  Client-centered therapy (developed by Carl Rogers)
        1.  Goal is to remove unrealistic conditions of worth that bar self-actualization
        2.  Basic principles
            a.    Unconditional positive regard prevents therapist from imposing additional conditions of worth in treatment setting
            b.    Empathic understanding puts the therapist in the client's shoes and provides nonjudgmental understanding

    B.  Existential therapy (e.g., Frankl and May)
        1.  A moral challenge to face life and take responsibility for one's problems
        2.  Emphasizes the need for meaning in one's life
        3.  Therapist uses phenomenological approach to enter into the client's experience

    C.  Gestalt therapy (founded by Frederick "Fritz" Perls)
        1.  Combines elements of psychodynamic and humanistic-existential treatment
        2.  Agrees with Freud that problems are unresolved conflicts from the past
        3.  But treatment focus is in the here-and-now and on how the client will choose to deal with his or her issues
        4.  Client is encouraged to act out old conflicts in the present and integrate them and their solutions into life (form a Gestalt, or a unified whole)

    D.  Humanistic-existential therapy: Pros and cons
        1.  Criticisms
            a.    Long and costly treatment
            b.    Unscientific abstractions are hard to test
            c.    Elitist (same as psychodynamic therapies)
        2.  Contributions
            a.    Stresses the emotional component of disorder
            b.    Techniques get to the root of a problem and can result in genuine self-knowledge
            c.    Demonstrates great respect for client's personal point of view
            d.    Some practitioners do serious work on scientifically validating their approach

IV.  The behavioral approach to treatment

    A.  Assumptions
        1.  Behavior may have been learned in the past, but it is maintained in the present
        2.  The target of treatment is the maladaptive behavior itself, not a hypothetical underlying problem
        3.  Treatment is built on practical application of basic principles of learning

    B.  Operant conditioning techniques
        1.  Contingency management is the manipulation of the consequences of behavior
        2.  Stimulus control involves bringing behavior under the influence of cues that signal when a behavior will or will not be reinforced

    C.  Respondent conditioning and extinction
        1.  Extinction removes reinforcers and thereby makes certain behaviors less likely
        2.  Systematic desensitization gradually makes one less responsive to troubling stimuli in three steps
            a.    Relaxation training
            b.    Establishment of a hierarchy of fears
            c.    Desensitization (combining feared stimulus with relaxation)
        3.  Flooding is like cold turkey extinction therapy
        4.  Aversion therapy makes one *more* responsive to stimuli that don't bother one enough (e.g., covert sensitization)

D. Behavior therapy: Pros and cons
   1. Criticisms
      a. It is superficial
         (1) Appears shallow because it does not encourage insight
         (2) It does not attempt to get at underlying mental causes, which can result in symptom substitution (this generally does not occur, however)
      b. It is manipulative because behavior therapists explicitly state their goals of behavior change
   2. Contributions
      a. It has produced many very effective treatment techniques
      b. Faster and less expensive than insight therapies
      c. Easy to evaluate because of clear concepts and goals

V. The cognitive approach to treatment: Cognitive restructuring

   A. Self-instructional training (developed by Meichenbaum)
      1. Concentrates on self-talk
      2. Cognitive coping exercises replace negative self-talk with positive self-talk

   B. Rational-emotive therapy (developed by Albert Ellis)
      1. Concentrates on belief systems about the self, the world, or other people
      2. Therapist disputes with client to replace irrational beliefs with more reasonable, productive ones

   C. Aaron Beck's cognitive therapy
      1. Irrational thoughts produce a "cognitive triad" of
         a. Self-devaluation
         b. A negative view of life experiences
         c. A pessimistic view of the future
      2. Socratic questioning leads to more rational thought

   D. Constructivist cognitive therapy (Michael J. Mahoney)
      1. Deals more with emotional components than other cognitive approaches do
      2. People construct their cognitive worlds through action and feedback
      3. Maladaptive behavior is result of imperfect construction
      4. Self-exploration teaches one about characteristic ways of doing things, and opens the door to better adaptation

   E. Common strategies in cognitive therapy
      1. Hypothesis testing checks to see if one's assumptions about the world are true
      2. Reattribution training changes maladaptive ideas about cause and effect
      3. Decatastrophizing looks at realistic rather than unrealistic outcomes of troubling situations

   F. Cognitive therapy: Pros and cons
      1. Criticisms
         a. Life is not always rational, and attempts to make it so may be misguided
         b. Sometimes problems more properly call for attacking the stimulus rather than our reactions to it
      2. Contributions
         a. Simple, straightforward treatment techniques
         b. Practical, effective outcomes for many problems

VI. Effectiveness: What works best?

   A. Therapies are constantly being challenged to prove their effectiveness
      1. Eysenck thought 66 percent of successes could be attributed to spontaneous remission (actual figure around 43 percent)
      2. Recent outcome studies show most therapies leave clients better off than *at least* 70 percent of untreated controls (some much better than that)

B.  Integration and eclecticism
1.  Effectiveness of any therapy is greatly determined by the quality of the relationship between client and therapist
2.  Establishment of hope in the client may be a common factor in all therapies
3.  In view of this, it makes sense to pay less attention to theoretical arguments and just use what works (eclectic approach), combining ideas and techniques as needed

## KEY TERMS
*The following terms are in bold print in your text. Define them and practice their definitions using the flash cards at the end of the chapter.*

action therapy (492)
aversion therapy (504)
client-centered therapy (498)
cognitive restructuring (505)
cognitive therapy (505)
constructivist cognitive therapy (507)
contingency management (502)
covert sensitization (504)
decatastrophizing (507)
dream interpretation (495)
ego psychology (497)
flooding (504)
free association (495)
Gestalt therapy (499)

hierarchy of fears (503)
hypothesis testing (507)
in vivo (503)
insight therapy (492)
latent content (495)
manifest content (495)
psychoanalysis (494)
psychotherapy (492)
rational-emotive therapy (506)
reattribution training (507)
resistance (496)
stimulus control (502)
systematic desensitization (503)
transference (496)

*Your text does not list the following terms as formal vocabulary; however, if you don't know what they mean, you will be unable to grasp the concepts of this chapter.*

antagonistic (503)
disconfirmed (505)
diversification (494)
eclectic (494)
elitist (498)

empathic (500)
eradicate (504)
grandiose (505)
orthodox (496)
paraprofessionals (505)

pragmatic (501)
repudiated (500)
resonating (498)
tenet (505)

## IMPORTANT NAMES
*Identify the following persons and their major contributions to abnormal psychology as discussed in this chapter.*

Aaron Beck (507)
Albert Ellis (506)
Erik Erikson (497)
Hans Eysenck (508)
Viktor Frankl (499)

Sigmund Freud (495)
Heinz Hartmann (497)
Michael J. Mahoney (507)
Rollo May (499)
Donald Meichenbaum (506)

Frederick (Fritz) Perls (499)
Carl Rogers (498)
Joseph Wolpe (503)

## GUIDED SELF-STUDY

1.  What are three goals of psychotherapy?

    a.

    b.

    c.

2.  How is psychotherapy different from the comfort and advice that one gets from friends?

## THE DIVERSITY OF PSYCHOTHERAPIES

3. All therapies can be grouped as (a)_____ -oriented or (b)_____ -oriented, or a

   mixture of the two. (c)_____ therapies try to have the person come to understand

   him/herself better so that he/she can change or better control problem behavior. (d)_____
   therapies teach new skills to directly alter behavior without any focus on motives that may lie
   behind it.

4. List which therapies discussed in the text fall under each of the following headings.

   a. Insight-oriented therapies:

   b. Action-oriented therapies:

   c. Insight-and-action combination:

5. Which approach is currently prominent?

Use the following terms to fill in the blanks for questions 6 and 7:

| | | |
|---|---|---|
| accountability | eclectic | science |
| alliance | intermediate | self-examination |
| art | novel experiences | World War II |
| caring | psychodynamic | |

6. Some therapists see psychotherapy as an applied (a)_____, in which manipulation of

   certain variables lead to predictable outcomes. Some therapists regard therapy as an (b)_____
   which depends primarily on the empathy and intuition that a therapist brings to the

   therapeutic setting. Most therapists today would take a/an (c)_____ position in these
   viewpoints. All therapy approaches more or less agree on three conditions that facilitate

   change in the psychotherapeutic situation. They are: a safe and (d)_____ human

   relationship with the therapist to form a therapeutic (e)_____ between the client and

   therapist, the exploration of (f)_____, and increased (g)_____ for the
   client.

7. Since the time of (a)_____, the field of psychotherapy has expanded tremendously. The

   field, which was once dominated by the (b)_____ perspective, is now very diversified.
   Many forms of psychotherapy exist and the therapists who use methods from more than one

   perspective are called (c)_____. Perhaps the biggest trend in mental health today is

   the drive for (d)_____; that is, therapists are being asked to demonstrate the effectiveness of their techniques.

## THE PSYCHODYNAMIC APPROACH TO TREATMENT

8. In psychoanalytic theory, the client does most of the (a)_____, and the analyst (b)_____

   what the client says, looking for possible connections with unconscious material. The analyst

   notices hints of unconscious material in the client's free (c)_____, and through the

   analysis of (d)_____ (which have both manifest and (e)_____ content), analysis of lack of cooperation from the client, or (f) _____, and analysis of (g)_____.

9. List the term that fits the definition.

   a. _____ Confronting and resolving conflicts to cause them to lose their power

   b. _____ When the therapist explains the significance of the patient's dreams

   c. _____ Verbalizing in as uninhibited manner as possible

   d. _____ Unintentionally reenacting old parent/child conflicts with the therapist

   e. _____ The unconscious meaning of a dream

   f. _____ Patient managing to interrupt his/her thinking by some diversion

   g. _____ Patient telling about a dream of wandering lost in an endless cave

10. What is the form of neo-Freudian therapy that is discussed in Chapter 19?

11. Fill in the following list of differences that identify the ego psychologists and set them apart from the Freudian perspective.

    The ego has its own (a)_____ and is independent of the (b)_____. Interpersonal relations, especially (c)_____-_____ relationships, are very important. Ego therapy uses the four basic Freudian techniques, but focuses more on the (d)_____ time instead of the (e)_____, and the therapist is more (e)_____ in trying to help the patient to cope.

12. List three shortcomings of psychodynamic therapy.

    a.

    b.

    c.

## THE HUMANISTIC-EXISTENTIAL APPROACH TO TREATMENT
Use the following terms in the blanks in questions 13-15 (one is used twice):

| | | |
|---|---|---|
| **act out** | **feelings** | **mirrors** |
| **befriends** | **freedom** | **positive regard** |
| **conditions of worth** | **Fritz Perls** | **psychoanalytic** |
| **control** | **here-and-now** | **responsibility** |
| **empathy** | **heroic partnership** | **self-actualization** |
| **existential** | **intuition** | **worth** |

13. In client-centered therapy, Carl Rogers uses unconditional (a)_____ to overcome the conditions of (b)_____ that have been put on the client. Rogers tries to fully hear the (c)_____ that the client is expressing and then he (d)_____ the feelings back to the client so the client can further clarify in his/her own mind what he/she is experiencing. Roger's goal is to use the therapist's (e)_____ (the ability to put yourself in someone else's shoes), and (f)_____ to help the client fully realize what his/her own feelings are and to respect them as part of him/her self.

14. The difference between the existential and humanistic perspectives is very apparent in their therapies. Each of these therapies aims at having the client see the (a)_____ that he/she has in life, but they interpret that freedom differently. Humanistic therapy sees freedom in terms of liberation from (b)_____, and once that liberation is accomplished, the client is on the road to (c)_____. The existential therapists, however, believe it is their role to help the client face the (d)_____ that goes with human freedom. Where the humanistic therapist warmly (e)_____ the client, the existential therapist forms a sort of (f)_____ with the client to help the him/her face the distressing, unalterable facts of life.

15. Gestalt therapy, developed by (a)_____, is an interesting take-off on (b)_____ concepts that are used from a humanistic- (c)_____ perspective. Unconscious conflicts are only relevant to the extent that they impact the living that you are doing in the (d)_____. Clients are encouraged to (e)_____ their conflicts in the therapeutic setting. Thus they confront their (f)_____, take responsibility for them, and learn to (g)_____ them rather than to be controlled by them. That way they can be more in touch with their own spontaneous emotional lives.

16. List the pros and cons of humanistic-existential therapy.

| Pros | Cons |
|------|------|
| a. | a. |
| b. | b. |
| c. | c. |
| d. | d. |
| e. | |
| f. | |

THE BEHAVIORAL APPROACH TO TREATMENT

17. Behaviorists believe that maladaptive behavior is maintained by the same principles of (a)_____ by which adaptive behavior is maintained. They do not look to the distant past because they believe current behavior is being maintained by (b)_____.

18. When the primary goal is to change overt behavior, the treatment is usually (a)_____ conditioning. To change emotions, (b)_____ conditioning is used. And to change thinking, (c)_____ techniques are used.

19. List the operant and respondent techniques discussed in this chapter.

    a.   Operant conditioning:

b.   Respondent conditioning and extinction:


20.  Draw a line from the concept on the left to its description on the right:

    a.   Stimulus control:                    Jumping into a feared situation all at once

    b.   Hierarchy of fears:               Pairing child porn with electric shock

    c.   Contingency management:      Arranging conditions to make behavior more likely

    d.   Systematic desensitization:    In real life

    e.   In vivo:                           Deciding what frightens me most

    f.   Flooding:                       Getting used to heights one step at a time

    g.   Covert sensitization:         Do this and I pay you; do that and I fine you

    h.   Aversion therapy:            Avoiding drug use by imagining the worst outcome

21.  Behavior therapy is (a)_____ in terms of cost and (b)_____ in terms of time than insight

therapies.  For effectiveness, behavior therapies have a (c) **good / poor** record.  Behavioral

therapies are criticized for being (d)_____ since they address only overt behaviors and not possible unseen causes.  The other side of that coin is behaviorism allows objective

precision that makes it suitable for (e)_____ investigation.  One criticism of behaviorism

is that some feel the clients' (f)_____ and (g)_____ are denied.

## THE COGNITIVE APPROACH TO TREATMENT

22.  Cognitive therapists believe the most important factor in human behavior is the person's

    (a)_____; therefore, to change a person's behavior one must change the person's

    (b)_____.  Techniques used to achieve these changes are called (c)_____.

23.  List three strategies common to cognitive therapies.

    a.

    b.

    c.

24.  Here are the cognitive therapies discussed in Chapter 19.  Note what name is associated with each one and give a brief synopsis of what happens in each.

    a.   Self-instructional training:

    b.   Rational-emotive therapy:

    c.   Beck's cognitive therapy:

    d.   Constructivist cognitive therapy:

25. List the pros and cons of cognitive therapy.

Pros:



Cons:



26. From "How to Choose a Therapist" (511):

   a.  When should you seek professional counseling/therapy?

   b.  How can you find a therapist?

   c.  What should you check out about your therapist?

   d.  According to this article, what is the most important of all as you consider selecting a therapist?

EFFECTIVENESS: WHAT WORKS BEST?

27. In 1952, (a)_____ claimed that patients who received psychodynamic treatment did no better than patient who received (b)_____. Since that time, it has become clear that almost any form of therapy is (c) **better than / same as / worse than** no therapy at all. One study (Sloane, Staples, Cristol, et al., 1975) showed that the rate at which people get better by themselves, also called the rate of (d)_____, was about (e)_____ percent. The recovery rate for people receiving therapy was about (f)_____ percent. When the NIMH compared cognitive-behavioral, psychodynamic, and drug treatments, (g)_____ treatment gets a slight advantage. There (h) **does / does not** appear to be a *significant* difference between the various approaches to treatment.

INTEGRATION AND ECLECTICISM

28. Just by looking at this subheading, what is this topic about?

29. Today the trend on perspectives is toward focusing on the similarities rather than the differences between psychotherapies.

   a.  List the attributes that the different psychotherapies hold in common.



   b.  Which attribute is speculated to be the most important?

## HELPFUL HINTS

1. A memory trick for three of the Freudian psychotherapy techniques is analysis of the "DiRT."
   **D** = dreams      **R** = resistance      **T** = transference
2. If you learned the strengths and criticisms of each of the perspectives back in their respective chapters, they will be the same strengths and criticisms for the therapies based on these perspectives. There will be some additional elements occasionally related to the business side, like $$$$$.
3. Students sometimes think that Rogers is giving acceptance to all behavior, no matter what it may be. This is not the case. He is not saying you should go about doing whatever you want. He *is* saying that feelings are feelings; they are not good or bad, they are just part of who you are. Behavior is your responsibility. You may have many feelings that would not be appropriate to act out.
4. Eclectic is a good word. Many people in student life have collected furniture from here and there. The name of that line of decor is "eclectic." (Have you ever seen a couch made from four tires and a door?)

## PRACTICE TEST
*Take the following test several times as you study the chapter. Write your answers on a separate sheet of paper and after each attempt, note in the tally box above each question whether your answer was correct or incorrect.*

| 1 | 2 | 3 | 4 |
|---|---|---|---|

1. The difference between insight therapy and action therapy is that action therapy
   a. aims at changing behavior, while insight therapy aims at self-understanding.
   b. is Gestalt therapy, while insight therapy is psychoanalysis.
   c. deals with motor problems, while insight therapy deals with affective disorders.
   d. deals with neurotics, while insight therapy deals with psychotics.

| 1 | 2 | 3 | 4 |
|---|---|---|---|

2. In the art versus science distinction, which of the following therapists is more likely to see therapy as applied science?
   a. Rogers      c. Wolpe
   b. Perls      d. Frankl

| 1 | 2 | 3 | 4 |
|---|---|---|---|

3. Today, more people are taking advantage of psychological therapy, and the stigma associated with such therapy has been reduced. The proportion of the population that now seeks mental health assistance in a given year is approximately
   a. 1 percent.      c. 10 percent.
   b. 5 percent.      d. 20 percent.

| 1 | 2 | 3 | 4 |
|---|---|---|---|

4. Free association, a Freudian technique, is based on the idea that
   a. free therapy is more effective than therapy that is paid for because the patient is less anxious about wasting time.
   b. apparently aimless talking can relax the patient and prepare him or her for more serious discussions later in the hour.
   c. reduced anxiety about multiple sexual relationships helps overcome superego dominance of the personality.
   d. unconscious conflicts can come to the surface more easily during moments of unguarded and spontaneous talking.

| 1 | 2 | 3 | 4 |

5. The manifest content of a dream is the
   a. hidden symbolic meaning.
   b. obvious story of the dream.
   c. part of the dream most likely to meet resistance.
   d. part revealed by transference.

| 1 | 2 | 3 | 4 |

6. A process whereby the patient relates to the therapist as if he were a father figure or other important person in the patient's childhood, and relives emotional experiences with him is
   a. transference.
   b. resistance.
   c. decatastrophizing.
   d. empathy.

| 1 | 2 | 3 | 4 |

7. Eugene avoids the topic of his younger brother. A psychoanalytic therapist might consider this an example of
   a. resistance.
   b. latent content.
   c. transference.
   d. failure to take responsibility.

| 1 | 2 | 3 | 4 |

8. In psychoanalysis, which of the following is *not* considered a component of therapeutic *progress*?
   a. Free association
   b. Transference neurosis
   c. Resistance
   d. Interpretation

| 1 | 2 | 3 | 4 |

9. An therapist like Hartmann or Erikson would emphasize which of the following?
   a. Insisting the patient take responsibility for his or her problem
   b. Examining id processes rather than ego processes
   c. Taking a more passive therapeutic stance than Freud
   d. Analyzing social relationships, especially those within the family

| 1 | 2 | 3 | 4 |

10. The Rogerian concept of unconditional positive regard refers to the therapist's responsibility to
    a. interpret the meaning of the client's statements.
    b. accept the client as he/she is without imposing additional conditions of worth.
    c. let the client know that he or she is "heard" and identified with.
    d. be genuine about his or her feelings in interacting with the client.

11. A therapist who talks in terms of self-challenge and confronting reality is most likely to be associated with which perspective?
    a. Freudian
    b. Existential
    c. Behavioral
    d. Cognitive

| 1 | 2 | 3 | 4 |

12. The concept of stimulus control refers to
   a. rewarding behaviors you wish to eliminate to gain voluntary control over them.
   b. consequences given for random behaviors at unpredictable times.
   c. environmental events that cue or elicit certain behaviors.
   d. rewarding behaviors that prevent the occurrence of unwanted behavior.

| 1 | 2 | 3 | 4 |

13. Contingency management means
   a. manipulating the consequences of a behavior in order to change the frequency of the behavior.
   b. professional management of patients on an individual contract basis.
   c. behavior management through the use of psychoactive drugs.
   d. hospital management in which psychologists and psychiatrists share policy-making responsibilities.

| 1 | 2 | 3 | 4 |

14. There are two ways of getting into a cold swimming pool—either jumping in quickly and getting it over with, or getting wet gradually, one toe at a time. The behavioral approach to dealing with feared situations that would be most similar to jumping in quickly would be
   a. systematic desensitization.          c. decatastrophizing.
   b. covert sensitization.                 d. flooding.

| 1 | 2 | 3 | 4 |

15. According to the psychodynamic view, if a treatment program deals only with overt behaviors, the problem will not go away, but will merely take another form. Why would this be the case?
   a. Because there are so many behaviors to work on, it is hard to get all of them.
   b. Because overt behavior results from deeper processes that are being ignored.
   c. Because clients don't know the difference between overt and covert symptoms.
   d. Because Freudian therapy does not usually produce any real behavior change.

| 1 | 2 | 3 | 4 |

16. If the problem does take another form, as in Question 15, what term is used to describe what happened?
   a. Incompatible behavior          c. Symptom substitution
   b. Cognitive restructuring         d. Covert sensitization

| 1 | 2 | 3 | 4 |

17. Rational emotive therapy was developed by
   a. Carl Rogers               c. Fritz Perls
   b. Donald Meichenbaum         d. Albert Ellis

| 1 | 2 | 3 | 4 |

18. Which cognitive theorist speaks of a "cognitive triad" of self-defeating thinking?
   a. Ellis                c. Beck
   b. Meichenbaum          d. Mahoney

| 1 | 2 | 3 | 4 |
|---|---|---|---|

19. Which of the following criticisms would apply to both the psychodynamic and humanistic-existential approaches to therapy?
    a. They are oversimplified and mechanical.
    b. They are difficult to test and evaluate scientifically.
    c. They do not adequately respect the individuality of the client.
    d. They do not get at true underlying causes.

| 1 | 2 | 3 | 4 |
|---|---|---|---|

20. The major theorists discussed in the chapter are inventors of their own brands of therapy, and tend to focus on one approach exclusively. The average therapist, on the other hand, may use ideas from many of these approaches. Such an individual would be called a(n) _____ therapist.
    a. metatheoretical
    b. eclectic
    c. ecstatic
    d. structuralistic

## ANSWERS
### Self-Study Exercise

1.  a. To remove or modify symptoms
    b. To mediate disturbed patterns of behavior
    c. To promote positive personality growth (492)
2.  There is a formal relationship for accomplishing the goals of therapy, the therapist has specialized training, and the client is paying for a professional service based on skills developed out of that specialized training (492).
3.  a. insight
    b. action
    c. Insight
    d. Action (492)
4.  a. Insight-oriented: Psychodynamic therapy, humanistic-existential therapy, and cognitive therapy
    b. Action-oriented: Behavioral therapy
    c. Insight-and-action combination: Some cognitive therapies emphasize changing behavior by analyzing the way you think and feel. Once you understand your thoughts and feelings (insight), then you can actively change what you think and what you do using the application of basic principles of learning (492-493).
5.  The most prominent trend today is integration of the two approaches, each perspective borrowing from other perspectives techniques that seem to work (493).
6.  a. science
    b. art
    c. intermediate
    d. caring
    e. alliance
    f. novel experiences
    g. self-examination (494)
7.  a. World War II
    b. psychodynamic
    c. eclectic
    d. accountability (494) See Hint 4
8.  a. talking
    b. interprets
    c. associations
    d. dreams
    e. latent
    f. resistance
    g. transference (495-496) See Hint 1.
9.  a. Working through
    b. Interpretation
    c. Free association
    d. Transference neurosis
    e. Latent dream content
    f. Resistance
    g. Manifest dream content (495-496)
10. Ego psychology (497)
11. a. energy
    b. id
    c. mother-child
    c. present
    d. past
    e. active (497)

12. a. The theory is difficult to validate scientifically.
    b. There is a multiplicity of psychodynamic theories.
    c. It is elitist; it limits itself to the rich, verbal, intelligent crowd (497-498). See Hint 2.
13. a. positive regard
    b. worth
    c. feelings
    d. mirrors
    e. empathy
    f. intuition (498-499) See Hint 3.

14. a. freedom
    b. conditions of worth
    c. self-actualization
    d. responsibility
    e. befriends
    f. heroic partnership (499)

15. a. Fritz Perls
    b. psychoanalytic
    c. existential
    d. here-and-now
    e. act out
    f. feelings
    g. control (499-500)

16. **Pros**
    a. Warm and empathetic
    b. Deals with whole person
    c. Provides sense of hope
    d. Respects patient's viewpoint
    e. Goes to root of problem
    f. Leads to self-knowledge

    **Cons**
    a. Long and costly
    b. Appropriate to neurotics only
    c. Benefits only YAVIS crowd
    d. Unscientific (500, Hint 2)

17. a. learning
    b. current conditions (501)
18. a. operant
    b. respondent
    c. restructuring (501-502)
19. a. Operant conditioning: Contingency management, stimulus control (502)
    b. Respondent conditioning and extinction: Systematic desensitization, flooding, aversion therapy, covert sensitization (503-504)
20. a. Stimulus control: Arranging conditions to make behavior more likely
    b. Hierarchy of fears: Deciding what frightens me most
    c. Contingency management: Do this and I pay you; do that and I fine you
    d. Systematic desensitization: Getting used to heights one step at a time
    e. In vivo: In real life
    f. Flooding: Jumping into a feared situation all at once
    g. Covert sensitization: Avoiding drug use by imagining the worst outcome
    h. Aversion therapy: Pairing child porn with electric shock (502-505)
21. a. cheaper
    b. faster
    c. good
    d. superficial
    e. scientific
    f. freedom
    g. uniqueness (505)
22. a. thoughts
    b. thoughts
    c. cognitive restructuring (505)
23. a. Hypothesis testing
    b. Reattribution training
    c. Decatastrophizing (507)
24. a. Self-instructional training: Meichenbaum—learn to talk to yourself in less scary ways
    b. Rational-emotive therapy: Ellis—therapist discovers what irrational beliefs you have and points out how irrational (unrealistic) it is to think that way
    c. Beck's cognitive therapy: Beck—therapist questions you to find your negative self-evaluations, views of life experiences, and views of the future
    d. Constructivist cognitive therapy: Mahoney—since client is always building his world around himself with his actions and reactions to the feedback that he gets from the actions, therapist tries to have client come to see how his thinking, feeling, and acting are building the world, and to learn how to change the parts he/she does not like (505-507)
25. Pros: Practical, forthright, detailed in manuals, professional therapist not always required, readily open to evaluation for effectiveness
    Cons: You can't always think yourself to mental health and sometimes changing your thinking is not the best approach to solving the problem

26. a. When talking your problems over with friends and family does not help
    b. By asking around—friends, physician, minister, priest, or rabbi, local college department of psychology, a hospital referral service, local women's center, even the telephone book Yellow Pages
    c. If therapist is licensed by the state, the therapist's qualifications, theoretical orientation, appointment policies and fees
    d. Your feelings about the therapist—are you comfortable with him/her? (511)
27. a. Eysenck                          e. 48
    b. no treatment                     f. 80
    c. better than                      g. drug
    d. spontaneous remission            h. does not (508-509)
28. The coming together of perspectives (510-511)
29. a. Provision of support, giving of information, raising the client's hopes
    b. Raising client's hopes for improvement in his/her mental health (510-511)

### Practice Test

| | | |
|---|---|---|
| 1. a (492) | 11. b (499) |
| 2. c (493,503) | 12. c (502) |
| 3. b (494) | 13. a (502) |
| 4. d (495) | 14. d (504) |
| 5. b (495) | 15. b (505) |
| 6. a (496) | 16. c (505) |
| 7. a (496) | 17. d (506) |
| 8. c (496) | 18. c (507) |
| 9. d (497) | 19. b (497,500) |
| 10. b (498) | 20. b (510) |

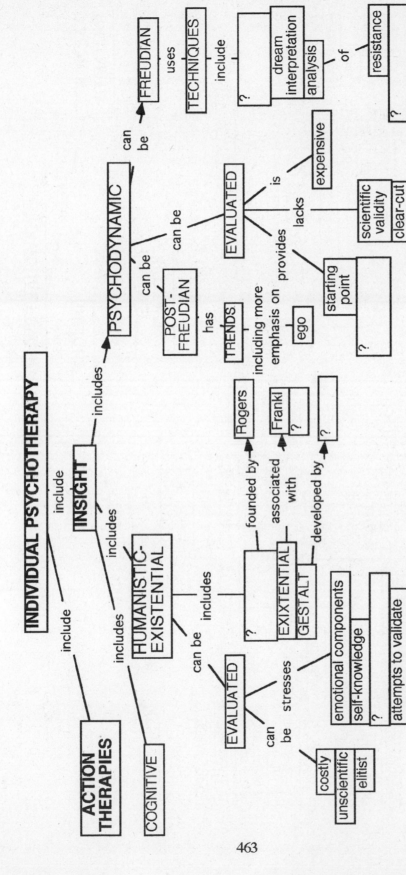

**CONCEPT MAP 19.1**

Fill out the boxes marked with question marks (?) with the concepts or words you think belong there. Suggested answers are on a following page.

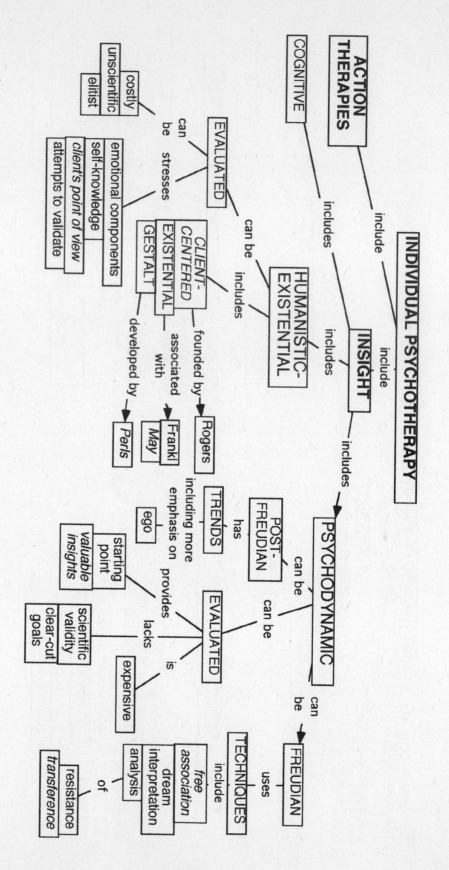

**CONCEPT MAP 19.1** The suggested answers are shown in *italics*.

464

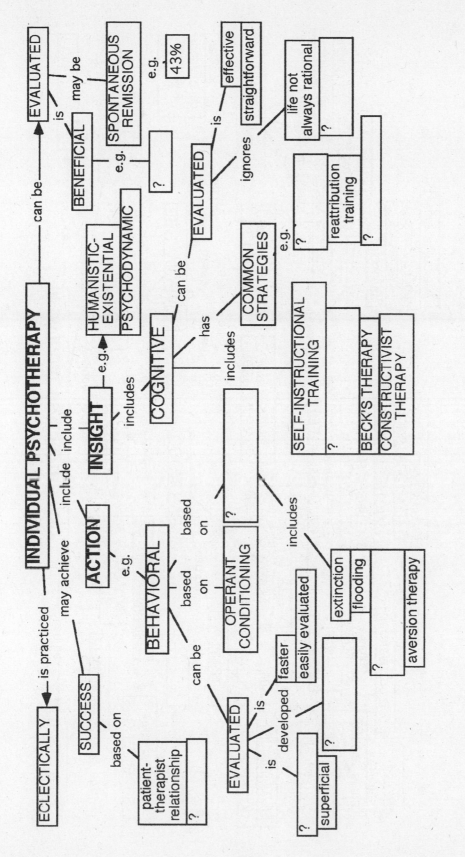

## CONCEPT MAP 19.2

Fill out the boxes marked with question marks (?) with the concepts or words you think belong there. Suggested answers are on a following page.

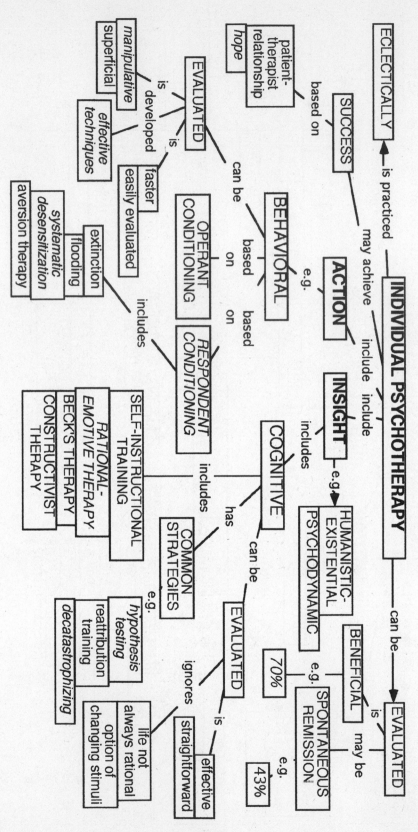

**CONCEPT MAP 19.2** The suggested answers are shown in *italics.*

466

(Cut out on the lines to use as Flash Cards)

| 19.1 action therapy | 19.8 covert sensitization | 19.15 hierarchy of fears |
|---|---|---|
| 19.2 aversion therapy | 19.9 decatrastrophizing | 19.16 hypothesis testing |
| 19.3 client-centered therapy | 19.10 dream interpretation | 19.17 in vivo desensitization |
| 19.4 cognitive restructuring | 19.11 ego psychology | 19.18 insight therapy |
| 19.5 cognitive therapy | 19.12 flooding | 19.19 latent content |
| 19.6 constructivist cognitive therapy | 19.13 free association | 19.20 manifest content |
| 19.7 contingency management | 19.14 Gestalt therapy | 19.21 psychoanalysis |

## DEFINITIONS (Cut out on the lines to use as Flash Cards)

| | | |
|---|---|---|
| **19.15** In systematic desensitization, a list of anxiety producing situations in the order of their increasing horror to patients | **19.8** Behavioral technique in which the effect of a stimulus is changed by pairing an imagined stimulus with imagined dire consequences | **19.1** Approach to psychotherapy that focuses on correcting problem behaviors by teaching the patient new skills |
| **19.16** Strategy used in cognitive therapy whereby clients are urged to test their assumptions in the real world | **19.9** Strategy used in cognitive therapy to help clients realize their fears are exaggerated by asking what would happen if worst fears were realized | **19.2** Respondent conditioning technique in which a patient's maladaptive response is paired with an aversive stimulus, e.g. shock or a nausea-producing drug; often used in the behavioral treatment of sexual deviations and alcoholism |
| **19.17** Procedure in which phobic patients are led through the actual situations that arouse their anxieties, usually accompanied by a therapist; the goal is to learn to relax in the presence of anxiety causing stimuli | **19.10** Psychoanalytic technique in which patients report their dreams and the therapist explores their symbolic content with the patient for unconscious motives and wishes | **19.3** Therapeutic procedure developed by Rogers in which the therapist provides a safe environment for the patient by mirroring the patient's own perceptions and offering unconditional positive regard |
| **19.18** Approach to psychotherapy that focuses on increasing patients' awareness of the motives underlying their actions so that, by understanding their behavior, they will be able to control it better | **19.11** Post-Freudian school of thought which is less deterministic and less biologically oriented; holds that the ego has its own energy and autonomous functions apart from the id | **19.4** Variety of cognitive therapy techniques that help clients increase coping skills, develop problem solving, and change the way they perceive and interpret their worlds |
| **19.19** In psychoanalytic theory, the unconscious material of a dream that is being expressed in disguised fashion through the symbols contained in the dream | **19.12** A respondent-conditioning technique in which extinction of fear is achieved by prolonged exposure to the feared stimulus in a situation that does not permit avoidance | **19.5** Method of treatment that focuses primarily on cognitive processes, or thoughts, seeing them as the causes of behavior; patients are encouraged to change behavior by changing underlying thoughts |
| **19.20** In psychoanalytic theory, the content of a dream as seen and reported by the individual | **19.13** Psychoanalytic technique in which the patient verbalizes whatever thoughts come to mind, without structuring or censoring the remarks | **19.6** Mahoney's approach to cognitive therapy; views emotional disturbances as reflections of people's imperfect attempts to adapt and develop; self-exploration helps clients develop better approaches |
| **19.21** Psychodynamic therapy method that relies on the techniques of free association, dream interpretation, and analysis of resistance and transference to give patients insight into their unconscious | **19.14** Perls' existential/humanistic form of therapy in which the patients act out past conflicts with the therapist in order to confront their feelings, take responsibility for them, and learn to control them | **19.7** Operant-conditioning technique in which the consequences of a response are manipulated in order to change the frequency of that response |

**CHAPTER TERMS** (Cut out on the lines to use as Flash Cards)

| | | |
|---|---|---|
| 19.22<br><br>**psychotherapy** | 19.29<br>*(You may fill in the remaining boxes with names, terms and definitions from text and lecture)* | 19.36 |
| 19.23<br><br>**rational-emotive therapy** | 19.30 | 19.37 |
| 19.24<br><br>**reattribution training** | 19.31 | 19.38 |
| 19.25<br><br>**resistance** | 19.32 | 19.39 |
| 19.26<br><br>**stimulus control** | 19.33 | 19.40 |
| 19.27<br><br>**systematic desensitization** | 19.34 | 19.41 |
| 19.28<br><br>**transference** | 19.35 | 19.42 |

## DEFINITIONS (Cut out on the lines to use as Flash Cards)

| | | |
|---|---|---|
| 19.36 | 19.29 | 19.22 Psychological treatment of emotional problems, in which the therapist aims to establish a relationship with the patient in order to remove or modify symptoms and promote positive personality growth |
| 19.37 | 19.30 | 19.23 Ellis' approach to cognitive therapy, which sees emotional disturbances as the result of irrational beliefs that guide people's interpretation of events |
| 19.38 | 19.31 | 19.24 Strategy used in cognitive therapy whereby the therapist helps the client change distorted ideas of cause and effect by realistically evaluating events for their causes |
| 19.39 | 19.32 | 19.25 In psychoanalytic theory, a defense mechanism used by the patient to avoid confronting certain memories and impulses; the patient may argue with the therapist, change the subject, miss appointments, and so on |
| 19.40 | 19.33 | 19.26 An operant conditioning technique in which a predictable relationship is established between a given stimulus and a given response by eliminating all other stimuli associated with that response |
| 19.41 | 19.34 | 19.27 Behavior therapy technique in which the patient, while in a relaxed state, progressively imagines increasingly fear provoking stimuli or is presented with the actual stimuli |
| 19.42 | 19.35 | 19.28 In psychoanalytic theory, the process by which patients identify the therapist with important people in their lives (usually their parents), and project onto the therapist their relationship with them |

## Chapter 20

# Group, Family, and Community Therapy

*LEARNING OBJECTIVES*
*By the time you are finished studying this chapter, you should be able to:*

**GROUP THERAPY**
1. List Yalom's 11 factors that promote therapeutic change in group settings, and specify the ones that are obtainable from individual therapy as well (516-517).
2. Describe psychodrama, and explain why it is a good example of psychodynamic group therapy (517-518).
3. Explain the focus of behavioral group therapy, and describe assertiveness training and social skills training (518-519).
4. Describe three varieties of humanistic group treatments (520-521).
5. Describe the nature and value of peer self-help groups (521-522).

**FAMILY AND MARITAL THERAPY**
6. Describe the communications and structural approaches to family and marital therapy (523-526).
7. Summarize research on the effectiveness of group, family, and marital therapies (522-523, 526-528).

**INSTITUTIONAL CARE AND COMMUNITY-BASED SERVICES**
8. Describe the token economy, and explain why it is a good example of a behaviorally-based therapeutic environment (529).
9. Define milieu therapy, and explain how it fits into the humanistic-existential perspective of psychology (529-530).
10. Summarize research on the effectiveness of institutional therapeutic environments (530-532).
11. Describe the rise and decline of the large mental institution and the logic behind community-based services (528, 530-533).
12. Describe four types of services offered in a well-developed community mental health system (533-535).
13. Describe the role of halfway houses, long-term care facilities, hot lines, and other innovative attempts to eliminate the need for traditional institutional care (535-537).
14. Describe three levels of prevention in mental health care (538).
15. Summarize research on the effectiveness of community-based mental health services (538-540).

*CHAPTER OUTLINE*

I.  Group therapy

　　A.  Characteristics
　　　　1.  Group therapies are based on the same theoretical perspectives as individual therapies—major difference is number of clients dealt with at one time
　　　　2.  Group therapies can be more efficient in terms of time and money
　　　　3.  Groups are more appropriate for certain kinds of problems
　　　　4.  According to Yalom, group therapies can provide the following benefits (* indicates a benefit of individual therapy as well)

a.  Hope*
b.  Universality
c.  Information*
d.  Altruism
e.  Corrective recapitulation of the family group
f.  Development of social skills
g.  Imitative behavior*
h.  Interpersonal learning
i.  Group cohesiveness
j.  Catharsis*
k.  Existential factors

B.  Psychodynamic approaches to group treatment
1.  Stress items 5(e) and 8(h) on Yalom's list
2.  In psychodrama (J. L. Moreno), clients act out their emotional issues in a theatrical setting with other group members
3.  Special psychodrama techniques show clients how they appear to others and may give insights into causes
    a.  Role reversal requires clients to switch parts
    b.  Double technique has the therapist play the client's role along with the client
    c.  In mirroring, group members portray one another

C.  Behavioral approaches to group treatment
1.  Stress items 3(c), 6(f), and 7(g) on Yalom's list
2.  Social-skills training teaches increased effectiveness in social situations:
    a.  Responding to authority figures
    b.  Job interviews
    c.  Asking for a date
    d.  Nondepressive behaviors for depressives
    e.  Nonpsychotic behaviors for psychotics
3.  Assertiveness training teaches how to stand up for one's rights without violating the rights of others, including such skills as:
    a.  Expression of feelings
        (1)  Verbally
        (2)  Nonverbally
    b.  Clear expression of disagreement
    c.  Use of the pronoun "I"
    d.  Expression of agreement when praised
    e.  Improvisation; spontaneity in living

D.  Cognitive group therapies
1.  Stress items 2(b), 3(c), and 7(g) on Yalom's list
2.  Most often used in combatting depression

E.  Humanistic approaches to group treatment
1.  Stress items 4(d), 8(h), and sometimes 10(j) on Yalom's list
2.  Encounter groups encourage unrestrained emotional expression to help the client vent feelings and show client how others react to him or her
3.  Gestalt groups deal with unfinished business from the past in emotional here-and-now interactions
4.  Large community groups (such as Marriage Encounter) may deal with more than 1000 people in alternating large and small group settings
5.  Distinctions between types of groups are becoming more blurred with time

F.  Peer self-help groups
1.  Stress item 4(d) on Yalom's list
2.  Based on the assumption that the best helper is someone who has been through it
3.  Pioneer was Alcoholics Anonymous (AA) in 1930s
4.  Hundred of such groups now exist for any imaginable problem or issue

G. Evaluation
   1. Group treatment in general is better than no treatment or a placebo, but
   2. There are methodological problems to effectiveness studies, and
   3. A general evaluation says little about specific types of group treatment
   4. Outcome studies of specific treatments show
      a. Behavioral treatments very good
      b. Humanistic/Gestalt treatments show mixed results
         (1) 33 percent report positive change
         (2) 38 percent report no change
         (3) 16 percent report negative change (remainder were dropouts)
      c. Best results occur when treatment is tailored to the needs and personality of the client

II. Family and marital therapy

   A. Families are natural candidates for group therapy because they are a natural group; problems of one member inevitably impact on other members

   B. Approaches to family therapy
      1. Communications approach tries to improve interpersonal communications and avoid double-binds
      2. Structural family therapy sees the family as involving interlocking roles which may or may not be productive in an individual's development
      3. Psychodynamic therapies focus on unconscious impulses and ego defenses
      4. Behavioral therapies may focus on specific goals such as:
         a. Preventing antisocial behavior in children, or
         b. Preventing relapse in mental patients returning home from institutional settings

   C. Marital therapy
      1. Approaches to marital therapy generally follow the same ideas as for family therapy
      2. Behavioral treatments try to change "coercive" interactions to "reciprocal" ones
      3. Cognitive therapists stress the ways partners think about each other
      4. Emotionally focused marital therapy tries to get at feelings underlying relationship
      5. Multi-family and multi-couple therapies have also had some success

   D. Evaluation
      1. Group-based couple/family therapies are more successful than focusing on "identified patients" because of the mutual impact family members have on each other
      2. Behavioral marital therapy can be effective against depression in either partner
      3. Insight therapies may have better long-term overall effects than others

III. Institutional care and community-based services

   A. The state institution
      1. Initially, mental institutions were seen as literal "asylums" in which a person could recover in a protected environment, but
      2. Institutions became overcrowded because recovery and release did not keep pace with admissions, and
      3. Institutions rapidly degenerated into poor-quality custodial care facilities partly because of their isolated locations
         a. Remoteness led to "out of sight, out of mind" societal attitudes
         b. Locations attracted few competent staff personnel
         c. Partial integration of patients into the community was impossible
      4. As a result, moves were made to provide alternatives for institutional care (see parts C through H, below), and to improve the therapeutic quality of institutional settings

   B. Therapeutic environments within institutions
      1. The idea of a therapeutic environment is to make all aspects of the institutional setting serve a therapeutic purpose
      2. Psychodynamic therapeutic environments stress providing remedial progress through the developmental stages (particularly for young patients)

3. Behavioral therapeutic environments stress learning appropriate behavior
   a. Token economies simulate real life outside the institution; one works for reinforcers by engaging in appropriate behaviors
   b. Social skills training and direct reinforcement of specific behaviors are also used
4. Humanistic-existential therapeutic environments stress:
   a. Independent living
   b. Democratic decision making
   c. Development of the self-concept (milieu therapy)
5. Evaluation
   a. Outcome for psychodynamic treatments unclear because of low numbers of cases
   b. Milieu therapy is better than custodial care
   c. Behavioral therapy is better than milieu therapy but generalization to outside world must not be taken for granted; follow-up is needed

C. The exodus to the community
1. Institutional populations began to decline in the late 1950s
2. New drug treatments introduced at that time made it possible for many institutionalized patients to be treated as outpatients
3. Inpatient populations dropped by half between 1970 and 1986

D. The community mental health center
1. Designed since the early 1960s to meet the needs of patients released from large institutions
2. Outpatient services is most commonly used service; provides counseling while patient lives in community
3. Inpatient services provide community-based hospitalization for those who require it
   a. Day hospital provides daytime services to those who can go home at night (quite effective approach in terms of efficiency and results)
   b. Night hospital is the opposite arrangement
4. Emergency services provide immediate care for those in crisis situations
5. Consultation services provide advice for other professionals in the community on dealing with clients in their care

E. Halfway houses
1. Provide residential treatment of a noninstitutional nature in a community setting for clients on their way out into the community
2. Best effect if small (15 to 20 residents)
3. Mental health professionals visit to provide services
4. May be self-supporting through therapeutic work programs
5. Useful in reducing recidivism (relapse)

F. Long-term care facilities
1. Provide long-term residential care outside of an institution for those not likely to be independent in the near future
2. Nursing homes often care for mental patients as well as the elderly
3. May be largely custodial in nature

G. Alternatives to hospitalization
1. Living with families as houseguests
2. Treatment in patient's own home by visiting professionals following an individualized treatment program
3. Most effective when mental health providers maintain close contact on continuing basis

H. Hot lines
1. Telephone crisis intervention staffed largely by trained volunteers
2. Deal with such problems as:
   a. Suicide
   b. Drug use
   c. Domestic abuse
   d. Troubled teens

3. Effectiveness in suicide prevention is questioned

I. Prevention
1. Primary prevention attacks the *causes* of disorder to keep disorder from developing (probably the biggest area where more needs to be done)
   a. Family planning and prenatal care
   b. Prevention of teenage pregnancy
   c. Academic mastery and psychosocial skills training
   d. Support for those in stressful situations
2. Secondary prevention intervenes early in a problem to keep small issues from becoming big ones
   a. Hot lines
   b. Emergency services
   c. Outpatient services
3. Tertiary prevention attempts to minimize the damage of major disorder
   a. Hospitalization
   b. Halfway houses
   c. Alternative noninstitutional treatments

J. Evaluation
1. Many community programs are effective, particularly in secondary and tertiary sense
2. But many others are not supported or funded sufficiently to do their best work
3. Cutbacks in institutional care result in early patient release, and inadequate community care results in readmission to the institution (revolving door effect)
4. Approximately one third of homeless people may be mentally disturbed individuals who have fallen through the cracks of the health care system
5. Some facilities actually abuse the system to maximize profits

## KEY TERMS
*The following terms are in bold print in your text. Define them and practice their definitions using the flash cards at the end of the chapter.*

assertiveness training (519)
behavioral rehearsal (518)
communications approach (523)
community mental health center (533)
day hospital (534)
encounter group (520)
family therapy (523)
group therapy (516)
halfway house (535)
hot lines (537)
large community group (521)
long-term-care facilities (536)
marital therapy (525)

milieu therapy (530)
night hospital (534)
paradoxical intention (524)
peer self-help groups (521)
primary prevention (538)
psychodrama (517)
secondary prevention (538)
social-skills training (518)
structural family therapy (524)
tertiary prevention (538)
therapeutic environment (529)
token economy (529)

*Your text does not list the following terms as formal vocabulary; however, if you don't know what they mean, you will be unable to grasp the concepts of this chapter.*

antidote (519)
continuum (518)
detriment (516)
disseminate (520)
heterogeneous (522)

mastectomy (521)
recapitulation (516)
recidivism (536)
resurgence (524)
satiation (529)

scapegoated (521)
stratagem (524)
tangible (529)

## IMPORTANT NAMES
*Identify the following persons and their major contributions to abnormal psychology as discussed in this chapter.*

Murray Bowen (525)
John F. Kennedy (533)

J. L. Moreno (517)
Gordon Paul (531)

Andrew Salter (519)
Irvin Yalom (516)

## GUIDED SELF-STUDY

1.  Other than individual therapy, what psychological therapies are available?


2.  Group therapy is listed as one of the most significant changes in psychological treatment in

    the last _____ years.

3.  The obvious practical advantage of group therapy is that it saves _____ and _____.

4.  Other than these two practical advantages from the previous question, what rationale makes
    group therapy intuitively sensible?


5.  Perhaps in the past, when thinking about group therapy, you have said to yourself, "No way
    I'd tell my personal problems to a group of strangers." There may be some good reasons for
    you to rethink that position. List the eleven therapeutic factors that group therapy may
    provide, according to Yalom.

    a.                                          g.

    b.                                          h.

    c.                                          i.

    d.                                          j.

    e.                                          k.

    f.

6.  To which of Yalom's factors does each of the following phrases relate?

    a.  _____ Getting rid of bottled up emotions

    b.  _____ Learning life is unfair

    c.  _____ Learning to smile more when interacting with others

    d.  _____ Enjoying being a giver

    e.  _____ Feels good to belong

    f.  _____ Interacting with the group the way you did with your family

    g.  _____ Learning your secret is no worse than anybody else's

    h.  _____ Learning that your feelings aren't good or bad, just part of who you are

    i.  _____ Concluding that maybe this is really going to work for you

    j.  _____ Watching others greet strangers and doing it the same way yourself

    k.  _____ Trying to express your assertiveness more in group

7.  Why do the different perspectives on psychology stress different factors? (This is not meant to
    be hard, so don't make it difficult).

8. What happens in a "traditional" psychoanalytic group approach?


9. _____ is a psychodynamic approach where group members act out their emotional conflicts.

10. List and explain briefly three techniques of psychodrama.

    a.

    b.

    c.

11. What is the point of all this "acting out"? (It was bad to have a kid acting out in Chapter 17.)


12. Most _____ group therapy is directed at specific behaviors or goals as defined by the group itself.

13. What is meant by the term "group process" on page 518?


14. Why is group process discussed under the behavioral groups?


15. What is range of the dependency on "group process" for behavioral groups?


16. So what does a group do if it does not depend on group process at all?


17. To employ group process, a behavioral group leader can do instruction and then have the group members interact to try out the technique, explore its utility, and then practice it to begin integrating it into to their personal behavioral patterns. This whole process is termed

    _____.

18. Two behavioral training goals that are well adapted to the group setting are _____

    training and _____ training.

19. In behavioral training groups, the therapist (a)_____ the clients about how to do a

    target behavior, (b)_____ it for them so they can see how it is done, and then has

    them (c)_____ the behavior themselves. The process of showing someone how to do

    something by doing it in front of him/her is called (d)_____.

20. Use the following terms in the blanks:

**agreement**          **extinction**          **nonverbally**
**disagree**             **I**                 **reinforcement**
**express**              **improvise**

In assertiveness training, clients are taught to verbally (a)_____ their feelings; show their emotions (b)_____ as well; speak up when they (c)_____ with someone; use the pronoun (d)"____" as much as possible; express (e)_____ when praised; and (f)_____, or live for the moment. In addition to the processes of modeling, rehearsing, and providing (g)_____ for improved behavior, assertiveness training also involves (h)_____, because clients learn that failure to do things "just right" will not be paired with disaster.

21. As far as evaluation is concerned, how effective are these behavioral teaching techniques?

22. What are the goals of humanistic group therapy in terms of Yalom's list? (See Hint 3.)

23. In their original forms, encounter groups encouraged (a)_____ displays of emotion, and (b)_____ groups focused on "unfinished business" from the past. Over the years, however, distinctions between the different types of groups have become (c) **more / less** clear-cut. Now, many of them are simply referred to as (d)_____ groups because of the focus on expressing one's emotions.

24. _____ is another name for the group leader in a humanistic group.

25. What is the "pressure cooker" technique for getting people quickly into a mode of sharing their feelings openly?

26. List and explain two other techniques that are used to get people to reveal their true feelings to other group members.

    a.

    b.

27. In effectiveness evaluations, humanistic groups rate as (a) **more / less** effective than other forms of group therapy. Research has not found a decisive pattern of success. A study of encounter group experiencers found that (b)_____ percent rated their group experience as beneficial; however, (c)_____ percent reported negative outcomes, and (d)_____ percent of *those* people could be called casualties. They reported that they felt increased psychological distress as a result of their group experience. One of the conclusions was that people with (e)_____ should avoid encounter groups and should be referred for other forms of (f)_____.

28. List any peer self-help groups that you know about.


29. Peer self-help groups are different from the other therapy groups that have been discussed in

    that they are not led by a (a)_____. The assumption with peer self-help
    groups is that the person who can best help and understand someone with a problem is

    someone who has (b)_____. Your text describes self-help groups as the

    (c)"_____ in the therapy market." Participants gain (d)_____ support, have a

    chance to air their problems, and collect (e)_____ on their particular problem.

30. Although some evaluations of specific types of groups have already been noted, we need to
    look at the evaluation of group therapies in general. List five questions your textbook says
    need to be answered concerning the therapeutic benefits of group therapy.

    a.

    b.

    c.

    d.

    e.

31. What are three of the methodological problems in evaluating group therapy effectiveness?

    a.

    b.

    c.

## FAMILY AND MARITAL THERAPY
32. In recent years family therapy has become **more / less** popular than in decades past.

33. Define the forms that family therapy may take: The strategic approach looks for the

    (a)_____ difficulties among the family members. Structural family therapy looks for

    the interlocking (b)_____ that family members play and urges them to become more

    (c)_____ in their interactions with each other.

34. A behavioral approach to marital counseling will try to move the couple away from

    (a)_____, which is reciprocal use of aversive stimuli, and toward (b)_____,
    which is mutual use of positive reinforcement to influence the other person's behavior.

35. How do behavioral family therapy groups help conduct-disordered children?


36. What particular process in behavioral family therapy is effective in preventing relapses among
    schizophrenic patients?

37. a.   How do marriage and family therapies do, in general, on the success meter?

b.   Which emotional problem in either partner of a relationship can be successfully treated with couples therapy?

c.   When comparing psychodynamic and behavioral marital therapies, which one seems to produce the most sustained effect after therapy is over?

38. In view of this, according to Snyder and Wills' (1989) study, if you are planning to make it to a silver or golden wedding anniversary, should you choose behavioral marital counseling or psychodynamic, insight-oriented marital counseling?

39. The _____ perspective has contributed the most to the development of group therapy.

## INSTITUTIONAL CARE AND COMMUNITY-BASED SERVICES

40. List three reasons that large mental hospitals were usually placed in the middle of nowhere, far from population centers.

a.

b.

c.

41. Why did the isolation of these large mental hospitals decrease their therapeutic potential?

a.

b.

c.

42. List some of the damaging effects of psychiatric hospitalization.


43. What is a therapeutic environment?


44. So, in general, how is each of the perspectives going to design its therapeutic environment?


Use the following terms in the blanks for questions 45 through 48:

| | | |
|---|---|---|
| extinction | reinforce | token |
| generalization | reinforcement | unconscious |
| identification | responsibility | very early |
| learning | same | young child |
| milieu | self | |
| phallic | token economy | |

45. The psychodynamic goal is always to deal with (a)_____ conflicts.  In seriously

troubled individuals, conflicts will have been formed at (b)_____ developmental stages, and therefore the ego and superego need development. When therapeutic environments have been based on psychodynamic perspective, the staff tries to provide the emotional

support and nurturance that a (c)_____ needs.  Ultimately, to develop the

superego, the individual needs to achieve (d)_____ with a (e) **same / opposite** -

sexed adult for the resolution of conflicts of the (f)_____ stage.

46. In behaviorism, the answer is always (a)_____. The therapeutic environment of a
(b)_____ economy allows for programmed, consistent (c)_____ of appropriate
behaviors and (d)_____ of inappropriate behaviors.

47. A good example of a humanistic-existential therapeutic environment is (a)_____
therapy, which focuses on personal growth of the individual by maximizing the individual's
independence and (b) _____ for his/her own behavior to build (c)_____-respect and
increase activity and interaction competency.

48. The most effective group therapy for getting patients ready for hospital release is (a)_____
_____. The problem is that the (b)_____ of these new more appropriate behaviors
to out-of-hospital circumstances does not tend to occur. To try to increase the likelihood of
this happening, patients are taught to (c)_____ themselves for appropriate behaviors.

49. In the 1950s, the discovery that certain types of (a)_____ made mentally ill people much
calmer, eliminating the need for hospitalization for many patients. These psychotropic drugs
began the "exodus to the community." There was also a growing awareness that isolation and
mere (b)_____ care were in no way therapeutic and even quite detrimental to
treatment. There was also the ever-present economic consideration: warehousing people in
mental hospitals is very expensive. In 1963, Congress passed the (c)_____
_____ Act. This law provided for one mental health center for every (d)_____
people in a geographic locale called a/an (e)_____ area. This formalized the
movement toward (f) **centralized / decentralized** facilities for the mentally ill.

50. Explain three levels of prevention (intervention) in mental health programs.

   a.  Primary:

   b.  Secondary:

   c.  Tertiary:

51. Spell out the specific contributions provided by each of the following mental health services:

   a.  Outpatient services:

   b.  Inpatient services:

   c.  Emergency services:

   d.  Consultation:

   e.  Halfway houses:

   f.  Long-term-care facilities:

   g.  Hot lines:

52. Go back to the list of seven areas of service provided by mental health clinics and mark to which level of prevention each belongs.

53. "Day hospitals" and "night hospitals" are forms of (a)_____ services where part of

the client's normal life is (b)_____. In (c)_____, treatment is provided

during the day and clients go to their normal homes at night. In (d)_____ the clients can maintain their normal daily activity of going to work or to school and then return for hospital care at night.

54. What side benefit was developed out of the introduction of psychological emergency services in hospital emergency rooms?


55. List two reasons consultations are helpful in the delivery of psychological services.

    a.

    b.

56. Describe the three experimental approaches described in your textbook for avoiding the hospitalization of people in mental health crises.

    a.   Denver:


    b.   Madison, Wisconsin:


    c.   Tucson's Treatment Network Team:


Use the following terms in the blanks for questions 57 and 58:

| | | |
|---|---|---|
| "revolving door" | function | long-term-care |
| custodial | halfway houses | night hospitals |
| day hospitals | halfway | night |
| day | hot lines | not enough |
| emergency services | state | one-third |

57. Mental health centers have made psychological help more readily available; this community

availability is definitely an improvement over the old large (a)_____ hospital system

because people do not have to wait until they cannot (b)_____ to be eligible for help.

Hospitalization within the community mental health care system in (c)_____ hospitals,

(d)_____ hospitals, and (e)_____ houses is more successful in avoiding recurrences

of the need for hospitalization.

58. The problem in the mental health care system is that there simply is (a)_____ of it. Some centers do not offer most of the seven areas of service listed above; their services are limited to psychotherapy and short-term hospitalization. That means there are no

(b) _____, _____, _____, _____, _____, and

_____ facilities. In some centers, some of these services are offered, but the quality

of service is nothing more than (c)_____ care. When people are released from hospitalization, community services are suppose to pick up responsibility for them in aftercare, but most often this does not happen and the individual survives out in the community until a crisis necessitates hospital readmission. This unsatisfactory state of affairs is called the

(d)_____ syndrome. Some of these people are the homeless. The estimate is that

(e)_____ of the homeless are the mentally ill people who are not being dealt with adequately in the mental health care system.

59. a.  Which of the three levels of prevention (intervention) of mental disorders has been the most neglected? (See your answer to question 52.)

b.  What was that level supposed to do?

60. What four recommendations have been suggested for beginning to move on this neglected level of intervention?

a.

b.

c.

d.

## HELPFUL HINTS

1.  Again, if the four basic Freudian techniques did not readily pop into your thoughts, you need to review textbook pages 495-496. The first time you encountered these methods was back in Chapter 2. Perhaps rereading that would help some of those old neural traces to click. Free association is not mentioned because the group interaction is the mechanism for revealing unconscious material instead of one client just talking ad infinitum.
2.  You will find that I ask about the effectiveness of each type group right after the other study exercise questions for that particular perspective. When I learn about a technique, I am ready to know right then about how well this "stuff" works.
3.  These questions on central goals of the different perspectives should be getting easier for you by now. They are the same questions asked in Chapter One when you were just being introduced to the perspectives for the first time.

## PRACTICE TEST
*Take the following test several times as you study the chapter. Write your answers on a separate sheet of paper and after each attempt, note in the tally box above each question whether your answer was correct or incorrect.*

| 1 | 2 | 3 | 4 |
|---|---|---|---|
|   |   |   |   |

1.  The main difference between group therapies and individual therapies is
    a.  group therapies are psychodynamic, whereas individual therapies can be of any theoretical outlook.
    b.  group therapies are more successful than individual therapies.
    c.  group therapies treat more than one person at a time.
    d.  group therapies are conducted by laypersons, while individual therapies require the participation of professionals.

| 1 | 2 | 3 | 4 |
| --- | --- | --- | --- |

2. Role reversal, mirroring, and the double technique are all components of
   a. Gestalt groups.
   b. psychodrama.
   c. assertiveness training groups.
   d. token economies.

| 1 | 2 | 3 | 4 |
| --- | --- | --- | --- |

3. Which of the following is the aspect of group therapy that a psychodynamic therapist would find most valuable?
   a. Corrective recapitulation of family group
   b. Imitative behavior
   c. Universality
   d. Group cohesiveness

| 1 | 2 | 3 | 4 |
| --- | --- | --- | --- |

4. Some people's problems are made worse by a lack of interpersonal skills. They may have anxiety about meeting people or they don't know what to say in a social situation. Which approach to group treatment would provide the most direct assistance here?
   a. A behavioral group
   b. Psychodrama
   c. Humanistic encounter group
   d. A Gestalt group

| 1 | 2 | 3 | 4 |
| --- | --- | --- | --- |

5. Which of the following approaches to group therapy is characterized by open, unrestrained emotional expression and feedback?
   a. Behavioral rehearsal group
   b. Distal relations group
   c. Assertiveness training group
   d. Encounter group

| 1 | 2 | 3 | 4 |
| --- | --- | --- | --- |

6. The leader in humanistic group therapy is often called a "facilitator." His or her role is to
   a. set an agenda for the group and make sure the schedule is followed.
   b. act as a participant without anyone knowing who he or she really is.
   c. provide interpretations to help group members understand their behavior.
   d. waver between being a leader and a participant and provide general guidelines.

| 1 | 2 | 3 | 4 |
| --- | --- | --- | --- |

7. Self-help groups such as AA and Weight-Watchers are
   a. dangerous for those who have not had private therapy first to get at the underlying issues.
   b. very popular but largely ineffective.
   c. perhaps the best bargain in the therapy market.
   d. declining in numbers since psychotherapy is now cheaper and more easily available.

| 1 | 2 | 3 | 4 |
|---|---|---|---|

8. Generally, attempts to evaluate the effectiveness of humanistic-type groups show that
   a. about two-thirds of participants are greatly helped.
   b. about one-third of participants report positive outcomes.
   c. about one-half of participants may become "casualties."
   d. less than half of participants finish the program.

| 1 | 2 | 3 | 4 |
|---|---|---|---|

9. The general goal of family therapy is to
   a. identify the family member with the problem and select him or her for individual treatment.
   b. deal with problems in the way family members interact with each other as a group.
   c. treat the parents and then teach them to treat the children.
   d. identify and prosecute child abuse and neglect.

| 1 | 2 | 3 | 4 |
|---|---|---|---|

10. Jill says the only way she can get Jack to mow the hill is to withhold sex until he does it. Jack says he can't get Jill to fetch a pail of water unless he refuses to give her any money. This is an example of a _____ marital relationship.
    a. coercive
    b. reciprocal
    c. skewed
    d. paradoxical

| 1 | 2 | 3 | 4 |
|---|---|---|---|

11. What general conclusions can be drawn about the effectiveness of group-based family and marital therapies?
    a. They are about as effective as practicing individual therapy on each person in the family.
    b. They are less effective than individual therapy because the fighting that occurs between participants prevents real progress.
    c. While effective, their increased cost and planning problems outweigh their advantages.
    d. They are more effective than individual treatment and produce longer-lasting results.

| 1 | 2 | 3 | 4 |
|---|---|---|---|

12. Which of the following characteristics best describes milieu therapy?
    a. Structured, organized, and highly scheduled to relieve clients of the stress of responsibility.
    b. Outpatient, community-based, involving work and interpersonal skill training in the real world.
    c. Low-keyed and democratic, stressing individual initiative and responsibility.
    d. Emotionally intense, aimed at retrieving past traumas and working them through in role-playing situations.

| 1 | 2 | 3 | 4 |
|---|---|---|---|

13. Patients who participate in token economies do not always maintain their good progress after release from the therapeutic setting. This may be because
   a. reinforcement contingencies in the outside world are not as stable and predictable as they are in a controlled therapeutic setting.
   b. patients learn to play along with the token economy system in order to achieve an early release before they are completely ready.
   c. the token economy is an artificial situation, because the outside world does not provide any reinforcers.
   d. the kinds of behaviors reinforced in an institution commonly have little relevance to living in the real world.

| 1 | 2 | 3 | 4 |
|---|---|---|---|

14. The decrease in mental hospital populations since the late 1950s is mainly attributable to
   a. improved socioeconomic conditions and quality of life in the country.
   b. the spread of community mental health programs that were instituted in the late 1940s.
   c. the development of drug treatments that permit outpatient treatment of many disorders.
   d. the redefinition of many disorders when *DSM-II* was introduced.

| 1 | 2 | 3 | 4 |
|---|---|---|---|

15. Edward does just fine when he can keep busy. He has a job and is good at it. It is when he has time on his hands that he gets depressed and anxious and needs some assistance with his problems. It sounds like Edward would benefit from
   a. traditional institutionalization.
   b. a halfway house.
   c. a day hospital.
   d. a night hospital.

| 1 | 2 | 3 | 4 |
|---|---|---|---|

16. Which of the following is a great advantage of community-based mental health services over traditional institutionalization?
   a. Family and friends provide therapy instead of paying professionals to do the same things.
   b. Drug treatments can be administered and monitored more easily.
   c. Maintaining the client's community ties allows a more normal life while treatment progresses.
   d. Law enforcement agencies can keep a closer watch for potential criminal activities on the part of the client.

| 1 | 2 | 3 | 4 |
|---|---|---|---|

17. The consultation service provided by some community mental health centers provides
   a. immediate admission for clients in emergency situations.
   b. advice and assistance to other professionals who may be already dealing with potential clients in the community.
   c. answers to mental health questions via hot lines.
   d. mental health professionals who visit clients at home on a call-as-needed basis.

| 1 | 2 | 3 | 4 |

18. The function of halfway houses is to
    a. provide an evaluation stage for patients on their way to inpatient facilities.
    b. serve as long-term residences for those who are not ill enough for institutional care but are unlikely to ever function on the outside.
    c. provide "recapitulation of the family group" for clients who have no families of their own.
    d. serve as a transition stage for clients going from inpatient care back into the community.

| 1 | 2 | 3 | 4 |

19. A psychologist addresses a local meeting: "What we need to do is provide jobs for the unemployed, shelter for the homeless, and get the kids off the streets and into schools and community activities. This may not sound like the practice of psychology, but believe me, it is." The psychologist is talking about
    a. primary prevention.
    b. secondary prevention.
    c. hortatory prevention.
    d. tertiary prevention.

| 1 | 2 | 3 | 4 |

20. Evaluation of community mental health programs reveals that
    a. these programs have reduced community mental disturbance to a trivial level.
    b. the ideas being tried are generally good ones but more needs to be done.
    c. these programs are uniformly unsuccessful and should be dropped.
    d. they are not as effective as larger institutions in providing for people's needs.

## ANSWERS
### Self-Study Exercise

1. Group therapy, family and marital therapy, community-based services (515)
2. 30 (516)
3. time and money (516)
4. Many psychological problems come out of interactions with other people, so working these problems out in an interpersonal context is "the real thing"; it is more natural (516).
5. 
   a. Hope
   b. Universality
   c. Information
   d. Altruism
   e. Corrective recapitulation of the primary family group
   f. Development of social skills
   g. Imitative behavior
   h. Interpersonal learning
   i. Group cohesiveness
   j. Catharsis
   k. Existential factors (516)
6. 
   a. Catharsis
   b. Existential factor
   c. Development of social skills
   d. Altruism
   e. Group cohesiveness
   f. Corrective recapitulation
   g. Universality
   h. Information
   i. Hope
   j. Imitative behavior
   k. Interpersonal learning (516)
7. If you said because different perspectives have different goals, you are right! (Chapter 1)
8. The focus of the group interactions is to explore all that regular Freudian stuff: Interpretation to uncover unconscious conflicts, working through transference, and dealing with resistance (517). See Hint 1.
9. Psychodrama (517)
10. 
    a. Role reversal: Members of the group switch the parts they are acting out
    b. Double technique: Therapist acts out client's role with him/her as client does it

c.   Mirroring: Group members play each other (517-518)
11. These different techniques allow the individuals an opportunity to see themselves more objectively and perhaps to gain some insights into their conflicts that up until then have been unconscious (518).
12. behavioral (518)
13. It is the interaction among group members, particularly their reactions to each other in the group setting, that can bring about change within individual group members (518, 520).
14. It is introduced here as a way of explaining what behavioral groups often do *not* concentrate on. It is intended to contrast behavioral and nonbehavioral groups (518).
15. The use of group process in behavioral groups ranges from almost none to extensive (518).
16. It is an instructional situation where all the people are in the room at the same time only because of time and cost effectiveness (518).
17. behavioral rehearsal (518)
18. social-skills; assertiveness (518)
19. a.   teaches
    b.   demonstrates
    c.   practice
    d.   modeling (518)

20. a.   express
    b.   nonverbally
    c.   disagree
    d.   I
    e.   agreement
    f.   improvise
    g.   reinforcement
    h.   extinction (519)
21. Behavioral groups that address behavior therapy, social-skills training, and assertiveness training are found to be very good (522).
22. The goal of humanistic therapy is always personal growth. In the group setting, learning intimacy and cooperation from others, learning about themselves and getting their feelings out in the open are the major issues (Yalom's numbers 4, 8, and 10) (520).
23. a.   unrestrained
    b.   Gestalt
    c.   less
    d.   experiential (520)
24. Facilitator (521)
25. Having a marathon where people spend hours and hours with each other to wear away the social facades and get down to the real people underneath (521)
26. a.   Eyeball-to-eyeball: Staring each other in the eye for a minute or more
    b.   Blind mill: Participants close their eyes and wander around the room communicating only through touch (521)
27. a.   less
    b.   33
    c.   16
    d.   8
    e.   serious psychological distress
    f.   therapy (523)
28. An organization mentioned by name in your text is Alcoholics Anonymous. But it also refers to many, many others: for dieters, stutterers, drug addicts, former mental patients, dialysis patients, cancer patients, families of cancer patients, spouses of alcoholics, children of alcoholics, parents of hyperactive children, single parents, widows, and widowers (521).
29. a.   mental health professional
    b.   had the problem him/herself
    c.   best bargain
    d.   social
    e.   information (521-522)
30. a.   Does group therapy really offer the therapeutic benefits that it is said to offer? This refers to Yalom's list.
    b.   Are these factors really responsible for therapeutic changes?
    c.   Do the changes in the behaviors of individuals in the group generalize to their outside lives?
    d.   Are these changes really helpful in outside life?
    e.   Can therapy hurt a person more than it help him/her? (522-523)
31. a.   Positive changes in attitude and self-concept do not necessarily translate into behavioral changes.
    b.   The ratings are done by the therapists and clients themselves, so they are not as objective (blind) as they could be, and they are based on self-reports instead of observed behaviors.
    c.   Group therapies as a whole are very diverse, so evaluations need to be done on very specific types of groups instead of just lumping them altogether (522).
32. more (523)
33. a.   communications
    b.   roles
    c.   flexible (523-524)

34. a. coercion
    b. reciprocity (525)
35. They teach the parents improved parenting techniques, such as the effective use of reward and punishments to encourage prosocial behavior (525).
36. Family members are taught new ways of expressing positive and negative emotions (525).
37. a. They are seen as generally successful (526).
    b. Depression (527)
    c. Psychodynamic (528)
38. Psychodynamic insight-oriented (528)
39. humanistic (520) (Hum-m-m-m, that's interesting—the one that has contributed the most to development of group therapy is the one that is less effective when evaluated!)
40. a. Ideally, people could rest from the stress of life by having a stay in the countryside.
    b. Land is much cheaper in the middle of nowhere.
    c. Nobody wanted mental patients for neighbors (528).
41. a. Low pay and remote locations do not attract many competent mental health professionals.
    b. Removing people so far from their normal living environments separated them from their social support network.
    c. With hospitals so far away, people did not go there until their problems were critical. Had services been closer, they would have been more likely to seek help earlier (528).
42. a. Loss of one's connections to real everyday life
    b. The temptation to give in to the "sick" role
    c. The social stigma of having been in "a mental institution"
    d. Loss of self-esteem for having needed "a mental institution" (528)
43. An environment where the circumstances of the patient's existence will help increase the likelihood of positive behavior changes. The individual is exposed to many different opportunities to develop more desirable behavior instead of merely practicing a skill in the very limited time of a daily "therapy session" (529).
44. By now I hope you can sing this tune—according to what they each think needs to be done to fix the abnormal behavior (Chapter 1).
45. a. unconscious
    b. very early
    c. young child
    d. identification
    e. same
    f. phallic (529, Chapter 2)
46. a. learning
    b. token
    c. reinforcement
    d. extinction (529, Chapter 3)
47. a. milieu
    b. responsibility
    c. self (529-530)
48. a. token economy
    b. generalization
    c. reinforce (540-541)
49. a. drugs
    b. custodial
    c. Community Mental Health
    d. 50,000
    e. catchment
    f. decentralized (530-533)
50. a. Primary: Preventing disorders from developing
    b. Secondary: Early detection and treatment to prevent minor problems from becoming major ones
    c. Tertiary: Minimizing and shortening existing disorders (538)
51. a. Outpatient services (including aftercare): Provide help without disrupting the patient's normal life (533)
    b. Inpatient services (day hospitals and night hospitals): Provide hospitalization within the community (534)
    c. Emergency services (including police referrals): Provide more immediate attention to people in mental health crisis during nights and weekends (534-535)
    d. Consultation: Provide mental health professionals' expertise on an as-needed basis to other professionals (teachers, physicians, police, etc.) who need psychological advice to carry out their services to people (535)
    e. Halfway houses: Provide an intermediate step within the community for transition from institutionalization to independent living (535-536)
    f. Long-term-care facilities: Provide long-term care for mentally ill within community (536)
    g. Hot lines: Provide emotionally supportive listening and information about resources available within the community (537)

52. Outpatient services (including aftercare): 2nd
    Inpatient services (day hospitals and night hospitals): 3rd
    Emergency services including police referrals: 3rd
    Consultation: 2nd
    Halfway houses: 3rd
    Long-term-care facilities: 3rd
    Hot lines: 2nd (533-538)
53. a. inpatient
    b. preserved
    c. day hospitals
    d. night hospitals (534)
54. Hospital emergency room medical staffs have become sensitized to the psychological needs of all their patients, not just mentally ill people (534-535).
55. a. Consultations are efficient ways of using mental health professionals' time. (You teach a teacher to deal with a disordered child and the next time he/she uses the same techniques successfully without having to even call in a mental health professional.)
    b. Behavior problems can be dealt with in the contexts in which they "normally" occur (535).
56. a. Denver: Foster care-like homes for those in crisis with access to psychiatric nurses as needed; for those needing close supervision there is an "intensive observation" apartment staffed by a psychology student and spouse; actual hospitalization as a last resort.
    b. Madison, Wisconsin: Treatment done within the community (without hospitalization) by tailoring programs to the specific needs of individuals in crisis—providing resources as needed and assisting the development of more adequate coping skills for the future
    c. Tucson's Treatment Network Team: A flexible treatment program for those with "chronic crises" but who would not participate if hospitalization was involved; a team member was assigned to the person to try to get him/her into a living situation that was as stable as possible and to intervene with whatever was needed—medication, crisis intervention, family counseling, and informal advice (536-537).
57. a. state
    b. function
    c. day
    d. night
    e. halfway (538)
58. a. not enough
    b. day hospitals, night hospitals, halfway houses, emergency services, hot lines, long-term-care facilities
    c. custodial (538)
    d. "revolving door" (540)
    e. one-third (539)
59. a. The primary prevention (intervention) level has been the most neglected.
    b. The primary prevention level is supposed to address community problems, such as racism, poverty, and drug use, that increase the likelihood that people may become mentally disordered (538).
60. a. Parent education that begins with family planning, prenatal care, and then continues with the provision of needed health and parent information
    b. Sex education to prevent teenage pregnancies and increase responsible decision making
    c. Mental health care at elementary school level to promote psychosocial skill development
    d. Help for people who are coping with stress that is near an unmanageable level, because stress definitely increases the likelihood of mental disorders (538)

## Practice Test

| | | | | | |
|---|---|---|---|---|---|
| 1. | c | (516) | 11. | d | (526) |
| 2. | b | (517) | 12. | c | (530) |
| 3. | a | (517) | 13. | a | (530) |
| 4. | a | (518) | 14. | c | (530) |
| 5. | d | (520) | 15. | d | (534) |
| 6. | d | (521) | 16. | c | (533) |
| 7. | c | (522) | 17. | b | (535) |
| 8. | b | (523) | 18. | d | (535) |
| 9. | b | (523) | 19. | a | (538) |
| 10. | a | (525) | 20. | b | (538) |

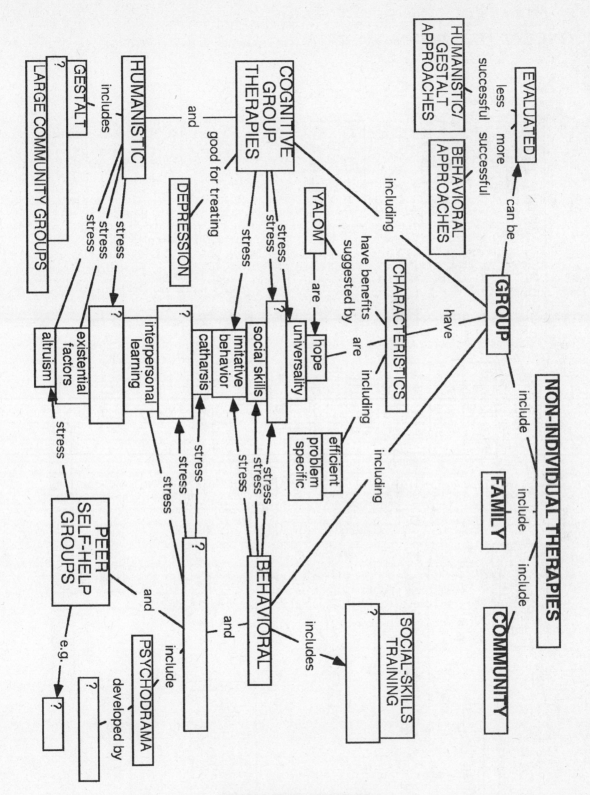

**CONCEPT MAP 20.1**

Fill out the boxes marked with question marks (?) with the concepts or words you think belong there. Suggested answers are on a following page.

491

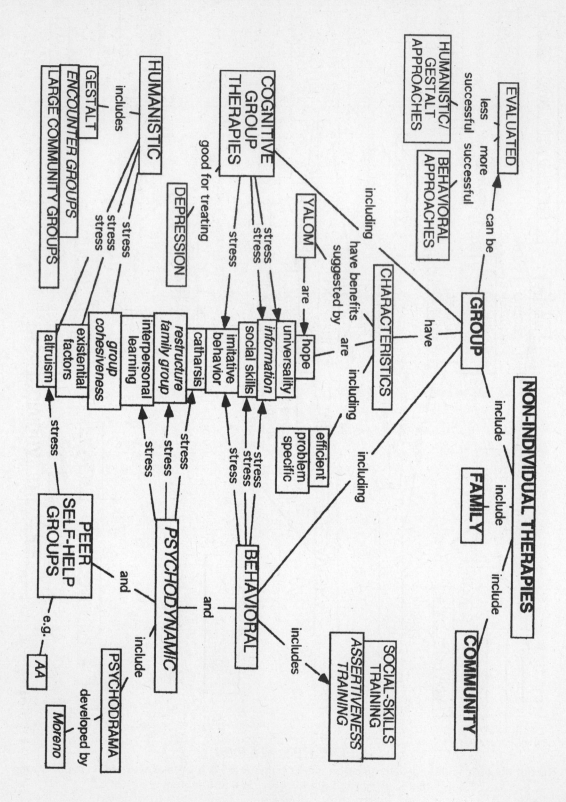

492

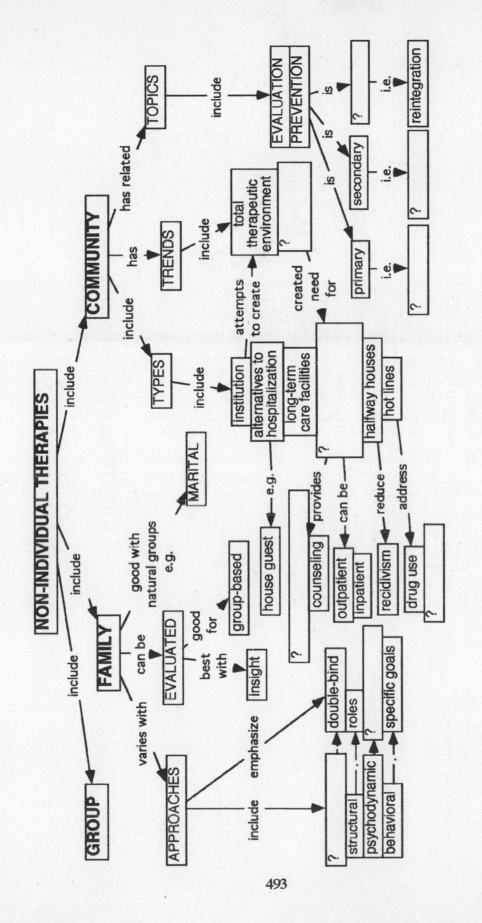

**CONCEPT MAP 20.2**

Fill out the boxes marked with question marks (?) with the concepts or words you think belong there. Suggested answers are on a following page.

493

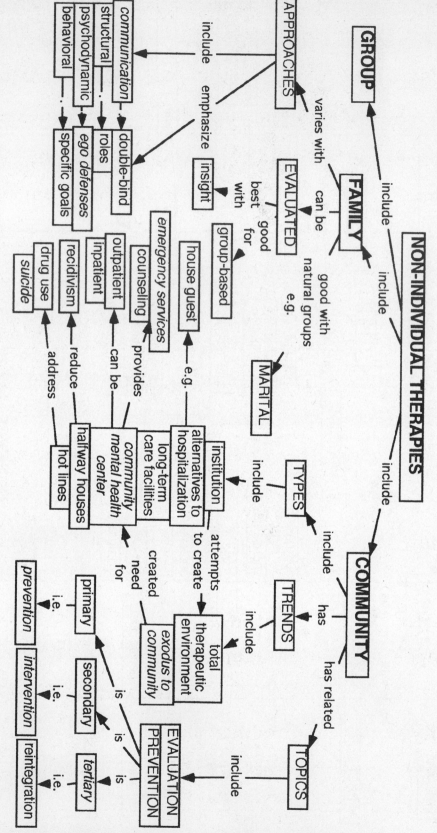

**CONCEPT MAP 20.2** The suggested answers are shown in *italics*.

494

# CHAPTER TERMS (Cut out on the lines to use as Flash Cards)

| | | |
|---|---|---|
| 20.1<br><br>**assertiveness training** | 20.8<br><br>**group therapy** | 20.15<br><br>**night hospital** |
| 20.2<br><br>**behavioral rehearsal** | 20.9<br><br>**halfway house** | 20.16<br><br>**paradoxical intention (1)** |
| 20.3<br><br>**communications approach** | 20.10<br><br>**hot lines** | 20.17<br><br>**paradoxical intention (2)** |
| 20.4<br><br>**community mental health center** | 20.11<br><br>**large community group** | 20.18<br><br>**peer self-help groups** |
| 20.5<br><br>**day hospital** | 20.12<br><br>**long-term-care facilities** | 20.19<br><br>**primary prevention** |
| 20.6<br><br>**encounter group** | 20.13<br><br>**marital therapy** | 20.20<br><br>**psychodrama** |
| 20.7<br><br>**family therapy** | 20.14<br><br>**milieu therapy** | 20.21<br><br>**secondary prevention** |

# DEFINITIONS (Cut out on the lines to use as Flash Cards)

| | | |
|---|---|---|
| **20.15** Partial-hospitalization system in which the patients go to work or school from nine to five and then return to the hospital for the night. | **20.8** Treatments of 8 to 10 clients at a time by a single therapist | **20.1** A form of social-skills training in which clients are taught how to assert themselves properly with other people and thus avoid being either passive or overaggressive |
| **20.16** (1) In existential therapy, a technique in which patients indulge or exaggerate their symptoms in order to prove to patients they can control their symptoms | **20.9** A residence for people who no longer require institutionalization but who still need some support in readjusting to community life | **20.2** Method of social-skills training in which the therapist tells clients how to perform the target behavior, models the behavior for them, and then has them practice the behavior in skits that simulate the situations they find troubling |
| **20.17** (2) In family therapy, a technique in which a family member deliberately exagger-ates maladaptive behavior forcing more functional adaptation | **20.10** Round-the-clock telephone services that people in trouble can call to receive immediate comfort and advice from trained volunteers | **20.3** An approach to family therapy in which family members are encouraged to tell one another what they actually feel and what kind of relationship they really want (also called strategic approach) |
| **20.18** Groups of people who share a special problem and meet to discuss that problem without the help or guidance of a mental health professional | **20.11** A type of humanistically oriented group therapy in which 50 to 2,000 people convene with several leaders for sessions lasting from one weekend to two weeks | **20.4** A facility designed to provide a variety of psychological services for everyone within a specified area |
| **20.19** The first level of prevention of psychological disorder, the goal of which is to prevent disorders from developing | **20.12** Facilities within a community that are designed to meet the needs of patients who will never, or not soon, be able to live independently | **20.5** A partial-hospitalization system in which the patients are hospitalized on a nine-to-five basis and then return home for the night |
| **20.20** Psychoanalytically oriented form of group therapy in which members act out their emotional conflicts together, often on a stage; clients are encouraged to reveal the roots of the problems, which can then be discussed with the group | **20.13** A form of group therapy in which both spouses are seen in an attempt to pinpoint their role expectations and communica-tion patterns; goals include an honest dialogue and better relating within the marriage | **20.6** Humanistic form of group therapy that emphasizes personal growth and increased openness and honesty in personal relations by means of free and candid expression within the group |
| **20.21** Second level of prevention of psychological disorder, the goal of which is to detect and treat disorders at an early stage, so that minor disorders do not develop into major ones | **20.14** Residential community therapy in which patients take responsibility for their behavior, participate in their rehabilita-tion, and help in making deci-sions (maximizing their inde-pendence, self-respect) | **20.7** Form of group therapy in which the members of a family are seen together on the as-sumption that the disturbance lies not only in the symptomatic individual but in the family unit as a whole |

**CHAPTER TERMS** (Cut out on the lines to use as Flash Cards)

| | | |
|---|---|---|
| 20.22<br><br>**social-skills training** | 20.29 | 20.36 |
| 20.23<br><br>**structural family therapy** | 20.30 | 20.37 |
| 20.24<br><br>**tertiary prevention** | 20.31 | 20.38 |
| 20.25<br><br>**therapeutic environment** | 20.32 | 20.39 |
| 20.26<br><br>**token economy** | 20.33 | 20.40 |
| 20.27 *(You may fill in the remaining boxes with names, terms and definitions from text and lecture)* | 20.34 | 20.41 |
| 20.28 | 20.35 | 20.42 |

**DEFINITIONS** (Cut out on the lines to use as Flash Cards)

| 20.36 | 20.29 | 20.22 A behavioral therapy that teaches people basic techniques for engaging in satisfying interactions with others |
|---|---|---|
| 20.37 | 20.30 | 20.23 A therapeutic approach in which family members are encouraged to fashion more flexible roles for themselves within the family unit |
| 20.38 | 20.31 | 20.24 Third level of prevention of psychological disorder, the goal of which is to minimize the damage, to both the victim and society, of a major disorder |
| 20.39 | 20.32 | 20.25 The arrangement of an institutional environment in such a way that all the patient's interactions with that environment will serve some therapeutic purpose |
| 20.40 | 20.33 | 20.26 Behavior modification procedure, based on operant-conditioning principles, in which patients are given a conditioned reinforcer such as tokens (which are exchanged) for performing target behaviors |
| 20.41 | 20.34 | 20.27 |
| 20.42 | 20.35 | 20.28 |

# Chapter 21

# *Biological Therapy*

## LEARNING OBJECTIVES
*By the time you are finished studying this chapter, you should be able to:*

**DRUGS**
1. Define psychopharmacology and describe the impact it has had in the treatment of mental disorders (544).
2. Describe the therapeutic effects and side effects of antianxiety drugs and be able to name the more commonly used antianxiety medications (544-547).
3. Describe the therapeutic effects and side effects of hypnotic drugs and be able to name the more commonly used hypnotic medications (547-548).
4. Describe the therapeutic effects and side effects of antipsychotic drugs and be able to name the more commonly used antipsychotic medications (548-550).
5. Describe the therapeutic effects and side effects of antidepressant and antimanic drugs and be able to name the more commonly used antidepressant and antimanic medications (550-553).
6. Discuss the relative usefulness of drug therapies and psychological therapies in the treatment of mental disorder (553-554).

**ELECTROCONVULSIVE THERAPY**
7. Describe electroconvulsive therapy (ECT) and its applications, and discuss the controversy surrounding this form of treatment (554-555).

**PSYCHOSURGERY**
8. Define psychosurgery, give three examples of psychosurgery, and discuss the controversy surrounding this form of treatment (555-556).

**EVALUATION**
9. Summarize your text's overall evaluation of the biological therapies (556).

## CHAPTER OUTLINE

I. Drug treatments (psychopharmacology)

    A. Antianxiety drugs
       1. Used to reduce tension and anxiety
       2. Also called minor tranquilizers
       3. About half are used to alleviate stress of medical illness; half in conjunction with psychological treatment
       4. Side effects and other unwanted consequences
          a. Daytime sedation
          b. Effect multiplies when combined with alcohol
          c. Tolerance and rebound effects
          d. Treats symptoms without treating causes
          e. State dependent learning may prevent coping skills learned under drug treatment from generalizing to undrugged state

5. Examples (Generic name [Trade name])
   a. Chlordiazepoxide [Librium]
   b. Diazepam [Valium]
   c. Chlorazepate [Tranxene]
   d. Oxazepam [Serax]
   e. Lorazepam [Aetivan]
   f. Alprazolam [Xanax]
   g. Meprobamate [Miltown]
   h. Buspirone [BuSpar]

B. Hypnotics
   1. Also known as sleeping pills
   2. Side effects and other unwanted consequences largely the same as with minor tranquilizers (see A 4 above)
   3. Examples (Generic name [Trade name])
      a. Flurazepam [Dalmane]
      b. Triazolam [Halcion]
      c. Tempazepam [Restoril]
      d. Zolpidem [Ambien]
      e. Quazepam [Doral]
      f. Phenobarbital [Luminal]
      g. Secobarbital [Seconal]

C. Antipsychotic drugs
   1. Used to relieve the major symptoms of psychosis
   2. Also called major tranquilizers or neuroleptics
   3. Seem to produce their effects by reducing dopamine activity in the brain
   4. Side effects and other unwanted consequences
      a. Apathy
      b. Constipation
      c. Blurred vision
      d. Dry mouth
      e. Muscle rigidity
      f. Tremors
      g. Tardive dyskinesia (untreatable)
      h. Abuse potential in connection with "patient management"
      i. Treating symptoms at the expense of finding causes
   5. Examples (Generic name [Trade name])
      a. Chlorpromazine [Thorazine]
      b. Thioridazine [Mellaril]
      c. Trifluoperazine [Stelazine]
      d. Fluphenazine [Prolixine]
      e. Chlorprothixene [Taractan]
      f. Thiothixene [Navane]
      g. Haloperidol [Haldol]
      h. Loxapine [Loxitane]
      i. Clozapine [Clozaril]
      j. Molindone [Moban]
      k. Reserpine [Sandril]
      l. Tetrabenazine

D. Antidepressant and antimanic drugs
   1. Used to elevate or stabilize moods
   2. Antidepressants produce their effect by blocking norepinephrine and/or serotonin activity
   3. Side effects and other unwanted consequences
      a. MAO inhibitors damage brain, liver, or cardiovascular system
      b. MAO inhibitors interact with some food to produce severe illness or death
      c. Tricyclics can produce side effects similar to antipsychotics, except for tardive dyskinesia (see C 4 above)

        d.    Tricyclics may take 2 to 4 weeks to become effective
        e.    For lithium, effective dosage is close to toxic dosage
    4.    Examples of antidepressants (Generic name [Trade name])
        a.    Tricyclics
            (1)    Amitriptyline [Elavil]
            (2)    Imipramine [Tofranil]
            (3)    Doxepin [Sinequan]
            (4)    Desipramine [Norpramin]
            (5)    Nortriptyline [Pamelor]
            (6)    Protriptyline [Vivactil]
        b.    MAO inhibitors
            (1)    Phenelzine [Nardil]
            (2)    Tranylcypromine [Parnate}
            (3)    Pargyline [Eutonyl]
            (4)    Isocarboxazid [Marplan]
        c.    Serotonin uptake inhibitors
            (1)    Fluoxetine [Prozac]
            (2)    Paroxetine [Paxil]
            (3)    Sertraline [Zoloft]
    5.    Examples of antimanic drugs (Generic name [Trade name])
        a.    Lithium [Eskalith]
        b.    Carbamazepine [Tegretol]

E.    Drug therapy versus psychotherapy
    1.    Drug therapy advocates predict the demise of psychological therapies
        a.    Drugs can be cheaper
        b.    Drugs can take effect sooner
        c.    Drugs can alleviate symptoms more effectively
    2.    Psychotherapy advocates say this is short-sighted and simple-minded
        a.    There is more to behavior than biology
        b.    Drugs ignore causes and simply treat symptoms
        c.    Psychotherapy can produce better long-term resistance to relapse
    3.    Best approach may be a combination of approaches
        a.    Drugs and psychotherapy together can produce a better result than either one alone
        b.    Drugs can reduce symptoms so patients can communicate and improve reality contact and thereby benefit from psychotherapy
        c.    Drugs and psychotherapy can each deal with their respective components of complex disorders

II.    Electroconvulsive therapy (ECT)

    A.    Electric shock (70 to 130 volts) applied to brain can be effective in quickly reducing depression

    B.    Affects norepinephrine and serotonin levels in the brain

    C.    Major side effect is memory loss
        1.    Retrograde loss affects memory of events prior to treatment (most serious effect)
        2.    Anterograde loss affects ability to learn new information
        3.    Limiting shock to right hemisphere lessens memory problems and is as effective as bilateral treatment

    D.    Much opposition to ECT has emotional as opposed to scientific basis, in part based on abuse potential

III.    Psychosurgery

    A.    Brain surgery aimed at reducing psychopathology in the absence of obvious organic brain pathology

B. Examples
    1. Prefrontal lobotomy
       a. Surgical separation of frontal lobes from lower centers
       b. Intent was to calm uncontrollable psychotic patients
       c. Often produced severe side-effect disabilities
       d. Developed in 1930s; largely obsolete today
    2. Cingulotomy
       a. Lesion in cingulate gyrus
       b. Same goal as in lobotomy: Disrupt emotion connections to frontal lobe
       c. More precise than lobotomy and effective in some drug-resistant obsessive-compulsive patients
    3. Stereotactic subcaudate tractotomy
       a. Specific brain structures destroyed to produce specific changes in behavior
       b. More precise and less damaging than older techniques

C. Psychosurgery is controversial and is used as a last resort therapy because effects are not reversible

IV. Evaluation

A. Biological therapies can be expensive, can have serious side effects, can be abused, and do not always get at the root of the disorder

B. But, they can be very effective in controlling symptoms, and may therefore make other forms of therapy possible

C. A prudent combination of approaches can deliver the benefits of both and avoid the worst pitfalls of each

## KEY TERMS
*The following terms are in bold print in your text. Define them and practice their definitions using the flash cards at the end of the chapter.*

antianxiety drugs (544)
antidepressant drugs (550)
antimanic drugs (551)
antipsychotic drugs (548)
cingulotomy (555)
electroconvulsive therapy (554)
hypnotics (547)
lithium (551)

MAO inhibitors (550)
prefrontal lobotomy (555)
psychopharmacology (544)
psychosurgery (555)
selective serotonin reuptake inhibitors (SSRIs) (551)
stereotactic subcaudate tractotomy (556)
tricyclics (550)

*Your text does not list the following terms as formal vocabulary; however, if you don't know what they mean, you will be unable to grasp the concepts of this chapter.*

incursions (554)
intractable (556)

lesion (555)
vociferous (554)

## IMPORTANT NAMES
*Identify the following persons and their major contributions to abnormal psychology as discussed in this chapter.*

Almeida Lima (555)

Egas Moniz (555)

## GUIDED SELF-STUDY

1. Biological therapies are those that treat the person's physical body in some way. What physical treatments are options for abnormal behaviors?

2. What are the most frequently and least frequently used medical treatments for abnormal behavior?

DRUGS

3. The study of drug treatments for psychological disorders is known as (a)_____.

Today, the use of drug treatments is extremely (b) **common / uncommon**, and while they can

be very effective, there are some problems, including (c)_____ results, unwanted

(d)_____ effects, and the issue of treating symptoms when the (e)_____ of the problem is still undefined.

4. Identify which drug category fits each of the following descriptive phrases. The categories are provided here, but you really should have a memory trick for a fast mental check list of the categories for test purposes (see Hint 1).

**Antianxiety drugs**       **Antipsychotic drugs**
**Antidepressant drugs**     **Hypnotics**
**Antimanic drugs**

a. _____ Also known as sleeping pills

b. _____ Also known as minor tranquilizers

c. _____ Used to relieve major symptoms of psychosis

d. _____ Two major types are MAO inhibitors and tricyclics

e. _____ Stabilizes mood in bipolar disorder

f. _____ Also known as major tranquilizers

g. _____ The most widely used prescription drugs in the world

h. _____ Can produce tardive dyskinesia as a side effect

i. _____ Lithium is the primary example

5. What is a synergistic effect?

6. What drugs are particularly noted for this synergistic effect?

7. What other connection is there between alcohol and antianxiety drugs?

8. What is "rebound" in connection with drug effects?

9. Taking antianxiety drugs to deal with stress has been compared to turning off a fire alarm to escape the noise. What is the point of that illustration?

10. Antianxiety drugs have been used to treat panic disorder, but not with great success. The

drug category that seems to work better with panic disorder is the _____.

11. Major problems with hypnotic drugs are daytime (a)_____ and the (b)_____ effect. Often, drugs that have less of one have more of the other. For example, Dalmane is bad for (c)_____, while Halcion produces more (d)_____.

Use the following words or terms for questions 12 and 13.

| | | |
|---|---|---|
| **tardive dyskinesia** | **management/control** | **dopamine** |
| **20 to 30** | **apathy** | **fatigue** |
| **relapse** | **Thorazine** | **schizophrenia** |

12. Antipsychotic drugs are used with great effect in the treatment of one of the most serious psychoses, (a)_____. A major breakthrough in this area was the marketing of a phenothiazine called (b)_____ in the 1950s. Attempts to understand how such drugs worked led to the (c)_____ hypothesis in connection with schizophrenia.

13. Problems with the use of antipsychotic drugs include a zombie-like state characterized by excessive (a)_____ and (b)_____, the potential for abuse by institutional staff who are less interested in treatment and more interested in patient (c)_____, and a variety of physical side effects, the most serious of which is (d)_____. This side effect is found in about (e)_____ percent of schizophrenics maintained on antipsychotic drugs. Finally, the drugs do not seem to "cure" the disorders they treat. When drug use is stopped, the patient will often suffer a (f)_____.

14. Answer true (T) or false (F) to the following statements about antidepressant drugs.

a. ___ MAO inhibitors are the most commonly used antidepressants today.
b. ___ MAO inhibitors can have serious side effects when taken with certain fermented foods.
c. ___ MAO inhibitors presumably work by increasing levels of dopamine in the brain.
d. ___ Tricyclics block the reabsorption of norepinephrine and serotonin.
e. ___ The big advantage of tricyclics is that they have an immediate therapeutic effect.
f. ___ Prozac not only works on depression, but seems to be an effective treatment of obsessive-compulsive disorder as well.
g. ___ Lithium is now generally used instead of MAO inhibitors to combat depression.

15. Identify the drug category to which of each of the following drugs belongs.

| | |
|---|---|
| **Antianxiety drug** | **Antipsychotic drug** |
| **Antidepressant drug** | **Hypnotic** |
| **Antimanic drug** | |

| | | | |
|---|---|---|---|
| a. _____ Halcion | | g. _____ Tofranil |
| b. _____ Prozac | | h. _____ Xanax |
| c. _____ Thorazine | | i. _____ Phenobarbital |
| d. _____ Haldol | | j. _____ Tegretol |
| e. _____ Lithium | | k. _____ Chlorpromazine |
| f. _____ Valium | | |

16. In discussing the relative merits of drug therapy versus psychotherapy, your text refers to two extreme positions taken by some therapists. Briefly summarize these extreme opinions.

   a.


   b.


17. A compromise position proposed in your text states that a combination of drugs and psychological treatment may be the best approach. Drugs seem to do a good job in the

   immediate control of (a)_____, and psychotherapy deals effectively with the original

   (b)_____ and the recent (c)_____ of the disorder. Also, combining psychotherapy

   with medications tends to reduce the (d)_____ rate when medication is discontinued.

ELECTROCONVULSIVE THERAPY
18. Electroconvulsive therapy, or ECT, has been useful to treat _____, particularly in cases where medications have failed.

19. Use the following words in the blanks:

   **language**                          **immediate**
   **right**                             **serotonin**
   **memory loss**                       **norepinephrine**

   Shock therapy seems to have its effect by altering levels of (a)_____ and

   (b)_____ in the brain. Unlike antidepressant drugs, the effect of ECT is (c)_____

   in time. The most serious side effect is (d)_____. This side effect can be reduced by

   stimulating only one side of the brain, the side that does not deal with (e)_____. In

   most people this is the (f)_____ side of the brain.

20. What is a shock treatment like? A mild trip to the electric chair????

21. Why is ECT such a controversial form of treatment?

   a.

   b.

   c.

   d.

PSYCHOSURGERY
22. Define the term psychosurgery.


23. Why has psychosurgery developed such a bad reputation?

24. What is the current status of psychosurgery as a therapeutic approach?

25. Name two psychosurgical techniques that have been developed since the days of the prefrontal lobotomy.

## HELPFUL HINTS

1. Drop the "anti's" in front of the drug category names so you don't have all those a's to use in a memory trick based on first letters of names of categories.
2. Remember from the chapter on addictions that withdrawal from barbiturates or alcohol needs medical supervision because they can be life-threatening bodily adjustments.

## PRACTICE TEST
*Take the following test several times as you study the chapter. Write your answers on a separate sheet of paper and after each attempt, note in the tally box above each question whether your answer was correct or incorrect.*

1. The study of drug treatments for psychological disorders is called
   a. neuroleptic research.
   b. chemotherapy.
   c. psychoneuroimmunology.
   d. psychopharmacology.

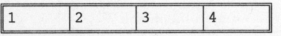

2. Which of the following is an antianxiety drug?
   a. Tofranil
   b. Thorazine
   c. Xanax
   d. Halcion

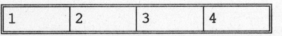

3. Some antianxiety drugs produce a reaction called "rebound" when they are discontinued after prolonged use. "Rebound" means
   a. the patient's symptoms go to their opposite extreme, that is, a highly anxious patient may become very lethargic.
   b. extreme muscle rigidity and other motor symptoms.
   c. a return of the original symptoms at a much increased level.
   d. a predisposition to become addicted to other drugs.

4. Antianxiety drugs are commonly members of a family of drugs called the
   a. benzodiazepines.
   b. MAO inhibitors.
   c. phenothiazines.
   d. tricyclics.

1 | 2 | 3 | 4

5. The use of antianxiety drugs has been criticized because they
   a. create hallucinations when used in large doses.
   b. encourage people to cover symptoms rather than solve problems.
   c. can lead to irreversible motor symptoms as side effects.
   d. cause manic behavior and sleep loss.

| 1 | 2 | 3 | 4 |
|---|---|---|---|

6. Which of the following drugs is a hypnotic?
   a. Halcion
   b. Mellaril
   c. Haldol
   d. Prozac

| 1 | 2 | 3 | 4 |
|---|---|---|---|

7. The first antipsychotic drug used in the United States, and still one of the most commonly used today is
   a. Prozac.
   b. Thorazine.
   c. Lithium.
   d. Valium.

| 1 | 2 | 3 | 4 |
|---|---|---|---|

8. What is tardive dyskinesia?
   a. A form of schizophrenia
   b. A permanent side effect of certain antipsychotic drugs
   c. A motor disorder now successfully treated with antimanic drugs
   d. A form of symptom substitution common to schizophrenia

| 1 | 2 | 3 | 4 |
|---|---|---|---|

9. Stelazine can do which of the following?
   a. Improve cases of generalized anxiety disorder
   b. Allow people with major depression to be treated as outpatients
   c. Reduce symptoms in schizophrenic patients
   d. Suppress withdrawal symptoms in alcoholics

| 1 | 2 | 3 | 4 |
|---|---|---|---|

10. Which of the following is *not* true of antipsychotic drugs?
    a. They can result in the transfer of hospitalized patients to out-patient care.
    b. They have been used in high dosages for "patient management" when staff are shorthanded.
    c. They can permanently reverse the biochemical causes of some psychoses.
    d. They can produce serious and possibly permanent side effects.

| 1 | 2 | 3 | 4 |
|---|---|---|---|

11. Which of the following classes of antidepressants is now seldom used because of potentially serious side effects associated with fermented foods in the diet?
    a. Serotonin uptake inhibitors
    b. MAO inhibitors
    c. Tricyclics
    d. Benzodiazepines

| 1 | 2 | 3 | 4 |
|---|---|---|---|

12. Antidepressants all seem to have their therapeutic effects by increasing the effect of
    a. dopamine.
    b. tetracycline.
    c. norepinephrine and/or serotonin.
    d. GABA and/or acetylcholine.

| 1 | 2 | 3 | 4 |

13. Which of the following would be useful in treating a patient with bipolar disorder?
    a. Valium
    b. Thorazine
    c. Tricyclics
    d. Lithium

| 1 | 2 | 3 | 4 |

14. Antipsychotic drugs seem to achieve their therapeutic effects by
    a. increasing serotonin activity in the brain.
    b. lowering the level of arousal in motor cortex.
    c. blocking dopamine activity in the brain.
    d. promoting the production of norepinephrine.

| 1 | 2 | 3 | 4 |

15. According to your text, the most hopeful outcome of the debate concerning the relative merits of drug treatments and psychological treatments is that
    a. drug treatments will eventually replace most forms of psychological treatment.
    b. drugs will be used to cure the less severe problems, but psychotherapy will continue to be used for the more serious disorders.
    c. drug treatments will fade because of a growing realization that they merely cover symptoms and do not cure the problem.
    d. a responsible combination of drug and psychological treatment will be used in most cases.

| 1 | 2 | 3 | 4 |

16. Electroshock therapy is used in the treatment of
    a. panic attacks.
    b. severe depression.
    c. schizophrenia.
    d. obsessive-compulsive personality.

| 1 | 2 | 3 | 4 |

17. One way of reducing memory loss associated with ECT is to
    a. shock the right hemisphere of the brain only.
    b. provide anesthetics before shock is administered.
    c. increase shock intensity to reduce shock duration.
    d. provide intense psychotherapy after treatment.

| 1 | 2 | 3 | 4 |

18. Which of the following is true of psychosurgery?
    a. It is rapidly replacing drug treatments for the most severe disorders.
    b. It is the old term for the prefrontal lobotomy.
    c. It is the best understood of the biological therapies.
    d. It is generally seen as a treatment of last resort.

19. A psychosurgical technique currently in use which destroys precisely located areas of brain tissue with radiation is
    a. stereotactic subcaudate tractotomy.
    b. split brain procedure.
    c. prefrontal lobotomy.
    d. multiaxial tomography.

| 1 | 2 | 3 | 4 |
|---|---|---|---|

20. Of the biological therapies discussed in the chapter, the most commonly used is
    a. psychosurgery.                c. diet management.
    b. drug therapy.                 d. electroshock treatment.

## ANSWERS
### Self-Study Exercise

1. Drugs, psychosurgery, and shock treatments (544)
2. Most frequent—drugs (544); least frequent—psychosurgery (556)
3. a. psychopharmacology      d. side
   b. common      e. cause (544)
   c. inadequate
4. a. Hypnotics (547)      f. Antipsychotic drugs (548)
   b. Antianxiety drugs (544)      g. Antianxiety drugs (544)
   c. Antipsychotic drugs (548)      h. Antipsychotic drugs (549)
   d. Antidepressant drugs (550)      i. Antimanic drugs (551)
   e. Antimanic drugs (551)
5. A synergistic effect is when a combination of drugs produces an effect greater than the sum of their individual effects (546).
6. Alcohol with barbiturates or benzodiazepines, with the alcohol and barbiturate combination being the more lethal of the two (546)
7. Sometimes antianxiety drugs are used while a person is going through alcohol withdrawal (546). See Hint 2.
8. Rebound is when symptoms return with even greater force after drug use is ended (546).
9. Relieving anxiety without dealing with the cause of the anxiety may be counter-productive in the long run, since anxiety, like a fire alarm, is a sign that something serious is wrong (547).
10. antidepressants (547)
11. a. grogginess      c. grogginess
    b. rebound      d. rebound (547)
12. a. schizophrenia
    b. Thorazine
    c. dopamine (559)
13. a. fatigue (or apathy)      d. tardive dyskinesia
    b. apathy (or fatigue)      e. 20 to 30
    c. management or control      f. relapse (549-550)

14. a. F      e. F
    b. T      f. T
    c. F      g. F (550-551)
    d. T
15. a. Hypnotic      g. Antidepressant
    b. Antidepressant      h. Antianxiety
    c. Antipsychotic      i. Hypnotic
    d. Antipsychotic      j. Antimanic
    e. Antimanic      k. Antipsychotic (545)
    f. Antianxiety

16. a. In the future, almost all psychopathology will be "biologized." Disorders will be treated by direct chemical intervention, and patients will save vast amounts of time and money that would have been wasted on psychological therapy.
    b. Managing symptoms through chemical intervention ignores the fundamental causes of disorder. Symptoms control leads to an artificial normality that is counterproductive in the long run (553).
17. a. symptoms              c. effects
    b. causes                d. relapse (554)
18. severe depression (554)
19. a. norepinephrine (or serotonin)      d. memory loss
    b. serotonin (or norepinephrine)      e. language
    c. immediate                          f. right (554)
20. A convulsion similar to an epileptic grand mal seizure is induced with electrical current while the patient is anesthetized. The patient has no experience of it at all (554).
21. a. ECT is a drastic measure considering that no one knows exactly how it works. It is like fixing a balky radio by hitting it with a hammer. While it may produce the desired result, it is still a highly suspect technique.
    b. ECT causes memory losses that in some cases turn out to be permanent.
    c. Many patients are terrified of "shock" treatment.
    d. There is potential for abuse in connection with patient "management" (554).
22. Psychosurgery is surgery on the brain designed to reduce abnormal behavior, even though there is no evidence of brain pathology (555).
23. The first famous psychosurgical technique, the prefrontal lobotomy, was a crude procedure that sometimes left patients in a vegetative state. Also, the use of such techniques as instruments of patient management left many questioning the legitimacy of the whole approach (555).
24. Currently, psychosurgery is more highly refined than in the days of the prefrontal lobotomy, but it is still seen as a measure of last resort because the techniques are still largely experimental and the effects are irreversible (556).
25. The cingulotomy and the stereotactic subcaudate tractotomy (555-556)

## Practice Test

| | | | | | |
|---|---|---|---|---|---|
| 1. | d | (544) | 11. | b | (550) |
| 2. | c | (544) | 12. | c | (550) |
| 3. | c | (546) | 13. | d | (551) |
| 4. | a | (544) | 14. | c | (549) |
| 5. | b | (547) | 15. | d | (554) |
| 6. | a | (547) | 16. | b | (554) |
| 7. | b | (548) | 17. | a | (554) |
| 8. | b | (549) | 18. | d | (556) |
| 9. | c | (549) | 19. | a | (556) |
| 10. | c | (550) | 20. | b | (544) |

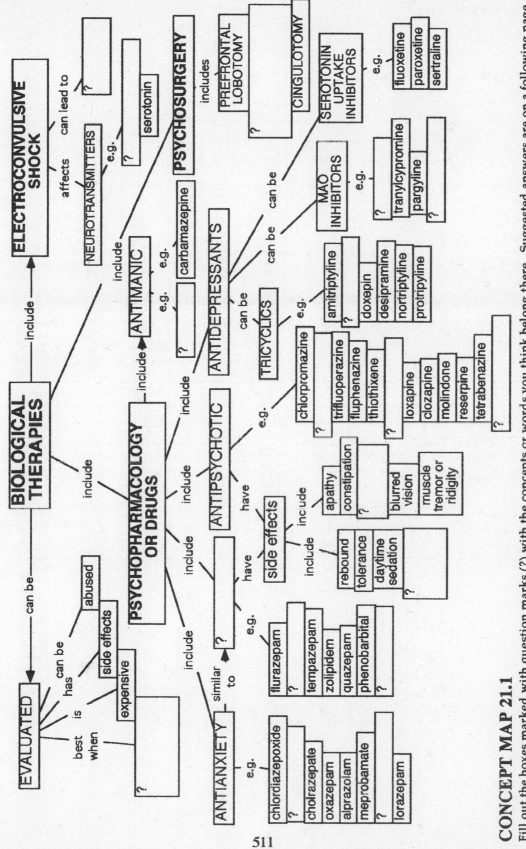

## CONCEPT MAP 21.1

Fill out the boxes marked with question marks (?) with the concepts or words you think belong there. Suggested answers are on a following page.

**CONCEPT MAP 21.1**

The suggested answers are shown in *italics*.

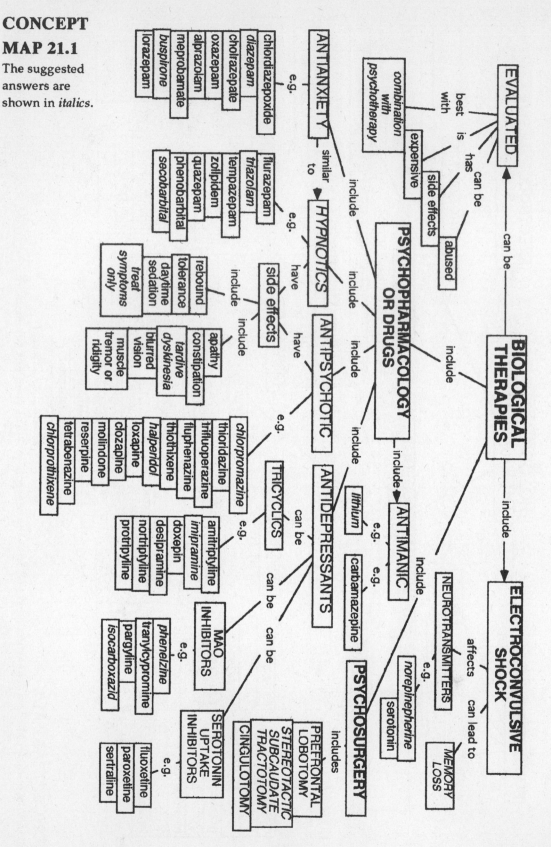

512

# CHAPTER TERMS (Cut out on the lines to use as Flash Cards)

| | | |
|---|---|---|
| 21.1<br><br>**antianxiety drugs** | 21.8<br><br>**lithium** | 21.15<br><br>**tricyclics** |
| 21.2<br><br>**antidepressant drugs** | 21.9<br><br>**MAO inhibitors** | 21.16<br>*(You may fill in the remaining boxes with names, terms and definitions from text and lecture)* |
| 21.3<br><br>**antimanic drugs** | 21.10<br><br>**prefrontal lobotomy** | 21.17 |
| 21.4<br><br>**antipsychotic drugs** | 21.11<br><br>**psycho-pharmacology** | 21.18 |
| 21.5<br><br>**cingulotomy** | 21.12<br><br>**psychosurgery** | 21.19 |
| 21.6<br><br>**electroconvulsive therapy (ECT)** | 21.13<br><br>**selective serotonin reuptake inhibitors (SSRI)** | 21.20 |
| 21.7<br><br>**hypnotics** | 21.14<br><br>**stereotactic subcaudate tractotomy** | 21.21 |

# DEFINITIONS (Cut out on the lines to use as Flash Cards)

| | | |
|---|---|---|
| **21.15** Class of antidepressants that seem to increase the level of certain neurotransmitters, including norepinephrine and serotonin | **21.8** A mood-altering drug used to control manic episodes | **21.1** Drugs used to reduce tension and anxiety; used by normal people during times of stress and by people undergoing psychological treatment for anxiety disorders, stress-related physical disorders, and withdrawal from alcohol and drugs |
| **21.16** | **21.9** First important class of antidepressants; assumed to block the action of monoamine oxidase, their mechanism has not been established | **21.2** Drugs used to elevate mood in depressed patients. |
| **21.17** | **21.10** Psychosurgical procedure for severely disturbed patients in which some of the connections between the frontal lobe and the lower parts of the brain are severed; very rarely performed today | **21.3** Drugs, principally lithium, used to prevent or treat manic episodes |
| **21.18** | **21.11** The study of the drug treatment of psychological disorders | **21.4** Drugs used to relieve symptoms such as confusion, withdrawal, hallucinations, and delusions in psychotic patients (also called major tranquilizers or neuroleptics) |
| **21.19** | **21.12** Surgery aimed at reducing abnormal behavior in the absence of any signs of organic brain pathology | **21.5** Psychosurgery technique to patients with severe obsessive-compulsive disorder in which an electrode is inserted into the cingulate gyrus and heated to create a lesion |
| **21.20** | **21.13** A class of antidepressants that work by blocking the reuptake of the neurotransmitter serotonin | **21.6** The administering of an electric shock to the patient, thus inducing a convulsion; used in the treatment of serious depression |
| **21.21** | **21.14** Psychosurgical technique for severely disturbed patients in which a small localized area of the brain is destroyed by radioactive particles inserted through small ceramic rods | **21.7** Drugs used to induce sleep (also called sleeping pills) |

# Chapter 22

# *Legal Issues in Abnormal Psychology*

## LEARNING OBJECTIVES
*By the time you are finished studying this chapter, you should be able to:*

### PSYCHOLOGICAL DISTURBANCE AND CRIMINAL LAW
1. Explain the purpose of the insanity defense (561).
2. Describe four tests for legal insanity presented in your text, specify the one most commonly used today, and explain why it is preferred over the others (561-562).
3. Discuss three objections to the insanity defense, and describe the concept of "guilty but mentally ill" as an alternative to "not guilty by reason of insanity" (562-566).
4. Discuss the purpose and controversial aspects of competency proceedings in criminal cases, making special reference to the role of antipsychotic medications in producing competence (566-567).

### CIVIL COMMITMENT
5. List four rights guaranteed to persons accused of a crime, and discuss how these rights either apply or do not apply to individuals about to be involuntarily committed for treatment (567-570).
6. Define "false positive" and "false negative" and relate these concepts to civil commitment (568).
7. List and describe four "standards of proof" that could be used in civil commitment proceedings, specify the one most recently advocated by the Supreme Court, and explain why it is preferred over the others (568-570).
8. Explain "dangerousness" as a standard for civil commitment and discuss the controversy surrounding it (570-572).
9. Explain the "Thank You" proposition and describe the role of expert testimony in civil commitment proceedings (572-573).
10. Summarize the arguments presented in the text both for and against involuntary commitment (572-573).

### PATIENTS' RIGHTS
11. Describe the cases of *Wyatt v. Stickney, O'Connor v. Donaldson,* and *Youngberg v. Romeo,* and discuss their impact on a patient's right to treatment (573-574).
12. Discuss the right to refuse treatment, and explain when that right may be denied (574-575).
13. List ten rights of mental patients relating to a humane treatment environment (575-576).
14. Discuss the potential conflict between the desire to protect patients' rights and the need to provide effective treatment (576-578).
15. Describe how recent legal decisions relating to abnormal psychology have affected the power of the mental health profession (578-579).

## CHAPTER OUTLINE

I. Psychological disturbance and criminal law

    A. The insanity defense
       1. Designed to protect from unfair punishment those who by reason of mental illness are not "morally responsible" for their actions

2. Legal tests of insanity
   a. Irresistible impulse (1834)
      (1) Could not control his/her actions
      (2) Does not answer question of what constitutes irresistible impulse
   b. M'Naghten rule (1843)
      (1) Did not know what he/she was doing, or
      (2) Did not know that the action was wrong
      (3) Limits excuse to those who are extremely out of touch
   c. Durham test
      (1) Unlawful act the product of mental disease
      (2) Depends on expert opinion
   d. American Law Institute definition (1962)
      (1) By reason of mental disorder he/she lacks substantial capacity to appreciate the criminality of behavior, or
      (2) Cannot conform behavior to requirements of the law
      (3) Mental disorder is not defined simply in terms of repeated antisocial behavior
      (4) Presently used in most courts
3. A new verdict: Guilty but mentally ill
   a. Intermediate step between "guilty" and "not guilty by reason of insanity"
   b. Allows recognition and treatment of mental disorder while still imposing punishment for action
4. Procedural aspects of the insanity defense
   a. Whose responsibility is it to demonstrate sanity or insanity of the client?
      (1) Hinckley verdict prompted federal rules requiring *defense* to prove *insanity*
      (2) Roughly three-fourths of states now require the same
   b. If acquitted through insanity defense, does the client go free or is he/she required to undergo treatment for the disorder?
      (1) Generally, acquittees may be institutionalized for treatment until it is demonstrated that they are no longer disturbed nor dangerous
      (2) Institutionalization may go on for longer than the prison sentence if he/she had been convicted
5. Criticism of the insanity defense
   a. How can a nonprofessional jury make a retrospective judgment about the mental state of the defendant at the time of the offense?
   b. Insanity is a fiction (Szasz) and the courts should judge people on their actions, not on their intentions or mental state
   c. Those acquitted by insanity defense may actually be confined (institutionalized) longer than if they had been found guilty (indeterminate sentencing)

B. Competency to stand trial
   1. Since people on trial are supposed to understand the charges against them and be able to participate in their own defense, someone deemed incompetent may be institutionalized until competent
   2. Deals with mental state at the time of the *trial*, not at the time of the offense
   3. Process can be abused by:
      a. Prosecutors who have a weak case and use it to get a defendant confined without conviction
      b. Defenders who have a weak case and use it to get a defendant out of reach of criminal prosecution
   4. Defendant runs the risk of indeterminate confinement except for recent rulings which require that if the person is unlikely to become competent in a reasonable amount of time, he/she must be released or committed through civil procedures (see below)
   5. Antipsychotic medication complicates the picture
      a. Without medication, defendant may
         (1) Never be competent, or
         (2) Appear "crazy" in court, thus
         (3) Biasing the trial toward the defense

b. With medication, the defendant may be
   (1) Subdued in court, and
   (2) Less able to participate in his/her own defense, and may appear
   (3) More "sane" than he/she really is, thus
   (4) Biasing the trial toward the prosecution

## II. Civil commitment

A. Procedures for commitment: What rights do potential institutional patients have?
  1. The right to a jury trial?
    a. A formal judicial hearing is usually needed before commitment, but
    b. Only fifteen states have a right to jury trial
  2. The right to assistance of counsel?
    a. Most states provide a right to counsel, but is the lawyer working as
      (1) An advocate, doing as instructed by the client, or as
      (2) A guardian, doing what is in the best interests of the client
    b. Most lawyers in this situation apparently take on the role of guardian
  3. The right against self-incrimination?
    a. Criminal defendants cannot be forced to testify against themselves, but does the silence of a person threatened with commitment mean
      (1) A wise decision not to self-incriminate, or
      (2) A symptom of disorder which then cannot be referred to
  4. The right to have charges proved beyond a reasonable doubt (standard of proof)?
    a. We can make two kinds of errors in deciding commitment
      (1) False positive (unjustified commitment)
      (2) False negative (unjustified release)
    b. False positives are worse than false negatives because loss of liberty is involved (therefore, "innocent until proven guilty")
    c. Possible standards of proof
      (1) Beyond reasonable doubt (90-95 percent)
      (2) Clear and convincing evidence (75 percent)
      (3) Preponderance of evidence (51 percent)
      (4) Medical standard (any evidence at all)
    d. Clear and convincing evidence seems to be the best approach because
      (1) While deprivation of liberty is involved,
      (2) We also want to be sure those who need treatment get it, and
      (3) If the decision to commit is wrong, it is likely to be discovered and the person will be released

B. Standard for commitment (grounds for commitment)
  1. Originally mental illness itself was sufficient
  2. More recently, dangerousness has been applied as a more rigid standard
  3. Dangerousness can be difficult to define; is it:
    a. Risk of physical harm to self or others?
    b. Risk of emotional harm to self or others?
    c. Economic harm?
    d. Harm to property?
  4. The determination of dangerousness (even if defined) is difficult because it presumes to predict behavior
  5. The more dangerous and the more likely the dangerous behavior, the more likely one is to be committed
  6. But if commitment is carried out, false positive are likely because of
    a. The rarity of many dangerous behaviors
    b. Lack of corrective feedback (if person is committed, we will never know if he/she was truly dangerous)
    c. Differential consequences to the predictor (false positives create fewer problems for the predictor than do false negatives)
    d. Unreliability of the criterion (the past does always predict the future)
    e. Powerlessness of the subject (if I decide you are dangerous, you can't do anything about it)
    f. The general lack of dangerousness among mental patients as a whole

7. The "thank you" proposition is sometimes put forward as an alternative to dangerousness, assuming that after treatment an involuntarily committed patient will be grateful that treatment was carried out
8. No matter what standard is used, the ultimate decision on commitment should be in the hands of the court, not mental health professionals, since social values ultimately determine who is and who is not to be confined
   a. The ease of getting someone committed varies from decade to decade (based on social values)
   b. Some argue that involuntary commitment should be abolished altogether (again a social value)

III. Patients' rights

A. The right to treatment
   1. *Wyatt v. Stickney*, an Alabama case, determined that institutions must provide:
      a. Individualized treatment programs
      b. Sufficient skilled staff to administer treatment
      c. A humane physical and psychological environment
   2. *O'Connor v. Donaldson* determined that mental illness does not justify involuntary custodial treatment
   3. *Youngberg v. Romeo* determined that patients are entitled to
      a. Conditions of reasonable care and safety
      b. Reasonably nonrestrictive conditions of confinement
      c. Training as may be required by these interests
   4. *Youngberg v. Romeo* also determined that the judgment of mental health professionals is "presumptively valid," meaning society should not second-guess them lightly

B. Other rights of mental patients
   1. The right to refuse treatment
      a. The "thank you" proposition argues against refusing treatment, but
      b. It also assumes that treatment is worth getting, but this is not always the case
      c. Current thinking is that "routine" treatment cannot be refused, but more controversial treatment may be
   2. The right to a humane environment includes (as a result of *Wyatt v. Stickney*):
      a. A right to privacy and dignity
      b. Nondiscriminatory opportunity for religious worship
      c. Satisfying and nutritious food (nutrition not to be withheld as punishment)
      d. Screened privacy in multi-patient rooms, with adequate storage for personal effects
      e. Privacy in bathing and toilet facilities
      f. The right to one's own clothing and personal possessions
      g. Visitation and telephone communication rights
      h. Unrestricted right to send and receive mail
      i. Outdoor privileges and exercise opportunities
      j. An opportunity for interaction with members of the opposite sex
      k. Reasonable pay for work voluntarily agreed to
   3. Behavior therapy has raised its own share of patients' rights issues
      a. Some believe that institutionalized patients should have the things listed above as a matter of course; therefore:
         (1) Time out procedures are limited
         (2) Token economies are challenged
         (3) Other specific behavioral strategies are criticized as manipulative
      b. Behavior therapists counter that by providing these things unconditionally, consequences in life are disconnected from behavior, producing a very damaging long-term effect on the patient and preventing behavior therapy from working
      c. All this is complicated by the fact that some patients *have* been abused by some staff under the guise of behavior therapy

IV. Power and the mental health profession

   A. The major outcome of most court decisions in this chapter has been to restrict the power of the mental health establishment

   B. This can be good if society wants to retain control over what is defined as abnormal and how people with abnormal behavior are dealt with

   C. This can be bad if reasonable, scientifically-based knowledge and treatment of mental illness is interfered with or prevented

   D. Diffusion of power plus informed consent based on education of the populace may go a long way toward fairness for all

## KEY TERMS
*The following terms are in bold print in your text. Define them and practice their definitions using the flash cards at the end of the chapter.*

civil commitment (567)
false negative (568)
false positive (568)

indeterminate sentences (566)
insanity defense (561)
standard of proof (568)

*Your text does not list the following terms as formal vocabulary; however, if you don't know what they mean, you will be unable to grasp the concepts of this chapter.*

consensual (577)
diametrically (565)
divulge (571)

due process (568)
exonerated (563)
free will (561)

incarcerated (566)
requisite (563)
retrospective (565)

## IMPORTANT NAMES
*Identify the following persons and their major contributions to abnormal psychology as discussed in this chapter.*

Kenneth Donaldson (574)
John Hinckley (562)
Daniel M'Naghten (561)

Nicholas Romeo (574)
A. A. Stone (572)
Thomas Szasz (566)

Ricky Wyatt (573)

## GUIDED SELF-STUDY

1. What are the three major areas where mental health and legal issues intertwine?

   a.

   b.

   c.

2. Of course, the law gets involved when a crime has been committed or when somebody's rights have been violated, but why does the law have anything to do with civil commitment?

PSYCHOLOGICAL DISTURBANCE AND CRIMINAL LAW
3. Psychologists debate the issue of free will; where does the criminal justice system stand on this subject?

4. Is there any exception to the law's view on free will?

5. What do we mean by a "legal test of insanity"?

6. Briefly name, date, and summarize the cases that have established the following important legal tests of insanity.

    a. "Irresistible impulse" decision:

    b. M'Naghten rule:

    c. Durham test (no date given):

    d. ALI's Model Penal Code:

7. Tell which test of insanity is used by each of the following.

    a. Federal courts:

    b. The majority of state courts:

    c. The rest of the state courts (except N.H.):

    d. New Hampshire:

8. As far as expert testimony by mental health professionals is concerned, the ideal test of insanity should be worded so as to put the burden of decision fully in the hands of the

    (a)_____, because they are the ones who are legally empowered to make the judgement about

    responsibility for the crime, not the (b)_____.

9. What incident led to a radical rethinking of the insanity defense, and why?


10. What two legal changes have occurred as a result of criticism of the insanity defense?

    a.

    b.

11. If a person is acquitted by reason of insanity, what happens to him/her after the trial? Detail the history of how this process has changed over the years.



12. List three criticisms of the insanity defense.

    a.

    b.

    c.

13. What are some of the difficulties with empowering a jury to make an insanity decision?

    a.

    b.

    c.

14. Statistically, there are more people in mental hospitals who were in trouble with the law but who never went to trial than people who went to trial and were acquitted on insanity defenses. How did all these other people get put away?

15. How are insanity and incompetency different?

16. Of what importance is the defendant's state of mind at the time of the trial?

17. Who brings up this competency question, and how can it be abused?

18. Detail the history of what happens to a person who is judged incompetent to stand trial.

19. By what means may people be *made* competent to stand trial?

20. Summarize the controversy surrounding the use of antipsychotic medications to make people competent to stand trial.


CIVIL COMMITMENT
21. The textbook authors consider the rights of the individual in a civil commitment proceedings in comparison to the rights of a defendant in a criminal trial. Why?

22. What percentage of admissions to public mental hospitals are involuntary?

23. Use the following words to fill in the blanks (one is used twice):

**advocate**          **guardian**          **time-consuming**
**counsel**           **jury**
**expensive**         **silence**

Fifteen states allow a person to have a (a)_____ in civil commitment hearings. The

argument against this is that jury trials are too (b)_____ and (c)_____ and that mentally ill people will be harmed by having their mental health issues debated openly. In

most states, the defendant in a civil commitment hearing has a right to (d)_____ (a

lawyer). The question then becomes, should the lawyer act as a(n) (e)_____, and pursue what is in the best interest of the client (whether he/she wants it or not), or act as a(n)

(f)_____, working for what the client wants (even if it is "crazy")? Most lawyers usually

end up acting as a(n) (g)_____. In criminal trials, (h)_____ cannot be held

against a defendant. This protection against self-incrimination (i) **is / is not** clearly established for persons in civil commitment hearings.

24. What three traditional standards of proof might be used in commitment decisions, and what level of certainty does each require?

    a.

    b.

    c.

25. What standard of proof for involuntary civil commitment was established by the U. S. Supreme Court? How does it compare to the standards in Question 24?


26. Which of the following is a "false positive," and which is a "false negative"?

    a.   The test says you are pregnant when you are not.
    b.   The test says you are not pregnant when you really are.

27. In the past, what were grounds for committing someone to a mental institution?

28. What circumstance is currently required for a person to be committed to a mental institution?

29. What are some of the debatable issues in this approach to involuntary mental hospital commitment?

    a.

    b.

    c.

30. Give examples of the following types of dangerousness.

    a.   Physical threat to self or other:

    b.   Financial threat to self or others:

    c.   Psychological threat to others:

31. The following factors tend to swell the number of false positives in the determination of dangerousness:

    a.   Lack of _____, because once a person is institutionalized, it is impossible to determine dangerousness on the outside.

    b.   _____ to the predictor, because locking up non-dangerous people results in much less bad publicity than freeing someone who is dangerous.

    c.   _____ of dangerousness criteria, and the resulting tendency to play it safe and overdiagnose dangerousness.

    d.   _____ of the client, who is in no position to influence the outcome of the case.

32. The "Thank you" proposition states that if a seriously disturbed person is forced into

    treatment against his/her will, that person will eventually be (a)_____ for the treatment after recovery from the problem. This is not always the case, but at least this reason for involuntary commitment has the advantage of stressing (b)_____,

which is not the case in decisions based on the criterion of (c)_____.

33. As in the case of the insanity defense, civil commitment rules have varied over the years.

In the decade of the (a)_____, laws were changed to make it harder to commit someone.

In the (b)_____, it became easier again. Now, in some states, one can be committed for

making (c)_____ of violence against someone, and in some cases, even dangerousness

to (d)_____ as well as people is sufficient. Regardless of the rule changes, however,

the type and number of people committed has (e) **increased / decreased / stayed about the**

**same**. People who ultimately make the decisions in a given case seem to operate as much on

the basis of (f)_____ as they do in response to the rules then in force.

PATIENTS' RIGHTS
34. A patient has a right to treatment; does he/she have the right to refuse treatment?

35. A mental patient also has a right to a humane environment. Included in this are (use the following terms):

| | | |
|---|---|---|
| **dignity** | **one's own clothes** | **religious worship** |
| **exercise** | **opposite sex** | **telephone** |
| **mail** | **personal belongings** | **toileting** |
| **meals** | **privacy** | |

a. The right to privacy and (a)_____

b. An opportunity for voluntary (b)_____

c. The right to nutritionally adequate (c)_____

d. The right to sleeping area providing (d)_____, a comfortable bed, a place for

(e)_____, a chair, and a bedside table

e. The right to privacy in (f)_____ and showering areas

f. The right to wear (g)_____ and use personal possessions

g. The right to visitation and (h)_____ communication

h. The unrestricted right to send and receive (i)_____

i. The right to regular (j)_____ and to be out of doors regularly

j. Opportunity to interact with members of the (k)_____

36. Which of the above rights may be abridged if the mental health professionals believe such abridgment is in the patient's best interest?

37. How can behavior therapy conflict with patients' rights?

38. In view of the *Wyatt v. Stickney* decision, when can electric shock treatment be used as a "punishment" for a mental patient?

39. What is the difference between how behavior therapists and the legal system see "time-out" procedures?

POWER AND THE MENTAL HEALTH PROFESSION

40. Mental health professionals are powerful in that they define what is (a)_____ and who

should be (b)_____ and for how long.  The people who are in this position are not

representative of the population as a whole; they are most commonly (c) _____, _____

_____.  The public are now trying to become informed consumers by insisting they have

information to make decisions for themselves, which is called (d)_____ _____.

41. What is the significance of each of the following precedent-setting cases?  I'm giving you page numbers after the dates to make things a little easier.

   a.  *Jones v. United States* (1983) [565]:

   b.  *Jackson v. Indiana* (1972) [567]:

   c.  *Addington v. Texas* (1979) [569]:

   d.  *Tarasoff v. Regents of California* (1976) [571]:

   e.  *Wyatt v. Stickney* (1972) [573]:

   f.  *O'Connor v. Donaldson* (1975) [574]:

   g.  *Youngberg v. Romeo* (1982) [574]:

   h.  *Knecht v. Gillman* (1973) [578]:

42. Check your vocabulary knowledge.  Fill in the correct term from among the following choices:

**Civil commitment**            **Informed consent**
**Confidentiality**             **Insane**
**Incompetent**                 **Standard of proof**
**Indeterminate sentence**      **Thank you proposition**

   a.  _____ Putting a person in a mental hospital against his/her wishes

   b.  _____ Providing treatment on the assumption that when cured the patient will be grateful

   c.  _____ The right to have information and to say "no"

   d.  _____ Loss of liberty without a specific time frame

   e.  _____ The degree of certainty

   f.  _____ "Crazy" when the crime was committed

   g.  _____ "Crazy" at the time of trial proceedings

   h.  _____ Therapist keeps a client's secrets

## HELPFUL HINTS

1. To review the psychological debate on free will, see the discussion of the humanistic-existential perspective in Chapter 2. This point of view developed in opposition to the determinism (lack of human free will) of the psychodynamic and behavioral perspectives.
2. Clarify with your instructor how much detail you need to know about the legal cases discussed in this chapter. Do you need to know the names of the cases to go with the principles they established, dates of the cases, and/or the individual details associated with each?
3. Shock used as aversive stimulation, or as punishment to suppress a behavior, has nothing to do with shock therapy, which is an electrochemical therapy used to reduce severe depression.
4. In connection with behavior modification and patients' rights, remember that behaviorists believe in the importance of *learning* as the way of acquiring behavior. B. F. Skinner once said: "People who help those who can help themselves can work a sinister kind of destruction by making the good things in life no longer contingent upon behavior." *Learning* requires a connection between what you do and what happens afterwards.

## PRACTICE TEST
*Take the following test several times as you study the chapter. Write your answers on a separate sheet of paper and after each attempt, note in the tally box above each question whether your answer was correct or incorrect.*

| 1 | 2 | 3 | 4 |
|---|---|---|---|

1. Which of the following is true of the insanity defense?
   a. It assumes that all behavior is irrational.
   b. It is only necessary if free will is responsible for normal behavior.
   c. It applies only to people who have been previously diagnosed as psychotic.
   d. It is intended to replace the concept of "guilty but mentally ill."

| 1 | 2 | 3 | 4 |
|---|---|---|---|

2. Which of the following expresses the criteria of the M'Naghten rule? A person is not to be held responsible for a crime if the person
   a. cannot resist the impulse to do wrong.
   b. does not know what he/she is doing, or does not know that the action is wrong.
   c. commits the act as a result of mental illness or defect.
   d. is already under treatment for a disorder that causes the behavior he/she is accused of.

| 1 | 2 | 3 | 4 |
|---|---|---|---|

3. What was the first legal test of insanity?
   a. The M'Naghten rule
   b. The ALI test
   c. The Durham test
   d. The concept of "irresistible impulse"

| 1 | 2 | 3 | 4 |
|---|---|---|---|

4. Which of the following objections to the insanity defense would most likely be made by someone like Thomas Szasz?
   a. The insanity defense is used to escape punishment by people who are clever enough to fake mental problems.
   b. Insanity doesn't exist and people should be held responsible for all of their actions.
   c. The judgments made by juries about the state of mind of the accused at the time of the offense are too subjective to be accurate.
   d. A successful insanity plea may leave a person worse off than conviction, since mental hospital stays are indeterminate in length.

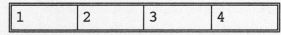

| 1 | 2 | 3 | 4 |

5. The issue of competency to stand trial can be abused by
   a. the prosecutor, who may be trying to get the case to trial in a hurry.
   b. the defense, who may think that a judge will be more sympathetic to a mentally ill defendant.
   c. either the prosecution or the defense, if one of them is stalling for time.
   d. the defendant's family, if they want him/her released from custody.

| 1 | 2 | 3 | 4 |

6. The main problem with providing legal counsel for someone who is being committed to a mental hospital is that
   a. most mentally disturbed people are unable to pay for a lawyer.
   b. the lawyer may have to choose between being an advocate of the client's wishes or a guardian of the client's best interests.
   c. lawyers are of no use to people who are not legally responsible for their behavior, since they cannot be brought to court anyway.
   d. legal counsel implies suspicion of guilt, but few mental patients are criminals.

| 1 | 2 | 3 | 4 |

7. The "catch-22" with competency to stand trial and antipsychotic medication is that
   a. with medication, the defendant looks sane, but without it he/she is incompetent.
   b. defendants may deliberately refuse medication so they can successfully use the insanity defense.
   c. who—defense or prosecution—is to decide whether medication is required?
   d. if medication is used in criminal proceedings, then it must be used in civil commitment proceedings as well.

| 1 | 2 | 3 | 4 |

8. "Innocent until proven guilty" is a key concept in criminal law. The goal is to avoid
   a. true positives.
   b. true negatives.
   c. false positives.
   d. false negatives.

| 1 | 2 | 3 | 4 |

9. Which of the following standards of proof can be said to require accuracy about 75 percent of the time?
   a. The medical standard
   b. The civil standard of "preponderance of evidence"
   c. The criminal standard of "beyond reasonable doubt"
   d. The standard of "clear and convincing evidence"

| 1 | 2 | 3 | 4 |

10. Assume you have a rich aunt you would like to get rid of legally. Considering the amounts of evidence you would have to generate to have her committed, which of the following standards of proof would be to your advantage?
    a. The civil standard
    b. The criminal standard
    c. The medical standard
    d. Clear and convincing evidence

| 1 | 2 | 3 | 4 |

11. "Dangerousness to self or others" is discussed in the test as a standard for commitment. This criterion is controversial because
    a. dangerousness, if applied to everyone, would mean that most criminals would be placed in mental hospitals instead of prisons.
    b. confidentiality prevents therapists from testifying about their dangerous clients.
    c. dangerousness is not objectively defined and cannot be easily measured.
    d. a person's degree of dangerousness is relatively stable, and once committed on those grounds, he/she may never be released.

| 1 | 2 | 3 | 4 |

12. Which of the following is *not* one of the factors that tends to inflate the number of people judged dangerous in dangerousness evaluations?
    a. Powerlessness of the subject
    b. Lack of corrective feedback
    c. Differential consequences to the predictor
    d. Use of antipsychotic medication during evaluation

| 1 | 2 | 3 | 4 |

13. The "thank you" proposition states that
    a. a person committed involuntarily will thank you for it after being cured.
    b. patients must be treated politely and with respect or commitment decisions may be reversed in court.
    c. society's gratitude for the removal of dangerous individuals justifies their commitment.
    d. once institutionalized, most patients can be treated in ways that will minimize complaints.

| 1 | 2 | 3 | 4 |

14. The case of *Wyatt v. Stickney* is a precedent-setting case in the area of
    a. patient's rights.
    b. competency to stand trial.
    c. the insanity defense.
    d. civil commitment criteria.

| 1 | 2 | 3 | 4 |

15. Behavior therapy techniques have been under the scrutiny of the courts because
    a. they do not agree with the deterministic assumption about human behavior that the courts take for granted.
    b. they are less successful than many other approaches to treating involuntarily committed patients.
    c. extinction procedures have been confused with punishment by some people.
    d. these techniques are often used instead of imprisonment and the prosecution does not think justice is being served.

| 1 | 2 | 3 | 4 |

16. The right to a humane environment includes all of the following *except* the right to
    a. privacy.
    b. wear your own clothes.
    c. leave the institution at any time.
    d. access to mail and telephones.

| 1 | 2 | 3 | 4 |

17. What is the generally accepted opinion concerning an involuntary mental patient's right to refuse medication normally used for the patient's problem?
    a. The patient can refuse if the refusal is made by a lawyer.
    b. The patient normally cannot refuse the medication.
    c. Only criminally insane patients cannot refuse.
    d. There are no judicial opinions on this issue.

| 1 | 2 | 3 | 4 |

18. In setting up a token economy in an institutional setting, what is a major issue that must be kept in mind?
    a. Whether or not the patient has been involuntarily committed
    b. Obtaining court approval since token economy is a nontraditional treatment
    c. Making sure that the patient's quality of life in treatment is equal to that of the median American
    d. Deprivation, when used in a token economy, can be seen as a violation of patients' rights

| 1 | 2 | 3 | 4 |

19. Why might it be a bad idea in the long run to insist that patients in mental hospitals be provided with everything they receive with no strings attached?
    a. Learning new behaviors requires contingencies of reinforcement.
    b. The cost of running the institution will go up, resulting in treatment cutbacks.
    c. The effectiveness of treatment goes down when patients are put into a position of power.
    d. Staff will no longer have any way of enforcing compliance with the rules.

| 1 | 2 | 3 | 4 |

20. As a result of the case of *Tarasoff v. Regents of California*, current thinking on the issue of patient-therapist confidentiality is that
    a. psychologists are under no obligation to discuss anything their clients tell them under any circumstances.
    b. psychologists can be prosecuted for divulging client information under any circumstances.
    c. psychologists must turn over their patient files to the authorities upon request.
    d. psychologists must break confidentiality if they reasonably suspect that the client may harm someone.

## ANSWERS
### Self-Study Exercise

1. a. Psychological disturbance and criminal responsibility
   b. Civil commitment
   c. Patients' rights (561)
2. Civil commitment means the state taking action to insist that a person be hospitalized for mental health care against his/her wishes. In this case, a person is losing his/her freedom, so civil commitment is very much a question of a person's legal rights (567).
3. It assumes all persons have free will, and that therefore a person can be blamed, held accountable, and punished for a behavior that society has defined as intolerable (561). See Hint 1.
4. The insanity defense is the exception for those people who, because of mental disturbance, are not judged to have free choice about their actions (561).
5. A "legal test of insanity" is the set of criteria which a defendant must meet in order to be declared insane. These criteria have been established in earlier, precedent-setting cases in which an insanity defense was attempted (561).

6. a. "Irresistible impulse" (1834): Person could not make him/herself do the right thing
   b. M'Naghten rule (1843): Person either didn't know what he/she was doing or didn't know the action was wrong
   c. Durham test: Excused an unlawful act that was the result of a mental problem
   d. American Law Institutes's (ALI) Model Penal Code of 1962: Person is not guilty if he/she lacks ability to understand the criminality of his/her behavior, or to act within the law. This does not include repeated criminal behavior and antisocial conduct (561-562).
7. a. A test similar to M'Naghten
   b. ALI test
   c. M'Naghten, some with irresistible impulse, some without
   d. Durham test (562)
8. a. jury
   b. mental health professionals (565-566)
9. The Hinckley verdict—acquitting someone by reason of insanity who did not appear psychotic brought the insanity defense to the forefront of public attention (563).
10. a. The development of a new verdict, "guilty but mentally ill," in some jurisdictions. It is an intermediate position between not guilty by reason of insanity and guilty. It is for the person who has a mental illness but does know what he/she was doing and that the behavior was wrong (563).
    b. The other change involves the question of which side has the responsibility to prove sanity or insanity. Since the Hinckley verdict many jurisdications have changed the rules so that now it is up to the defense to prove insanity. Before, the burden fell on the prosecution to prove sanity (563).
11. Prior to the 1970s, he/she was automatically committed to a mental hospital. In the 1970s, mental health laws were changed to require commitment proceedings to determine if he/she was still mentally ill and dangerous. In the 1980s, things were tightened up again (after Hinckley) and automatic commitment for an indeterminate period is again possible (565).
12. a. It is difficult for a jury to determine if a person was insane at the time of the crime.
    b. "Insanity" doesn't exist; all behavior is purposeful for the person engaging in it.
    c. Innocent by reason of insanity can lead to an indeterminate stay in a mental institution, which can be worse (longer) than if the defendant were sent to prison (565-566).
13. a. Guessing what was in another person's mind is a very subjective process.
    b. The jury has to make a retrospective judgement, trying to guess what the defendant's state of mind was at the time of the crime.
    c. The testimony presented by psychological professionals is often conflicting and is also a retrospective judgment (565-566).
14. They were judged incompetent to stand trial (566).
15. The difference is a matter of time. Insanity refers to the person's state of mind while the crime was being committed, and competency refers to the person's state of mind at the time of the trial (566).
16. If a person cannot understand the charges against him/her and respond to his/her lawyer to help build the defense, then the person cannot be put on trial (566).
17. Either the prosecution or the defense. Sometimes competency is abused as a delay maneuver if either side feels they have a weak case (566).
18. In the past, he/she could spend years locked up in a mental hospital trying to get his/her legal rights back. Now, since a 1972 Supreme Court decision, he/she cannot be held in limbo forever. He/she must be either officially committed (because he/she is mentally ill and dangerous) or released (567).
19. By use of antipsychotic medications (567)
20. a. Does medication actually give defendants adequate access to their thinking skills? Are they really as mentally fit with medication as they would be if they were not mentally ill?
    b. Antipsychotic medications often make people groggy and passive, which is no way to go to your own trial.
    c. Is it fair to make a person look less crazy than he/she is? Perhaps if the jury saw the person without medication, it would have no doubt he/she is seriously disturbed (567).
21. In both cases, the person is at risk of losing his/her freedom whether, in prison or in a mental institution (567).
22. 55 percent (567)

23. a. jury
    b. expensive (or time consuming)
    c. time consuming (or expensive)
    d. counsel
    e. guardian
    f. advocate
    g. guardian
    h. silence
    i. is not (567-568)
24. a. "Beyond a reasonable doubt": 90-95 percent certain; used in criminal trials
    b. "Preponderance of evidence": 51 percent or more; civil proceedings
    c. Medical evidence standard: Any evidence whatsoever; medical diagnoses (568-570)
25. "Clear and convincing evidence," corresponding to about 75 percent sure; this is lower than "beyond a reasonable doubt" for criminal judgments and higher than the 51 percent of the civil standard (570).
26. a. False positive
    b. False negative (568)
27. "Mental illness" or "need of treatment" (570)
28. Dangerousness to self, others, or property (570)
29. a. How should dangerousness be defined?
    b. To what extent can future behavior be predicted from past behavior?
    c. How accurately can one anticipate rare events where clearly established odds are not available? (570-571)
30. a. Homicide, suicide, physical attack
    b. Patient claims voices are telling him/her to burn his/her financial assets
    c. Patient stalks a victim whom he/she believes to be Satan and terrorizes that individual with threats, or as a parent he/she locks a child in its room for days at a time trying to keep it away from the evil in this world (570)
31. a. corrective feedback
    b. Differential consequences
    c. Unreliability
    d. Powerlessness (571-572)
32. a. grateful
    b. the patient's welfare
    c. dangerousness (572)
33. a. 1970s
    b. 1980s
    c. threats
    d. property
    e. stayed about the same
    f. intuition (573)
34. Involuntary patients can be required to submit to "routine" treatment, which may typically be medication. More controversial treatments, such as ECT, require permission from the patient, next-of-kin, or the court (575).
35. a. dignity
    b. religious worship
    c. meals
    d. privacy
    e. personal belongings
    f. toileting
    g. one's own clothes
    h. telephone
    i. mail
    j. exercise
    k. opposite sex (575-576)
36. "f" (personal possessions); "g" (visitation and phone communication); "h" (mail) (575-576)
37. Behavior therapy is reinforcing people for behaving more appropriately. But many of the most ready reinforcers are items on the patients' rights list; that means they cannot be used as earned rewards since they must be provided automatically (576-578). See Hint 4.
38. In extreme cases, electric shock (an aversive stimulus) can be used to suppress serious self-abusive behaviors (577). See Hint 3.
39. For behavior therapists, time-out is eliminating the possibility of reinforcers in order to extinguish undesirable behaviors. The court looks upon it as solitary confinement and as a situation that could be easily misused (577-578).
40. a. abnormal
    b. institutionalized, or treated
    c. affluent white males
    d. informed consent (587)
41. a. Insanity acquittees could be automatically hospitalized until they were no longer dangerous, and if necessary, they could be hospitalized longer than the jail time for the crime for which they were acquitted (565).
    b. A defendant in a criminal trial cannot be held as "incompetent to stand trial" indefinitely; as soon as the possibility of becoming competent in the foreseeable future is eliminated, the person must be formally committed to a mental institution or released (567).

c. The court set a standard of proof at "clear and convincing evidence" (75 percent) for involuntary commitment decisions (569).
d. The limit on client-therapist confidentiality is when the welfare of public is at risk (571).
e. The court ruled that if a person is locked up because he/she needs treatment then adequate, individualized treatment in a humane environment must be provided (573).
f. The court gave indirect support for right to treatment because it said a person cannot be locked up for custodial care just because of mental illness (574).
g. The court subtly shifted emphasis from absolute patient's rights to support for mental health professionals' decisions about what is best for the patient (574). See Hint 2.
h. This is an instance of patient abuse being labeled as behavioral therapy (578).

42. a. Civil commitment (567)
    b. Thank you proposition (572)
    c. Informed consent (579)
    d. Indeterminate sentence (566)
    e. Standard of proof (568)
    f. Insane (561)
    g. Incompetent (566)
    h. Confidentiality (571)

## Practice Test

| | | |
|---|---|---|
| 1. b (561) | 11. c (570) |
| 2. b (561) | 12. d (571) |
| 3. d (561) | 13. a (572) |
| 4. b (566) | 14. a (573) |
| 5. c (566) | 15. c (576) |
| 6. b (568) | 16. c (575) |
| 7. a (567) | 17. b (575) |
| 8. c (568) | 18. d (576) |
| 9. d (570) | 19. a (576) |
| 10. c (569) | 20. d (571) |

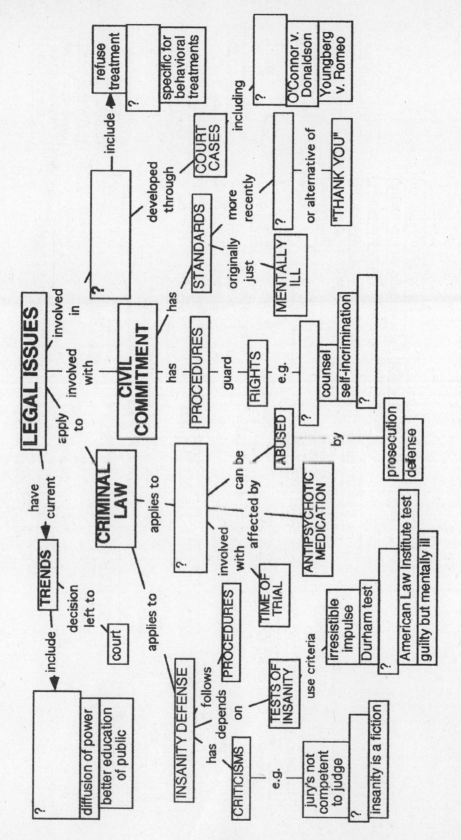

## CONCEPT MAP 22.1

Fill out the boxes marked with question marks (?) with the concepts or words you think belong there. Suggested answers are on a following page.

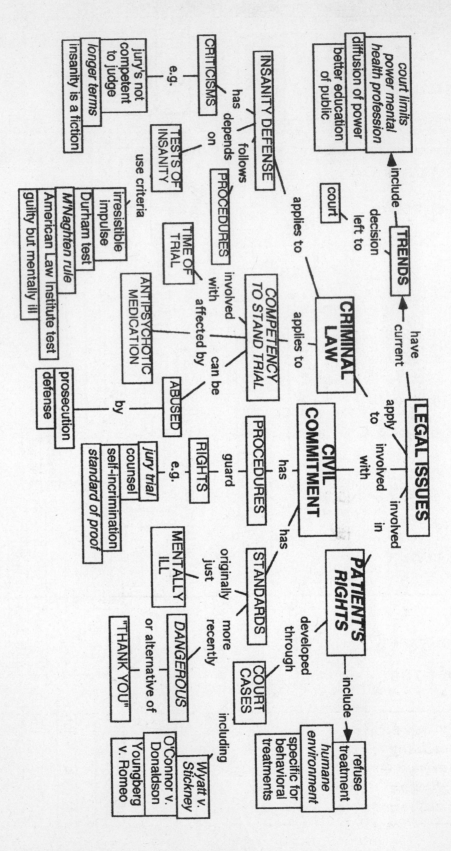

**CONCEPT MAP 22.1** The suggested answers are shown in *italics*.

534

| 22.1 civil commitment | 22.8 | 22.15 |
|---|---|---|
| 22.2 false negative | 22.9 | 22.16 |
| 22.3 false positive | 22.10 | 22.17 |
| 22.4 indeterminate sentence | 22.11 | 22.18 |
| 22.5 insanity defense | 22.12 | 22.19 |
| 22.6 standard of proof | 22.13 | 22.20 |
| 22.7 *(You may fill in the remaining boxes with names, terms and definitions from text and lecture)* | 22.14 | 22.21 |

# DEFINITIONS (Cut out on the lines to use as Flash Cards)

| 22.15 | 22.8 | 22.1 The commitment of a person to a mental institution because the state has decided that he or she is disturbed enough to require hospitalization |
|---|---|---|
| 22.16 | 22.9 | 22.2 (1) An incorrect diagnosis of no illness. (2) In commitment hearings, a failure to commit when commitment is justified and necessary |
| 22.17 | 22.10 | 22.3 (1) An incorrect diagnosis of illness. (2) In commitment hearings, an unjustified commitment |
| 22.18 | 22.11 | 22.4 A period of incarceration with no limit, often given to those defendants acquitted by reason of insanity |
| 22.19 | 22.12 | 22.5 A legal plea in which the defendant admits to having committed the crime but pleads not guilty, stating that because of mental disturbance he or she was not morally responsible at the time of the crime |
| 22.20 | 22.13 | 22.6 In commitment hearings, the degree of certainty required in order to commit someone to a mental institution; must be "clear and convincing" evidence that the person is mentally ill and dangerous |
| 22.21 | 22.14 | 22.7 |